Introduction

Africa, Motors, and a History of Development

FRANK TAYLOR'S CAR may not be the only Nissan with headlights from the former Yugoslavian company Saturnus (see figures I.1 and I.2). I would not be surprised to find other Nissan rally bodies sporting these pre-1970s Saturnus headlamps, popular among rally drivers for their strong beams, reaching two to three times farther than other lights in darkness. But add its Toyota engine and its Ford Escort dashboard, and Taylor's rally car becomes a one-of-a-kind vehicle that tells a unique story about Africans and mechanical creativity. That story ends with a championship. Driven by his son and navigated by his wife, the vehicle earned TayComm Rallies, the family's rally team, a first-place finish in the 2018 national competition for two-wheel drive. But let's begin the story by taking a big step back in time. Since the combustion engine's invention in the late 1800s, car manufacturers and users from the Global North, a geography that claims the motor vehicle as its own, have considered automobiles and Africa incompatible. Cars, most colonial officials believed, signaled the cutting edge of industrial progress, born of centuries of scientific and technological advances. Their ideas about Africa evoked the complete opposite. "The image of Africans as irrational took root in the Enlightenment and took off during the imperialism that followed," writes Gabrielle Hecht. "Europeans built political philosophies premised on the radical Otherness of Africans. Armed with Maxim guns and industrial goods, they saw artisanally produced African

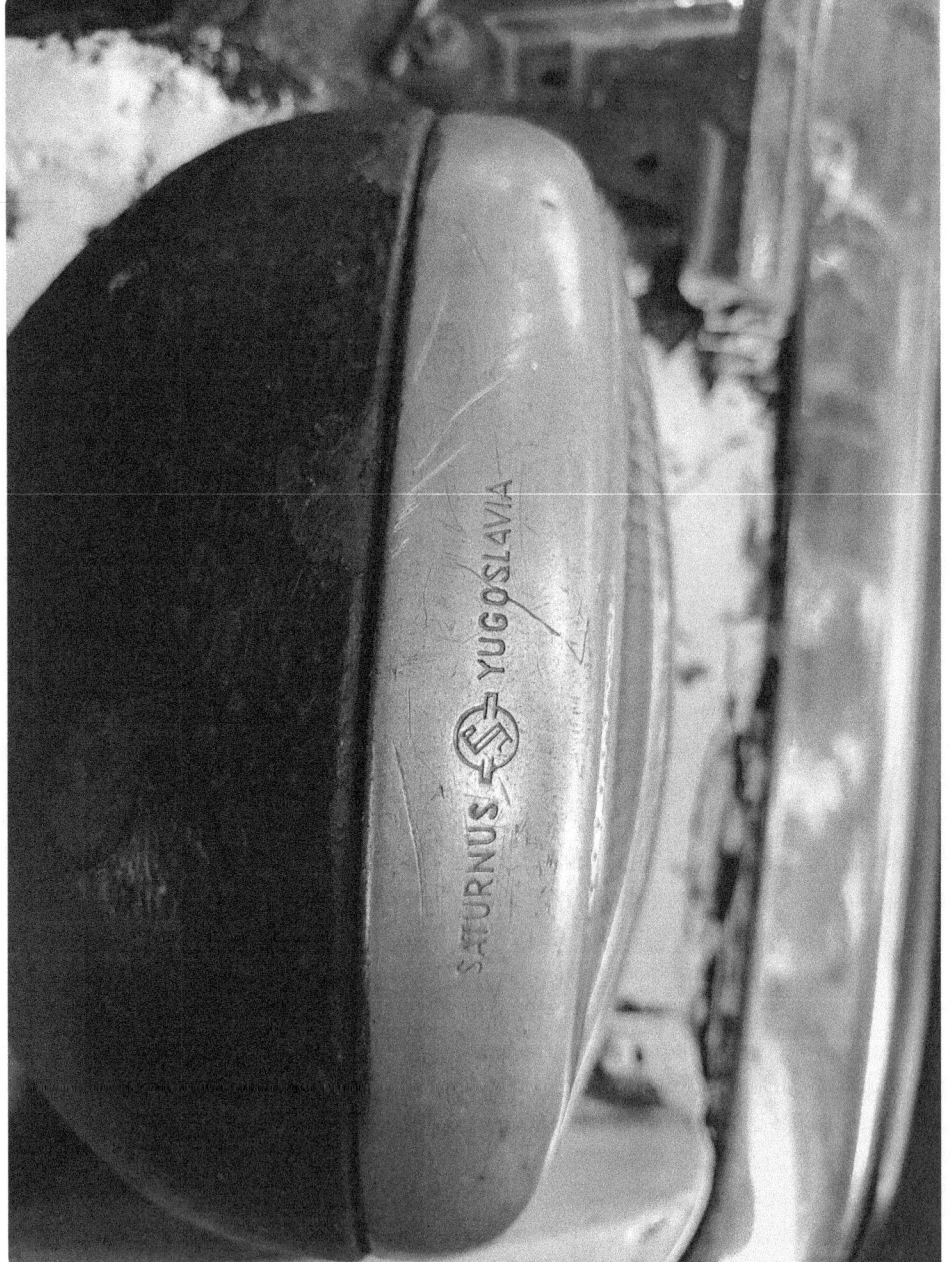

AFRICAN MOTORS

Here and overleaf: Apprentices from the Ufuidi soccer team learning and working in a state garage.

AFRICAN MOTORS

TECHNOLOGY, GENDER, AND THE HISTORY OF DEVELOPMENT

Joshua Grace

DUKE UNIVERSITY PRESS   *Durham and London*   2021

Printed and bound by CPI Group (UK) Ltd, Croydon, CR0 4YY
Project editor: Annie Lubinsky
Designed by Matthew Tauch
Typeset in Arno Pro and Futura Std by
Westchester Publisher Services

Library of Congress Cataloging-in-Publication Data
Names: Grace, Joshua, [date] author.
Title: African motors : technology, gender, and the history of development /
Joshua Grace.
Description: Durham : Duke University Press, 2021. | Includes biblio-
graphical references and index.
Identifiers: LCCN 2021000751 (print) | LCCN 2021000752 (ebook)
ISBN 9781478010593 (hardcover)
ISBN 9781478011712 (paperback)
ISBN 9781478021278 (ebook)
Subjects: LCSH: Automobiles—Tanzania—History—20th century. |
Automobiles—Social aspects—Tanzania. | Technology—Social aspects—
Tanzania. | Economic development—Social aspects—Tanzania. | BISAC:
HISTORY / Africa / East | TRANSPORTATION / Automotive / History
Classification: LCC TL119.T35 G74 2021 (print) | LCC TL119.T35 (ebook) |
DDC 629.22209678—dc23
LC record available at https://lccn.loc.gov/2021000751
LC ebook record available at https://lccn.loc.gov/2021000752

Cover art: Top photo: Woman with ice cream exiting a
modified British Zephyr. Bottom photo: Brian Ibrick (right),
son (middle), and unidentified individual performing
mechanical work. Photo from the collection of Brian Ibrick.

CONTENTS

ACKNOWLEDGMENTS

This book began with a breakdown. In 2007 our 1992 Dahaitsu Feroza, the first car we had purchased in Dar es Salaam, Tanzania, needed more serious attention than previously thought as its engine missed a cycle and overheated. Our mechanic, Abdu, said the cylinders in the block needed to be rebored and then paired with resized pistons. It sounded serious and expensive to me. As part of a generation of Americans for whom shop class had been deemphasized and even denigrated, I knew very little about cars. And so I was surprised that Abdu described this as a fairly routine fix that would actually improve the vehicle and its value. My very American approach to vehicles—which privileged factory originality and might have led to the engine being scrapped—left me skeptical, but because other research had to stop, I asked to hang out in the garage over the week it took to fix the vehicle. Unlike some of the engine work explored in this book, the reboring occurred at the Department of Engineering at the University of Dar es Salaam. But the rest of the work occurred in a garage whose density of people, things, and activity took me by surprise even though I knew garages were a common fixture of life in the city. That rebuilt engine purred, and Abdu joined me to stand by his work when we sold the vehicle (albeit for the same price as we purchased it). That process led me to archives, to roadsides, and back to garages to try to understand the history that allowed the Feroza to find new life.

Like that fixed Feroza, this book had many hands in its construction and in the many repairs necessary to get it working and keep it going. Laura Fair coaxed this project out of me and then provided steady guidance, patience and encouragement, methodological creativity, honesty, and much more. I could not have asked for a better adviser in matters of academia or life; not a week passes when I don't think of a personal or academic lesson or inspiration Laura provided. The late David Bailey first accommodated my interest in the history of technology through individual studies I enjoyed and grew from immensely. I had always hoped that I could give him a copy of this finished book and that it would find its way into the unending stacks and piles of books one navigated upon entering his office. I'm thankful to have the many questions he asked me then—and that I failed to answer and still likely cannot now—as a memory of him and those times. Walter Hawthorne, Peter Alegi, and David Wiley supported this research throughout my time at Michigan State University. I'm particularly grateful for their close reading of my work. I started studying cars just as Lewis Siegelbaum published *Cars for Comrade: The Life of the Soviet Automobile*, and I greatly appreciate the time and resources he shared with me. Greater East Lansing's *babu*, Mwalimu Deo Ngonyani, was the heartbeat of the academic Kiswahili-speaking community at Michigan State University. Much more than a linguist and language teacher, Deo is a fabulous historian in his own right and has provided valuable feedback and answered many questions over the years. He and Philomena embody the Kiswahili term *karimu*.

My introduction to African expertises came in undergraduate classes with Mwesiga Baregu and Ruth Meena at the University of Dar es Salaam in 2003 and 2004. They and my classmates first introduced me to concepts about knowledge production and power that ultimately shaped this research. That same year, Tony Waters taught and mentored me in the classroom and through many conversations at Hill Park, ultimately encouraging me to take the steps that led to this book.

In graduate school, I was fortunate to take classes both with and at the University of Michigan as well. A joint seminar between the University of Michigan and Michigan State University on African socialism and communism was ideal for this project, as the latter half of the book attests. Many thanks to Kelly Askew and Laura Fair for helping make this a class for which I still commonly check my notes or pursue questions about Tanzanian socialism. Thanks to Gabrielle Hecht and Paul Edwards, I benefited from a rich program in science and technology studies (STS) at the University of Michigan. Gabrielle and Paul graciously welcomed me into their introduction to STS course. Important parts of this book would not be possible without the grounding their course provided and the questions they encouraged students to ask. The same goes for Gabrielle's seminar Technologies, Natures, Bodies and for the inspiration and ideas she brought as a committee member both during and after graduate school. Her feedback, encouragement, and example have been critical at each step. My thanks to Todd Shepard for coming up with the title *African Motors*.

Tanzania acted as a second home to us during this project. Patrick Kahemele and Nawanda Yahaya were the best friends I could have hoped for as an undergraduate student at the University of Dar es Salaam. Later, when I was a researcher, times with Nawanda in Morogoro and with PK watching soccer all over were some of the best of my life. Both opened their homes and their budding families to me. I cannot wait to get all the kids together when travel is possible again. The Carvalhos have been an anchor for us in Dar es Salaam for over a decade now. There are too many good times and too much good food to recount, but we treasure them all. The same goes for Jane, Gunnar, and Mimi, who also opened both home and family to us. We were lucky to meet Happy, Wendy, and Nancy during language training. We also had a wonderful academic family in Dar es Salaam that provided fellowship, laughter, and encouragement along the way: Tony and Dagmar Waters, Ken Hosea, Ngesa Ngesa, Andreana Prichard, Kristin Philipps, Paul Bjerk, Priya Lal, Amy Nichols Belo, Julie Weiskopf, and Gerrard Alolod.

I offer my deepest gratitude to the men and women across Tanzania who took time to talk with me about their lives, many of whom continue to ask about the status of the project almost ten years later. Finally, *safari imeisha* (the journey is over)! Idrissa, who accompanied me on travels to Tabora and Kigoma, understood this project in a way few did. His companionship during travel, his curiosity, and his gentle demeanor led to new insights and opened doors I considered firmly shut. A passionate taxi driver with deep and entrenched opinions about Tanzania's car history—and about routes and vehicles themselves—Idrissa fell on hard times when his engine died. I wasn't sure what to think when he suggested he help me do research in exchange for me paying to fix his engine, yet I was lucky to find friendship with an individual who was surely among the sharpest historians of Tanzania's technological past. Idrissa helped put me in touch with Mjomba Kondo, who later welcomed me into his garage and welcomed the idea of me being an apprentice of sorts. I hope this book shows my appreciation for the time and ideas Kondo, Jitu, Saidi, and Idrissa shared with me.

I was lucky to begin rewriting this book surrounded by fantastic colleagues at the Department of History at the University of South Carolina. Writing groups with Tom Lekan, Kay Edwards, Matthew Melvin-Koushki, Nicole Maskiell, Ann Johnson, Jessie Barnes, David Kneas, Connor Harrison, Monica Barra, and Meredith DeBoom sustained and inspired me through various stages of redrafting the manuscript. I could not have done this without them. Tom Lekan read an entire draft of the book—some parts multiple times. His gentle advice, support, knowledge of East African history, and friendship were critical to making it better and getting the project across the line. Kay Edwards was a constant source of wisdom, advice, encouragement, and fellowship. She helped steer me away from needless detours and toward a completed manuscript. Ann Johnson, the department's other car historian when I arrived at the University of South Carolina, passed away before I finished the manuscript. I hope this book nevertheless reflects the encouragement she gave me as a young scholar and even a fraction of the rigor and creativity she brought to the field. Allison Marsh, Matt Melvin-Koushki, Carol Harrison, and Tom Brown have been a source of laughter, advice, fun, and support since 2013. My deep gratitude goes to four department chairs—Larry Glickman, Dean Kinzley, Jessica Elfenbein, and Christine Ames—for their unwavering support.

I was lucky to have a chance to sharpen my ideas through workshops and invited talks. The Learning How workshops at the Max Planck Institute for the History of Science provided an opportunity to think more deeply about knowledge politics. Francesca Bray's incisive commentary helped me situate chapter 2 in broader literature. I scribbled down many ideas from Nina Lerman about knowledge and social mobility in the in-between moments of coffee breaks. Dagmar Schaffer pushed me to center materiality more in chapter 2—a push I needed and from which the chapter benefited greatly. The fantastic work of my colleagues—Stewart Allen, Whitney Laemmli, Kate Smith, Johanna Gonçalves, Caitlin Wylie, Anna Harris, and Melissa Van Drie—showed me how much more I could do with the topic. A talk at the University of Oregon's African Studies Center gave me a chance to first articulate ideas about African history and automobility's "machinic complex." Thanks to Melissa Graboyles, in particular, for offering smart and encouraging feedback. Likewise, a Baraza at the University of Florida's African Studies Center, and questions from Brenda Chalfin, in particular, helped me sharpen ideas about the garage as an archive and about the impact of material austerities. I was lucky to share ideas at the Africanizing Technology workshop at Wesleyan College coordinated by Laura Ann Twagira and to participate in the Shifting Baselines Workshop at the Max Planck Institute for the History of Science, coordinated by Wilko Hardenberg and Thomas Lekan. A workshop at the University of Virginia arranged by Ellen Bassett provided a forum to explore the urban parts of this book with Jennifer Hart, Brad Weiss, and Ellen.

A number of friends and colleagues have greatly enriched the content of this book and the process of writing it. Jill Kelly and Brandon Miller made life in East Lansing a joy; I deeply miss weekly meals and going to dive bars with them. The same goes for Lindsey Gish and Matt Park, both of whom helped me frame this project. In the small world of car historiography in African history, I'm lucky to be able to learn from and share ideas with Jennifer Hart. More than learning from her work, Jennifer shaped my thinking on the problematic language of informality at a critical juncture of the writing. Many conversations with Kate de Luna have spilled into the text, too. She showed me ways to think about concepts, terms, and language in ways that greatly enriched my thinking about Kiswahili as a technical language, including its longer histories. Laura Fair, Kristin Phillips, Andreana Prichard, Breanne Grace, Amy Nichols Belo, Priya Lal, Julie Weiskopff, and Paul Bjerk are fantastic scholars of Tanzania whose work has inspired me and whose fellowship has been a source of joy for the past fifteen years. I've been lucky to share the early career book journey with Tasha Rijke-Epstein and Robyn d'Avignon. Both provided helpful conversations about STS and African history at important points in the writing.

In Columbia, South Carolina, I have many to thank for fellowship, food, ideas, and entertainment, including the Wu-Palmer family, the Shah-Fuente family, John Lane and Tom Lekan, Kay Edwards and Sunny, Matt Melvin-Koushki, the Coenen Snyder family, the Henderson-Platt family, and the Mandsagers. Our families in Oregon, California, Nebraska, and Colorado offered welcome respites from work and have always shown us what matters most in life. The final stages of this book have come in tighter quarters than I could have imagined. That means I owe Bre, Silas, and Benny—and Andrea, Spencer, Miles, Jack, and Yogi—a great deal of thanks for their patience, encouragement, and love.

I owe so much to the research infrastructure in Tanzania and the United Kingdom. My thanks to the Tanzania Commission for Science and Technology for granting research clearance and to the Tanzania Gender Networking Programme and Sokoine University of Agriculture for providing letters of support throughout the research process. Staff at the main branch of the Tanzanian National Archives (formerly in Dar es Salaam) have worked in difficult circumstances for a long time. I appreciate their dedication to Tanzanian history, their patience with numerous file requests, and their help tracking down missing files. The same goes for the regional branches in Dodoma and Mwanza. The NBA room at the National Library in Dar es Salaam provided more than I could have imagined. Its staff has wonderfully preserved a historical collection of reports, novels, and periodicals. I thank the Tanzanian Petroleum Development Corporation for granting access to its archives and to libraries at the National Transport College, the National Development Corporation, and the National Bureau of Statistics for the same. Staff at Ujenzi did not find any historical documents, but they spent weeks looking, and I appreciate their effort and the time I spent there. The Zanzibar National Archives helped fill in some of the missing parts of the colonial archive from across the channel. It was a joy to work there. In the United Kingdom, I thank the staff at the British National Archives, the Imperial War Museum, the Liddell Hart Centre for Military Archives at King's College, Archives and Special Collections at the School of Oriental and African Studies at the University of London, the London Museum of Science Archive at Wroughton, and the collections at Rhodes House at Oxford University.

I couldn't have done any of this without generous research funding. I first began exploring this car history on the back end of a Fulbright Fellowship administered by the Institute for International Organization. Many thanks to Jermaine Jones for his wonderful leadership of this program. At Michigan State University, I received generous support from Title VI Kiswahili language fellowships administered through the African Studies Center and the Center for Gender in a Global Context. In the wake of congressional budget cuts that ended the Fulbright-Hays Program for 2011–12, the Andrew W. Mellon Foundation stepped in to generously fund prospective recipients. This book would not exist without that lifeline of support. The American Council for Learned Societies generously funded a writer year that saw the completion of this manuscript. The College of Arts and Sciences, led by Lacy Ford and Joel Samuels, provided critical support for summertime writing and funds for completing the manuscript.

Duke University Press has been a joy to work with. I'm so thankful to have had a chance meeting with Elizabeth Ault at the 2015 African Studies Association. Elizabeth pushed me to write the book I had envisioned even when I hesitated to do so. Her vision for the book enabled me to find mine. Editorial associates Kate Herman and Ben Kossak kept the project ticking along. Thanks to both of them for their attention to detail; the same goes for copyeditor Kimberly Miller. Two anonymous reviewers gave important feedback on the initial, longer manuscript. I'm thankful for their critiques and encouragement; they've made this a much better book. Tim Stallman put my vague ideas about maps into something that brought historical sources to life. Thanks to Jason Begy for the index.

I dedicate this book to my best friend, Bre, with love and thanks for the past seventeen years of life. She has been a constant source of joy, inspiration, love, grace, steadiness, and brilliance. Bre read more of this project than anyone else and listened to me during the highs and lows of writing and research. I'm so lucky to call her a partner in life. Silas and Bennett spent their first years with this manuscript in the background of their lives. They've questioned how long it took me to complete and somehow tied this book's publication to getting a dog. So there you go, Si and Benny—you get a dog now. You both have brought me more joy than I knew possible.

I.1–I.2 *Yugoslavian headlights on Frank Taylor's champion Nissan rally car. (Photos by author.)*

technologies as proof of a primitive existence. 'Africa' became seen as a place without 'technology.'"[1]

Indeed, as car use grew in East Africa in the early 1920s, colonial motoring literature described an almost insurmountable technological gulf between European motorists and African societies. The Royal East Africa Automobile Association (REAAA), which published pamphlets of its motor trials for colonial and metropolitan audiences, paired motoring maps and pictures of vehicles with images of unstable stick bridges, mud houses, unclothed women, and superstitious "witch doctors."[2] In 1927 the association's director, Frederick Galton-Fenzi, helped a journalist from the *New York Times* sell this mythical technological absence as a desirable travel experience for American car enthusiasts. The article detailed auto tours over "roads [that] have been pushed right through the heart of the tropical jungle. Herds of giraffe are frequently seen and many varieties of antelope." The REAAA assured readers that when one is motoring over "old paths and elephant trails," bamboo bridges "feel insecure, as the bridge sways," but they do not merely hold. They also feel like "motoring over a carpet stretched in midair." As for their African audiences: "The natives are terrified at first, but within a day or so they are filling the tank and holding out one hand for a tip. At present they are providing tea and bread and butter for tourists in their little refreshment stands, but soon, if we are to believe Mr. Galton-Fenzi, there will be shacks devoted to hot dogs and coffee."[3]

Portrayed as confused, shocked, scared, unclothed, or stationary assistants whose work, despite their quick appropriation of station culture, is limited to helping motorists with fuel, coffee, and hot dogs, Africans and their built worlds appear in these sources as worlds apart from European and American cultures of technology. As Michael Adas demonstrates, the ability to invent and produce machines created "perceptions of the material superiority" of European cultures that supplemented and reinforced, but did not replace, colonial hierarchies of biological race. The presence or absence of tools of industrialization like motor vehicles, railways, and wheels—including the new cultures of space, time, and speed they created—provided a "measure of men" that "[distinguished] civilized people from savages and barbarians."[4] Cars, for example, required fuel sources, engines with a variety of hardened metals, and tires made from rubber. While the rubber may have come from the Congo Free State (and later, the Belgian Congo) as raw material, tapped under brutal conditions, it was transformed into a finished product through the know-how and tools found in American and European factories. In this version of history, Africa at best provided the raw materials for a variety of production processes that evidenced Europe's "material superiority" over colonized societies.

An early biofuel scheme during World War I clarifies this view of Africa and other colonies as spaces of absolute technological lack. When German U-boats cut off oil supply lines to the Middle East during World War I, a committee tasked with finding energy alternatives proposed creating "Alcohol for Motor Fuel" from farms in British colonies. With a seemingly endless supply of vegetation, "tropical" colonies offered fuel solutions because "the natural increase of native population is retarded by civil war, pestilence, and disease, so that large areas are available, almost for the asking."[5] The project never gained traction. But it exemplifies a sociotechnical chasm many British thinkers and automobile enthusiasts took for granted.[6] Fed by travel writing that described "tropical" societies as technological voids, the plan suggested that non-European societies could not produce significant agricultural surpluses, let alone the "revolution in engineering" the car represented.[7] At best, with British aid, its land could supply metropolitan fuel needs. There are no considerations of when such passive contributions to metropolitan needs would lead to an African motoring society. European and American motoring cultures were still in their infancy at this time and still largely confined to the upper classes. With such limited diffusion at home, in these sources it appeared unthinkable that Africans could adopt, let alone shape, a motoring culture.

And yet they did. From a fleet of 14 colonial cars in 1914, the number of motor vehicles reached 30,000 by Tanzanian independence in 1961 and grew to nearly 600,000 by 2000. During the same time, the total miles of roads grew by a factor of ten, and the number of registered Tanzanian drivers increased from 6 to an estimated 400,000.[8] Some might correctly read those as low numbers in a comparative context and suggest that Tanzania makes an odd place for studying cars and society. But that would miss an important point: Tanzanians shaped vehicles and car culture without feeling a need to match—or appropriate—Northern trends of use. For much of the independent period, users and planners explicitly aimed to avoid those trends by putting automobiles and society together differently—a phenomenon most have either missed or misread, as a photo (figure I.3) taken during the East African Safari Rally in 1977 demonstrates. In the photo two independent Africans feature only as bystanders as a machine made in Europe, the United States, and East Asia flies by. Like the REAAA pamphlets, the car's presence evokes a world history of technology in which other societies innovate to move forward while Africans stand hopelessly still, mired in

I.3 *Two Maasai men watch a vehicle whiz by on a dirt road during the 1977 East African Safari Rally. Rally organizers intentionally sought out rough sections of road to test both vehicles and drivers. (Author's collection.)*

the same technological state, or simply looking on as others innovate, as shown in the upper right of figure I.4. Though clear change has come to automobiles in the fifty years between Galton Fenzi's 1920s promotion of European and American motoring in East Africa and the rally, nothing African, whether the people or the road, seems to have changed at all.[9]

This brings us back to Taylor and his rally-winning vehicle, a combination of different makes and models from around the world. He attached the Saturnus lights for their beam strength, and the Toyota engine for its durability and power. The Ford dash had less of an impact on performance, and Taylor simply trusted his judgment and skill to make the parts work together not just as a functioning vehicle but as a rally-winning automobile. He assembled it at home in a garage mechanics call *bubu* ("muted" or "silenced") or *nyumbani* ("home"). The son of a British agricultural officer and a Chagga mother, Taylor initially learned about mechanics working with his brothers on sisal estates in the 1970s. "I admired that job. I really loved it."[10] After working as a long-haul trucker, he opened three garages with his brothers in Dar es Salaam. In 2012 at the home garage where he

1.4 *An advertisement from Columbus Shock Absorbers and Levelers of Dayton, Ohio, that equates 3,100 miles of driving in East Africa to 60,000 miles of "normal driving" in the United States. (Author's collection.)*

made the rally vehicle, he told me, "This is about love. I feel happy. This is my hobby. I don't just do it to get money; I like my job."[11] Although Taylor possessed financial resources few Tanzanian mechanics had, his approach to cars nevertheless drew from a long history of African garage work that valued modification because it made cars work, was enjoyable, and offered mechanics an opportunity to change themselves and their livelihoods, too. Far from being passive observers of global technological trends, mechanics like Taylor have poured themselves into shaping automobiles and parts from several different nations—and even different time periods—into their own African vehicles.

African Motors charts the myriad ways users, makers, and maintainers like Taylor transformed motor vehicles from a tool of imperial rule into an African technology.[12] Covering 150 years from the 1860s to the 2010s, it follows the auto mechanics, drivers, passengers, and oil traders who built their lives and their communities around the automobile and its accompanying infrastructure, including roads, repair garages, urban transport systems, and oil economies—a suite of systems often called *automobility*. Automobility takes car scholarship beyond motor vehicles themselves to the myriad technological systems and sources of labor, knowledge, and energy that allow a driver to produce movement by stepping on a gas pedal. Mimi Sheller and John Urry, two of the field's founders, refer to these inputs as a "machinic complex." Automobility, they write, is "constituted through the car's technical and social interlinkages with other industries, including car parts and accessories, gasoline refining and distribution, road-building and maintenance, hotels, roadside service areas and motels, car sales and repair workshops, suburban house building, vehicles as new retailing and leisure complexes, advertising and marketing, urban design and planning."[13] Largely a product of a rich field of scholarship on European and American mobilities since the late 1990s, some of the specifics of these "technical and social interlinkages" translate poorly to historical experience in East Africa.[14] For this reason, I approach automobility not as a theory but as a historical method that encourages scholars to open the black box of car-based mobilities in order to explore the various ways African users put car, road, energy, and society together.[15]

In particular, scrutinizing the details of who and what made things move and how centers the multitude of users, spaces, knowledges, and things that made automobiles an integral part of everyday life in Tanzania by the end of the twentieth century. In the following pages, tracing the history of this vernacular machinic complex takes readers to some of the traditional sites of automobile scholarship, such as garages, oil trading, and urban transport. But it rests on the nineteenth-century caravan paths and vernacular labor institutions, such as *gereji bubu* ("muted garages"), through which motorized transport took root in the early to mid-1900s among laborers on both plantations and city streets. For instance, mechanics like Taylor often refer to bubu garages as a *kiwandani*. Generally translated as "factory" in recent decades, the term emerged between the fourteenth and fifteenth centuries to describe a place of social exchange and/or work just outside Swahili homes.[16] That precar vernacular institutions and spaces shaped automobiles does not simply confound the dichotomy, and supposed incompatibility, between East Africans' longer technological histories, on the one hand, and automobiles, on the other.[17] It also gestures toward a broader historical point: because car and society can be put together differently across places and times, African history provides an opportunity to explore and reflect on alternatives to the better-known forms of automobility that took root during the twentieth century.[18]

Moreover, and this is the book's main theme, such a vernacular complex, machinic or not, opens new avenues for writing African-centered histories of development. In addition to establishing the fact of African mechanical creativity—evident in Taylor's car—automobility helpfully situates such creativities and competencies across different technologies and technological spaces, practices, scales, periods, and identities in Tanzania's past. *African Motors* uses these multiscalar competencies to anchor a history of development in users' and makers' own experiences and ideas about not just automobile use, oil, or mass public transit but also expertise, gender, mobility, and well-being.[19]

The Kiswahili word for "development," *maendeleo*, makes this link between cars and development more explicit.[20] *Maendeleo* comes from the verb "to go" (*kwenda*) and its cognate, "to continue" or "to progress" (*kuendelea*); the addition of *ma*, denoting the plural, gives the term a literal translation akin to "progresses," "continuations," or "improvements." Moreover, the addition of the causative (*sha*) turns going (*kwenda*) into *kuendesha gari*, literally "going by car," while *kuendeleza* is one of the Kiswahili verbs used to describe maintenance—literally, keep something going. Though originally referring to spatial movement, like its English equivalent, *maendeleo* denotes a metaphorical movement from one socioeconomic condition to another.[21] In the 1940s, African intellectuals translated and popularized the term as "civilization" and connected it to "improvement," progress, and, during the fight against colonialism, the opposite of disorder.[22] By independence in 1961, the term had become "the new watchword of public discourse," and its usage more closely approximated midcentury concepts of development rooted in economic growth, rising production, and expanded social services.[23] During this period, politicians applied it to those who loved maendeleo (*mpenda maendeleo*)—and thus answered the state's calls regarding production and social ordering—and those who opposed it (*wapinga maendeleo*). Heeding the state's call helped "drive the nation" (*kuendesha taifa*)—literally causing the nation to go places it had not under colonial rule.[24] *Maendeleo ya haraka* ("fast development") asserted a need for this to occur quickly, while the more steadying phrase *songa mbele* ("move forward") encouraged steady forward movement.[25]

Maendeleo not only found use among elites in public discourse but also worked, and was shaped, by everyday users.[26] Hawa Ramadhani, one of the few women drivers in the decades after independence, titled her unpublished memoir "The Life and Development of Hawa Ramadhani" ("Maisha na maendeleo ya Hawa Ramadhani"), while her male colleagues spoke in interviews of their careers as mechanisms to "drive" themselves (*kujiendeleza mwenyewe*) by offering mobile networks and resources they could depend on in good and bad times alike.[27] In such personal contexts, *maendeleo*'s meanings and actions overlapped with a more extensive language about well-being that included "searching for life" (*kutafuta maisha*) and blessing (*riziki*), the achievement of respect (*heshima*), adulthood (*mzima*), ability/heft/capacity/power (*uwezo*), or claims to be civilized (*mstaarabu*).[28] These terms also provided individuals and communities with a language of debate and critique in historical newspapers or interviews. The same drivers, passengers, and mechanics who used *maendeleo* and the associated verbs to discuss personal achievements also used the term to identify the specific institutions and actors who kept development from happening in desired forms or kept it for themselves in Tanzania's history. Maendeleo's lexicon thus points to a more exciting   and likely denser—history of development, as Laura Fair has shown, than top-down or rise-and-decline narratives of development allow.[29]

Moreover, anchored in literal acts of spatial movement and their relationship to concepts of well-being and power, *maendeleo* and its root verbs gesture beyond a search for local equivalents to development as a transnational concept rooted in the twentieth-century West—or as process that arrived with European rule—and toward a host of vernacular practices, technologies, and ideas about movement, its meanings, and its longer histories.[30] It thus provides ways to explore development as a historical process Africans made, unmade, remade, and even maintained in specific technological ways.[31] In his seminal *Encountering Development: The Making and Unmaking of the Third World*, Arturo Escobar showed that representations of non-Western societies as simple, weak, and backward fueled the "making" of development "as a discourse" rooted in Western/Northern ways of knowing and doing. The "unmaking" came later, he asserts, as the promises of development failed to arrive or to last. With *kwenda* and its built worlds, *African Motors* takes inspiration from, and retools, Escobar's language for "making" and "unmaking" development. Its premise is quite simple: built worlds of mobility reveal how African users made development in their own ways, how these ways had to be maintained or transformed under new circumstances, and, finally, how unmaking in the form of failure or breakdown could lead to new things. And thus Taylor's car offers a material metaphor for a history of development in which things and ideas can be taken apart and put back together differently.

This nexus of making, unmaking, and repairing reflects a broader process contained in the book's title, *African Motors*. As already noted, the invention of the continent in the late 1800s as an undesirable place in need of European guidance rested on assumptions about its technological lack. "Africa" excels at craft and curios, things and skills found in much earlier episodes of European history, colonial officials charged, but needed centuries to approach anything close to a vernacular motoring society. Similarly, as both the engine that moves cars forward and an industrial sector, "motors" historically signal a society's technoeconomic worth, potential, and maturity. Places that produce their own automobiles have useful knowledge, institutions, and skills. They have obvious technological histories and large economies that count in world histories of development. Conversely, places that did not invent motors or motoring economies, such as Tanzania, are defined by lack and by their need to follow the steps toward technological maturity established by a motoring core. Following these steps, moreover, does not guarantee arrival at a technological place of grace.[32] As Johannes Fabian observes, placing others behind in linear temporalities of progress often implies that catching up is not possible because something about that society keeps change from either occurring or occurring correctly. The reasons a society originally fell behind, whatever they were, meant it would likely always be behind.[33]

African Motors charts alternative understandings of both of the words in its title, and it explores the long, often intimate relationship between them. Africa and African, though rooted in an "invention" of the continent as dark, primitive, and backward, were also repurposed and redefined by historical actors who used and repaired automobiles and who saw nothing incommensurate about their racial and cultural identities and automobility. As the opening two chapters illustrate, drivers, travelers, and mechanics rejected the racial presuppositions of European rule, including the idea that Africans could not or would not shape built worlds of movement or the automobile itself. Indeed, drivers and mechanics alike asserted that the combination of an African user and an automobile enhanced both person and vehicle. More practically, because automobile use was not dominated by any of Tanzania's 120 ethnic identities—and because independent citizens remade this term—African (*mwafrika/waafrika*) provides a broad category used by historical actors to establish the presence of machinic agency and identities throughout society during three periods: late precolonial, colonial, and independent.[34] Similarly, my use of *motors* departs from studies that limit technological worth to invention and to mass industrial production in official (*rasmi*) spheres and to knowledge that comes from these historical epochs.[35] Instead, I use the term to argue that the unofficial and uncertified, as well as acts of maintenance and repair, provide sites, institutions, bodies, and ideas for locating systems and cultures of mechanical expertise in Tanzania's past, such as Taylor's home garage.

MATERIAL MAENDELEO AND EFFECTIVE GENDER: CREATIVITY, SILENT AGENTS, AND THE POLITICS OF ABSENCE

Had we watched Taylor turn Saturnus, Nissan, and Ford into a rally-winning vehicle, we likely would have heard elements of a Kiswahili technological lexicon that largely predated the car's invention. Although, as chapter 2 details, mechanics never thought it practical to translate the automobile and its parts into Kiswahili—as some technical schools thought prudent—a dynamic vernacular about actions, thoughts, and things not only drove garage work but also applied to other topics explored in this book. This lexicon informs three main themes:

1   Creativity, innovation, and making: ubunifu/kubuni, kutengeneza/ matengenezo
2   Vernacular technological institutions: bubu, mtaani, chini ya mwembe/ mti, pembeni
3   Scarcity and absence: uhaba, upungufu, hamna, adimu

The first theme comes from a word for creativity and innovation, *ubunifu*, derived from the verb *kubuni*. Although it is most commonly translated as "creativity," its usage defies distinctions in contemporary Western lexicons that situate invention, production, and building as agentive activities associated with white and masculine pursuits—and consequently as connected to disciplines of science, technology, and engineering—while marking repair/maintenance, craft and artisanship, and the appropriation of outside ideas as nonwhite and feminine.[36] Indeed, Kiswahili speakers use kubuni to talk about a range of activities, including invention, fixes large or small, and the act of building/constructing itself. For our purposes, the term captures everything from the complete remaking of an automobile in garages, where mechanics laid claim to "creative" (*mbunifu*) as an identity premised on their creativity (ubunifu), to acts of routine maintenance (*kudumisha, kutengeneza,* or *kuendeleza*) of vehicles or urban transport systems that nevertheless required extensive thought, labor, and resources and that, in some cases, led to new or parallel systems on citywide and national scales.[37] *Ubunifu* is paralleled by *kutengeneza,* a verb for "making" that similarly covers both production and repair—two acts captured by the word *matengenezo.* Historic elements of Kiswahili technical worlds, both terms anticipate recent calls in science and technology studies to take consideration of historical agency beyond invention and mass production to the intellectual and physical labor necessary to repair and maintain. Steven Jackson calls this process "broken world thinking," and like the dual meaning of matengenezo, he emphasizes the productive nature of repair. Instead of a simple return to a previous state of function (the before of breakdown), repair often makes something work again by making it work differently. No matter how small, those changes constitute a creative, productive act.[38]

In this book, repair's productivity helps situate technological agency across time and place and for a range of things and activities. Though it may seem obvious, automobility's "machinic complex" never presented itself to African users as a finished project with a bounded and tested manual, so to speak, for prospective users to simply appropriate by following preset guidelines forged elsewhere. Instead, from garage to street to oil economy, users cited the changing circumstances for both creating and maintaining car-using societies across place and time since the early 1900s. For example, mechanics observed and responded to changes in car design (such as increased electric wiring or the inclusion of fuel pumps); after interviews, they gave me pieces of paper and sent phone text messages listing models they had repaired to establish their ability to competently react to the challenges of repair as new models arrived and/or as parts became scarce. Both issues—changing models and dynamic parts worlds—meant maintenance might always (and repeatedly) require mechanics to produce cutting-edge knowledge to get pistons pumping and wheels moving.[39]

The same breakdown-creativity process also applied to a much different technological world: oil economies. Not only did quadrupled fuel prices in 1973 press an already capital-stretched nation to explore unconventional means to simply maintain the previous year's oil supplies or to attempt to replace oil's role in their economy with another energy source. It also placed Tanzania's national oil company in an undesirable position in global energy economies as bureaucrats tried to obtain petroleum without sustained—that is, economically maintained—financial resources. Chapters on driving, urban transport, and road making lead to a similar conclusion: invention and manufacture did not close the design process; on the contrary, maintenance and repair proved the primary task through which a variety of African users, fixers, and maintainers forged vernacular cultures of automobile use, amplifying and constantly repeating a process Madeline Akrich calls the "de-scription of technological objects."[40] Akrich offers *de-scription* as an alternative to *inscription*: the sociotechnical composition of things created through invention, design, and manufacture. Inscription anticipates particular types of users and thus locates technological power at sites of invention. She shows that technology transfer requires de-scription by users capable of translating something designed far away (where the script is born) into existing sociotechnical matrices.

In this book, such de-scripting occurred most often through routinized acts of matengenezo. Even more, this maintenance/repair sometimes removed the social and technological scripting about how cars and their parts should be combined, oil obtained and moved and used in economies, or human-machine networks of movement created across space. By this, I mean that social and technological elements of inscription from sites of car production in Europe and the United States, and later in Japan, Korea, and India, failed to cohere into something that traveled intact to East Africa and presented itself to prospective users as a script. On the contrary, breakdown and remaking occupy a central part of this narrative because African communities so commonly witnessed automobile dysfunction during the car's early history in colonial Tanganyika. Consequently, the first generations of men who became mechanics and drivers did not read automobiles as a measure of European superiority that needed to be translated from colonial culture into African life. Rather, seeing fragile technologies regularly rendered helpless (as a large colonial photo archive attests), mechanics took their place at the proverbial design table to make and remake technologies that clearly needed assistance. Noting that this nexus of unmaking and making drove his passion for mechanical work, Taylor later adopted this open approach to vehicle design to make his rally car in the era of independence.[41]

The details of matengenezo make it possible to write an African-centered history of automobiles that matters on its own terms—thus sidelining the implications of northern invention narratives. The latter privilege northern places, institutions, inventors, and ways of knowing. Traditionally, such narratives approach a Southern society which uses something from the North as copiers, appropriators, and followers and thus as places defined, at best, by their ability to receive ideas and things forged elsewhere and *after* inscription—after Northern ingenuity sets historical processes in motion.[42] Such narratives gain power by overlooking the technical details of the mechanical work that produced cars like Taylor's. Though no doubt invented and originally manufactured in other places, most of the cars mechanics saw in the 1910s and 1920s had been remade so many times that the original script had been lost. In broader historical terms, then, African mechanics made, designed, and tested vehicles coterminous with, not after, users around the world who contributed to car culture by (re)making automobiles in shops, on farms, in junkyards, along streets, and on assembly lines, as a rich historiography demonstrates.[43] This should overturn narratives in which Africa is merely a backdrop to design, as chapter 2 explores, and in which Africans merely watch, instead of shape, world technological histories—as earlier photos suggest.[44]

African automobile design acts as the heart of this book's argument about creativity and agency, but automobility, by definition, asks us to take analysis beyond the car itself and therefore leads to one of this book's main contributions: composed of different technological registers, automobility's machinic complex provides a multiscalar history of African creativity.[45] In addition to mechanics like Taylor who made a variety of African vehicles, urban bus passengers in Dar es Salaam initiated debates about making mobile systems in their socialist city work better. They then set about building a network of vehicles to make it happen. Long-haul truck drivers did the same in the 1970s and 1980s. When state distribution (*usambazaji*) networks slowed to halt, they used their regional and national mobility to create networks of distribution that brought important goods to Tanzanian homes in a period of scarcity. Similarly, oil traders at the Tanzania Petroleum Development Corporation (TPDC) found ways to keep hardship from becoming worse in the wake of price hikes in 1973 that left Tanzania, as an oil importer, with few options for creating self-reliance during the second decade of independence. In other words, as it pertains to car history, creativity emerged among individuals as well as collectives of different sizes; it can be found in rural and urban spaces as well as among those who inhabited both, such as drivers; and it makes up histories of good and bad times alike.[46]

Instead of homogenizing creativity, locating ubunifu in multiple technological registers helps account for its diversity and its uneven efficacies. Because fixing a car is different from fixing an urban transport system or an oil economy, the improvisation that made and repaired African cars in city garages did not produce similar national-scale results for the TPDC.[47] Sometimes creative work failed owing to wrong choices. At other times it came up against structural obstacles that made success unlikely or significantly altered previous technological horizons.[48] But such failures do not void the thoughtfulness or complexity of innovative work. Indeed, in some cases, failed creativities provide opportunities to scrutinize automobility's affordances as a social and technological system that became synonymous with development and well-being in much of the world. Despite myriad forms of innovation at the TPDC, the OPEC (Organization of the Petroleum-Exporting Countries) crisis made the fulfillment of the technopolitical imaginations of the 1960s much less likely in Tanzania because so many basic tasks, including those linked to rural modernization, required petroleum and a machinic complex of roads, pipelines, and railways to move it. Here the corporation's struggle to innovate out of an oil crisis it did not, and likely could not, control exposes the sociotechnical breakdowns that accompanied one manifestation of automobility-as-development (and a fairly minimalist one, at that). Such limits to ubunifu and matengenezo certainly suggest a need to take seriously the constraints for sustaining technological nation building in the second decade of independence. They also bring variation to actor experiences of economic decline and the possibilities that came out of them; technologically speaking, decline was rarely a linear process.[49]

Creativity acts as a bridge to our second theme: the centrality, depth, and complexity of the so-called informal. *Informality* entered scholars' lexicon in the late 1970s when researchers recognized that official reports and statistics failed to capture the breadth of economic and political action.

Studies of economic informalities expanded the types of actions, actors, and spaces scholars and policy makers considered in their evaluations. But in many studies, informality acted as a form of making do. It signaled a constrained agency circumscribed by precarity that, in a best-case scenario, needed to give way to something better because it was an undesirable telos.[50] Though much fewer in number than studies of economic action, studies of informalized technology took a similar approach, with researchers writing about it as "localized learning." Economist Joseph Stiglitz has argued that such localization mitigated against the knowledge "spillovers" that many economists associate with specialization in official economic and educational institutions.[51] He had no problem identifying pockets of creativity in postcolonial economies. But he also argued that creativity's existence outside official channels such as schools and institutes made it incapable of driving economic and technical change on national scales. It therefore did not constitute a vernacular basis for building meaningful and large-scale sociotechnical worlds that could have political and economic impact.[52] Clapperton Mavhunga observes that this two-step process of identifying skill and then denigrating it began in the colonial period when officials marked all vernacular knowledges as the equivalent of informal, simply because they were not European.[53]

In this study, the main problem with the formal/informal divide is not definitions of informality per se but the determination of when and how things count as *formal* in histories of development—and therefore as useful, powerful, effective, and desirable and as an end point (telos) of change.[54] Historians of science and technology know this issue well. The core of both historiographies uncovers the emergence of terms such as *science, technology,* and *engineering* to mark a broad set of ideas and practices as exclusive domains of upwardly mobile white men between the eighteenth and twentieth centuries. Sharing common sets of ideas and practices with the mechanical arts and *techne,* disciplines associated with engineering, technology, and science nevertheless claimed monopolies on "useful knowledge" and the institutions and practices that generated this status.[55] Development ideologies have performed similar work by invoking mythic histories of science and technology from Europe and the United States as the foundation of universal ideologies of economic and social well-being. The best-known expression of this view of "knowledge as power," as it is often called, is probably Harry Truman's 1949 Point Four Program speech. Truman announced that science and technology opened development to all peoples regardless of nationality or race. As a discourse of progress making universal claims, however, it rested on incredibly narrow definitions of the types of knowledge, bodies, and things that counted as powerful, a phenomenon that Bruno Latour calls "particular universalism" and that Tania Li notes accounts for a sliver of the practices and things associated with development.[56]

In this context, *African Motors* demonstrates that a variety of vernacular institutions created deep bodies of car-based knowledge and action. These places, things, and knowledge worlds go by several terms in Kiswahili. At the most general level, actors call these spaces "muted" or "silent" (*bubu*— the term I use most often for clarity), "not official" (*siyo rasmi*), "place of work"/"factory" (*kiwandani*), and "street" (*mtaani*). Technologists can also describe more particular places—"under the mango tree" (*chini ya mwembe*), "in/on the corner" (*pembeni*), and "street" (a specific *mtaani*)— as well as actions: "secretly" (*kisirisiri*) and "cleverly" (*kiujanjaujanja*).[57] Terms such as *siyo rasmi* and even *bubu* sometimes mark bodies of knowledge as distinct from an official sphere, no doubt. But that distinction carries a much different meaning from the many academic and professional uses of *informality*.[58] As general categories, "silent," "not official," and "street" signaled that a garage, car, or action was likely not registered and perhaps illegal; it was there, a fixture even, and yet not advertising itself in the same way as a government workshop or technical institute. Yet there was nothing pejorative about this and, at times, nothing consequential. Indeed, historical actors often saw colonial and national institutions, the normative formal, as the weak, the shallow, and the uncertain, while describing "under the mango tree" and "street," more specific categories of bubu, as the deep and complex, the exciting and cutting-edge—in other words, as a space of knowledge generation and spillover.[59]

They also saw these spaces as a durable part of everyday life and even as an end point of a process of sociotechnical change. Recall Taylor's winning rally car. He, like many of the mechanics in the following pages, approached knowledge and things formed on streets, under trees, and at homes as both the beginning and the end of historical processes of sociotechnical change. This should not surprise us because, historically speaking, mango trees, street sides and corners, and kiwandani have proven themselves as places of thought, innovation, and work for centuries. They echo Jane Guyer's astute observations about monetary institutions in Nigeria, where, given the historical instability of banks, the question is not why large numbers of people invest in unofficial institutions but rather why anyone would trust their money to formalized institutions given the region's entropic economic histories: "Trusting the rational-legal framing of economic life can be dangerously irrational for individual actors. In some sense, it is the formalities that seem to work at face value that become the most challenging of all to understand."[60] James Scott makes a similar point in the conclusion of *Seeing like a State*.[61] Using the term *metis*, he gestures toward deep and flexible bodies of expertise and world-making rooted in citizens' everyday lives instead of in the state and market institutions that take center stage in many stories of twentieth-century development.[62] The connection between metis and bubu histories in this book is not just that expertises come from unexpected places, bodies, and institutions, but also that such knowledges spread across place and endure over time in ways that challenge the "discursive creation of a 'top' consisting of planners, governmental agencies, and international agencies that is then set against a 'bottom' of ordinary people," as Ato Quayson puts it.[63]

Beyond explaining mechanics' function, expanding the institutions and places of expertise carries important implications for gendered constructions of technological personhood. Reworking Jamie Palmer's term *ineffective masculinities*, *African Motors* uses these vernacular categories of car work to chart alternative regimes of expertise and personhood. In a study of American perceptions of Cuban political leaders, Palmer observes that media outlets in the United States presented the latter as "deficient yet not feminine" in ways that foreclosed the possibility of them meeting "the expected, if ideal, standard of hegemonic masculinity." She adds that US news outlets described Cuba's political elite as "simultaneously (a) *hypermasculine*, that is, motivated by anger, violence or idealism and (b) *hypomasculine* or displaying inadequacies in either their professional efforts and/or their physical characteristics."[64] A similar process has played out in Tanzania's twentieth century. Both colonial and national authorities saw some promise in bubu and mtaani technological identities but still described the mechanics as hypomasculine because they had not learned or practiced in the formal spaces/institutions that marked sociotechnical change as legitimate or ideal. Simultaneously, at least three types of African technologists—mechanics, drivers, and oil traders—also appear as destructive and violent hypermasculine figures whose gendered technological identities have harmed their communities.[65]

Personifying technological misuse, the latter two social groups, drivers and oil traders, play central roles in narratives of modernization's failure during the 1970s.[66] As epidemiologists blamed the former for spreading HIV-1 through a motorized culture of sexual privilege, creating the nation's worst public health crisis of the independent period, oil-trading bureaucrats occupied a fraught location in analyses of economic downturn. Citizens and scholars alike suspected that the demise of state institutions resulted from ministers and bureaucrats using national resources to enhance their own status as powerful men by purchasing luxury items such as cars. Instead of investing in their own communities, they pursued a masculine status they did not deserve and could not achieve without using corrupt means that harmed others. In Palmer's language, this ineffective Tanzanian masculinity desired too much technological power (hypermasculinity) while not offering the national community enough in return (hypomasculinity). By answering such constructions of "ineffective men" with their opposite, effective men, I am not arguing that all African technologists who worked in ministries or with vehicles in bubu spaces were excellent at their jobs.[67]

Rather, effective technological masculinity means that for men to make claims on social mobility over their lifetimes, their knowledge, tools, spaces, bodies, and minds needed to work/function in a manner that allowed them to pursue gendered adulthood by gaining trust and followers.[68] The details of credibility vary in each occupation, of course. But throughout the century this book explores in the greatest detail, the 1900s, the aim of men remained consistent: to use access to motor vehicles and their accompanying infrastructure to attain social mobility or security. This is where effect and affect intersect: creating identities as mature men who could care for themselves and others rested on an ability to care for technological things through repair and maintenance.[69] African men not only accessed this dual form of care most easily in bubu and mtaani spaces but also considered it the best for creating gendered respectability at both home and work—in some cases, a redundant phrasing. As in Jennifer Hart's study of Ghanaian drivers, cars gave men opportunities to pursue a variety of ideas of manhood across ethnic, religious, and political lines, what she calls *plural masculinities*.[70] The technological basis of these plural and dynamic masculinities is what I call *effective manhood*. In most cases, the men in this book defined manhood through a "normative framework" of masculinity rooted in an ability to build houses and families, collect things and knowledge, and care for dependents, who then cared for them as they aged.[71] Owing to the density of automobiles in towns, this process often involved rural-to-urban migration. Interlocutors described it through two Kiswahili phrases: "to build life" (*kujenga maisha*) and "to search for blessing" (*kutafuta riziki*). Regardless of the phrase used, working gender required things that work.

This book's main contribution to gender scholarship comes in the *how*, *where*, and *what* of this work as it pertained to technological personhood. I have already referenced parts of the how and where through the significance of vernacular institutions located on street sides and at homes. Needless to say, men building lives did not stumble over the absence of certificates, degrees, or books in their pursuit of gendered adulthood. A big part of that comes from the what: the dense thinginess of their claims to both expertise and gendered personhood.[72] Men inhabited and built their lives around particular hard materialities of car use that provided the literal substance of their claims to expertise and social mobility. In part and scrap worlds like Taylor's garage, mechanics staked their reputations on the ability to turn used or broken parts into something new and functioning—even if just until its next repair or maintenance checkup. Scrap piles and the things that could be made out of them, in this sense, provided the literal stuff of a mechanical masculinity that could always be made and maintained (in the social sense) as long as there were enough broken things that needed to be, and could be, transformed.

Similarly, drivers and passengers built "risk cultures" around details of the surface conditions of roads and their inhabitants, whether spirits, cattle, or humans.[73] They also relied on the hardware of cars themselves. Distrusting colonial mechanisms of evaluation, African drivers hitched their reputation to the condition of the automobiles they drove. They felt a functioning car validated the care and skill of its driver in ways that colonial departments with racialized pay scales could or would not. This process, which distributed drivers' personhood onto a technological thing, was by no means unique. Citizens and leaders during the independent era linked new forms of community and personhood to the construction and maintenance of new built worlds. This included buses, regional trucking networks, and that building block of decolonization that made all of these things go: oil. In each case, different users and builders attached gendered ideals of themselves and others to specific parts of the material worlds they inhabited.[74]

In turn, these hard material things provide a technological lexicon of gendered work and creativity. *Modification, overhaul, short-* and *long-term fixes, experimentation,* and *maintenance* were uttered in oral histories and written in documents to reference some form of technological work. But they provide critical insights into gender history as well. Whether one was maintaining a car, an oil economy, or one's body while moving at rapid speed on roads, maintenance required forms of care, caution, and competence not associated with working-class Tanzanian masculinities at any point in the twentieth century.[75] Nevertheless, keeping things in working order—or getting them there—and maintaining or achieving a gendered respectability went hand in hand. The same goes for overhaul, modification, and experimentation. Both occur when something—and, generally, many things—break. Yet dysfunction, instead of a disappointing end point of failed modernizations, provided opportunities for users to redesign and remake not only built worlds but also themselves. As already noted, Jackson calls this productive and generative approach to maintenance or repair "broken world thinking."[76] In the following pages, it applies to gender as well.

Precisely because things broke in good and bad times alike, both men and women who labored to reconstitute technologies and networks also reshaped, and sometimes completely overhauled, what counted as respectable gendered personhood. As they built and repaired cars and systems, some made claims to expert knowledge that directly challenged dominant ideas about who could create or acquire useful automotive knowledge. Others used motorized mobilities to maintain their and their family's social standing in difficult economic times as poverty rates worsened. Taylor, who loved his job, shows that we should not reduce this process to socioeconomic need. Yet the following chapters demonstrate that technological repair, maintenance, and overhaul facilitated gendered mobility and security for those who described themselves as individuals lacking economic, social, or educational resources. There were, of course, limits to this gendered work. Because both colonial and national institutions considered car work men's labor, maintenance, repair, and care have largely been structured—and maintained—as masculine labor. This book highlights the way women challenged ideologies of immobility by taking to the roads as walkers, passengers, and drivers. But it also demonstrates that a masculine culture of repair and use has persisted—a form of social maintenance that excludes, structurally distancing much of Tanzania's population from reworking social and technological function since at least the early 1900s.[77]

For the third theme, related to the combination of austerity and material absence, *African Motors* shifts gears from locating agency to exploring the various forms of infrastructural constraint that accompanied automobility. Motor vehicles, though most often considered a tool of colonial industrial power, gained administrative popularity in the 1920s because they produced dry-weather mechanized mobilities on roads cleared by conscripted laborers whose work significantly reduced the government's infrastructural costs. Unlike railways, sometimes called "the permanent way," automobiles became a tool of empire because they operated on "temporary" infrastructure that Tanganyika's British government chose repeatedly not to make into all-weather roads (as chapter 1 shows in detail).[78] Important in their own right, decisions to not build also set the context for debates about the possibilities and limits of technological nation building after colonial rule. In contrast to the technological optimism and spectacle found in several varieties of Cold War modernization, Tanzania's nationalist leader, Julius Nyerere, approached infrastructural projects ambivalently. He understood that creating new economies and social services that were postcolonial in a literal sense—in that roads, bus systems, and oil economies produced a type of citizenship that did not exist during the colonial period—required the construction of technological systems and a commitment to their maintenance, both costly projects.[79]

Indeed, in 1962, just a year after independence, Nyerere tried to persuade Tanzanian citizens that they had not fully grasped the true nature of nation building. Arguing against an idea he cast as popular opinion, he said nation building was not a literal project in the construction of new built worlds. "To build a nation," Nyerere declared, "is not just a matter of producing tarmac roads. . . . To build a nation in the true sense, a task into which we must throw ourselves wholeheartedly, is to build the character of its people—of ourselves; to build an attitude of mind to enable us to live together with our fellow citizens of Tanganyika, and of the whole world, in mutual friendship and co-operation."[80] The absence of things, though noteworthy after his pivot toward character, did not stem from an antitechnological approach to development. Nyerere liked machines (and tarmac roads), linked oil refineries to self-reliance, and called for creativity with each.[81] I argue, instead, that Nyerere's unease about nation building–as–hardware cannot be fully understood without exploring what Noemi Tousignant calls the "problem of capacity."[82] Delivering new built worlds on a national scale after decades of colonial infrastructural austerity would have linked the nationalist project to an extremely costly, difficult, and likely long—at least longer than most expected—technological project.

I highlight these absences across temporal divides not only because they are found throughout colonial and independent archives but also because they shaped the possibilities and constraints of nation building in underappreciated ways.[83] For Nyerere and other political leaders, infrastructural absence in earlier periods meant that the decisions they made in the first decades of independence were connected to and hemmed in by administrative cultures of austerity from colonial rule even as they, African nationalists, hoped to make up for what was not previously constructed as part of a "civilizing mission." This positionality—thinking with and through absence—inverts foundational scholarship on the ways technology shapes society. In the history of technology, large technological systems such as electricity or automobile infrastructure gain social and political power—sometimes called *momentum*—through the huge number of material, economic, political, and social investments that allow them to work and become part of everyday life—in other words, through their presence.[84] Thomas Hughes describes these systems as "both socially constructed and society shaping." The latter part refers to the momentum that dense networks acquire after long periods of construction, maintenance, and use.[85]

African Motors explores a process in which decades of not building permanent infrastructure also gained momentum by shaping political imaginations and policies decades after decisions not to build had become a bureaucratic norm.[86] *Uhaba* ("scarcity"), *upungufu* ("shortage"), and *hamna* ("none"), three commonplace words for "absence," play a role in each chapter, sometimes even providing the foundation of creativity. But I explore the momentum of absence most thoroughly through the impact of the 1973 petroleum crisis on national oil economies and pursuits of technological self-reliance. I take seriously Nyerere's belief that an incredibly meager infrastructural "colonial inheritance" combined with the quadrupling of petroleum prices to narrow Tanzania's pursuit of technological sovereignty into a twelve-year period between 1961 and 1973. To be clear, I am not slamming the door on the possibilities of a postcolonial infrastructural sovereignty or linking the challenges of independence exclusively to historical processes that began in previous eras as underdevelopment theory once did. Historians have rightly pointed out that dependency theory robbed African actors of agency during the independent period by locating historical possibility in processes originating during the slave trade and the colonial period.[87]

Yet absences, as well as concerns about overcoming them, shaped actors' positionalities in important ways.[88] In addition to influencing Nyerere's definitions of "self-reliance" and African socialism, bridging technological gaps created during colonialism informed one of the most popular phrases of the early independent period. "We must run while others walk," or *mbioni* in Kiswahili—the locative of the noun for being in a race—emerged in the early 1960s as a rallying cry to literally build the nation in ways British and German colonial governments had not over eight decades. This infrastructural hurry came not only from a desire to deliver to citizens the promises of nationalist campaigns but also from fears that technological capacity and protection of sovereignty went hand in hand in a political context in which Rhodesia announced its Unilateral Declaration of Independence in 1965 and in which popular leaders such as Patrice Lumumba had been assassinated by world powers a few years earlier.[89] Moreover, and more to Nyerere's original point, tracing out absences and the processes through which leaders and technologists attempted to overcome them situates the imperatives that accompanied technological nation building as a project tied to oil and costly infrastructure—in other words, a form of automobility. Decades before John Urry wrote that "the car is simultaneously immensely flexible *and* wholly coercive," Nyerere had identified the hard limits of automobility as development.[90] He did so not just with cars but also with petroleum's place in "modern agriculture" for a predominantly rural society—an important and often overlooked component of automobility's machinic complex. I thus hope to provide a hard material (and technological) dimension to one of the departure points of Tanzanian history since the 1960s: that colonial rule's creation of dependent economies in East Africa shaped the form, debates, and tools of maintaining sovereignty in subsequent decades.[91]

I call the sum of these three themes material maendeleo, to emphasize the thinginess of *maendeleo*'s root and connected verbs—*kwenda* and *kuendelea*. Building on rich scholarship in African history and studies, I explore the social, cultural, and political dimensions of maendeleo with a specific focus on the way that everyday movements took on larger political meanings—or, as Anna Tsing observes, the possibility of spatial movement becoming political movement(s): "movement as mobility and mobilization."[92] But let me make a seemingly strange case for a more detailed technological approach to development histories. I say "strange" because an avalanche of scholarship on development theory and discourse—including the brilliant "postdevelopment" critiques of the topic that inspire this work—has used tech-based terms such as *technology*, *technocrats*, or *technicist* (hereafter aggregated as *tech-*) to make points about modernization and development. Much the way Antina von Schnitzler points out that apartheid was literally technopolitical—in that it was imagined and enacted through infrastructure—the pairing of *tech-* and development occurs so often as to be redundant and perhaps even alarming.[93] I appreciate the reasons this occurs: many writers have associated technology as a set of both tools and ideas—and successful use of it: the heart of this narrative—with the idea that midcentury forms of modernization from the Global North represented the highest form of social and economic life.

Yet little work on development has paid close attention to how tools, systems, and their users work, especially from African perspectives.[94] This "black boxing," an approach that minimizes both the social and material complexities of technological systems—which become "opaque to scrutiny from the political system"—not only stands in contrast to the centrality of technopolitics in development as both theory and practice but also forecloses alternative configurations of tools, knowledge, power, and well-being.[95] But if we take Mavhunga's approach to technology as ways of knowing, doing, and moving—a definition not tied to developmental histories linking powerful knowledge to specific places, times, and institutions—a different technological history of maendeleo emerges.[96] Instead of a *tech-* approach that leads to developmentalism or ignores situated actor perspectives, material maendeleo illustrates that Africans actively shaped the things and ideas of twentieth-century development, whether a car, an oil system, or a definition of an expert (*fundi stadi*/sana or *mtaalum*). In turn, their continual ability to put spaces, ideas, and things together differently alerts historians to alternative ideas about well-being. For instance, the opening chapters show not only that the material foundation of a vernacular machinic complex lay in walking paths but also that the incorporation of automobiles into life did not lead to mass car consumerism or a thorough motorization of African life.[97] Instead of incorporation— can Africans appropriate development and its tools?—this leads to a focus on how development has been done differently.[98]

There is not a single materiality or technology in the following chapters. We look at paths, dirt and mud, engines and bodies, piles of used parts, calloused hands that certified mechanical knowledge, systems of urban transport, oil and pipelines, and motoring landscapes composed of spirits and incredibly specific road conditions. In each instance, I do not use materiality as something distinct from the social, political, economic, and cultural but rather as a *method* for exploring processes that are simultaneously human centered—and thus dense with evidence for more traditional social and cultural histories of Africa[99]—and not those in which the details of technological systems and their hardware take center stage.[100]

The latter, what Timothy LeCain calls the "matter of history," should not be understood as a division between human and technological worlds.[101] Rather, Hughes's oft-cited phrase about large technological systems—that they are "socially constructed and society shaping"—applies to the range of materialities explored here. A key contribution of this book is to show that both social and technological shaping applied differently for garage work and urban transport—where things could be reworked into viable, even desirable, worlds of sociotechnical interaction—than in oil trading, whose hard limits I referenced earlier. I am intrigued by how some built worlds offered possibilities for decentralized groups of users to repair and remake systems—sometimes at quite large scales—whereas the dysfunction of others (again, oil carries most of this narrative) led politicians to think less about technological reconfiguration than the intransigence of historic global economic inequalities.[102]

Focusing on things, in this sense, goes beyond recognizing the limits of human agency or their distribution in technological systems (actants), as much scholarship in science and technology studies has shown. Methodologically, it helps unearth overlooked and othered built worlds and spaces of innovation and action, thus rooting histories of technology and development in local processes and epistemologies, what Donna Haraway calls "situated knowledges."[103] That, in turn, shifts the focus from the centralized and containerized top-down approaches to cognition that have informed much of the history of development as well as scholarship on infrastructure, as Chandra Mukerji observes. She makes the case for a "distributed cognition" and "distributed reasoning" in the construction of large technological projects. As I show in the following chapters, this distribution and its materiality not only matter to the details of mechanical function but also provide the foundation for writing social and cultural histories of technology and development through the "unaccountable intelligence," as Mukerji calls it, that was nevertheless critical to basic function.[104]

BUBU HISTORIES AND ARCHIVES: METHODS AND CHAPTER OUTLINE

Oral history and archival sources inform all six chapters of *African Motors*. In Tanzania I conducted over two hundred oral interviews in Kiswahili with men and women drivers, passengers, migrants, roadbuilders, and mechanics. I did not use a single approach to oral history in the following chapters because words related differently to interlocutors' perceptions of credibility depending on the technological action involved. Mechanics, though happy to talk at length about their life histories and creativity, generally mistrust words divorced from action or materiality. In the garage, "driver of words," an undesirable title, refers to a person who makes baseless claims about innovation without showing through action—or with material evidence—that they can do so.[105] Drivers and passengers who had mobilized contraband economies (*magendo*) in the 1970s, on the contrary, extended the verbal strategies they had used to pass through police checkpoints into the interview by openly lying about their involvement in extralegal activities in initial interviews before opening up about their involvement in subsequent meetings.[106] Given this variety, I include a methodological discussion in each chapter. When possible, I paired oral histories with the personal collections Karin Barber terms "tin trunk archives" and with historical demonstrations of past repair work that I video-recorded and pictured.[107] I also joined a bubu garage in Dar es Salaam as an apprentice in order to better understand the social and technological worlds of car repair.[108]

This combination of oral history, personal archives, and mechanical fieldwork moves the history of development beyond a focus on theory, discourse, and elites to the perspective of multiple types of African automobile users.[109] It also performs additional epistemological work regarding the politics of archives and technological agency. Neither colonial nor national archives provide much detail about car repair or driving because the colonial and national bureaucrats who created much of the documentary archive that historians read were often highly constrained technological actors themselves. In most cases, they could not repair their own vehicles and did not possess deep knowledge about regional trucking networks or urban infrastructure.[110] Composed of both people and things, bubu spaces like Taylor's garage thus offer the densest historical archives about the social and material details of technological work. In addition to providing sites of oral history, they offered built worlds composed of vehicles, parts, and roads—much of them absent from documentary evidence—that brought the words of oral history to life. Critical for social and technological historians alike, in this book, bubu archives shift focus from "the development apparatus"—or the official spaces and actors of development found in written documents and archives—to "archives that Africans themselves have produced" and the "alternative epistemologies" they contain.[111]

Bubu, I must stress, is neither completely hidden nor necessarily hard to find. In fact, its most common political use refers to widely agreed-upon social facts. *Miradi bubu*, what novelist Gabrielle Ruhumbika translates as "invisible projects" in his book of the same name, stood in for the transnational back channels that, many believed, allowed corrupt ministers and bureaucrats to gain personal wealth through public projects during the latter years of socialism, leading directly to its demise. For this reason, the term *miradi bubu* has become a staple in neoliberal accusations of corruption. In both cases, *bubu* refers to social truths that gain explanatory power precisely because something is not being said, shown, or advertised by those in positions of power—or, as Ruhumbika puts it, is being made invisible. In this sense, its usage by interlocutors in this book comes closer to "muted" than to "mute"; it comes from a choice to make things heard or not in specific political conditions or with specific political goals. In turn— and this is where we can pivot from invisible projects to bubu garages— bubu suggests that not all meaningful action speaks, speaks loudly, or even needs to speak to matter to those who already know. Bubu thus rarely turns up in the archive while also gesturing to deep bodies of knowledge, complex histories, and a multiplicity of places that do not advertise themselves yet provide plentiful historical material to reconstruct pasts.

I also draw on eleven different archives in the United Kingdom and Tanzania. In the United Kingdom, documents about road and vehicle experimentations in colonial Tanganyika provide critical insight into East Africa's unsung role in metropolitan car and road design, while collections from regional engineers and the district officers responsible for touring and building roads allow us to dismiss outright colonial ideologies of African technological backwardness from German and British officials' own experiences of vernacular infrastructural agency. In Tanzania I combined research at three branches of the Tanzania National Archives (Dar es Salaam, Dodoma, and Mwanza) and at Zanzibar's National Archive with materials found at former socialist parastatals. Questions at Usafiri Dar es Salaam, a national bus company that played a significant role in urban socialist modernization, yielded unarchived operational documents on the floor in an unused office, while requests at the TPDC led to an incredibly organized collection of documents about post-OPEC-crisis oil trading. I believe I am the first to see or write a history of the TPDC with this archive. In both cases, documents at parastatals open the black box of state labor to help us better understand the work lives of the bureaucrats whose actions became a focal point in discussions of postcolonial failure after the 1970s.[112]

Six thematic chapters move chronologically from the 1860s to 2015. Chapter 1 introduces readers to the main components of this book's machinic complex: cars, roads and paths, and African walkers and drivers. In addition to showing that colonial automobility relied overwhelmingly on vernacular ideas and labor, it provides the basis for the book's argument about cars as a tool of technopolitical austerity. The chapter concludes in cities where African drivers forged their own institutions of training and validation on street corners and loading docks. Extending this urban African culture of vehicle use, the second chapter provides an eighty-year history of car repair in these same cities and townships. Though colonial and, later, national officials aimed to create male African car experts who trained in and abided by European industrial standards, government and private garages nevertheless provided both the most, and the most accessible, opportunities for young African men to remake themselves and cars and to forge alternatives cultures of expertise. In addition to providing details about the men and cars overhauled in garages during both the colonial and national periods, this chapter explores what I call an *infrastructure of expertise*: the specific material worlds, embodiments, and accompanying pedagogies through which mechanics created, recognized, and validated expert knowledge even as they built cars and lives as men. Both chapters unearth materialities and built worlds that confound the discourse of incommensurability between Africans and automobiles explored earlier in this introduction.

A history of urban mobility in Dar es Salaam during the socialist period, chapter 3 narrows the book's focus to technologies of nation building and citizenship after independence. It illustrates that details about automobiles, including their types and condition, provided city residents evidence to engage their state over the nature of postcolonial and socialist citizenship in state-controlled newspapers. As the marquee infrastructural project of socialist urban modernization, the city's bus system expanded to create new mobilities in what planners and residents hoped would be a newly decolonized and socialist city space. When it struggled to meet demand, urbanites not only wrote about their frustrations with lost time, immobility, and mashed bodies trying to get a seat but also built an alternative that, despite its illegality, helped them fulfill state demands by becoming more efficient workers and more humane socialists, they argued. I call this back-and-forth discursive and material process *technological citizenship* and use it to establish the relationship between infrastructural repair and political repair. Chapter 4 extends technological citizenship to the link between refined petroleum and rural modernization. It moves the farthest away from the automobile to demonstrate that rural modernization did not offer a respite from automobility's infrastructure and from the need to refine and move large amounts of petroleum throughout the country. The chapter may seem out of place given not only its focus on oil and refining but also its jump from streets and garages to the world of bureaucrats.

Yet it provides a critical vantage point for assessing the intersection of infrastructure, energy, and pursuits of national-scale self-reliance from the 1960s through the mid-1980s. Arguments about economic contraction in the 1970s, including much of the "state failure" literature, rest on assumptions that a big, bloated state bureaucracy ruined postcolonial economies—and an otherwise clear path to economic sovereignty—by pursuing costly technological projects willy-nilly, enriching themselves instead of literally spreading the wealth to fellow citizens.[113] Yet these assessments relied on abstract evaluations of technology that minimized or completely ignored oil's articulations with rural modernization as well as the impact of global oil markets on petroleum-importing agriculturally based economies like Tanzania. This chapter, which ends with the state voicing its concerns about getting oil and other basic commodities to communities around the nation, sets the stage for chapter 5. A social and cultural history of postcolonial driving from the 1960s through the 1980s, this chapter uses oral histories to illustrate that both men and women created mobile lives on regional roads over decades in order to produce domestic, settled lives at home for their families. Such *motorized domesticities*, as I call them, required not only intimate knowledge of regional transport landscapes but also what drivers and passengers called a "cowardly" approach to motor mobilities.

More than sketching out a culture of independent motor travel, this chapter explores the economic turbulence of the late 1970s from the street level. As Tanzania's socialist state struggled to circulate oil and goods after the late 1970s, networks of truckers and passengers filled in. The state lumped most of these actions into categories of economic sabotage. But those who distributed salt, food, soap, and clothes made the case for the importance of their movement not just to families but to a larger socialist family that was struggling and that, they argued, could be remade through new forms of distribution. The conclusion, "Motoring Out of Time," shows that an African motoring age blossomed just as automobility, and "southern" automobility in particular, morphed from a national achievement reflecting technological maturity into a global threat. Through stories about terrorism, climate, and pollution, it weaves many of the accomplishments from the chapters into the international development discourses that pathologize the nation's motoring culture as an undesirable alternative to modernity. Building on the vernacular machinic complex sketched out here, I take on these disqualifications and argue that Tanzania's approach to maendeleo provides historical alternatives to the relationship between cars and societies.

This book covers about 150 years and much of what constitutes present-day Tanzania but does not have the space to cover many places, times, or themes equally or in as much depth as they deserve. I did not begin this journey aiming to take on this temporal or geographic scope but rather stumbled into such a framing by casting a wide net in the collection of archival and oral evidence. In doing so, I got happily stuck in places such as Morogoro and Tabora where I had not intended to spend much time but found deep interest among driver and mechanic communities in the project. The trade-off to this approach is incomplete regional representation. I have nevertheless tried to write a sort of interscalar history by moving between micro, mezzo, and macro scales to establish general patterns across space and time.

ONE

Walking to the Car

A Popular History of Mobility and Infrastructure

in Tanganyika, 1860s to 1960

THE SAFARI BWANAS, or "Lords of Travel," arrived on the streets of Dar es Salaam in 1953 to celebrate the coronation of Queen Elizabeth II (see figures 1.1 and 1.2). Coordinated by the Public Works Department (PWD) of the colonial government of Tanganyika, the float features the colonial government's first registered vehicle—GT 1, a 1923 two-ton Albion truck manufactured in Glasgow—and three white men dressed immaculately in white safari gear, accompanied by six African porters. The float provides a clear rupture with nineteenth-century stories of overland travel. In contrast to European men who were carried by porters, sometimes in *machela* (a cloth one lies in like a hammock, carried by at least two people), and who became sick and died, pictures show the "safari gentlemen" in complete control owing to the vehicle's autonomous movement—reading, lounging, and drinking whiskey in the truck's bed, with a "giant wooden sword in hand to ward off hostile tribesmen."[1] The porters, wearing cloth around their waists, follow GT 1 in a straight line. The first three carry oversized books on their heads, including *How to Build* and *The Laws of Tanganyika*.[2] The last three porters cart the "essentials of life" for touring colonial officials: whiskey, baked beans, and quinine. All of this follows a sign announcing "Hatari," or "Danger," and the year, 1925. A local newspaper

1.1–1.2 *The Public Works Department's representation of colonial automobility. "Africa through a Lens: Tanzania,"* CO 1069-160-66 *(left) and* CO 1069-160-74 *(right),* BNA, *London.*

described this year as a period of British rule "when men were men and Africa was very dark."[3]

The Albion's beams are not lit because it is daytime, but one can imagine the exhibition unfolding within the context of much of the travel writing about Africa published during the late nineteenth and early twentieth century: a "dark continent" pierced not by the metaphorical light of David Livingstone's three Cs—Christianity, commerce, and civilization—but literally by the front beams of a vehicle hastening Africa's material transformation through the movement of people and things.[4] The float thus offers a classic example of the role of travel writing in "producing 'the rest of the world'" as a primitive and helpless other, as Mary Louise Pratt writes.[5] It also visualizes what Michael Adas terms "machines as the measure of men"—a process in which societies that invented and manufactured technologies like automobiles began to see themselves as superior to those that had not.[6] Indeed, for many colonial officials, missionaries, and motoring enthusiasts, the contrast between wheeled and wheel-less societies provided a clear indication of the nature of technological change in Tanganyika and beyond. Those with knowledge and tools (and wheels!), the "Lords of Travel," would lead it and impose it with swords, if necessary, on those "hostile" to their mission. Africans participate in this change only as "superannuated" porters. Their presence, seemingly unnecessary for actual movement, nevertheless drives a colonial narrative of progress in which Africans follow a motor vehicle into a better future built by European know-how.[7]

But it was all a joke. According to the *Tanganyika Standard*, this "delightful piece of pure fun" helped the PWD win an award for creating one of the coronation's two most humorous floats. How did the presentation of complete social and technological order—as if officials had turned the streets of Dar es Salaam into a museum exhibition in London—become a farce and "pure fun"?[8] Why did the combination of road, car, and porter act as a confessional technology for the PWD to publicly admit its limited ability to turn hatari and "darkest Africa" into something else? Finally, how might African societies have interpreted the PWD's comedic take on colonial automobility given their critical role as porters and guides, pushers and pullers of vehicles, road builders, and government drivers?

This chapter answers these questions through two contrasting narratives of European and African mobilities. The first establishes the role of road, wheel, and car in European abolitionist and colonial interventions. It shows that cars became a tool of empire in the 1920s because they allowed administrators to produce mechanized movement without constructing or maintaining permanent road infrastructure—a phenomenon I call *the maintenance of impermanence.* To explore this process, the first half of this chapter centers the journeys through which administrators collected taxes, made maps, collected and composed "tribal" histories, installed and surveilled local leaders, made roads, and heard grievances, among other tasks. These, of course, are common topics in colonial archives and histories. But by centering the production of mobility behind these processes—the travel *in* the writing of the documents that now make up Tanganyika's colonial archive—I highlight European officials' reliance on the goodwill, ideas, and forced labor of African communities for their mobilities. In addition to revealing the complex worlds of movement into which cars entered in East Africa, this reliance inverts the sociotechnical model visualized above.

The second narrative, a popular history of walking and motoring, roots an African automobility that emerged during the colonial era in mobilities and built worlds that predated the car or European rule. By walking from rural to urban areas on indigenous infrastructure and newer colonial routes, labor migrants and traders produced the most visible form of autonomous movement in colonial archives—a mobile agency confirmed by oral histories as well. By the 1930s, migrants and traders, though not vehicle owners themselves, had become the largest group of technological actors to make the car and road a part of everyday life in the colony. The chapter ends with a microhistory of an African driving culture anchored in loading docks, street corners, and plantations—all destinations of labor migrants. In these spaces, manual laborers-turned-drivers created their own institutions of industrial training and competency. One of these drivers, Vincent Njovu, operated GT 1 before its starring role in the Safari Bwanas float and claimed the vehicle as "the love of his heart" in his biography, *Dereva wa Kwanza Tanganyika* (*The First Driver of Tanganyika*).[9] He offers just one example of the African car men who forged new forms of technological personhood through partnerships with colonial machines. If, from a colonial perspective, machine use provided a "measure" of a society's potential in colonial discourses of race, drivers demonstrate that these technological measures of humanity can be rejected and reworked with the very same technologies.

Before starting, we require a short note on the "ways" that serve as the proverbial stage for this history. The meanings of *path, track,* and *road* changed in colonial archives over the period covered in this chapter. Writers in the mid- to late 1800s used the terms interchangeably, but distinctions between roads and paths/tracks solidified following the introduction of wheeled carts, railways, and then automobiles. By the early 1900s, authors used *paths* and *tracks* to highlight infrastructure that worked poorly for wheels and motorized movement and to suggest that African infrastructure lagged behind Europe's. To avoid these colonial distinctions—and following Clapperton Mavhunga's use of the multiple meanings of the vaShona term *nzira* ("ways")—I use the Kiswahili word *njia*, to refer to "ways" as material and spatial routes of movement (one Kiswahili dictionary describes njia as "an area used for passing") as well as to its secondary use as "ways" of doing, deciding, and learning, or what Mavhunga terms "*nzira* as a site of creativity and work."[10] As the next section illustrates, such njia undercut a history of wheel, road, and *gari* (the most popular Kiswahili word for "automobile") that associates vernacular njia with slavery and technological weakness and thus views them as justifying European rule.[11]

CARAVANS, SLAVERY, AND GARI: HOW ROAD AND WHEEL BECAME HUMANITARIAN

From the 1860s, traveling Europeans described East Africa as a place whose societies did not have the tools or knowledge to help themselves. As Gabrielle Hecht demonstrates, assumptions about material absence in Africa played a critical role in inventions of the continent as a "primitive" place requiring "humanitarian" assistance from industrial European societies.[12] When it came to slavery in East Africa, however, abolitionists struggled to create clear distinctions between societies possessing useful things and those lacking them. In fact, abolitionists' entire justification for intervention—the ubiquity of slavery and its geographic growth into central Africa—rested on the presence of an impressive network of caravan njia spanning over a thousand miles from the Swahili coast to "the interior"— the latter an expanding sphere of enslavement and trade located to the west of Lakes Tanganyika and Nyasa.[13] "Slavery was not the major form of labor mobilization for caravans along the central routes," Stephen Rockel writes, emphasizing African men and women's ability to shape cultures of travel and exchange as they pursued social mobility through movement in the latter half of the 1800s.[14] But even though historians have found more nuanced descriptions of caravans and porters in European sources, caravan mobilities gained political visibility for their reputation as both "slave traffic" and "slave transit."[15] Given the difficulty of witnessing acts of capture many miles away in central Africa, European travelers cited caravans with slaves—slaves being transported to the coast or slaves who worked in caravans—as evidence of slavery's pervasiveness.[16]

David Livingstone, for example, cited bodies discarded on the sides of the southern caravan route north of the Ruvuma River as evidence of slavery's ubiquity. The accompanying picture (figure 1.3) shows a gun-toting porter dressed in coastal garb leading slaves along an earthen path flanked by tall grasses; with their necks fastened by "slave sticks," they are unable to outrun their captors. Shortly later, Livingstone writes, he encountered a caravan leader warning slaves against escaping by executing one of the captives and by leaving some to die on the side of a path.[17] Though some slaves are not bound, all are too weak to escape, clear evidence to readers that these individuals had not traveled to the coast of their own free will. Livingstone believed the violence he witnessed on this route had frightened other roadside communities, leading to depopulation over large stretches. He complained that this made securing food and water more difficult for his large retinue of porters.[18]

The notion that caravan infrastructure facilitated massive social upheaval rested on a contradictory evaluation of Tanganyika's built worlds of

SLAVERS REVENGING THEIR LOSSES.

1.3 An illustration of David Livingstone's description of slaving caravans. Notice the narrow path and the dress of those leading the caravan—styles which linked them to the coast and to European assertions that caravan mobilities stemmed almost entirely from the mobile activities of Araba merchants preying upon African communities in the "interior."

mobility. European travelers complained incessantly about caravan travel as they attempted to "open up" Africa. They blamed existing njia for their immobility, foul moods, ill health and the closing off of "the interior," the center of slave production, to humanitarian mobilities.[19] Yet the caravans of Swahili and Arab patricians produced enviable forms of movement using the same njia and porters. Travel writers granted Zanzibar-based slave trader Hamed bin Mohammed bin Juma bin Rajab el Murjebi (sometimes called Tippu Tip) the ability to cross great distances with enviable ease, even providing help to European travelers in the form of food, directions, and labor.[20] Frederick Lugard granted the same mobile agency to "Muscat Arabians," who "penetrated into the then totally unknown interior, and began that system of slave buying and slave catching which, until their advent, had never assumed such proportions on the East coast." Social decline followed, he asserted, as slaves adopted coastal ideas and languages and as concubinage created a mixed-race population.[21] Without mentioning caravan infrastructure, Lugard connected exogenous mobilities westward from the coast to mass enslavement and to ethnic and racial impurity. Several years later, James Christie, a physician researching the spread of cholera in Zanzibar, added the spread of disease to the pathology of caravan mobilities.[22]

In an 1889 publication, *Tropical Africa*, Henry Drummond provided a slightly different portrait by writing that the "true mode of native travel" predated European arrival and the intensification of slavery: "No explorer in forcing his passage through Africa has ever, for more than a few days at a time, been off some beaten track. Probably nowhere in the world, civilized or uncivilized, is better supplied with paths than this unmapped continent. Every village is connected with some other village, every tribe with the next tribe, every state with its neighbor, and therefore with all the rest."[23] Drummond noted routes' "persistent straightforwardness in general" and their hardness, having been beaten down under travelers' feet for "centuries"; even a path through an "almost uninhabited" region was "so beaten, and so recently beaten, by multitudes of human feet, that it could only represent some trunk route through the continent."[24]

Drummond wrote about existing built worlds without contradicting a technological tenet of humanitarian discourse: the effectiveness of paths "everywhere," and their use by slavers, required a robust technological intervention capable of replacing the economic and social networks that caravan infrastructures sustained. This is where the road and the wheel came in. Livingstone boasted to a slave-trading chief in southern Tanganyika "what the English would do in road-making in a fine country like this." Not far from the desolate landscape he describes above, Livingstone shared a vision in which "British" "roads" wide enough to carry carts pulled by animals provided a foundation for "railway, ships, plowing oxen."[25] Livingstone pitched European-style njia as a technological solution for not just ending slavery but repopulating and remaking African societies and landscapes ravaged by slavery. As wagons and their goods displaced walking-caravan economies, roads would relocate labor from head porterage and captivity to farming and trading communities located, ideally, in resettled villages along new thoroughfares.

This plan envisioned mass cultural transformation following the introduction of new mobilities and things. This included the ox plow, a tool to increase output in postslave economies, as well as a number of other heavy items whose circulation in African space had previously required huge teams of porters to move from coastal ports to westward regions, including organs, books, Bibles, glass bottles of drugs, food, clothes, equipment for industrial and domestic training and clinics, and, most of all, steamships to extend geographic influence across the lakes.[26] Finally, earthen roads provided the material foundation for future infrastructure, including telegraph lines and railroads.[27] By changing how and on what people and things moved in East Africa, abolitionists aimed to effect an astounding amount of social and economic change across the region. And thus the imperial language of "opening up" Africa did not come from closed Africa but from concerns about creating specific European-serving mobilities. Colonial sources concede that African societies already moved over distances long and short. But these njia did not facilitate the forms of European control that abolitionists, missionaries, or officials had in mind.[28]

The idea that wheels could transform African landscapes hit bumps immediately. Initially used on existing caravan routes, animal-drawn carts (gari) imported from South Africa and India got bogged down even as their animals—including oxen, camels, mules, and elephants—suffered, dying of thirst and starvation between caravan stations and of sleeping sickness from tsetse flies across large stretches of Tanganyika.[29] Undeterred, advocates of wheeled transport called for new road construction to circumvent slave routes and known tsetse fly areas—where pack animals died from sleeping sickness—and to provide food and water (and thus more comfortable travel) for new economies.[30] In 1875 the Imperial British East Africa Company and its Scottish financier, William Mackinnon, commenced the East Africa Road in Dar es Salaam with the hope of reaching Lake Nyasa six hundred miles away. After four years of work and nearly £15,000—and despite having the support of the sultan of Zanzibar, who both controlled overland trade routes and supplied laborers from nearby and from Aden—the project ended in 1879 with only seventy-three miles completed, 250 miles short of Lake Nyasa. The company's engineers blamed the "tropical" landscape for the slow pace of construction and the project's rising cost. They praised laborers for their ability to find economical traces for the road but complained about demands for higher wages, requests to stop work during harvests, and desertion.[31]

The road's failure prompted debates among European travelers in East Africa about the wheel and the road as humanitarian technologies. According to Joseph Thomson, who wrote two volumes about his travels in the early 1860s, proponents of wheeled transport harbored unrealistic expectations about infrastructural interventions. Agreeing that European-style njia "gave a distinct impetus to material advancements and helped on the work of civilization," Thomson wrote that boosters of rail and wagon mobilities underestimated the cost of these projects while overestimating their economic and social impact: a "road is not of the slightest value to a porter" or their communities. "The ordinary native pathway serves all [the porter's] purposes as well as any fine road that can be made." He concludes his two-volume travelogue by asking, "What better means of transport is there than that of the native porter?"[32] An unlikely contributor to imperial road debates, Thomson, a geologist from Scotland, joined the East Central African Expedition in 1878 with the hopes of finding the source of the Nile. When the expedition's leader died of illness a couple days into the journey, Thomson took charge of the caravan while admitting his inability to identify African built worlds, including the difference between "tropical jungle," "tall grass," and "matted bushes," on the one hand, and "beaten path," on the other.[33]

Openly conceding his reliance on African guides and porters to read this landscape—"the headman may practically do what he likes with his pupil"—Thomson felt that European mobilities within east-central Africa had created a "pitiable spectacle" in which "the European has been lowered immensely in the eyes of the native."[34] Because caravans, including his own, relied at least in part on slave labor, missions of "peace and goodwill" had merely brought more violence to a region where movement was already entangled with the very forms of coerced labor abolitionists aimed to end.[35] Thomson, who journeyed and wrote after the East African Road's demise, concluded his second volume with an ironic statement about infrastructural humanitarianism: "Not a station has yet been fixed which deserves the name, not a traveller assisted (the would-be helpers themselves require to be helped), and not a single desired object attained. Clearly," Thomson concludes in his discussion of roads, "Europe has found Africa a harder nut to crack than it expected."[36] After abolitionists met at the 1888 Brussels Conference, the 1890 *Slave Trade and Importation into Africa of Firearms, Ammunition, and Spirituous Liquors (The General Act of Brussels)* championed "construction of roads, and in particular of railways . . . with a view to substituting economical and rapid means of transportation for the present system of carriage by men" in Chapter 1, Article II, before dedicating the subsequent chapter to controlling and replacing "caravan" trade in Chapter 2.[37] But even as other enthusiasts of British colonialism linked European infrastructures of mobility to "good business for British trade" and to the spread of "British Civilization," across the continent caravans and their leaders continued to move on older routes in eastern Africa.[38] The aforementioned el Murjabi amassed much of his wealth at the height of enslavement in the Congo in the 1880s and 1890s, when European njia were supposed to have cut off caravan routes between central Africa and the coast by providing wheeled transport.[39]

The Kiswahili name for "automobile" (*gari*) first entered the regional vocabulary in this context. *Gari*, Hindi for "cart" and "vehicle," likely traveled with South Asian migrants who set up shops along new and old trade routes, using wheeled carts pulled by bullocks and donkeys (figure 1.4).[40] Later used by missionaries and German settlers after the formal onset of colonial rule, animal-drawn gari moved slowly along existing routes of travel, often with the assistance of guides and porters, and more easily along a handful of new German njia.[41] Geographically limited by njia that did not anticipate it and by the tsetse fly, which undercut European transport imaginaries, the term gari nevertheless worked its way into a vernacular transport lexicon.[42] Whereas in 1884 a Kiswahili English dictionary listed *gari* solely as meaning "carriage," another from 1902 translated "car" as both *gari dogo* ("small cart") and *gari la fahari* ("car of luxury"). Moreover, this dictionary lists "caravan" both as *msafara*—a common translation for "caravan"—and as "big car" (*gari kubwa*). The latter suggests that caravans both aided wheeled transport and sometimes filled in completely for wagons in an environment in which the German colonial government largely pursued a policy of widening, not replacing, caravan njia.[43] Next in line, the railway, which paralleled much of the main caravan route across the territory to Ujiji, took the name "cart of smoke" (*gari la moshi*).[44]

1.4 *Bullocks and carts, or gari, on a street in Dar es Salaam in the late 1890s or early 1900s. Image courtesy of the Melville J. Herskovits Library of African Studies Winterton Collection, Northwestern University. Dar es Salaam. Object 12-7. February 27, 2018. http://hdl. handle.net/2166.DL/inu-wint-12-7.*

The first written record of African communities calling the automobile *gari* occurred in 1907.[45] That vehicle, specially built with a raised chassis by the Süddeutsche Automobilfabrik Gaggenau GmbH (South German Automobile Factory of Gaggenau Ltd.) in Germany (still featured on Mercedes-Benz's website), arrived in Dar es Salaam to carry Paul Graetz from German East Africa across central Africa to German Southwest Africa.[46] A retired officer from the colony's military, Graetz supported railways and linked them directly to "civilization." But he believed it would take decades to expand rail networks—which touched less than 5 percent of the population—and he thus pitted motor vehicle against porter on the central caravan route.[47] Skeptics called the trip "impossible." Graetz responded by predicting that he would arrive in Tabora, nine hundred kilometers from the coast, in three days.[48] He claimed that the car, which he called the "mystery of Europe" (*rätsel au Europa*), inspired fear and awe among bystanders. In Dar es Salaam, he asked Africans "several times where the strength of the engine came from—from the gasoline or the water—I have only received the answer '*Sijui Bwana Kubwa, Kazi ya Wazungu*' ('I don't know, sir. The work of Europeans?').".[49] On the journey's second day, Graetz overtook a westward-bound caravan that had departed Bagamoyo, a coastal entrepôt, days earlier. Noting that the automobile had reduced travel time by 80 percent, the German claimed victory.[50]

Graetz and his "mystery" spent the remaining 820 kilometers in Tanganyika utterly reliant on caravans and local communities. The help was likely arranged by *Mzee* (a Kiswahili term for *elder*), the traveling party's cook who played an equally significant role repeatedly mobilizing assistance through language translation. Porters pulled the vehicle from rivers at least three times. After the first instance, a hundred Africans, likely requisitioned by German-appointed leaders, pushed the vehicle and carried its contents to the other side of the river and to the next town thirty kilometers away. The next crossing turned porters into the car's savior. As water flooded the engine, Graetz writes, "We were desperate for salvation when through the foliage of the trees we saw a long caravan coming down the valley, the heavenly help sent us": "brave Wanyamwezi" who pulled the car out of the river with ropes and straps.[51] Members of nearby communities also dislodged the vehicle from boulders, cleared brush in front of it, made bridges, and shared their drinking water when the car's radiator ran dry.[52] After running into tree stumps in tall grasses in Ugogo, Graetz "picked an old Mgogo" man to navigate the local landscape. Neither scared of nor mystified by the vehicle as Graetz anticipated, the man did "nothing more than to drive an automobile through Ugogo, he did the same regardless of the speed of his job, regardless of the sound of the engine, regardless of the impact of the car. He was sitting on the front seat, his long thin arm stretched far forward in the desired direction of travel."[53]

Even with this help, Graetz arrived in Tabora after nearly five months instead of three days. Then, on the last stretch of caravan infrastructure leading to Ujiji, the automobile gave out. Sixty men and a "caravan of water-bearing women" from a nearby community, the Wavinsa, made rope out of bark to pull the vehicle "horribly slowly, not half as fast as a pedestrian."[54] The trip from Dar es Salaam to Ujiji, a walking journey taking between five and seven weeks, took Graetz over five months.[55] Motoring over njia meant for walking, the motorist nevertheless blamed the "primal and majestic power" of the "tropical" environment for his late arrival. "The path," Graetz writes, "shows only traces of human activity. But the effect of nature is everywhere."[56] We take on this cliché about "tropical" roads later, but more important here is that European communities within German East Africa did not seem to care about the vehicle's loss to porterage. Still rattled by the Maji Maji Rebellion between 1905 and 1907, which spread on vernacular njia, a German miner in Morogoro whom Graetz took on his first car ride—"astonished at the progress of the old world"—remarked that "'such a carriage would probably be able to prevent an insurrection.'"[57]

The miner correctly identified the punitive nature of njia for wheeled transport during this period. Within a decade of Graetz's journey, the colony had short-distance roads that could be traversed by wheel and motor in some coastal areas and connecting dense sites of European settlement. One of these near Dar es Salaam received the nickname "Pokea Mwenzio," or "receive your partner." The invitation extended to complete strangers, Mrisho Sulemani Minchande told me. Travelers feared that visibility on this road could lead to forced labor—a fear borne out by an iconic picture of German roadbuilding in which chained women pound a road.[58] *Gari* entered Kiswahili's mobile lexicon through colonial efforts to save Africans from slavery by replacing caravan mobilities with European njia—ways of animal, rail, and car movement charged with power to transform social and economic ways. Yet, in the few places gari and European njia appeared, they owed their existence and function not to autonomous, self-generating movement contained in an engine driven by mysterious mechanisms but to human labor that was often coerced. Meanwhile, African guiding, porterage, and caravans remained the most reliable forms of transport in much of the colony in ways that profoundly shaped colonial motoring culture in subsequent decades.[59]

"MANPOWER REINFORCING HORSE-POWER": CARS, ROADS, AND THE MAINTENANCE OF IMPERMANENCE, 1919–1961

Twelve years after Graetz's journey, the League of Nations placed German East Africa under British rule as a mandate territory in order for it to receive "tutelage" from "advanced nations who by reason of their resources, their experience or their geographical position can best undertake this responsibility."[60] At this point, cars gained administrative importance for what they were not: porters or railways.[61] Porterage, in addition to its ties to slavery, played a huge role in World War I campaigns in Tanganyika. Though the war brought both the largest number ever of vehicles—including many Ford Model T's—and pack animals (with high rates of death), porters, who numbered nearly one million, still dominated mobilities for both

European armies in what Michael Pesek aptly calls "the war of legs."[62] Even as porters and other laborers in the British army also widened roads for troops and heavy equipment while pursuing German troops, motor transport units produced less reliable movement than existing options.[63] With huge desertion and death rates during the war, British officials also struggled to engage porters when the conflict ended. The government responded with conscription. In the first half of 1928, over half of the total days porters worked for the government came from conscripted labor.[64] Article 5, Section 3 of the League of Nations Mandate explicitly outlawed forced labor. But it allowed administrators to conscript porters for "essential public works and services and then only in return for adequate remuneration."[65] At £3 per ton-mile in the 1920s, porterage initially cost more than railways (two pence after construction) and feeder roads (one-sixth of a penny per mile). But rail rates rose—and varied by region—making porterage a cheaper, if not ideal, option.[66]

Additionally, railways offered a partial geographic answer to the challenges of replacing vernacular with colonial mobilities. After repairing the Central Railway Line in 1927, the British government extended the railway to Lake Victoria in 1928, and the line from Moshi arrived at Arusha in 1929, "freeing many thousands of natives from the former necessity for carrying their produce great distance to market."[67] However, even before a global recession took its toll in the early 1930s, officials doubted they could finance more construction, leaving almost everything south of the Central Line unreachable by regular motorized transport. Other administrators noted that rail carriage still required porterage.[68] "To bring down to railhead or to a lorry passable road 100 tons of produce a month over a distance of 100 miles, the work of two thousand men would be absorbed," one wrote.[69] With limited funds and a desire to reduce porterage, officials in both the United Kingdom and Tanganyika looked to automobiles to produce mechanized mobilities in areas "which until recently seemed likely to remain unexploited."[70] "Motor lorries in substitute of portery" became an official transport policy in the mid-1920s.[71]

Aside from porterage's link to slavery and its costs, automobile boosters believed motorized transport would create a more efficient "plantation industry" in the new British territory. A 1927 report described porterage as both "wasted energy" and "wasted labour" whose "abolition" would boost "native-grown crops."[72] "Carriage of produce on the heads of natives still subtracts valuable time from productive employment," the labor commissioner asserted in support of his belief that "too much has been spent on railways, too little on roads."[73] In addition to supporting motorized traffic, the government instructed officials to arrange denser settlements of the human population around new njia. Echoing Livingstone's statement from sixty years earlier, administrators linked this combination of population density, infrastructure, and new mobilities to an export cash crop economy and to a technologically driven process of social evolution in which more productive African farmers could adopt the tenets of "civilized" life by settling along new routes. Speaking to the Royal African Society in London, L. S. Amery, Secretary of State for Dominion Affairs and Colonies, and W. Ormsby-Gore, Under Secretary of State for the Colonies, asserted that a "native may ride in a railway train, but it never occurs to him to construct one; but when the native becomes the owner of a motor-car he realizes that the whole value of that car to him depends on the existence of roads."[74] Here a car's ability to move over a variety of locally made njia presented a situation unthinkable with trains: car ownership among Africans would spur economic activity while also releasing the administration from the costly infrastructural requirements regular motoring necessitated.[75]

Instead of producing freedom from forced work, British colonial automobility rested on officials' power to regularly throw colonial subjects into road construction, maintenance, and roadside assistance. When Governor Donald Cameron visited the southwestern regions of the colony in 1925 in "very ancient, old pre-war Buicks," the trip required "hundreds of tribesmen" to push the governor's vehicle through the Igali Pass toward Tukuyu. One "domestic servant" estimated that local communities pushed the governor's convoy 480 kilometers. This constituted a quarter of the party's 1,600-kilometer journey, much of which ran through hilly terrain.[76] District and provincial officers' personal papers tell a similar story. In the early 1920s, most government safaris—safari was an official government term appropriated from Kiswahili and officials submitted official safari diaries—occurred on foot with "long lines of porters strung out" to carry equipment and to guide the trip; the number of porters generally depended on the amount of luggage.[77] Newly arrived or transferring officers, especially those with families, required hundreds of porters to relocate their personal belongings.[78] After crossing the colony on the central railway, ninety-nine porters carried Joe and Cicely Harris and their luggage—which included a two-and-a-half-year supply of canned food—about five hundred kilometers from Kigoma to Sumbawanga.[79]

Tax collection, a more common occurrence, took between 2,200 and 5,000 porters in the 1940s.[80]

Annual administrative mobilities—whose occurrence created many of the documents in colonial archives—used, and often combined, all forms of mobility, including walking, cycling (with bikes sometimes tied to the side of a car for other parts of a journey), motorized movements on trains and motor vehicles, and water vessels.[81] This movement generally occurred over the seven-month dry season, and thus began with the repair of "waterlogged" njia by wage and conscripted labor, as shown later.[82] Donald Barton, the district officer (DO) of Dodoma, writes that a three-ton Native Authorities truck transported "domestic impedimenta and a forty-four gallon drum of water" to Farkwa. "On arrival we unloaded and the driver departed; he would return to pick us up on Saturday morning."[83] Local administrative staff then arranged a walking safari, including porters drawn from individuals who had defaulted on their taxes. Edward Lumley, a DO in Kigoma, felt these walking tours allowed officials to better know their districts. But he, too, traveled on a motorcycle with his "servant sitting pillion" in order to cover more ground even as porters hauled loads to the nightly camp.[84] Lumley also thought the vehicle elevated his status. "It was the first internal combustion vehicle that the Waha had ever seen, and while it initially aroused their curiosity it did not make them gasp with wonder. They just shrugged their shoulders and said 'white man's magic!' This explained everything. There was nothing to be amazed at, the white man could do anything."[85]

When Lumley traded his motorcycle for a used sedan, he told a very different story about technology and power. Motoring over rough roads "with the aid of villages on the way, *manpower reinforcing horsepower*, I managed to get the Standard through to Malagarasi" (emphasis mine). At a river of the same name, the car sank when a raft made of canoes sprang a leak. Lumley returned to his station by foot, a journey of two days, thinking his Standard would stay at the bottom of the river for "a long time." He was wrong: "It happened that some Waha living near the river, skilled swimmers, had by a fantastic feat of diving into twenty feet of water brought the car ashore by means of ropes made of tree bark tied to the front axle. . . . The technique employed was to sink upright poles into the bed of the river close to the front wheels. They shinned down these poles with the ropes in their teeth and tied them to the axle."[86]

Lumley developed a hernia in his groin from the walk home, forcing him to seek immediate medical attention in Mwanza. "As I was now unable to walk any distance and my Standard was out of action it was decided that I would sit in the car *and be drawn by a team of Africans*" (emphasis mine) eighty kilometers to Mwanza with the car in neutral. He placed "as many of my loads as possible" in the car, and the pulling commenced toward Biharamulo over "non-existent roads." The "team" also had to build a bridge en route by cutting trees and placing them across the water. In Mwanza, mechanics and a doctor repaired both Lumley and his vehicle.[87] Lumley's *Forgotten Mandate* continues without any reflection on his decision to use these individuals as the equivalent of a team of draft animals. Perhaps this silence stemmed from the regularity with which African laborers salvaged—and, at times, constituted—colonial automobility. A. H. Savile, a DO in Handeni, recalled a colleague, John Ransome, who required communities in his district to come "with alacrity" when they heard four successive gunshots. He fired these shots anytime his car became stuck. Savile witnessed John do so when their car became stuck in an "uninhabited" area. They then sipped whiskey while waiting for men to push them out of the bog. Savile then remarked, "I think you will agree that was an example of what can happen in a well-administered district." John died years later, Savile notes, from a heart attack he suffered while pushing his vehicle out of the mud.[88] One could spend weeks at Oxford reading similar stories.

Porterage thus persisted in the 1900s not in spite of automobiles but because of the limiting dry seasonal and spatial technological intervention that rails, roads, and cars produced. In addition to supplementing new motorized technologies such as railways by bringing goods to and from stations, porters mobilized transport economies and basic administrative tasks in areas without motorable njia (most areas distant from the coast) and throughout Tanganyika after rainy seasons.[89] In 1927, the government used 32,678 porters (13,300 conscripted) before a steady increase brought the numbers to nearly 49,000 (21,000 conscripted) in 1929 and 60,000 (22,000 conscripted) in 1930. Published numbers disappeared when the department temporarily closed during the Depression. In the 1940s, annual "requisitioned" porters ranged from 3,800 to over 11,000. While these numbers track with increases in motor traffic during and after the war, reductions in porterage were likely balanced out by increases in African road labor (which we explore in the following).[90] For at least the 1920s and 1930s, porter conscription was both common and highly unpopular, but some African men created labor regimes around this persistent need for hauling and guiding that recall Rockel's description of porters as "professionals." Savile described his porters as "an elite body of men who were always on call and never did any other work, such as the maintenance of roads and buildings, etc."[91] Such "voluntary" porters also pursued designated tasks within the caravan—whether guiding or carrying a specific load—and they set limits on daily mileage. Knowing their importance for the DO's every move, Savile records that the porters joined the chef, a talented ventriloquist, in mocking the DO through impromptu plays at daily camps.[92]

There is no doubt railways and automobiles fundamentally altered the porterage of the late 1800s by pushing much of that labor to new forms and sites of work (such as coastal plantations, as Sunseri details), but key elements of porterage persisted due both to the needs of newer transport systems, their limited geographic reach and seasonality, and because of the efficacy and desirability of historic forms of movement.[93] Notes about speed and time in administrative documents speak to this continuity. While on some stretches of njia, especially near larger towns, cars sustained speeds of 25 miles per hour, this appears seasonal, and motor movements also fell to similar, and sometimes lower, daily average speeds, and thus overall distance, than walking. Walkers, both officers and porters, regularly went twenty to thirty miles per day, A. H. Savile wrote. Car travel seems to have averaged six to ten miles per hour if they did not encounter a major obstacle—as Lumley records for a twenty-hour trip from Kilwa to Lindi—which likely halved the walking time but only because African "servants" dug multiple "diversions into the forest that ran along our route."[94] It seems such speeds were achieved without heavy baggage—and thus, "light" instead of "heavy" traffic—which was often carried by porters.[95] Of course, the same engines that, in Lumley's case, worked through the night in ways porters usually did not, caused much longer delays when they broke down or met obstacles such as ravines, high grasses, mud, or waterways that porters traversed more easily. In such cases, motor transport moved more slowly than walkers and increased reliance upon African labor.[96]

Some officials blamed this situation on the colony's roads, citing the difficulty and cost of creating all-weather surfaces in "tropical" climates as well as the lack of haulage alternatives, such as pack animals, owing to tsetse flies. Many bridges, too, were seasonal and washed away with heavy rain.[97] Yet regional engineers and district officers understood seasonal infrastructure not as an insurmountable tropical outcome but largely as an administrative decision rooted in two policies. First, "railway preference" forbade the construction of motorable roads that challenged the railway's monopoly on haulage. This meant njia running parallel to tracks did not receive classification—they needed to feed, not compete with, the rails—while nonrail carriage and goods licenses were restricted to places without "the permanent way."[98] As Walter Rodney observes in *How Europe Underdeveloped Africa*, Tanganyika's colonial governments funded transport schemes oriented toward export while providing "minimum investment"—and counting on human labor—to shore up internal trades that received little capital.[99] When African drivers fueled one such trade, as we see later on, the government narrowed definitions of goods and passenger "carriage" in an attempt to redirect energy and revenues back to the railway even though car transport was no doubt possible and growing from the late 1920s. However, the flexible nature of car-based mobilities facilitated African initiatives in ways that challenged the transport monopolies Tanganyika's colony economy relied on.[100]

Second, engineers in Tanganyika published successful soil-stabilization experiments in the *Journal of the Institute of Civil Engineering*. Instead of blaming "tropical Africa," they identified an unwillingness to pay for construction and maintenance as the main deterrent to all weather and heavy haulage car-based mobilities. Each mile of J. Lynch's road experiment cost £3,000, with an additional £300 per mile for maintenance each year. By the mid 1950s, estimates commonly reached above £5,000 as the administration prioritized "high standard on a limited mileage," a policy that saw average cost per mile reach £18,000 between 1950 and 1955.[101] Lynch added that reoccurring annual maintenance—and maintenance alone—could make a "good all-weather road" for £100 to £200 per year per mile, before noting that the government spent, at most, an average of £20 per mile on roads through the end of the 1940s.[102] DO Lumley put this figure at £2.[103] Either way, the average almost certainly did not cover the transport of all-weather material to construction sites with heavy equipment or human labor, a costly part of building and maintenance that left officials using materials located closer to a work site that were less suitable for soil stabilization.[104] Administrative documents do not hide the government's decision to pursue road impermanence. A PWD circular from 1933 stated that the global depression forced the "government to economize in every possible way."[105] The department considered construction unlikely, adding that "maintenance of roads, bridges, and buildings has been kept at the lowest possible figure."[106]

Anticipating denials for their funding requests, engineers and DOs focused on what they could do *without* financial support.[107] The 1933 circular directed regional engineers and DOs to arrange camps along categorized roads for permanent "gangs" to perform what the PWD called "stitch-in-time" maintenance. "Stitch-in-time" requested that road laborers respond to a district's immediate needs after heavy rains, for harvests, for administrative tours, or for official government visits. As the name suggests, officials considered this patchwork repair done cheaply with local resources; transporting rocks or soil for long-term road stabilization was out of the question. In 1937 the PWD published new regulations dividing responsibilities between two types of "headmen." The "traveling headman" took directions from the European road foreman and relayed them to "gangs" over a fifty- to sixty-mile stretch of road. He also inspected each group's progress, made sure they accomplished a "fair day's work," and walked over each route monthly. The "section headman" oversaw ten miles of road, ensured that gangs dug gravel pits for resurfacing at least twenty-five paces from the road, and had to "try and prevent native cultivation on the land from coming too near the road."[108] As one of the few PWD policies translated into Kiswahili, these directions turned the maintenance of impermanence into a technical problem for African headmen and their laborers to address through a "fair day's work."[109]

The DOs took notice of this delegation, too. The district commissioner of Kigoma complained in 1942 that "stitch-in-time" turned recurrent maintenance work into the "prime cost of the road" while leaving administrators completely reliant on African maintenance labor for their district's mobility.[110] Administrative officers had an official name for this process: "field engineering." A common practice in the battlefield, an officer in the King's African Rifles in Tanganyika defined it as the construction of "bridges, culverts, etc." from "materials and tools likely to be available in the bush on safari or in the field."[111] For example, when communities asked DO Darrell Bates to build a road, the government denied his request. Bates constructed a road "on the cheap" by reallocating funds marked for "Repairs to Typewriters" and "Latrines and Washhouses" and by using materials found nearby. His foreman, Ali, made the road trace and, with the help of two "talented masons" conscripted from the district jail, built bridges by placing timber on "old girders and spare rails" found alongside the railway. Rollers made out of "empty cement barrels, filled with soil," smoothed aggregate—a free gift from Bates's friend at the railway—into a "mud free" road.[112] Frank Longland, a longtime administrative officer, published a variety of such techniques in the government press's eventual best seller, *Field Engineering: A Handbook on Simple Construction*—later included in colonial officer training at Oxford University.[113]

More than improvisation induced by austerity, DO experiences of field engineering relied on—and seemingly *counted* on—African knowledge of landscapes. In *Forgotten Mandate*, Lumley praises "the African's . . . wonderful sense of locality." When surveying a road near Burundi, he credited Africans with the ability to "identify its exact course on the ground when we crossed the river to survey the escarpment."[114] On the same project, Lumley used elephant tracks on a hill to create a trace for motor vehicles. "His tracks give you easy grades cause he avoids steepness in his travels and his routes never exceed a grade of about one in sixteen, and this is the grade at which I was aiming."[115] When updating an old German road survey to build a road for tsetse fly relocations, Tlawi, another of Bates's assistants, threw a stone at a pack of buffalo to "see them run"—offering a possible route for the road's trace.[116] The same applied to some river crossings as local water vessels, often with planks placed over them, served as vehicle ferries.[117] Yet African knowledge alone was not enough.

Because the League of Nations considered roads part of "essential public works and services," the mandate allowed DOs like Bates—who used two hundred men for the above project—to conscript labor for maintenance and construction.[118] They did so under the Native Authority Ordinance and section 9 of the Hut and Poll Tax Ordinance: "Forced labor may be exacted from persons who have not paid their hut or poll tax and who have not, in the opinion of the collector, taken reasonable steps to procure the means of payment."[119] Men and women who defaulted on taxes worked at makeshift road camps for up to forty days. The same ordinances gave district officers and their staff discretion to cancel taxes in case of a famine or familial hardship or to accept barter in lieu of cash payment. But some admitted they did not. "I must confess," Lumley writes, "that I did not press defaulters for their tax" because "without this tax labour I could not have undertaken the construction of a road of this length, for the district vote would never have run to it." "Government was always stingy with money for roads," and without default labor "our problems would have been almost insoluble."[120] Thus, in the late 1920s, 80 percent of Biharamulo's road and bridge construction and maintenance used default labor. In this northwestern part of the colony, some officers also used "unpaid communal labor"—in which they offered beer and beef instead of payment—through the late 1930s.[121] Knowing communities disliked it, officials said it created an "economic equilibrium" for districts during the depression.

On a territory-wide scale, PWD officials estimated a need for seventeen thousand laborers annually to keep roads passable at "basic sufficiency."

They also complained that fewer laborers came forth each decade.[122] It is not hard to understand why. In addition to taking time needed to work on plots after the rains, road labor was strenuous—requiring digging and haulage of heavy material—and occurred, officials admitted, in remote places few wanted to go, let alone stay for several weeks.[123] If many district and provincial administrators used conscripted labor, not all agreed with its role in the territory's infrastructural economy. In addition to taking "away from the labourer all incentive" to work for a wage—the very justification for replacing porterage with mechanized transport—DO Philip Harley argued that "forced labour to 'keep them up' have reduced [roads] for the most part—nay, one and all, to mere tracks. They represent the sum total of 'our necessity for conscripted labour.'"[124] Or as Lumley put it, "no amount of repair work could have a lasting effect."[125]

Several individuals I interviewed held similar views about roadwork. Musa Mlenga, born east of Iringa in 1919, recalled being "forced" (*kulazimishwa*) to do roadwork at least once a year, usually after heavy rains.[126] Saidi Rashidi Matei of Ruaha Mbuyuni added that "if you want to go get water you have to ask; if you're late, they cut money."[127] Though Matei, like several others, recalled payment of up to ten shillings, "the road did not help anything" because there were "few cars" and "we all went by foot"—a charge that officials had created a disciplinary regime around an inappropriate technology.[128] Men and women interviewed in Chogo village near Handeni raised a similar point by noting that, far from making their lives better, roadwork made up one part of a disciplinary regime built around "the period of taxes" (*wakati wa kodi*). In addition to tax collection and possible roadwork, villagers who did not have colonial-style pit latrines were forced to dig one. When men were not home during "the period of taxes," Mahija Hamza Chagga recalled, women stood in for them for both latrine digging and roadwork.[129]

Interviews regularly came back to the pointlessness of this technological labor. In a rural area about sixty miles east of Iringa, one woman underscored what these seasonal njia did *not* bring: goods she could purchase through circulating markets. "My clothes were like rope," she recalled, suggesting that "temporary" infrastructure did not bring a commodity economy that made earning wages worthwhile.[130] Women near Handeni talked about roadwork as just one of two forms of forced labor by recalling a song about carrying their district officer—"The big man, we got him, we got him" ("Bwana mkubwa tunae tunae"). Because "that *mzungu* did not have a car, if you were caught [not paying taxes], you had to help carry him to the next village," Chagga said. She called these unfortunate people "his gari." Halima Bakari Mkomwa, who repaired the road for a governor's safari, used a similar phrase to describe those who carried his luggage. "Their [colonial officials'] cars were people" ("magari yale ni watu")—a literal example of delegatory process captured by the phrase "people as infrastructure."[131] Almost the entire burden fell on rural communities. Though most car use occurred in urban areas, administrative motoring, tax collection, and trade required huge amounts of labor at least once a year from rural communities.

Fearing the League of Nations could use the absence of permanent road construction to question Tanganyika's progress as a mandate territory, the government openly justified infrastructural impermanence. A 1945 report, "Road Policy in Tanganyika," used comparisons to two industrialized societies, the United States and Queensland, to assert that social and economic progress did not require costly infrastructural investment. "It should be noted," J. R. Farquharson argued, "that in USA, the most highly motorized nation in the world, earth roads still constitute almost 60% of the public highways." Farquharson's analysis contradicted his own data, as the statistics on dirt roads in table 1.1 demonstrate.[132] Table 1.2 shows the late, but small, increase in bituminized road before independence in December 1961.[133] In a special independence-day issue, the *Tanganyika Standard* advised new leaders of the direct link between development and transport—an axiom of postwar modernization theory—calling on the new nation to improve its famously bad road networks.[134] Yet this call— which asked a sovereign African government to do what two colonial governments had not—missed the attractiveness of colonial automobility as an "imperial formation" that assumed and pursued impermanence— an infrastructural process akin to what Ann Laura Stoler calls "states of deferral."[135]

The point is not that bituminized motorable roads are an objective good but that maintaining infrastructural impermanence over decades necessitated and created a "technopolitical regime."[136] Hecht defines this as "shorthand for the tight relationship among institutions, the people who run them, their guiding myths and ideologies, the artifacts they produce, and the technopolitics they pursue."[137] Keeping impermanent njia passable in Tanganyika required legislation that sanctioned conscription and default labor in the name of a "public good" and careful, albeit contradictory, distinctions between porterage as slavery requiring "abolition" and porterage as labor to salvage colonial mobility. It necessitated memos to

TABLE 1.1 J. R. Farquharson's Road Comparison

Type of road	USA (total miles)	USA (% of total)	Queensland (total miles)	Queensland (% of total)	Tanganyika (total miles)	Tanganyika (% of total)
Concrete or blocks	112,000	3.8	43	–	0	–
Bituminous	335,000	11.3	1,440	1.2	60	0.4
Gravel and stone	774,000	26.1	3,708	3.9	1,600	10.0
Soil-surfaced and formed	760,000	25.0	32,000	26.0	14,000	89.6
Unimproved	984,000	33.0	81,000	68.0	14,000	89.0

SOURCE: "Memorandum by JR Farquharson on Road Policy in Tanganyika Territory," MC/106, "Road Policy in Tanganyika by Mr JR Farquharson, OBE," TNA.

care for default labor (so that bodies could be conscripted again after the next rains), technical guides such as Longland's *Field Engineering*, PWD memos that aligned maintenance routines with the colony's austere technopolitics, and a "guiding myth" that said Africa resisted technological change. It joined the annual rituals of administrative power to dry weather mobilities, ultimately binding the end of the long rains around May to conscripted road work, tax collection, and the visibility of touring administrative officers. Finally, this regime required a technology of what Sara Barry terms "hegemony on a shoestring": a vehicle that worked well enough when combined with African labor and seasonal njia.[138] When lorry tonnage increased from 10,297 tons per year in 1921, to over 15,500 in 1925 and to over 30,000 tons in 1930, the PWD argued that it was doing its job to remake Africans' material worlds.[139] With most administrative movement occurring during the dry season—and with huge amounts of labor required to turn njia into passable condition for motoring—cars thus produced a different "sense of power" from what Brian Larkin calls a "colonial sublime" in his historical ethnography of infrastructure in Nigeria. "One intent of infrastructural technologies in colonial rule was to provoke feelings of the sublime not through the grandeur of nature but through

TABLE 1.2 Road Statistics: 1925 to 1960 (in miles)

	Main road	A class	B class (earth roads)	C class (native tracks)	Total metaled	Total earth roads	Roads passable for light motor vehicles during dry season
1925	NA	62	5,187	5,013	62		
1930	2,552	757	9,153	3,770	84	16,435	13,187
1935	2,649	985	9,890	6,807	86	20,539	17,184
1945	2,932	2,280	10,724	7,053	NA	NA	NA
1948	2,958	2,472	10,687	8,321	NA	NA	
1950	3,039	3,055	10,493	NA	NA	NA	NA
1960	3,774	5,176	10,833	NA	NA	NA	NA

SOURCE: Rolf Hofmeier, *Transport and Economic Development in Tanzania: With Particular Reference to Roads and Road Transport* (Munich: Weltforum, 1973), 323.

NOTE: Most A-class and main roads were not all-weather and thus unsuitable for heavy traffic. "NA" indicates "not applicable."

the work of humankind" in projects that showed mastery over nature.[140] Similar aspirations exist in some colonial documents, but few administrative actors on the ground saw a subliminal horizon; indeed, Bates, after opening a road trace intended to entice villages away from tsetse fly areas, concluded, "I tried to imagine it dotted with thatched huts and cattle and spirals of blue domestic smoke. But I couldn't."[141] This thread of not building, but rather maintaining impermanence, continues in chapter 4 through the anxieties national politicians felt in having to make up for the lost time of an unhelpful colonial "inheritance." Given these details, it is certainly no wonder Tanzanian economist Justinian Rweyemamu, writing about a decade after the end of British rule, coined the phrase "perverse capitalist industrial development model" in 1973 to describe historical situations "unlikely to lead [ex–colonial countries] to the self-generating and self-sustaining stage of development" cited in many Northern economic models.[142] For now, engaging the proverbial clutch, we switch gears from officials' struggle to move or to envision new infrastructural horizons to the vernacular njia that made the car an African technology by the end of colonial rule.

THE IRONIES OF AUTONOMOUS MOVEMENT: MIGRANTS, JOYRIDERS, AND VERNACULAR BUILT WORLDS

This second safari narrative explores a historical process I call *walking to the car*. It starts with the thousands of labor migrants who walked, and sometimes rode, between worksites and homes, before ending with a microhistory of an African driving culture forged in urban street spaces shaped by these very migrancy networks. Most of the tens of thousands of traveling laborers—forty-five thousand in 1937—did not become government drivers. It appears that no more than a couple thousand Africans did so during the interwar period. World War II changed that. In addition to forcibly conscripting African drivers and their assistants—leading to 9,460 licensed drivers by 1946—the war put pressure on the colonial government to improve its main highways and left thousands of used vehicles for private and government use.[143] By this time, however, drivers and migrants had already created large-scale cultures of movement within and across colonial borders, a form of what Clapperton Mavhunga calls "mobility as creative work."[144] Mobile creativity at this scale certainly contradicts stereotypes about African immobility, what James Ferguson calls the "myth of permanence." Here it also situates migrants as technological actors who held real, albeit unexpected, amounts of infrastructural power in the colony. "Whatever the causes," Ferguson writes, "the high level of spatial mobility of Africans has often confounded modern colonial and post-colonial apparatuses of knowledge, bound as they generally have been to modern Western assumptions about the use and political control of space."[145]

In Tanganyika, evidence suggests that "the causes" stemmed from the robustness and varieties of existing built worlds—including the mobilities they facilitated—and their continued strength and relevance after the introduction of motorized transport.[146] When the aforementioned Governor Cameron opened a railway extension to Lake Victoria, including feeder roads for farmers to transport their crops to stations, he said the project gave communities "more time to cultivate [their] fields instead of walking long distances to a market." He exhorted the audience to "grow more cotton, more groundnuts, more sim-sim, so that the construction of the railway and the roads may be justified." A "typical peasant" responded, "'We know all that, we realize it; what we want from you is not words but rain in due season.'"[147] The response—which clearly stuck with Cameron—recalls Steven Feierman's work on the centrality of rain to power in northwestern Tanzania and Todd Sanders's study of rainmaking in the region Cameron visited. Rain movements, and a community's ability to mobilize them, created social health and political legitimacy, what Sanders describes as "acting upon the world in order to changed it"—or what Mavhunga calls "hydrological mobility." The exchange also reveals that cars and trains came into existing modalities of movement capable of combining old and new—and that, far from finding them mysterious, Africans made sense of them quickly.[148]

This vignette only scratches the surface of the myriad mobilities in East African history. The banana, an Asian crop, arrived in the lakes region in the first century AD, followed by beads two centuries later.[149] Before nineteenth-century caravan trade, marketplaces facilitated exchanges of iron, salt, food, knowledge, and other items among neighboring communities and chiefdoms.[150] As long-distance caravans emerged, communities along main routes created sociotechnical systems to maximize benefits through tribute; promoted stability through *utani*, or joking relationships based on familiarity, which created reciprocity among groups where antagonisms might arise; and shared in overlapping forms of urbanization across three hundred miles.[151] During German rule, the Maji Maji Rebellion occurred on njia small and large, spreading across almost half of the colony.[152] Several years earlier, the Hehe chief Mkwawa defeated German troops by leading them along a dead-end njia meant for one purpose: ambush. The Swahili author Mtoro bin Mwinyi Bakari described detailed cultures of mobility in which travelers read landscapes and animals around them as good or bad omens for a journey and sometimes placed offerings at crossroads before departing. Doing so stemmed from mobility's link to enrichment and maturation ("Go abroad so that you may have experience") and to risk ("The foot that travels always gets bit").[153]

With this thick sociotechnical landscape in mind, the rest of this chapter explores pre- and postcar vernacular articulations of movement and infrastructure. Though we shortly arrive at the towns and peri-urban areas where automobiles became a core part of African street life, doing so too quickly risks diminishing a technopolitical threat that haunts large sections of the colonial archive: long-distance African walking. Historians have shown that colonial authorities turned their attention to the mobilities of labor migrants because colonial economies relied on this movement. When local labor deserted plantations, mines, and cities—or simply chose better-remunerated labor elsewhere—it created shortages that ultimately made the long-distance mobility of communities from distant "labor reserves" an integral part of Tanganyika's economy.[154] Under British rule, governments and labor recruiters spent three decades trying to control this movement by introducing legislation criminalizing desertion and mechanisms, such as tax tickets and possibly travel passes, to enable officials to identify travelers. They also associated migrants' control over mobility with destructive processes: the spread of diseases, weakened bodies less capable of work, the loss of both tax revenue and labor time, desertion and labor shortage, and "detribalization," a colonial shorthand for social instability as individuals from different areas moved and lived together.[155] In Jacob Shell's words, African walking constituted a "subversive mobility."[156]

Few colonial officials paid as much attention to the technological basis of migrancy as labour commissioner Major Granville Orde-Browne. Like his colleagues, the commissioner thought Africans lacked the historic cultures of long-distance movement required for "modern" economies.[157] Yet Orde-Browne uniquely rooted existing mobilities in vernacular walking njia that, he admitted, offered migrants more and sometimes better options than colonial transport and that would raise the percentage of recruited contract labor. Believing such long-distance journeys to be a new phenomenon for African travelers—and thus, a danger to travelers and roadside communities—Orde-Browne sought to replace walking routes with a new colony-wide system of migrant automobility composed of new roads, vehicles, and rest camps (the first at Kilosa was called a control camp) complete with tick-resistant cement floors, kitchens, dispensaries, and even literature translated into Kiswahili. In contrast to tired and diseased bodies at plantations, enticing walkers onto specific colonial-built njia and camps, and eventually into vehicles, offered the technological means to create a stronger laborer whom the government could more easily tax, control, and heal in its own infrastructures of movement.[158] The government built the road–rest camp system slowly during the late 1920s and 1930s, and, in many cases, recorded large numbers of visitors into the 1950s.[159] But the expected turn to contract labor through and because of motorization did not occur: "It formerly seemed probable that the popularity of the contract would rapidly increase, with the result that a far larger use would be made of motor and rail transport."[160]

Instead, the commissioner continued to describe a complex and incorporative world of mass movement spanning the colony and crossing colonial borders.[161] Using terms often deployed to denigrate njia—including "native paths," "bush roads," or "tracks"—Orde-Browne describes migrants making sociotechnical calculations to avoid authorities, and thus taxation or detection after desertion, as well as to seek *kipande* (noncontract work with payment after thirty days) or "casual," day-to-day work agreements. They negotiated the latter with employers instead of signing long-term labor contracts as "recruited" labor.[162] Some of these routes included better-known caravan njia—sometimes flanked by roads or rails—but the commissioner correctly believed that migrants repurposed local and regional routes for intra- and interterritorial travel.[163] As they did so, communities responded to travelers' needs by selling portable food such as dried fish, by offering temporary labor for individuals needing more resources, and by providing lodging in extra rooms and houses.[164] When the commissioner, with the help of department officials, mapped these routes through interviews with migrants, he concluded that "the exact tracks were unknown" and "various." He nevertheless produced a map showing thin lines of colonial transport power—generally straight lines—with red, curved walking itineraries encompassing most of the colony's space. The latter concedes that migrants held infrastructural, and thus geographic, power when it came to one of the administration's biggest concerns: securing labor through movement.[165] "The journey"—rather, Africans' many njia—"appears as the crux of the matter; if it were not such a prominent feature of the situation the need for the contract would be far smaller."[166]

A similar concession appears in Orde-Browne's research on the contract labor over which recruiters and the government hoped to exercise more control. Workers from central and western regions signed contracts with labor recruiters in order to finance and profit from their journey to Zanzibar. Higher wages made the island a preferred destination among some migrants. In some cases, they got there by first agreeing to work for plantations on the mainland, with recruiting agencies paying laborers' annual taxes and offering free transport to the coastal region via rail or road. But after earning wages for a short time, the commissioner learned, these contract laborers deserted, moving by foot and by boat to Zanzibar. Some financed this leg by selling their former employer's tools.[167] A similar process occurred in the lakes region, where myriad njia allowed both workers and information about wages and living conditions to move almost un-checked across territorial boundaries. "The worker may not be very intel-ligent," Orde-Browne wrote, but he will "compare conditions in the two countries" and even pursue "more congenial employment under another name."[168] Not surprisingly, desertion—"unlawfully leaving Employer's service"—was the most common offense committed under the Master and Native Servants Ordinance.[169] Orde-Browne concluded that work had to be done on the meanings of the contract because "it is obvious that any sort of free transport, without obligation or means of discrimination between travelers, would speedily be killed by 'joy-riding' for the African is an enthusiastic traveler, as is witnessed by the large numbers who travel third class on the Tanganyika Railways for pleasure."[170]

Though at times enhancing the government's power and reach, colo-nial technological interventions also offered additional options for mi-grants to construct routes. James Giblin shows that government-approved "headmen" (*wanyapara*) tasked with aiding labor recruiters by leading workers on routes sanctioned by the government allowed travelers to use older walking paths to control their journeys and resources.[171] Interest-ingly, when the government started collecting statistics on whether labor-ers were traveling to or returning from work, road-camp statistics show large discrepancies favoring the former (travelers going to work), suggest-ing that laborers intentionally avoided such colonial spaces upon leaving employment.[172] Even with the popularization of bus travel in the 1940s and 1950s, the sticking issue was less official versus vernacular njia than the act of purchasing tickets. Research found that migrants and their families preferred to buy their own tickets in order to guarantee the "casual" na-ture of work and thus opportunities to leave.[173] Indeed, control over one's movement, whether buying a bus ticket or walking vernacular njia, likely contributed to the dominance of casual over recruited labor. The latter, which rested on colonial motorized transport technologies, produced only a quarter of laborers at its highest point.[174] The rest seemingly used more flexible itineraries of movement they felt empowered to use. Shabani Mohamed Swedi, a *manamba* (labor migrant) who later became a driver, never deserted because his overseer (*mnyapara*) respected him, but he recalled with whole-body laughter a common scene in which overseers taking the daily roll discovered laborers had left after looking inside their rooms to find no one there.[175]

Oral histories point to similar conclusions about this "mixing" of move-ment and control over livelihoods. Maliko Karumba of Kigoma traveled throughout his youth in the 1930s. He initially went to sisal plantations near Korogwe in hopes of getting "something to live by," whether "clothes" or "cows." After marrying, he traveled north across the border to Uganda, working at six different farms. Though Karumba traveled by train and lorry to Korogwe, he went on foot most often, a journey of twenty-nine days. He did the latter with other young men "in groups of ten or twenty," eventually becoming the "leader" (kiongozi) of such parties. As the leader, he traveled on "indigenous" njia (njia za kienyeji) because he wanted to avoid the requests for tax found on colonial rails and roads and because he considered British transport technologies an inferior infrastructural network: they simply did not provide as many options for travel as vernacular njia. He learned about the latter through his own experience traveling with laborers as a young man. For example, when the two older men who led him to sisal plantations came to intersecting paths, they would say, "Take this way, that one's not good." Like caravan communities before them, travelers protected themselves with medicine that they brought with them and that they incorporated from pathside communities.[176] Karumba recalled one variety of plants that ensured safe passage through a forest and another from a different community that protected them against lions.[177]

Karumba's mobility thus drew from and knit together long-standing modalities of movement from along his journeys into a culture of long-distance travel forged and passed down through generations of migrants.[178] This allowed him to create social security at home by keeping as much of his earnings as possible, and the variety of routes allowed him to respond to changing wages within the colony or across its borders.[179] Such flexibility of movement and its social product was not possible everywhere or at all times. Juma Said Mlela worked on a sisal estate south of Tabora in Kisengi before spending twenty-five years in Tanga doing similar work. In places both near and far to his home, he feared the consequences of traveling alone. "Slipping through and leaving" (kupenya na kutoroka) an estate, though technically possible, was only one part of a journey, he said. Avoiding deadly animals required a group, and desertion came with legal risks for oneself and one's family that, he said, included imprisonment for oneself and possible charges for one's father.[180]

Women born in the late 1930s and 1940s also discussed the importance of travel to their livelihoods. It was especially important for creating social networks on their own terms between initiation (kuvunja ungo) and marriage: "You were initiated, and then you were married; and that was it. Those days our parents didn't think to educate girls."[181] Through connections to older women in their families and to friends in urban townships, some maturing women joined networks of mobility and trade.[182] Amina Musa of Tabora, for example, used remedies her grandmother, an Mdigo from Tanga, had learned decades earlier through her own travels. Following the death of her husband in 1941, Musa spent four years walking from Tabora to Dodoma, with a group of eight other men and women, to collect *ubuyu*, a fruit from baobab trees in the hills just outside the latter town. Her group often walked along the Central Line and used njia (*vichochoro,* or footpaths) made by animals when such routes appeared. She carried cassava and potatoes as "travel food" (*chakula cha njiani*). The journey there took twelve days. Once in the forests, she said, "I could protect against bad people and wild animals; if they're around, you spread [the medicine] on your skin and they can't see you."[183] Musa did this for four years before becoming tired. Hadija Mahomedi combined colonial rail and road travel with African infrastructure to transport cloth from Dar es Salaam to areas where commodities were difficult to purchase. "In those days," she recalls, "cloth was a blessing, and so women accepted me when I came to sell it."[184]

Operating in what Husseina Dinani calls a "complex world of marriage, divorce, and mobility," Mahomedi's grandmother had migrated from Songea in southwestern Tanganyika to Kilwa Masoko on the coast and ultimately to Dar es Salaam in the 1920s—the last move to flee an abusive relationship.[185] Mahomedi said her grandmother traveled with friends because solo mobility invited suspicion, including the possibility of *uchawi* (a form of power often associated with harm to another individual or community) being used against a traveler.[186] Finding few opportunities in Dar es Salaam, she relocated to a sisal plantation at Ruvu, where she sold beer to laborers on Sundays; she eventually sold enough to buy a house in Dar es Salaam. Mahomedi was born on that very estate in 1942, and Mahomedi's mother and grandmother told her the family's travel history and taught her to brew sorghum (*mtama*) beer, called *koba.* After marrying in 1955, she moved to Dar es Salaam with her husband, where she sold koba at Keko, a city market. She described Keko as more than a place to sell goods; it was a repository of knowledge and social capital where she "got locals" (*kupata wenyeji*) who helped her mediate short- and long-term challenges.[187] When Mahomedi divorced her husband in the late 1950s, she used social capital from the market to sell *kaniki* cloth (a durable indigo-dyed cloth from India shown in figure 1.5) with four other women. Stating that travel and business posed risks for a woman's respectability, she and others used the very item they sold, kaniki, to create respectability. Mahomedi said

1.5 *Hadija Mahomedi demonstrating one way she wore sewn kaniki on the road. Mahomedi later became a car owner by winning a running race sponsored by the independent government. (Photo by author.)*

women sometimes sewed two kaniki together to create a blanket for sleeping or clothes for travel; it was also a mark of piety for Muslim women entering towns: "You couldn't show your face when you walked into town. You needed to have a *buibui* [hijab]." Not particularly fond of the travel itself, Mahomedi said mobility allowed her "to search for blessing" (*kutafuta riziki*) and create an urban livelihood in Tabora: "I built a house and could care for my children."[188]

The government considered these mobilities a technopolitical threat because about a quarter of migrants ended in cities—a process one official termed "the drift to the towns."[189] Indeed, the intersecting tensions about motorization and migrancy in Tanganyika crystallized around concerns that large-scale vernacular movements had allowed technological change to occur within urban instead of rural areas. Believing Africans came to town to avoid work—and, moreover, that urbanization led to detribalization—some officials returned migrants to their hometowns and called for a more restrictive pass system to keep the problem from occurring.[190]

The mandate, however, guaranteed freedom of movement. Other officials noted, "Wholesale repatriation will be expensive. . . . Once it became known that free passages home were to be had, one can picture the Tanga authorities being inundated with a crowd of applications, each one of whom could produce evidence of having originated from an upcountry district. There is no more enthusiastic 'joy-rider' than the African native."[191] A district officer in Dodoma expressed similar concerns. "Because of its central position on the Railway and the Great North road, [Dodoma] becomes a halting point" for migrants expelled from other cities, who used colonial transport networks to find a new home.[192] The expansion of private and government bus services between the 1930s and the 1950s made this job even more difficult because anyone who could afford the fare could return to cities after repatriation. In fact, the growth of bus services connecting urban, peri-urban, and rural communities in the postwar era coincides with the most active period of forced returns from Dar es Salaam.[193]

When passengers arrived in the city, they encountered a nascent motoring culture created by urban Africans. W. Fryer, Dar es Salaam's DO, complained in 1931, "There was a time not so long ago when one of the first concerns of the majority of natives was to get if possible money to pay his tax," before suggesting that the "younger generation between 20 and 35 years of age who have grown up in the Dar es Salaam district prefer to travel by motor car, accompanied often by their wives, to walking and putting aside the cost of the fares for the payment of their tax and fulfillment of their just obligation to the government." Aided by motorized mobilities, African urbanites spent "money in other directions" at the expense of government revenue, he concluded.[194] Officials in Tanganyika had hoped to use vehicles to free up rural labor by shifting work—"energy"—from human transport to increased agricultural production in a sedentary space. This process attached production "efficiency" and social change to assumptions that labor freed from porterage—"wasted energy"—would acquiesce to colonial cultures of technology, movement, and production. Instead, these farmers selectively appropriated the car, a symbol of luxury across Europe by 1931, using it to sell their goods and use their income as they pleased. Like Orde-Browne, Fryer linked African technological initiative to fiscal irresponsibility, but they disagreed on the virtues of each modality. The former wanted to replace mass African walking in rural areas with colonial motor transport, whereas the latter bemoaned the loss of walking in cities.

Both cases invoked a problematic distinction between walking and wheels, including motoring, that also informs historical scholarship.[195]

"Traditional wisdom holds the wheel to be one of mankind's cleverest inventions" and an inevitable feature of technological progress, historian Richard Bulliet writes. He calls a tendency to explain the absence of wheels as "a failure to recognize a great invention" fundamentally ahistorical because it assumes wheels' usefulness and desirability across time and space.[196] Evidence here demonstrates that sociotechnical distinctions between wheeled and wheel-less societies mislead because they underestimate the cultures of space and time created by walking and overestimate the sociotechnical changes required to adopt motorized movement. For African users who were already moving across distances on an expansive and dynamic network of paths and roads, adding motorized transport to journeys, when available, did not present a social or technological challenge. Instead, walking provided a social and material foundation for the integration of mechanized movement into preexisting and dynamic itineraries of African movement. As maps 1.1–1.3 show, vernacular njia clearly influenced the geographic traces of both road and rail movement even as migrants found ways to skirt these routes on other paths not known to officials.[197] It took the colonial government until the postwar era to begin to even match the geographic scope of nineteenth-century caravan routes—and often with very low traffic densities.[198]

Mobile Africans' power matters because, distinct from Jennifer Hart's research on drivers and entrepreneurs in colonial Gold Coast, African car ownership remained incredibly low throughout the colonial period in Tanganyika. Outside of a handful of farmers in Arusha, Moshi, and Bukoba, the issue of African car ownership centered around debates about chiefs receiving government loans from the Native Administration to purchase vehicles.[199] Officials begrudgingly conceded to these requests, albeit insisting on secondhand vehicles, in order to enhance a chief's prestige. The chiefs sometimes purchased vehicles of their own choice by contributing their own resources.[200] Meanwhile, estimates put South Asian ownership of buses and trucks at 80 percent of colony totals. Private, corporate, and European government ownership made up the rest.[201] Each of these groups undoubtedly shaped car culture by helping drive vehicle numbers from twenty-five to eight thousand during the interwar period. (World War II mobilization drove much of this growth.)[202] In the 1920s, for example, Karimjee Jivanjee expanded a family trading business in Zanzibar into ownership of agricultural estates on the mainland, including six sisal estates. He followed this act several years later by opening two car importing businesses, both named International Motor Mart, in Dar es Salaam

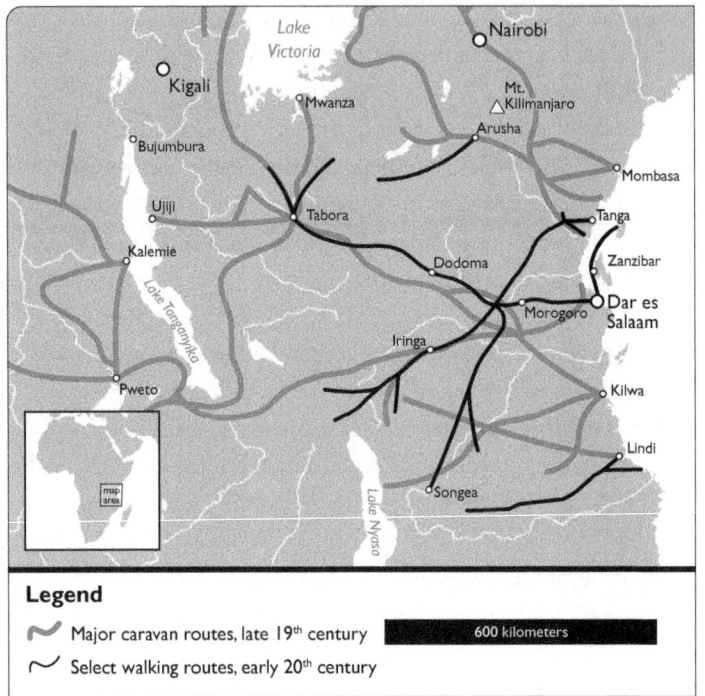

MAP 1.1

Legend

〰 Major caravan routes, late 19th century

⎰ Select walking routes, early 20th century

600 kilometers

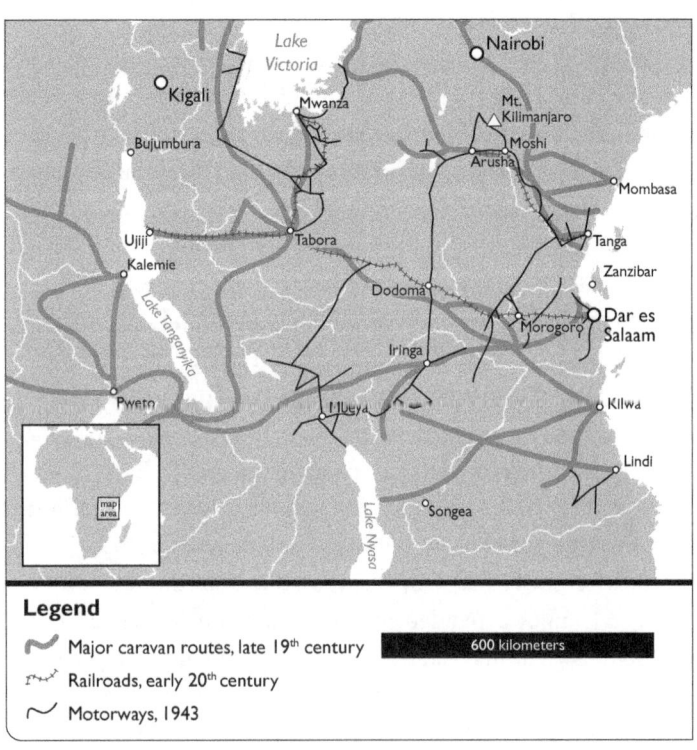

MAP 1.2

Legend

〰 Major caravan routes, late 19th century

✦⌁ Railroads, early 20th century

⎰ Motorways, 1943

600 kilometers

MAP 1.3

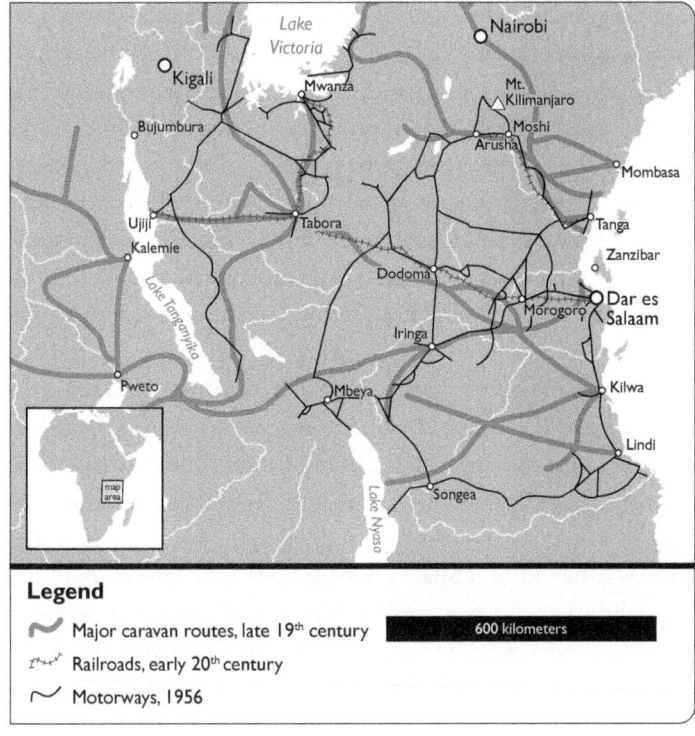

Lake Victoria

Nairobi

Kigali

Mwanza

Mt. Kilimanjaro

Bujumbura

Moshi

Arusha

Mombasa

Ujiji

Tabora

Tanga

Kalemie

Zanzibar

Dodoma

Morogoro

Dar es Salaam

Iringa

Pweto

Kilwa

Mbeya

Lindi

Lake Tanganyika

Lake Nyasa

Songea

map area

Legend

〰 Major caravan routes, late 19th century

⌇ Railroads, early 20th century

⌢ Motorways, 1956

600 kilometers

MAPS 1.1–1.3. *Map 1.1 combines major walking networks from nineteenth-century caravans and labor migration routes of the twentieth century. Though not comprehensive for all walking, it shows the expansive nature of walking geographies and their influence on motorized transport, shown in maps 1.2 and 1.3. Apart from the northern route to Kenya, most motoring occurred within urban and peri-urban areas, and all of the longer routes remained seasonal. Maps created by Tim Stallman. Based on Sheriff,* Slaves, Spices, and Ivory, *191; Deutsch,* Emancipation without Abolition, *2; Tanganyika Territory, "Annual Report of the Labour Department 1943,"* BC/9, ZNA; *and Tanganyika Territory, "Annual Report of the Labour Department 1955,"* BC 25/3, ZNA.

and Tanga, before distributing motor gasoline and kerosene for Caltex, a Texas-based company.[203]

The Jivanjee story offers one of the clearest links between rising motor vehicle numbers and production and extraction regimes in the colony, especially large-scale agriculture on plantations rooted in imported machinery and mechanized transport. War and its aftermath were the other driving factors. World War II mobilization combined with a postwar wave of colonial development schemes aiming for increased output through wider application of industrial farming techniques to quadruple vehicle numbers from 5,000 in 1939 to nearly 20,000 in 1951.[204] The individuals, companies, and events that pushed this quantitative increase help us understand why the motor vehicle first became a part of African life. But that is different than giving importers and owners power to shape mobile cultures at scale in Tanganyika, as maps 1.1–1.3 illustrate by showing the influence of walking networks on the geographic contours motorized traffic took. Neither automobile ownership (or the access to credit it required) nor political power were the sine qua non of technological power in Tanganyika, a story we continue through a microhistory of African driving culture—itself a product of migration and urbanization.[205]

AFRICAN CAR MEN AND THE "STREET-CORNER STATION": CITIES, INDUSTRIAL MEASURES, AND VEHICULAR VALIDATION AT THE PWD

In both oral and archival evidence, the path to a driving career went through manual labor in one of three colonial spaces: the PWD, the King's African Rifles (which often ended with joining the PWD), or proximity to machines on city streets or at plantations. Quickly supplanted by cities in terms of the density of machines and vehicles, plantations and large farms were some of the first places to build labor around engines—including the combination of machine and vehicle. Drivers' backgrounds thus varied widely, from sisal workers, road laborers, a golf caddy, and a guitar player in a rumba and jive band to fish sellers, farmers, and carpenters.[206] Vincent Njovu, who earned the title "the first driver of Tanganyika," was one of the few drivers—if not the only one—with a secondary school education.[207] But his chance to drive came from letters of recommendation he earned working as a houseboy in Dar es Salaam after permanently migrating there after World War I.[208] At least one government driver, Alifeo Martin, hailed from Nyasaland; he either emigrated from there as a manual laborer or after the war stayed in Dar es Salaam, where he began driving in 1928.[209] Mwinyigoha Mfaume earned chances to drive through his father's connections with colonial departments.[210] Saidi Kamtawa, the Tanganyika African National Union's first driver, left a sisal estate in Kilosa to work as a fuel station attendant in Dar es Salaam before becoming a turner for two years.[211] In each case, transforming contact with automobiles into the status of *dereva* ("driver") required either movement to or linkages with urban areas—the center of the colony's motoring economy.[212]

Mrisho Sulemani Minchande received such an opportunity through manual work he performed near his home, forty kilometers southwest of Dar es Salaam.[213] He joined a local road gang in the late 1920s: "We got ten cents per day, and this was a lot of money. . . . You got money to pay the tax and you get clothes to wear for one and half or two shillings; kaniki for three; kanga for three. If you don't work, where do you get clothes? And those who don't pay their taxes are forced to clear roads for forty days." Minchande also worked around a motor vehicle for the first time. Through months of loading and unloading vehicles, he created a bond with a driver who offered to train him as a "turnboy" (*taniboi*), a driving assistant whose position the colonial government funded because early vehicles did not have self-starters. (Many of these vehicles remained in service through World War II.) Minchande spent three years as a turner on PWD road projects, transporting trees from Mkuranga to the outskirts of Dar es Salaam in an eight-ton Bedford truck. He turned down a chance to become a driver because his uncle, a driver, had a drinking problem that his father blamed on the job's status and expendable wages.[214]

Other young men jumped at a chance to get their own car. The PWD promoted between two and three turners to driver per year through its testing and certification system, one of the most common avenues to promotion.[215] To get to this point, turners received a regular "labourer's rate" as they helped load and unload, crank the engine, and clean the vehicle at the end of the day. Though most motoring happened in town, a turner's main responsibilities came beyond the city limits. If a vehicle broke down or got stuck, they assisted in repairing or dislodging the vehicle. If more pushers were required, they went to get help; if a part was needed, they stayed by the vehicle to guard it and its cargo. If both the driver and the turner had to leave the vehicle and seek help on foot, the latter carried tents, rations, and water. Finally, owing to fears of being stranded on temporary roads after heavy rains, drivers refused to travel alone "for fear of lion," an official wrote, defending the extra expense. For these tasks, a turner received daily wage rates plus six and ten shillings for short and long trips, respectively. They sometimes gave a portion to drivers in exchange for training.[216]

Justified by colonial officials because of the design of early vehicles and seasonal road conditions, the relationship among a *taniboi*, driver, and vehicle quickly became an African institution known as *utingo*. Interchangeable with the Kiswahili word *utaniboi*—also a reference to the work of turning vehicles—*utingo*, which some dictionaries translate only as portering, originally described the back-and-forth (*kutinga*) act of loading and unloading (urban porterage) before taking on a connotation as a specific form of driver training sometime in the 1920s. It seems neither drivers nor their assistants internalized the racialized infantilization that accompanied the use of *boi* in colonial departments to reference individuals who would have considered themselves *kijana* (youth) or *mtu mzima* (adult). Some still use the term *boi* as an institution of technical learning and mobility.[217] Nevertheless, utingo gives better insight into the vernacularization of vehicles and driving because it references the specific spaces (loading docks and street sides) and activities (loading and unloading, as figure 1.6 shows) where African men created a car culture premised on their own status and social mobility.[218] In addition to supplementing their salary with monetary gifts from their assistants, utingo gave drivers a type of technological status they did not have in departments. Within the PWD, African drivers occupied the bottom rung of racialized pay scales that gave over 300 shillings to European drivers and between 185 and 250 shillings to Asian drivers, while putting a ceiling of 175 shillings on pay for "native drivers" (though most earned much less).[219]

But on the many trips they took away from the department, drivers held technological authority over turners and over the many young men hoping to become drivers themselves by loading and unloading vehicles. Ironically, this technical authority came from licenses they earned after passing a driving test. Licensing may seem an obvious requirement. But before the growth of training programs after World War II, colonial officials complained that driving was one of only two forms of African labor in which the government certified workers through a required test and license. The other, a civil service exam, made the applicants finish secondary school and thus a colonial curriculum with European cultural norms. But in the case of driving, utingo, a vernacular street institution, provided prospective trainees a route to an officially sanctioned form of technical status through manual labor in settings controlled by other African men of

1.6 *A picture from a farm, likely a mission, showing how loading and offloading—utingo—offered young access to vehicles and their drivers. Drivers described this scenario for city streets and plantations, too. "Men and boy loading sacks on truck, Tanzania [s.d.],"* *Evangelisch-Lutherisches Missionswerk Leipzig e.V., impaunpub_Volume3/*IMP-LPZ-*ALBUM-04-1098.tif.*

similar backgrounds. For young men who started as urban porters, learning "just to change a gear" brought "big respect [heshima]," recalled one driver, while ascending to the status of dereva was a dream.[220] Jumanne Sisia, who later purchased a taxi, using it to help nationalist leaders visit communities in the Tabora region in the late 1950s, took up utaniboi after working as a "room boi" at Tabora hotel. He described the new work as a "big honor" (*fahari kubwa*) and as "something praised among the youth."[221] As the following incident illustrates, he was not alone in connecting utingo to upward social and technological mobility.

In 1935 a group of porters who had loaded and unloaded lorries in the PWD since 1924 took issue with an order from a "Head Driver to clean WC's to which we replied that this was *not our work* and that that to do this kind of sanitary work there are special men provided by the Department" (emphasis mine). A motor superintendent fired the porters "on the spot." Their letter asks the director to "reinstate us on our work for which we spent half of our young age and to seek other work at this juncture would mean that we have wasted for naught the youth blooming age of our life." This "blooming age" likely referred to maturation as a process through which men ranging from their teens through their forties garnered resources that allowed them to create lives as adults (*mtu mzima*) by marrying, building a house, and having children. The director sided with the motor superintendent and driver. But the episode demonstrates that young men who loaded and unloaded had clear ideas of how "our work" should lead to upward social and technical mobility, not to degrading tasks that replaced proximity to an important machine with excremental labor.[222] Given the limited numbers of drivers employed in the colony, young men did not obtain utingo automatically by simply working on docks and street sides. Nevertheless, utingo offered young men in "casual" and "spot" labor unique opportunities for social mobility through one of the world's preeminent machines.

Utingo also offers clues about what young men working on streets thought about vehicles and motoring economies. In addition to the term *gari*, former drivers called automobiles a "tool of fire" (*chombo cha moto*). This translation of the vehicle sidesteps the history of the car as gari—a wheeled technology of colonial intervention—by integrating vehicles into a longer history of masculine work that includes fire, metal, and claims to power that Peter Schmidt has described in detail for iron smelting.[223] Important linguistically here is not just fire (*moto*) but also the derivation of the word "tool" (*chombo*) from verbs of inserting (*kuchoma/kuchomeka*), firing (*kuchoma*), piercing/stabbing (*kuchomeka*), and even pulling out (*kuchomoa*). These actions echo the creation of metals through smelting and smithing in previous centuries as well as their use in hunting and roasting meat, along with social reproduction through sex, as Kathryn de Luna illustrates.[224] Translating this to the car, drivers controlled a "tool of fire" with pedals and a steering wheel and also "inserted" different gears— *kutia gia*—into the heart of the engine: the fire itself. Moreover, when they started and turned off vehicles, their actions came from a language of "lighting" (*kuwasha*) and "extinguishing" (*kuzima*) fire. Far from a mystery, cars and their specific modes of use fit an existing masculine lexicon of technological power. And they were fairly accessible on the street.

As manual laborers defended their pursuit of utingo, government officials cited this nexus of urban manual work and mechanical learning as the source of a widespread culture of vehicle misuse. In his postwar *Survey of Dar es Salaam*, J. K. Leslie bemoaned the "freedom" of the "street-corner-station" where porters (un)loaded a vehicle's cargo. These street "spot jobs" offered young male porters—whose back-and-forth (un)loading constituted the root of the word *utingo*—steady income for working only a few hours per day, he wrote. Leslie thought this problematic because it allowed young "casual" laborers to meet their needs in a city without submitting to a colonial culture of time or technological discipline.[225] Moreover, street corners gave those who facilitated this process—drivers—technological respect and influence, Leslie complained. Mwinyigoha Mfaume, a resident of Dar es Salaam whom Leslie's research assistants interviewed for the *Survey*, had been charged with overloading, speeding, and using a government vehicle to ferry passengers for private gain while he was supposed to be serving in the governor's convoy. Mfaume made it clear to Leslie's research assistant that he drove in order to make as much money as possible. The driver wanted to electrify his house, upgrade its roof to corrugated steel, and then quit. Leslie concluded that Mfaume, driving only for money, had no incentive to value his career or the rules of the road as a driver.[226] And thus Mfaume overloaded the vehicle, drove quickly, and carried goods and people illegally, pursuing his own ideas of technological and social respectability.

Had Leslie researched driving records across the colony, he might have pointed to a huge archive of traffic violations to validate his point. Lists of traffic fines enumerate a variety of breaches: speeding, "reckless and dangerous" driving, overloading, using public vehicles to "ferry passengers," operating dilapidated vehicles, allowing an unlicensed individual to operate a licensed driver's vehicle (an important form of driver training), driving on closed roads, using forged driver's licenses, "stealing goods in transit," and driving without insurance.[227] As Jennifer Hart demonstrates, such violations tell us more about colonial social ideals for how vehicles should be accessed, used, and regulated, especially in urban spaces, where colonial officials could better surveil drivers, than about the actual nature of driving skill itself.[228] Indeed, the above list of violations does not reflect a problematic appropriation of automobiles by African drivers ill prepared to sit behind the wheel. It points instead to debates over the nature of that appropriation and to the fact that drivers, their assistants, and passengers felt empowered to forge their own culture of transport from roadside or plantation utingo to the open road. Growing lists of fines thus evidence an appropriation in the process of occurring, albeit not on colonial terms.

The PWD records support utingo's effectiveness at turning "spot" laborers into competent drivers. The head of the Transport Department noted that that department was "fortunate in possessing a good class of Africans for its drivers," adding that "it is gratifying to be able to state that no driver of this department has been convicted by the local courts during the last six years for any cause in connection with his duty as a motor driver." The next year, the department promoted seventy-two African drivers; that year, only a single accident occurred, and an investigation found the driver faultless.[229] Officials often described driver conduct and efficiency as "good," and the thirty-five-year-old Abdallah Bakari was "also able to carry out minor repairs on vehicles." Mohamedi Saidi, for example, turned his role as an engine turner into a driving career. Saidi turned for sixteen years from 1930 to 1946 (likely from fourteen years of age to thirty); at the age of the thirty, he took an appointment as a lorry driver at over two shillings per day, "inclusive of cost of living allowance."[230] He then became part of a select group. Only eleven African employees worked as drivers at the Transport Department in 1923. This number vacillated between the mid-30s and 60 in the 1920s before reaching about 130 a decade later.[231] Similar promotions occurred in driving ranks at the King's African Rifles. In 1936 four second-class drivers earned promotion to first-class, three third-class drivers to second-class, six learners to driver, and six recruit drivers to learner.[232]

Evaluations and subsequent promotions came from intense mechanical scrutiny of the relationship between vehicle and African driver.[233] Because departments did not have the staff to follow their drivers around, European supervisors at the PWD evaluated "proficiency" by looking at the condition of the vehicle itself when it returned from journeys.[234] One review read, "To my knowledge, over the last ten months, he has always kept his vehicle in good condition and both clean and greased. It is usual for him frequently to check his own tyre pressures and personally carry out weekly maintenance on his truck without specific instructions. He has never had a traffic accident to my knowledge. He very much considers it his duty to supervise the loading of his truck." Twenty-six-year-old Adam Ibrahim's promotion went straight through the garage: "The mechanic advises me that this man is a first class driver and can be recommended in compliance with para 2 of Gov. Circular no. 21 1946." Additional regulations in the 1940s formalized this relationship between driver skill and vehicle condition. They added that "neglect" of basic car maintenance, including "water and oil level, tyre pressure, etc.," would "render [African drivers] liable to make good the cost of any repairs" out of their own salary.[235]

Consider the case of longtime driver Alifeo Martin of Karonga, Nyasaland, who was "the regular driver of GT 4." Martin broke his hand when the engine backfired, causing the starting crank to spin violently into him. (He was likely giving his assistant an opportunity to sit in the driver's seat to start the vehicle, an important part of training.) The motor vehicle superintendent, J. G. Gardner, "personally checked the time and found it to be at normal setting." He subsequently "stripped" the vehicle and found nothing to suggest that the backfire originated from driver neglect. This was good news for Martin. Had Gardner found a defect, he could not have written, "I consider it was an accident which could not have been anticipated and so avoided."[236] Martin received a full salary during his recovery and returned to his post. The same occurred for a PWD driver whose brakes failed at a bridge, causing the vehicle to fall over the rail into a river. A mechanical investigation by a European mechanic concluded that the driver's claim of attempting to stop well before the bridge could be trusted because of "a fault in the brake system" common to this make and model around the world.[237] For others, inspection led to demotion. Kibwana Mohamed, "formerly a driver of GT Lorry 403," served a seventy-day prison sentence for speeding, "carrying 5 passengers in the cab of that vehicle," and "lacking independent brakes." Though he did not lose his license and was reengaged by the PWD, officials offered him only a position as a "machine boy."[238] From the status of driver, he thus returned to the demasculinized position of "boy."[239]

In each of the above cases, colonial records combined the African driver identity and the vehicle or station into a car-driver hybrid: "Idi Tambwe driver of GT 525" or "driver of the Mahenge Station lorry."[240] Vincent Njovu gained the title "first driver of Tanganyika" not because he was the first driver in Tanganyika—he definitely was not—but because he was the first to drive GT 1: the first new vehicle imported and licensed by the British government (featured in Safari Bwanas, though Njovu was not driving during that event). As already shown, this car-driver approach brought intense scrutiny to users by binding their technological identity to an automobile's material condition. Operating on rough roads with old vehicles and at the discretion of a mechanic, this certainly entailed risk. Yet this method of evaluation also offered men who had moved from urban porter to turner to driver a unique form of mechanical personhood as they became an extension of the vehicles they operated—a form of what Tim Dant calls "the driver-car" assemblage. "Neither the human driver nor the car acting apart could bring about the types of action that the assemblage can; it is the particular ways in which their capacities are brought together that bring about the impact of the automobile on modern societies," he writes.[241]

Similar configurations of human and machine created different social, economic, and political opportunities for African men in Tanganyika—what I call *effective technological masculinity*. Becoming car men gave African drivers uniforms, paid leave, and steady wages through which they built families and purchased homes and farms. Njovu bought houses in Dar es Salaam and Arusha; he retired to his home near Mbeya, where he purchased a farm. Working for the PWD for over thirty years, he traveled the continent on paid leave and retired as the governor's personal driver. Drivers also played roles in dual economic networks: one for the government or private transport as a salaried employee and another transporting goods and people on the side.[242] Between 1931 and 1932, the railway estimated losses of £25,000 in revenue to the popular economies mobilized by these drivers.[243] A 1934 amendment to the Carriage of Goods by Motor (Prohibition) Ordinance thus targeted the combination of automobiles and head porterage. Office commentary stated that the update "extends the meaning of the words 'convey or knowingly cause to be conveyed by means of a motor vehicle'... to include conveyance of goods from one place to another *partly* by motor vehicle and *partly* by other means, e.g. head porterage" (emphasis mine).[244]

The update did not stop lorry traffic or the formation of vernacular economic networks. A complaint at the Arusha Chamber of Commerce said that African farmers were using their vehicles for much more than the produce their "private" licenses allowed and that they had expansive networks across the western portions of the colony.[245] Stan Pritchard, the traffic inspector for Tanganyika Road Services—a branch of East Africa Rail and Harbor in Nairobi—spent much of his time investigating "thieving from our lorries" on the Itigi-Mbeya road. In one case, gold bullion from Lupa made it all the way to a dhow on the coast before being found; officials never figured out how it got there. Pritchard's lengthy investigations found that drivers and mechanics had devised ways to remove the entire back panel of "supposedly thief proof" vans by removing bolts from the bottom—and that they had connections to villages and township shops across the area to sell goods.[246] While the Arusha cases complained exclusively about private vehicle licenses driving an alternative commercial network, the other two bemoaned the particular combination driving and porterage (walking) as a network the government struggled to know or control. Driving thus offered young men an opportunity to combine urban identities and skills forged predominantly in towns with the creation of economic networks that extended across the rural routes they drove—a form of urban-to-urban and urban-to-rural agency that produced at least two outcomes.[247]

First, in terms of drivers' own life cycles, they invested resources in families and homes where they retired, a process through which they passed from the youthhood mentioned by PWD porters above into a form of adulthood premised largely on rootedness in place. Unlike Mfaume, who finished his family home in Dar es Salaam, many retired to peri-urban and rural areas, where their resources went farther and where they farmed into their old age. Second, forging these networks helped drivers shape political movements. Njovu funded visits by Julius Nyerere to Mbeya during nationalist campaigns, while, decades earlier, the driver Mtumwa Makusudi, who traveled between Dar es Salaam and Bagamoyo, helped found the latter's African Association. Two of the three founding members were drivers.[248] Saidi Tanu, Nyerere's driver, literally drove a figurehead of the independence movement around Tanganyika in an effort to unite the colony's different groups into a party and potential nation. In addition to the regular obstacles to motoring, some colonists they met along the way wanted their political, and thus spatial, journey to fail. Additionally, their first car broke down often. It took another vehicle, a Jeep popularly called DST-72 (its license plate number), to facilitate Tanu's movement of Nyerere throughout Tanganyika. After ten years of independence in 1971, Tanu and DST-72 initiated celebrations by driving Nyerere to the party headquarters, casting their motoring—and the combination of African driver, anticolonial politician, and vehicle—as vernacular African history.

Tanu's fondness for DST-72 and Njovu's love of GT 1 lead to a final point: drivers rooted their technological masculinity in a human-machine relationship because cars treated them better than colonial officials did. Elias Mwaifani, who worked for the PWD in Mbeya, recalled, "The British would say, 'Stop here.' He then got out, popped the bonnet, and had a whole meal and tea to himself as I sat in the vehicle. You couldn't ask for food and you didn't ask what he was eating." Upon arriving at a destination, officials stayed at guesthouses while Mwaifani stayed with the car at "PWD 'parking.'"[249] Mwaifani felt more like a servant than a driver, a status reflected in racialized pay scales that clearly valued European and Asian labor over African employees' work regardless of their licensing and labor—a constant across racial categories. A group of African drivers raised this very point in two letters to protest their conscription into Britain's World War II campaign. They first accused the government of "[showing] an affection toward Indians" who escaped conscription. "Are we only drivers, or are we as fowls and they human beings or are they men of spirit by themselves?. . . It would be better if they, like us, were also pressed into the service—*for have they not licenses as we have?*" (emphasis mine).[250] Another letter added, "Beware of all us drivers to whom you have been so hostile, constantly fining us. . . for drivers are what you want, not money. It is we drivers who will be of more use to you in this great war."[251] Njovu's memoir asserts that some drivers received a large payout in exchange for their service. But officials still misinterpreted the drivers' anger, believing that Africans feared Indians would take their spots.[252]

To the contrary, PWD drivers highlighted the irresolvable contradictions produced through the colony's racialization of industrial identities: European, Indian, "native." Technological status rooted in certified skill and testing did not make sense as long as racial categories—instead of demonstrable skill—determined pay and status, they asserted. As it stood in the 1940s, the measure of men in colonial departments had more to do with European categories of race than with licensing: a vetting process through which all drivers passed or failed as mechanical equals whose competence could be judged through vehicle inspections.[253] The episode thus provides a glimpse into African drivers' views of the cars they drove and into the reasons they pursued long-term relationships with them. Automobiles could be learned and understood in vernacular institutions and could vouch for drivers' skill and humanity within a colonial department that structurally devalued their labor. In other words, automobiles acted as technologies of trust because they helped diminish "the arbitrariness of colonial power" and because, as Hart observes of the colonial Gold Coast, their mobile nature helped men "negotiate the plurality of masculinities in operation" during the colonial period.[254] As they earned wages and drove colonial economies, they also mobilized urban and rural vernacular economies while investing in their own rural livelihoods later in life. In sum, more than bringing meanings to motor vehicles and other colonial technologies, as Luise White has demonstrated, drivers forged industrial cultures of training and validation between street corners, government departments, and the vehicles themselves.[255]

There is no doubt that automobiles and the njia they required brought changes to colonial Tanganyika. When Saidi Tanu and Julius Nyerere traveled from Tabora to Dar es Salaam in just under twelve hours, they accomplished what Paul Graetz had not fifty years earlier by completing in one day a journey that took caravans several weeks. But this compression of space and time through motor travel occurred only in certain seasons, along certain routes, and required huge amounts of labor. Moreover, this anticolonial motoring was possible because vernacular njia—both "ways" as routes and "ways" of doing and knowing—provided the sociotechnical infrastructure for cars to become part of African life. Neither migrants nor the "street-corner-station" aligned with the farcical and idealized colonial visions of automobile use evident in the Safari Bwanas float. But their labor and movements gave the car its popular rooting in African spaces and livelihoods, especially in cities, where users approached the vehicle as a technology they could remake through vernacular institutions and itineraries of manual labor.

This process of walking to the car should not signal the arrival of a motor age or a desire for building a car-based African society. Motor vehicles and seasonably motorable roads became parts of vernacular networks in some parts of Tanganyika (often in conjunction with other modes of mobility), yet this inclusion did not displace precar forms of movement and in some cases magnified the latter's importance for creating livelihoods under colonial rule. With the end of British rule in Tanganyika in 1961, an independent government certainly faced questions about what to do with a technology tied so closely to British colonial identities; with connection to forced labor of Africans; and which, without such colonial regimes of violence, had not created economically or socially self-reliant forms of movement—issues examined in chapter 3. Having journeyed from the broad spaces of mobility to urban street corners (and to the PWD), we stay there to examine the emergence of African mechanics, their African vehicles, and the forms of street knowledge that made both of them work.

TWO

Overhaul

Making Men and Cars in Repair Garages

ONE OF THE FIRST historical records of motor vehicle repair in Tanganyika foreshadows the contradictory location of African mechanics in twentieth-century narratives of expertise. It comes from British lorry driver William Campbell's memoir of World War I's East African theater and from the repair of his differential gearbox, in particular. Having just watched his assistant successfully fix the differential "all right after I had started him," a common arrangement for apprentices, Campbell added that his "boy" "had not the remotest idea of the object," echoing exclusionary discourses we have already seen. Indeed, the driver thought African assistants stupefied by the "magic" of vehicles because their design was "incomprehensible" to them, especially the engine: "a complete mystery to him." When Campbell concludes, "We came to like our black workshop companions for their unaffected, innocent simplicity," he describes not only an African "boy" too naive to understand or modify the vehicle itself but also an individual unchanged by knowledge acquisition and practice even as the apprentice touched, took apart, and successfully reassembled the differential gear.[1] Like British education officials who made technical policy in Tanganyika after the war, Campbell distinguished between Africans' ability to competently fix vehicles, on the one hand, and a theoretical comprehension of internal combustion rooted in classrooms, books, and certification, on the other. In this context, no matter how much Campbell's assistant expanded his repertoire during the war, he had to work through colonial institutions and the theory and book-based knowledge they offered to move beyond the denigrated status of a "boy" or "companion" for whom machines were "incomprehensible."[2]

A brief detour through the history of car repair exposes the false theoretical standard Campbell imposed on his assistant. In American and European cities, early car owners looked to blacksmiths and plumbers to repair vehicles because of their familiarity working with metal and small engines. On farms, rural users reimagined early vehicles as plows, washing machines, and mills, what Ronald Kline and Trevor Pinch have termed "users as agents of technological change."[3] In the 1930s, when manufacturers displaced much of consumers' power to tinker with automobiles, design and repair remained a tacit exercise heavily reliant on fingertip knowledge for the creation of both skills and technologies.[4] In the United States and Europe, none of this technological agency required the theoretical comprehension that Campbell deemed necessary for African repair assistants or the colonial and national education that officials later normalized through apprentice programs and international technical assistance.[5] Yet this myth of repair shaped expectations during and after the colonial period about who could or should obtain automotive expertise, including how, where, and with what they should do so.

This myth also has shaped expectations about the car itself, including what, exactly, might constitute an African automobile.[6] Drawing on the assumptions of "tropical" roadlessness explored in the previous chapter, designers in Europe attempted to create vehicles that required neither all-weather roads nor the African labor required to make roads or push stuck vehicles. The Science Museum Library and Archives at Wroughton, an old military base about 80 miles west of London, includes the records of one such effort by Frank Mott. A car designer and tester for Birmingham's Morris Commercial Vehicles, Mott traveled to Nairobi, Kenya, in 1926 to investigate customer complaints that the company's standard vehicles worked poorly on the colony's roads. After addressing problems with the vehicles' drivetrains, Mott's managing director sent word that the company had a new idea. He called it a roadless lorry. By *roadless*, designers meant a vehicle "intended to carry a full load over any type of soft ground that a man can walk over, and negotiate obstacles which no other vehicle could look at." A truck with "caterpillar" tracks, as figure 2.1 illustrates, it was a joint project of Morris and the Roadless Traction Limited. Its connection to colonial Africa came via the Imperial Cotton Growers Association,

2.1 *A Morris one-ton truck similar to the one in which Frank Mott attempted to motor around Mount Kilimanjaro.* © *British Motor Industry Heritage Trust.*

which was looking for heavy haulage solutions for roadless regions. Similar models had already been tested in the Anglo-Persian Oil Company's oil fields, where the tracks allowed engineers to carry heavy equipment over wet sand during the rainy season.[7]

Morris directed Mott to perform a motor trial that intersected with a conference of East African governors in Nairobi in order for attendees to see the technological virtues of a machine that did not require roads, thereby minimizing infrastructural investments. To do so, Mott aimed to motor south from Voi, crossing into Tanganyika to round Mount Kilimanjaro before heading northward across the Kenyan border to the conference in Nairobi. The vehicle did not make it. On a stretch near the Tanganyika border, though "quite good as Kenyan roads go," the "roadless" truck stopped moving, its tracks filled with mud. Mott abandoned the trial and railed the machine to Nairobi without crossing into "roadless" Tanganyika. The engineer blamed the trial's failure on the uniqueness of East African mud and its tensile strength, in particular: "I am afraid it is difficult for you to appreciate the consistency of mud and its nature—particularly when it is partly dried and mixed with grass." Mott called for more tests in England on a course that approximated the mud he encountered in southern

Kenya. He even suggested a recipe: a foot of blue Staffordshire clay mixed with "tough grass." Having never reached "roadless" Tanganyika, Mott left Kenya in 1926. Neither he nor the Morris ever returned.[8]

Tanganyika's status in Europe as a "roadless country" nevertheless made it a destination for colonial car trials. Funded by the 1929 Colonial Development Act, which aimed to stimulate metropolitan industries, the colonial government purchased a hundred-ton motor vehicle that manufacturers called a "road train," which was a tractor-like vehicle with one or two large trailers. The ability to move a hundred tons of goods at a time made the purchase of a "road train" economical for frugal colonial governments that balked at constructing permanent transport infrastructure. In 1932, after a short trial in Dar es Salaam, the Public Works Department (PWD) railed the road train to Isaka in central Tanganyika, where it got stuck. As it "bogged down" twice over only forty-seven miles, crews spent a total of ten days dislodging the vehicle. "A corduroyed track [log road] had to be constructed to enable the train to be turned and return to base, during which return journey it again became stuck in the mud." The engineer concluded that normal motor vehicles had no problem traversing the very same road. Roadless-train trials continued, without success, until the late 1940s.[9] Though officials never received a metropolitan-designed African car that fit their needs, repeated failure did not disrupt an idea that outlived the colonial period: East Africa was, at best, a place to test vehicles designed elsewhere because its combination of mud, heat, and dust made mechanical success so unlikely.[10]

This chapter turns that assumption on its head. Anchored in government workshops and city garages over the course of seventy years (1910s–1980s), it demonstrates that automobile repair facilitated two interrelated forms of overhaul: one gendered and one technological. First, young African men charted alternative regimes of mechanical expertise by migrating to towns, where they joined workshops in which tacit knowledge gained through touch, smell, sound, and movement was considered the most important marker of mechanical competency. Instead of learning in classrooms or through books, apprentices learned by repurposing parts and vehicles on the shop floor; instead of passing tests and obtaining certificates, they staked their careers on the ability to react to changing economies of repair and to know about a dizzying number of models and makes. Often located under trees and at homes, their shops were not always easy to identify as garages, as their Kiswahili name, *gereji bubu* ("muted garage"), suggests. Yet they created an accessible infrastructure of expertise through which unschooled men saw cars exposed, learned by doing, and found incentives for having what Douglas Harper describes as "a mind that is not locked into established ways of seeing and doing."[11]

I define an infrastructure of expertise as the thinginess of knowledge production and acquisition. It includes the material places and spaces, things, and bodies—whether an institution or a mechanic's corporeal body—that shaped learning, innovation, and assessments of a knowledge's credibility and desirability.[12] I use it not only to expose claims like Campbell's about the need for African technologists to prove competence on a theoretical plane in buildings and with books and tests but even more so to establish the robustness and attractiveness of the alternatives mechanics created and saw in the piles of scrap parts and bodies of broken cars that alerted them to the presence of useful knowledge.[13] Since the mid-1900s, scholars and policy makers have largely defined expertise and, by extension, "knowledge as power" through institutions and certifiable knowledges deemed formal that require a particular infrastructure of buildings, doors, libraries, and desks.[14] But African mechanics have long approached expertise's "knowledge infrastructure," to use Paul Edwards's term, differently.[15] They saw scrap parts, shops without doors and walls, patched-together vehicles, and minds that learned through the senses and through experience as the most complex regime of car repair available to prospective mechanics. Young men did so because this infrastructure matched the vehicle and parts landscapes that mechanics inhabited in ways that manuals and books did not. It also offered them a unique opportunity to become respected adult men by establishing their own styles of repair, by collecting and repurposing used parts, and by training others to do the same—a form of what this book calls *effective masculinity*.[16]

The second form of overhaul involves changes to the vehicle itself through everyday acts of repair and maintenance. As American historian Kevin Borg observes, garages subsist and thrive on dysfunction. He describes the auto shop as a place "where the weaknesses of technology are laid bare; where progress is stalled, repaired, and sent back on the road; where technological failure is the stock-in-trade and the ideal of the well-oiled machine meets the reality of our entropic world."[17] He calls this "technology's middle ground," noting that repair garages are situated between producers and consumers and are often staffed by individuals who do not own, design, or manufacture the machines they fix.[18] Yet, without their knowledge and labor, neither automobiles nor the economies they produce work. My argument here is slightly different. More than "technology's middle ground," repair shops in East Africa—and the act of maintenance and repair—provided mechanics with opportunities to substantially remake automobiles as technologies, echoing Harper's observation that "making and fixing are parts of a continuum."[19] Steven Jackson calls this process "broken world thinking." As part of a broader call to view maintenance and repair as sustaining (in that systems keep working) and generative (in that systems change through maintenance and repair), Jackson writes that "the instances of breakdown that occasion [maintenance and repair] are not separate or alternative to innovation, but *sites* for some of its most interesting and consequential operations" (emphasis mine).[20] We turn now to the reasons that centering such "sites" as places is so critical to histories of African innovation.

GARAGE AS ARCHIVE: CRAFT, MECHANICS, AND THE THINGINESS OF METHOD

When African home garages first emerged in townships in Tanganyika in the late 1930s, both their presence and the men who worked in them flew in the face of colonial education policy about the relationship between Africans and industrial technologies.[21] They did so for two reasons. First, officials approached craft or "handycraft," which they considered widespread in Tanganyika, as distinct from the skills and cultures of labor necessary to create industrial societies like those found in Europe or the United States. Even though administrators commonly complimented the "manipulative skill" and "no little ingenuity" of African artisans (*mafundi*) "in their traditional crafts," they did so believing that craft and artisanship, on the one hand, and mechanics, on the other, occupied two distinct temporal moments in human technological history: the former came in the centuries before the Industrial Revolution—at best setting the stage for it—while the latter propelled and sustained it.[22]

Frederick Lugard enshrined this distinction in his blueprint for colonial rule, *The Dual Mandate*, by arguing that carpentry and other artisanal trades could be learned through "manual training" on the job by almost any colonial subject. But the same did not apply to learning mechanics. Car work required theoretical instruction at technical institutions where students with form 6 education lived and studied day and night in dorms. It also necessitated pay incentives to attract a colony's best students because highly educated colonial students almost uniformly picked clerical work over a career in a workshop, he said.[23] "Education Policy in British Tropical Africa," a 1925 memorandum the Director of Public Works of Zanzibar cited in 1928 to "formulate a defined policy with regard to industrial education," formalized this distinction by directing that "instructions in village craft must be clearly differentiated from the skilled mechanic."[24] By this time, a pilot mechanical apprentice program had run for four years in Zanzibar. Entering at the age of ten, all students took courses in masonry, carpentry, leatherworking, and smithing. But only those who excelled at both a craft and their schoolwork—especially arithmetic and English— had the opportunity to learn mechanics and advanced metalwork. This select group worked in PWD shops by day and took math, drafting, and language courses during the evenings. They received small stipends, a portion of which was banked for them to pay for tools. And they slept in school dorms so that they had time and space to study, distant from the home life officials thought antithetical to industrial values. Within five years, officials shuttered the program because even the best students could not find employment in garages. Two mechanics became drivers for the PWD. One died shortly after, and the other earned less than more experienced drivers even after passing the apprentice programs. Another went on to the railway workshops, the only success for a group trainers consider the "best."[25]

Teachers in the program and engineers for the government told their superiors that the distinction between craft and mechanics found in "Education Policy in British Tropical Africa" did not apply in the real world.[26] Regardless, between 1930 and 1950, British educational policy in East Africa narrowed its focus on official colonial educational and theoretical knowledge, including a five-year Motor Mechanics course at the Central School in Dar es Salaam and an insistence that soldiers returning from World War II receive official education, complete a three- to five-year apprenticeship in a European-owned garage, and then pass trade testing based on standards from the United Kingdom—this in spite of practical knowledge gained during the war.[27] Like for Zanzibar's pilot program, officials struggled to convince African men with English language skills or military training in mechanics to undergo lengthy programs and certification processes because they found work elsewhere. And some of those who joined took issue with the program's demands. Angered that the school took money from their stipends to pay for tools and classroom equipment, students at Dar es Salaam's new technical institute went on strike in 1953 and were summarily removed from programs and dorms even as officials sought answers to the event.[28] Unlike in the pilot program in Zanzibar in the 1920s, postwar educators did not doubt the distinction between craft and mechanics.

Instead, postwar officials cited a sharp divide between craft and mechanics to explain their perceptions of students' limits and failures. For example, they concluded that the strike revealed students' unpreparedness to adopt and make sacrifices for the industrial values that drove European industrialization. Several other reports came to similar conclusions. An aptitude assessment in 1951 concluded that technical planners "had in mind the machine shops in Pittsburgh, Manchester, and Frankfurt instead of the more attainable model of the 'average' English town. We must therefore beware of too ready an assumption that the same machines, the same technique and the same industrial lore as serve the western world will necessarily serve this patchwork tract of scrub and settlement."[29] Philip Mitchell suggested that if Europe and the United States had not skipped steps leading from craft and artisan guilds to mechanical institutes, doing so in East Africa was out of the question. England's mechanical institutes, he argued, came through "the Industrial Revolution," not "old craft guilds and their apprenticeship system." With mafundi, which administrators usually translated as "artisans," East Africa had only elements of the latter but needed its own "Industrial Revolution," a process that took centuries, to create a society and economy that looked anything like England with its mechanical institutes.[30] David Edgerton calls this mythical approach to technological history "the linear model."[31]

Culture—not skill, intelligence, or biological notions of race—bore the brunt of administrative critique.[32] G. W. Hatchell, an instructor, complimented students' skills in drawing and in English before complaining that "they will throw up their employment on the least provocation or on no provocation at all." Students did so, he argued, because extended-family networks offered financial assistance in times of need and thus provided a safety net if students quit. Moreover, industrial child rearing had not yet taken hold in most African homes, he said, making expectations about work and time discipline difficult to instill in students in classrooms or on shop floors. Finally, he blamed classroom training for creating haughty students who, because they were an elite minority, did not value "the dignity and vital importance of skilled work with hands, which too few Africans recognize as the true spur to social advancements."[33] Alfred Emms, the assistant director for technical education in Tanganyika, agreed but doubted anything could be done. He cited a "widespread" perception among students that handwork and "perspiration" were "lower class" labor without "heshima," or "respect." Apprentices, he argued, must be taught not to use skill as a means of attaining a higher "post" but instead to seek the "pleasure" of becoming a "skilled craftsman" who is content with mastering their "technical field" instead of chasing quick social mobility. "Training in a manual skill is reasonably simple but a manual skill alone is insufficient without . . . moral qualities," Emms concluded.[34]

By centering particular details about an idealized industrial culture, administrators wrote about the potential for African skill in a distant future—likely decades or centuries away but possible nonetheless—while maintaining a clear distinction between African and European societies as groups occupying different temporal positions in linear histories of technological change. One report stated that "[the African student] has, so to speak, one foot in each of the two worlds, in the traditional African world and in the unstable world of imported civilization. It is important that neither foot should be moved, or the balance is precarious." Anthropologist Johannes Fabian calls this move "temporal distancing" and writes that it results in a "denial of coevalness": "By that I mean *a persistent and systematic tendency to place the referent(s) of anthropology in a Time other than the present of the producer of anthropological discourse*" (italics original).[35] For our purposes, the temporal distancing found in archives worked through the separation of craft and mechanics and, consequently, of head and hand work. Educators used these distinctions to argue that students who struggled in or failed out of mechanical apprentice programs needed more time to adopt industrial values because they came from craft-based societies moored in a version of Europe's deep technological past.

In turn, this use of the craft-mechanics distinction foreclosed the rapid form of technological change Lugard proposed for colonized elites in *The Dual Mandate*. It did so by scaling up and temporally elongating the requirements of sociotechnical change. Policies in the early 1920s envisioned a select group of Africans transformed rapidly through their time in European colonial institutions, an approach that allowed an educated elite to skip steps from craft to mechanics in a decade. By the postwar era, officials used technologists' individual failures to identify much larger, time-consuming societal changes they thought necessary *throughout* the colony before the same African elites could become competent technologists. Unlike Lugard's original use of the distinction, in which he sought to attract the best students to mechanical careers, its use in subsequent decades turned craft into an imposed phase of linear technological change that all of society needed to pass through before an African industrial identity, as defined by European observers, would be possible.[36]

This leads to our second point: thinking that Africans were best suited to rural life, the colonial government located its plans for a slow and controlled sociotechnical evolution in villages distant from almost all of the colony's garages. As David Arnold observes for colonial India, "rural society was one of the principal locations, arguably *the* principal location, for colonial ideas of both technological inertia and 'improvement.'" In Tanganyika cars still played a role in rural education—just not any part associated with actual movement or mechanical function.[37] W. H. Percival's 1937 "Handyman Course," for instance, used the discarded cans and boxes in which gasoline was shipped to and around the colony to remake rural technological actors and their material surroundings. Aiming at African boys who had finished primary school in Kiswahili but would not advance to secondary school, where English was the medium of instruction, Percival found application for the box and can in every part of a rural homestead. "Furniture from Petrol Boxes" tasked students with making a long list of household items, including a "simple chair," a meat safe, a bookcase, a cupboard, and a clothes rack. A unit on smelting and blacksmithing encouraged pupils to turn gasoline cans into toilets, rattraps, drawer handles, window hinges, drawers, a cooking stove, and small cooking pots. In the garden, gasoline cans became planter boxes, sundials, "rustic seats," and, when pounded flat, thatched roofs.

The syllabus thus allowed the simplest form of motoring scrap to construct a new technological subject across rural Tanganyika: a "handyman" who owed his new status and transformed homestead to the slow incorporation of industrial scrap and skills into African life. To appreciate the amount of sociotechnical work Percival asked can and box to perform, recall Campbell's description of "workshop companions" in the opening vignette. Though his assistant successfully repaired the rear differential, Campbell does not link his achievement to cultural or technological progress. Quite the opposite, he uses the fix to suggest that the vehicle's mechanical properties constituted a mystery to an African mind and, moreover, that what his assistant did with his hands could not communicate esoteric knowledge to his brain. He remained a "boy" with "unaffected, innocent simplicity." And yet, with the introduction of can, box, and curriculum, Percival envisions a transformed homestead, an ability "to produce citizens with wider capabilities, a measure of independence, and a keener appreciation of craftsmanship," and a man—not a boy—made by the colonial curriculum.[38]

Combined with the industrial training programs described above, village education helped create an infrastructure of expertise—composed of buildings, curricula, sites of labor, and the gendered bodies of students—through which administrators envisioned technological change in Tanganyika as a top-down process directed by the colonial government. Both approaches considered changes in rural family life critical to the development of an acceptable African industrial culture; both worked through official education structures and required literacy, books, and classrooms. Finally, both programs targeted men exclusively. Colonial officials wrote about "customary" women's work as purely "manual" and therefore divorced from the types of cognition machine work required. They suggested, moreover, that introducing African women to nonmanual labor compromised the tenets of indirect rule—an approach to governance that anchored policies in officials' perceptions of African "custom."[39] While the most immediate effect of this policy was the masculinization of both technology and cognition in colonial departments, divorcing manual labor from head work denigrated most men's claims to knowledge mobility, too, because their journeys mirrored those of the drivers in the previous chapter: labor migrants and "casual" laborers seeking proximity to a vehicle.

The only voice in archival documents to endorse these men came from the garage and an automobile expert. According to C. W. Stevenson, the director of public works and an engineer, shop-floor training had already paid dividends in government shops. "It is not clear what is implied by the term, 'trained African,'" he wrote in 1936 as he explained to the Department of Education that secondary students from Makerere University, the best in East Africa, needed the same "experience" and "practical" training that uneducated day laborers gained through decades of the manual on-the-job training that Lugard had condemned for mechanics in 1922. Stevenson noted that, more than creating a false standard of mechanical skill, a preference for official training drove up the costs of workshop labor. Though less skilled than manual laborers, certified mechanics expected high salaries and left when they did not receive them.[40]

The director's comments also allude to an epistemic challenge that historians of technology face with written archives. On the one hand, many of those who produced them did not or could not fix vehicles themselves. On the other, colonial officials' technological ideal—paper-based expertises rooted in books, classrooms, and certification—simply leads to a historical dead end because they do not reference the spaces, bodies, minds, or itineraries that created automotive expertise in the colony. The same issue applies to the independent period.

For these reasons, I treat garages and their contents as the most authoritative archive for telling stories of African car repair. I do so in four ways. First, I use oral histories to chart interlocutors' path to garage life and to establish genealogies of mechanical knowledge passed from mechanic to apprentice, what interlocutors call "inherited mechanics" (*ufundi wa kurithi*). Historically, this phrase is a bit redundant. *Ufundi*—an amorphous term for knowledge mastery by a practitioner, who earns the title *fundi*—refers to almost any specialized form of knowledge or mastery of action, including carpentry, sewing, spiritual matters, soccer, hunting, and mechanics. Kathryn de Luna shows that *fundi* came from the Mashiriki verb "to teach" (*-tund*), adding that it spread geographically through its connections with social mobility (especially as a form of status claiming during enslavement).[41] The verb "to teach" (*kufundisha*) in Kiswahili describes the causative process of transmitting knowledge to a *mwanafunzi*—literally, the offspring (*mwana*) of the teacher—who acquires both knowledge and status through this inheritance before they do the same, as fundi, for others. I do not approach these inheritance transmissions as unchanging or monolithic but as evidence of broad historical commonalities found across multiple generations of mechanics and across geographic space—in other words, evidence of the knowledge specialization and spillovers often denied vernacular expertises and institutions in most development literature.[42]

Second, when possible, I paired oral histories of repair with actual demonstrations of the fixes and modifications that older mechanics had performed decades earlier. This led not only to elaborations of the actions of mechanical labor but also to an axiom of scholarship in science and technology studies: that material details matter for understanding how both things and social groups work.[43]

For example, during a recording in Tabora, one mechanic, Kassim Jaha Abdullah, refused to proceed with a demonstration of brake repair, aghast at the materials his young assistants had brought him for his re-creation:

> This is not history! We didn't have nuts like these; we couldn't even find nuts. We had to make them out of cans and scrap metal. How can I stand here and tell our friend, "We did this and this and this," when it isn't true? And what does he know? He'll take this information home and share it

with others who are smarter than he is, and they will say, "That doesn't seem possible." Things have changed since those days.[44]

Abdallah insisted on material specificity because details about the parts or scrap available in changing economies shaped mechanics' technological options for repair and, by extension, their reputations and careers. He feared that using what the apprentices had brought could expose him as a fraud not only to his local peers but also to a transnational community of mechanics, of which he considered himself a member.

Third, Abdallah's words also speak to a similar concern regarding technical authority: that the density of things and people surrounding us in the garage demonstrated expertise, not the words said in an interview or found in books or certification documents. Successful mechanics attracted customers and students and collected stunning amounts of spare parts and broken vehicles that spilled out of their spaces of labor (*kiwandani*) and into sitting rooms and chicken coops. They also documented their own lives through pictures they either kept in the garage or proudly displayed in albums and on living-room walls. In other words, the stories I heard in garages and the certificates mechanics produced were not supposed to validate them. Instead, they were one part of an infrastructure of expertise in which the ability to collect people and things over decades and to transform them signified mechanical credibility to both apprentices and customers alike.[45] Crawling into and under the vehicles I saw in garages in 2011 and 2012 did not always offer direct links to decades-old pasts, no doubt. Yet as the chart and pictures in this chapter attest, vehicles carried literal material traces of creativity that helped bring oral histories and picture archives to life. In one case, an interview with a bus-owning family about a simple fix—collecting heavier front springs and using them throughout the vehicle to protect against rough roads (a process occurring during the interview)—led the sons of the family to call me as I traveled on one of their buses, en route to Kigoma from Tabora. After the bus's conductor brought his phone to me and said, "They want to talk to you," the brothers wanted to know if the relentlessly bumpy trip had validated their history about springs from the day before.

Fourth, I joined a street garage in Dar es Salaam as an apprentice. Owing to my limited research time, I experienced only a month of uninterrupted training for a process that takes several years (I returned at least once a week while in Dar es Salaam). Still, the opportunity to learn by doing, to follow parts, and to document repairs I observed or in which I participated informed subsequent oral interviews. Questions about more recent approaches to repair resulted in detailed explanations of changed conditions or in histories of methods of repair that became commonplace in bubu garages. The apprenticeship also revealed details about everyday garage life rarely visible in oral histories. In the interview format, mechanics stressed their intelligence (*akili*) by recounting their mechanical creativity during their careers. Though an important foil to the devaluation of African skill throughout the twentieth century, akili narratives diminish the bulk of daily activity in a garage. This includes the role of routine maintenance for training apprentices and the careful orchestration of bodies required to remove and replace heavy parts during modification.[46]

My status as the lowest member of a garage assuaged several mechanics' fears that I was a spy from American car companies who had come to steal their ideas—a clear indication of how bubu mechanics assess their own place in global car economies. A quick call to my head mechanic, who said something like, "He only helps fix brakes. He can't do anything with your ideas," often made interlocutors chuckle and established them as the mechanical expert during interviews. We turn now to the beginning of a process through which mechanics came to see themselves as auto experts with worldwide credibility.

FROM *BOIS* TO MEN: MANUAL LABOR AND SHOP-FLOOR EXPERTISE IN COLONIAL GARAGES

After World War I, the Transport Department (incorporated into the PWD in 1930) acted as the center of motor vehicle repair in Tanganyika.[47] The Transport Department classified these workshop laborers as casual and, consequently, offered few of them more than daily-wage contracts. But it still attracted a class of dedicated workmen who spent decades pursuing the highest status they could achieve in the department without official education: automobile mechanic.[48] Young men also joined private repair shops located in the colony's townships and on its plantations, the latter one of the first spaces where manual laborers worked side by side with machines. In the early 1920s, only a handful of garages or machine shops existed in the entire colony, with most found at sisal plantations. A decade later, each major township had repair centers. By the postwar period, the Department of Labour counted more than 262 registered garages, likely overlooking many unregistered shops, and at least 3,954 African men were employed as mechanics or fitters.[49] Beyond this numerical growth, garages offered young African men accessible technological spaces to reframe expectations about class, gender, and useful knowledge. Through proximity to broken machines in urban spaces, they built lives as city men in ways that confounded colonial theories about who drove sociotechnical change, where they did so, and how.

Prospective African mechanics entered workshops between their early teens and late twenties. They gained access in three ways. The first route, and the most common at government garages, was through a family member or friend who had a good reputation at a workshop. When the PWD needed more labor, the department asked trusted African laborers to work through familial contacts. Fadhili Ramadhani entered the PWD workshop in Tabora at age eighteen or nineteen through his father's connections as an engineer's assistant. He started as the department's gatekeeper, but "they liked me," he explained. He then began a five-year apprenticeship at the motor workshop.[50] The second method was for young men to prove themselves as competent and dedicated manual laborers. At the Transport Department, members of road gangs, porters, and even craftsmen gained opportunities to drive—the first introduction to mechanical knowledge—and assist in repairs by performing manual work for years and sometimes decades. The same occurred at private garages. Porters (*wapagazi*) who loaded and unloaded trucks were sometimes asked to move vehicles short distances or to help African drivers and headmen start them. Simply learning to start vehicles helped manual laborers seek training as drivers while also providing them more access to spaces of maintenance and repair.

Ramadhani Saidi Malambo turned his role as a taniboi ("turnboy") into garage work in the late 1950s. "If the car needed repair, I took it to the mechanics at the garage. I watched the way they fixed it; they did this and that, this and that. And this was how I learned ufundi."[51] This proximity to machines was also an integral part of Omari Kibwana's transition from a laborer on a sisal estate in Iringa to a mechanic at the age of sixteen. In his case, an African foreman in charge of the farm's truck and tractor equipment chose him as an assistant and paid him five shillings a month to help fix Bedford, Austin, and Ford trucks and tractors. "In those days you didn't need anything to enter a shop," he said.[52] In 1946 Suleiman Saidi Sitembo followed friends to Morogoro township from the village of Mkuyuni. "I came to the city without a brother, a sister, or an uncle, but I had friends. For my first job, I sold *vitumbua* [a pastry] for a woman named Kibibi; I received two shillings a month and slept at her place. My pillow was straw, and my bed cement. I got news there was an Asian man with a garage. I went to join, but I didn't receive a salary: you don't pay and aren't paid." He joined three other Waswahili (plural for people who identify as or are identified as Swahili) learning in the garage and referred his friends whenever there was an opening.[53] Kassian Duma, who grew up near Iringa two hundred miles southwest of Morogoro, dropped out of school after form 3. He had no money, and his father had already died. He traveled to Iringa in search of work (*kibarua*) and joined a garage owned by a Greek emigrant, where he learned welding.[54] In Tabora, Shabani Ramadhani traded domestic work for work as an "office boy," cleaning offices and arranging files, at the PWD before using his access in the department to make his way to the garage.[55]

These young men entered shops as cleaners, fitters, or learners, titles that translated to the shop floor as the English-Swahili hybrid *boi* ("boy"). Though the aesthetics of repair garages varied, prospective mechanics often learned in makeshift workshops constructed with constrained budgets. In these spaces, young men encountered a wealth of broken machines. The Transport Department, and later the PWD, struggled to keep more than 50 percent of government vehicles roadworthy. This stemmed not only from the age of the vehicles—which were commonly more than ten years old—but also from the proliferation of vehicle types. With ten different manufacturers in 1922 and twenty-two in 1926, the PWD found purchasing and keeping stores of standardized parts "uneconomical."[56] Consequently, government workshops reused old cars and parts and often made their own spares. Even for good vehicles, they used secondhand parts to perform a complete overhaul every five years; underperforming or worndown vehicles found themselves turned into spare parts or auctioned for use elsewhere. All of this matters because it required as much labor as garages could afford and thus created a form of manual day labor that not only exposed young African men to the details of breakdown, repair, and overhaul but also offered these men a rigorous pedagogy in which improvisation and flexibility were standard.[57]

Before participating in seasonal overhauls, new garage laborers started by cleaning parts. A former apprentice from a government garage in Tabora recalled his experience this way: "The head mechanic always wore white, from his leather boots up to his wrists. As a *boi spana* [literally, a spanner (wrench) boy] your job was to clean parts with petrol and a rag. When you finished, you alerted him, and he would swipe his finger inside the part and rub it on his uniform. If you dirtied his clothes, you had failed. If no stain showed up, he shook your hand. This was no small thing because it was every boy's dream in the garage to someday wear the white uniform."[58] The white uniform may seem distant from a learner meticulously cleaning parts. Yet simple acts like cleaning offered casual laborers entrance into a world of esoteric mechanical knowledge where they learned about parts and their particularities by make, model, and year. Even if they were just cleaning a carburetor, they would likely take an hour, if not hours, looking it over, touching inside—double-checking their work before it was inspected by their supervisor. With rag in hand, they ran their fingers over crevices and into holes and over valves—cleaning dirt and grease but also revealing details of the thing they held. Perhaps they did the same with pistons and their rings; on a lucky day, they peered into engine blocks and wiped them clean after reboring. Over months and years, cleaners learned the names of parts and their relationships to other parts of the vehicle.

From cleaners, they became learners and assistants. At this point, the most important figure in the garage was not the head mechanic but an African headman who translated languages, shared expertise (whether their own or instructions that came from a head mechanic), directed work, and set the rules for his students: "We respected the foreman. We had to arrive at work exactly at 7. First, you arrange all of the wrenches, and then you wait to be told by the foreman what work you will do." "It wasn't like school," Kibwana explained about machine work on the sisal estate. "It was: do this, take that off, put it back on; no, not that way, it's not right. You do this until a person understands this or that. We didn't open books."[59] Like their counterparts at the PWD, aspiring mechanics in private garages and on plantations did not speak English, so they learned using mnemonic strategies. Bushiri Ali, who learned in Iringa, incorporated part names into a song as vehicles were taken apart and put back together: "*Gereji boi* meant you knew how to do things. As a garage boy, you spend the entire year learning the names of things, by which I mean you couldn't write, so you didn't. You get experience by seeing with your eyes [*kuona kwa macho*] and by singing. You sing: *stata, stata, stata,* until it gets in your brain. But you don't write."[60] Though car parts retained their English names, the song served important pedagogical work that guided Ali through the tasks of repair and made the vehicles' many parts knowable not just as things but as relational pieces that served specific purposes in the process of repair and automobile function.

Such shop-floor pedagogies came from African foremen. According to Ali Bushiri, European supervisors divided labor according to specialties: one apprentice learned fixing gearboxes, one attaching engines, one washing, and so on. But African headmen "mixed" them up so that, after ten years in a garage, a fundi would be "complete, that is, knowing all machines."[61] Kondo Mfaume called this the "full idea" (original in English) of the car.[62] At this point, a cleaner-turned-learner could start making a claim on the status of *fundi*—a capacious Kiswahili word that describes a holder of skill and expertise in almost any task and that does not follow the craft-mechanics divide.[63] Historians of the 1800s and early 1900s have shown that the term *fundi*, and its connection to learning and knowing, was closely connected to claims on masculine social mobility by slaves seeking to become clients (and thus, not slaves) through skill acquisition, whether hunting elephants with rifles or guiding and protecting caravans. Like the foreman's "full idea," these earlier aspirations to skilled mobility produced specific sociotechnical innovations that allowed subordinate men to exercise some control over economic activities and the learning associated with them. In garages, a new fundi likely still had their work inspected by a foreman and head mechanic. But cultivating, possessing, and asserting the "full idea" allowed claims on importance within shops.[64] Indeed, colonial records illustrate that fundi gained authority not by their ability to pass tests but by their daily competence during periods of overhaul that peaked during the rainy season, when cars flooded into workshops because most roads were impassable.

Repair records from government vehicles speak to the variety of fixes apprentices saw, assisted with, and learned as they developed this "full idea." Easier tasks included replacing bushings and lines for brakes or doing metalwork, such as making bodies (which was sometimes done with scrap wood) or repairing chassis. Intermediate tasks delved further into the engine, such as replacing the connecting rods that attached the piston to the crankshaft, or involved the steering (such as the kingpins) and drive mechanisms (such as the axle). The most advanced projects involved reboring the engine and setting oversized pistons and rings. This common operation exposed apprentices to the heart of the engine and to a variety of techniques, including precise machine work. An apprentice at most workshops from the 1920s to the 1940s would see each of these fixes done on cars from multiple manufacturers, including Bedford, Albion, Morris, Chevrolet (Canadian), Dodge, Ford, Morris, Cubitt, and Cross-ley.[65] They worked on a range of years and types, from large vehicles such as lorries, dump trucks, and garbage vehicles to sedans and motorcycles. And they encountered different systems of combustion, including kerosene, gasoline, and diesel. A lucky PWD fundi might see all of these fixes in just one rainy season.

As a standardized approach to maintenance, annual overhauls required laborers to see automobiles not as technologies finished at the point of manufacture but rather as vehicles that needed continual (re)constitution by parts from various models and required men's touch and ideas to continuously make them commensurate with operating conditions or part availability—an amplified process of what Madeline Akrich terms the "de-scription of technical objects."[66] It is worth recalling that many of the cars used in colonial Tanganyika—and certainly most of the vehicles mechanics saw in repair garages—had long lost their original composition, or inscription, from their manufacture in Europe or the United States. Indeed, repair records describe a seasonal process of reinscription in which the PWD and its staff made entire fleets of vehicles that functioned well in Tanganyika. Repair records do not provide any detail about African mechanics' and headmen's roles as designers and innovators in this process. But knowing the critical role of these men upends the process of car design explored above. Instead of vehicles designed in Europe for a stereotyped "tropical" and "roadless" Africa—a process that actively sought to replace African labor with a reliable colonial machine—and only tested in Tanganyika, these vehicles went in and out of garages that relied on the learning that took place at the intersection of African minds and hands.

Moreover, instead of the above distinction between heads and hands, workshops relied on an embodied intuition built on touching things. Scholars have described this process in a number of ways. Harper calls it "working knowledge," while Christopher Henke uses "body centered." Tim Dant and Stefan Krebs describe "sensual knowledge" and "sensory skills," respectively. All establish a strong link among embodied sensing and intuiting (seeing, touching, and hearing); mechanical knowledge production, whether learning or innovating; and the skilled motions needed to repair a technology.[67] Sociologists Harry Collins and Robert Evans call this form of knowledge production "expertise by experience" and make the case for removing qualifying adjectives such as *lay, folk,* or *popular* from the way we write about it. "We say that those referred to by some other analysts as 'lay experts' are just plain 'experts'—albeit their knowledge has not been recognized by certification."[68] Mechanics from the colonial and national periods used a near-exact phrase in Kiswahili—*utaalum wa uzoefu,* or "expertise of experience"—which they anchored in the "test of doing."

No doubt, one could theoretically take courses at government schools and then learn by experience in the PWD garage. But to do so, and to privilege this itinerary, overlooks where useful automotive knowledge resided in the colony.[69] Shop-floor training acted as the ground zero for mechanical expertise because it offered the densest space of things and actions pertaining to vehicles. Even more, it matched the specific repair landscape of government or private fleets in ways that allowed maturing men to make claims on not just an abstract mechanical expertise but even more so the specific forms of African car making that had already proven themselves in local contexts within Tanganyika.

The places and itineraries of overhaul mattered to mechanics because they hoped to enter garages as boi and leave as men. For Suleiman Saidi Sitembo, who became the boss ("big man," or *mkubwa*) at Babu Garage in Morogoro in the mid-1950s, dedication to automobile repair brought a monthly salary of thirty shillings as well as increased status: "If someone runs a garage, everyone knows him."[70] I pressed Sitembo on these comments by asking about the presence of racial discrimination (*ubaguzi*) during work. He said it was there but then shifted the conversation from racially based insults to the merits of technical competency: "They'd say: 'Your mom was born from a horse and a dog.' You can go to the police, but there's nothing they can do. I was lucky to get the chance for [the owner] to see that I know my work. Then they treated me like their child."[71] Sitembo's claim to move from being less-than-human to becoming the "child" of the garage owners through technical work may seem odd. But his use of ufundi to narrate social mobility was common in oral histories of colonial mechanics. Kondo Mfaume described mechanical work as "a respected position because we could fix a car."[72] In this short phrase, the "we"—young African men—gain "respect" through the status of the car as either broken or fixed. If achieved, the latter offered a mechanical state that made the fixer's background as a "native," casual manual laborer less relevant, as it did with drivers in the previous chapter.

Pay at garages rarely equaled even the bottom end of colonial salaried labor. But mechanical work allowed men to generate enough wealth to marry, to rent and build homes in urban areas, and to have children even as they performed labor they valued personally. In the evenings, some went out on the town, enjoying the cinema, going to dance clubs, or playing soccer. They sported stylish clothes and bought gifts for friends and family while rooting themselves in urban and peri-urban spaces by building homes. In Sitembo's case, his salary as the "big man" at Babu Garage was fifteen times what he had made selling vitumbua after immigrating to the city.[73] Mechanical work also facilitated claims on social status that few manual laborers could make. Mbaraka Kassim, who began training in garages in Zanzibar in 1935, placed his success on an equal footing with that of educated colonial clerks: "Even though I didn't go to school, I was able to become as successful and popular as the African clerks in town. I went to movies and bought nice clothes. If people saw me walking on the street, they would say, 'That guy is a mechanic!'"[74] For men like Kassum with limited or no access to colonial education, garages offered an accessible space through which they navigated the hegemonic markers of gendered personhood in the colony through earnings, access to one of the world's most important technologies, and social networks that provided access to both.

Like drivers, mechanics faced hard limits on their social mobility through car work. At the PWD, government pay structures valued race and official education over shop-floor competency. The highest-paid African received 140 shillings per month and 1 shilling per hour overtime, less than the lowest-ranked Asian, who received 150 shillings per month and ten cents more per hour of overtime.[75] But most mechanics were left out of the permanent establishment that would have led to receiving such pay, or uniforms, including the white one. One official described them as "labourers and other such menials." In a 1939 letter to the department, mechanics charged the government with ignoring its own rhetoric about technological hierarchies by valuing the department's drivers over the mechanics. Though the PWD considered both forms of work "casual labor"—meaning laborers could be let go "at any time with nothing more to show for their long service than the regular receipt of their wages from month to month"—drivers occupied posts that officials called "permanent," and they received monthly salaries, paid leave, uniforms, and traveling allowances, as chapter 1 illustrated.[76] Mechanics who had served for up to fifteen years had lower pay, received pay per hour and not per month, and had neither uniforms nor paid leave. The motor superintendent concluded that "two very competent boys" had already left for this reason and called on his superiors to reward "skilled workers" with paid leave and uniforms. Neither was offered, only a badge of service for workers who had spent ten years in the workshop.[77]

Perhaps some of these men, like Kassum, opened a garage in their own neighborhood. In 1942 Kassum left a private garage where he had worked for seven years in order to open a home-based garage in the Ng'ambo neighborhood of Zanzibar Town.[78] He fixed used cars owned by African, Asian, and Arab traders and acquired apprentices of his own whom he instructed in exchange for their labor. In Tabora, Jumanne Mrisho worked at a garage during the day as an apprentice but learned during the evenings with a mechanic whose reputation (*sifa*) was that he had not studied. Mrisho brought his other friends to these evening sessions.[79] Working in garages that lacked much of the equipment of government and private workshops, and for businessmen with tight budgets, mechanics extended the overhaul techniques standard in colonial garages. They also developed new methods for diagnosing and fixing automobiles. When World War II exacerbated spare-parts shortages, a driver in Tabora recalled that an African mechanic who worked out of his home found a solution to a steering column that had stymied European mechanics in private garages.[80]

As apprentice programs based on international standards struggled to attract and motivate students in the late 1940s and 1950s, neighborhood garages provided accessible yet rigorous sites for acquiring mechanical expertise for young men with limited financial and educational resources. In them, mechanics started to remake themselves and vehicles outside of European technical authority and institutions. Frederick Cooper demonstrates that colonial officials across Africa saw casual labor as an obstacle to social and economic development because it was deemed unreliable and unskilled. Indeed, a main goal of postwar development was decasualization through increased wages and benefits—programs that coincided with government apprenticeship programs and industrial trainers' desire to see a specific form of technical culture in British East Africa.[81] But for young African men, the casual nature of auto repair provided opportunities to learn important skills because there was no threshold for colonial education and because they saw it as neither temporary nor unskilled. The result was not only an alternative infrastructure of expertise but also a culture of industrial masculinity that combined hand and head work, marking both as important parts of learning, creativity, and social mobility. This occurred first in colonial workshops before becoming the basis of African mechanical identities in home and private garages.[82]

I argued in the introduction that calling these spaces or practices *informal* overlooks that such garages were part of an institutional landscape that was always broader—and could be made broader still—than the things colonial rule brought and valued as powerful knowledge. Here it is worth recalling that two common Kiswahili nouns for "school" come from German and English: *shule*, which is used on the mainland, a former

2.2 *An African mechanic repairs a truck near Pare sometime between 1929 and 1940. "Autoreparatur in Maore, Südpare," Evangelisch-Lutherisches Missionswerk Leipzig e.V., impaunpub_Volume3/IMP-LPZ-ALBUM-01-1421.tif.*

German colony, and *skuli*, used on Zanzibar, a former British protectorate. My point is that we need to take care with language about useful knowledge, lest the Kiswahili verb for learning—*kujifunza*—occur only in spaces whose lexical foundations come from colonial rule and institutions. During the colonial period, casual laborers-turned-mechanics showed that both men and cars could be put together differently and that useful knowledge came from unexpected spaces, bodies, minds, and institutions (such as the setting visible in figure 2.2).[83] We now explore how these knowledge debates continued as an independent generation of African mechanics made cars their own.

"MANPOWER": MECHANICS AND THE POLITICS OF REPAIR IN INDEPENDENT STATE GARAGES

After independence in 1961, the new government nationalized the PWD as the Department of Works, or Ujenzi. Over the next two decades, Ujenzi expanded opportunities for official technical education to new regions and social groups by offering evening training classes in each of Tanzania's townships. In contrast to colonial programs, which failed to provide African students incentives to finish certification—and which relied upon teaching from the United Kingdom—Ujenzi's vocational training, its large new workshops, and its competitive salary attracted attention from young men with a wide variety of educational experience.[84] A survey conducted in 1966 showed that a miniscule 1.6 percent of Tanzania's young men with secondary education considered "motorcar mechanics" their first choice for a profession. But as a second-choice career, mechanic was ranked behind only doctor, engineer, and lawyer as a desirable profession.[85] The survey did not include women nor the vast majority of Tanzanians who did not pass on to secondary school. Yet oral histories show that state garages ignited the technological imagination of individuals who viewed the state's new technological spaces as places to become men and to gain resources for growing old by turning physical labor into mental authority and wealth.[86]

More than creating men, Tanzania's state aimed to produce specific forms of "manpower." As a marriage of education and economic planning that gained popularity among planners in the 1950s, manpower formalized the idea that growing and productive economies required specific sets of training and skill: economies that had them grew, while those that lacked collective skill fell behind. Proponents of manpower planning drew heavily on theories of human capital popularized by the economist Theodor W. Schultz. Citing Adam Smith, Schultz argued that humans and their skills should be treated "explicitly as a form of capital."[87] He argued, for example, that higher levels of education explained why Japan and Germany had recovered more quickly than Great Britain from World War II. The same applied to the American South, Schultz charged, where segregated education had harmed economic growth by leaving large parts of the population undertrained. As for the continuation of embodied expertise as masculine: with skill as capital, planners expected a return on the costs of training experts. Although women were no doubt capable of learning, their role as mothers (and thus time away from employment) greatly reduced their return on investment, some planners argued. Only months after winning independence in 1961, Julius Nyerere welcomed the Ford Foundation to conduct a manpower survey, declaring: "No problem facing this Government is more urgent than that of increasing the supply and improving the organization of highly qualified manpower needed for economic and social development."[88] Given the racially segregated nature of colonial education, no one was surprised at the skill gaps the surveyors found. A government Manpower Division subsequently formed to address this gap.[89]

In manpower terms, auto work required a combination of low-, mid-, and high-level skill. *Low-level* served as a catchall term for manual work. Surveyors approached this category as purely physical and thus regarded these workers as in need of direction from garage foremen and managers. Conversely, mid- and high-level work required the ability to make administrative and technical decisions, to give orders, and to train unskilled employees. Midlevel mechanics directed work and teaching on the shop floor, whereas high-level managers ordered parts and vehicles, signed off on the repairs proposed by foremen, and managed the entire garage staff in an office. Manpower planners thought garages needed only small numbers of these two categories because they could train and certify the best workers from Tanzania's huge pool of low-level labor.[90] Labor counted as skilled in these assessments—and therefore as manpower—only if it could be categorized through certification and therefore enumerated to meet the anticipated demand of future economic forecasts. Out of the 8,000 skilled workers thought to be needed to reach economic goals for 1980, demand of "motor vehicle mechanic" remained high, ranging from 74 to 154 more positions needed annually in government ministries between 1975 and 1980. Legislation in 1974 gave the Ministry of Labour and Social Welfare responsibility to coordinate training to meet these needs through a National Vocational Training Programme.[91]

In the 1960s, most young Tanzanian men did not question this narrow definition of skill or its graded categories of manpower. In fact, these standards connected the new nation to global circuits of knowledge and evidenced a legitimate state willing to lead technological change. Ujenzi's regional workshops featured foundries, lathes for modifications to parts, and a special mobile team that traveled the country in a Land Rover to take on the hardest repairs. The campuses had libraries, dorms, and soccer fields. Ujenzi also taught in Kiswahili on the shop floor, provided evening and morning classes, and even paid for the trade tests through which workers moved from Grade 3 (315 shillings a month) to Grade 2 (420 shillings) to Grade 1 (460 shillings). (After the second grade, mechanics became "pensionable."[92]) It was, in Hamisi Salum Luwango's words, a "good life" (*maisha mazuri*).[93]

Both Omar Seif Ngomadodo and Suleiman Seif Saidi built their lives through this new technological structure. Starting as a taniboi at the Arusha PWD in 1954, Ngomadodo followed a short career as a driver in southeastern Africa by operating buses for both of Tanzania's national bus companies. One of these, Dar es Salaam Motor Transport, paid for his studies at a nearby technical school, where he achieved the top grade of motor mechanic. He worked in state garages until they were dissolved in 1988.[94] Suleiman Seif Saidi first learned ufundi in the military, before studying at the national vocational school in Changombe, where he took a range of courses, including Technology, Workshop Practice, Calculations, Technical Drawing, Science, English, Swahili, and Political Education. He worked for Dar es Salaam Motor Transport and KAMATA (Kampuni ya Mabasi ya Taifa, a national bus company) in engine overhaul until 1991; he "did modifications with the lathe, boring, and surface machines. If there was the possibility to modify, we did it."[95]

A handful of mechanics, such as Mohamedi Kibwana Kondo, entered government motor depots through family connections.[96] But most recalled that "you couldn't even get an interview without showing a certificate from school," which most young men lacked.[97] Sports, especially soccer, provided an avenue to circumvent these standards. Hamisi Hamadi "Mau," who grew up in Kigoma, asked the Ujenzi shop manager several times whether he could join the garage as an apprentice. Refused on each occasion, he called the experience humiliating because it exposed his lack of education and social standing. But Hamadi, a soccer manager, had a keen eye for talent and connections to players. After Hamadi's club, the Soccer Tricks, beat competition from Bujumbura, Burundi, in the city's national stadium, the same manager walked onto the pitch to offer him a trade: build a team for Kigoma Ujenzi in exchange for an apprenticeship. The deal brought not only Hamadi to the shop floor but also the players he needed to build a team. They called the team "Ufundi" (pictured in figure 2.3). Once in the garage, they aimed to move from Grade 4—a learner "without education—to Grade 3, "at which point you were considered a fundi," through trade testing at regional and national technical institutes. Between 1973 and 1976, the group shown in figure 2.4 passed from Grades 3 to 2, ultimately earning an opportunity to train at Ujenzi's college in Morogoro, a technological pilgrimage they documented with pictures that still hang on their walls.[98] Others took the same path through the Vocational Training Centre opened in 1960 in Dar es Salaam, where motor mechanics was one of three original training programs—and where one student happily recalled combining classroom instruction with work in their Tanzanian teacher's personal garages.[99]

2.3 *The Ufundi sports club of Ujenzi managed by Hamisi Hamadi "Mau" in 1973.*

2.4 *Apprentices from the Ufundi soccer team learning and working in a state garage. The photo gives a sense of the joy and pride mechanics found in being with each other and around machines while working for their nation.*

Once an obstacle to social mobility, certification became a rite of passage to technological adulthood. It provided financial security and social status and allowed them to enter the ranks of "those with certificates" (*wenye vyeti*).[100] Scholars in science and technology studies, such as Collins and Evans, have challenged claims to certified expertise removed from the messiness of embodied work and tacit learning.[101] But for these maturing mechanics—each of whom stressed the importance of embodied knowledge for learning itself—paper certificates issued by national and international institutions meant "you rented a room and still had money to save," as Fadhili Ramadhani put it.[102] Certification, such as the one pictured in figure 2.5, also granted holders access to the newest models and the best machinery. Hussein Almasi took a three-month course on British motorcycles at Changombe in Dar es Salaam: "[The government] took care of everything (food, lodging, and transport), and we got to learn about a motorcycle we knew nothing about."[103] In sum, maturing men sought testing and certification precisely because they removed knowledge and credibility from their (aging) bodies and the shop floor. They placed validation and credibility instead in state institutions that offered higher pay, pensions, classes, and immediate access to new vehicles.

At the same time, state garages challenged mechanics' ideas about technological personhood. Neither mechanics (Grade 1 to 3) nor their apprentices (Grade 4) had authority to make decisions about the means or method of repair. Instead, bureaucrats who "could not even fix a door handle," as one fundi complained, received mechanics' suggestions on a paper card assigned to each car and then made the decision in an office. The hierarchy for decision-making descended from manager to inspection officer to assistant mechanical inspector to subinspector to foreman and, finally, to fundi. Consequently, if a mechanic's superiors considered repairs uneconomical, they denied the request by writing on the card BMR ("beyond mechanical repair"). Unfixed, the car was later sold at auction (*kupigwa mnada*).[104] Noting BMR's economic wastefulness, mechanics said it grew out of managers' technological ignorance, and it left the shop-floor labor with a devalued and mindless form of labor. "Take-off-put-on," the Kiswahili phrase for replacing a worn-out part with a new one, left no room for mechanics to experiment on shop floors or to attempt part or vehicle salvage.

A mechanic living in Kigoma recalled that problems with technical authority extended to international training and certification programs, too. When a European instructor for his trade-testing class experienced

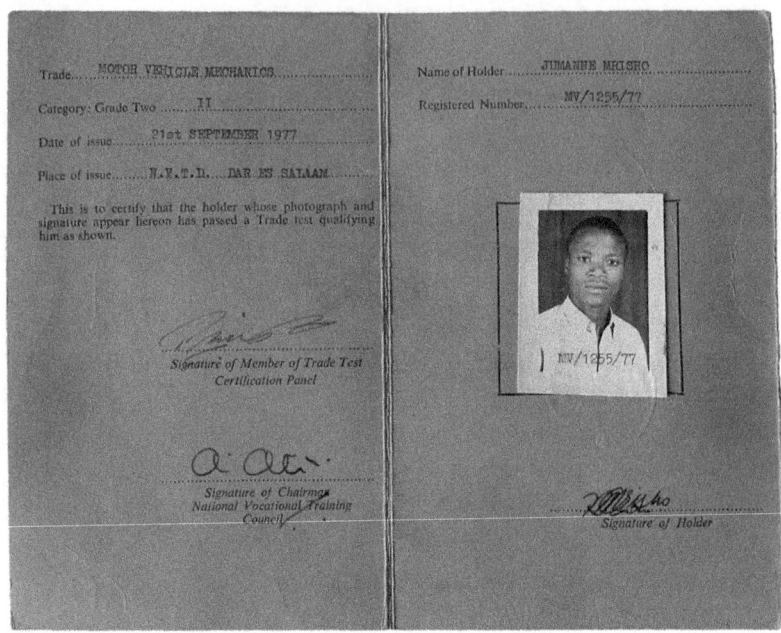

2.5 *An example of a trade certificate from Jumanne Mrisho issued in 1977. Mechanics produced these repeatedly in interviews but also used them to talk about the limits of social mobility in government repair shops.*

car trouble out of town, Yusufu Ulimwengu came to help only to find his teacher stymied by a simple carburetor problem. Ulimwengu quit the next day, rhetorically asking me in the interview, "How can I learn from someone who didn't know that?"[105] Shabani Ramadhani obtained his Grade 3 certificate before tiring of a system he described as "blaa blaa": "A person comes, and you do the test. To prepare, you study theory, not the practical you already have. . . . If you pass, you are promoted and your salary is increased. For the second grade, I passed in the wheel-alignment test, but then [the teachers] came again [for another test], and I just said, 'I don't want this test.' It was all white people at the tests and colleges. The country was run by them."[106] Hussein Almasi described a similar experience. After using his position on Morogoro's regional soccer team to get a position at Ujenzi and a Grade 3 license, he found that "there [in the garage] you're below people. If you want to do something to raise yourself, you aren't able." He left in 1978 for a bubu garage that specialized in modifications so that he "could become self-reliant [*kujitegemea*]."[107] Almasi grounded "self-reliance"—a tenet of Nyerere's African socialism (*ujamaa*, or

"familyhood")—in mechanics' ability to direct their own work and validate themselves as experts through knowledge they already held or could
generate with things on hand.

His definition was likely shaped by the consequences of economic
instability in garages. After the mid-1970s, economic contraction led to
crippling shortages of new spare parts in state garages. Combined with
managers' decisions to not authorize modifications, an absence of new
spares meant mechanics simply had little work to do. Consequently, much
like vehicles marked "BMR," mechanics found themselves "marked redundant" (*kupigwa redundancy*) and let go.[108] Some, like Almasi, left the state
garages completely. Kassian Duma recalls, "The ministries were shaky; we
all knew we needed to go 'outside' for work. We all knew the job [*ufundi*],
and there was business."[109] Hamisi Salum Luwango opened an auto shop
specializing in welding in Morogoro with three of his colleagues: "We
were all in the [state] workshops. The government closed them along with
factories in the 1980s; that's why we're here in this 'indigenous' [*ya kie-
nyenji*] garage. It's a good life in the government workshop. There was
a dispensary, a representative from the Red Cross, you got clothes and
overalls, shoes and boots, you got a travel allowance."[110] For all of these
reasons, the soccer team in Ujiji combined day labor in state spaces with
work in their neighborhood in the evening.[111] They trained their sons and
neighbors and supplemented their income—and they enjoyed the labor,
as figure 2.6 shows.[112] Moreover, this strategy gave government ministries
time to recover economically so that mechanics could later claim their
pensions.

The decline of the state garages lingered in the minds of the mechanics I interviewed because of the technological opportunities they believed
their superiors had overlooked. Haji Hamisi Haliyamtu stated frankly that,
had he been a manager, he "would have allowed modifications" because
it would have salvaged state vehicles and, by extension, garages and mechanics' careers.[113] F. Kabura, a mechanical engineer who worked in motor
manufacturing in West Germany for ten years, came to a similar conclusion when he returned to Tanzania. Shortages of new parts "forced" the
"responsible engineer" to creatively "make [their] own parts" and to be
"continuously involved in investigations analyzing sources of breakdowns and faults."[114] The overwhelming number of makes and models
state mechanics had to modify, he argued, had kept them from developing deeper knowledge and replicable standards that could be implemented across government institutions. But if the government limited the

2.6 *State mechanics in Ujiji on a street where they all lived. They repaired cars and trained young men after work.*

variety of makes and models it imported, engineers could focus on those specific makes and models to turn into a national fleet. The opposite happened over the next decade as markets liberalized and used and new parts proliferated.[115]

Kabura and Haliyamtu did not think this was inevitable. According to mechanics, state cars were not BMR and could have been turned into national, or at least local, fleets; government had the manpower it needed but, instead of using it creatively, marked it redundant by disallowing the fixes that could have created social and technological self-reliance. Even during times of scarcity—and in some cases precisely because of it—government garages were within reach of achieving a mechanical version of *kujitegemea* ("self-reliance") in which ideas from the shop floor provided examples of technology in use that could be scaled up or standardized around the nation. Some mechanics even denied that spare-parts shortages ever existed because they did not view broken parts as constituting *uhaba*, or shortage. Interestingly, Kabura concluded his article—written in a time of part scarcity—by identifying the main problem in garages not as crippling material shortage but as a culture of authority that denigrated handwork and knowledge production that occurred outside of offices—in this case, in a garage: "The biggest problem for an engineer in Tanzania seems to be social acceptance within an enterprise. . . . There is still some confusion regarding the concept and role of an 'engineer'; even some managers consider an engineer as being a 'spanner-boy' who tightens the nuts."[116]

It is understandable why mechanics like Kabura and Haliyamtu equated their ideas and actions with Nyerere's definition of kujitegemea while also feeling disappointed, even betrayed, by the managerial approach to self-reliant knowledge they encountered in government spaces. The president had intentionally defined self-reliance specifically in 1967. "Self-reliance is not some vague political slogan . . . For a community, self-reliance means that they will use the resources and skills they jointly possess for their own welfare and their own development."[117] These earlier statements may not have anticipated the situations mechanics would encounter a decade later as the nation faced a series of economic crises, and yet this hands-on approach to kujitegemea had wider purchase. In 1978, an editorial in the *Sunday News* stated: "Self-reliance must also mean confidence in our own creative ability. The weakness here is caused by our half-baked elite, having been placed in a position of responsibility—but are scared of workers and, therefore, unwilling to learn from their experience."[118] Such statements recall Ato Quayson's caution about what constitutes a top or bottom in hierarchies of knowledge that inform scholarship. When it came to fixing cars in Tanzania in the 1970s, the individuals most capable of effecting change were largely ignored and yet continued to forge technological alternatives to personal and collective self-reliance.

"SPANNA MKONONI": "LEAVERS," STREET KNOWLEDGE, AND SELF-RELIANCE IN GEREJI BUBU

Neither gereji bubu nor their mechanics counted in manpower surveys—and, consequently, in assessments of national skill—because the spaces were unregistered and their laborers often uncertified. But the state was aware of their existence, and it argued publicly that the garages threatened national development. An article for *Nchi Yetu* (Our Nation)—a publication of the Ministry of Culture—titled "Capitalism Must Be Battled: Experts Complain about Street Garages" charged unregistered garages with taking "strength" away from socialist "unity" (*umoja*). It also ridiculed bubu mechanics' claims to credibility through experience:

One depressing example is if you walk just a few streets of our cities right now, you will see sections where decrepit cars and motorcycles are scattered here and there. There is one of these for every twenty houses, and he [the owner] claims he is a mechanic and that he has an ability based on experience and that he can work anywhere and anytime. They use the well-known phrase "Experience never grows old." We agree that experience never grows old, but this experience must be placed within a specific structure so that one can bring real success for the nation together with our children.

The article concludes that "the 'experience does not grow old' method being used by some of these mechanics endangers our nation."[119]

President Nyerere took a slightly different approach in a 1974 Workers' Day speech before the National Labor Union. He recalled a visit to a "small factory" (*kiwanda kidogo*) called Kameco in the Keko neighborhood of Dar es Salaam. Describing the expertise (*ufundi*) of the mechanics as *utundu-utundu*—a term with the dual meaning of being creative and also mischievous or child-like—Nyerere said, "They did not get customers. Who would believe you could give your car to a Swahili person of this type (*namna hiyo*) and they would fix it?" Even with government support for small industries, the garage struggled until its remaining members switched from car repair to making knives and clothes. Instead of questioning the believability of their expertise, as the president did with cars, he declared their decision a success and noted they were sold by a national company. "If I brought these clothes to you all and told you they were made in Germany, you would believe me." Though, in this exchange, it is hard to conclude that Nyerere thought urbanites of "this type" could not fix vehicles, the speech provides clues about state distinctions between desirable and less worthy urban technological identities and pursuits. Learning *utundu-utundu* by individuals of "this type"—likely having minimal schooling—could lead to the creation of high-standard home goods but not to a fixed car. As an example given in a speech titled "Everyone Must Work" ("Kila Mtu Afanye Kazi") suggests, this subtle distinction allows utundu-utundu knowledge to count as work for the nation for homewares but not for vehicles.[120] The cartoonist BataKing echoed these views with his classic character Bwanyenye. When his friend asks if the cars along Nyasa Street are a "college for those who fix vehicles," Bwanyenye calls him an "idiot," adding, "I have heard this is a car graveyard where motor vehicles come after they have died."[121]

Reports by members of the National Vocational Training Programme provide the clearest suggestions for why "manual" and experience-based training in places like Nyasa Street ran afoul of national, and thus socialist, priorities. Distinguishing hand work from theory and mental labor—what interviewees often termed *akili* and linked to manual labor—S. R. Makutika, the Labour Commissioner, feared technical authority would remain in the hands of "the owner himself or an expatriate." More than a connection to Tanzania's colonial past, Makutika feared manual labor imparted incomplete knowledge because, he asserted, copying a superior's actions might leave the learner clueless as to the rationale behind their trade. "Formalized" vocational training, he concluded, could address this problem.[122] Though each critique recalls the craft-mechanics divide from the colonial period, both episodes came out of specific concerns about young Tanzanian men whom officials and scholars called "school leavers." While, in some cases, leavers had left school early, the term generally referenced urban youth who had completed primary education (through standard seven) but did not find the urban employment they desired, if any at all.[123] This was, in part, a success story of independence. Tanzania's expansion of primary education led to increased social mobility for educated urban workers until the late 1960s, at which point the leavers looking for jobs greatly outnumbered employment or secondary school opportunities. The state's solution: take a less-skilled job or emigrate to an ujamaa village.[124] Nyerere's form of African socialism envisioned young people farming in rural communities where they not only contributed to national development through agricultural production but also created self-reliant forms of personhood that allowed individuals, families, and new socialist villages to sustain themselves. As the next chapter shows in more detail, cities emerged as the opposite of such socialist self-reliance. The president and many officials considered them places of loitering—and thus certainly not sites of work and nation building—and of unending need where individuals struggled to care for themselves or their families.[125]

City streets (pl. *mitaani*) thus appear in official discourse as self-reliance's opposite and, consequently, also as evidence of possible future demise. Those who dwelled on mitaani in state sources became beggars, thieves, and drug and alcohol addicts—drags on socialist society.[126] The poem "Kabwela Mji si Wako" (Loiterer, the city is not yours)" made this connection between street-based jobs and social and economic security explicit. It described jobs such as portering or selling bananas (which often occurred alongside or by walking streets) as an "absurdity" (*upuuzi*), whereas village work with a hoe is considered "work" (kazi). Kabwela, a popular term to refer to someone who was "poor and exploited" and "who deserved sympathy and assistance," as James Brennan details, will not find that assistance or sympathy—or meaningful work connected to socialist belonging—on city streets, the poem says.[127]

The idea, then, that young male leavers could make a claim on expert mechanical knowledge, even creating a category of expertise through the same term, *mtaani*, flew in the face of what politicians called "the politics of self-reliance" (*siasa ya kujitegemea*). It did so, in part, because both street knowledge and mechanics fit uncomfortably into Nyerere's approach to education. In rousing speeches, the president made impassioned pleas to respect and theorize from rural communities, respecting them as agricultural experts, while repeatedly attacking the arrogance of bureaucrats and managers who rooted their authority in university degrees, offices, and external connections. These same positions, though, did not translate to discussions about the spaces and forms of learning that had led to the existence of a robust culture of vernacular mechanical knowledge by the independent period. In a 1974 speech that reprised his more well-known essay "Education for Self-Reliance," Nyerere asserted that "the problem of integrating education with [African] society cannot be solved by abandoning formal education structure. We cannot go back to an exclusive dependence on the traditional system of what I previously called 'learning by living and doing.'" Echoing the *Nchi Yetu* article above, he suggested that even African industrial learning-by-doing could not and should not take hold in Tanzania because such industries and skills had first arrived as "imported capitalism" during colonialism. Letting them continue, he added, "would leave us so backward socially, and technologically, that human liberation in the foreseeable future is out of the question." In other words, even as it attempted to replace foreign with Tanzanian manpower, Nyerere's government saw a need for "knowledge imports" from abroad to address gaps administrators saw in higher-level manpower that, they argued, should not be filled through existing vernacular networks.[128]

Yet the broad category *mtaani* emerged as a vernacular category of technological self-reliance for urban communities sometime in the mid-1900s. First used to describe communities built around spaces of movement, for most of the 1800s and a good part of the early 1900s, *mtaa* denoted "neighborhoods" or "wards" in Swahili towns.[129] It is not clear when *mtaa* and its locative, *mtaani*, started to include and then largely reference the actual spaces of the street or a form of street life. Certainly, as manual laborers, prospective drivers had accessed vehicles on and alongside streets since the 1920s. Moreover, in the early 1900s, colonial governments used the term *mtaa* to denote individual street names in Kiswahili. This created a town grid of *mitaa* ("streets") that, linguistically, overlapped with the public spaces and activities that predated early uses of the term to mean "quarter" or "ward." One could thus speak of Mtaa wa Pugu ("Pugu Street"). By the early independent period, the term referenced a broader street life that connected homes, markets, and sites of leisure to the spaces of movement that connected the people who used them, whether they lived close by or a bus ride away.[130] And this is how we should understand mtaani as a literal sociotechnical place (*-ni* forms the locative in Kiswahili) of mechanical training. At times, learning and work occurred on or alongside motorable streets. But, just as frequently, mtaani referenced an urban technological space that gained power both by what it was—a network that combined everyday activities, leisure, and expert labor—and by what it was not: the type of bounded, walled space that authorities associated with expertise.

In contrast to the authorities, aspiring mechanics and their parents thus considered street garages spaces that turned young boys into respectable men capable of supporting themselves and a family. Interchangeably known as *bubu* ("mute") and *mtaani* ("street"), such garages had offered accessible spaces of training in neighborhoods since their emergence in the late 1930s among African mechanics. Because they were largely unregistered and existed at mechanics' homes, under trees, or in alleyways, gereji bubu functioned as open community spaces where local boys could be supervised and taught useful trades beginning as young as age nine.[131] Some young men sought out mechanics on their own by "begging" or "asking for advice" (*kuomba shauri*) about their lives, a Kiswahili phrase that signals deference to hierarchy. But most agreements came between mechanics and parents who, as mechanic Vitusi Kihanga put it, "are crying, they don't have anything" to "educate" their children.[132] According to Juma Katigiro, accepting "primary school leavers" and "failures" "who had nowhere to go" was a new "tradition" among mechanics, who understood parents' concerns because of their own experiences.[133] Bubu mechanics certainly wanted and needed labor. But they also saw their garages as institutions where young men could mediate economic uncertainty by learning a trade, as they once had.

Apprentices, generally called "youth" (*vijana*), spent at least two years (and more commonly three to six years) learning about vehicles and garage life by assisting their head mechanic, whom they called "uncle" (*mjomba*). Instead of a salary, they received a small percentage of the profits.[134] Suleiman Abdallah Mwenda moved from Morogoro to Dar es Salaam in 1964 and started training in "mechanical" "on the streets" the next year. "We took apart engines. Otherwise, how are you going to learn?" After seven years, with "wrench in hand" (*spanna mkononi*), he started looking for work as a "full mechanic." Two years passed before he found a group of mechanics in Dar es Salaam with similar aspirations. After agreeing with the local party branch about the use of land, they built a workshop in 1976 in which each fundi had his area of the garage and his own specialty—Mwenda was Peugeot expert.[135] Similarly, Peter William Mabula finished primary school in 1971 but could not find work. So he joined a bubu garage in a home on Rihani Street: "I stayed there for a year and half with about ten others. You are tested by what you can do; there's no theory. You're just thrown into work. . . . It's just you and your ambition [*bidii*]. VETA (a vocational school) was there, but it served the government, and we didn't have money to enter."[136]

In oral histories, mechanics emphasize three elements of their journey from a "spanner boy" (*boi spanna*) or youth (*kijana*) to two titles of authority in mute garages: fundi (which could mean "mechanic," specifically, or simply someone possessing skill) and mjomba ("uncle"). First, recalling Stephan Miescher's observation that "apprenticeships were sites where young men and young women became aware that certain crafts and occupations were gendered," interviewees describe a masculinized form of labor in which bodies replace machines.[137] Because vijana often worked in garages without jacks, engine hoists, or lathe machines, most things they did required copious amounts of lifting, scrubbing, grinding, and pushing. "One of the tests for a new boy was if his back was straight and his chest was out when we were carrying engines in the garages," a mechanic in Dar es Salaam recalled. "We didn't have a hoist, so we hooked the engine to scrap water pipes and hoisted those on our shoulders. If you saw a boy do this [he bends his back and brings his chin to his chest], he wouldn't survive."[138] Because removing or replacing heavy parts such as transmissions or engine blocks could maim or kill others in the garage, these moments provided opportunities for young men to gain superiors' trust by demonstrating their seriousness about repair.

I found myself in such a situation as we removed the transmission from a Nissan Patrol without a hoist. Our supervisor, a young fundi, loosened the bolt holding the transmission to the engine and frame from above as I and several young vijana prepared to reverse bench-press the transmission from below. Given the weight of the transmission, we all needed to do it together or risk serious injury as it fell on us. The young man next to me had earned the nickname Kenge, referring to a lizard considered an annoyance for stealing eggs from chicken coops. He, too, seemed committed to this name, challenging anyone above him with insults—even snapping his fingers centimeters from a fundi's face. But on this occasion, he focused on the task as a committed member of the garage. Young men who reliably did so found themselves close, or at least closer, to head mechanics as the latter performed specialized tasks—a critical opportunity to learn and to participate. Even as vijana physically lifted and pulled themselves closer to specialized knowledge, they performed women's work, including sweeping, cooking, and cleaning clothes and rags. One mechanic escorted his head mechanic's children to and from school.[139]

Apprentices' mechanical failures stayed with them through nicknames drawn from their failures. I asked about this process while replacing brake pads and drums on a Toyota Land Cruiser. My supervisor, Saidi, said that a student could be called a range of insults, from "idiot" (*mjinga* or *fala*) to *msenge*, a term usually applied to gay men that is also used to demasculinize men who are assumed to be straight. But in the case at hand, one might be called the "brake idiot" (*fala wa breki*). Weeks later, an overheating Toyota Corolla came into the workshop. We needed to remove the radiator from the cross frame of the car, but the nut and bolt that connected it to the vehicle's frame were stuck—I thought possibly even melted. Saidi put a wrench on the nut so that it stood straight up and told me to loosen it with one Bruce Lee kung fu–style chop—a request shaped by Lee and kung fu's popularity in independent Tanzania.[140] With an open hand, I hit the wrench as hard as I could. It went flying, the nut did not move, and pain radiated from my hand. Another student whom we called Jitu Balotelli—a combination of the Kiswahili term for "giant" and the name of the Italian soccer player Mario Balotelli, whom he liked—reset the wrench and loosened it with one kung fu blow. He had reearned his nickname, and I had earned mine: *nuti*. Apprentices thus shaped their own names and identities within the garage as they moved from the status of "youth" toward that of fundi, or mechanic. Jitu occupied an intermediate position. He had not given himself the name Jitu, but he had gained enough respect in the garage to modify it with Balotelli. Like previous generations, he will likely rename himself when he passes from the status of youth to that of fundi or uncle.

Second, and to inch toward this status, vijana collected tools, which allowed them to leave the garage when ready. Though some were able to buy a new or used wrench with the small amounts of money they sometimes received from assisting with repairs, many started their collections by salvaging tools from scrap (*scrappa*)—often by joining the head of a broken wrench to a sturdy piece of scrap metal.[141] The more wrench sizes a student had, the more likely he was to assist in repairs or work on his own. Young men later added screwdrivers, jacks, and hammers and even collected used tires, wheels, and engine blocks to serve as jacks and resting places for cars and people alike. Becoming an uncle required something more: a willingness to teach apprentices and share knowledge in return for labor. It was thus not uncommon for youth to become fundi in their late twenties and thirties but not to become an uncle until decades later, when they had enough customers and respect to train others. Having one's own space helped men become *wajomba* ("uncles") by providing space to work and teach. But it was not necessary. At least two types of gereji bubu, mtaani ("street"—usually the side of the road; sometimes called *pembeni*, for "corner") and *chini ya mwembe* ("under a mango tree"), required only that the mechanic have hand tools and knowledge. For example, Juma Katigiro opened a shop under a mango tree in 1967: "It wasn't big. We didn't have anything—a machine for welding, gas, or anything. I had a wrench in hand [*spanaa mkononi*] and my strength [*nguvu zangu*]." After business grew, Katigiro moved to a larger plot in 1972, purchased welding equipment, and welcomed students.[142]

Third, apprentices and their families saw gereji bubu as spaces of innovation capable of transforming boys into men through access to useful, and even cutting-edge, knowledge found near their homes. Supervised at all times by a head mechanic or more experienced students, apprentices started with routine maintenance such as changing brakes and replacing oils, greases, and lights. Part modification acted as the core of their curriculum. Simple fixes, like plugging a hole in a carburetor by melting scrap metal onto it, or body modifications requiring welding taught useful skills they could use in and outside of the garage. However, deep knowledge of ufundi required a garage to undertake repairs of transmissions, differentials, gearboxes, and engines. Mechanics announced these types of repairs, and they expected all serious vijana to participate as much as possible. Beginners contributed to these modifications through physical labor. They removed and hoisted heavy parts, ground and polished metal (sometimes for days), and cleaned parts for reassembly. But as they saw vehicles exposed, they learned how parts worked together. If they remained in the garage, vijana earned opportunities to try their hand at some of the more careful work that modification required. To move out of the garage, an apprentice had to be able to carry out routine maintenance and usually needed to specialize in modification of at least one area of a vehicle.[143] This training and work occurred in Kiswahili with one important exception: vehicle part names. In contrast to national and international development experts—who erroneously saw the English names of parts as obstacles to learning and therefore translated every part of the car into Kiswahili—mechanics easily, and happily, learned common words like *injeni* ("engine"), *carbureta* ("carburetor"), and *difu* ("differential"). "You can't order whatever they translated a filter as at a store. It's a *filta* [filter]," my head mechanic said.[144] Moreover, words incorporated from English gave mechanics the kind of niche lexicon that expertises are built on.

Modifications varied from garage to garage, and sometimes competing mechanical lineages discounted each other's work, telling me, "They're not a mechanic [*yule si fundi*]." Yet bubu garages held in common an understanding of automobiles and their parts as open technologies that could be modified and fabricated as dictated by consumer demands, economies of spares, or even the location of a repair, as I show later.[145] Known broadly as *ufundi wa kienyeji*—literally, "indigenous mechanics"—modification-as-pedagogy provided generous leeway for students and mechanics to establish their own styles and methods of repair. It was also the root of their passion for work. A reoccurring theme in oral interviews with mechanics was the restless state of their minds as they "wracked their brains" (*kichwa kinauma*) for a solution to a problem. Men claimed either that they could not sleep when a job was unfinished or that dreaming provided a means of mechanical creativity. Others relished time spent with friends and loved ones thinking through technological challenges. Indeed, the location of many bubu garages at homes allowed mechanics to mix work, leisure, and domestic life—raising kids, fixing cars, and enjoying neighbors in the same space. Either way, the final step for boys to become men was to have cars on their mind and to have the hand skills and tools to turn their visions into technological reality and a social opportunity for themselves and others.[146]

Mechanics trained in gereji bubu did not consider this to be making do or second-best. Calling the garages "their schools," mechanics distinguished themselves from *wasomi* ("the educated") by talking about the difference between books, paper, and words, on the one hand, and knowledge and "action," on the other.[147] They referred to the latter as *vitendo* and *utendaji*, both rooted in the Kiswahili verb *kutenda* ("to do or act"). Others called it *practico* ("practical"). "Practical is better because it is the exact thing [*kitu kamili*]. It's action that is 'production' [original in Kiswahili] itself. . . . You can't be a driver of words [*dereva wa maneno*] and fix anything."[148] Suleiman Abdallah Mwenda talked about the connection between touching and knowing "in one's head" by sight and by action: "Practical and theory are different. Practical is mechanics of action, while a book mechanic needs to open a book to remember what to do. I know everything in my head: for example, the wrench size for a Peugeot starter."[149] Mohamedi Naso described this as "getting expertise at your hands [*mkononi*]."[150] Even Francis Mwakatundu, whose father trained at colonial technical institutes, learned through "physical, totally physical labor" (*physical*, original in Kiswahili).[151]

The hands that created this knowledge were not just any hands, as Shailja Patel captures beautifully in *Migritude* when speaking of her father's career: "I always wanted / tough mechanic's hands like his / *credentialled by* each / ground-down finger nail each palm-line seamed with grease" (emphasis mine).[152] "Getting expertise at your hands" thus occurred in places and with things that smashed and dirtied them and sometimes bent a finger out of shape—but all the while linking thing and cognition together in a body part that, as Patel writes, also acted as a metric of credentialing. The point here is not that all rough and calloused hands reflected such credentialing; many, if not most, forms of labor in Tanzania created callouses, cuts, and bruises. But office work, as Tanzanians often say (and told me), rarely did. And thus politicians' smooth, soft hands were sometimes used to question their commitments to working-class causes—including stipulations that every politician voluntarily farm each year. Smooth hands, in this case, represented the social power to distance oneself from physical labor. But not all smooth hands were powerful or desirable. For mechanics, tough, worn hands signaled the authority of a technologist who had forged expertise through "practical" head and hand work—that is, through the forms of action/acting (*utendaji*), they contrasted not just with book and classroom knowledge but also with the manager's office and the car card in state garages. Calloused hands, and the places and processes through which mechanics earned them, marked boundaries of mechanical expertise and allowed bubu mechanics "control over the most important aspects of their work" and influence over definitions of specialization as a "path to status."[153]

These were not exclusive categories, and some mechanics used practico to ascend official (*rasmi*) technological hierarchies.[154] Trained at home by his father, Ndeko Jamii used practical education to get a position and theoretical training through the car workshop at the East African Railways and Harbours Corporation. "Practical education was very valuable at this time because you can then sit for and pass a trade test from Grade 3 to 1."[155] David Mfume, who learned ufundi first on bicycles and then on his father's car, studied until form 4 and then joined Iringa Super Garage, which he turned into a position at Ujenzi. Through studies and tests at Changombe, he combined his practical background with theory: "I knew everything. I could fix petrol, diesel, all kinds; it was all the same to me."[156] Hamisi Salum Luwango studied the modification of brakes, springs, and tools on the streets of Morogoro before joining the heavy plant in the same city—a government workshop—and then heading to the Changombe training center in Dar es Salaam. "The point of certificates is to move up levels. . . . In those days you got a big salary," and bubu helped get mechanics there.[157]

One indication of the efficacy of transforming bubu into certified work came in a 1983 pamphlet titled "Youth and Work" ("Kijana na Kazi"), published by the Association of Tanzanian Christians in a series titled "Upbringing and Youth." The section "Ways to Get the Work You Prefer" (*unayoichagua*—literally, "that which you choose") offers two avenues of success: submission of written letters or word of mouth. For the latter, it gave urban auto mechanics as *the* example of how young people who had little or no school credentials to put on a letter of application to technical schools could seek knowledge: "In this case, you are able to walk around to various garages that are near you (even those below trees on the streets) and try to get learning opportunities [*nafasi ya uanafunzi*] from those who work in this area." Much like in oral histories, in "Youth and Work," the dichotomies that fueled debates about knowledge—street and school, head and hand, learning by doing and learning through official structures—sat not as opposites but rather as different strategies for pursuing desirable work based on an individual's background and the potentialities that surrounded them. Moreover, much like mechanics themselves, the pamphlet prioritized individual and community-level notions of self-reliance and the practical measures young people could take to achieve them over manpower categories that sought to create and measure self-reliance on a national scale, thus distant from the metrics of personhood found on streets and in garages.[158]

Most of the men I interviewed anchored self-reliance in a gendered form of personhood that combined knowledge, people, and things into mechanical families.[159] As a fundi aged, apprentices took over the most laborious aspects of car repair and modification, allowing their mjomba to generate income from a supervisory role—sometimes into their seventies and eighties—even as younger mechanics and laborers inherited the mjomba's knowledge through work (hence the term *inherited mechanics*). For this to not only be possible but also bear fruit, mechanics collected used parts and broken cars that they stored in various areas of their houses: living rooms, chicken coops, or even the trunks and seats of cars parked outside. "We got cars from the police and from bigwigs [*watu wakubwa*] in the government" who sold vehicles at auction.[160] Another added, "We had people come to us and say this is scrap. For us it wasn't scrap; we see it as a spare to fix."[161] As national spare-parts shortages reduced the state's ability to import necessary parts for state and private vehicles, bubu shops became centers of repair for state and private vehicles alike—a strategy that literally paid off. Mtokambali Hassan Saidi said modification was the type of "ufundi that made life go" because parts shortages created opportunities for mechanics talented at salvaging and rebuilding vehicles.[162] The economist Ngila Mwase found that "home-made" spares rose significantly in value after import restrictions were passed in 1977; even after 60 percent import duties on new spares, he found that bubu parts sold for three times as much.[163]

Knowing the general consensus about economic decline after the mid-1970s in scholarship on Tanzania, I expected stories of near-insurmountable struggle in interviews. Instead, bubu mechanics showed pictures of themselves and their families eating ice cream, listening to radios, becoming political figures, and rebuilding valued machines. Given the demasculinization associated with not having things during this period—*huna kitu* ("you have nothing"), as Emily Callaci observes for Dar es Salaam—building one's life and livelihood around parts that could be transformed by the knowledge one held and the labor one could get provided a steady basis for social security and, sometimes, power, found at the intersection of wealth in knowledge, people, and things. Mohamedi Naso and Musa (who requested his surname withheld) each opened gereji bubu at their parents' home so they could care for them in their old age as the mechanics continued to work. Another mechanic described this as "restful work" (*kupumzika na kazi*)—literally, "resting and/with work"—a process through which the transformation of people (in this case, trained apprentices) and things (parts and cars) allowed aged bodies to use their minds to remake built worlds.[164]

Mechanics like Musa and Naso talked about wealth and economic security in two ways: first, as a network of men they had trained—and that they continued to train and direct in repairs during old age—whom they could call on for assistance; and second, as cars and parts that they could repurpose and, at worst, sell as scrap metal.[165] Wealth in people, knowledge, and things thus went hand in hand. Wealth in knowledge (knowing how to fix and modify) attracted laborers who not only could help transform dysfunction into function as they labored for aging mechanics but also saw wealth in things as an incentive to join the garage. In turn, these forms of wealth helped bubu mechanics marry, build families and homes, educate their children, and, in some cases, have cars of their own.[166] "Tools (*vifaa*) are what allow a person to rise up in life" and "get maendeleo," Mohamedi Naso said. Though mtaani and kiwandani were both sites of expert knowledge generation through bubu experiences, only the latter suggested a dense material world of things (such as tools and parts) a mjomba collected and could make available for vijana—a relationship visible in wealth of both people and things in figures 2.7–2.9.[167]

Known primarily as sites for primary school leavers, gereji bubu also helped expand respectable technological masculinity for men like Brian Ibrick and Frank Taylor. Ibrick grew up in an elite family in Moshi during the late colonial period. He finished secondary school, was fluent in English, and could have chosen a professional or trade career through familial networks. Ibrick's path to garage life went through a music career on the road. As a young man, he toured East Africa as the guitar player and singer in a Jimi Hendrix–style band. Worried his son would die a penniless alcoholic, Ibrick's father arranged for his son to apprentice for an Italian company building an oil pipeline in Tanzania. After two years of training as an apprentice, Ibrick received a chance to prove his competence when an engine "knocked" in a remote area. His Italian supervisor wanted to go back to the workshop to get a spare part, but Ibrick asked for the opportunity to stay and fix it with the parts at hand. He succeeded, and his supervisor offered him a raise that would have put him on the road to a salaried position. Instead, he opened a bubu garage in his home in Dar es Salaam, where he trained friends and family members and became a staple of the city's music scene under the name Brian Tshaka. An advertisement from 1983 described his style as a mix of Jimi Hendrix and Sam Cook.[168]

2.7–2.8 An engine kept in a sitting room in a mechanic's home in Tabora and an example of the arrangements of photos among the soccer mechanics in Ujiji. Note the intersection of family, knowledge, and things. (Photos by author.)

2.9 *A part of Frank Taylor's collection of spare parts—some of which went into his winning rally car.* / 2.10 *Brian Ibrick, the muungano, and R. Diwani on the front page of the* Daily News. *Ibrick keeps some of his personal archive, including this newspaper article and some musical instruments, in the trunks of vehicles in his garage.*

2.11 *The muungano's engine block came from this Vanguard near Moshi.*

He is best known, though, for creating what the *Daily News* called the "first ever car to be created in Tanzania," a praise which earned Ibrick's car a picture on the front page of the newspaper (figure 2.10).[169] It was constructed at his home, as pictures show, and he called it the *muungano*, or "union," because he formed it out of "pieces and pieces" of twenty-seven different vehicles, including motorcycles; bearings from small rail-cars found at sisal estates; an engine block, piston, and crankshaft from a scrapped Vanguard (pictured in figure 2.11); pistons from a Land Rover; an electric pump from a Ford; and a speedometer from a truck. The finished product so impressed the party's Youth League commander, R. Diwani, that he made an impassioned plea to reconsider the urban technopolitics of ujamaa: "This admirable piece of workmanship serves as a pointer to the kind of future we can have if we shall take seriously the question of organizing imaginative and inventive minds." The author added that Diwani "lashed at the bureaucratic tendency of glorying certificates."[170] A year after the article appeared, "the long arm of the law" fined and jailed the "ingenious Ibrick" for having an unregistered vehicle and lacking insurance. After he had spent almost six months in jail, multiple government offices, including the military, recruited Ibrick to their workshops, citing his unique "talent." He adamantly refused, and according to his son, "Cool Brian," the incident left him bitter for quite some time. One night, Cool

2.12–2.13 *Ibrick's bubu garage in the mid-1970s (left) and in 2012 (right). The only remaining part of the muungano is a fence post just behind the small truck on the left side of the photo on the right.*

recalls, he awoke to a sound only to find his father outside dissembling the vehicle with a hacksaw. His father then buried most of it near the garage for the trouble it had brought him. Part of the frame is used today as the post for the gate to the garage (and apartment complex) shown in figures 2.12–2.13.[171]

The burial marks a sad ending for Tanzania's first car, a vehicle that had grown up with both the mechanic and his son. But as Diwani's reaction shows, there is more to the muungano than its untimely and unnecessary death. It showed urban residents that creativity came from unlikely spaces, bodies, and minds and could also be used to build a different present and future—"the kind of future we can have," as Diwani put it. Figures 2.14–2.22 and figure 2.23 show the process through which the muungano came to life, but as we see in the following, it was only one type of Tanzanian car constructed in bubu spaces by making things with different origins work together.

AFRICAN CARS AND PARTS: MODIFICATION, RESURRECTION, RISK, AND CREDIBILITY

In addition to the muungano, Tanzanian mechanics "made" a variety of African vehicles composed of repurposed and redesigned parts. The technological form of these African automobiles depended on their use and their location—and thus the local or regional availability of spares and heavy machinery for modification and fabrication. Though owners' preferences certainly mattered, mechanics said they rooted modification, and their conversations with owners about it, in details about which types and models of parts worked together and which parts and models they considered reliable enough to stake their reputation on.[172] Fadhili Ramadhani described modification as a process that took time because it needed to be reliable: "Say you have a Bedford, and there is a Morris spare; you have to use it because parts aren't available. The gearboxes of Bedfords were really annoying, especially in the [mountainous] areas around Dodoma. It breaks, you take it out, but where do you get another one? There is no deceit here [*haina ujanja*]. If the gearbox dies, that's it. So we put in Morris

----

2.14–2.22 (*opposite*) *Ibrick's muungano in the making. It took two years. Ibrick started it in Moshi but finished it in Dar es Salaam after moving.*

2.23 *Ibrick's finished muungano at the downtown* AGIP *gas station.*

gearboxes, but these were much harder to find than the Bedford."[173] The same occurred with engines in older Ford and Chevrolet models that had few or no spare parts available.[174]

In this manner, modification relied on a mechanic's ability to not only read a dynamic landscape of used parts but also make parts from different makes and models commensurate with a broken vehicle. Bushiri Ali found the Isuzu one-ton engine reliable and liked to transfer it to truck bodies when their engine died. Abba Kazuge put a Scania engine into a Mercedes Benz bus, while Hussein Rashid Chambusu hopes to carry on this tradition by swapping a gasoline for diesel engine in his 1955 Bedford truck.[175] Depending on the size of the frame, this could require lengthening the front half of the frame (*kurefusha shoo*). Others did the same with early-model Toyotas and Mercedes. Various makes and models of carburetors (especially on popular Peugeot sedans) and differentials were also interchangeable "as long as you could make them fit"—which was often by making spacers out of pliable scrap metal (often tin or aluminum) able to fill spaces and help hold two parts together by bending over the conjoined pieces. A common tactic for moving passengers and cargo on the rough roads between Tabora and Kigoma saw mechanics replace lighter rear stock springs with heavier front versions. This saved bus and lorry owners losses from taking their vehicles off the road. To facilitate each of these fixes, mechanics identified certain models of vehicles that "agreed" to modification more than others, including Bedford, Land Rover, Peugeot, and, later, Isuzu.[176] One of the most popular was the Land Rover 109. The 109's engine and gearbox were not always reliable, but they could be replaced with Japanese models available in the late 1970s.

Not all vehicles needed to function the same—that is, to achieve equal mechanical reliability. Sedans used as taxis in small towns—where speeds remained low—and trucks used only seasonally to haul harvests did not always require such durable fixes because they could be used and repaired as needed owing to their proximity to garages and their lower speeds of operation. Indeed, the only mechanic I interviewed willing to take on a cracked engine block, a death knell for an engine, answered that it depended what the owner needed it for. He said that he had filled in cracked blocks for customers who used them for short, slow haulage of goods with the understanding of the possibility of breakdown.[177] A bus owner, of course, could not take this risk, and the mechanic would have replaced the entire block. Far from placing any used part on any vehicle, modifiers thus assessed how a particular part fit a car and the owner's needs. A worn part not suitable for buses and heavy vehicles on long routes over rough roads could find use within a township, village, or region. In some cases, this meant vehicles had close relationships with garage and mechanic. But this occurred by design. Continuous repair allowed owners to get the most out of parts and thus avoid further costs, as mechanics kept a close eye on other areas of the vehicle.

The material results—African cars born out of a variety of uses, environments, economies (including part availability), and styles—had two main traits: (1) They were the product of *unionizing*—a translation from *kuunganisha* ("amalgamating, joining, or uniting") with which I have taken some license, also inspired by the name of Ibrick's muungano ("union"). *Unionizing* refers to mechanics' practice of joining many parts not built to function together—and thus often presenting obstacles to their amalgamation—into a working thing because those same parts achieved mechanical union through the labor of joining (as figures 2.24–2.28 show). While this process differed based on location, as we see below, the physical and intellectual labor of fitting pieces together in ways that allowed each to function facilitated the ontological transformation of scrap into an African vehicle. (2) Unionizing (repeatedly) created something new through "resurrecting" (*kufufua*), a term mechanics likely used because they were not the first to create something out of most vehicles they saw and because

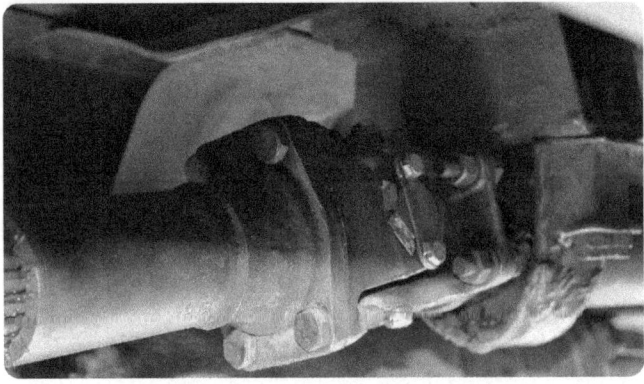

2.24–2.28 *Examples of car and part modification. Clockwise from top right: Putting a new engine in a different model or make required changes to the frame inside (next to the driver's seat) and outside (the metal seam near the top is a new front) of this bus in Tabora; Jumanne Katigiro demonstrating the manual repair of a Land Rover crankshaft (refinishing its corroded surface) using branches as a vice, rope, sandpaper, and kerosene; a drive shaft connected to a transmission of a different model with scrap metal used as a spacer; same from other side of the vehicle; and the metal housing necessary to put a Peugeot carburetor into a Datsun.*

their creative work came from breakdown. If manufacturing constitutes the birth process of a vehicle, mechanics' use of "resurrection" insists that production comes out of death, too, and thus, that death is not final. And for good reason: in addition to changing the material composition of a part or vehicle, modification required the skill to see parts from different years, makes, and models work together as a single, resurrected thing. Harper calls this seeing "beyond the elements of a technique to its overall purpose and coherence" and considers it an ultimate form of mastery.[178] Though mechanics standardized their approach to kufufua as much as possible within their garages, the dynamism of part economies regularly produced unique resurrections. In this sense, mechanical labor was not about the application of transnational standardized and institutionalized "best practices" found in vehicle or teaching manuals but about an ability to establish highly localized (in that part availability varied geographically) and even temporally limited (in that an assessment may not apply in the near future) best practices based upon a mechanic's assessment of technological possibility and constraint.[179] This took, one mechanic recalled, "a lot of intelligence" (akili nyingi).[180]

This process also helped create competing bubu identities in the independent period: mikoani, or "upcountry mechanics"—though most lived in or near small towns—and those from pwani, or "the coast," also called mjini ("city/town"). Mikoani mechanics criticized their urban colleagues as "take-off and put-on" (kufungua na kufunga) laborers because the latter had much greater access to spare parts and machinery. Places near coastal economic centers used lathe machines that drastically simplified part modification by removing much of the labor of metal grinding. This allowed them to fabricate custom parts and to tie proper modification, in their minds, to use of such equipment—a specific example of what I have called an infrastructure of expertise.[181] Conversely, mechanics in the central and western regions had to be as creative in their methods of fixing as in the fixes themselves. When salvaging a crankshaft, for example, Jumanne Katigiro created a lever system that used only rope, sandpaper, kerosene, and a tree branch. It required lots of labor and time to refinish the part and then even more to affix the resized crankshaft to the pistons (see figures 2.24–2.28). To refinish and resize engine blocks, a common but laborious form of maintenance, some mechanics in these areas wrapped thick tree branches about the size of a piston in sandpaper and twisted until they achieved the size needed for the new pistons.[182] For refinishing the top of engine blocks, one mechanic attached sandpaper to a sheet of scrap glass and used it to level engines that had been warped by overheating, a tactic he had learned from his father, who, he said, came up with the idea when he found leveling metal surfaces without lathe equipment tedious.[183] But not all mikoani fixes had utilitarian uses in mind. Mabula's modified Zephyr, pictured in figure 2.29, included radio speakers on the car's exterior, fire extinguishers, and faux rocket boosters. It served as Tabora's most popular wedding vehicle throughout the 1980s.[184]

Pwani mechanics tended to dismiss mikoani improvisation as unreliable. Most said, for example, that performing modifications without a lathe, as just demonstrated, could risk the owner's life and the mechanic's reputation. Coastal mechanics instead built their reputations on two conflicting tasks: keeping cars as original as possible by repurposing used parts and, conversely, performing modular and complete rebuilds that combined parts from different makes and models. They used the first approach for customers who insisted on keeping their vehicles as stock original as possible, an increasingly difficult prospect as shortages of new and used spares for specific models worsened. The latter grew out of the large stocks of used and spare parts that mechanics kept or that they found nearby. These generally involved modular fixes, as my mechanic Mjomba Kondo described previously. But they could also take the form of Ibrick's sleek

2.29 A stylistic example of modifications done to a British Zephyr. The black boxes on the left are stereos.

TABLE 2.1 Fixes by Part, Problem, Method, and Place

Car part	Cause	Method	Place	Other details
Frame	Accident or owner redesign	Welding, pounding, straightening	All	
Chassis	Too short, not heavy enough, or cracked	Welding	All	Done to make trucks more durable or on Land Rover 109s to make them multipurpose
Springs and Stabilizers[1]	Broken, not heavy enough, change for preferred or more available type; weld different stabilizing shafts together	Welding	All	A modification done on heavier vehicles in areas with bad roads by putting more durable front springs on both front and back. In smaller vehicles, fixing broken stabilizing shafts.
Engine frame[2]	Insert larger or different engine due to breakdown or preference	Welding and joining	All	
Differential[3]	Broken or unreliable type	Joining and fitting	All; most often up-country	Bedford especially reliable; Isuzu liable to fail
Radiator[4]	Cracked or leaking	Find crack and fill with scrap; swap		
Engine[5]	Recurrent problems	Swapping	All	Isuzu one-ton and older Mercedes models especially reliable; change from gasoline to diesel to reduce costs6
Pistons[7]	Knock or a miss; damage to shaft; certain ring sizes unavailable	Rebore shaft with a lathe	In or near cities	
		Manually resize piston grooves[8]	Up-country	

Car part	Cause	Method	Place	Other details
Crankshaft[9]	"Play" in cycles causing a miss or knock	Swapping or repurposing	Up-country	Requires a resized main bearing (below)
Main bearing (on which crankshaft moves)[10]	Cracked	Cut from scrap metal such as a frying pan	Up-country	
Gearbox	Recurrent problems or switching with engine	Swapping	All	Land Rover 109 especially liable to problems
Engine block[11]	Cracked	Fill with melted scrap metal	Up-country (and rarely)	Afterlife: As table or jack in the garage Scrap metal for making nuts and bolts
Bumper	Accident or redesign	Cutting, welding, and pounding	All	Material: Use scrap metal or *bati* (corrugated galvanized iron or steel roofing material)
Gas tank	Accident or make larger	Cutting, welding, and pounding	All	Material: Use scrap metal or *bati* (corrugated galvanized iron or steel roofing material)
Carburetor[12]	Engine swap; not working	Swapping	All	
Bearings[13]	Stripped	Cut; place support under	Up-country	A temporary fix to add support
Voltage	Change in car designs; brighter lights; more amps	Change alternator and battery	All	Particularly done by mechanics who learned in the 1940s and 1950s
Brake shoes[14]	Loose, broken, need resizing	Bend to size; resurface	All	
Brake pads/discs	Worn		Up-country	

Car part	Cause	Method	Place	Other details
Muffler	Worn	Cutting and welding	All	
Bushings[15]	Worn	Cut from scrap tires	All	A secondary repurposing economy outside of or connected to the garage
Nuts and bolts[16]	Replacements	Made from scrap metal such as engine blocks		Also a secondary economy serving garages

1. Mtokambali Hassan Saidi, interview, Morogoro, March 13, 2012.

2. Erick Anthony Baharia, interview, Tabora, April 10, 2012.

3. Mtokambali, interview; Omari Kibwana, interview, Dar es Salaam, May 14, 2012.

4. Kibwana, interview.

5. Hadi Maganza, interview, Dar es Salaam, March 16, 2012; Kibwana, interview.

6. Hussein Rashid Chambusu, interview, Tabora, April 14, 2012.

7. Abba Kazuge, interview, Tabora, April 15, 2012; Maganza, interview; Fadhil Ramadani, interview, Tabora, April 14, 2012.

8. Kazuge, interview.

9. Juma Katigiro, interview, Morogoro, December 12, 2012.

10. Mathias Kayega, interview, Morogoro, December 10, 2012; Musa (surname withheld), interview, Iringa, December 20, 2012.

11. Kibwana, interview.

12. Kassim Jaha Abdullah, interview, Tabora, April 2, 2012; Katigiro, interview.

13. Katigiro, interview.

14. Kibwana, interview.

15. Fausten Mallya, interview, Iringa, December 15, 2012.

16. Fadhili Ramadhani, interview.

roadster or Taylor's rally cars.[185] In sum, while the chart in table 2.1 represents a large portion of the fixes I heard about, not all mechanics would perform them or perform them in the same way.

Some recalled modification as an undesirable "risk" (an English term used in a Kiswahili conversation) in an increasingly complex technological landscape that offered fewer guarantees to mechanics or their customers than during periods with fewer vehicle types and more spare part availability.[186] Kondo Mfaume, who had a good reputation for modification, warned that others' fixes could have a "short life" and thus be "very, very dangerous" for mechanics because they built their careers on reputations of "no breakdown."[187] Peter William Mabula and John Samuel got little joy out of modification because "innovators (*wabunifu*) grew out of a bad state of things [*hali ya shida*]" when "life wasn't good" across the nation and because the proliferation of makes and models made specialization difficult. Vehicles with too many modifications were sometimes called *spanna mkononi*—the same phrase used by mechanics to discuss their own self-reliance—by members of the public skeptic of too much improvisation.[188] In this context, mechanics insisted on modification taking a modular form. They cut parts out of old vehicles but kept them as stock as possible so that the part's reliability was a matter of its make and model, not of their own skill or fault. Others, like my head mechanic, Mjomba Kondo, described this risk as a natural part of their ufundi career. Kondo, who began training in the mid-1970s as these crises shaped repair options, said, "We change with the times. If the government orders cars from Japan, we learn about cars from Japan. A mechanic learns like a doctor; so we must learn to change with the time. We learn about Japanese cars because it is the current system [*mfumo wa sasa hivi*]. My responsibility is to fix and to teach but also to know the way things change."[189]

To do so, many mechanics made changes to the garage itself. In larger shops like the one where Kondo trained, specialization was paramount, and the boundaries of expertise respected. It had mechanics dedicated to car types, one each for Volkswagen and Peugeot, as well as mechanics who performed solely one task, including welding, wiring, and engine work. The latter, the highest status, generally referred to everything from a rear differential through the gearbox and engine to the radiator. This scope meant that many fundi mechanico (a term reserved for those who specialize in engine work) specialized in particular makes and models or forms of modification and, in some cases, that certain areas—such as Temeke in Dar es Salaam—were known for their automotive specialties: Datsun, Toyota, and Land Rover.[190] Some mechanics added manuals to their shops. Mtokambali had manuals for a 1958 Chevrolet Passenger Car and a 1987 Land Rover TDI, for example. And most conducted research on new models, often seeking out a "sample," to identify their changes and assess their commensurability with existing parts and repair practices. Importantly, few claimed to have the "full idea" of a vehicle as their predecessors had during the colonial period. Indeed, by the 1980s such a statement signaled the immaturity of an individual unwilling or unable to work in a shifting technological environment in which credibility and knowing the boundaries of one's expertise went hand in hand precisely because of the variety of Tanzanian cars and parts to be made or repaired.[191]

The idea that Africa required specially designed vehicles began with European engineers like Frank Mott, but, using tacit knowledge to become automobile experts, African mechanics in the colonial and postcolonial periods repeatedly usurped expectations that design would or should be an outside-in process. Far from a mystery to these men, cars could be not only known but also overhauled and redesigned from engine to body, even spurring debates among bubu mechanics about whose variety of car/part sat at the cutting edge of Tanzanian auto work. The African cars they made ranged from the sleek space-age design of Brian Ibrick's muungano to vehicles joined together in bubu shops during spare-parts shortages. By continually demonstrating that vehicles could be put together differently, they also showed that men could be constituted differently as automobile experts through an infrastructure of expertise that was simultaneously accessible and rigorous. As the following chapters illustrate, the work of repair and salvage—as well as the hope that postcolonial states would create a new form of technological citizenship—was not confined to garages. The following chapters move firmly into the independence period to explore the relationship between technology and citizenship through multiple practices and registers. We begin by stepping into the lines and buses of urban mobility in independent Dar es Salaam.

THREE

The People's Car of Dar es Salaam

Buses, Socialism, and Technological Citizenship

IN 1979 AN ANONYMOUS RESIDENT of Dar es Salaam published a poem about the city's bus parastatal, Usafiri Dar es Salaam (UDA), and a bus journey that never happened in the English newspaper the *Daily News*:

> It is perhaps just a common 'plaint.
> O UDA bus!
> What is this mess? We wait and wait, Till we are late.

> At every stop there is a crop of men and women,
> Young and old, anxious students, worried clerks, and shopping maids
> Stand and sit and stand again, but in vain
> There is no bus, that's the strain.

> At last, when it comes, the wayward bus
> Is fully packed and there's a rush
> Who can board it? Gates are jammed,
> Shoes are trampled, bush shirts torn
> Pushing, pulling, kicking, cursing, shouting, shrieking folks are rammed.
> Leaning shelters badly leaking, helter skelter public seeking
> Safer spot, Oh, what a lot!

Listless drivers, rude conductors
Some are hazy, others crazy, pinching cents to fill their coffers!

Buses creaking cannot start
Some are old, others slow, flat tyres would not go
Most of them are out of order making journey harder and harder

Lo, you see another sight!
—a common sight
Buses trail in one direction but don't come from opposite direction.
You wait and wait, till you frustrate
And return home, Your discretion![1]

Dedicated readers of English and Kiswahili newspapers likely saw nothing strange about a bus poem and nothing petty about its detailed complaints about urban immobility. From the late 1960s to the early 1980s, Dar es Salaam residents filled reader-contribution pages with stories of lost time, disorderly bodies, broken technologies, and a range of emotions—from hope and gratitude to anxiety, anger, and fear—about their personal and collective futures, all from riding buses.

Moving us completely into the independent period, this chapter explores the politics of automobiles—including personal sedans, farming trucks, presidential Jeeps, and urban buses—from 1961 through the latter years of Tanzanian socialism in the mid-1980s. It uses periodical sources, oral histories, and official documents to excavate the reasons urban mobility took center stage in public conversations about socialist modernization. It makes two arguments. First, it demonstrates that seemingly insignificant material details mattered to poets and letter writers because the city's bus network provided a system through which "urban ujamaa and citizenship were given form," as Laura Fair writes of the city's drive-in movie theater.[2] Immobilized bodies, creaking wheels, flat tires, torn shirts, and reckless driving may seem like petty complaints made by overdramatic passengers who had nothing better to do than complain about commutes. But for most residents of Dar es Salaam, city transport systems merited decades of public discussion because infrastructures of mobility had long been integral to urban life—and, by extension, to residents' right to the city—and because writing about the condition of buses provided a form of everyday technopolitics for evaluating and engaging the state. A state capable of transforming urban mobility through new routes and vehicles showed that it could turn the promises of nationalist campaigns into a material reality. Conversely, residents worried that a state that could not maintain city buses or move bodies efficiently in an enclosed urban space might not be able to build and maintain a nation on a much larger scale because, as Keith Breckenridge observes, "the state is very much a thing, or, perhaps more accurately, it is a constellation of things: roads, hospital, telecommunication lines, computers, filing cabinets, weapons, bullion (to name a few)."[3]

At first glance, this might seem like a familiar story. Broken and breaking technologies have served as evidence of the declining fortunes of African-initiated modernization schemes since at least the 1970s. That story usually goes something like this: as African states attempted to deliver the promises of independence, they offered technological promises in the 1960s that they did not have the capacity to keep, or rather to maintain as functioning systems, by the end of the next decade. Regardless of the reasons for this failure—whether unstable global economies, corruption, inappropriate technological choices, or misplaced ambition—the limping and broken vehicles that proliferated in the late 1970s reflected a changed political environment with drastically reduced horizons for technological, economic, and political change. Breakdown, dysfunction, and fears of decline are thus part of the following story. But unlike the conventional technological narrative of this period, they are not its end because things can be repaired and remade.[4] Indeed, this chapter demonstrates that partial technological function and dysfunction, as well as the anticipation of both, acted as a catalyst for citizens to engage with government ministries over the nature of socialism as an infrastructural project that could and should be repaired and remade instead of scrapped or left to deteriorate in difficult times.[5]

This brings us to the second point: automobile users in Dar es Salaam both shaped and built systematic, large-scale alternatives to the state's more centralized urban mass mobility.[6] In the mid-1970s, when broken buses kept residents from work and social obligations, a vernacular system composed of privately owned vehicles known as *thumni-thumni* filled in. State and party officials immediately condemned these buses as capitalist exploitation by wealthy car owners. However, Dar es Salaam's operators and passengers made a case for thumni-thumni's socialist qualities and for their ability to help repair and supplement, rather than replace, urban uja-maa's built world during a period of crisis. A prime example of what Priya Lal calls "creative engagements with ujamaa thought," they won their case in 1983.[7] By doing so, passengers and letter writers overturned one of the original axioms about technology and African independence: that private motor vehicle use created inequality even as it ruined the nation's pursuit of economic self-reliance. Now known as *daladala*, these buses have become a focal point of urban neoliberal politics since the mid-1990s.[8] Indeed, they have been perhaps the most visible and influential technology of Bongoland, as Dar es Salaam is often called, in the twenty-first century.[9]

But they first emerged as a populist socialist technology, a people's car, organized around residents' efforts to create a socialist built world of movement that aligned with their everyday routines. In much the way rural and urban socialists repackaged and shaped ujamaa's ideological lexicon, a key theme of scholarship on this period, Dar es Salaam bus and car users reworked transport systems into material networks that aligned, as closely as possible, with an actually existing form of urban African socialism they could perform every day.[10] With both points, this chapter takes a new approach to cars in independent and socialist Dar es Salaam. With few exceptions, private automobiles—or cars like sedans that facilitate private motoring—in this city's past have gained attention for tempting, corrupting, destroying, and exploiting.[11] In most cases, these automobiles symbolize national-scale processes—both as state discourse and as populist critique—even when only one or a handful of vehicles feature in the stories and ideologies they influence. I thus certainly explore the social and political meanings of these highly visible and symbolic vehicles in public discourse.

But I must also note that cars, especially private vehicles, have rarely been systematically important in the city's history for their everyday use value or for the impact they could make on users as hard material things in larger numbers—that is, as a network instead of as a political or cultural status symbol.[12] Indeed, a striking element of the transformation of daladala from private automobile to people's car is that although individually, party officials argued the vehicles symbolized capitalist behavior, decadence, and decline, when put together by residents into a system, they offered a new form of socialism on wheels. The point in tracing out such histories is not only to recover technological details of national politics and everyday life. As Eden Medina puts it, focusing on technological systems can help open the "black box of politics"—in this case, a box that sometimes limits the hard material possibilities of urban ujamaa.[13] We begin the story of this remarkable transformation by looking at debates about automobiles, decolonization, and socialism during the first eight years of independence.

TECHNOLOGY, CITIES, AND
INDEPENDENCE: *NAIZI* TO *GARI LA*
TANU, 1961 TO 1969

Cars were difficult to disentangle from colonial rule because nearly everything about them—from those who used and purchased them to the manner in which roads were built with default tax labor—had been used to
create and justify hierarchies for over five decades of German and British rule, as chapter 1 illustrates. In 1963 Frantz Fanon expressed these
concerns in *The Wretched of the Earth* by linking the "mediocrity" of a
newly independent Algerian "bureaucratic bourgeoisie"—"which turns
its back more and more on the people as a whole"—to the "chromium
plating on big American cars."[14] That same year, President Julius Nyerere
connected motor vehicles to a political culture of "pomposity and ostenta-
tion" in Dar es Salaam. At the time, high-ranking government officials and
guests moved through towns on closed streets with police escorts securing the way. Sandwiched in between police motorcycles and sedans, these
car "caravans" (*misafara*) were usually composed of luxury vehicles from
Rolls-Royce or Mercedes-Benz. Though they were designed for security
purposes—an issue that animated national debate after Nyerere's would-
be successor, Edward Sokoine, died in his msafara in 1983, as chapter 5
explores—Nyerere felt these mobilities created new political hierarchies
in Dar es Salaam in the name of "Presidential Pomp." "Whenever [the pres-
ident] decides to go out, whether to dinner, a dance, or even to visit some
friends, the normal flow of traffic has now to be interfered with," leaving
other road users "cleared out of the way (like so much unsightly rubbish),"
much as street sweepers did with trash. Nyerere warned that, more than
being an inconvenience, "this sort of pomposity has nothing to do with the
people, for it's the very reverse of democracy."[15]

Beyond his own mobility, Nyerere feared "pompous" car use could become a political norm across government service. In a 1965 speech to the
National Assembly, he scolded bureaucrats and ministers for disobeying a
presidential order to reduce ministerial expenditures on government cars;
they were classifying luxurious add-ons as "'spares' so that its price can
be within the limit [he] set."[16] Tanzania could not control the drought or
dropping commodity prices that had led to slowed economic growth that
year, he argued. But it could make choices that were more likely to lead
to self-reliance: "For instance, we must choose between buying another
car for the President or a tractor for a maize farm. The more we buy of the

goods to enjoy, the less we can buy of the goods which will produce wealth in the future."[17] This choice between "goods to enjoy" or "goods which will produce" was not restricted to the national scale. The same year as Nyerere's speech, a poem in the *Civil Service Magazine of United Republic of Tanzania* connected a group of African professionals known as *naizi*—a Kiswahili shorthand for the "nationalizers" who took over government positions from colonial officials—to questionable public behavior in Dar es Salaam. "Nationalizers and Their Ways" ("Naizi na Visa Vyao") accused bureaucrats of enhancing their status by living off loans they could not or did not intend to repay. The eighth stanza reads, "At the end of the month, the nationalizers crash into each other's cars / The nationalizer then rents a Benz so he can be happy [*kuhepi*] with Amina / The nationalizer does not pay his debt, he is an expert at bribery."[18]

The poem ends by stating that motoring naizi "ambush" girls on narrow footpaths (*vichochoro*) in city neighborhoods even as their wives wait at home for them to return from work. It thus suggests the following image: a suit-wearing and car-driving African professional uses his status and motor vehicle to steal young women away from their homes. Some readers questioned the validity of this description with poems of their own. Others piled on, cautioning their colleagues against becoming *wabenzi*, literally, a "people of the Benz." Indeed, *Civil Service Magazine* provided a "model budget" of five hundred shillings monthly that warned professionals away from not only cars but also scooters. "While you are waiting anxiously for your next promotion in order that you can buy a scooter, the purchase of a bicycle with a Government loan would be a sound investment." Doing so would save not only twenty-six shillings per month of the forty allocated for bus travel but would "come in handy for your children when they are fit to use a bicycle to go to school."[19]

In this manner, technology, and motorized transport in particular, performed important ideological work in the construction of respectable Tanzanian bureaucrats. Unlike naizi who lured young women away from families with costly vehicles as their wives and children waited hopelessly at home, men who chose bikes over cars and scooters built sustainable families in which their children inherited the fruit of bureaucratic labor—in this case, a bike that helped to educate a future generation of professionals by carrying them to school. Furthermore, with minimal transport needs, bike-owning bureaucrats would not be tempted into corruption and could simply serve their community.[20] Powered by legs instead of gasoline and needing only a path instead of tarmac roads, bikes emerged as the technology of mobility for bureaucrats who cared deeply about both their own family and future and that of the nation. Even if bikes were manufactured elsewhere, their lower cost kept most of a bureaucrat's spending in-country. In a statement in 1965, Nyerere argued that, in addition to the monthly burden of repaying car loans, the problem with car ownership was that large sums of Tanzanian money went to car-manufacturing nations when "our nation is still an infant that has not reached the point of having many luxury cars as it now does."[21] A year earlier, the government had added a registration tax for private automobiles to discourage this trend.[22]

Such anticar discourses departed significantly from colonial ideologies that doubted Africans' racial and cultural preparedness to create motoring societies. No one doubted Tanzanian bureaucrats' ability to appropriate automobiles or to fashion identities around them as the German and British colonists had. Indeed, most imagined the opposite. Politicians charged that naizi motorists risked appropriating motoring culture too completely, thus creating a situation in which African car users dragged the complete package of colonial technopolitics into the independent era.[23] Nyerere said as much in a 1975 speech in China:

> Our idea of government and statehood was permeated by the idea we had seen at work—the colonial example. Thus, for a time, an African riding in the back of a chauffeur-driven car was to us a sign of our independence. We expected members of our government to act like the bosses we had known, and took pride in their doing so. Gradually, however, we began to realise that the replacement of white faces by black faces was not what the independence movement had been for.[24]

Car use among an independent professional class of naizi could thus make it appear that few structural changes had occurred since the end of empire.

But some city residents disagreed with the president's assessment. A fruit of independence "symbolic of [citizens'] drive for modernity," as Fair writes, or an indication of "up-to-date people" (*watu wa kisasa*), as Callaci shows, the number of registered cars—which grew by about nine thousand each year from 1960 to 1965—offered tangible evidence of how quickly life had changed under a sovereign African government.[25] The important part for new car owners was not only the vehicle itself—which certainly enhanced their mobility and class standing—but also the structural changes that allowed a debate about the politics of African car ownership to materialize so quickly after independence. To purchase a vehicle, naizi first had to gain access to bank loans and adequate salaries in ways not possible under colonial rule. Such loans did not fit the "model" family budget described above. But they offered membership in a new technoeconomic community of independent Africans who showed that Tanzanians could competently do what British officials had done before them and reap the rewards of their labor. The car owners I talked to did not purchase an expensive Ford Cortina, as the protagonist in one novel about corruption did, at 20,000 shillings, but found used vehicles starting as low as 1,700 shillings. They said they had no problem registering them, especially if it was their only vehicle. In the mid-1960s, then, debates swirled about the best way to create urban mobilities that were postcolonial in a literal sense. While, for Nyerere, doing so meant ridding Dar es Salaam of pompous car-riding politicians and bureaucrats, other city residents claimed motoring as a right to forms of urban and political citizenship long denied them.[26]

Tanzania's official turn to socialism in 1967 intensified this debate, a form of what Paul Edwards and Gabrielle Hecht call the "technopolitics of national identity."[27] The Arusha Declaration (AD), which formalized Tanzania's intent to build a socialist state around the idea of ujamaa, or "familyhood," first mentions motor vehicles in the document's second section, "The Policy of Socialism," under the subheading "The Major Means of Production and Exchange Are under the Control of the Peasants and Workers."[28] The list of the major means of production and exchange includes land, minerals, energy, transport networks, factories and machine tools, and banks and insurance. But unlike in other socialist and communist countries, in which controlling the "major means of production" was an unambiguous goal that justified huge industrial expansion, the AD explains that focusing on the "major means of production" as actual tools of development could undermine economic self-reliance and even create inequality. A section titled "Let Us Pray and Heed to the Peasant" connected the technological inputs required for urban automobility to the exploitation of the nation's rural communities: "Tarmac roads, too, are mostly found in towns and are of especial value to the motor-car owners. Yet if we have built those roads with loans, it is again the farmer who produces the goods which will pay for them. What is more, the foreign exchange with which the car was bought also came from the sale of the farmers' produce."[29] With cars and tarmac roads as the opposite of praying and heeding to peasants, classic hierarchies emerged not between capitalists and workers, or feudalists and farmers, as much Marxist thought suggested, but rather through a "position where the real exploitation in Tanzania is that of the town dwellers exploiting the peasants."[30]

Because urban car users not only preferred tarmac roads but also needed a continuous supply of oil and spare parts, they became an obvious technology of this "real exploitation" despite the country's low rate of car ownership (and thus, the focus on popular transport and buses here). From 660 people per vehicle in 1948, vehicle ownership grew to 275 and 164 people per vehicle in 1957 and 1964, respectively. The rates in 1964 were similar to those in Uganda (164 people per vehicle) and below those in Kenya (95 people per vehicle).[31] Motor vehicles made it difficult to "pray and heed to the peasant" because car owners were predominantly located in cities, with about 60 percent of the nation's total in Dar es Salaam alone. In addition to having 33 persons per vehicle in 1967—as opposed to 164 people per vehicle nationwide in 1964—the Coastal Region that included Dar es Salaam had the most cars per mile of "classified" road at 17.4.[32] Beyond numbers, the type of vehicle mattered, too. Most Tanzanians owned midsize or small sedans, not the large vehicles more easily integrated into agricultural modernization.[33] Public service vehicles such as buses were only 5 percent of the fleet, and agricultural vehicles reached their highest points, 6 and 6.5 percent, in 1967 and 1970 respectively. In sum, using foreign exchange earned by farmers to build costly infrastructure for a small and declining demographic of urban motorists who lived in about a third of the nation and whose vehicles did not contribute directly to national production goals made even less political sense after the AD than it had in conversations about naizi.

Yet targeting urban motorists and automobility also simplified a more complex technological problem that socialist planners and politicians faced: the magnitude of technological nation building in the *rural areas* where most of the nation lived.[34] Outside of cities, the politics of road-building centered on which types of roads would maximize the geographic tentacles of development. A clear break from colonial railway preference and its export aims, the first two five-year plans (1964–74) prioritized the expansion of cheaper "feeder" roads for their ability to reach more communities than main trunk roads, or highways.[35] The Tanzania-Zambia highway (Tanzam), built at a cost of almost $59 million, including almost $30 million in aid, ultimately garnered more attention than this feeder policy. But according to the National Development Corporation, the project became a priority because of the regional politics of liberation—aiding in transport to Zambia after Rhodesia's Unilateral Declaration of Independence—not out of a desire for tarmac roads. Indeed, the corporation's magazine, *Jenga*, a dense site of capital-intensive technological iconography, presented the

Tanzam highway as the type of project the nation could neither afford to construct nor maintain at scale; sections cost up to $850,000 per mile. In addition to the costly construction of tarmac roads, maintenance made them a foil to the material politics of self-reliance. About 60 percent of the bitumen used in the 1970s went toward maintenance of existing roads—routes that reached few parts of the country because of their high costs and whose maintenance made extensions less likely.[36] In contrast, feeder roads, in addition to being low-cost, aligned well with ideologies of self-reliance.

"Farming roads," a process in which villagers of all social ranks worked together in a line to clear or cut new roads with hoes, became a defining technological act of ujamaa's rural implementation and national iconography. Politicians celebrated road farming as evidence of not just self-reliance but also the "single heart" (*moyo mmoja*) communities forged through this infrastructural "effort" (*juhudi*). Newspaper and party pamphlet editors published pictures of politicians leading lines of villagers opening up new rural socialist roads with hoes raised overhead; they enumerated the miles of new and repaired roads (1,285 and 1,173 miles, respectively, for an unspecified year) for each district; and they published poetry to the hoe (*jembe*), the tool around which this "effort," "heart," and their product, roads, were built.[37] Without forced conscription or its connection to taxation, one of the most despised parts of colonial life had become an iconic act of communities pursuing socialist maendeleo by answering the "call of the president." A man in Tabora described braving danger from wild animals to create a new road trace. After walking and mapping the route, he presented his case to regional officials, who helped raise voluntary labor and register the road. While he told this history as a personal contribution to national development etched into the landscape, it also offered a seemingly ideal example of the development Nyerere had envisioned: initiative from below amplified by government offices.[38] For a farmer willing to collectivize and "adapt himself rapidly to an advanced system of agriculture," the government even offered road clearance "at its own cost."[39]

Still, road farming came from a position of infrastructural concern. Though the state repeatedly presented rural life to Dar es Salaam's residents as a foil to the costliness of their urban habits, agricultural modernization on a national scale also required the construction of a technological capacity Tanzania would not have for at least several years, by the most optimistic projections, if not a couple of decades.[40] We explore this through oil's role in rural modernization in the next chapter. This matters here because it suggests that ujamaa's technological minimalism—though only one part of a more complex political culture of technology—emerged not because Nyerere preferred it over more capital-intensive alternatives or because he had always been stridently antiurban. Rather, it suggests he felt Tanzania had few other choices than to gather people together in villages and increase production, and thus exports, with low-capital tools like hoes and feeder roads.[41] Indeed, in 1962 Nyerere's first description of ujamaa justified the pursuit of a rural-based African socialism in two ways: because of the difficulty of providing social services to a "scattered" populace and because of what he called a "low level of technology."[42] "While other people can aim at reaching the moon," he remarked that same year, "our present plans must be directed at reaching villages."[43] To do so required sustained investment in new transport infrastructure—investments so large that "reaching villages" across the nation remained both a top political priority and an unlikely infrastructural reality.[44]

Nyerere thus championed a technological minimalism that embraced "traditional knowledge" and "improvement of the tools we now use" as the path for "moving into the future."[45] In addition to their low cost, the president associated hoes, axes, and ox plows with two pillars of African socialism: collective work (*kazi*) performed by all able-bodied villagers (as equally as possible) and self-reliance (*kujitegemea*). Combined with affordable, ready-at-hand technologies, collective work enabled village communities to achieve self-reliance—a term referring to communities' ability to sustain themselves and contribute to national development using their own resources, including knowledge, tools, and labor. Mechanized technologies such as tractors, motor vehicles, and factories would achieve different results, Nyerere wrote. The president feared that, in addition to its capital costs, mechanized equipment required personnel and a bureaucracy to import and distribute costly spare parts and fuel around the country—thereby empowering a technical elite of foreign and national experts at the expense of the country's farmers. Almost every step of this process contradicted the emphasis of the Tanganyika African National Union (TANU) on work (*kazi*), sweat (*jasho*), and land (*ardhi*) as the foundation for national development. A critical component of these expressions was Nyerere's belief that Tanzanian social units—whether the nation or a village—needed to "graduate" from the hoe to the ox plow to the tractor without skipping a step in this linear model of technological change. He wanted this graduation to occur "with the maximum possible speed," citing a need for increased production, but the president insisted on gradual change out of fear that new technologies would cause "massive social disruption" by undermining economic self-reliance and thus any chance for technologies to build equality.[46]

Consequently, hoes, villages, ox plows, and walking, not cities and cars, took center stage in ujamaa's discourse about technological change for most of the 1960s. Both the hoe and the ax found their way onto the party's flag, and unlike poems that castigated naizi motoring, periodicals published numerous hoe praise poems, including "The Hoe Is the Weapon of the Nation" ("Jembe Silaha ya Nchi").[47] As Lal records, mass walking to and between ujamaa villages became a literal performance in traveling the "long road to socialism," as Nyerere called it. The press covered the president's own 133-mile walking journey, on which he was joined by other political leaders, to Mwanza from his birthplace, Butiama; pictures of his cracked, blistered feet still hang at the National Museum in Dar es Salaam.[48] None of this meant that mechanization should not eventually take place on a national scale or that certain communities were not already prepared to move into a technological future without massive social disruption. After all, roads had been farmed in anticipation of motorized mobilities; ministries and parastatals also supported vehicle assembly projects, including with Land Rover and Bedford, for a "Make It Here in Tanzania" campaign.[49] Instead, mechanization required that communities demonstrate their readiness for new tools through increased production and through collective decision-making among a village's leadership.[50]

For example, villages could earn or purchase trucks for transporting bulk goods, known as "TANU cars" (gari la TANU)—and only trucks, not sedans—by reaching or surpassing production goals and by showing that their output would be enhanced by a motor vehicle.[51] In at least some cases, these gari la TANU were not exclusively for a village's own use but were rather entrusted to regional party leadership for broader development goals—thus the car's party name. For instance, an ujamaa village growing sisal in Tanga Region collected contributions of 2,355 shillings that they entrusted to the TANU district chair; the latter then gave the money to the regional party chair to purchase vehicles for the region. The district chair offered this process as an example of how collective farming among rural socialists could lead to technological changes for the entire regional citizenry through increased motor mobilities that not only contributed more to the national economy, but also potentially brought more goods and services to Tanga through revenue generated. The chair hoped farmers yet to collectivize would see the vehicles as an incentive to join collective farming efforts that were the foundation of ujamaa. A cooperative, or an *ushirika*—from the Kiswahili verb for "to participate"—offered a more common route to acceptable socialist vehicle use, especially if cooperatives served most of the country, as did the Tanganyika National Transport Co-operative Ltd.[52] In these cases, drivers and owners in rural areas combined their car resources to create small vehicle fleets that served specific regional needs. In contrast to the AD's description of urban motoring, in which cars and tarmac roads created "real exploitation" by draining economic surpluses created in rural areas, this vehicle use could create a rural automobility that enhanced ujamaa and therefore did not threaten economic self-reliance.[53]

Indeed, such lorries likely used farmed roads maintained by local labor. And they came near the end of a sociotechnical process that required that villagers first become familiar with a variety of tools—whether hoes, axes, or ox plows—whose use aligned neatly with ujamaa's emphasis on land, work, and sweat. In sum, cars could—and ideally would—play a role in ujamaa as technologies based in rural economies and whose presence came as the result of hard work and infrastructural self-reliance. Inasmuch as gari la TANU evidenced a society that used roads and vehicles, ideally these technologies enhanced village life and fed back into self-reliant forms of production that celebrated automobility between different villages as well as between villages and factories.[54] Each element of this nascent rural automobility made an urban *and* socialist automobile difficult to envision during most of the 1960s. But only three years after the AD, the Second Five Year Plan (SFYP) created a people's car for Dar es Salaam.

SOCIALIST CARS, URBAN MOBILITY, AND TECHNOLOGICAL CITIZENSHIP: UJAMAA'S "COMMUNAL ASPECT," 1969 TO 1979

In 1969 the SFYP altered the AD's sociotechnical model. While insisting that the state's prioritization of rural modernization had not changed, the plan nevertheless proposed infrastructural investment in ten cities, including "Greater Dar es Salaam," to spread the "secondary effects" of urban life to surrounding ujamaa villages. These effects included better access to social services such as piped water, electricity, and education as well as the extension of roads to encourage trading among rural communities and between villages and towns.[55] Several years later, Nyerere called this urban-rural technological network of social services a "communal aspect" of socialism.[56] He did not provide a formal definition of the term. But in the wake of the SFYP's infrastructural expansion, he suggested technological systems had brought something specific to ujamaa: forms of citizenship determined not by income or political status but by the state's ability to distribute goods and services around the country through government-owned corporations, or parastatals, and the infrastructure they built and maintained.[57] Unlike the AD, which warned against costly forms of technological change imposed from above, the SFYP justified state-driven infrastructural growth by framing it as an incentive for Tanzanians to voluntarily join ujamaa villages. Despite the party's focus on rural modernization since 1967, higher wages in cities drove urban immigration rates to near double digits in Dar es Salaam even as rates of voluntary villagization, a cornerstone of Nyerere's vision for African socialism, remained low.[58]

Framing the plan around alarming urban immigration rates, as Nyerere and the authors did, suggests they saw the potential for infrastructure to do something that ideology alone had not: convince most of the nation's citizens to root themselves in rural areas and commit themselves to the state's vision of agricultural production—albeit one modified by new built worlds. As roads, electricity, pipes, buses, and schools extended outward from towns into rural communities, Tanzanians would not have to choose between the state's vision of self-reliant rural livelihoods, on the one hand, and access to the social services and markets that citizens associated with independence—but that they found primarily in cities—on the other. Infrastructural expansion thus allowed planners to address the shortcomings of rural villagization schemes while reaffirming the state's role in creating equality as a socialist project. Initially, the plan did not provide a clear road map for its implementation beyond linking socialist citizenship to a stronger technological state. But it justified large capital outlay in parastatals and ministries that increased the state's assets by almost eight times to make the infrastructural "communal aspect" a material reality of what Callaci calls "ujamaa urban."[59] One example of a hard material urban "communal aspect" came through plans for towns along Uhuru ("Independence") Corridor based upon the infrastructure—a highway, oil pipeline, and railway—present over a 500-mile stretch by 1973. The idea was that small towns could easily mix agricultural and industrial production while citizens accessed the social services rooted both in the movement of petroleum and goods—movements that were not built just for town dwellers but also intimately connected to efforts for national and regional economic sovereignty.[60]

This urban infrastructural investment also came with new warnings and demands. Because the changes laid out in the SFYP meant embracing the types of expertise and technologies that had been characterized as threats to Tanzania's economic self-reliance and egalitarian principles for much of the 1960s, bureaucrats' technological choices as both professionals and individuals became a topic of public concern throughout the next decade. Though Nyerere had previously stated his belief in those "who have had the privilege of higher education" guiding "the masses through the complexities of modern technology," the plan included a stern warning against "tractorization"—a wasteful process in which clueless bureaucrats who lived in cities ordered mechanized equipment because they thought it best, not because communities wanted or needed it.[61] The same applied to the city's new bus parastatal. Speaking at Saba Saba, an annual trade fair in Dar es Salaam, the president explained:

> Something foundational for our economy, like buses, should be our buses and not those of some official who says, "That's my bus." Your bus? And the driver inside, the same person may say, "That's my driver." Your driver? Is it possible for you to have your own driver? A driver is only able to be a driver of the socialist community, not "your" driver. A driver is the same as a teacher: a teacher is of the community; a doctor is of the community; and a driver is of the same socialist community.

Nyerere concluded his address by stating that an *mjamaa*, a person who follows the principles of Tanzania's ujamaa socialism, could never say "my bus," for such a person "believes that the work of [the party] is to build a classless society," even with vehicles.[62]

The SFYP renewed scrutiny of the role of motor vehicles in urban socialism precisely because most new parastatals and ministries located their head offices in the city. Controversy over bureaucrats' personal access to motor vehicles began in 1969 with the Karadha loan scheme, a program for civil servants to purchase used automobiles through the national bank. Two state newspapers, the *Standard* and the *Nationalist*, argued that car loans for civil servants contradicted the "TANU creed and the objective of building a socialist society," and they began a campaign to have the program canceled. Contributors to the newspapers argued that Karadha was dangerous because the technological rewards of socialism accrued to a minority.[63] Motoring civil servants benefited directly from imported spare parts, "consuming millions of gallons of petroleum," and the maintenance of tarmac roads—all an "unnecessary drain on foreign exchange" according to the article "Combat Conspicuous Consumption"—while farmers waited for resources, and city residents waited in long lines to board overcrowded buses.[64] In 1970 the National Executive Committee canceled Karadha and raised import taxes on vehicles for those who, in Nyerere's words, held "doggedly" to the necessity of private car ownership.[65]

One year later, the TANU changed one of its guiding documents—the leadership code *Mwongozo wa Tanu*—by adding prohibitions against car ownership to the restrictions on "landlordism" and business ownership for civil servants spelled out in the AD.[66] When oil prices quadrupled between 1973 and 1974, the State Motor Corporation took over the importation and distribution of all vehicles and parts—retroactively acquiring many private cars purchased after 1966—while the Motor Vehicle (Restriction of Use) Order put police on Dar es Salaam's streets to enforce a weekend driving ban aimed at reducing oil consumption.[67] These policies reduced car ownership and the share of the gross domestic product used on motor vehicle infrastructure. For example, the growth rate of premium automobile fuel fell from 7.5 percent in 1972 to 2.99 percent in 1974, as that of regular fuel sank from 7.5 percent to −7.75 percent over the same period.[68]

They also helped create the independent era's most infamous car user: a corrupt motoring bureaucrat who chose his own well-being over national development. For example, John Rutayisingwa's 1979 novel *Ngumi Ukutani* narrates the demise of Double Nyaritwa, manager of the Ministry of Palm Oil, through his quest to become a motor vehicle owner. Double begins the novel as a faithful national servant, husband, and father of three children. All of this changes when he purchases a luxurious Ford Cortina: "The moment he got his vehicle, the character and direction [of Double's life] changed."[69] Instead of dedicating himself to his work and family, Double revels in the attention he receives from young women, none of which was due to his physical appearance: "If he wanted to get [the girl], it wouldn't take much. The car would do the work." And it does. Friends of Double's first girlfriend, Diana, advised her to date men who have "heft [*uzito*]—someone like Double who can own a Ford Cortina" and not "men without cars or men who own bad cars like Honda and Volkswagen."[70] Aisha, an eighteen-year-old schoolgirl, was also "pulled" (*kuvutiwa*) to Double by the car. When she reveals her pregnancy to him, Double scrambles for resources because car maintenance and gifts for girlfriends have left him broke even though he has stopped giving money to his own family. Double offers a secret tender for cafeteria food in his ministry cafeteria to a wealthy

Asian financier. He is subsequently arrested and convicted of corruption. The Cortina acts as a fulcrum in a decline story that is simultaneously personal and national.

The car plays this important role in the book because it continues to function perfectly as a technology even as everything around it breaks down, including Double, his family, his ministry, and his friendships. Indeed, *Ngumi Ukutani* suggests that managers had to choose between two types of maintenance in their lives: the economic and social maintenance of their own families and national communities, on the one hand, and the mechanical maintenance of the automobiles that brought them prestige, on the other.[71] Naizi, of course, had faced similar warnings during the previous decade; other sources similarly linked disreputable masculine behavior to the combination of political authority, cars, suits, bars, and young women.[72] But the SFYP added a critical component to concerns about elite motorists like Double: that beyond creating "real exploitation," managers could destroy the nation's chance at socialist infrastructural development by enriching themselves using resources earmarked for the "communal aspect"—a process novelist Gabriel Ruhumbika termed "the silent empowerment of the compatriots" (*miradi bubu ya wazalendo*).[73] When economic contraction set in after the OPEC (Organization of the Petroleum Exporting Countries) crisis of 1973, citizens and some officials interpreted working managerial sedans on Dar es Salaam's streets as the opposite of a tool of nation building. Because officials like Double chose not only which projects received funding—and, consequently, who received new equipment or whose infrastructure was maintained when it broke down—but also which did not, their seemingly unchanged access to functioning automobiles stoked fears that the SFYP had succeeded only in creating two tiers of technological citizenship. The one for bureaucrats functioned while that for the masses fell apart.

For these reasons, the TANU carefully crafted President Nyerere's relationship to automobiles and self-reliance. It largely did so through the state vehicle DST 72—a Jeep built sometime in the early 1950s. In 1974, for example, a state-owned newspaper, *Mfanyakazi* (The Worker), featured a picture of Nyerere stepping out of DST 72, with the caption: "This car, which still runs up to the present, was used by the president during the fight against colonialism."[74] Saidi Kamtawa, Nyerere's longtime driver, received the vehicle through the TANU in 1958. He used it to transport the president for many, though certainly not all, of Nyerere's daily tasks. The president had access to a stable of state luxury cars—including Mercedes-Benzes and a

Rolls-Royce—and he used government Land Rovers on many up-country visits. But DST 72 gained attention in state media sources and carried him in national parades because it was one of the few automobiles, if not the only one, that aligned with ujamaa's technopolitics. In addition to its anticolonial credentials, the Jeep had been completely overhauled by students at Dar es Salaam's National Institute of Transport in 1975. That it did not require the tarmac roads the AD associated with "real exploitation" cemented the Jeep as one of the few mechanized technologies that reflected multiple types of self-reliance and African initiative: it had fought against colonialism, it was maintained and overhauled by independent Africans, and it did not require costly externalities. An ideological anomaly, the Jeep's historical national use value and its technological details (heavily used and maintained by a national institute) justified the president's public motor vehicle use even as he lambasted the idea of car ownership in 1980: "If I had a private car on my salary right now I would be bribed (nitahongwa). I will have to look elsewhere for money to run it."[75]

By the mid-1970s, reducing private car ownership and use in cities had become a staple of urban socialist planning. For example, when the government decided to move Tanzania's capital from Dar es Salaam to centrally located Dodoma—a move meant to create a decolonized national space and a "rural capital," as Emily Brownell shows, located at the center of the nation—the city was designed for pedestrians.[76] Once completed, the nation's new parliament functioned—or at least could or should function—without, or with reduced, private vehicles in a manner difficult to enforce in Dar es Salaam. Similar approaches found their way into plans for the latter's redesign. The city's 1979 Master Plan built on two earlier events—the party's crackdown on private motoring and the OPEC crisis, both occurring in 1973—to remake mobility around falling rates of private vehicle traffic. The total percentage of private vehicles on roads had fallen from 18 to 13 percent since the beginning of the decade. In its place, the plan called for expanded pedestrian routes and bus mobilities. It envisaged both growing bus mobilities—constituting nearly a quarter of all movement by 1999—in tandem with growing biking and walking on pedestrian-only avenues. To achieve this vision, the plan called for policies prioritizing the importation of buses over private vehicles, and it imagined new, less capital-intensive socialist moorings built around the party's ten-cell house system. The idea was that city neighborhoods composed of cells could create their own pockets of self-reliance if each was provided with a market, a dispensary, and a school system, thereby rendering mechanized mobilities superfluous for most daily activities.[77]

Importantly, it seems the state adopted these plans not just because of OPEC's impact or ujamaa's technopolitics but also because of the strain high urbanization rates placed on existing systems of mobility. Already marked as the antithesis of ujamaa's kujitegemea, urban socialism nevertheless produced a number of practical approaches to creating more economically self-reliant forms of a mobile and growing city. In an important concession of the state's failure to reverse these urbanization rates, the plan suggested that municipalities recognize squatter plots as an accepted part of urban life. Of course, accepting this growth came with concessions that, it seems, urban residents largely welcomed: sacrificing any vision citizens had of expanding private car mobilities in favor of the growth of pedestrian and bus mobilities. These were not carless cities by any means, and not all of the plans came to fruition. But each plan imagined built urban worlds structured around the forms of movement the state considered most economically self-reliant: walking, biking, and busing. We explore the larger implications of the official imaginaries of self-reliant urban mobility in the following. First, we look at these same issues from the perspective of city residents.[78]

Among Dar es Salaam's residents, cars and their use took on political meaning because intracity mobility had been an integral part of urban citizenship for decades. When J. K. Leslie conducted a social survey of the city in the mid-1950s, bicycling and walking dominated transport. But change was already occurring. In 1949 the colonial government formed the city's first bus system to facilitate the daily movement of laborers between African neighborhoods and a growing industrial sector to the southwest of the city center.[79] In 1952 Dar es Salaam Motor Transport (DMT) estimated its annual numbers at 7 million passengers, or 600,000 per month for a population of just 72,000—just over eight bus trips per month for each city resident.[80] Though the company had a horrible reputation among passengers, by independence in 1961, the motorized mobility that DMT provided had become a defining feature of daily life in Dar es Salaam. Kariakoo, the sociopolitical center of Dar es Salaam, received over 60 percent of passengers and acted as a transit point for residents to reach any part of the city.[81] Civil servants boarded buses to reach ministry offices in the city center, teachers went to school, and workers traveled to factories. Businessmen and businesswomen traveled to food markets in Kariakoo to buy produce before taking another bus to sell their goods in smaller city markets. When the workday ended, buses connected social networks across the city and ferried passengers to soccer matches, cinemas, religious obligations, hospitals, and late nights at bars and discos; the latter, nightlife, peaked at the end of the month.[82] Residents moved to the extent that the novelist M. G. Vassanji called buses "portents of life in the city."[83] Though walking and biking remained important forms of mobility throughout this period, owning a bicycle required economic means beyond some I interviewed, while the pressure to arrive on time for work and social engagements across a growing city made bus mobilities an integral part of social and economic life.[84]

Owing to the cost of operating municipal transport, Overseas Motor Transport, DMT's original owner from the colonial era, operated the service until the London and Rhodesia Mining and Land Company Ltd. (Lonrho) purchased a majority stake in the company in the early 1960s. Despite Lonrho's obvious connections to apartheid, the state lacked the financial resources to create nationwide transport services and thus allowed the company to invest heavily in national transport in both rural and urban areas.[85] After the SFYP, the state nationalized DMT in 1970 under the newly created parastatal National Transport Corporation (NTC). More than taking DMT out of Lonrho's hands—and, in the vice president's words, tackling the "structures of colonialism and capitalism" within Tanzanian society—the NTC tasked DMT with creating a socialist culture of urban mobility based on efficiency and respect.[86] Drivers and conductors underwent training supervised by TANU party officials detailing how they should treat different members of the city's socialist community. In contrast to the chaotic boarding procedure of previous operators, the nationalized company allowed elderly, pregnant, and disabled customers to enter through their own door in the front while everyone else lined up to board through the rear entrance. One driver recalled instructions to go the extra mile for drunk passengers by taking them directly to their homes.[87] In 1974 the NTC translated the name of DMT into Kiswahili, renaming the parastatal Usafiri Dar es Salaam, or UDA. The parastatal hoped its buses provided motorized spaces where urban residents learned socialist values as they interacted with state technologies, professionals, and each other on a people's car that facilitated the state's evolving vision for socialist change.

Further, UDA also provided a socialist vehicle for the city. In contrast to socialist and communist countries in which providing a people's car was a design and manufacturing process, in some cases explicitly attempting to match Fordist elements of the West, the limited reach of vehicle assembly projects in Tanzania (with most attached to Western car companies) meant ujamaa's people's car would come from outside the nation.[88] From 1975 to 1983, the parastatal purchased 220 buses from communist Hungary's publicly owned company Ikarus to replace the British Leyland and Albion vehicles of the British-based company. A 1963 Council for Mutual Economic Assistance (COMECON) agreement that aimed to coordinate central and eastern European socialist and communist production—better facilitating the "building of Socialism"—gave Ikarus resources to expand its manufacturing and sole export rights among nations in the Eastern Bloc. The company responded by building some of the first and, in some car circles, some of the best mass-transit buses in the world. It captured markets across Latin America and Africa, even joining forces with Los Angeles's Crown Coaches in 1979 to produce the Crown Ikarus.[89] Nyerere visited the Hungarian bus factory in Budapest in 1969 amid talk of building a factory in Tanzania; it never happened. But the president returned with a bus outfitted for medical services.

Within several years, two types of sleek, cutting-edge buses from the company's 200 series (figure 3.1) provided a space for Dar es Salaam residents to enact urban ujamaa on city streets with some of the best technologies of mass transit available. Unlike the Ford, Peugeot, Volkswagen, and Mercedes sedans produced in western Europe and the United States and linked to managerial corruption, Ikarus buses painted in a striking dark red and deep yellow, known by their popular Kiswahili names *karusi* (or *karusi sanyasanya* and *kumbakumba* for the articulated versions), not only came from socialist technological ingenuity and transnational socialist relationships but also brought pleasure to those who rode them. Watonga, the protagonist of Charles Mloka's 1985 novel *Mjini Taabu*, took "complete pleasure" (*starehe tupu*) in boarding and then riding while standing on a packed *kumbakumba*. On the way to a dance hall, she concludes that "town is the place where our compatriots get the fruits of independence. In villages it is 'Freedom and Work' (*uhuru na kazi*) while in cities it is 'Freedom and Pleasure' (*uhuru na starehe*), or what urbanites call 'enjoy' (*enjoi*)."[90] As this chapter's opening vignette suggests, UDA and its karusi struggled to meet both the NTC's charge for building a socialist urban citizenry or Watonga's vision of mobile "Freedom and Pleasure." Within several years, less than half of its fleet was roadworthy.[91]

But the standard narrative of parastatal failure overlooks UDA's huge impact on city life. Two years after its nationalization in 1970, UDA served

3.1 *The only picture of an articulated Ikarus found at* UDA *headquarters in 2010. This model was nicknamed* karusi sanyasanya—*collect-collect—for its ability to clear out stations as it moved down a route.*

nearly 70 million city residents annually, increasing only one year later to 86 million, the equivalent of 180 bus trips a year for each of the city's 500,000 residents. By the end of that decade, the bus parastatal estimated that it regularly served over two-thirds of the city's population, with one government study estimating that buses had displaced walking and biking as the most common form of intracity mobility.[92] Even in the early 1980s, with half of its fleet broken, UDA moved between 100 and 120 million passengers every year, a fourteen-fold increase from the mid-1950s. It accomplished all of this even as the population tripled between 1967 and 1977, growing from 300,000 to nearly 900,000 in large part owing to immigration; this placed a heavy strain on UDA's equipment in a global environment in which the transfer of capital-intensive technologies and resources—buses, parts, and fuel—saw operating costs skyrocket after the oil crisis of 1974.[93] Between 1974 and 1983, the parastatal received only 35 percent of the requested foreign exchange through national budgets to use on repairs and purchases; not surprisingly, by the late 1970s, UDA's documents show acute spare-parts shortages.[94] Even a critical study of the parastatal by a British transport consultant suggested foreign firms should not jump at the chance to replace the Tanzanian parastatal, should they get it, because fuel costs alone

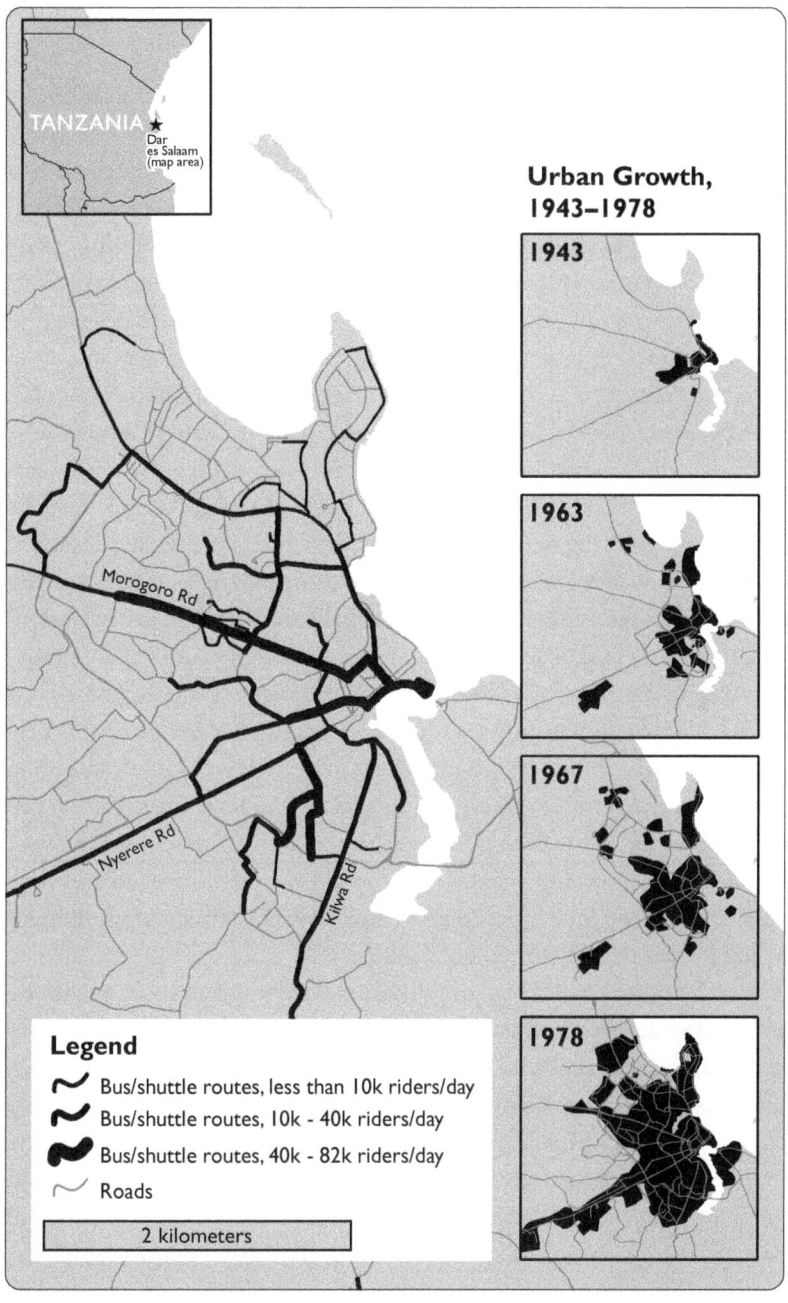

**Urban Growth,
1943–1978**

1943

1963

1967

1978

Legend

〰 Bus/shuttle routes, less than 10k riders/day

〰 Bus/shuttle routes, 10k - 40k riders/day

〰 Bus/shuttle routes, 40k - 82k riders/day

〰 Roads

2 kilometers

MAP 3.1 *Bus routes both facilitated and were shaped by the city's growth. By 1979, UDA buses generated new concepts of space and belonging in a city where mobility had once been restricted by racialized zones of movement and residence. Maps created by Tim Stallman based on Marshall Macklin Monaghan Ltd., "UDA Bus Routes and Ridership," T9; and "Urban Growth 1945 to 1978," 15, in Dar es Salaam Master Plan, Tanzania (September 1979).*

rendered public or private businesses economically unsustainable.[95] Yet
the parastatal managed small profits in 1979 and 1980.[96]

As map 3.1 illustrates, by moving passengers during hopeful and difficult
times alike, the parastatal turned Dar es Salaam into a postcolonial space
in a literal—material—sense. During the colonial period, racial zones had
divided the city into European (Zone 1), Asian (Zone 2), and African
(Zone 3) populations, disallowing most urban African mobilities to or
within Zones 1 and 2 for at least the first half of the twentieth century. Early
bus transport largely sustained this geography because it was designed to
move workers from racialized residential zones to spaces of labor on the
edge of the city. Yet, as the map shows—and much as in Kenda Mutongi's
history of transport in Nairobi—bus routes facilitated the city's growth.[97]
By the late 1970s, a hundred UDA bus routes cut across these former demar-
cations and connected peri-urban settlements to Dar es Salaam's historic
center through a ring route that encircled the entire city.[98] With subsidized
tickets almost every resident could afford, UDA opened most of the city
to most of its residents in ways that radically transformed urban mobilities. Residents had little say in these routes' design. But in the newspapers they made their voices heard about the placement and number of bus
stops because neighborhood stations connected their homes to this new
infrastructural community.[99] More than easing their commutes, spreading
stops throughout the city slowly chipped away at preexisting spatial hierarchies. Referring to the former European zone, a letter writer called on UDA
to place more stops in Oyster Bay because it was "no longer an exclusive
area" and was "no longer occupied by an exclusive car owning community
as was the case during the colonial period."[100]

For the letter writer, bus mobilities offered practical solutions to the
continuing decolonization of city spaces by simply opening Oyster Bay
to popular urban mobility in ways not possible in previous decades. In
this sense, UDA's coordination of road, bus, and station allowed Dar es Salaam residents to think about and experience their city in a new way, and
they tried to influence its form. For a new generation of urbanites who had
not lived under colonial rule, however, UDA buses were not only a natural
part of urban built worlds but also an integral part of city space and time.
"Sudi, a Short Story by Pili," published in the *Daily News* in 1980, had its
protagonist get lost in her thoughts as she rode in an Ikarus to simply clear
her mind after a difficult stretch of life: "Luck was on my side. I got the UDA
as soon as I reached the nearest bus-stop. While I sat there holding tightly
the handle-bar and while the rickety Ikarus dangerously negotiated the

sharp streets of Dar es Salaam, my whole two years association with Sudi began to unfold before me like a motion picture."[101] As residents grappled with UDA's struggles and possible demise in the late 1970s, their anger, concern, and sadness stemmed from a recognition that the parastatal had transformed urban life on a previously unimaginable scale, had raised expectations about how the city should work, and had become part of the cultural fabric of Dar es Salaam regardless of its shortcomings.[102]

For both the state and passengers, I call this process *technological citizenship* because competing ideals about independence, socialism, and urban or rural life linked citizenship to a range of technological things that signaled the presence of an mjamaa, a good socialist, or their opposite.[103] On the one hand, Tanzania's state constructed ideal socialist citizens through rural technologies that found little application to urban life and that positioned most technological users in cities, regardless of their intentions, as anchors who held back difficult nation-building projects that involved a majority of Tanzania's population and geography. Inasmuch as the SFYP expanded the boundaries of this construction, it came with disciplinary mechanisms that linked urban socialist citizenships to demands that Dar es Salaam, its parastatals, and its managers prove their technological worth to the national community by using things responsibly and increasing output. On the other hand, residents of Dar es Salaam approached decolonization, socialism, and their relationship to a sovereign African state through technological systems capable of transforming both their city and their everyday lives. The expansion of UDA thus provided a material form and a daily ritual through which they could engage, critique, and shape the nature of urban ujamaa over the next decade.

UDA: SOCIALIST TIME, ORDER, AND INSTITUTIONS

To reconstruct the daily experience of riding buses, I use letters to the editor and poems passengers sent to state media sources. Depending on editors' preferences, contributions about buses appeared daily or biweekly in Kiswahili and English newspapers from 1969 until 1982.[104] Some residents tired of the relentless discussion of public transportation in newspapers. One passenger wrote, "Too much of anything is harmful. This [bus talk] is now becoming monotonous."[105] For many, however, the importance of transportation to urban life and nation building justified the emotional outpouring facilitated by newspapers' public forums. By citing what they saw or experienced aboard buses and by expressing a desire to see their socialist city work better, passengers transformed flat tires, ailing buses, and bad driving into issues for collective concern about the direction of national development. As historical sources, reader-contribution pages have helped historians highlight points of engagement between citizens and their states while also emphasizing the subjectivities of citizenship based on gender, class, and age.[106]

Complaints about infrastructure do not jump off the page like marriage or dress in public discussions and debates about what constituted an African national culture in the city. Yet newspaper editors' perception of infrastructure as an apolitical, or at least less political, realm of urban socialist life—that technology should work so society and economies function as best as possible—transformed everyday technological breakdowns and shortcomings into perhaps the most sustained public discussion about the nature of urban ujamaa during the 1970s and early 1980s. As Andrew Ivaska observes, the substance of reader contributions changed significantly with the nationalization of Tanzania's newspapers in 1972, ending the type of public debate evident in his rich examination of national culture during the "long" 1960s.[107] Nyerere and the TANU continued to encourage public debate and discussion. But the party censored newspapers and sacked editors who published content deemed detrimental to the state's national and international image, creating an archival grain full of strident antiurbanism, as Callaci notes.[108]

This grain, however, is precisely the reason the hard material details of urban commutes, when put into letters and poems, not only provided an acceptable outlet for citizens to voice their hopes and fears about progress or decline directly to their state but also included hard-hitting accusations of corruption later in the decade. Certainly, not all residents wrote with explicit political engagement in mind. But writing about their everyday experiences with state buses for over a decade created a politically acceptable topic in state-controlled newspapers that residents later used for more direct debate and engagement over definitions of socialism. Party leaders and residents certainly did not agree about the relationship between socialism and city life. But the groups seemed to share a belief that the regular function of systems was part of an infrastructural ideal all parties hoped to achieve and maintain—an example of technology as "congealed social interests."[109] Consequently, as long as technological dysfunction hindered the free flow of urban life—keeping infrastructure from becoming an invisible material platform of social and economic pursuits whose reliable function makes it a taken-for-granted aspect of life—UDA provided a literal infrastructure of complaint, what Claudia Gastrow calls "aesthetic dissent"—"a site for the opening of political contestation"—that censors continually allowed to be published.[110] We can surmise that this occurred because censors, and many others in state ministries, considered residents' expectations about infrastructural function quite reasonable and unlikely to pose a political threat. Indeed, letters in the first half of the decade combined complaints with suggestions for improving urban socialist mobility. But by 1977 the complaints and suggestions had morphed into exasperation, anxiety, and open critique of UDA and the government.

In these ramped-up critiques of UDA, passengers–turned–letter writers did not stray from state discourses about efficiency, discipline, and order.[111] Following the SFYP's investments in urban infrastructure, the state expected increased output from Dar es Salaam's residents and repeatedly asked for evidence that an industrial culture of work was taking hold in the city.[112] In addition to the infrastructural costs already mentioned, scholars have noted the perceptions of town dwellers as "lazy" and dependent—the opposite of self-reliant villagers.[113] This did not mean that Dar es Salaam could not become part of the larger socialist community. But it did tie urban citizenship to "the worker" (*mfanyakazi*): an individual equally committed to labor and to fighting exploitation (*unyonyaji*).[114] As Tanzania's economy failed to meet its growth goals and as shortages of goods and services became normal following the oil crisis and drought from 1973 to 1974, definitions of exploitation expanded from the more obvious enemies of socialism—African and Asian capitalists, urban loafers, and even some politicians—to encompass the urban worker's daily activities. For example, following factory wage increases in 1974, Nyerere warned residents that taking higher pay without increasing their output could be considered a form of exploitation that was "equal to a businessman selling a half kilo of maize flour for the price of a kilo."[115]

Such subtle distinctions between work as nation building and work as exploitation brought increased scrutiny to socialist definitions of discipline (*nidhamu* and *utii*), efficiency (*bidii, kasi, ufanisi, uhodari kwenye kazi*), and production (*maarifa*). In 1962 Nyerere wrote in "Ujamaa: The Basis of African Socialism, "I do not use the word, 'worker', simply as opposed to 'employer' but also as opposed to 'loiterer' or 'idler.'" But in the case above, he expected urban laborers to achieve a balance between their wages and their output or risk contributing to a culture of exploitation.[116] Amid these concerns, the TANU Executive Committee held a two-day seminar in 1973 "to debate and precisely translate" the term discipline (*nidhamu*), because it feared that decreasing factory and farm output stemmed from inadequate descriptions of industrial work culture. When *Mfanyakazi*, a state-controlled newspaper and the nation's most popular periodical, reported on the seminar, it titled the article "The Discipline We Follow Will Not Be the Whip," a clear reference to colonial violence. It also included a picture of an overloaded UDA bus with passengers and a conductor hanging out the door. "Who is lacking discipline, the passengers or conductors?" asks the author in the caption before answering, "*All are at fault*" (emphasis mine).[117] The National Institute of Productivity opened a year later to make these issues a formal part of socialist governance.

Instead of challenging the state's heightened expectations about work and efficiency, passengers wrote about the difficulty of fulfilling the heightened obligations of urban socialist citizenship—that is, of becoming the type of efficient worker Nyerere described in 1974—in the 1970s in the context of technological breakdown, scarcity, or both. Whether or not they read *Mfanyakazi*'s accusation that bus users "are at fault," writers shifted blame from the passengers and operators hanging off the vehicle to the state's ability to construct and maintain technological systems that made urban socialist citizenship an attainable goal for the city's residents. By repeatedly addressing two topics—the difficulty of boarding a bus and the socialist society evident once inside—bus riders not only connected the state's technological power and responsibilities to a collective experience of everyday life in Dar es Salaam but also engaged and shaped state discourses about time, work, and community in ways that showed their commitment to making the city and its socialist institutions work better. Much of the following journey relies on the periodical sources just discussed, but the writers who signed their names were almost exclusively male and literate. For these reasons, I also conducted thirty-four oral interviews while walking old UDA routes on Dar es Salaam's streets and using pictures, poems, and cartoons to jog memories about daily life. We now turn to these daily journeys.

The first UDA buses pulled into neighborhood stops around six in the morning, but the journey of a Dar es Salaam passenger began long before the first vehicle arrived. Several residents recalled awakening around four o'clock in the morning (or earlier) to get a place in line (often sleeping again once there) or to place an object, popularly known as a "buoy" (*boya*), to hold their place so they could continue sleeping or enjoy their morning tea at home.[118] But this strategy was an option only for those who lived near a

Tunangojea mabasi Bwana. Je, Foleni hizi zinasaidia au zinawapotezeeni muda na kuwaleteeni uchovu?

NI KWELI FOLENI MBAYA AU HUDUMA MBAYA?

3.2 *An example of an orderly* UDA *foleni. Though often linked to lost and wasted time—and thus to* UDA's *struggle to meet the needs of a growing urban populace—some residents appreciated the foleni for the social order they believed it represented.*

bus stop. The rest walked to stations where they regularly waited for over two hours in lines known as *foleni*, as shown in figure 3.2, to get on board. Some claimed waits up to four hours, and others, like the poet from the opening vignette, gave up and returned home.[119] For the thousands who worked in the city's downtown and industrial center, this wait occurred again during the evening.[120] The orderly queuing of city residents at stations successfully replaced the chaotic boarding procedure of UDA's colonial predecessor and even elicited praise from passengers in letters. But as the residents began to recognize, it also linked their daily mobility to the state's ability to purchase and repair its fleets of vehicles, creating what Brownell calls a "landscape of deferral."[121] When Shadrack Swai, a reporter for *Nchi Yetu* (Our nation), asked a worker what he did while standing in line, the potential passenger answered by asking, "Do these lines really help, or do they just waste our time and make us tired?"[122] With a growing urban populace, increased demand for mobility, and shortages of equipment and fuel, stations and their long queues became places where government shortages structured the rhythm of everyday life for city residents.

Between 1973 and 1980, passengers frustrated by foleni wrote about the consequences of lost time for both personal and national development. For their personal lives, workers cited lost jobs, owing to late arrivals, and physical danger, even death, from postponed hospital trips. A student added, "The best way to get to school early is to walk. If you wait for UDA, chances are you will get to school at the end of the first lesson."[123] One teacher explained his embarrassment about routinely arriving at school later than his students, emphasizing that the challenges of training the nation's future workforce were compounded by his inability to personify the principles of nation building for Tanzania's youth.[124] Foleni even became part of cultures of romance. In the song "The Bus Stand" ("Standi ya Basi"), the jazz band Toma Toma Jazz Band placed UDA buses at the center of a husband's accusations of infidelity against his wife. "My wife, every night you come home late with tired eyes," the song begins, before the husband demands to know "what makes you late." The woman, whose part is sung by the entire band, responds in the chorus, "I'm late because of the bus stand," later adding, "My husband, you know the problem with buses; have compassion on me."[125]

In most letters, "the problem with buses" was their influence on urban and national development and, in particular, the consequences of collective immobilization. In "Too Much Time Wasted," Mikundi E. N. B. argued that reductions in bus stops "wastes hundreds of productive man hours" for workers along the Pugu Road industrial corridor and thus contributes to "the deterioration of the national economy."[126] In "UDA Good at Inventing Excuses," Nicholas Kiwale, a worker at the Tanzania Audit Corporation (the institution that collected data about labor power at national corporations), asked readers to imagine the consequences of the city's daily waiting for the national output. "If all institutions whose employees depend on UDA for their daily movement to and from work were to compile statistics of the number of man-hours lost due to late-comers, the result from just one year would surely be alarming." Further, Kiwale argued that the worst effect of waiting was an accepted culture of "slowing down" among the city's residents. More than the quantifiable hours lost through inefficient transport, he said, daily interactions with transport reduced workers' expectations of their own labor. For Kiwale, this slowing down was not a choice but rather came from bodies and minds made tired through constant waiting.[127] Unlike the jubilant hours-long lines Fair describes for the city's drive-in theater, writers described bus foleni as "torture," "[disheartening]," and "tiring," leaving workers with "no morale left for work" and "dwindling hope."[128] One writer even connected waiting to the economic downturn in 1979. "When the transport system fails, the economy is likely to collapse in one way or another. . . . UDA has got trained manpower yet what we achieve from it is poor services and therefore the retardation of our economy."[129] Accordingly, newspaper contributors began to play with UDA's Kiswahili acronym by calling the bus company "Unyonge Dar es Salaam" ("weakness of Dar es Salaam") or "Uchelewashaji Dar es Salaam" ("makes-you-late Dar es Salaam").[130]

In writing about work and time, letter writers likely knew about the state's emphasis on efficiency after the SFYP, their president's warnings against "idleness," and one of the AD's core statements under "Conditions of Development": "Everyone wants development; but not everybody understands and accepts the basic requirement for development. The biggest requirement is hard work."[131] But none of these policy documents or the paternalist discourse that followed captured the complicated reality of urban life for workers who wanted to build the nation but could not even get aboard a bus. In socialist Romania, anthropologist Katherine Verdery describes similar experiences of governance as power "constituting itself through the effects of austerity," creating what she calls the "'etatization' of time": a condition in which state distribution patterns structure the flow of everyday life.[132] Passengers described a similar form of state time and power on Dar es Salaam's streets. Whereas the Kiswahili phrase *kupiga foleni* ("to line up") evidences the intentional power of a teacher over students or a commander over soldiers, station foleni came from a less intentional power of austerity emanating from increasingly common government shortages after 1973.[133] This subtle distinction mattered in letters because it shifted the blame for "slowing down" and "retardation" from urban citizens perceived as lazy to the state's technological missteps.[134]

By the middle of the decade, some passengers rebelled against the foleni in preference for free-for-all boarding that "made it appear as if citizens were battling each other" by "[exercising] their potential in athletics, football, judo, bumping and so on and so forth. It is not entertaining at all. While you are at these stops you can easily detect dwindling hopes of fathers, mothers and their children expecting this bus labeled 'UDA.'"[135] A resident of Manzese described "the exchange of fists among passengers themselves, passengers against UDA workers (conductors, drivers and inspectors)" as commonly "hazardous incidents."[136] One passenger even drew attention to the socialist-inspired rules that were supposed to apply inside the vehicles. Posted at the front of each bus near the driver was a sign that read,

"Please help the handicapped, pregnant women, mothers with children, and the elderly." But instead of deference and respect for the aged, handicapped, and pregnant, the author described getting a seat as "the biggest nightmare" because most of the seats were "dominated by the young and healthy who would be most disinterested in giving up their seats after such a big fight." As for the populations listed on the sign, "in the end, the old, the sick and many others you may care to name, are left standing breathing relief that they are at least still alive and kicking, not to mention those who cannot get into the bus at all." The writer concluded by reminding readers to have a "human attitude toward each other. . . . This is sadly lacking in the Dar es Salaam bus rider. The rules of the jungle only apply here."[137]

Despite widespread concern about the "rules of the jungle," attempts by the Traffic Police to enforce order at stations and on buses largely backfired. Periodic stings in 1977 fined 100 Tanzanian shillings and even arrested some passengers who pushed their way through crowds to ultimately stand or hang from bus doors.[138] Passengers, such as one who signed their letter as "Helpless Victim," responded by writing letters defending themselves and the "thugs" who annoyed them by citing the consequences of the lost time caused by UDA's "inefficiencies."[139] Jonah Karuga argued that passengers took drastic actions because they feared losing their jobs and that, ironically, police stings wasted even more work hours without addressing the root cause of lost time: shortage and possible state inefficiencies. He argued that workers were "caught between the jaws" in having to choose between work security (and raises) and a large fine."[140] "Laws should not be for the purpose of harassing people," passenger Mohamed Ally Ramadhan told a reporter who asked about the stings, "but always a reflection of the concrete situation that exists at the material time."[141] In "Passengers Don't Hang on UDA Buses for Fun," E. G. Munuo, who listed their address as the High Court, noted that workers "have to report to work in time at any cost," an impossible situation given bus shortages.[142] "Disillusioned Citizen" agreed by sharing their own experience with lax enforcement of car insurance laws for motor vehicle owners. The writer continued that if bus-riding residents were asked, "What is the law the reply would be: 'Law is the instrument through which the poor are harassed by the police, sent to court, fined quickly or jailed while the rich offender's position is protected.'"[143]

The question raised in state newspapers was not whether social and technological dysfunction was evident on city streets but, rather, why, and who was responsible for its emergence and for restoring order?

Periodical sources provide two distinct answers. Publications that followed the party ideology connected UDA's problems to a long-standing culture of vagrancy, begging, and crime anchored in the city's colonial past and in more recent migrations during the independent period. For example, in "What Is This Life in Dar es Salaam?," *Nchi Yetu*, the publication of the Ministry of Culture, connected the unprofessional conduct of bus operators to the figure of the male urban loafer. The article suggests that boys who came of age in Dar es Salaam's urban environment made poor professional parastatal men because they had sustained themselves through begging and crime for much of their lives.[144] For these reasons, they could not be trusted with community resources even after training at government offices—let alone help facilitate an urban culture of discipline and efficiency, or what Jamie Palmer terms "ineffective masculinity."[145] The same periodical implicated bus riders, too. It scolded them for instigating petty conflicts and for failing to pay fares.[146] In both cases, *Nchi Yetu* authors used UDA buses as proof that leaders had been correct about the unlikeliness of implementing urban socialism and about the desirability of rural over urban life.[147]

Passengers, in contrast, argued that sociotechnical disorder could not be reduced to generalizations about the city's past or its supposed antagonism to socialism. Instead, they pinpointed the specific contours of gender, class, and institutional authority that became evident in details about why certain social and technological systems functioned while others did not. In detailed letters, passengers blamed the poor condition of the fleet on reckless driving; they accused conductors of showing "lack of work discipline" by overloading buses, inciting violence, stealing fares, or simply failing to create conditions that allowed care and efficiency to prevail.[148] They also provided suggestions to UDA, such as training conductors as waiters, introducing penalties for operators, or, as one writer offered, creating buses exclusively for women at the city's main stops so they could avoid the "problems" (*taabu*) altogether.[149] Others visualized these complaints in popular cartoons that portrayed conductors as greedy, unintelligent, or incompetent youth creating discord among a socialist family in which Nyerere was considered the "father" (*baba*), the ministers as "elders" (*wazee*), and the citizens as "relatives" (*ndugu*). Given the state's role in directing technological change after the SFYP, caricatures of UDA conductors switched the context of disorder from discourses of urban pathology rooted in the antisocialist tendencies of cities to the government's inability to train disciplined employees or to take seriously passengers' written suggestions for solving the day-to-day problems of city life—in other words, to achieve official definitions of socialist familyhood.[150]

Similarly, passengers noted the technological disparity between functioning government sedans and broken UDA buses. Using the "ST" prefix designated for government vehicles, (*Serikali ya Tanzania*; Government of Tanzania), passengers labeled these cars *sitaki tabu* ("I don't want misery") vehicles because those who "are in a position high enough to warrant the use of 'Sitaki Tabu' can never know the tribulations, the dilemmas, horrors, struggles for almost survival of a Dar es Salaam bus rider."[151] Referencing the politicians and parastatal managers who used sitaki tabu, one passenger explained that "they do not seem to bother about the suffering of the masses" because of the state vehicles they had at their disposal. Had "these big shots" been forced to travel on city buses, the problem would have been solved long ago.[152] Another agreed, writing that newspaper forums had provided more than enough suggestions for improvements to be made. Yet, because UDA buses were the "transport . . . used by the proletariat," the leaders "have their ears blocked."[153] Managers are "concerned with their own material gains. They may know that their targets are not being achieved, but they may be interested in driving in good cars and craving for other privileges which are beyond the reach of the ordinary worker."[154] Meanwhile, a passenger asked, "Did a bomb fall on the 41 buses" taken out of service? And they wondered why UDA and NTC would not allow driving cooperatives like Co-Cabs to service residents if the point of socialism was to serve people.[155]

Bureaucratic motoring mattered to city residents because it regularly worked. Its function, far from suggesting the need to diminish the resource-heavy technological acts associated with parastatals—part of Nyerere's and the party's critique of urban motoring—suggested that the same efforts needed to be directed toward mass mobility.[156] As Callaci and Brownell show, who moved and how had become a metric for power in Dar es Salaam, with the powerless left waiting, walking, or begging for lifts.[157] But there was another dimension to this infrastructural hierarchy that increasingly fueled resentment: parastatals and ministries could clearly take technological resources from afar and turn them into a functioning, well-maintained system, even under economic duress. In other words, the selective maintenance of function for these leaders and the "social separation" it created, and not solely the presence of brokenness and dysfunction, increasingly drove residents' critiques.[158] Scandals broke in newspapers between 1980 and 1981 when the practice of hiring private car operators (and thus, not collectivized entities) at government ministries and departments became public. "A personal car, itself a status symbol, has become an end rather than the means" in government work, a reporter wrote, even as most of the country dealt with scarcity and fought dysfunction.[159]

By 1977 passenger letters had morphed from critique and suggestion to open accusations of managerial exploitation.[160] Writing about a price increase for UDA fares in 1980, one passenger remarked, "It is most unfortunate and indeed a pity that most of our institutions have decided to depart from the goals and aims for which they were nationalized, namely to serve the 'people' [*wananchi*] as efficiently as possible."[161] Others publicly accused UDA of various forms of corruption: "earning [of] money at the disservice to the commuters," "grab," "misappropriating," and "willful mishandling of Government's property"; they set "operating costs" in quotations to show their disbelief about what managers were doing with the parastatals' income.[162] In 1977 a poet compared UDA to a dhow being tossed by waves in the Indian Ocean:

[UDA] ride passengers like animals, like horses
If an institution falters, call it UDA
This shame has cornered us, the failures of us black people [*makosa yetu weusi*]
In the days of Jesus, government institutions didn't fail as they do now[163]

Broken buses signified something more than broken technologies. They suggested that a state institution did not have either the capacity or the will—as accusations of corruptions alluded—to make Dar es Salaam work in such a way that residents could build an urban socialist community.

That scared citizens like M. Mtenga because Nyerere had signaled the state would not revive failing parastatals, and "the common man," not managers, would "feel the pinch" of lost services—or as E. M. Saga put it, there is a "devil killing our institutions."[164] Concerns poured into newspapers after UDA's "sister" company at the NTC, the National Road Haulage Company (NRHC), was simply left to die with questions left unanswered about who would take up NRHC's important role in rural transportation.[165] As NRHC folded and UDA shortages shaped city life, the price of bus tickets rose in 1980 to meet the rising costs of transportation, the parastatal asserted.[166] Some writers, like Obilla, did not believe this explanation. "The present system of operation is not people-oriented" but a way for "UDA personnel to find an easy means of earning money."[167]

In this context, residents thus approached their "city as a sociotechnical process." Stephen Graham and Simon Marvin argue that networked systems like urban transport have the potential to create new communities—or "networked societies"—when they work because they signal the existence of a political system that can construct and maintain material worlds. Conversely, the same infrastructure can turn the minutiae of everyday life into discourses of exclusion through "networked fragility," a condition in which infrastructural failure "brings panic and fears of the breakdown of the functioning urban social order."[168] Indeed, residents took issue with infrastructural decline not because it produced technological absence but because it produced dense broken and breaking material worlds that shaped urban life in undesirable ways through lost time and colliding bodies. In this sense, bus riders implicated their state in the technological construction of an urban public culture increasingly shaped by shortages and by the social and economic implications of slowed mobilities and tired bodies and minds.[169]

Yet we should not read inevitable failure into the technological experiences of the 1970s. Passengers gave UDA time to get things right by waiting in foleni for at least three years and by offering operational advice for over a decade. As economic and infrastructural decline seemed less likely to reverse in the late 1970s, residents' expectations of postcolonial citizenship did not diminish. Indeed, their engagements and debates with the state over urban socialist citizenship spilled out of newspaper columns and into the streets and alleyways, where they addressed their state's infrastructural fragility by redefining the socialist politics of motoring. Indeed, precisely because residents had experienced decline as a technological process, they also believed it could be addressed, if not reversed, through technological means they controlled.

REMAKING SOCIALIST CARS: APPEARING BUSES, SHORTAGE, AND TECHNICAL REPAIR AS POLITICAL REPAIR

As passengers engaged their state in newspapers, some residents created a technological alternative to state-controlled urban mobility. In the early 1970s, minibuses began "appearing" around the city's bus stations. *Mabasi ya kuzuka*—literally, "buses that appear"—received this name for their ability to appear in public spaces and subsequently disappear again.[170] More commonly called *thumni-thumni*, meaning "fifty cents" (the cost of a ride), these buses were illegal for much of the 1970s because, the state asserted, they used private vehicles to compete with parastatals like UDA.[171] Yet many residents considered thumni-thumni an important technological alternative to formal state infrastructure as shortages immobilized the city. These urban citizens had reason to think that thumni-thumni could play a role in ujamaa's urban story.[172] In the face of crippling shortages between 1977 and 1980, Nyerere called for workers to be "unorthodox and innovative in their determination" to fix socialism as the nation "tightened its belt" and began its "National Economic Survival Programme" to revive production. Newspapers featured stories about the ingenuity of Tanzanian factory workers who turned metal scrap into working machinery and who remade spare parts that were ordinarily imported at great cost. The president suggested that workers explore using shea butter as an industrial grease: "In this particular case it may not be possible, but there may be other instances of shortage where similar questions lead to a positive result."[173] Perhaps seeking to encourage such innovation, the president stated that "inadequate public services" and the increased demand they reflected are "an indication that the country had forged ahead in its development effort."[174]

In this context of technological experimentation, thumni-thumni passengers made a public case for the socialist qualities of private vehicles. Oral history interviews with former drivers, owners, and passengers showed a system with four characteristics. First, thumni-thumni fares were double the UDA prices, but they targeted areas of shortage where regaining time lost standing in foleni was worth paying the extra cost. Second, the vehicles were owned privately (often by civil servants) and registered in ways that sidestepped the socialist politics of car ownership. Most owners registered thumni-thumni as taxis, allowing them to operate and carry passengers any day of the week, including during Sunday driving bans. One man who already owned a vehicle registered his bus in his wife's name, knowing the party was unlikely to trace the vehicle to his home.[175] Before registering vehicles, individuals had to purchase them, of course, and they had a number of places from which to choose. In addition to dealerships, newspapers ran ads listing used cars—including those sold by the state—or one could buy from a friend or a garage. It certainly helped that used vehicles like Volkswagen Beetles, Kombi vans, and even Land Rovers were associated with neither socially destructive luxury nor the state (through a license plate). A common complaint in newspapers was that state vehicles, identifiable by license plates, were used for private gain. But private vehicles providing a state service did not create much, if any, populist critique in printed sources. Similarly, in oral interviews, every resident interviewed credited thumni-thumni with "making transport easier" by reducing transport wait times for the entire city (UDA and thumni-thumni passengers alike).[176] This was a "big benefit" (*masilahi makbuwa*) to daily life because people could "arrive at work on time."[177]

Third, almost any vehicle could be a thumni-thumni. State newspapers identified Volkswagen minibuses as the preferred vehicle of operators, but residents used Land Rovers, saloon cars, and even trucks to transport passengers.[178] This mixing of vehicle types and models for passenger service was not new but rather the innovation of transport co-ops and collectives in the early 1960s celebrated by the state for turning private technologies into a public good.[179] Fourth, instead of operating on main roads, they plied vernacular routes through unpaved neighborhood thoroughfares called *uchochoro*. More footpath than road, uchochoro made up the intimate, unmapped grid of neighborhood life, allowing drivers who knew the city's uchochoro to navigate large portions of the city without detection. When they appeared out of the cover of neighborhood infrastructure, drivers either knew the daily location of traffic officers or took the opportunity to get to know them as "comrades" (*ndugu*) by at the least offering a ride.[180]

One driver who had been stopped by the police argued that the exchanges with police provided opportunities to create useful networks of reciprocity and "understanding" (*maelewano*). He gave the following example: giving a small gift, in his case, a fish from the harbor, to a policeman created an ally (*ndugu*) who could be helpful if there was a family emergency that required immediate assistance from the police. He used the Kiswahili word *ndugu*, which broadly translates as "relative" but during the socialist period meant "comrade." As I asked follow-up questions, he suggested I had misunderstood ujamaa as a lived experience. Like others I subsequently interviewed (and those in "saboteur" networks in chapter 5), he distinguished between ujamaa as a political term defined by the state and ujamaa as a sociotechnical network through which city residents could take steps toward meeting the basic demands of city life.[181] For the latter, thumni-thumni not only worked quite well but also fell within the bounds of socialist technological use precisely because they created bonds of reciprocity. Aili Mari Tripp describes a similar situation with an illegal bus and a police officer: "Realizing they would be in trouble, the passengers, who up until that moment had been perfect strangers, spontaneously transformed themselves into one big, happy family on its way to a wedding and started singing, clapping, and making shrill, ululating sounds, as is the custom for people on their way to celebrations. The police, unable to charge the driver for operating a bus on a commercial basis, had no choice but to let them go."[182] Whether or not thumni-thumni regularly turned Dar es Salaam's residents into "one big, happy family," the contrasting affinities created by UDA and thumni-thumni are difficult to ignore. Unlike for the former, which was characterized by dehumanization, conflict, and loss of the will to work, riders and drivers of thumni-thumni spoke of "efficiency," "understanding," comfort, "respectability," and the creation of socialist relationships with ndugu ("comrades") through road networks.[183]

In 1979 newspaper editors at the *Daily News* published a series of letters on economic reforms that included a case for the legalization of thumni-thumni. Passengers' arguments mirrored Nyerere's speeches about innovation and shortage: thumni-thumni, though private and illegal, offered an existing system of mobility that could be formalized at no cost to the state with machines and labor found around the city. Regardless, state and party officials accused the writers of contradicting "the national agenda" regarding the state's monopoly on social services.[184] Bus passengers wrote back, incensed. They argued that thumni-thumni were not competition for UDA but rather a complementary system of technology to assist the government until "it could become more efficient." They added that UDA could even ensure that private bus owners acted according to socialist standards by controlling the licensing of all new buses.[185] Once UDA stabilized, writers concluded, the parastatal could regain its monopoly and thereby dissolve thumni-thumni operations.[186] Three passengers pointed out that the state had used this exact approach with private hospitals and doctors in Tanzania throughout ujamaa. Yet a private doctor who healed bodies was not considered antisocialist.[187] Between 1979 and 1982, most public discussion on the topic ceased. Then a writer who identified as "Patriot" remade the above case for thumni-thumni with the caveat: "I very much hope that talk of finding alternative ways and means of meeting transport needs of this city . . . would not be interpreted as pro-capitalism."[188]

Patriot's frustration likely came from writers' limited success in redefining what counted as a socialist technology during an economic crisis. Whereas state media sources continued to link private vehicles to anti-ujamaa activity—including the pursuit of political prestige, the wasting of scarce resources, and, consequently, the destruction of the nation's economic well-being—thumni-thumni passengers who wrote to newspapers suggested two criteria for assessing a vehicle's socialist qualities within the context of shortage: it needed to help residents fulfill their obligations to become *wafanyakazi* (workers) through daily mobilities, and it needed to assist the state by relieving pressure on its struggling services.[189] In sum, they argued that something's use value to both citizens and the state, not its predetermined place in ideology, determined its political value to city users.[190] This did not make thumni-thumni passengers private vehicle enthusiasts. Leaders and citizens alike continued to associate sitaki tabu such as Double's Cortina with political decline and economic exploitation. But not all sedans had to be used this way, writers argued. In the right hands, private automobiles had already been used to achieve "comradery" amid infrastructural crisis on Dar es Salaam's streets.[191] And, writers thought, they could do so even more.[192] A similar theme came through in oral histories as residents pushed back against my characterization of thumni-thumni as "prohibited" (*marufuku*). Residents emphasized that the vehicles themselves were legal and registered. And though using these cars as passenger vehicles was technically prohibited, they argued that using a legally registered vehicle to address widespread city needs by transporting others—and not just one's family and friends—aligned with ujamaa's socialist ethic.[193]

Such "broken world thinking," as Steven Jackson puts it—or what Brian Larkin has called "repair as a cultural mode of existence"—needs to be recognized for what it was between the late 1970s and early 1980s: an effort by residents to repair a socialist city and its services with the assumption that parastatals and the services they offered were there to stay.[194] While there was no guarantee that their solutions would work, city residents were not anticipating the failure of their state or the arrival of free markets as a remedy to socialism's limitations. Instead, they thought deeply about what Stacey Langwick calls "practical alternative materialities" to help make their city work better during crisis in order to salvage a state institution that provided urban technological citizenship on a scale that thumni-thumni could not in the late 1970s—indeed, on a scale that no institution had achieved when UDA achieved its peak ridership in the mid-1970s.[195] Let me put this differently. Passengers did not endorse the self-help approaches to urban planning popularized in the 1970s that called for a reduction of state power, as officials feared. Nor did they valorize the local as a solution to the shortcomings of centralized urban planning, a theme often found in scholarly critiques of modernization.[196] Instead, Dar es Salaam residents called for a hybrid approach in which the state and private operators addressed urban infrastructural crises together, with the latter answering to the former. In sum, technological repair also acted as a form of political repair for urban ujamaa.

And they succeeded. In 1983 Prime Minister Edward Sokoine legalized thumni-thumni, later called *daladala*, to bring relief to the city's residents. Daladala went on to become the most common form of urban transport after privatization (*ubinafsishaji*) and are thus most often analyzed against the backdrop of neoliberalism.[197] However, it is important to emphasize that this staple of postsocialist Dar es Salaam first emerged as a technological mobilization within ujamaa as a means through which city residents reframed the possibilities of urban socialism as a social and technological project. Sitting between the hopes of the 1960s (with independence in 1961 and the declaration of socialism six years later) and the despair of the 1980s (with neoliberal reforms occurring in the early 1980s), the 1970s in Tanzania can appear as a precipitous economic and political decline ending with externally imposed structural adjustment and failed technological systems. This narrative overlooks that Dar es Salaam residents engaged their state not in spite of decline and dysfunction but because of it. Moreover, they provided a technological solution to make the city and socialism work better during a difficult period.[198]

Just months after the mini buses' legalization, Prime Minister Sokoine died in a car accident. In an impromptu act of appreciation, daladala operators ferried an estimated ten thousand residents to his funeral procession at no charge. One of Sokoine's biographers used this act to establish the politician's populist credentials.[199] It was also a unique moment in Dar es Salaam's history of socialist motoring: automobiles that only months earlier had been marked antisocialist transported thousands of residents to the city center to pay their respects to one of Tanzania's most respected socialist leaders—indeed, the man many had hoped could renew the optimism of earlier decades. In the broader context of socialist and independent motoring in Dar es Salaam, this public mourning showed that everyday users had remade the people's car without rejecting the efforts of leaders like Nyerere and Sokoine to create socialism as a state-led project. And yet, friction over the technopolitics of socialist repair and maintenance had burst into the open in ways that have shaped urban politics to the present, as discussed in this book's conclusion. Magnifying a process evident among mechanics in chapter 2, the state's call for a collective approach to repair in the context of economic crisis challenged the party and government's respective claims to holding technological power and to directing sociotechnical change. While, in the 1960s, Tanzania's leaders had focused on technology's relationship to the means of production, the next decades saw the means of maintenance and repair take an equally prominent place in national politics.

Letters, poems, and oral histories about urban infrastructure in Dar es Salaam evidence the important role of technology in creating communities of belonging and in meeting expectations about the material fruits of independence. By discussing the different forms of technological citizenship evident on Dar es Salaam's streets, bus riders turned quotidian experiences of waiting in line, boarding buses, and dealing with the mechanical condition of city's automobiles into a decade-long conversation about socialism and city life during a period of increasing scarcity. But residents were not paralyzed by this "infrastructural fragility." The illegal buses that appeared and disappeared on the narrow, unpaved paths of city neighborhoods show that decline was met with social and technological ingenuity and with debate over the manner in which technologies gained socialist or pro-capitalist qualities. In addition to buses, the urban socialist cars sanctioned by the state in the 1970s, Dar es Salaam residents made the case for treating a wide variety of personal vehicles as the automobiles of urban *wajamaa* ("socialists"). The next chapter demonstrates that urban automobiles received a disproportionate amount of public attention in the broader context of automobility's role in national development. We now turn to the oily technopolitics of rural modernization.

FOUR

Oily Ujamaa

Petroleum, Rural Modernization, and
"Effective Freedom" before and after
the "OPEC Bombshell"

THE FIRST OIL CRISIS of East Africa's independent period came eight years before the Organization for the Petroleum Exporting Countries (OPEC) sent global energy prices soaring in 1973. In 1965 Rhodesia's Unilateral Declaration of Independence created an apartheid state on Zambia's border. The Organisation of African Unity immediately called for an embargo of Southern Rhodesia's economy. Julius Nyerere agreed with no hesitation. But when Zambian president Kenneth Kaunda did the same, Southern Rhodesia cut off shipments of energy and minerals to and from the landlocked nation, halting two huge contributions to its economy: the importation of fuel and the exportation of copper. Because no equivalent infrastructural link existed between Tanzania's coastline and Zambia, Nyerere helped coordinate a massive British, American, and Canadian airlift that moved fourteen thousand metric tons of oil per month from Dar es Salaam to Kinshasa and then to Ndola, Zambia. A couple of years later, Tanzania formed a joint trucking company with Fiat and the government of Zambia. Operated by Tanzanian and Zambian drivers, the Italian trucks hauled between 4 and 7 million gallons of oil on a rough dirt road that earned two distinct nicknames: "Hell's Road," for what many journalists and drivers described as "the worst road in the world," and "Zambia's lifeline," a crucial link to the Indian Ocean. Built by the British in 1957 as part of postwar development, the route claimed over a hundred drivers' lives and caused large amounts of oil leakage out of drums and bladders damaged on the rough roads.[1]

In 1968, three years after the Unilateral Declaration of Independence, Nyerere and Kaunda jointly cranked open the valves of a $16 million pipeline that sent oil flowing from Dar es Salaam, where they stood, to Ndola, Zambia. The presidents subsequently followed the oil to Ndola, where they hailed the petroleum's arrival as an important step in the fight against imperialism. Here Nyerere gave an impassioned speech linking the pipeline to "real independence." In just over ten minutes, he used the words *freedom* and *free* twenty-three times. In the first twenty-two instances, he juxtaposed freedom to both *slavery* and *dependence*, terms he used interchangeably. Given Africa's colonial past, he began, "We know that a destitute man can sometimes get a good meal, clothes and shelter by selling himself into slavery." But after this point, "he will receive just those things which it is in the interests of the master to give him. He will receive nothing else." The same held true for new nations, Nyerere argued. A nation that "has sold its freedom for economic assistance" can no longer claim to pursue development. "Development will be incidental to the needs and desires of the master."[2]

In 1968 neither Tanzania nor Zambia had reached this servile state, but the president warned that the end of colonialism, though a "great triumph," had only led to "a paper independence." Because colonialism had left little in the way of skills and infrastructure to help nations sustain themselves, the independence movement had "achieved political power and the trappings of sovereignty; but our real power was much more limited than sovereign independence normally implies." The pipeline provided a "means" to create "real independence" by "achieving practical power to implement the theoretical freedom we possess." Only months after the Prague Spring, Nyerere compared Zambia's and Tanzania's technological response to Rhodesia to the "nonmilitary" protest in Czechoslovakia against the Soviet Union, an "occupying power." Czechoslovakia offered a template of action for the East African nations not because Rhodesia and the Soviet Union were equivalent but rather because, in both cases, the aggrieved nations, Czechoslovakia and Zambia, stood no chance of winning a military victory against a regional aggressor, Nyerere claimed.[3]

Like the protesters taking to Prague's streets calling for peaceful reform, the transnational pipeline offered a positive example of what the president called "effective freedom": a political condition capable of vanquishing oppression because it "comes from self-reliant economic strength" and can therefore spread "like a bush fire: it will sweep the racialist and colonialist out of control as it ignites the spirit of the oppressed peoples." Describing the pipeline as "a weapon in the struggle for African freedom and unity . . . a shield against threats to our own progress," Nyerere stated that because of this "one commodity," oil, and its ability to move through pipes, Tanzania's and Zambia's "freedom is enlarged."[4]

Moments later, he made his twenty-third, and final, reference to *free*. After calling on citizens of both countries to *"guard this pipeline, and guard it well"* (italics original), Nyerere spoke directly to Kaunda: "Mr. President, as a symbol of the unity of our two countries, let us go forward together and jointly turn the tap which will make this oil—Zambia's oil—flow freely from Dar es Salaam." Even though this petroleum came from distant oil fields, went through refining processes in Dar es Salaam, and then traveled across Tanzania to Ndola, it was "Zambia's oil." And it was literally so: the Tanzanian-Italian Petroleum Refinery (TIPER) moved a mixture of spiked crude mixed specifically for Zambia's economy. As long as these systems worked and were guarded well, no apartheid state could make a claim on Zambia's new oil or its "enlarged" freedom.[5]

A new infrastructural materiality played a critical role in this movement from paper to real independence. Before it took the names "Hell's Road" and "Zambia's lifeline," the route from Morogoro to Zambia was not merely the longest and costliest road in Tanganyika's colonial past; it also served as the bulk of the colony's Great North Road—Cecil Rhodes's infrastructural imaginary of a trans-African highway connecting British power from Cape of Good Hope to Cairo. But neither the geography nor the materiality of the Great North Road served African liberation. The road turned north toward Kenya at Dodoma, a reflection of the scope of British imperial ambitions, not toward an ocean outlet that would serve new nations' economic interest. Moreover, its rough and temporary materiality served the needs of regional liberation so poorly that world powers undertook massive airlifts of oil and copper.

The same did not apply to the pipeline as Nyerere described:

The oil coming out of this pipeline today was put into the eight-inch diameter pipe on 29 July, at Dar es Salaam. It has travelled 1,058 miles, at an approximate speed of 1½ miles per hour. It has gone up and down hills, crossed rivers, through populated areas and across undeveloped bushland. Slowly but surely the oil has moved forward through this pipeline to Ndola. Now it has arrived, and Zambia's oil supply is assured; Mr. President, her nightmare of stringency and worry about this commodity is over.[6]

Nyerere's description recalls Christopher Jones's term "landscapes of intensification."[7] For widespread use, Jones shows, energy required a geographically expansive infrastructure to reliably deliver it from nodes of production to users. Crossing rivers and mountain ranges and tying "undeveloped bushland" to "populated areas" across a thousand miles and two nations, TAZAMA (Tanzania-Zambia Mafuta [Tanzania-Zambia Oil Pipeline]) acted as the first step in creating an intensified landscape of liberation across Tanzania. Translating into Kiswahili as "look" or "watch," the acronym even provided a useful material metaphor: look or watch (*tazama*), one could say, at the material things that have led to a more "effective freedom."[8]

The pipeline was only the first step in Nyerere's pursuit of "real independence." Over the next four years, Tanzania's government added an asphalt highway (constructed by USAID [United States Agency for International Development] in 1970) and a "freedom railway" (built by China in 1972). Sixty miles wide and 1,125 miles long, the resulting "Dar corridor" served "real independence" in a number of ways. Tanzanian planners viewed the corridor as a new foundation for regional national development, in addition to providing Zambia an "outlet to the sea." Members of the National Development Corporation hoped to use the road, railway, and pipeline to entice communities to settle along a nearly three hundred–mile stretch of the corridor, gaining access to goods and services that had not yet been extended to many rural areas.[9] To fully appreciate this link among services, goods, and infrastructure, recall an interview from chapter 1. A woman who lived about eighty yards off this Dar es Salaam highway said that she disliked colonial roadwork primarily because she could not do anything with the small wage she received—not even buy new clothes. Within just two decades, however, the corridor facilitated multiple forms of mobility, including of people, goods, and oil. It thus offered citizens material evidence that independence had produced forms of "effective freedom" not realized or even pursued during the colonial period—a form of what Brenda Chalfin terms "technologies of sovereignty."[10] Moreover, it reflected

Nyerere's and Kaunda's skill in navigating Cold War politics, using aid from East and West to further their own visions for African liberation.[11]

But what does a pipeline have to do with agricultural development, the bedrock of ujamaa's African socialism? And what happened to Nyerere's celebration of small-scale technologies, sweat and work, precolonial values, and an orderly sociotechnical evolution that "did not skip steps"?

This chapter answers these questions by establishing the close relationship between refined oil and the form of rural modernization Tanzania's leaders pursued between 1961 and the mid-1980s.[12] As described in the previous chapter, party officials sold rural and urban development as distinct technological projects—confining automobility and its costly machinic complex to the latter. With their dense infrastructure, demanding citizens, and corrupt motoring bureaucrats, cities constrained Tanzania's quest for economic self-reliance in ways that farmers' hoes and plows did not, Nyerere argued. Indeed, the president asserted that ujamaa's emphasis on simple tools, hard work, and land offered a technological alternative to the capital-intensive forms of development championed by modernization theorists from the Western and Eastern Blocs, even drawing the likes of E. F. Schumacher, a booster of "intermediate technologies" and the author of *Small Is Beautiful: Economics as If People Mattered*, to visit Tanzania to see these processes for himself.[13]

Yet this technologically minimalist approach to African socialism overlooks a central component of ujamaa from its inception: rural modernization was also a form of automobility that required a machinic complex composed of fossil fuels, on the one hand, and an extensive infrastructure of pipelines, railways, and roads connecting refined oil to communities across the nation, on the other. By pairing oil with rural modernization—or with antiapartheid liberation—the president did not unwittingly stumble into a technological condition that clashed with ujamaa's ideological commitment to bottom-up change or to the role of hoes and hard work in small villages. As what one scholar calls "lifeblood," oil was "a way of life" integrally linked to various forms of production and consumption that societies around the world took for granted, whether a predominantly manual form of agriculture, as in Tanzania, or thoroughly mechanized sites of production.[14] Timothy Mitchell calls this "carbon democracy," observing that much of what has been understood as "the economy" has assumed an ability to control the movement of oil through what Mimi Sheller and John Urry call a "machinic complex."[15]

Using documents from the archive of the Tanzania Petroleum Development Corporation (TPDC) archive, this chapter turns its attention to three specific parts of automobility's machinic complex: oil, the things that moved it (such as TAZAMA), and the things that transformed petroleum into a commodity commensurate with the "real independence" and "effective freedom" of which Nyerere spoke. It does so for two reasons. First, it establishes petroleum's centrality to ujamaa's rural modernization. As noted earlier, ujamaa gained international attention in the 1960s and 1970s because Tanzania's leaders announced their intention to create alternatives to dominant forms of economic and technological well-being. When ujamaa failed to sustain this economy or culture of technology, ultimately requiring leadership to address balance-of-payments issues in 1979, critics charged that one reason the nation needed this assistance was because its leaders had abandoned the original infrastructural approach of the Arusha Declaration (AD). Instead of small tools and a small bureaucracy, both of which reflected Nyerere's insistence on a voluntary, bottom-up villagization through technological "self-reliance," the state had expanded its infrastructural power and its bureaucratic size, with devastating consequences.[16] In 1973 forced villagization moved nearly 80 percent of the nation's rural populace into state-planned villages. It used heavy machinery and oil and turned government vehicles into symbols of bureaucratic oppression among rural communities.[17]

When economic turmoil hit just four years later, the link among technologically heavy bureaucracies, arrogant experts, faltering economies, and exploited farmers provided an argumentative framework to explain socialism's seeming failures: ujamaa had become technologically inappropriate even by its own standards.[18] But this link among costly infrastructure, bureaucrats, and economic decline overlooks key parts of ujamaa's technological history. Though Nyerere talked a lot about small technologies, he never sold ujamaa as an economic system completely detached from large technological systems (LTSs) or bureaucracies.[19] My intent in following this thread is not to dismiss or diminish forced villagization's place in Tanzania's 1970s or any other forms of state oppression that occurred during this time. But given the role of technology and bureaucrats in declensionist narratives of the 1970s—narratives that subsequently informed broader theories of African state failure and that assumed the viability of infrastructural alternatives not taken—we need examine the technological details about such alternatives.[20] Second, for this reason, centering oil and its machinic complex demonstrates that ujamaa's status as an alternative to dominant forms of modernization always passed through petroleum and its infrastructural and bureaucratic imperatives. Historically, these imperatives matter because they raise questions about the technological possibilities and constraints of nation building from the perspectives of some of the historical actors responsible for literally building the nation—in this case, oil technologists at the TPDC and high-ranking ministers and politicians, what Leander Schneider calls "the world of officials."[21] These individuals held concerns not just about which technological systems aligned with Tanzanian socialism—the core element of the above critique—but also about the *when* of infrastructural self-reliance: the time needed to build and maintain infrastructure across national and regional space in ways that safeguarded Tanzania's political and economic sovereignty. The OPEC crisis of 1973, which quadrupled oil prices, magnified concerns about this infrastructural clock by shifting capital to increasingly costly shipments of petroleum and thus away from the construction or maintenance of systems that refined and moved it.

Two years later, and only seven years after his rousing speech about mobile oil constituting "effective freedom" capable of spreading like a "bush fire," Nyerere connected OPEC's price hikes to the end of a technological era of nation building and decolonization. This era had begun with independence in 1961, twelve years earlier, but had ended far earlier than expected and fallen far short because of the new dynamic OPEC introduced beginning in 1973. To explore the reasons Nyerere shifted from one form of technological determinism (with freely flowing oil equated to "enlarged" freedom) to another (in which petroleum prices compromised Tanzania's pursuit of "real independence," turning the nation into what he called a "fourth world country"), we look at the surprising link between oil and ujamaa's concepts of self-reliance alongside a technopolitical form of common sense found among leaders: infrastructural change had to happen at running speed.

"WE MUST RUN": AFRICAN SOCIALISM, PETROLEUM, AND LTSS IN AN "OIL SHORT" COUNTRY, 1961 TO 1973

In addition to its presence in the colonial economy, oil possessed two other qualities that made it a practical source of ujamaa's energy. First, it offered an economical alternative to other popular options, including hydroelectric, coal, and nuclear power.[22] Between Tanzanian independence in December 1961 and the beginning of the OPEC crisis in August 1973, the average price per barrel *fell* from $23.90 to $19.40.[23] Second, distributors transported oil along a modular infrastructure of road and rail; the bulk of roads were dirt. Though this was not ideal for creating economies of scale, as Hell's Road to Zambia demonstrates, petroleum could nevertheless reach users without the construction of the costly centralized networks of distribution required by the alternatives. This was especially important in Tanzania. Officials noted that colonial governments had never built a geographically expansive rail network capable of delivering bulk goods such as oil throughout the nation's regions—tying them together as one entity through a mechanized system of movement.[24] Combined with Tanzania's limited capital to spend on technological projects, oil's modular mobilities not only offered practical solutions to energy concerns but also aligned with a gradual infrastructural scale-up that fit neatly with the AD's cautious approach to LTSs. As rural communities not only gained more access to petroleum but also used it to increase their output—in both cases guaranteeing a market for oil—the state could justify expanding its distribution networks.

Tanzania still pursued other forms of energy generation. A 1962 survey funded by the Food and Agriculture Organization recommended construction of a large hydroelectric dam at Stiegler's Gorge. But World Bank funding never materialized, despite repeated requests. In the meantime, the government constructed three smaller dams. Kidatu dam near Dodoma, as well as two others built near Arusha and Tanga between 1967 and 1975, "considerably reduced the amount of gasoil required for electricity" in these regions because electric power plants ran on petroleum.[25] But demands from other regions and energy sectors almost immediately nullified these reductions. In addition to increased operations by Tanzania-Zambia Railway Authority (TAZARA) railways, the construction of a fifteen-megawatt power plant in Mwanza required fourteen thousand tons of gas oil per year.[26] Oil thus played a critical role in Tanzania's economy even as the nation expanded its nonpetroleum energy sources. It provided electricity, and thus fueled factories, in areas where coal and hydroelectric energy were not available or prohibitively expensive. It also had a complete monopoly on motorized mobilities and greases for factories. One TPDC document summed this up by describing "petroleum products as the main sources of energy for Industrial and Agricultural Development."[27]

We can see oil in ujamaa's productive processes if we begin with that classic image of African socialism: farmers and their hoes. After work, sweat, and land paid dividends by creating a surplus from sold crops, wajamaa, in Nyerere's speeches, bought equipment such as tractors, trucks, fertilizers (often processed at refineries and shipped with diesel), and milling machines that, in turn, officials connected to the increased output needed for economic growth.[28] Once harvested, some of these primary resources traveled via vehicles powered (and engines greased) with refined petroleum to ports for export. Other finished products moved within the country to a factory, often powered by gas oil, to become a finished product marketable within Tanzania through government-run cooperative stores in towns and large ujamaa villages. The government brought attention to this process through campaigns that advertised "Always made here" (hutengenezwa hapa) and, for domestically made kitchen utensils, "luxury in the kitchen" (fahari ya jikoni).[29] Indeed, in 1966 Nyerere linked such "Buy Tanzanian" campaigns for "consumption goods" to the nation's ability to save foreign exchange and therefore pursue or enlarge investments in social services or industry, adding, "We shall want to buy more and more machinery and other things for development."[30] Some Marxist-Leninists who critiqued this process thought Nyerere erred by not jump-starting the production of both raw and finished materials with state technologies earlier, thereby allowing fluctuating primary commodity prices more influence on the nation's economic trajectory.[31]

But for the point at hand, transforming a primary product like shea butter (mafura) into soap sold in cooperative stories used at least four types of refined oil before it became a socialist commodity. Trucks powered by diesel and gasoline (type 1) moved mafura to a factory, perhaps over roads made from residual fuel oil (RFO), a byproduct of petroleum refining used to construct asphalt roads (type 2). Factories processed mafura using gas oil (type 3) to provide electricity and industrial lubes (type 4) for machines. The mafura then moved to stores via motorized transport. If a village used mechanized equipment, the soap would require even more of the first type of oil. The same applied to social services. In addition to kerosene, a staple for lighting in homes and schools, larger villages and towns had hospitals with stand-by generators using diesel and gas oil;[32] mobile clinics ran on gasoline and diesel.[33] Food and other staples also came via motorized networks. Between 1965 and 1971, national oil consumption grew by 8.1 percent per year. This included increases in gas oil (10 percent), motor spirits (7 percent), and lighting kerosene (5 percent). In 1973, just before the OPEC crisis, gas oil and lighting kerosene, two staples of rural use, grew by another 15 and 10 percent, respectively. Jenga, a periodical

4.1 This visualization of ujamaa's productive and distributive processes also aligns with the presence of petroleum products in rural modernization schemes, including the role of heavy motor vehicles such as large trucks and buses, mechanized farming, factories, schools, workshops, and community centers. "Vyama vya Ushirika Tanzania: Jana, Leo na Kesho— Shughuli za Chama cha Ushirika," Ushirika Nyongeza, July 7, 1974, xi.

of the National Development Corporation, called this process "the rural revolution."[34]

The director of the TPDC, Sylvester Barongo, a geologist who had earned a doctorate at the Colorado School of Mines, interpreted this growth "as an indication of the country's economic progress. Increasing consumption of lighting kerosene shows that more and more rural areas are having some illumination at night and the consumption of illumination kerosene is likely to increase with increasing Ujamaa/permanent villages. Gasoil/diesel is used in transportation and its high growth rate is indicative of growing distributive activities."[35] Small villages with minimal agricultural output and services required five to eight drums of mixed products (1,500 liters) per month. A more mature ujamaa village that sold crops and offered social services, however, consumed about thirteen times more, including eighty-four drums (16,800 liters) of gasoline and twenty-four drums (4,800 liters) of diesel.[36] In other words, oil use provided a parastatal like the TPDC with an important indicator of a village's pursuit of African socialism. Villages that needed petroleum in increasing quantities had likely heeded the state's call to band together, to work harder, to provide services, and to use tools that did not leave them still using hoes "like their ancestors," as Nyerere once quipped.[37]

Moreover, ujamaa's brand of socialism gave Barongo every reason to boast about the "growing distributive activities" he associated with increased oil use and "transportation." Like many socialists, Nyerere distinguished capitalism from socialism not by production but through the state's role in distribution: "Socialism is essentially distributive."[38] With the slogans "Help us build ours" ("Saidie tujenge chetu") and "leaders in the nation's business," the State Trading Corporation took a central role in what it called "the distribution revolution": a process in which the state centralized imports and exports in order to take business out of the hands of the few—the economic condition at the beginning of independence—and make it work for the entire nation.[39] Increased use of gas oil, diesel, and kerosene between 1967 and 1973 was an encouraging sign for Tanzania's socialist experiment because it reflected the state's growing ability to move things, including oil, across a growing national network of roads (both bitumen and dirt), trucks, pipes, and rail cars to rural communities—that is, a nascent machinic complex capable of getting one of the world's most important energy sources to places where it had had minimal impact in previous decades.

More specifically, literally moving oil and other goods through national space aligned with one of Tanzania's iconic postcolonial political slogans: "We must run while others walk." This phrase found its way into Kiswahili as *mbioni*, meaning "on the way" as well as being the locative state (*-ni*) of heading somewhere with intent; indeed, *mbio* translates as *speed*. Kivukoni College, the party's hub for ideological training, adopted *Mbioni* as the title of its journal and sometimes included a man running with a torch, a symbol of independence, on the cover.[40] This literal act of running as independence was only one part of a socialist Kiswahili lexicon that bound literal and metaphorical movement, as well as speed, together. In addition to "driving the nation" (*kuendesha taifa*)—the causative of the Kiswahili verb for "going," to emphasize displacement from a starting point—leaders encouraged citizens to pursue "quick development" (*maendeleo ya haraka*) by collectivizing in villages. In most circumstances, this haste came not from a preference for speed but from anxiety about two issues. First, nationalist politicians felt pressure to deliver on the promises of decolonization for their citizens by providing new forms of livelihood. With little to show from colonial development, Tanzania started independence from behind and needed to run to catch up, Nyerere asserted.[41] "First," Nyerere said in a speech to university students, "it must be realized that we are in a hurry."[42] Second, doing so in a sustainable manner, Nyerere thought, necessitated a "modern" economy capable of scaling up production and protecting against foreign influence. This, in turn, required the type of "practical power" Nyerere associated with the pipeline and "real independence" in the opening vignette. And yet, as C. D. Msuya, a parliamentarian and the minister of finance, noted, "The country inherited a poor rudimentary stagnant economy with inadequate communications."[43]

This juncture of technological speed and self-reliance—indeed, technological speed *as* self-reliance—is where we need to get detailed about Nyerere's hybrid approach to socialist nation building. The president believed Tanzania would not get centuries to build up a technological base for production, as industrial powers around the world had. Rather, Tanzania, like other colonies, was thrust into a particularly challenging situation: creating self-reliance while competing against other nations and corporations that had a huge head start. Nyerere considered this postcolonial situation so unique that he said there was "no model" in Marxist theory for his country "to copy."[44] And yet he turned the absence of a viable model into an opportunity for Tanzania to avoid the errors of orthodox socialism: "European socialism was born of the Agrarian Revolution and the Industrial Revolution which followed it. The former created the 'landed' and the 'landless' classes in society; the latter produced the modern capitalist and the industrial proletariat. . . . The European socialist cannot think of his socialism with its father—capitalism!"[45] As a technological process, industrialization produced rampant exploitation while crystallizing inequalities that had to be addressed through subsequent socialist and communist phases. To follow this Marxist model, Tanzania would require decades, and likely centuries, to pass through the feudalist and capitalist phases (industrialization occurs in the latter), all in the name of creating class conflicts, *before* ever having the opportunity to address inequality.

Why move Tanzania from a largely agricultural society to an exploitative industrial system—a process that would require either huge state investments or dependence on foreign capital—to simply satisfy the notion that human equality was best achieved through the Euro-American phases of history and was rooted in class exploitation? Nyerere thus eschewed the sequential phases of orthodox Marxist development: tribalism, primitive communism, feudalism, capitalism, socialism, and communism. And he made the case for combining what he thought his society did best— agriculture (found in the precapitalist phases of Marxist development)— with LTSs (from the capitalist stage) to make precolonial qualities relevant and useful in contemporary political economies. His belief that this could be done came from North Korea, where he noted that a predominantly agricultural society had nevertheless achieved impressive amounts of rural electrification—and without capitalism as its "father."[46] Some Marxist-Leninists saw this as an unworkable theoretical hybrid combining antagonistic phases of Marxist development—tribalism and capitalism. But Nyerere sold it as a form of scientific socialism that approached the "problems of a particular society from the standpoint of that society."[47]

A clear articulation of this policy came in "Socialism: The Rational Choice": "Remnants of feudalism and primitive communism do, of course, still exist, in the world; but neither of these are viable systems when challenged by the organized technology of the twentieth century." Nyerere continued by stating that, in actual practice, new nations did not have much of a choice regarding their technological preferences because they inherited certain trade patterns and because regional and world economies valued particular types of production and exchange. "When Britain experienced its industrial revolution at the end of the eighteenth century, it was enough" to achieve global economic power. But Nyerere doubted "little Tanzanian capitalists" could compete with Ford or Nippon

Enterprises. Unlike Henry Ford, who could begin his trade with bicycles and "build up his capacity hit by hit," Nyerere noted that Tanzania was expected to achieve what amounted to centuries of change for industrial countries (who often had the benefit of colonial resources) in just decades and in an environment that, unlike in eighteenth-century Britain or early twentieth-century car manufacturing, was already full of industrial competitors. Nyerere asserted that, technologically speaking, industrial capitalism was neither desirable nor necessary because its prominent place in Marxist stages of history assumed that progress required mass exploitation and violence, both elements of colonialism new African leaders were eager to avoid, as David Ottaway and Marina Ottaway observe. Additionally, even socialist and communist forms of industrialization, including China, raised concerns about cost and self-reliance.[48] After waxing poetic about Romania's accomplishment in a speech in Bucharest, Nyerere cited Tanzania's absence of oil as the reason "we cannot copy your economic development methods and procedures."[49]

The president thus pursued a technological mix that made sense for his nation's own history and desires as well as within the context of existing patterns of global capitalism. That Nyerere and others felt compelled to enact changes quickly but with defined technological limitations provides an interesting approach to what Paul Virilio calls *dromocracy*: the notion that political power comes through the production and control of movement. This, in turn, often involves discourses that attach social progress to acceleration and speed—leading Virilio to reframe "power-knowledge" as "moving power."[50] While there is no doubt that Tanzania's leaders felt a need for speed, we should not collapse ujamaa—and its rural automobility, in particular—into broader dromocratic discourses. "We *must* run" was an imposed condition; ujamaa did not endorse quickness for its own qualities. In fact, Nyerere noted that pursuing development quickly by immediately importing industrial equipment cost much more—and thus statements in the AD distinguish money, tools, and maendeleo.[51] Further, technologies that moved quickly, such as automobiles, cost more to operate and maintain at higher speeds. Most important, the state's dromocratic discourse often encouraged the type of intentional plodding and pacing necessary for long trips. Leaders described the nation as a "long caravan heading toward socialism" ("msafara mrefu kuelekea ujamaa") and encouraged communities to "press" or "forge" ahead: "songa mbele."[52] In this sense, the "must" can be read as referring to the need to keep pace in a long race in which going too quickly and falling too far behind both posed dangers. In the essay "Groping Forward," the president argued that some-times the goal was to just keep moving: "Society, like everything else, must either move or stagnate—and in stagnation lies death."[53]

That technologies small and large went together in Nyerere's philoso-phy of technology and movement leads us back to oil and its infrastruc-ture. After four years of planning, in 1965 Nyerere opened the nation's first and only oil refinery, the TIPER, through a joint-ownership project with the Italian firm Agip at a cost of about 110 million shillings (nearly $16 mil-lion), including loans repayable to the construction firm ENI through the refinery's operating profits.[54] Tanzania fully owned its 50 percent share by 1967.[55] The nation's leading periodical, *Mfanyakazi* (The worker), cel-ebrated the refinery's completion by describing it as an infrastructural im-perative not just of development but of quick (*haraka*) development: "As one of the nations [in the world] developing quickly, [Tanzania] is doing everything it can to be able satisfy itself [*kujitosholeza*] with the important needs that any developing country must have. One of these must haves is an oil refinery."[56] Speaking before the National Assembly in 1966, Nyerere linked it to a process of "[doing] as much as possible to reduce the de-mands on foreign exchange" for gasoline and diesel imports.[57] What nei-ther Nyerere nor the newspaper mentioned was that an oil refinery was particularly important for an "oil-short importing nation" like Tanzania. "Petroleum-short"(or "oil-short") referenced petroleum's small share of the national energy profile. Moreover, without known reserves of petro-leum, Tanzania, like most African nations, imported all of its oil.[58] Short-ness mattered to leaders like Barongo because oil made up a huge part of Tanzania's "energy mix," including 95 percent of its commercial energy.[59]

In this situation, constructing a refinery allowed the state to import crude—that is, unrefined oil—at cheaper per-barrel prices than the refined products they had previously purchased. In Tanzania's case, TIPER reduced the nation's reliance on Kenya's Mombasa factory, run by multinational corporations—which continued to distribute in northern regions—while adding oil exports to Zambia and other neighboring nations that offset between half and two-thirds of Tanzania's oil imports.[60] Additionally, the price difference between bulk crude and domestic sales allowed Tanzania to reinvest profits back into the refinery, into distributional networks, and into exploration. The Department of Commerce intended to add bitumi-nization and fertilizer plants to TIPER—a common approach with small refineries. When used domestically or exported, both products saved or generated foreign exchange for the national economy. Moreover, both

Barongo and Nyerere described the refinery as a "toolbox" through which professional Tanzanians, through the partnership with Agip, would later operate it themselves. From infrastructure to energy and knowledge, few technological systems more thoroughly permeated the state's pursuit of technological and economic self-reliance, leading the TPDC to call the refinery the nation's "technical back-bone."[61] Dividends generated by refinery profits helped the government repay two-thirds of its loan by 1973; there was no end date to the loan because repayment varied based on annual profits. This situation allowed 41.4 million shillings of investments in the refinery between 1966 and 1972 and an investment budget of 1.7 million shillings in 1973.[62]

In 1969 the government created the TPDC "to promote the development of the petroleum industry and the production of petroleum" and to "carry on the businesses" of prospecting, refining, and distributing petroleum.[63] In doing so, it gave the TPDC one of the most ambitious projects of the independent period: to create an indigenous petroleum economy in Tanzania, a place with no known oil reserves and almost no institutional experience in the petroleum business, as a critical sector of a socialist economy. *Indigenous*, a word used frequently in forums about oil and development, had two meanings: first, to coordinate the exploration and extraction of "petroleum," within national borders (to see if Tanzania could join the ranks of energy-rich nations); and, second, to create the technological capacity to direct and oversee the importation, refining, and distribution of petroleum products. Because unrefined oil had few economic uses, a nation with no known oil reserves, like Tanzania, could create an indigenous petroleum economy through technological power alone—what a recent volume calls an "oil assemblage"—by turning crude into a variety of finished products and then distributing them. The TIPER and TANZAM, built in 1965 and 1968 respectively, constituted important steps toward this goal.

But even after the TPDC's creation in 1969, multinational companies still controlled importation and national distribution because each of these acts of mobility—ship transport to Tanzania's coastline and then distribution within the country—required sustained investments in equipment and infrastructure Tanzania could not yet make. In 1970, and "in accordance with [the] country's Socialist Philosophy," the government purchased a 50 percent stake in both British Petroleum (BP) and Shell—it already had the same stake in Agip—while transferring operation of these companies' stations to local cooperatives and district committees.[64] The nationalization of already existing networks provided a practical means of quickly expanding state input over the oil economy. It took another seven years for the TPDC to take control of importing. The move came after a 1976 report by Justinian Rweyemamu confirmed long-held suspicions about multinational oil companies overcharging Tanzania for imports.[65] More than a reactionary move, the TPDC's growing role in Tanzania's oil economy aimed to reverse a consumption trend encouraged by multinational companies: the growing use of light distillates in the 1960s such as gasoline used in small motor vehicles. While such fuels increased companies' profit margins, using foreign exchange for this purpose did not match the priorities of a socializing economy like Tanzania. The TPDC thus focused on expanding the supplies of middle distillates such as gas and fuel oil used for mechanized farming, industries, and heavy vehicles.[66] This is where growing indigenous technological capacity intersected with the government's socialist aims: fuels imported, refined, and distributed matched ujamaa's social and economic priorities. Transforming crude oil into refined products at the TIPER for use in Tanzania occurred across a wide geographic space and went through a variety of technical systems, as table 4.1 shows. When the parastatal took full control of importation in 1977, before a shipment of crude headed to Dar es Salaam's port, the TPDC entered into bilateral agreements with an exporting nation or company. Then the National Bank of Commerce (NBC), in conjunction with Tanzania's Central Bank, opened a line of credit with an international bank such as Barclays, Citibank, or Bank of America. Without any ships of its own, the TPDC arranged for a shipping company, often from India, to deliver the product to Dar es Salaam's port. At this point, the parastatal oversaw the refining process at the TIPER. Lacking its own distribution network, the TPDC sold the TIPER's refined products to multinational companies, which, despite being pushed out of the procurement process, distributed the products within Tanzania's borders. Cash payments from these sales then moved from the distributing companies to the TPDC's account and finally to the NBC, where they could be used to start the process all over again. The government's role as a consumer gave Agip, Shell, and BP about half of the market share; Esso and Caltex made up the rest.[67]

In the 1970s and early 1980s, the TPDC never equated oil's indigeneity with controlling every step of this process. But it hoped to raise Tanzania's influence in regional oil markets by purchasing a shipping fleet, by gain-

TABLE 4.1 Indigenizing Oil

Place	Relationship
Italy	Refinery construction Pipeline construction Oil marketing company Exploration (Agip) Loans for construction Personnel
United Kingdom	Banks for lines of credit News about the spot market
United States (New York)	Banks for lines of credit News about spot market
United States (North Carolina)	Contractors to build the freedom road to Zambia
India	Tankers to ship crude from source to Dar es Salaam Source of rumors about oil trade Consultants for oil exploration Technical Education and Conferences
China	Freedom Railway—mechanism for moving oil in bulk along Uhuru Corridor
Kenya	Refined products from Mombasa to northern Tanzania
Libya	Processed and crude light oil
Iran	Processed and crude light oil Bilateral agreements for barter
Iraq	Processed oil products
Kuwait	Processed and crude light oil Hub of the spot market
United Arab Emirates	Processed oil products

Place	Relationship
Oman	Processed and light crude oil
Yemen	Processed oil products
Algeria	Crude oil for barter
Angola	Crude oil for barter

ing more control over domestic distribution (including truck fleets and gas stations), by expanding its refinery, and by developing natural energy sources, if found. The TPDC had good reason to consider these achievable goals. When it started operations in 1973 under the direction of Barongo, Tanzania had made important strides toward infrastructural self-reliance. In addition to its refinery and a pipeline, a new railway, TAZARA, opened in 1973 with a forty-six tanks for distributing oil. In just eight years, the nation had greatly expanded its machinic complex and the role of oil in social and economic life. From year to year, economic trends were uneven. But the overall arc of growth—including growing usage of oil—gave politicians and TPDC leadership reason to expect the next eight years to follow a similar pattern.[68]

But just months after the parastatal's office opened, an event it called "OPEC's bombshell" landed. In August 1973 members of OPEC wrested some control of oil markets away from multinational corporations, greatly increasing the influence of nationalized command economies over production and distribution. By the end of the year, oil prices rose from $19 to nearly $80 per barrel.[69] Barongo and his staff anticipated that price increases would place a huge strain on "developing non-oil producing countries." But they also supported the nationalizing countries—especially former colonies—and saw opportunities for the crisis to drastically reshape regional and global economies.[70] Their hopes were not unfounded. Oil-producing countries in the Middle East reached out to newly independent countries in Africa, stating unequivocally that the embargo was not intended to hurt their economies and that they would cut out the powerful "marketing companies" to deal directly with "consumer countries"—an arrangement that seemingly benefited both exporting and importing nations.[71] Moreover, the shah of Iran spoke of creating aid programs with "surplus funds"; Algeria stated, "The Arab countries would not hesitate to assist the developing countries"; the prime minister of Kuwait stated, "It is our duty to improve the conditions . . . of friendly developing countries of Africa."[72]

Encouraged by these statements, in its first post-OPEC-crisis memo, "Petroleum Products," the TPDC laid out new forms of economic cooperation with oil-exporting nations newly flush with capital: "There appears to be room to develop economic programmes which complement each other in the two economies." It started with a proposal for bartering, including oil exchanges for beef, cereals, and shoe and hide products, or "the possibility of establishing a furniture factory."[73] This way, Tanzania would not have to use foreign cash reserves on oil, industrial equipment, or fertilizer, and the investing nation was guaranteed access to both raw resources and a market of consumers. A more ambitious plan involved turning Dar es Salaam into a bunkering port for the Western Indian Ocean. This, in turn, hinged on the reciprocal embargoes of South Africa and Israel that East African and Arab nations wrote into oil contracts. These embargoes limited the strategic ports where shipping companies could bunker oil as they moved between Atlantic, Indian, and Pacific Ocean economies. With the obvious choice, South Africa, off the table because of apartheid, the TPDC suggested that an "Arab" OPEC nation invest in another larger refinery in Dar es Salaam and pipelines that ran thousands of miles to central and southern Africa.[74] In addition to seeking to starve South Africa's oil economy, the TPDC tried to sell expanded markets for Red Sea and Persian Gulf oil exporters. The memo concludes by calling for unity among "developing" nations to "face this situation united."[75]

A huge expansion through a global crisis may seem unrealistic in hindsight. But for the same reason that the TPDC supported OPEC's nationalizing economies, it saw increased prices as a practical opportunity to turn transnational ideologies of liberation calling for collective action among former colonies—first at Bandung in 1955 at the Asian-African Conference and after the crisis at the 1978 South-South conference in Buenos Aires, which adopted the Plan of Action for Promoting and Implementing Technical Cooperation Among Developing Countries—into an infrastructural reality capable of creating new flows, economies, and technological dependencies. Building a bunkering port in Dar es Salaam, including expanded refining capacity and new pipelines, would have given OPEC nations economic and technological influence in East Africa. In turn, it provided a rare opportunity for the TPDC to pursue the infrastructural acceleration championed in "we must run" through a unique postcolonial relationship not envisioned in any of the AD's warnings against foreign aid: former colonies—not former colonizers and multinational corporations—who could provide technical assistance and loans. If the surplus value of the crisis could be used to change the way oil moved regionally through new ocean routes and land infrastructure, former colonies could build networks of decolonizing energy flows without the majors. The suggestion thus envisioned a radically different form of the "web of sociopolitical relations required for hydrocarbon extraction and production," as Hannah Appel puts it, formed through the technological possibilities opened up by decolonization and a global oil crisis.[76] No OPEC nation took Tanzania up on its offer, however, and price hikes quickly took an economic toll.[77]

Nevertheless, ujamaa's oiliness in this formative period of nation building reveals a different relationship among the state, petroleum, technology, and cultures of development than is described in much of the literature on energy in Africa. Petroleum in postcolonial Africa is often associated with resource curses ("Dutch disease"), dependency, spectacle, and rampant political corruption through a gatekeeping state more focused on monopolizing resources through relationships with multinational entities than distributing them domestically.[78] Most of this literature comes from petroleum-exporting nations—a minority on the African continent. In Tanzania the link between socialism and oil demonstrates that petroleum did not require a gatekeeping state or spectacle to take an important place in postcolonial cultures of technology.[79] Moreover, instead of resource excess, ujamaa's oil politics were anchored in anxieties about material absence, a shortage of time to bridge an infrastructural gap with more powerful countries, and the need to find a modular middle road to address this condition through oil's domestic mobilities on trucks and dirt roads. The challenge the TPDC faced when it started operations in 1973 was not running per se but rather sustaining that literal and metaphorical movement from the first decade of independence in a less friendly political economy. In ways Nyerere had not anticipated, Tanzania's time to accelerate—that is, to get running—had ended even earlier than he had anticipated.

THE "OPEC'S BOMBSHELL": LTSS, ACQUIRED CHARACTERISTICS, AND LOST MOMENTUM AFTER 1973

By 1975 oil imports, only 7 percent of Tanzania's overall energy profile, used about half of the country's export revenues and represented a quarter of its import bill. As table 4.2 illustrates, to import the roughly 1 million tons the nation purchased in both 1972 and 1973, the TPDC paid over double the price in 1974, more than three times the cost in 1977 for about three-quarters of the load, and by 1983 eight times the 1972 and 1973 costs for only 745,000 tons.[80] Similar trends repeated between 1977 and 1984, as table 4.3 shows. After paying 550 million shillings for 675,000 metric tons in 1977—five times the price that yielded 814,000 tons five years earlier—NBC paid over 2,357 million shillings, more than quadruple the cost, for the same amount seven years later, in 1984. Though oil imports constituted only 10 percent of Tanzania's total value of exports in 1972, in 1982 they made up 60 percent.[81] Consequently, though petroleum use rose by 8 percent, 1 percent above the TPDC's goal to achieve economic growth, for the first twelve years of independence (1961–73), net national usage did not meet this 1973 pre-OPEC-crisis level again until the late 1980s. For those like the TPDC's staff who believed development required increased use of oil, this amounted to losing a decade's worth of time to expand or sustain the nation's economy.

Nor did conditions stabilize after 1974. Operating costs in the region escalated to the extent that the remaining multinational companies drastically reduced their activity in East Africa. Though, at first glance, the departure of these majors fulfilled a key aim of the parastatal's creation regarding technological sovereignty, including the indigenization and

TABLE 4.2 All Oil Product Imports (in metric tons and millions of Tanzanian shillings)

	1972	1973	1974	1977	1979	1981	1983
Amount	1,067,000	1,067,739	1,039,683	866,140	881,278	747,517	745,261
Cost	268.7	277.2	680.6	862.6	1,482.0	2,051.0	2,311.7

SOURCE: Compilation of data from TPDC, "Takwimu za mafuta yaliyoingizwa nchini kwa kipindi cha mwaka 1974–1984," M01156, TPDC; and "Summary of Imports," Petroleum Products Import/Export Summary (Crude, WP, RFO), 1970–1983, M01168, TPDC.

TABLE 4.3 Crude Oil Imported for Refining at TIPER (in metric tons and millions of Tanzanian shillings)

	1972	1974	1977	1979	1980	1981	1984
Amount	814,396	859,673	675,036	570,701	694,195	466,114	675,893
Cost	102.0	455.6	549.9	774.5	1,250.2	1,109.6	2,357.4

SOURCE: TPDC, "Crude Oil Imports Summary, 1972–1986," M00409, TPDC.

socialization of oil infrastructure, TPDC documents cite a more "complex financing" issue. Despite their questionable pricing tactics, multinational corporations like Caltex had provided ninety-day interest-free loans to the Tanzanian government, a safe investment because companies knew they would make money distributing the very oil for which they had given a loan. When these companies started to pull out of Tanzania's market in 1974, the TPDC had to not only find new loans but also secure "a permanent source of supply" of crude because the majors had offered both as a package. The parastatal had intended to take each of these steps as it gradually nationalized the industry. But whereas the majors fled from the region's higher-cost post-OPEC-crisis operating environment, the TPDC continued with its original charge—to make a self-reliant and indigenous oil economy—in the context of drastically higher prices and operating costs and with steadily decreasing amounts of capital for purchases of any kind.[82]

After the original bombshell, escalating oil costs came from two more sources: further price increases and reduced purchasing power. In 1978 tensions between Iran and Iraq led OPEC to raise prices by 14.5 percent, a hike the parastatal called "unethical behavior by OPEC" that "has sent our forecasted bill off gear completely. We are now faced with not only fantastic high prices of white supplies, but also with uncertain sources of supply."[83] The war hit Tanzania especially hard because the light Arabian crude from Iran had provided between 40 and 60 percent of its imports since 1963. Worse yet, the Ministry of Energy and Natural Resources had just negotiated a rare long-term contract for 400,000 metric tons of light fuel, but "the load from Iran . . . has not been possible because of frequent Iraqi aerial attacks on Iranian seaports including the loading terminal of Kharg Island," which scared most shipping companies away. "For those adventurers willing to risk their vessels, the War Insurance Premium is very prohibitive—nearly 2.5 percent of the hull value."[84]

In this context, the simple technocratic term *procurement* signified a new bureaucratic task. Here is how Barongo described the process in an interview:

> [Purchasing] was difficult because . . . we didn't have immediate cash, so we entered into an arrangement like this. We secure at this point (Y1), and then pay at this point (X1) six months later for shipment Y1. But because six months is a long time in terms of how much the country consumes, you have to secure another one about two months later at Y2 for payment at X2. Now, before you complete payment for Y1, you would probably have secured another one (Y3) for payment at X3. . . . When you reach that point (X1), you are not paying for one but for three at that time, because you have not paid for one. And you are carrying interest . . . and you have used that oil completely. Every three months you are putting three cargoes, but you have only paid for one. The first one overlapped two months and for the third a month . . . so you have two months free of payment, but then you have these staggered payments. So it was very difficult, and therefore the debts accumulated over time.[85]

Compounding debts thus made it less likely that the NBC could secure a line of credit for a future load.

The less obvious effects of price increases manifested in the TPDC's decreasing ability to move petroleum in both international and national spaces. According to TPDC documents, the Majors reacted to the nationalizations of global oil markets by flexing their distributional muscles: refusing to provide shipping services between the OPEC exporters who had just nationalized their economies and consumers like the government of Tanzania. Indeed, a 1973 document, "Petroleum Products," the parastatal's first summary of the bombshell, lists as its first priority "the establishment of a reliable communications network" with the distribution networks previously controlled by the Majors.[86] The TPDC hired the National Shipping Company of India to deliver much of its petroleum as it sought World Bank financing to purchase its own fleet, requests the bank repeatedly denied. Limited options for distribution also hurt national markets. The TAZARA "freedom railway" opened in 1973, adding rail services to a corridor that already included a highway and an oil pipeline. Its huge influence on petroleum distribution is visible in the refined products carried by the central line (a colonial railway) and to the southern highlands via TAZARA.

TABLE 4.4 Regional Distribution of Refined Products

Region	Amount (metric tons)
Central Line (spanning central Tanzania) and Southern Highlands (southwestern Tanzania)	347,113
Dar es Salaam area	128,384
Zanzibar and Pemba	8,273
Northern and Lake Zone (northeastern and northwestern Tanzania)	87,238
Mtwara and surrounding areas (southeastern Tanzania)	26,287
Tanga (northeastern Tanzania)	29,821

SOURCE: TPDC, "Distribution of Refined Petroleum Products: Problems and Possible Solutions," D.401/1-16/75, M00841, TPDC.

Unfortunately for the TPDC, the project's completion in 1973 served as a high-water mark for constructing and maintaining LTSs capable of moving refined petroleum around the national space. The parastatal estimated that its rural economy required 170 large railway tanks per day, but TAZARA maxed out at 46 and averaged only 23.[87] At one point, nearly half of its wagons (179 out of 405) sat idle needing repairs even as refined oil waited for distribution in Dar es Salaam's port.[88] Such shortages limited distribution along rail routes, but "up country stayed without products for weeks." This led to issues in networked systems: the electricity parastatal in Dodoma ran out of fuel, as well as shortages of a "common man product" like kerosene, used in villages and towns alike. Shortages were further exacerbated by the small number of fuel stations and storage for villagers to easily access the petroleum when it arrived.[89] Equally critical, though, was the inability to extend motorized transport networks, especially rail, to areas without steady access to the two main distribution veins (the central railway line and TAZARA) in the wake of the OPEC crisis. Over half of oil distribution in Tanzania occurred on two rail lines, the central line and TAZARA, including valuable exports to Zaire, Rwanda, and Burundi. Communities living at a distance from these routes, though constituting about half of the nation's population, received less than 20 percent of all refined products. Indeed, the Northern and Lake Zone region started to rely on Kenya for its oil while, in southeastern regions, falling oil availability likely fueled resentment about the concentration of infrastructural strength in central and northern areas, as Priya Lal covers.[90]

The TPDC repeatedly reminded its home ministry of the social and economic costs of these distributional failures by stating the obvious: oil touched every part of ujamaa's economy. Recurrent diesel shortages for trucks, for example, meant harvested coffee crops—a valuable source of foreign exchange—did not move to markets and cashew nut processing machines did not run. Washed-out dirt roads that might have been paved with RFO inhibited the transport of cotton in Mwanza and Shinyanga. The same road problem prevented the nearly sixty thousand tons of manure that Tanzania's economy relied on from spreading around the nation; at times, half of this amount sat in silos after rains because fuel was unavailable. When crop failures brought aid, in the form of corn, from both the United States and the Soviet Union, it, too, required diesel (and dry weather) to reach recipients. Industries also felt the pinch. Two textile factories in northwestern Tanzania required thirty thousand liters of gas oil per month to sustain production; when this amount could not be delivered, the factories shut down.[91]

The "Report on the Plan for Saving the Economy" asserted that steadily decreasing consumption of oil between 1979 and 1981 led to the closures of four soap factories: Lake Soap, Kirani Industries, Tip Soap, and Kamal and Mirakai. The estimated domestic soap demand, at 200,000 cartons per month, should have kept these factories open. But production at two of the factories fell to just 15,000 cartons by November 1981. Similar shortages occurred in the production of bike and car tires, corrugated sheets for housing, cotton wool and sanitary napkins, house utensils, construction equipment, toothpaste, and agricultural implements. In addition to the absence of fuel sources at factories, the report blamed oil shortages for shrinking productivity in villages—in particular, the diminishing possibilities for mechanized agriculture—and for crops that never made it to factories. When the report concluded that "of all the problems standing in the way of pushing our economy forward, one of the biggest is getting oil for our machines to function," that applied to equipment in rural and urban areas alike.[92]

Up to this point, Tanzania's biggest machine, the TIPER, had functioned brilliantly. Despite processing 6 million barrels of oil per year, it started to fall behind the demands of Tanzania's economy.[93] This should have been good news. It meant the nation's economy had matured since the refinery's construction in 1965 to the point that the TPDC and other ministries could justify planned refinery expansions through proven domestic production and consumption. Instead, the TPDC shelved an expansion that would have given the TIPER the capacity to refine the middle distillates that Tanzania's economy needed. It delayed, and ultimately canceled, plans to build a bituminization plant to process RFO into road material, for an estimated savings of 18.29 million shillings per year over import costs and profits from 4.3 to 17.2 million shillings a year. The TPDC described the cost of not building this plant by citing a 700 percent increase in the export price of processed RFO used in asphalt from $7.20 to $50 per barrel after 1973, a huge increase in costs for road construction.[94] By the late 1970s, annual refinery maintenance was no longer possible. "A maintenance crew used to come from Agip. They'd be here from twenty to thirty days, replace the worn-out parts, and for the next eleven months you'd be operating a virtually new refinery."[95] Instead, as funds for maintenance dried up, the TPDC took the refinery offline to wait for money to purchase spare parts and pay labor.[96]

Only seven years after OPEC first raised prices, Tanzania's future looked bleak as external debt rose from $49 million in 1977 to $539 million in just five years.[97] A memo from Reginald Green, an adviser to the Ministry of Finance, asserted the economy would "collapse between late 1981 and 1982" without major changes. Green acknowledged the rise of "proto-magendo" markets, using a term for the illegal parallel economies that arose, at least in part, owing to the state's shrinking ability to distribute goods or services, and he feared the economy could become "full magendo."[98] (Chapter 5 explores some of these networks from the perspective of drivers and passengers who produced mobilities during this period.) Procuring oil became so difficult that obtaining 40 to 60 percent of the minimum required for the national economic recovery became a success because getting none was a real possibility.[99] The situation from July to December 1981 was described as "generally, not that bad" even though the TPDC listed only ten to twenty days of supplies of the middle distillates that Tanzania's economy needed. I asked Barongo whether the country ever ran out of petroleum. He answered no but added, "Oh yeah, many, many times we went to the brink."[100] In ideological terms—which, as shown above, Barongo understood well—Tanzania could neither refine nor distribute enough oil to fulfill its charge to create equality and growth through distribution.

In *Carbon Democracy: Political Power in the Age of Oil,* Timothy Mitchell calls the OPEC crisis a crisis "that never happened" because it only minimally reshuffled the international technopolitical hierarchies already in place before the summer of 1973.[101] Barongo and his staff might agree with Mitchell's main point: that the crisis ultimately left much about the structure of oil markets unchanged; it could have and should have done more, their archive suggests, in the name of infrastructural decolonization. And yet the "OPEC's bombshell earned its name at the TPDC for altering the landscape of socialist nation building at a time when the central components of the state's technological power had either just matured, gaining elements of what historian Thomas Hughes calls "technological inertia," or just begun operation. This link among oil prices, infrastructural acceleration, and time—in terms of both a need to hurry up and a feeling that the OPEC crisis had caused the compressed temporality of "we must run" to run out prematurely—allows us to revisit an axiom in the history of technology: that beyond their social construction, LTSs like oil trading and refining are also "society shaping."[102]

Beginning with his 1983 classic comparative history of electrification, Hughes has argued that LTSs gained a "momentum" or "soft determinism" in which "durable physical artifacts project into the future the socially constructed characteristics acquired in the past when they were designed."[103] In the United States, Germany, and England, electrification did not require just unique individual or cultural genius, as narratives of Euro-American technological exceptionalism suggested. Instead, it took input and investment from governments, corporations and financers, educational institutions, and other technologists who found solutions to the problems that emerged as systems matured. By creating unity out of this diversity, "systems builders" such as Thomas Edison helped give LTSs "momentum." By this, Hughes meant that sunk costs, already-built worlds, and entrenched modes of operation—among many other factors—can create a technological path dependence that constrains and shapes efforts to pursue alternatives. And thus things shape social and political possibility.[104] To do so, however, LTSs tend to require a combination of time and capital.

Indeed, Hughes called electrification "econotechnical"—"inseparably technical and economic"—and labeled systems builders like Edison "inventor-entrepreneurs" who bridged gaps between technological and economic feasibility, on the one hand, and demand, on the other. This econotechnical approach gave *Networks of Power: Electrification in Western Society, 1880–1930,* its bite as a comparative history. Differences in electrification infrastructure on a national scale among Germany, the United States, and the United Kingdom revealed that, far from being monolithic entities, built systems gathered "acquired characteristics" through the societies and political economies in which they were built. The assertion that LTSs took on characteristics from the dynamic political economies in which they emerged may seem obvious. But it nevertheless holds important implications for understanding the changing contours of technological nation building for systems builders like Barongo and his staff. More than simply constructing new things, technologists required time and money to turn ujamaa's nascent machinic complex into a system that could reliably build socialist economies as society-shaping technologies with momentum.

Instead of the speed of "we must run," ujamaa's oil infrastructure took on the "acquired characteristics" of the "bombshell."[105] This came in the form of decreased maintenance at the TIPER, national and international distribution problems, shelved plans for refinery expansions and new distribution mechanisms, and empty or at least emptier tanks in machines around the nation. In turn, these acquired characteristics suggest that the

TABLE 4.5 "Not That Bad": July–December 1981

	Stock (metric tons)	Daily consumption (metric tons)	Days to last
Liquefied petroleum gas	387	16	24
Aviation fuel	0	7	0
Synthetic oil	5,841	209	27
Gas oil	11,405	750	15
Industrial diesel oil	2,972	149	19
Furnace oil	4,846	450	10
Kerosene	5,936	200	29

SOURCE: "Taarifa kuhusu hali ya mafuta nchini," Kamati ya Waziri, Makatibu Wakuu wa Mipango ya Kujinusuru Kiuchumi—Matatizo ya Mafuta Nchini, 1981, M01896, TPDC.

TPDC found itself facing a type of technological momentum—that is, path dependence—that worked not through multiplying presences, as with Hughes, but through proliferating absences that they struggled to turn back. These growing absences required repetitive and dynamic "articulation work" to keep things working as well as possible. In turn, unlike infrastructure that exercises power through its invisibility—receding into the background of everyday life—these oil systems occupied a messier middle ground between stabilization and failure.[106] They combined function (in some places and times and with some things) with struggle, disappointment, and an altered infrastructural horizon in which the avoidance of collapse was an incredible accomplishment. Before exploring the larger implications of the bombshell's acquired characteristics, we first turn to the TPDC's attempts to reverse this momentum through bureaucratic ingenuity.

"SAVE FUEL, SAVE THE NATION": BUREAUCRATIC INGENUITY AND THE TECHNOPOLITICS OF "SAVING ONESELF" (KUJINUSURU)

In 1974, using the mantra "Save Fuel, Save the Nation," the Tanzanian government implemented petroleum rationing in nearly every aspect of daily life, including a reduction in Usafiri Dar es Salaam (UDA) bus operation in Dar es Salaam, better care and loading procedures for city buses, and the closure of places of leisure at 10 p.m. to save gasoline and electricity (gas oil). It also endorsed energy alternatives such as replacing gas oil with fuel oil in electricity generation, using coal instead of diesel for tea processing, using steam engines instead of diesel engines on trains, and suppressing the importation of gas stoves and insisting on coal for home and industry.[107] Though these "best practices" (*matumizi mazuri*) decreased automobile fuel usage (by 7.73 percent for premium and 18.3 percent for regular), saving fuel for the nation did not provide the TPDC with more operating capital for purchases.[108] Instead of spending more money on oil, the rescue policies shifted oil to critical areas of production to jump-start economic output. Consequently, in 1980 the TPDC received just over half of the 1,785 million shillings of foreign reserves it requested for crude imports. The government said it would use these savings to help make the next planned purchase between July and August. But when this time arrived, it provided only 1,200 million shillings instead of the 1,440 million requested.[109]

So began "survival" (*kujinusuru*—literally, to save or rescue oneself), an official policy designed to move Tanzania through a constraining economic period.[110] As one architect of the policy put it, the point of the program was to buy time and then hope for good fortune: "Faced with collapse in 9 to 12 months any survival strategy that does not consolidate and rebuild use of existing capacity is of no value. At the least it wins time for maneuver or a stroke of good luck—eg a first in Brazil, an oil strike

TABLE 4.6 Select Industries: January–June 1981

Exporter	Product	Percentage of minimum needed to rescue economy
Coffee Authority	Green coffee	54
Sisal Authority	Sisal fiber	35
Mwadui Diamonds	Diamonds	71
SUDECO	Sugar	30.6
Shell and BP (state owned)	Gas and oil	8
Tantimbers	Timber products	13
Tanzania Tea Blenders	Tea	28
T.C.C.	Cigarettes	32.4
Tanganyika Packers	Corned beef	126
General Tyre	Tires and tubes	30
Tanzania Saruji	Cement	3.8
Total		44.5

SOURCE: "Taarifa ya utekelezaji wa malengo ya kujinusuru kiuchumi uuzaji mazao nchi za nje, Januari 1981–Juni 1981," Kamati ya Waziri, Makatibu Wakuu wa Mipango ya Kujinusuru Kiuchumi— Matatizo ya Mafuta Nchini, 1981, M01896, TPDC.

in the delta—without its own viability depending on good luck."[111] The TPDC received a clear, albeit difficult, role in economic survival: to gain steady, and ideally increasing, access to petroleum without reliable access to foreign exchange. It had at least four mechanisms to do so: the spot market, commodity swaps, oil swaps, and exploration.

The first mechanism, the spot market, involved a "freely competitive market in which a very small part (below 10 percent) of OPEC's exports" were traded.[112] Composed of small companies and individual holdings, the spot market offered smaller cargoes for higher prices per barrel. This provided a good option for the TPDC because it did not require as much total capital from the NBC as the much larger loads the parastatal preferred to arrange. Nevertheless, the per-barrel price was much higher, and thus the spot market offered a comparatively bad value in per-barrel costs. Moreover, most players in this market were located at centers of finance and oil exportation distant from Dar es Salaam. Engaging it required connections, which, in turn, meant filtering requests from consultants that came through the TPDC's telex machine.[113] As a short autobiography of Nasser Al Salem, the founder of Warba National Contracting Co., illustrates, consultants established themselves as experts with considerable industrial expertise and connections: "I joined the Kuwait National Petroleum Co., April 20 1968 in the personnel department. I worked there for 15 months and was then transferred to the International Marketing Dept. in London. Subsequently, I worked in that department for almost eight and a half years." Al Salem goes on to list a vast international record: he worked in various places from New York to Pakistan and sat on national committees and boards of international business. He ended the message by giving the TPDC insider information about spot oil he had gleaned having "just returned from New York."[114]

When done by telex, this process took many things, from pricing to shipping, out of the TPDC's hands. A contact in London, George Kremer, provided two possible oil sources: "oil brokerage firm of international repute in London" and a "royal contact I have in Saudi who has his own company." This prince, whom Kremer considered "a serious person [who] can effectively perform" after "checking up," offered to arrange "direct" deals with Petromin of Saudi Arabia for a commission of fifty cents per barrel. Kremer considered this "the cheapest and the best chance we have of obtaining oil."[115] The parastatal also sent its own staff to Kuwait, Iran, and Iraq to gain knowledge about regional spot hubs. The TPDC director of finance, Roy Chowdhuri, traveled throughout the Middle East to inquire about and then secure loads of fuel.[116] In Kuwait City, Kuwait, and Baghdad, Iraq, he communicated possible sources for crude with offers that often expired the following day even though the prices were "unbelievably high."[117] Competition for spot-market cargoes not only led to higher prices (such as $27 per barrel) and higher premiums ($2 per barrel), but also required quick decisions in a context in which prices changed daily.[118] "Many countries are around and spot cargoes when available are grabbed by the highest bidder at unbelievably high prices," Chowdhuri messaged in 1978 before adding, "*If cargo is a must* from here may I have your okay to go up 2 dollars per barrel, repeat two dollars per barrel, over yesterday's approved rate if absolutely necessary. Otherwise you can indicate the ceiling up to which I can bid." Barongo replied, "Price considerations irrelevant as absence of crude is more costly." Albeit at "unbelievably high prices," this spot action kept the nightmare scenario of economic recovery from occurring: the complete absence of oil at the selected industries.[119]

The TPDC also bartered raw goods produced in Tanzania for crude oil, preferably a desirable type of petroleum it could refine at the TIPER. An official policy of the Ministry of Energy stated, "These fuel shortages have forced us to think about long-term methods for getting oil on terms we can rely upon year after year. One way to do this is to explore possibilities for entering long-term contracts (five years or more) with friendly nations like Algeria and Iraq so that we get a certain amount of oil and they get coffee, meat, sisal ropes, etc. (Barter Trade)." Citing a provisional agreement with Algeria to exchange an unspecified amount of oil for twenty thousand tons of coffee and two hundred tons of frozen meat, the policy concluded that bartering provided a means of "using the resources we have to get out of day after day and month after month of not having oil."[120] Historical evidence of these negotiations is scant, but they involved big players who had the authority to grant resource concessions without parliamentary approval, such as future Tanzanian president Benjamin Mkapa and the minister of energy, water, and natural resources, Al Noor Kassum.[121] When I interviewed the latter, he said swap arrangements happened above his pay grade, and he suggested I read his memoir—the very basis of the questions I had asked him.[122]

Another strategy, swapping petroleum, temporarily caused an international scandal. In 1983 the *Observer* of London charged Barongo and Kassum with secretly selling millions of dollars of RFO, the waste product of refining used in asphalt, to South Africa in exchange for heavy greases the TIPER did not process (again, owing to the shelved expansion plans).

Beginning in 1978, the newspaper said, Barongo agreed to receive $1,500 for each shipment, while Kassum negotiated a far larger sum of thirty cents per ton exchanged. Following a detailed investigation by the government of Tanzania and its admission of an unintentional link with South Africa, Marcotrade admitted it had forged the papers that set the scandal in motion. The two men later reached a settlement out of court with the *Observer*, which also issued a public apology in the bottom corner of page 34.[123] "Categorically and with indignation," the government confirmed its ideological position against apartheid with a play-by-play recounting of events involving multiple international companies, several countries, and the type of tangled story that had become everyday life for the staff of the TPDC such as Barongo. It all started with good news. The TPDC had secured a rare bulk shipment of 100,000 metric tons of Cabinda crude from Angola at competitive market prices. But Tanzania's refinery could not process Cabinda crude because planned expansions to refine middle distillates had been shelved.

The TPDC thus bought the shipment with the intention of exchanging it for a package of crude and refined products to refine at TIPER. After securing the Cabinda crude, the TPDC asked five multinational companies to bid on the shipment and, with the help of the NBC, awarded the contract to Singapore-based Marcotrade in exchange for Iranian light crude; the TPDC sweetened the deal by adding RFO from the TIPER to the Cabinda load. To initiate the swap, the NBC and Marcotrade established lines of credit through international banks to confirm the origins and sizes of each shipment. According to bank documentation, none of the oil had come from or through South Africa. The government further asserted that its bureaucrats had arranged the deal by the books. The value assigned to each oil type followed internationally recognized standards published in *Platt's Oilgram*, a periodical that assesses and sets standards for global energy prices, and the Tanzania Harbours Authority approved the deal.[124] The incident speaks not only to the creativity and work of national technological survival but also to an element of oil economies that has largely gone unnoticed. Inasmuch as political power came from the ability to move oil, as Mitchell argues, we must add that this movement had another requirement that imposed restrictions on oil-short countries: that oil had to match specific infrastructural capacities in ways that necessitated the Cabinda swaps.[125]

Each of these strategies bought time for the fourth: pursuing "good luck" through exploration. In the context of survival, the TPDC reevaluated projects they had previously passed over, such as the Songo Songo gas mine—a long-term project whose drilling led to a project-ending explosion in 1976.[126] "We looked at that data again and thought what may not be enough for Agip [to make money] may be enough for Tanzania," Barongo said. "Tanzania is not a giant that requires that much. So we negotiated with an agency."[127] After drilling two wells (SS1 and SS2), the parastatal received funding from the World Bank to search at two sites, where they found gas. The economic payoff was decades out, but it offered signs of an indigenous energy sector that did not exist a decade earlier and gave the staff hope that they were making a difference. If they staved off collapse in the short term, Tanzania had capital resources for the future. The TPDC planned to use the Songo Songo gas to process fertilizer.

Much more good luck came in 1979. The Ministry of Energy and Natural Resources gambled on the hunch of a Tanzanian geologist who believed his nation had undiscovered mineral wealth. Using $65 million—the equivalent of six months of oil—the ministry ordered a geological survey by satellite of the entire nation. The geosurvey found large reserves of natural gas, copper, and mercury, as well as numerous sites with uranium. Tanzania became mineral rich overnight. The discovery led to an uncommon outlook on development for a period defined by decline, emergencies, and recovery. Kassum wrote that "all of these could be the foundation for developing the country, building an industrial base and extending the agricultural sector. The prospect was exciting."[128] He added that the TPDC and the ministry had shown "ingenuity" in their approach to scarcity.[129]

Kassum's assessment echoed a statement from Barongo's 1976 essay on oil and socialism. "There is an old adage," he wrote, "'Oil is found in the minds of men,' and the history of exploration almost anywhere in the world adds substance to the phrase. As often as not it is new ideas just as much as new technology that set off a successful exploration programme."[130] The "old adage" came from Wallace Pratt's 1943 book *Oil in the Earth*, which addressed concerns that oil production could not keep pace with consumption unless new reserves were found. He called for new and creative strategies to find more oil and create alternatives.[131] By the 1970s, few followed Pratt's estimates of available crude, but even geologists who estimated much higher availability, such as the chief geologist at BP, H. R. Warman, expressed concerns in 1972 about what M. King Hubbert in 1956 called "peak oil": the notion that searches for new petroleum sources would have diminishing returns.[132] By citing Pratt, Barongo wrote Tanzania's specific concerns about oil-shortness into a wider history about the relationship between twentieth-century human societies and their energy sources. In the same way that Pratt called on ingenuity to bridge the gap between needs and known reserves, the TPDC had found submerged resources that could "be the foundation for developing the country" in an extreme context of oil-shortness.[133]

More than a moment that does not fit linear narratives of decline, this road to discovery reveals a different form of labor LTSS may require. Put simply, Hughes's language about "building" and systems builders—as well as this literature's focus on phases of achieving "systematic power" (even as "precarious achievements") or its destabilization—does not reflect the technological work of economic survival.[134] Instead of pouring themselves into projects that made infrastructure more reliable and robust—gaining the momentum at the heart of Hughes's writing—the TPDC developed strategies to stave off disaster by doing everything possible to maintain two minimums whose failure would spell economic ruin: minimal amounts of oil imports to keep the economy afloat and minimal distribution via transport networks that themselves could not be expanded and only partially repaired. Without momentum in its own built systems to repair or construct, the TPDC's labor was thus dominated by efforts to push back against the econotechnical trends that quickly gained inertia after the OPEC crisis. Here the technological momentum that shaped society—and threatened to do so in even more drastic ways—came not from systematic presences but from systematic absences and shortages that kept the parastatal from pursuing the form of "effective freedom" Nyerere had earlier envisioned. We turn now to competing interpretations of the OPEC crisis's impact and to competing narratives about the role absences played in ujamaa's demise.

"GIVE US TIME": THE CHRONOPOLITICS OF LTSS IN "AN OIL-SHORT WORLD"— THE TPDC, ROBERT MCNAMARA, AND JULIUS NYERERE

This final section explores three interpretations of post-OPEC-crisis nation building through the TPDC and Barongo, Robert McNamara and the World Bank, and Nyerere. It shows that views of LTSS and their users played a critical role in the creation of divergent views about technological possibility, achievement, and failure during the first two decades of independence as historical actors explained why the promises of the 1960s had not translated into sustained experiences of self-reliance through the end of the 1970s. As used here, *chronopolitics*—the politics of time—brings attention not only to the different ways the above individuals talked about the speed of creating technological capacity (and therefore the duration needed to reach a desirable end point) but also to when events such as the OPEC crisis constituted an epochal rupture or not. I conclude the section by linking Nyerere's thoughts about technological constraint to Hughes's classic work on LTSs and technological momentum.

First, the TPDC: The parastatal did not always receive funding earmarked for annual reports. But when it did, the directors described a healthy corporation. Though the reports commonly started by noting that "foreign exchange remained [a] severe constraint," Barongo and Kassum boasted of "financial strength" and a "very sound financial base." Much of this came from petroleum's value as a commodity. Despite the economic contraction, the nation still used enough for the TPDC to fund about half of its annual budget from its profits even after returning a huge portion of its income to the government. Levels of profit varied based on price controls set in the Ministry of Commerce. In 1982 the Price Commission's petroleum subsidization cut into the corporation's earnings, leading to intra-parastatal cuts. Even then, the TPDC's consistent nongovernment revenue allowed it to pay down debts. It consistently earned high marks for its ratio of liquid assets to debt and thereby continued its pursuit of an indigenous energy economy through "external co-finance" through Agip, other multinational corporations, and the World Bank.[135]

With "balanced dependence on foreign credit" and its own profits, the parastatal's status in the late 1970s and early 1980s aligned with the AD's insistence on a technological self-reliance that nevertheless used aid if done sustainably—sometimes called "maximum self-reliance."[136] In one report, Barongo pointed out that this "financial strength" made the TPDC one of the largest taxpayers in the country—the largest in 1985—and allowed it to support "loss-making" ventures that were nevertheless critical to the national economy, such as oil trucking fleets that sustained damage on bad roads as they distributed petroleum. The director also bragged about a socialist work environment defined by the parastatal's efforts to train and care for its staff. The TPDC covered all health-care costs at Aga Khan Hospital; it offered automatic contributions of fifteen thousand shillings for any family bereavement; it began, but did not finish, a housing scheme for its workers in Mikocheni (where the archive is now located); and it offered incentives of up to three thousand shillings for drivers to increase efficiency in petroleum distribution.[137]

Three decades after Barongo published these reports, I asked him to reflect on the TPDC's successes and failures during ujamaa:

> The initial period helped to build up a knowledge base in the country. Then you can begin from that knowledge base to do bigger things. Of course, when we were still importing, we were in talks of buying [an] importing ship, or ships, or *components of self-reliance*. We felt it would be easier if we owned the ship, but then maybe you own it on a continental basis; owning one ship is not good enough, you need three. You need the refineries in Mombasa and Msumbiji [Mozambique] to team up together to secure the shipping tankers. But it was only a paper on the drawing board. . . . So the *element of self-reliance* was not strong enough. But in terms of building the knowledge base and manpower there was [something]. . . . When the liberalization [of economies] happened, many of those companies were based on people who had knowledge from the refinery [from the 1970s]. (emphasis mine)[138]

Barongo carefully distinguished between two different types of self-reliance. One, a technological capacity he called "the material component of self-reliance," did not fully move from "a paper on the drawing board" to an actual "element of self-reliance" owing to cost.[139]

Still, the TPDC excelled at self-reliance as the ability to learn, react, and potentially change the "material element" in the future through economic survival programs, he claimed. Because the TPDC opened its doors in the wake of the OPEC crisis, assessing, reacting, learning, and innovating made up the entirety of its existence. This knowledge, far from disappearing with ujamaa's demise because it lacked application to nonsocialist periods or was defined only by economic emergency, acted as the foundation for national energy economies in subsequent decades. Indeed, in recent decades, it provided the literal substance for debates about how capital sources should best be used for maendeleo in places like Mtwara, as Lal observes.[140] Partially an example of what Jean-François Bayart calls "extraversion"—a process in which external "borrowings are also acts of reappropriation and reinvention"—because of the transnational nature of oil economies and infrastructures, navigating petroleum shortness after the OPEC crisis was also in part simply a matter of inventing and innovating because there was no manual for pursuing development without oil.[141] They thus inhabited the cutting edge of living with and through oil-shortness, and according to Paul Rweyemamu, manager of TIPER, TPDC's contacts with oil-exporting countries developed after 1973 enabled Tanzania to survive economic turbulence created by subsequent price hikes.[142]

We cannot generalize about other government institutions from the TPDC's experiences. Only one of many parastatals, it had unique access to steady revenue because of oil's integral role in the economy.[143] The TPDC nevertheless provides an important counterweight to an influential explanation for economic contraction in Tanzania: that it stemmed from inefficiencies in parastatals and government ministries that could and should have been avoided with better economic and technological decision-making by a bureaucratic elite. This argument came from different groups across the ideological spectrum as they attempted to explain the decline. Tanzanian intellectuals, with many drawing from a Marxist or Marxist-Leninist approach to state-building, thought the parastatals, though necessary, had forgotten their mission to serve workers. Critical in their own right, none of these Tanzanians went nearly as far as the World Bank. It used the idea of the bloated parastatal and the OPEC crisis's impact to call for a restructuring of Tanzania's public sector through structural adjustment policies, as we see below. In both cases, arguments assumed that the 1960s and 1970s offered paths to technological nation building from which bureaucrats had diverted their nations by pursuing infrastructural projects that enhanced their ministerial power instead of aligning with citizens' needs. Doing so brought technologies people did not want or could not use while sapping financial resources.

This leads to our second form of infrastructural chronopolitics. A World Bank "Economic Memorandum on Tanzania" based on consultant research in 1980 separated the impact of oil prices and a list of significant "external events" from the state's role in economic decline: "Undoubtedly, a series of adverse external events—including the price rise since 1974, the collapse of the East African Community in early 1977, the war with Uganda in 1978–79, and in 1980, another year of poor rains—have further aggravated the existing problems and made more urgent the need for restructuring the economy. But the *underlying weaknesses* are of a more long-term nature and related primarily to the structure and nature of the *domestic* economy" (emphasis mine).[144] No matter the impact of other events, export reductions stemmed from longer-term public sector "inefficiencies" caused by a socialist state that needed to get out of the way of economic growth.[145] As Howard Stein details, the economic precarity across the Global South caused by the second wave of oil price increases in 1979 helped set the stage for the initiation of structural adjustment as a policy that tied lending to the implementation of specific market imperatives.[146]

On February 11, 1980, the World Bank president, Robert McNamara, traveled to Nyerere's birthplace, Butiama, to personally deliver news about the World Bank's intention to "structurally adjust" the nation's economy to address balance-of-payments deficits. In Nyerere's sitting room, McNamara conceded that the bank had not seen the increased prices coming and that "the deficits faced by oil importing countries" were "much larger than . . . the Bank staff had expected and could be dealt with only by reducing imports—and the rate of growth—or by a larger flow of assistance." He also called the post-OPEC-crisis world "permanent in character and requir[ing] permanent changes by oil exporting countries." With the Organisation for Economic Co-Operation and Development (OECD) economies in recession—and thus little likelihood of increased aid—and oil exporters unlikely to change the structure of petroleum economies, he offered only one option: "to restructure the economies of these countries combined with additional financial resources. The actions that were necessary would be difficult but had to be taken to overcome the problems caused by the permanent changes in the international environment."[147] McNamara used the same language a month later when meeting with Amir Jamal, the minister of finance: "Rapidly increasing oil prices and slow growth rates of OECD countries were permanent changes . . . and required permanent adjustments by all of them."[148]

The bank's redundant use of *permanent* to refer to post-OPEC-crisis economic change allowed it to frame technological nation building between 1961 and 1973 as a binary: either Tanzania had done enough to survive the bombshell of 1973 by avoiding a balance-of-payments problem, or it had not. And because it had not, it needed to recognize that the OPEC crisis had fundamentally changed the global economy in at least two relevant ways: wealthier nations had less aid to give, and costly state projects and institutions that were more viable before the crisis were no longer sustainable in a context of runaway operating costs, the bank president charged.[149] The bank's chronopolitics made much of the historical context before its declaration of "permanent changes" invisible, including colonialism, the infrastructural efforts of "we must run," and its own admission that a combination of external forces and internal reforms (attempts to reduce expenditures on bureaucracy) were not enough to reverse global economic trends of the 1970s.[150] Finally, it left unresolved the tensions between the bank's belief since the 1960s that some entity needed to quickly undertake and coordinate infrastructural construction and maintenance in Tanzania and the World Bank's unease with the nation's growing public sector. "Although it is clearly necessary for Tanzania to 'run while others walk,'" one memo states, "President Nyerere may have pushed too far" regarding government support of nation-building projects—or what the World Bank sometimes called "overcommitment."[151] According to McNamara's assistant, who took notes of the meeting, Nyerere agreed that something needed to be done to help "oil importing countries" to "move."

But the Tanzanian president took a different approach to the cause of the crisis and any possible solutions:

> A massive push was needed for *take-off*. One measure advocated by some was to cut development expenditures. But where could these cuts be made when education, health services, water, etc. were still at minimal levels and many people went without these services. Pointing to the state of the Musoma-Butiama road (". . . which could not be the worst in the country since it leads to the President's home . . ."), Mr. Nyerere stressed the dilemma faced by Tanzania; enormous needs and limited resources. (emphasis mine)[152]

McNamara was best known in Tanzania as the architect of an unpopular American war in Vietnam—a war in which millions of gallons of oil fueled the United States' military. It is unclear how much Nyerere knew about McNamara's role as a president at Ford Motor Company in 1960 and his reputation as a penny-pinching technocrat obsessed with efficiency. The East African president likely did not know that muscle-car enthusiasts scoffed at his promotion of the Mustang, a much less powerful vehicle than previous models (but a gas-guzzler in its own right). Nevertheless, we can surmise that Nyerere meant his gesture toward the Musoma-Butiama road as a critique of McNamara's technological moralizing. Despite a career built on society-wide access to cheap fossil fuels, the American, Nyerere felt, had accused him of building an inefficient state when most services were already at bare minimums: "enormous needs and limited resources."

Seven years before McNamara visited Butiama, Nyerere had crafted a different narrative about the possibilities of technological sovereignty before and after the OPEC crisis in two speeches to foreign audiences. In "The Economic Challenge—Dialogue or Confrontation," a speech given to the Royal Commonwealth Society in November 1975, Nyerere argued that Tanzania paid doubly for increased oil prices. In addition to higher costs for its own petroleum, Nyerere explained, nations like Tanzania helped offset the bill of rich industrialized countries, which responded to changes in the global economy by adjusting the prices of their finished goods and shipping "to meet the extra oil costs involved in their manufacture." This, in turn, drove up costs for infrastructural consumers like Tanzania, a point Nyerere made through the changing amount of sisal necessary to purchase a tractor. In 1965 a tractor cost the equivalent of 17.25 tons of sisal. This increased to 42 tons in 1972 and nearly 66 tons in 1975. In other words, for increased agricultural production to translate into economic growth, it had to surpass the compounded rise in the associated costs of producing and exporting a product, making technological self-reliance through expanding production incredibly difficult for oil-short nations.[153]

Because "modern agriculture requires the use of oil," Nyerere continued, Tanzania was at risk of becoming a "fourth world country." Regardless of whether the OPEC crisis had made industrialized nations richer, Nyerere pointed out that it had exacerbated capital flight from new nations to the industrialized world. Citing Nobel-winning economist Jan Tinbergen and McNamara himself, Nyerere told the audience that 80 percent of global economic growth was occurring in the Global North:

> There is nothing accidental about this situation. At any one point there is a certain amount of wealth produced in the world. If one group of people grab an unfair share of it, there is less for others. When Tanzania's oil bills went up from about Shs. 200/- million in 1973 to Shs. 750/- million in 1975, that was a reduction in our wealth and an increase in someone else's wealth. Tanzania has less money to spend on things other than oil; the oil producers have more. The amount of wealth has not changed—only its distribution.

This new system required two changes of mind: industrialized countries needed to address inequality within their nations without passing on a greater burden to the developing world, and less-developed nations needed to recognize that in such a world of shared burdens, the "western style or level of consumption" was off the table. He thus marked an end to a particular vision of "developmental time," as Hannah Appel puts it, that would gradually see Tanzania's socialist economy grow, make, and consume more.[154]

He said as much to his own citizens. In a 1976 speech to Dar es Salaam leaders, after scolding urban government and parastatal workers for below-capacity commodity output, he told the audience that they were at the point of choosing which commodities were "of necessity"—*vya lazima*—to import in the context of economic survival. It started with a familiar topic, UDA:

> Stop yelling at me about UDA. These buses don't run on water; they run on oil. And where will I get oil? We don't have money in this country, and oil is incredibly expensive right now. I'm buying oil with cotton, cashews; if possible, I just won't order clothes for the country because we have clothes factories. If possible, I won't order cement because we have cement factories. I'll do all of this so that we save enough money to buy all of your oil [*hayo mafuta yenu*] for UDA. And you: you are all of the workers in these factories. And it is you who are able to stop all of this talk about which commodities are not necessary [*vitu visivyo vya lazima*].

Though some of this talk repeated the president's earlier critiques of urban citizens and their economically unsustainable lifestyles, Nyerere also made a new, rather striking admission within the context of ujamaa: owing to increased oil prices, not even the state's model of agricultural communities, the basis of African socialism's "driving of socialism" (*kuendesha ujamaa*), as he put it, produced self-reliance. It had cost the state sixty thousand shillings to produce raw materials that fetched only thirty thousand as exports.[155] In other words, at this point, Nyerere found it difficult to think about self-reliance through urban *or* rural socialism. Or, as he put it in a 1974 speech in New Zealand, "The truth is that under the existing world systems of international exchange the poor countries have to run hard in order to stand still."[156]

At a luncheon in London in 1985, the president took a broader historical view. As he had in 1975, Nyerere began by presenting the OPEC crisis as a rupture that had stalled and then reversed his nation's technological progress: "During the 1960s most of Africa's newly independent countries—including Tanzania—made a promising start on economic progress. In the 1970s, and especially the last half of the decade, we ran into difficulty; the 1980s have so far been a period of economic disaster." With Africa the victim of a "malfunctioning world economic order," he made the case that Tanzania had already seen these types of conditions before: "With *no reserves to begin with*, our nations have, to varying degrees, had to withstand two major oil price shocks, high inflation in the developed countries from which we buy most of our imported goods, extreme reserve currency exchange rate fluctuations, a combination of very high interest rates and world depression, and two long periods of draught" (emphasis mine). Here a temporal timeline that began with Tanzania's austere "colonial inheritance"—"with no reserves to begin with"—never deviated from a historical pattern of underdevelopment from that period and carried through to structural adjustment policies. The prices of 1973 magnified, but did not alter, the problems his government faced in building an economy without resources in the wake of a technologically austere form of empire.[157]

Before he toasted the lord mayor and the Corporation of London, he added, "I want to plead with you: do not force this confrontation upon us. Give us time. Give us time and resources to grow out of our crisis of debt and development."[158] By asking for time and resources, he reminded the audience of the constraints he faced in creating sustained economic and technological growth from 1961 to 1973. The president inherited a nation that did not have the economic capacity to produce foreign exchange for capital investment and that needed a wide variety of projects to be completed for basic postcolonial services to be delivered. His crowning infrastructural achievement, the Dar corridor, moved bodies, goods, and oil in the name of regional and national liberation.[159] With technical assistance, the project took eight years, and it was completed during the same year that OPEC posted increased prices. But it served only three major regions of the country, leaving the state in a situation in which it needed to not only maintain the Dar corridor but also expand transport infrastructure to the rest of the country at a time when doing so was unlikely. The president's plea for more time recalls Paul Edwards's observation that infrastructure is not just an if (of success or failure) but also a when—a product of time and the possibilities allowed therein.[160] For Nyerere, infrastructure's when came down to both the efficacy of speed and "the slowness of speeding up" technological power.[161] Whereas running had led to progress through the 1960s and early 1970s, by 1974 a viscous political economy meant "poor countries [had] to run hard in order to stand still"—that is, to not fall behind.

More specifically, by invoking these time periods together—colonial and post-OPEC-crisis—Nyerere suggested that the intervening period of "we must run" had not provided a temporality in which Tanzania could overcome the momentum of the absences of empire once they were compounded by another series of shocks. Gabrielle Hecht calls this process of moving across periodic boundaries and imagining rupture by citing troubling continuities "conjugation," because the the word "enacts continuity and change *simultaneously*" (emphasis mine).[162] Nyerere did not argue that the OPEC crisis had made technological or economic liberation impossible—the state and the TPDC had changed far too much about oil politics for such a reductive argument—but that it made achieving these goals less likely by magnifying the impact of other events. Put differently: in a conjugated infrastructural time, events acted by accumulation to slow ujamaa's infrastructural speed. For example, when a 1977 famine reduced exports and forced the government to ask the World Bank and International Monetary Fund for financial assistance, Nyerere noted that the oil crisis had given bad weather the ability to become an actant in Tanzanian development by pushing the nation's faltering economy to the brink.[163] When the country was already hemorrhaging foreign exchange to get only a fraction of the amount of oil from earlier years, the famine further drained already-stretched financial resources.

Amir Jamal made a similar point with Tanzania's war with Uganda. By dispelling a communist threat in East Africa, Tanzania had hoped neighboring and Western countries would help finance the war. They were wrong.[164] Instead, the victory cost an estimated $500 million in foreign exchange, equivalent to four years of oil supply or to improvements that could have been invested in expanding refining capabilities.[165] To be clear, I am not excusing failed policies such as Ujamaa Vijijini (forced villagization) or offering another monocausal explanation for the economic contraction. As Nyerere suggested, external events like OPEC's bombshell set the stage for failure but certainly did not act alone.

Rather, Nyerere's speeches drew on and overlapped with other modes of thinking about technological constraint, decolonization, and automobility. By hinting that technological nation building had not been possible in the short window between 1961 and 1973, Nyerere echoed a core tenet of underdevelopment theory—namely, that new nations inherited their precarious economic and technological positions from the colonial period and that this status influenced their pursuit of sovereignty. In contrast to much of this work, which required capital and an exploitative regime to be *present* to initiate extraction, Nyerere asserted that things not built earlier could also set in motion arcs of underdevelopment because they later imposed a need for infrastructural speed. Historians have pointed out that underdevelopment theory sometimes turned Africans in the independent era into automatons whose options and ideas had already been constrained by centuries of underdevelopment.[166] Not so here: Nyerere's socialist technopolitics turned undesirable colonial underdevelopment into a technological hybrid aimed at avoiding the mass immiseration of industrial capitalism in orthodox Marxism. That the OPEC crisis constrained this hybrid shows not only that underdevelopment was an ongoing process but also that "agency and underdevelopment were connected features of an Africa unequally tied to other parts of the world," as Lisa Lindsay observes for Atlantic slavery.[167]

Moreover, Nyerere's post-OPEC-crisis thoughts aligned closely with transnational scholarship, activism, and policy grappling with oil-shortness. In 1979 "The Future of the Automobile in an Oil-Short World," later published as *Running on Empty*, included a lengthy description of the impact of the OPEC crisis on global mobility: "Scarcely a day passes without the international press carrying news of some additional restriction on the use of cars—the adoption of gasoline rationing in Tanzania, a lowering of highway speed limits in Portugal, or the establishment of 'bus-only' lanes on Los Angeles freeways."[168] Questioning the viability of the very technomobilities that twentieth-century modernizations required, it concluded, "The basic needs development strategy and its ever-growing global auto fleet may be in conflict."[169] A year later, a commission led by Willy Brandt, mayor of West Berlin, published *North-South, a Programme for Survival: Report of the Independent Commission on International Development Issues*. It, too, acknowledged that postwar development approaches required the "use of cheap oil" and called for a specific program "protecting poorer oil importers" (as larger economies transitioned to new energy sources).[170] Finally, a joint World Bank–United Nations report on privatization belatedly acknowledged what Nyerere, Jamal, and Barongo had said all along: "Complex interrelationships between the use of petroleum products, economic growth and foreign exchange resources pose a difficult issue of choice for the Government: how to achieve an optimal balance between the import of petroleum products and the import of other inputs necessary for economic revival."[171] As a 1981 document in Robert McNamara's World Bank archive put it: "An era of low cost energy has ended."[172]

I do *not* want to romanticize an oily—or, rather, oilier—ujamaa that could or should have been.[173] As a modernist project designed in the name of economic growth, Nyerere's African socialism included various forms of paternalism and violence that set his government in conflict with rural Tanzanian citizens on small and big issues alike. Furthermore, though quite distinct both quantitatively (in terms of per-capita use) and qualitatively (in that ujamaa envisioned a much different relationship between automobility and society), the relationship between oil and "effective freedom" does not provide a technological alternative capable of diverting concepts of development from rising petroleum use as a metric of social health—the latter a form of what Julie Livingston has recently called "self-devouring growth."[174] Yet keeping open the possibilities for an ujamaa that was not destined to fail (even in difficult times) and whose infrastructural limitations and failures are not reducible to bureaucratic shortcomings brings us back to the critical relationship between African sovereignty and economic growth in a context in which both—sovereignty and growth—went through fossil fuel systems. In turn, the possibilities of using energy like oil to secure sovereignty (and earlier visions of what the nation could be) were shaped by decades of not building under colonial rule and by both the limits and possibilities of infrastructural catch-up after independence, especially events between 1973 and 1979. In 1986, under a new president, Ali Hassan Mwinyi, Tanzania's inability to buy oil contributed directly to its surrender to International Monetary Fund policies.[175]

This entanglement of oil and sovereignty should also lead to a reappraisal of a technological counterfactual that gained popularity after the mid-1970s: that better and more appropriate technological roads to self-reliance had appeared in real historical time and had been ignored by a class of power-hungry bureaucrats whose decisions destroyed the nation. While, historically speaking, evidence to make this argument about "the work of state" is still forthcoming—and may be for quite some time—this element of decline narratives sidesteps some of the most critical technological details of postcolonial and postwar nation building: that self-reliance and "real independence," including ujamaa's rural modernization, went through oil and its LTSs. This counterfactual also ignores the various constraints and creativities that characterized oil procurement in the 1970s and in the wake of empire as Tanzania's political class pursued infrastructural acceleration through Nyerere's Marxist technological hybrid while breezing past the susceptibility of a place with comparably small amounts of oil use to petroleum's price increases.

This chapter has offered a view from the parastatal and presidential perch to examine technological capacity and citizenship on a national scale. The final chapter continues this thread by jumping into truck cabs and buses with drivers and passengers on regional roads. It shows that concerns about a "proto-magendo" economy expressed by ministers during the emergency meetings in the early 1980s were not only correct but also late in their recognition of the vernacular economies that had already helped sustain communities years earlier. But what these ministers called "sabotage" the drivers and passengers considered an actually existing form of socialism based on distributive networks that they and others needed to meet the demands of home. If, from Barongo's and Nyerere's standpoint, the OPEC crisis constrained Tanzania's ability to build a socialist family, road users nevertheless created automobile networks through which they mediated economic uncertainty and established actually existing forms of ujamaa during an economic emergency.

FIVE

Motorized Domesticities

Car, Road, and Home in Independent Tanzania

IN 1975 RICHARD MACHARY, a journalist for the Ministry of Culture's *Nchi Yetu* (Our Nation), detailed the strategies "smugglers" used to "[outsmart] immigration officials at the border." The text of "Cleverness Passing Contraband through Borders Has Grown" started beneath a large picture of a woman's braided hair, shown in figure 5.1, because "beautiful women" hid goods in various parts of their bodies to bring them in and out of Tanzania. "Valuable gems are inserted into girls' braided hair. When this girl gets to the border, the immigration officer inspects only her handbag and suitcase, thinking these are the only places to hide things. The woman's body is completely ignored." Machary's sources told him that besides hiding things in their hair, women placed diamonds and gold in secret compartments in the heels of their shoes and in oversized watches. They also rolled things in cloth that mimicked a tampon and "placed them in their private places" ("sehemu za siri za msichana") so that "it just appeared they were having their monthly period." As the section title, "Beautiful Women Used," attests, Machary did not think East African women possessed the ability, desire, or need to devise these strategies on their own. Nor did he credit other Tanzanian "criminals" (*wahalifu*), whom the article blames for

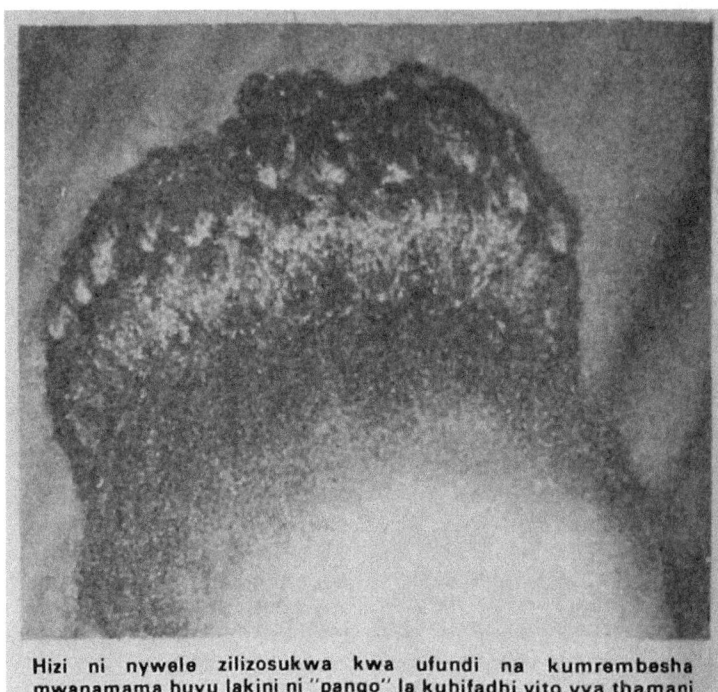

Hizi ni nywele zilizosukwa kwa ufundi na kumrembesha
mwanamama huyu lakini ni "pango" la kuhifadhi vito vya thamani

5.1 *Photo from Richard Machary's article. The text reads, "This hair has been expertly braided to beautify this woman but it is a 'plan' to hide valuable things." Richard Machary, "Ujanja wa Kutorosha Mali ya Magendo Mpakani," Nchi Yetu, November 1975, 20–21.*

stealing the nation's wealth and for using women in vulnerable socioeconomic conditions, with this cross-border "cleverness."[1]

"Hard-core criminals [*majambazi*] learn from watching movies and then use these strategies to move goods," Machary wrote, linking economic "sabotage" to capitalist Hollywood. "For example, a picture called 'The French Connection' demonstrates methods for hiding drugs in various places within a car."[2] In this 1971 film, Gene Hackman's character helps smuggle heroin from Turkey to France and then to the United States via Canada by hiding the drug throughout the vehicle. After watching the film, Machary explains, Tanzanian smugglers put diamonds and gold in tires or placed clothes in empty oil tankers, as in the case of one shipment from Horororo village in Tanga to Mombasa, Kenya. For larger items such as ivory, "they made sure" they could be moved "without being known." Machary did not provide an example of how this secretive movement worked, but he "got wind" of "prostitutes" transported across the border using caskets: "[The smugglers] told the officers they were going to bury the bodies. But when they failed to produce death certificates, the officers became suspicious. That's when they opened the caskets to find several prostitutes inside." The police had already responded by attempting to control road mobilities. They sometimes lined both sides of the streets into and out of border towns, and they erected checkpoints on routes across the country.[3]

Most sources identified smugglers as working-class men struggling to become adults in a context of economic uncertainty. Unlike the naizi and wabenzi from chapter 3, these men did not own vehicles, wear suits, or use their power to gain social status. Instead, they helped secretly load and unload contraband items such as ivory, clothes, and sugar, and they sometimes drove. State and church media sources publicly condemned men's participation by linking their actions to a "boss" class who had no interest in addressing the economic uncertainties Tanzanians faced after the mid-1970s. "This is wealth," the young man carrying a tusk in the cartoon in figure 5.2 states, while the onlooker editorializes, saying this national wealth benefits only a "boss." In figure 5.3, a magendo ("contraband") sugar transporter declines a request to take a sick child to the hospital.[4] More than taking sugar revenues from the national economy and people's homes, the drawing suggests that magendo fundamentally changed the individual who participated in it. Helping a young girl get to the hospital while possessing the means to do so should have been an easy decision even for an mjamaa (a socialist) whose morals had been compromised. A redeemable socialist would have used the moment to perform a metaphorical U-turn: not only helping the girl but then repenting of his economic sins. In one of the earliest descriptions of ujamaa in 1962, Julius Nyerere said "I would like to see that wherever two or three of us meet," whether in a bar, bus, school, market, farm, or office, "the place becomes a classroom for discussing and learning about ujamaa."[5] Here, however, magendo made that metaphorical classroom of socialist advancement through interaction with a fellow citizen in need an impossibility.

This intersection of magendo, roads, and motor vehicles marked a turning point in the state's approach to automobility. Instead of an objective tool of development needed in increasing quantities for building the nation and turning socialism's distributive (usambazaji) logic into a material reality, after the middle of the decade, roads and the motorized mobilities they afforded also appeared as places where citizens contested the state's authority and compromised—if not destroyed—its efforts to

5.2–5.3 *Two examples of the intersection of motor vehicles, magendo, working and lower class masculinity, and a perception of the absence of ujamaa values in everyday interactions.* M. M. Komba, Chakubanga wa Mwenge, 1979–1991, TNL.

build a self-reliant economy that pursued social equality. The link between the latter ideals and usambazaji was clear. Usambazaji provided government officials a practical tool to equally distribute the spoils of socialist maendeleo across national space (and through set government prices). For this reason, magendo mobilities posed a direct threat to the state's technological, and therefore economic, power to create equality—in other words, socialist "sabotage." Periodical sources and politicians alike blamed the sabotage on shadow figures, "rogues" and "bosses." But magendo's publicized mobilities were rarely produced by these individuals. Women on buses and men loading vehicles with contraband suggested that, rather than being a crime of a wealthy minority, magendo had already or could later become a bottom-up rejection of socialism by everyday users willing to be used by corrupt individuals who offered temporary economic relief.

In 1982, seven years after Machary's article, the state declared that "theft of public property has become the order of the day" and began a six-month operation on roads to end it.[6] But magendo was not the only national-scale destructive act associated with road transport. A couple years later, epidemiological research on HIV/AIDS placed roads and male African drivers at the center of HIV-1's rapid spread throughout east-central Africa in the late 1970s and early 1980s. By the time Nyerere stepped down from the presidency in 1985, regional motor mobilities had been credited not only with creating a saboteur economy in which people rejected their state but also with facilitating the infection of thousands of diseased and dead bodies. Reading state and public health sources, one can easily come away with the impression that the cultures of automobility that emerged on Tanzanian roads during the first decades of independence had harmed rather than benefited both their users and the nation. I call this phenomenon *automobility as failed modernization,* and I conclude this chapter by sketching its emergence in national and international public discourse between 1975 and the early 1990s.

Yet this chapter focuses on a different set of sources and thus different historical processes. In oral histories, the men and women who took to the roads as drivers and passengers characterized motorized travel as a technological act through which they created community across the national space and as a gendered process through which they built and maintained lives as adults in good and bad times alike. Decades later, they framed their stories about mobility not through assumptions about destruction and decline but rather through a common list of benefits I heard after asking, "What did you get out of traveling?" They built houses, married, had children and educated them, and cared for family. Roads certainly took men and women far from their homes, put them in danger of physical harm through accidents, and even created a corpus of stories about things drivers feared because they could not understand or control them. In many cases, travel also led to actions that could be interpreted as magendo. But as I show in the following, they traveled with home on their minds and also considered themselves integral parts of a national family not in spite of their mobility but because of it.

Such motorized domesticities came in two interrelated forms. The first involved a mobile homemaking in which drivers and passengers brought resources from far away to physical houses where they built lives as settled and respectable adults through decades of movement. Similar to passengers who moved up and down stretches of the Tanzania-Zambia Railway, as Jamie Monson describes, motorized movement offered some opportunities for social security while, for others, it was a "necessity for survival."[7] The second—a capacity to dwell safely in and on technologies known for social, physical, and spiritual risk—required care of their vehicles, crew, cargo, and body as well as respect for the known and unknown dangers of road travel. John Urry calls this process "inhabiting the car." He points out that car-based societies and the circulations they require rest on the ability of certain groups to continually "inhabit" spaces and technologies in which continual motion, not habitation, is assumed.[8] Building on Urry's work, this chapter unearths the cultures of risk and well-being that drivers and passengers forged on Tanzanian roads from the early days of national road travel in the early 1960s—as drivers first began to make homes on the road—to debates about the meaning of family and mobility as magendo and HIV/AIDS brought increased scrutiny to road use and mechanized movements.

Cars and roads may seem like strange technologies for evaluating ideas about family and home in Tanzania.[9] But recognizing that "the domestic domain opens up in two directions," as Karen Tranberg Hansen writes, provides insight into the "significance of domesticity in the changing constructions of space, activity, power, and gender in Africa."[10] We can add technology to this list as well. Making home on the road led men, the huge majority of drivers, to reject the dominant masculine category ascribed to them, *dume*—a word that features in the Kiswahili word for "patriarchy" (*mfumodume*)—in favor of the opposite: the coward (*mwoga*). In turn, driver-cowards' strategies for inhabiting road and car center details about the logics and strategies of automobility and broader ideas about creating home and family, from multiple user perspectives.[11] This chapter focuses on two aspects of these user perspectives: the machinic embodiment of care that men and women drivers created on national and regional roads in the 1960s and 1970s, and the details and meanings of movement for broader ideas about nation, socialism, and home, especially during times of economic crisis.[12] We begin by exploring a distinction many drivers made in interviews: the difference between "driver" (*dereva*) and "not a driver" (*si dereva*).

"DRIVER" AND "NOT A DRIVER": CAREFUL COWARDS ON THE ROAD

Key elements of driver training continued from the colonial to the independent period. Prospective drivers still learned by entering utingo (the vernacular institution of driver training) as turnboys and in rarer cases through driving schools. Moreover, a career on the road similarly attracted young men with limited education or technical training. The drivers I interviewed came to *udereva*, the Kiswahili word for a driving career, from backgrounds that included music, manual labor, a gas station attendant, migration to urban areas, garage work, or from having no job at all. They often did so in their late teenage years or their twenties.[13] But unlike in the colonial period, when the word *boi* in *taniboi* applied exclusively to young African men who cranked vehicles—thus infantilizing them as boys regardless of their age—most drivers used the term after 1961 as a form of gender exclusivity. *Boi* linked roadwork to men's sanction to not only make livelihoods away from home for long periods of time but also to do so by moving through uninhabited places for long stretches of a workday. Between 1969 and 1972, men occupied between 97 and 98.7 percent of the "Transport, Storage, and Communication" workforce of thirty-one thousand, whereas they constituted between 91 and 94 percent of the official wage economy. Six years later, when women's role in the official economy had grown threefold, to 12 percent, their role had shrunk by 1 percent in "Transport, Storage, and Communication."[14]

Far from linking just any man to a driving career, public sources anticipated a particular masculine body behind the wheel, as a Safari King cigarettes advertisement demonstrates through its visualization of the Kiswahili term *dume* in figure 5.4. *Dume* often translates simply as "male" but also connotes idealized forms of manliness rooted in physical

5.4 Combined with text declaring *dume* (manliness) has entered town, the image of this 1977 Safari King advertisement visualizes the idea that only certain types of bodies (and only certain types of male bodies, in particular) mobilized economies across the nation during the first decades of independence. Safari Kings advertisement, *Uhuru*, July 28, 1977.

strength or other types a power. Featuring a driver with muscles bulging as he changes a tire, the advertisement declares, "Like it's never happened before—the manliness [dume] is now in town." The advertisement suggests that part of being a dume, or a man's man, is not only an ability to change a vehicle tire—quite a simple task, as chapter 2 shows—but also the sanction to move across vast distances through uninhabited spaces with a large machine and heavy loads. On this particular journey, the vehicle sustains minor damage, but the driver, a dume, guides it back to a safe sociotechnical space—in this case, the city—where he fixes the truck. He gains status as manly in a new way—"like it's never happened before"—by arriving "now in town" after successfully guiding the vehicle through liminal space.[15] His ability to move between settled and unsettled space recalls myths of origin in which hunters gained political power in the deep past by bringing meat from the unsettled bush, a place of danger, to a settled village.[16] But instead of the political power created through mobility in myths of origin, truck drivers in advertisements gain a unique form of respectable working-class masculinity during a political period, ujamaa, in which connections to motorized mobilities commonly evoked the opposite.[17]

Indeed, other than Nyerere's unique relationship to his Jeep in chapter 3, this motorized dume advertised the only car-based identity during ujamaa capable of helping rather than harming the national community. Unlike naizi and wabenzi (whose relationship with vehicles provoked accusations of corruption) or the "saboteurs" from this chapter's introduction (who worked secretly with truck owners and whom media sources called to contribute to the national development through farming), here the combination of truck and working-class man leads to increased social status for the driver as well as to an assumption of broader social health. A driver in a Fiat truck advertisement speaks of himself and the truck as "us"—a team working together. He can do so because, distinct from naizi and wabenzi, both urban categories, both advertisements tie the driver's mobility to the sanctioned circulation and consumption of goods across national spaces—in these cases, big loads constrained only by laws limiting the amount of road carriage and cigarettes manufactured domestically. Another advertisement that placed a passenger bus against the backdrop of a huge boxing glove illustrates that the masculinization of driving applied to vehicles carrying people, too. By tying motorized movements to one of Tanzania's most popular working-class masculine pastimes and to physical strength, the ad naturalizes the notion that passengers trust their lives to the type of men who pursue boxing for leisure and driving as a profession. As a socially constructed ideal driver, this dume possessed physical strength as well as a desire, need, and/or duty to navigate dangerous spaces to pursue social mobility.

Unlike the dume's sanctioned pursuit of risk in the name of national well-being, women's motorized bodies upset gendered expectations about mobility and power. Consider this description of Bibi Titi Mohamed, the former leader of the Tanganyika African Nation Union's Women's League, whose car use during the fight against colonialism was later used by a party secretary to justify treason charges against her: "Bibi Titi was a particular kind of woman—the kind who obviously no husband would put up with [because] she was riding around in a TANU Landrover with men for months on end . . . There are many educated women in politics, and this is acceptable because they have drivers who bring them home at night."[18] Here the very thing that makes the dume so manly—the open road's distance from a permanent dwelling—turns an anticolonial hero into a suspicious figure because not even a male driver can take her "home at night," literally putting her in her gendered place, a bounded domestic sphere.[19]

In spite of playing a crucial role in national mobilization during the 1950s—a role that required spatial mobility and the capacity to mobilize resources—women in postcolonial Tanzania were expected to be good wives, mothers, teachers, and farmers, that is, good producers and reproducers.[20] In contrast to an iconography that celebrated men's physical and social mobility as nation builders, advertisements depict women as mothers of the nation whose labor ties them to their homes and to reproductive labor, as the popular greeting to pregnant women, "You are carrying tomorrow's nation," attests. Rarely present in advertisements with mechanized technologies, women dominate food and soap advertisements, often accompanied by the children for whom they act as the primary caregiver. When present in advertisements that include automobiles, women accompany men in technologically passive roles, sometimes appearing as the reward for luxury car ownership (i.e., a car-owning man gets a certain type of woman). Should these women—part of an upwardly mobile social group that can afford personal vehicles—drive, the automobiles shown (sedans) would likely limit their mobility to an urban area, not permitting them to traverse the dume's open, and quite bumpy, road.[21] In sum, trucks and regional road mobilities came into direct conflict with constructions of domesticity and identity that assumed women's immobility in/at a home where they cared for a family.

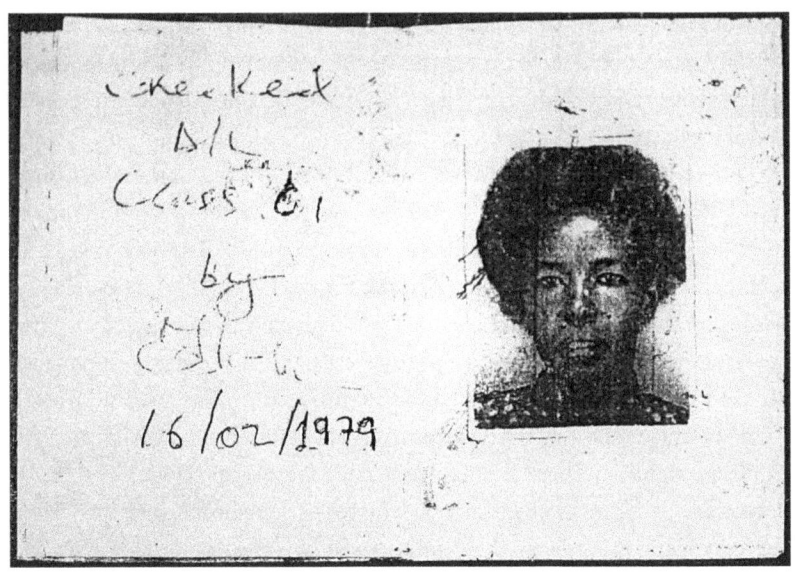

5.5 *Hawa Ramadhani's 1979 license.*

After nearly three years of networking with drivers, I talked to only two women who had worked on regional highways between the 1960s and 1980s. Zakia Maomba, who goes by her driving name, Bibi Benzi, or Grandma Benz, learned at her home, a garage in Zambia. Her father owned a trucking company, and Benzi traveled regularly to see her mother outside of Morogoro. On one of these trips, she fell in love with and then married a Tanzanian mechanic who worked at her father's garage. Despite her father's initial anger about their relationship, the new couple received a truck as a wedding gift. Benzi drove, and her husband performed duties as a turnboy and mechanic.[22] Hawa Ramadhani, pictured on her license in figure 5.5, also learned at home, albeit from German nuns at a mission in the 1950s. She worked for government parastatals in Dar es Salaam, including Usafiri Dar es Salaam (UDA). She left the city to work on regional roads transporting food.[23] Though these women were a minority among drivers, their lives reveal gendered road travel as a relational process learned and shaped by both men and women who were actively constructing livelihoods on the road in ways that did not align with hegemonic expectations about movement. Dominant ideas about movement and bodies certainly made Ramadhani and Benzi highly visible, and sometimes particularly problematic, agents of car-based mobilities. But the drivers also shared a core set of assumptions with male colleagues about the skills, values, and strategies that distinguished dereva from si dereva.

Critically, neither men nor women made claims on the masculine figure dume. Instead, drivers distinguished between two categories of technomobile conduct in oral histories: driver (*dereva*) and not a driver (*si dereva*). More than the licensing that legally sanctioned one's place behind the wheel—a tool colonial drivers used to assert racial parity—claiming the status of driver hinged on an individual's ability to turn motorized movement into adulthood by correctly reading the changing material and social land-scapes of the road. This first required care for one's body and for the vehicle as it moved through space and encountered unknown obstacles. Owners fired drivers who damaged vehicles or cargo, and those who sped reck-lessly or ignored warnings about the people and things they encountered along the way needed luck to survive. "Carefulness" (*makini*), a word both men and women used in interviews, mattered because drivers aimed to use their career to make claims on broadly held notions of adulthood by mar-rying, purchasing houses and land, having children and educating them (*kuwasomesha watoto*), and gaining access to household staples they col-lected en route.[24] Drivers simultaneously called this process "searching for blessing" (*kutafuta riziki*), "building life" (*kujenga maisha*), and maende-leo. "Maendeleo," Hassan Saidi said, "is you yourself being able to plan (*kupanga*) your life and this comes from what income and other things you can get (*mapato*). You cannot plan your life without mapato."[25] Si dereva was simply the opposite: an individual who died in an accident or who through reckless behavior squandered opportunities to age well.[26]

Drivers achieved the status of dereva by becoming not a dume, but rather a mwoga: a coward. According to Kiswahili proverbs, "the coward leaves with laughter while the hero leaves with cries," "the fierce [*mkali*] get weeping while the fearful rejoice," and "the timid crab withdraws its claws."[27] A mwoga thus treads carefully, is wise, and learns. They know they are not in control. Drivers thus talked about a set of "soft" techno-logical virtues for proper road conduct that sit uncomfortably with the "hard" industrial masculinity of the motorized dume.[28] As Paul Edwards notes, this "hard/soft split . . . plays a major ideological role" in postwar discourse of technological worth, often shaping gendered access to and valuations of industrial work. The former, coded as masculine, produces, intuits, and moves things for a growing economy. The latter, coded as fem-inine, assists, nurtures, and cares, often from an immobile position. But in the actual act of technological labor, this gendered distinction breaks down. "Neither men nor experts in formal thinking hold a monopoly on scientific abilities. Women are fully capable of all the tasks of science and computer work. Equally, men have their own kinds of softness and intuition."[29] Edwards's observation also applies to constructions of gender on Tanzania's roads, where users' actions rarely fit binary constructions of hard or soft, male or female.

A hegemonic industrial masculinity did not align with drivers' experiences or aims because the roads they traveled on required much more than the dume offered: physical strength, a machine, and sanction to move freely.[30] "First," narrations often began, "there is the bad condition [hali mbaya] of roads." Despite growing infrastructural investments, trucks moved along a transport infrastructure not designed for large (and wide) vehicles and heavy traffic. In the early 1980s, 85 percent of roads were dirt, 14 percent gravel, and only 8 percent paved, mostly in urban areas.[31] The length of tarmac roads fell slightly from 1972 to 1979, decreasing from 2,625 to 2,423 kilometers, as the categories "gravel" and "others" increased from 4,909 to 5,731 kilometers and 26,188 to 45,000 kilometers, respectively.[32]

Retired drivers described highways, barabara, as constantly emergent infrastructures whose surfaces changed owing to weather and the passage of other vehicles. Operators learned about some elements of these roads through experience, including a sharp turn; a steep descent; the presence of clay that, when wet, made passage impossible; or places where blurred lines between pasture and road resulted in livestock on truck routes.[33] But other features required the full attention of one's mind and body during passage. Even at slower speeds, new potholes, hardened tire ruts, fallen trees, or wandering cows caused accidents that not only stranded drivers far from help but also destroyed equipment and goods and endangered the driver's life and livelihood.[34] Broken springs, tired engines, cracked radiators, worn-out clutch plates, and body damage counted as normal wear and tear on Tanzania's roads. But companies and owners could easily interpret overturned or smashed vehicles as evidence of a driver's lack of care and caution. Creating a livelihood behind the wheel thus required drivers to approach roads not as finished infrastructure but as lively materialities that could never be completely known because of subtle, yet important, shifts in their form. Ibrahim Moses thus described a roadboy as an identity distinct from a driver who learns at a technical institute because a roadboy sees and learns from the landscape itself, knowing when to climb aggressively and when to stop.[35]

In this material context, the definition of speeding (*kasi kubwa*), or driving too fast, changed based on the specific road conditions. Speeding happened, of course, but it reflected inexperience and/or immaturity, not simply the surpassing of posted kilometer-per-hour limits—which, in some cases, drivers recalled as difficult given the surface conditions. Instead, speeding suggested the status of si dereva because it meant an individual had not taken the time to know the road materialities well enough to appreciate the risks of constant rapid movement for themselves, the vehicle, and others' property. In fact, material obstacles to rapid movement played an important role in drivers' narrations of their careers. Smooth roads, which have become more common in recent decades, create danger not only by luring drivers into a sense of false control but also by removing the modes of awareness through which previous generations avoided and survived calamity.[36]

Bad road conditions thus created good drivers by necessitating a form of machinic embodiment connecting eyes, mind, arms, and legs to both vehicle and road.[37] Constantly scanning surfaces and roadsides for danger, the driver stood ready to react with legs, arms, and hands—stomping on pedals, holding gears and wheel, and bracing for impact if necessary. Conversely, drivers argued, smooth roads allow drivers to relax, and thus operators have lost the ability to quickly react when the unexpected occurs. One such accident killed Minister Salome Mbatia in 2007. Some linked its occurrence to the road's smooth surface and the false sense of security such surfaces provide while traveling at high speeds.[38] While these accusations say little about younger generations of drivers, they underscore the role of rough, uneven, and potholed materialities in drivers' own descriptions of automobile care and professionalism. Far from being an obstacle to development, the bad condition of roads created a good technological subject: a skilled mwoga driver more likely to survive road mobility and build a home and family.[39]

In interviews, drivers established their skill and care through a single statistic: the number of times they had been found at fault for an accident. A few claimed "zero accidents" over their career. But most admitted to crashes and talked about their ability to navigate accidents when (not if) they happened and to be found without fault—a skill captured by the stative Kiswahili verb *kunusurika*, meaning to "escape narrowly."[40] (Readers may remember this verb from economic survival programs in the previous chapter.) Drivers judged at fault for accidents had stamps placed on their licenses by a police officer. After retirement, the clear license booklets that my interlocutors produced during interviews did not reference the absence of accidents during a career. Instead, it offered official verification that they had prepared themselves for the regular unknowns of road travel, a skill connected to their pursuits of gendered respectability long before we met. In addition to reflecting the driver's own safety, a clear license booklet demonstrated to owners or a company that a driver had cared for vehicles and cargo. Doing so certainly required some physical strength to hold steering wheels steady on bumpy roads for hours at a time and push heavy gears or stiff brakes.[41] Ramadhani described strength as a prerequisite for the job and compared her own to that of a man.[42]

But the same drivers described strength as useless if not accompanied by an acute awareness produced by eyes constantly scanning roads and an active mind. Talking to me in their sitting rooms, drivers imagined themselves back in their truck cabs as they narrated: feet forward on pedals, left hand on the gearshift (because vehicles travel in the left lane of the road), right hand on the wheel, and, critically, eyes scanning with an active mind ready to react to danger. This may seem only a slight alteration from the dume's muscular body. Yet interlocutors connected their safe passage over thousands of miles to an alternative mwoga machinic embodiment that privileged mind and senses, especially sight, over strength because of fears about what potholes, tire blowouts, and wandering livestock could do to the bodies of trucks and drivers alike.[43]

Motoring with care took a toll on operators' bodies over decades of travel. Ramadhani said scanning roads and squinting had damaged her sight; pushing resistant clutch pedals had left her left leg weakened.[44] Regani, too, had a bad leg, a damaged shoulder, and a weakened arm—each the result of car and road vibrations felt through the steering wheel. Others described ailments in eyes, legs, and arms.[45] Now retired, drivers presented these maladies not only as the cost of driving but even more so as the cost of driving well. Julie Livingston uses the term *debility* to describe the "impairment, lack, or loss of certain bodily abilities" that comes not just from misfortune but even from comparatively privileged positions in labor economies.[46] In interviews, drivers' worn and now-retired bodies evidenced technological care over a career in which most whom I interviewed had passed from the status of youth (*kijana*) to adult (*mtu mzima*). Because driving well slowly damaged their bodies, they felt they had to make the most of a limited time frame to bring resources home. Many aimed to achieve this social mobility from their late teens and early twenties to their fifties, which most considered a short window owing to claims on their resources.

Young men still acted on their gendered privilege on the road. "We were young, had money, and we drove. The women loved us," one said. Although I never interviewed someone who did it, drivers recalled colleagues who had networks of lovers they visited at stations or homes along their routes. Others found companionship and the "comforts of home" at guesthouses and truck stops: "It was easy. After you arrived, you paid for your room. If you left the key with the manager, this meant you wanted a woman waiting for you in your room after you'd eaten. You made love, and maybe she would wash your clothes."[47] Drivers knew that stops on higher-traffic routes along the Kenya-Tanzania border and along the Tanzania-Zambia Highway (TANZAM) offered these services. Some used them, and they spoke frankly about sexually transmitted diseases, such as gonorrhea (*kisonono*) and syphilis (*kaswende*). They described them not only as a known and treatable part of this landscape but also as a cost of creating relationships over distance as they inhabited road networks. Some large trucking companies provided medical care and condoms at their regional offices in later decades.[48]

Yet other drivers avoided truck stops for these very reasons. Men with families, including spouses, children, and aged parents, said they tried to leave as much of their travel allowances at home as possible before starting their journey. This left little for "enjoyment" (*starehe*), they said. Moreover, starehe lengthened their travel time and thus reduced the number of trips they could take.[49] Others mentioned religion. No matter how we phrased questions about the allure of truck stops, some Christian and Muslim drivers insisted they had not taken part in extramarital relationships, choosing instead to find places of worship and prayer on their journeys. Regardless of their reason for avoiding stays at truck stops, doing so required young assistants and drivers to learn how to cook on a small charcoal stove they carried in the back of the cab and with food purchased along the way. In addition to saving their travel allowance, they returned home with food for their families (often with more charcoal for cooking). This not only allowed drivers' families to avoid any shortages—whether owing to famine or rationing systems—but also, they said, created a more diverse and nutritional diet for loved ones. Steady access to diverse foods at low prices was the most common answer to my questions about the benefits of a driving career. Mohamed Shabani Mketo contributed to a regionally diverse spread at home by picking up rice in Mwanza, honey in Shinyanga, and potatoes, onions, and oranges in Mbeya. After food, the ability to see their country and region, what one termed a "fantastic awakening," came in a close second.[50]

Others forged ties with communities in which they initially arrived as strangers. In each town Juma Ramadhani visited, he sought *watani* (people associated with his ethnicity's utani) through word of mouth, asking for a place to stay in exchange for a gift from his travels. During the precolonial era, such utani, or "joking relationships," connected distant communities along trade routes and provided a template for proper social and economic activity. In the context of independent automobility, joking relationships helped drivers create secure bonds through a social institution that had allowed trade and movement to occur for centuries. After years of traveling, Juma Ramadhani had created a geographically disperse social network that allowed him to move safely and comfortably around the country.[51] Saidi Abdallah, an Mzaramo, did not have to look for his *mtani* (person from his ethnicity's utani), an Mnyamwezi who owned the guesthouse where the driver stayed in Mwanza. Asked, "What ethnicity are you?" Abdallah responded, "Mzaramo." The owner answered, "And I'm your father." He then gave Abdallah a room to rest in before taking the driver's bags to his own house, where he later welcomed him for dinner. Abdallah stayed at this man's home on each subsequent trip.[52] Drivers like Abdallah rested, talked with individuals they considered peers and friends, and ate home-cooked meals. In at least one case, a driver married a woman, a daughter of a man he befriended through utani.[53] But drivers also provided something, too. They brought goods the state rationed by a card system—such as salt, sugar, clothes, oil, flour, and rice—and regional delicacies unavailable in local markets that enhanced a family's food options.[54]

Hawa Ramadhani and Benzi found fewer places and strategies for making a home on the road. By the time Ramadhani drove on regional routes, she had divorced her first husband, who questioned her role as a driver at ministries in Dar es Salaam; she also left kids at home with her family when she traveled. She and her family commonly faced accusations of sexual immorality, one of her children recalled in an interview.[55] Not surprisingly, Ramadhani avoided truck stops for all but the necessities, opting to sleep on the roadside instead. She credits this for her personal "development" (maendeleo): a process that allowed her to build two houses, buy two farms, and open shops in Morogoro. She later married a fruit seller from Kilwa Masoko whose produce she had transported. Benzi, whose husband traveled with her as a turnboy and mechanic, did not mention regular questions about her ability or moral standing as a woman driver in her written memoir.[56] But Ramadhani recalled that men drivers regularly asked Bibi Benzi's husband, Babu Benzi, for permission to marry her. He answered, "Bring the cattle," to which they responded, "We only have chickens at home."[57] Ramadhani, who chuckled telling the story, considered it a joke—and one that could be turned against drivers' masculinity because they claimed to lack the necessary resources for such a marriage.

As the only case I heard of in which an assistant had any authority over the driver's life, it points to questions from the traveling public about Benzi's standing within her own truck. These questions derived not from actions on the road but simply from assumptions that husbands had power over wives. In both cases, to continually inhabit the road, women physically carted their husbands along in the cab even though they served technologically inferior, if not completely passive, roles in the production of movement.

That men's presence diminished but did not completely displace fears about women's place on the open road helps situate the gendered contours of the coward driver. In contrast to mwoga men who hoped to build a family in the near future through distant travels, a mwoga woman driver made a settled family first, and even when she sanctioned her movement with a husband sitting beside her in the truck, she still faced accusations of not fulfilling her duties at home, as Ramadhani's family recalled.[58] Men felt sanction to be young, as they put it, using their late teens and twenties to enjoy their mobility and to see other regions and countries— enjoying the comforts of home on the road as they did so, before turning their attention to building a settled home later in life. National gender ideologies that marked women's mobility as deviant thus influenced the type of cowardice Ramadhani and Benzi performed. For men, one reminder to be a mwoga came not from ideologies formed in dense areas of population but from the vulnerability they felt traveling between settled spaces, a corpus of stories to which we now turn.

"IT IS SAID": SEEING RISK LIKE A DRIVER

More than fuel, food, sex, and rest, truck stops offered young drivers wisdom about the risks of motor travel. As far as I can tell, only one form of conversation turned into a corpus of stories widely known and shared by individuals who inhabited the roads. Describing "something(s) of awe/wonder" (*kitu cha ajabu*) or a "wondrous occurrence" (*miujiza*; also "miracle"), this corpus likely emerged as regional trucking routes grew in the 1960s and young men saw things they could not explain and shared their experiences over food and drink. Not all had experienced these events, and thus stories often began with the Kiswahili phrase *Inasemekana* (It is said). To explore more about these stories than emerged in individual interviews, a research assistant who lived along the road to Iringa asked drivers pulling into a truck stop in 2012 about stories they had heard or had been told on the road (this collection is cited as Ndiuma Station Stories). I then incorporated general aspects of these stories of awe into interviews with retired drivers. I cannot confirm that only men experienced these *miujiza*. Hawa Ramadhani passed away before I had a chance to follow up with her, and I lost contact with Benzi's family before I knew about this corpus. In her written vita, Benzi uses the word *miujiza* to describe an accident with livestock in which she fled from Maasai pastoralists while her husband ran to the police station for help.[59] For these reasons, I cannot assert that the following stories are exclusively masculine.

Yet mobile men clearly linked their motorized movement to a gendered landscape of risk. For example, a driver pulled over to the side of the road between stops to get some sleep. He woke up to a huge snake that extended far above the trees around him. Scared, he left at once and did not stop driving until his nerves had calmed. On another trip, he added, "I was taking wood from Tabora to Shinyanga when I heard *pooooo*. Both tires in the back had punctures. But it was only so that I would stop in a bad place [*sehemu mbaya*]."[60] He decided to continue, and when he reached the next station, both tires were full. Omar Seif Ngomadodo said, "You can't pass through mountains at night because there are strange things in the dark."[61] Drivers knew Kitonga pass near Iringa not only as a dangerous and narrow mountain road but also as a place where mechanical failure occurred so commonly that they needed to give offerings to mountain spirits before attempting an ascent or descent. Heeding the advice of local communities, they threw an item of value—whether fish or money—onto the side of the road before this segment of their journey.[62] A mountain on routes in Chiweta, Malawi, required drivers to bathe "with water" before they ascended it. If they had intercourse after this bath, they had to bathe again before the mountain allowed them to climb it. Large trees, especially baobab and mango, also act in cha ajabu (of awe/wonder) histories: "There's a region in Dodoma where there is a baobab tree that workers cut down to build a road, but the tree regenerates itself. It is said this tree has powers."[63]

Things blocking the way play a central role in these stories as well. "You may see those cows ahead, [or] you can see a really tall person or normal woman [in the street], if you avoid them, you wreck your car and there is no person" and "your car overturns."[64] Ngomadodo recalls seeing a group of people dancing in the road at the Ngerengere Bridge near Morogoro. "They want food, and that's why cars overturn trying to avoid them. I passed right through them and then didn't see a single one behind."[65] Another driver described a similar experience nearby: "Once, on the road to Ngerengere from Mpanda at 1 a.m., I encountered people dancing in the road. So I sped up—you know, they want food, and this is why people who try to avoid them get in accidents. So I ran them over, and they disappeared."[66] Drivers used the same tactic if they saw people carrying a casket who direct them to veer off the road and thus avoid the funeral procession.[67] Some versions of these stories replace people with livestock, particularly cows, "who don't have herders or anything with them." In Malawi, near Chiweta, drivers must pass under jumping cows. "If you try to pass and you hit them, the car breaks."[68] At Tanangozi, a weigh station southwest of Iringa on the road to Mbeya, trucks broke down owing to a grave "in the middle of the road. . . . Even electricity cannot pass above the grave; you have to find another way. This was not caused by the deceased but by the deceased's family. The grave was later moved out of the road," and cars could pass again.[69]

The grave story echoes others in which roadside communities obstructed motorized movements by blocking or luring drivers from their intended path:

> There's a part of Tanga called Tanga Uvuo. One driver heard the sound of a drum. He stopped his vehicle to follow the drum sound. He hears it just in front of him, but every time he gets closer, it moves farther in front of him. Now far from his car, he sees light from a light bulb. When he gets close, the light moves out into the distance. The driver comes to realize that he has encountered wondrous people. They are naked, and no one is even looking at the drum. The driver then runs to his vehicle and leaves as quickly as possible.[70]

Three figures on or near roads appear most often in cha ajabu histories: women, livestock, and elders (*wazee*).

The stories urged extreme caution with women whom drivers did not know. "There's a place called Lugoba-Chalinze where you can be bewitched. If you are driving a car and you see a beautiful girl in the middle of the road, if you avoid her you get in an accident, but if you hit her you'll be safe."[71] In another version of the story found at Makanya-Buko, a "beautiful woman" "can change the road if she wants. So you see that you're passing on a good road, but, surprise, you are driving in the bush and you get in an accident without ever knowing."[72] Here the literal act of chasing a woman leads to an accident that could strand one far from a road. One man I interviewed failed to heed this advice when a woman asked for assistance in a remote area. He feared sleeping with her or even near her, so they slept in different parts of the truck. She disappeared the next morning.[73] Women presented danger in urban and rural areas alike: "At Tunduma, there was a driver who met a young girl. They agreed to sleep together. When they arrived at the room, they do their thing. Surprisingly, the young woman has medicine [*dawa*] in her breast. As the driver sleeps, she robs him of everything."[74] Corporeally embodied or phantom, inasemekana stories position all women in road spaces as a risk to men's well-being.

Men told similar stories about livestock roaming rural roads without herders. For young men at the center of economic networks, unguarded cattle—symbols of wealth and coming of age for men in much of colonial and precolonial East Africa—could represent the dangers of wealth accumulation. One story makes this link among wealth, cattle, and a loss of personhood explicit: "It is said that at Tunduma, if you encounter a bank note, you turn into a cow, and if you turn into a cow, you'll find there is a rope around your foot and a herder behind you who takes you to be slaughtered. And everyone only sees you as a cow."[75] The story describes a remarkable transformation: from seeking money in a vehicle by moving across national space, the driver finds himself bound by rope to a herder who intends to use his flesh to nurture others or to mark a socially significant event such as a wedding—the type of occasion when a cow would be slaughtered. Drivers told their assistants that anyone who stopped or tried to avoid the livestock, like the visions of women, would be killed by a spirit or through an accident as they pulled their car to the side of the road at high speed. Men seeking social mobility thus lined up their vehicles to hit these unherded livestock, and they stepped on the gas.

Sightings of women and livestock thus gave drivers sanction to throw motoring caution to the wind. Senior drivers instructed their younger colleagues to step on the gas pedal to intentionally strike something with their vehicle that, from a distance and at speed, they thought a harmful spirit because of stories they had heard at stops. Though men claimed to pass through nothing, intentionally hitting things in the road at high speed seemingly signals the opposite of a driver-coward moving carefully and timidly across road materialities whose physical features they tried to know in detail. But here increasing speed provides a technological strategy to avoid acting on their sexual privilege or recklessly pursuing the economic aspirations sanctioned for dume in public discourse. These were not split-second decisions but rather acts ritualized through the stories young drivers heard at stations as they ate or waited for fuel and as they learned about the distinction between "driver" and "not a driver." The point is not only that speed could be a mwoga's friend. "It is said" stories suggest that immobility (stopping) in particular places brought its own types of risk. When a mwoga accelerated to avoid these encounters, he did so because hitting something, and possibly somebody, at high speed was preferable to slowing down or stopping in a place where they would be vulnerable—where neither the speed of their vehicle nor reciprocal human relationships could help them.[76]

Drivers blamed the final group, "old people" or "elders" (wazee), for causing accidents, diverting journeys, and killing travelers. A story from Tanga at Mwembe Basha, an area with a large mango tree, linked wazee to people being "eaten a lot"—"and it occurs mostly to men"—after becoming "suddenly tired" as they passed by "even if you try to guard against it." "It is said," the story continues, "that there are some elders up on the mountain, and this is their doing—their sorcery."[77] These same elders caused traffic police watching the road to fight each other over nothing. "Only later did they recognize that strange things happen at this place."[78] At other times, these old men asked for lifts. "There's a part of Shinyanga where a driver met an elder who asked for a lift. The assistant said, we don't take people. Now every time they go to the bathroom, they meet this elder whom they did not give a ride, but when they get back in the car, they don't see him. When they go forward and stop and look back, they see the man on the road below them saying, 'Thank you, I arrived. Continue with your journey.'"[79] Drivers tell a similar story between Tanga and Handeni after refusing an mzee (elder) transport. But instead of hitching a ride, as in the previous story, the elder alters the materiality of road infrastructure as they choose between a wet and a dry route. "When they followed the dry way, they think it is better, but, amazingly, the car refuses to go and acts stuck as if it is in mud. They call their boss on the phone. He comes, but every time they try to move it, it becomes more stuck. It's there up to today."[80]

Because wazee acted as the gatekeepers of road sections, sometimes playing with road materialities and authorities (including traffic officers) and at other times eating those who passed by, drivers did not have a single strategy for dealing with them. Some claimed safe passage ensued if drivers avoided eye contact; others said they had to be dealt with through some kind of offering.[81] Unlike for women and livestock standing on or near roads, I never heard a story that involved running over wazee. On the contrary, elders' advice could help produce mobility, as the driver of a Scania truck recalled:

> From Mpanda there is an area called Katavi after the name of a mountain. You can go there with your car, but it will refuse to go up the mountain if you are carrying something that isn't allowed by the spirits [mizimu] who guard the mountain. One time I was carrying manure from Mashamu to Dar es Salaam. When I arrived at the mountain, the car refused to go. So then there's these old men who tell us, "Hey, you guys, you're carrying cow manure. Dump it, and you'll go right up." So we unloaded the manure, and the truck worked again.[82]

In spite of losing his cargo, the driver "survives" with his vehicle and body intact to drive another day. The old men, for their part, mediated between the spirits and drivers by offering a spirit-based mechanical solution to the vehicle's immobility even as they provided cow manure for a nearby community.[83]

Aspirational young men seeing women, livestock, and elders on the road provides an expected, if not cliché, set of characters in tales of masculine social mobility. Accumulating livestock and marrying a wife or wives, and likely using the former to do the latter, have long been critical to the passage of men from the category of youth to adult.[84] In many cases, elders stood in the way of this passage by attempting to control resources, including livestock, as well as rituals such as circumcision and marriage through which young men could claim status as senior.[85] For this very reason, drivers' instruction to run over and through women and livestock, the very resources through which they could make claims on mobility and status, suggests a cautionary logic in these tales. So, too, does the contradictory role of elders. Feared and visible for their meddling, they nevertheless play a mediating role that salvages automobility when the unexpected occurs. In these scenarios, the driver does not act as a machinic dume boasting an industrial masculinity that is clearly distinct from that of previous historical epochs but rather heeds the demands and advice of wazee whose infrastructural assemblage—trees, mountains, and access to spirits—trumps the hard materiality of automobility.[86] Here the driver-coward inverts long-held expectations of hegemonic masculinity, eschewing the most obvious symbols of social mobility while paying respect to those who often stood in the way of young men's power.

Drivers did not share these stories as fodder for academic thick description but because cha ajabu and miujiza stories defied explanation, came with dire consequences, and thus stuck with men who recognized that they moved across landscapes they neither comprehended completely nor controlled.[87] Just as a tire could blow or an engine overheat, elders in trees could stop cars, women could change roads, and mountains could refuse mechanized passage. In this context, the "it is said" (*inasemekana*) of cha ajabu stories informed a logic of risk through which drivers established and mediated various forms of vulnerability on roads, sometimes even identifying particular places and structures where danger was densest. Contrary to the images of the dume, whose muscular body and place within a machine granted social mobility and status as one of the primary actors in national discourses of movement, stories about the unexplainable and about known unknowns reminded drivers that they passed through and likely slept in roadside places where their connection to a machine did not connote power or well-being.

Only one former driver called them "just stories" and told me to forget them—this after giving a long interview about them. But most drivers, even those who questioned their own experiences, saw no ontological friction between automobile movement and the notion that spirits could play an active role in their mobile lives.[88] Even the driver who dismissed cha ajabu as "just stories" knew what to do if they occurred and had listened to them carefully enough over his career to provide one of the widest set of stories I heard. He had since changed his mind about their efficacy, but his younger self knew that roads and what dwelled in and around them did not care what he believed or consider his machine powerful. A successful "search for blessing" required an ability to accumulate wealth by navigating regional automobilities in which risk to a driver's body and vehicle extended to his family's and his future status, a reality that turned his vehicular violence toward women and livestock phantoms into an act of wisdom that showed a driver had matured—that he was thinking not only about his immediate well-being but about a possible future for his family and home.[89]

Combined with the aforementioned attention to road materialities and speed, cha ajabu experiences helped create a "risk culture" among male drivers during the first two decades of independence. Ulrich Beck argues that risk culture does not require the actual presence of danger but rather rests on an anticipation that something could happen in the future that merits preparation and thought at a present moment. The "culture" part comes when a number of individuals pool their experiences and responses into an organized set of rules that prescribes proper behavior in order to sustain survival in a context of near-constant danger.[90] Becoming a man on the road, even the type of muscular dume pictured in advertisements, did not exclude fear, vulnerability, or care. Indeed, such manly technological identities relied on qualities normally associated with postcolonial femininity because a "driver," unlike "not a driver," used transport networks to build lives as settled, respectable men over decades of road travel. This culture of risk provided a foundation for drivers to protect themselves on the road as automobility grew in the first decades of independence. After the mid-1970s, it also provided a mechanism through which drivers and their communities created socialist bonds in difficult times.[91]

THE MEANS OF DISTRIBUTION: DRIVERS, PASSENGERS, AND ECONOMIC EMERGENCY FROM THE ROAD

After the mid-1970s, drivers became a go-to source for household commodities for Tanzanian citizens.[92] Regional Trading Centers (RTCs) and Cooperative Stores (*Maduka ya Ushirika*) rationed household staples such as sugar, salt, corn, toothpaste, and soap. And the stores themselves faced shortages as the State Trading Corporation, the parastatal responsible for distribution (*usambazaji*), struggled to procure and move basic goods— something it admitted in its magazine in 1970.[93] Beyond UDA's disheartening foleni in Dar es Salaam, citizens around the country complained about waiting in foleni at RTCs for hours only to receive much less salt, soap, flour, or cloth than they required, or none at all.[94] Friends who grew up during this era told me, "You looked for a driver" because they were the most reliable source of basic goods; Emily Callaci notes that they even distributed novels.[95] One study estimates that this second economy, often overlooked in macroeconomic analyses, grew from 6.6 percent of the gross domestic product in 1975 to 31.4 percent in 1986. Moreover, a whopping 85 percent of families used unofficial economies to meet basic household needs.[96]

But months into my research, I had little to show from drivers themselves about what friends described as a quotidian act of socialism in the late 1970s and early 1980s. The few drivers who provided fantastic narratives about navigating checkpoints and distributing goods for desperate families looked like anomalies until a taxi driver, Idrissa, who later became a research assistant, asserted that any driver who denied selling on the side had to be lying. Idrissa had witnessed it himself as a child, and he had heard drivers talk about it among themselves. He claimed it was one of the worst-kept secrets of the later years of ujamaa. We tested his hunch in Dar es Salaam, Tabora, and Kigoma. We met with drivers for a first interview, in which most denied anything associated with magendo. We said goodbye but continued to reach out through phone and text conversations. Whether the next day or the next week, most of these drivers eventually admitted they had participated in acts that the government could have seen as an economic crime. They initially lied out of uncertainty about telling their stories to an unknown American researcher. Most agreed to another interview because, as Idrissa and others had believed, their actions were open secrets. Some asked for private audiences at their homes. But others told these stories in crowded taxi stands near bus depots.

This section uses these follow-up interviews to establish the details and logic of automobile exchange during the latter years of African socialism as drivers became the socialist means of distribution for many citizens. It uses twenty anonymized interviews conducted in Dar es Salaam, Morogoro, Tabora, and Kigoma.[97] Following Basil Owomero and arguments from the drivers themselves, I do not use state-based categories of licit and illicit economic activity but rather center a vernacular language of economic emergency based in need, family, giving, and mutual compassion—all core elements of ujamaa's humanism.[98] As James Ferguson writes in *Give a Man a Fish: Reflections on the New Politics of Distribution*, groups "largely excluded from *any* significant role in the system of production, may often be found engaged in tasks whose fundamental purpose is not to produce goods at all but to engineer distributions of goods produced elsewhere by making claims on the resources of others."[99] What he calls the "labor of distribution," I term the *means of distribution*. As the state lost its ability to both produce and distribute basic goods—and thereby live up to its claims that the government acted as "tools" of development—individuals who had or could find the means to move found themselves at the center of economic and technological debates about which forms of distribution constituted ujamaa in uncertain times.

Driver distribution networks worked as follows: long-haul truckers who visited the Republic of Congo (later, Zaire), Burundi, Rwanda, Uganda, Zambia, and Kenya procured items simply by shopping and bringing them across the border. Truckers had done this since the first days of independence. As the availability of goods worsened in the latter half of the 1970s, citizens began to ask drivers for items at truck stations, on the edge of villages, or even in hostels. "Everyone knew drivers had things, they just had to be discrete [*kisirisiri*] about approaching you. Then you give it to them on the side [*pembeni*]." As drivers and driving became associated with goods, regional truckers—that is, those who rarely crossed international borders—started to procure and move goods domestically. Some obtained large quantities of salt, sugar, and maize at RTCs and government-sponsored stores by getting extra ration cards that they could produce if questioned about their loads. They picked up the goods at night and transported them to places of need where staples fetched higher prices. For those willing to cross borders, rice and corn shortages in Kenya and Zambia, for example, provided opportunities to make a large profit when domestic supplies were adequate. The state responded by suspending the use of these cards and by placing roadblocks (*vizuizui*) on domestic routes to inspect cargo.

Drivers and passengers had several strategies for passing roadblocks. They placed small quantities of food—such as salt and sugar—and clothes under their seats. Larger quantities had to be hidden in the cargo and moved at night. Large sacks of corn and rice provided the perfect disguise for hiding T-shirts and sacks of sugar, salt, or soap. So did *dagaa*, a dried fish moved in bulk from the lakes of western Tanzania toward the coast. "You put whatever you are moving below," one driver described, "and you top it off with dagaa. The smell is strong, and no one is going to search through it." Despite taking great care to hide items, drivers also downplayed the threat posed by police and border patrol agents. To avoid a search, drivers recalled, they greeted police officers or the border patrol and discreetly passed them money. The amount depended on the size or content of the cargo, ranging from ten shillings to a thousand shillings, according to my interviews. One recalled the price of passage through two roadblocks between Dar es Salaam and Chalinze as ten shillings in the late 1960s. Another credited a social network he had put in place for years as a driver. He "never had a problem on the road" transporting used clothes, girls' skirts, and women's wear from Kigoma to Arusha: "Before I started this business, I had lots of friends along the way. You give them some money or a beer, and there: you have a friend."

If drivers could not avoid a search, bargaining ensued over the amount of illicit cargo to hand over. "Without a permit [*kibali*], you can't pass [a roadblock]. You can either take the stuff out for inspection, or you give him money [*toa hela*]," a man said who moved rice between Dar es Salaam and Nairobi in the mid- to late 1970s. Getting the loads out of the country posed risks but was also not uncommon: "You give a thousand shillings. In those days, that was a lot. Even five hundred or six hundred is enough." For goods like soap and sugar, he added, "If they take the loads out of the back, they take some for themselves and then give permission" to go. Then he went to Nairobi and sold the produce in a "free market" (*biashara huru*).

On trips southwest from Morogoro to Iringa and Mbeya, the owner of the truck driven by Michael Menze simply told him, "There is someone on the way you'll pick up with magendo goods. They don't have a license [to sell goods]." After picking up this "someone" and his goods, Menze navigated cross-district transporting as follows: "From district to district there is always a roadblock. So you get caught. . . . They come and say, 'Kibali' [a trading license]. We don't have one. 'Come, let's talk' [*njoo, tuzungumze*]. The businessman goes to the side and gives anything [*chochote*], that is, money, and they open the gate." Menze repeated this process at Korogwe and then by nightfall at Chalinze. At other times, the trader simply gave the driver money to give at each roadblock. For a truck full of contraband items, Menze said the total amount could be as much as five thousand to ten thousand shillings per journey—upward of $1,000 during the late 1970s. Other drivers also downplayed the danger of cross-district and cross-border roadblocks. One who regularly brought goods back from Kenya under his seat said sugar, salt, and other daily items offered little risk even if a driver was caught at a roadblock. "If you have really bad luck, the government nationalizes everything. But this didn't happen very often." Police officers needed these same items for their own homes, he said.

As these oral histories of police encounters evidence, exchanges were grounded in a language of shared economic struggle. Those seeking goods said, "We have a problem" or "Help me and I'll help you" ("nisaidie nikusaidie") to signal their interest. Things not distributed along the route, or given to a truck owner, were taken home, where drivers and families exchanged goods by word of mouth. They communicated availability through everyday conversations among neighbors about shortages. If someone lacked an item, "you simply say we have that at home. Come on over. Then they come to your house. . . . [But] once you're known [by police], you have to stop." Most exchanges took place at night, a risk because "the police worked at night, not during the day" to control suspected magendo. For this reason, some wives of drivers controlled the distribution, and they legitimized evening exchanges as family visits to homes.

Because drivers could easily connect the distribution of household goods to the sustenance of a socialist family, their decisions to sell other items, such as petroleum, offer more insight into the nature of this process and their views of ujamaa's economy. Before their journeys, offices and companies allotted drivers gas; as long as they went and returned as required, owners asked few questions about how they spent their money. Selling small amounts of fuel to car owners and gas stations on their journeys—called "hitting the snake" (*kupiga nyoka*), after the hose needed to suck petrol out of a gas tank—helped supplement drivers' salaries.[100] The men who did this said it carried minimal risk and that they needed to do so due to low salaries and the increases to the cost of living in the 1970s and early 1980s. Some government drivers even coordinated their activities with colleagues. With the assistance of civil servants who provided official vouchers for petroleum, drivers obtained gasoline at government pumps; they sold it on the road and shared their earnings with the civil servant and the pump attendant.

Consider the narrative of a policeman in Tabora who escorted political figures, including President Nyerere. During our first interview, he vehemently denied selling gasoline, but later in the week, I asked him for the "real" (*halisi*) story:

> DRIVER: First, just let me say that our salaries weren't enough. When we got a trip, the bosses got and arranged everything, not the drivers. Now about the petrol: when we got a trip, we were allocated a bunch of petroleum, but normal citizens were getting nothing; private car owners didn't have any. So you get to a place where you are sleeping for the night. During the evening, people come to you and say, "We have a problem. We don't have any fuel. Can you give us ten to fifteen liters?" So you have empty pockets, but you have just received an opportunity [*riziki*: literally, blessing]—no one is around, and the boss is sleeping in a nice house. Our salary was low, and our necessities high. So we sold the petrol. We received 100, 150, or 200 liters for a trip. So you look at your journey and figure out you will use only seventy liters. That means thirty to seventy are extra (in English); so you take a little for your own needs [*kujipongeza*—literally, "to congratulate oneself"]. But you never took so much that you would arrive with an empty tank; otherwise, they would ask, "What have you been doing with the car?"
>
> JG: Where did you sell it?

DRIVER: Just as you would suspect. Any village you go to will have a fuel shortage. At this point you don't know to whom you will sell. Sometimes two or three people would come to you, and you would end up selling to them. You know, the big men are helping themselves to good food and beer over there, and you can't even get a soda. As they sit and drink, you do your thing.

JG: How much did you sell for?

DRIVER: This changed depending on availability. When there was a huge shortage, you could get a high price. But when there wasn't, you would just sell for a normal price. Just so you can help yourself and get a soda.

IDRISSA: Was this normal? Were there lots of drivers who did this or just a few?

DRIVER: Completely, so much so that we drivers would talk among ourselves and ask, "How many liters do you have 'extra' [in English]? 'I got forty.' 'Okay, some guy is coming, what do you say?' So you give him three or four liters. It wasn't just me; it was a normal thing. And those days a driver who didn't know how to sell petrol was not a driver. I'm not going to hide this: every driver, whether in the government or a parastatal, did this.

Neither drivers nor their families became rich. But their ability to access and distribute goods through transnational movement made them increasingly important technological actors in a national economy that still required distributional labor. In fact, the minority of drivers willing to transport large amounts of contraband items for traders and vehicle owners said crackdowns like the vizuizui had the unintended result of placing drivers in a desirable position vis-à-vis the truck owner (*tajiri*—a wealthy person) and the person selling goods for the first time. Drivers usually received bonuses and gifts from the owner of the cargo they transported but only a small wage from the vehicle owner—if anything at all. Widespread shortages altered this relationship as car owners tried to capitalize on scarcity through drivers' willingness and skill at negotiating roadblocks and borders. "Someone can tell you, 'My goods are in a certain place,'" one driver explained. Playing middleman between the seller and the truck owner, the driver then agrees with the tajiri on the use of the vehicle and receives a bonus from the seller upon delivery. A driver who moved goods across the Kenyan border provided a similar description of driver-owner relationships: "The tajiri gives you money for the trip and money for your pocket—he has to win you over [*kubembeleza*]" because of the risk. "Then you load the clothes or whatever else, and then you put in the magendo." If caught, drivers tried to blame both other parties.

Interlocutors linked these actions to familial security and social mobility, as an oral history told among drivers in Morogoro illustrates. A driver and his boss were on the road to Dar es Salaam with a load of elephant tusks when their truck broke down. Normally, a driver with illegal goods negotiated for passage with police officers he knew and trusted at a checkpoint, but a broken-down vehicle full of contraband goods was too difficult for a police officer to let go. For this reason, the driver told his owner to flee, adding that he would claim the ivory as his own and take the punishment. He asked only that the owner look after his family. After three years in jail, the man returned to Morogoro to find his family living comfortably in their own house, and he subsequently received a compensation that he used to buy trucks for his own business. Most drivers distanced themselves from this explicit type of magendo (a term they would use in this situation) or mentioned regret for their roles in it. But the story suggests that for some young men trying to build their lives, truck-owning patrons provided steadier social and technological networks than the state for building social security in a difficult time. Drivers who knew this story well noted that this individual paid for his crime—as a citizen must—while caring for his family in a unique way.

Men, though the vast majority of drivers, did not monopolize these movements or exchanges. As passengers, women used buses and hitch-hiking to acquire goods to sell out of their homes and at regional markets. The key to their mobility was a network of buses put in place by the government, known as KAMATA (Kampuni ya Mabasi ya Taifa [National Bus Company]), and regional buses owned by local cooperatives and parastatals. These allowed women to travel to places with free markets (*biashara huru*) such as Kenya and Zambia, where they procured goods and packed them into their suitcases. Before they reached the Tanzanian border, they gave the driver money for safely navigating any checkpoints. Others worked within domestic markets. In 1961 Eliza Malewa, a recently widowed woman living in Kigoma, sold the gold jewelry given to her as a wedding gift in order to buy large quantities of cloth from a factory in Mwanza, a city on Lake Victoria eighteen hours away by bus. From Mwanza, she traveled across the country to her uncle's home near Kariakoo, the central market in Dar es Salaam, where she stayed until she was out of cloth. In Kigoma, Rehema Mwalongo, recently divorced, met canoes bringing used clothes across Lake Tanganyika from Burundi and then distributed the clothes at a bus stop to drivers and passengers, who took them to markets where access to external goods was limited. These women described travel as an important strategy for creating social security at home as they matured and navigated social and economic uncertainty. Widowed and divorced, respectively, Malewa and Mwalongo took to the road to create an economic foundation they could use for the rest of their lives—often as capital (*mtaji*) for starting a local business.

At least one married couple viewed women's mobility as a way to increase their financial security in difficult times. Desta Juma, who identified herself as a farmer in Tabora, convinced her husband that the business opportunities opened through travel were mutually beneficial. At first, she gave all her earnings to her husband, but she later began to hide portions of her earnings in tin cups around the house for her own use. This type of masking could also characterize relationships among neighbors who traveled together. Zenabu Mkomwa, who told her oral history among some of her grandchildren, surprised the small audience when she revealed that she had used an alias while traveling. She drew a hard distinction between appreciating the companionship of traveling together and having those same individuals know where one lived and what one did with one's resources.

Over a six-month period from 1982 to 1983, the government tried to squash the saboteur economies it partially blamed for the economic decline. Nyerere ended the campaign by placing such saboteurs outside of the socialist family.[101] He, the party, and the state did so not just by establishing that illegal acts had occurred or did occur—hardly a contentious topic—but also by offering an unambiguous moral vision of commodity directionality, that is, of the relationship between economic health and things going out or coming into the nation. That vision followed this pattern: criminals, an *Nchi Yetu* article charged, were illegally exporting things that could sustain Tanzanian families, including corn, beans, cooking oil, sugar, all forms of clothes (including cloth diapers and school uniforms), and glasses, as well as commodity items that undercut the nation's economy, including tires and radios manufactured in Tanzania, sheep- and goatskins, rhino horns, and elephant tusks. The latter implicated magendo in poaching. As these valuable items left, often through the Tanzania-Kenya border, khat, a popular and denigrated East African stimulant, entered. In sum, magendo drained Tanzania of the fruits of national labor, making the pursuit of familyhood all but impossible, while offering, in return, an addictive stimulant. This source thus tied magendo to a thoroughly destructive process of regional dependency: Tanzanians produced for foreign African markets and got khat in return.[102]

Still, official definitions of anti-ujamaa economic behavior remained opaque. Outside of the clearer examples that have been mentioned— transporting tusks or, to a lesser extent, moving goods from RTCs or selling motor oil—individuals did not always know whether their actions crossed a political line distinguishing socialism from antisocialism, even when they likely crossed a legal line. Some state sources expressed wariness about prosecuting citizens for gaining access to basic goods. Indeed, most speeches and jail sentences focused on a classic purge figure of socialism: the kulak who turned state enterprises into an opportunity for personal wealth.[103] Other sources, including the unabashedly moralizing *Nchi Yetu* article above, tacked between the specific, and quite obvious, examples of socialist immorality—such as selling rhinoceros horns and elephant tusks—and much vaguer, but no less frequent, assertions about police confiscating "bags" and "sacks" of valuable goods. In the latter case, the police reported the value of the items confiscated, but the contents remained a mystery—an eerie silence in public reports that established moral clarity by communicating which commodity had moved and what its directionality of movement was.[104] Indeed, those who sold items for any extended period feared being swept up into this broader, vaguer category of magendo even when they only sold cigarettes and did not consider this an immoral activity. One man stopped doing this after two years for fear he might appear to the police as a potential state competitor, a category associated with sabotage. During a period when having cigarettes, salt, or a shirt could be read as treason, individuals struggled to clearly read the distinctions between sabotage and national familyhood.[105] The result was a silent (*bubu*) economy that was easily found and known but that did not advertise itself, lest a misreading occur.

That silence disappeared in the oral histories I heard, as drivers and traders forcefully pushed back against any characterization of their actions as economic crimes. "People like us can't be saboteurs; you have to have a lot of money to be a saboteur. We were just workers. And because of how bad things were, we were helping citizens," one driver remarked, aligning with Judith Scheele's term "licit smuggling."[106] "It helped citizens because there was nothing to buy," another added, "but the 'business of magendo' [*biashara ya magendo*] was available." One driver called it a "blessing." In addition to "selling" (*mauzo*) goods, they "exchanged" (*kubadilishiana*) items, "helped one another" (*kusaidiana*), navigated and helped avoid "poverty" (umaskini), or engaged in "small" activities or business (*shughuli ndogondogo* and *biashara ndogondogo*) that fit neatly into broader understandings of ujamaa. In this sense, drivers and passengers legitimized distributive activities by linking them to important processes of social reproduction, including food for children and soap for cleaning, clothes for school and weddings, and commodities of style and status like, cigarettes and stylish clothes.[107] "Nyerere used to tell us to tighten our work belts, but we couldn't even buy clothes," one man recalled. To get "cents to use," he drove to Mwanza Textile Factory to secretly purchase *kitenge* and *khanga*, two popular types of cloth used for a variety of everyday activities, and then sold them for nearly double the price out of his home. He sold the cloth for only one year because of the risk of imprisonment.

The distinction between magendo as a destructive national act and the distribution and exchange of goods as a personal and familial strategy for security revolved around both the rationale for and scale of what one had and did. Drivers did it, they said repeatedly, because they needed to and because they could. "You do it," one driver said, "so that you don't have to rely on the tajiri." "You have transport and money," another explained. "If you get a chance [chance originally in English], you have to do it [*lazima ufanye*] because it will give you a chance to live well." A driver for the government health ministries who siphoned gas recalled, "You had to because your salary wasn't sufficient." His actions did not constitute magendo or sabotage (*kuhujumu*), he argued, because they came after a period of price increases known as *mwendo wa kuruka* (literally, "the speed of jumping"). Though sufficient in previous years, his government salary did not keep up with the speed of inflation and the needs of home. And shortages at cooperatives left citizens no choices, one driver argued. "A cooperative store is about cooperating to open our own store. But your [government] stores died suspiciously [*kiujanjaujanja*] because certain people profited at the expense of the people." Drivers and passengers thus recognized that state definitions of magendo included items they carried and exchanged, while also refusing to accept that meeting needs with those goods constituted economic sabotage: a high crime capable of impacting the nation's bottom line. "We drivers were just used [*kutumiwa*]; it was the rich who drove magendo." Another defined *wahujumu*, or saboteurs, as those with "lots of money. A driver can't be *mhujumu*," he stressed, "because he doesn't own enough; he's just a worker [*mfanyakazi*]."[108] One answered my questions about driver networks by anchoring magendo, a term he used, in the colonial period, and thus to actions that had been a legitimate part of driving culture long before concerns about national sabotage.[109]

Drivers did not seek to become the means, or tools (*vyombo*), of distribution for Tanzanian citizens, nor did they seek or enjoy the economic conditions that led to this position. But their roles and logic highlight alternative configurations of ujamaa based not only on innovations within the contexts of economic emergency but also on the details of socialist ideology itself. Distribution, not production, distinguished a socialist from a capitalist society, Nyerere said. With socialism as "essentially distributive" as long as drivers and passengers moved, distributed, and did not become tajiri themselves—thereby owning the means of production and distribution—providing families with what they needed and creating self-reliance for themselves fell well within their, and many other, understandings of socialism.[110] Claiming a place within such a distributional ujamaa, or at least defending departures from the top-down "distribution revolution" that the State Trading Corporation envisioned, was risky but not ideologically difficult. Many drivers and passengers saw their actions as reconstituting networks in a time when economies and technologies did not work as well as anyone had hoped because government vyombo had neither the means of production nor the means of distribution to do so. As Ferguson observes, providing a sociotechnical alternative for distribution at a time of crisis, then, "was less about creating new goods and services than about raising the denominator in a distributional process."[111] Indeed, the minister of communications and transport, A. H. Jamal, suggested that regions deal with shortages by having "*all* those who deal with transport . . . put their efforts together pertaining to ideas, money, and planning" (emphasis mine).[112]

The actions of both drivers and passengers, as well as Jamal's statement, recall Laura Fair's observation that the "road leading to socialist development was never definitively mapped out" for most of the nation's population.[113] Like the road journeys themselves, an actually existing ujamaa took twists and turns, hit unexpected bumps, slowed and sped up, had happy and relieving arrivals at destinations, as well as frustrating breakdowns. But rather than anticipating the need for ujamaa's end and the arrival of privatized markets and rather than being defined as solely physical, social, and political risk, road travel during ujamaa created forms of socialist familyhood when official mechanisms struggled to do so. This raises a question: if men's and women's mobile bodies could be part of restorative circulations of familyhood, why has motor travel been so thoroughly linked with destruction, risk, and death?

RISK WITHOUT BLESSING: AUTOMOBILITY AS FAILED MODERNIZATION AND THE REASSEMBLED DRIVER

This final section examines how public portrayals of motor mobilities turned the combination of the Tanzanian man, travel, and automobile into an assemblage of death and decline beginning in the late 1970s. Up to this point, road travel attracted little public attention outside of large construction projects, insurance-sponsored road-safety weeks, and some calls from citizens to focus more attention on road safety. While there was a sense that Tanzania's road culture could be improved, road mobilities were not connected to, let alone a cause for, national scale catastrophe. Total recorded road accidents and deaths reduced between 1975 and 1979 and rose only slightly over the next decade.[114] But as economic and political fortunes soured after the mid-1970s, roads gained new clout not as technologies of desirable circulation but as tools of public commentary to discuss uncertainty and decline, even for people who did not travel on them. As the circulatory veins of the national body, roads connected settled communities to faraway places and uninhabited areas and therefore brought the unknown and uncontrollable, as Brad Weiss shows for Haya communities.[115] Mobilities some associated with magendo initiated this process in the mid-1970s by challenging the state's monopoly on both distribution and the technologies facilitating it. By associating transport exclusively with risk, two other events, both connected to magendo, turned road travel into a national and international technological metaphor for failed modernization through the misuse of tools other societies had supposedly used to create social and political health.

First, on April 24, 1984, Prime Minister Edward Moringe Sokoine died in a car crash after a Land Rover hit his government sedan head-on on the hilly roads outside of Morogoro. A fierce opponent of saboteur economies who was considered by many to be Nyerere's successor, Sokoine had just delivered an ultimatum to the National Assembly in Dodoma about economic mismanagement that some believed would have led to the largest government shake-up in years. Sokoine's last words to the ministers— "Tutakutana Dar es Salaam" ("We will meet in Dar es Salaam")—figured prominently in rumors that his death was not an accident but had been coordinated by a wealthy stratum of Tanzanian society that had grown rich off of socialism's demise. Details of the accident fueled these suspicions. The driver of the offending vehicle lacked a license and was a member of the antiapartheid African National Congress, which lived and trained in camps nearby.[116] The accident also required that a vehicle pull onto the road after the lead motorcycles of Sokoine's convoy had already passed, not only cautioning bystanders to stay put but also alerting them to the imminent passing of a politically powerful figure.

When Nyerere, who was commonly called Mwalimu (teacher) privately received Sokoine's body at the statehouse, the president's brother, Joseph, "broke down and wailed," before saying to his brother, "Mwalimu, have you no security? Your prime minister dies in a road accident?" In a radio address that night, Mwalimu himself refused to dismiss rumors about Sokoine's death by remarking to a national audience, "Let's believe it is an accident."[117] But his brother's wording—"have you no security?,"—implying that the state did not control the national infrastructure—better captured the sense of danger road mobilities increasingly evoked. If a prime minister traveling in a caravan died, then who could be safe?

A couple of years later, epidemiological research on HIV/AIDS turned roads from spaces of economic sabotage and political chaos into technologies of mass death. As national and international officials scrambled to find solutions to East Africa's HIV/AIDS epidemic in the mid-1980s, they wanted to explain how and why a virus (HIV-1) from west-central Africa first became an epidemic nearly two thousand miles from its origin.[118] Researchers' perception of magendo economies shaped the resulting epidemiological narrative. In the context of economic hardship, researchers approached sex work not only as a transaction but also as the specific outgrowth of shortages in goods, employment, and money. They therefore assumed it occurred most often at rest stops or the distribution sites in transport networks. As a result, this literature argued, groups who moved within regional distribution networks formed relationships based on the exchange of sex for goods or money at transit points before unwittingly carrying HIV back to their own families and communities. Originally theorized in Peter Piot and colleagues' work in Zaire, this process was described succinctly in a 1991 article in *AIDS and Society*: "Most of the goods distributed throughout East Africa are transported by truck. Truck stops along these well-traveled routes offer rest and relaxation for the truckers which often translates into the purchase of sex."[119] Researchers considered African drivers, like gay men in the United States, "'the sort of people who get this illness.'"[120] Indeed, Piot later wrote in his memoir, "In many places HIV mainly affects gay men, or truck drivers, or drug users."[121]

Research conducted between 1986 and 1992 provided epidemiologists with the evidence to characterize long-distance trucking in East Africa as a "portal of entry for the AIDS virus to and from African communities," on the one hand, and a high-risk activity on par with homosexuality, prostitution, and drug use, on the other. One found that 40 percent of drivers ($n = 45$) and 23 percent of turnboys ($n = 23$) who passed through an unnamed "transport depot" in Kampala tested positive for HIV-1; the study also found *Treponema pallidum* antibodies suggestive of syphilis in over sixty percent of drivers and over a quarter of turnboys. Research at Tanzanian truck stops and "nearby communities" in 1992 provided similar conclusions. Nearly 13 percent of truckers tested positive for HIV-1, while the station itself had 27 percent and 56 percent infection rates for men and women, respectively.[122]

Critically, none of these studies doubted Tanzania's need for automobility. Road, car, and station feature in these publications as objective technologies of movement that facilitate economic growth. When HIV became part of these circulations, the technologies themselves (car, road, and station) escaped critique even as a transnational African masculine culture of driving drove arguments about HIV-1's spread.[123] Survey questions about drivers' sexual "knowledge, attitude, and practices" (KAP) suggested that drivers either had not yet recognized their culpability in the spread of HIV-1 or refused to address it through changed behavior. Nearly 89 percent ($n = 18$) of seropositive drivers had never used condoms; the same applied for 100 percent of turnboys ($n = 6$). Similarly, 96 and 82 percent of seronegative drivers and turnboys respectively had never worn a condom. While nearly half of both groups reported over fifty sexual partners, only half described their activity as high risk.[124]

Through KAP, researchers distinguished among the mobile sexual practices of men and women in a context of economic uncertainty. According to reports, "itinerant market women" and "barmaids" engaged in casual sex and movement, in the case of the former, to "supplement" incomes. Women's sexual vulnerability and mobility stemmed from economic need in a period of crisis. But the same did not apply to drivers. Researchers pointed to their unique access to consumer goods (indeed, HIV shared a name with a shirt style from Burundi known as Julianna, which was distributed almost exclusively by drivers), their steady salary, and their ability to partake in magendo economies, sometimes even trading goods for sex.[125] Drivers had casual sex not out of economic need, these reports asserted, but because their occupation took them away from home for long periods. Furthermore, though researchers did not use the word *custom* or *tradition*, they described a monolithic culture of African masculinity that sanctioned men's rampant, and newly mobilized, promiscuity. Because drivers hailed from nations across east and central Africa, researchers did not associate their KAP with a particular national or ethnic origin but with a gendered culture of movement and power across eastern, central, and southern Africa.[126] Two earlier studies included men that identified as Tanzanian.[127]

In 1991 a team of national and expatriate researchers with the Truck Drivers AIDS Intervention Project aimed to reshape this driver masculinity. The project declared that "the most efficient way to reduce the spread of HIV is for those at greatest risk to modify their sexual behavior." It trained petrol pump attendants, barmaids, and prostitutes at trucking stations in Tanzania to educate drivers through their daily itineraries. Flora Myula, a barmaid at Ndiuka near Iringa, said, "We serve them beer, and when they start making advances, then we arm ourselves with our education tools and discuss with them all facets of the pandemic and how it can be avoided." In addition to 3,000 stickers, workers distributed 325,000 condoms, 15,000 condom instructions, and 10,000 posters in six months.[128] If he carried a message on his truck and condoms in his pocket, a driver's spatial agency and sexual privilege moved from a high-risk sexual activity that exploited women's economic vulnerability and destroyed families on a transnational scale to an acceptable technological act as long as he consistently used a condom. In this way, public health campaigns aimed to reassemble male driving subjects.[129]

Given the technologies at play in this narrative—including road, car, and the oil needed to move the vehicle and driver through space—the condom, a thin, flexible sheet of latex, performs an incredible amount of work creating sanctioned male African mobilities. Condoms did nothing to address the structural economic foundation of epidemiological narratives that cast "barmaids" and "itinerant market women" as victims of drivers' sexual and economic privilege. But they safeguarded the transactional relationships that emerged out of economic difficulties while providing a new embodied assemblage of acceptable African male automobility in which condoms mediated acts of intimacy and exchange. Given African drivers' KAP and their seeming refusal to change them, the authorities concluded that nonepidemic male automobility required covered penises to stop men's HIV-contaminated semen from infecting not only barmaids but also homes throughout the country. Simultaneously, such interventions normalized the mobile dume, as long as his penis was covered, in ways that conflicted with drivers' own understandings about risk and well-being on the road.

Drivers with whom I talked provided a different narrative of HIV-1's emergence. Though acknowledging their colleagues' role in the pandemic and sometimes counting dead colleagues on their fingers in interviews, they emphasized the newness of the virus itself, not the combination of East African masculinity and motorized technologies, as the historical rupture that made AIDS a pandemic.[130] Because HIV not only was unknown but also took several years to manifest, they argue, drivers unwittingly spread the virus between the late 1970s and the mid-1980s, when knowledge of it became public. Those still alive consider reckless their deceased friends who refused to believe the AIDS campaigns of the early 1990s. Drivers spoke of a period of uncertainty in public health messages before asserting an acceptance of condom use. But they also consider those unlucky who contracted and spread HIV-1 during the 1970s and much of the 1980s, before the virus's existence was known and when its causality was still a hypothesis, as Steven Epstein shows for the United States.[131] Finally, death, though a harsh consequence for drivers and assistants who could not have known about HIV, was also an accepted part of road landscapes that were made up of known and unknown risks and that, as a consequence, called for their users to be cowards.[132]

These events have helped create an impression not only that Tanzanian motor travel is uniquely destructive but also that this status stems from the dissonance between African cultures and the dictates of automobility. But in the car's wider history, Tanzania's socialist period fits a larger pattern: risk, death, destruction, and debates about proper movement are one of the key features of twentieth-century histories of motoring around the world.[133] "In risk societies," the late Ulrich Beck writes of a North American and European context, "the consequences and success of modernization become an issue with the speed and radicality of processes of modernization."[134] Here the consequences of something like automobility do not stem from the supposed dissonance between tradition and modernity—that is, from the failure of traditional cultures to become fully modern, as epidemiologists intimated—but from the success of modernization itself as it spreads, becoming a more integral part of societies. In Beck's terms, the types of risk and death associated with ujamaa's failure do not evidence absent skills or rampant misuse, as epidemiological narratives suggest, or lack of control, as Joseph Nyerere described roads after Sokoine's death, but rather a form of maendeleo forged by users on the nation's roads through gendered cultures of adulthood, movement, and home. The point is not that the latter removed the risks of motor travel, but that they provide insights into the reasons individuals took such risks; into how they identified and mediated danger; and into how they built communities to and by navigating other forms of risks (including economic instability) while doing so.

Instead of being a technology of decline, a range of automobiles that included buses, lorries, and long-haul trucks offered actually existing tools of socialist distribution that allowed everyday economic and technological actors to make decisions about a critical act of ujamaa. Even as the official form of familyhood became less tenable, networks of exchange that connected homes, roads, and even factories allowed car users to address social insecurity and, in a handful of cases, to thrive because of their social location in infrastructures of movement. Within limits, it also allowed users to redefine what counted as familyhood during and through their travels. Beyond their contributions to understanding the latter years of socialism, these forms of motorized movement and sociality provide a crucial historical context for understanding motoring's growth after the end of ujamaa. Open borders made many more used vehicles available for purchase after 1985 and thus helped usher in a period in which Tanzania's motor culture, though present for decades, became so difficult to ignore that observers raised alarms about the pace and number of vehicles found on the nation's streets by the end of the 1990s. We look at these claims in a moment. Let me conclude by pointing out that these vehicles came into a logic of movement and gendered adulthood forged during the 1970s and 1980s, when most observers associated automobility exclusively with failure—debates to which we now turn.

Conclusion

Motoring Out of Time: Tanzanian Automobility

in Unsustainable Times

THIS CONCLUSION EXAMINES Tanzania's motoring past in a changing geopolitical context of automobility. Unlike during much of the twentieth and early twenty-first centuries, the creation and maintenance of national motoring cultures no longer offers indisputable evidence of successful modernization: the world has simply run out of time for fossil fuel–based mobilities to exist at their current scale, let alone expand, as they are in much of the world. In 2007 transport accounted for 23 percent of energy-related greenhouse gas (GHG) emissions. Automobiles produced about 75 percent of these gases, in addition to having a high annual growth rate. The Intergovernmental Panel on Climate Change (IPCC), a project of the United Nations Environment Programme and the World Meteorological Organization, identified at least two worrisome aspects of this 23 percent figure. First, international institutions and nations do not have a theory of growth capable of operating without continuous fossil-fueled movements because "economic development and transport are inextricably linked. Development increases transport demand, while availability of transport stimulates even more development by allowing trade and economic specialization. Industrialization and growing specialization have created the need for large shipments of goods and materials over substantial distances; accelerating globalization has greatly increased these flows."[1] Julie Livingston calls these entanglements "self-devouring growth."[2]

The second issue magnifies concerns about automobility's known destructiveness: "The world is not yet motorized because of low incomes," the IPCC report states. Moreover, "if and when these areas develop and their population's incomes rise, the prospects for a vast expansion of motorization and increase in fossil fuel use and GHG emissions is very real."[3] Car ownership levels in fast-growing car countries like India and China are nowhere close to per-capita ownership in the United States, but the expanding geography of ownership has produced profound results. Though it took over a century—from the late 1800s to around 2010—to reach the first billion automobiles, we are predicted to reach two billion sometime from 2020 to 2035, likely taking only a quarter of the time as the first billion.[4] The first billion—located predominantly in the Global North—signaled vitality, social health, and technical sophistication.[5] The second billion, spurred by expanding geographies of ownership, has magnified the environmental dread that arrived only at the end of the first billion. Even as time runs out to reverse emissions trends, more people than ever are using motor vehicles. In this context, places like Tanzania that combine low overall ownership rates with higher rates of automobile growth in *recent* decades—namely, since the World Bank (WB) and the United Nations recognized climate change as a phenomenon in 1992—have become disproportionately visible in discussions of mobility and sustainability.[6]

A major concern about this growth pertains to projections about *how* it will occur in the Global South. Increased car consumption in the Global South, climate experts fear, has involved and will involve used vehicles in places that not only are experiencing high rates of urbanization but also have less regulated economies and cultures of technology use. Combined with the Volkswagen emissions scandal, Gabrielle Hecht's description of European Union oil subterfuge—shifting dirtier blends to Africa so that Europe can meet its emissions goals while profiting from energy exports—should derail any assumptions that traditional Northern industrial manufacturing acts as a foil to supposedly dirtier and more harmful Southern vernaculars.[7] Moreover, some of the specific environmental fears about climate change and motorization in Tanzania started to become a reality through the structural adjustment policies (SAPs) created and implemented by the WB and the International Monetary Fund. After 1985, WB-led privatization brought regional extensions of asphalt roads—a policy that generally overlapped with socialist-era goals. And yet, as Thomas Lekan shows, when

President Jakaya Kikwete approved the construction of a "hard-packed" road through the Serengeti (from Arusha to Musoma)—a request made by communities who lived in and near the park—Northern conservationists protested the possibility of a game park becoming more motorized.[8]

The same outrage applied to the Serengeti road, however, has not been aimed at the removal of the regulatory apparatus from ujamaa that limited car ownership and importation through extended periods of Tanzania's independent period. Private ownership grew slowly during the 1980s—returning to late 1960s levels of importation—before taking off in the late 1990s and early 2000s, reaching an estimated 380,000 registered vehicles in 2007. Some estimates suggest Dar es Salaam's vehicle fleet tripled during the 2000s with national growth rates reaching 10 percent by 2010—jamming city streets, where most vehicles reside. Still, only 6 percent of Dar es Salaam families own a vehicle—over 60 percent take public transport—and just over 1 percent nationwide.[9] In addition to low national rates of ownership, Tanzania's per-capita carbon output, at 0.2 metric tons, still pales in comparison to 15.5 metric tons in the United States or 8 metric tons in the European Union. Yet, according to WB estimates, the 0.2 figure not only surpasses the nation's previous high in 1972 for total carbon output but also reflects major increases in use of liquid gases such as gasoline and diesel that have accompanied private car ownership increases since the mid-1990s. A previous high of 3,025 kilotons of carbon dioxide emissions from liquid fuels in 1973 had nearly halved by 1980 (1,727 kilotons). From 1995 (3,142 kilotons), this amount has then climbed steadily, reaching 6,182 kt in 2012.[10] Still, when I read these statistics, I recall Andreas Malm and Alf Hornborg's critique of the term "Anthropocene"—that particular historical processes created climate change and not just the human species writ large—and that the most environmentally destructive segment of world population, Western elites like Robert McNamara (World Bank president and former president of the Ford Motor Corporation), pushed policy changes that led to reversals of intentional efforts by Tanzanian leaders to keep motorization rates low.[11]

Thus, Tanzania's small, yet growing, carbon footprint has caused little concern on its own. Terrorism, traffic, urban pollution, and high accident rates have combined with climate to create a broader constellation of national and global risks associated with the expansion of vernacular automobilities in Tanzania since the 1990s. The result is a thorough denigration of the nation's motoring culture at its quantitative peak. Recall that European motorists doubted Africans' ability to appropriate the motor vehicle throughout the colonial period; colonized subjects could assist in, but not lead, the formation of a motoring culture. While the previous chapters have thoroughly undercut this supposed incompatibility of Africans and automobiles, a version of this belief persists even as, and perhaps because, Africans have undeniably made cars their own. My goal in these final pages is not to question automobility's destructive nature. A rich interdisciplinary scholarship shows that motor vehicles and their systems harm societies, natures, bodies, and climates. It also notes the difficulty of replacing car mobilities with another sociotechnical system once motor mobilities have become a norm. "Automobility we might say is neither socially necessary nor was its development inevitable," John Urry wrote, "but having got established it seems impossible to break from."[12]

Instead, I am interested in how societies have remade, and can remake, the social and technological interlinkages that compose the car's machinic complex. In the first section, this involves questioning which and whose historical models of technological life will come to the fore as we use history to imagine different futures and excavate alternatives not taken. Tanzania's 0.2 metric tons of carbon emissions per capita still pollute and destroy. But the quantitative gap between 0.2 and 15.5, the US number—or even the differences within Tanzania's own history of liquid-fuel use from the 1970s to the 2000s—also reflects qualitative differences about the ways societies create ideal worlds and react to historical changes. In other words, precisely because self-devouring growth "seems impossible to break from," and thus because it is unlikely to end suddenly in most of the world, Tanzania's car history provides practical ways to think about the possibilities of excavating, and theorizing from, alternative pasts—roads not taken or simply less seen—and of working toward alternative futures. Since the early 1900s, Tanzanian users have continually configured their own relationships to motor vehicles without much of the ideological and material baggage that has shaped the automobile's Northern histories or that are now becoming frightening norms in India. This central component of African automobility should denaturalize the notion that Northern societies offer the most useful knowledge and experience for creating better worlds of mobility. That, however, rests on recognizing that not all historical unsustainabilities are the same, as well as, in this case, challenging the denigration of African car cultures during the socialist and privatized eras—topics to which we now turn.

ALTERNATIVE HISTORIES OF UNSUSTAINABILITY: SOCIOTECHNICAL REPAIR AND THE WHAT-IFS OF TANZANIAN AUTOMOBILITY

Let us start with a brief recap of Tanzania's motoring culture. From the early 1900s to the 1950s, walkers and passengers integrated motorized transport into existing modalities without anticipating or desiring societies in which cars, fossil fuels, and wide roads dominated life and labor. At the same time, mechanics creatively repurposed parts in ways that took repair and maintenance out of the constraints of a precarious making do or a second-best to factory mass production. In a different technological register, planners struggled with unsustainable energy costs and spent a decade looking for ways to create better economic livelihoods for citizens without steady or increasing access to petroleum. Drivers, for their part, created forms of moral distribution on paved and unpaved roads alike. And their experience on the streets led to gendered identities premised around fear and care—perhaps a more constructive gendered baseline for making identities that depart from homogeneous masculine notions of speed and growth. Finally, decades before mass public transit took center stage in efforts to reduce private vehicle ownership and emissions in the name of global sustainability, residents of Dar es Salaam asked for and literally waited patiently for buses, a form of mobility that would reduce automobile ownership in their city. When this faltered, they built a collective system out of private vehicles and defended to skeptical officials the possibility of creating socialist collectives out of individual technologies.

None of this was done to pursue environmental sustainability. The environmental movement that linked industrial societies to planetary-scale destruction was only in its infancy in the 1970s, while the Tanzanian groups I highlight here were far more concerned with sustaining and remaking the economies (small and larger) and built worlds they associated with sovereignty, urban culture, or gendered adulthood. But as automobile historian David Kirsch observes, scales of use and an ability to re- or unmake sociotechnical systems—two major components of the remaking described below—matter when assessing the environmental impact of automobiles. Cars have polluted and destroyed as linked parts of sociotechnical systems—most often as constituent parts of mass-consuming societies that destroy environments in myriad ways. Greatly reduce the number of cars—or usage—and they do much less harm. While that does not make cars themselves clean (or green!), it brings needed attention to the will and capacity of societies to unravel damaging sociotechnical systems when they are identified as such.[13] As Matthew Patterson observes, "A world where cars represented individual freedom . . . did not and does not exist 'naturally.' The world can be remade without the car at its sociotechnical heart."[14] While that seemingly aligns with the IPCC narrative, I highlight the way Tanzanians' experience with automobility's unsustainability foreshadowed the more recent and environmentally focused efforts to remake worlds of movement.[15]

Tanzania's first two decades of independence, and its response to the OPEC (Organization of the Petroleum Exporting Countries) crisis, in particular, offer important clues about unmaking automobility in the way Patterson envisions. In most parts of the world where socialism took root, it provided a critique of the private motor vehicle as a symbol of class inequality. As chapter 3 pointed out, with ujamaa Tanzania went one step further than other socialist nations by not just denigrating private vehicle ownership but also doubting that the Fordist production techniques central to most modernization schemes could or should be adopted by new nations. After the OPEC crisis, these socialist priorities combined with the new imperatives of oil's clear economic unsustainability to produce six years of falling car ownership rates from 1973 to 1979. Planners, politicians, and international consultants aimed to regularize these decreasing rates in Dar es Salaam through a 1979 master plan that invested heavily in walking and busing—going as far as to rearrange housing and market space throughout the city. Its vision for peak-hour morning traffic in 1999 included 36 percent on foot, 24 percent on public buses, 13 percent on employer buses, 15 percent on bicycles and motorcycles, and only 12 percent in private vehicles. Only some of the plan came to fruition, including much of Dar es Salaam's pedestrian infrastructure, because privatization policies started shortly after the plan's publication. But the existence of other relationships among society, technology, and modernization's limits is precisely the point. Already skeptical about the car's place at the "sociotechnical heart" of development schemes, the 1970s made one thing very clear to Tanzanian planners: even a minimal commitment to automobility as development had endangered the nation's sovereignty. Consequently, they sought to normalize minimal use.[16]

In this sense, the SAPs of the WB and the 1979 master plan reflect divergent historical possibilities for addressing economic unsustainability. Championed by a former president of the Ford Motor Company, SAPs clearly linked growth, energy use, and growing mobility to social health through a political structure that reduced the state's regulatory role in sectors such as transport. Conversely, the master plan built on Julius Nyerere's and ujamaa's skepticism about the car's central role in postcolonial life by constructing built worlds that assumed historically low and falling car ownership was achievable and desirable. Moreover, the plan's restructuring of movement and built worlds was largely consistent with an urban culture in which sociotechnical remaking, often through breakdown and repair, was standard. We can thus begin to see the contours of a postcrisis automobility that involved reduced fossil fuel use within a built environment that encouraged less motorized intracity mobilities, growth in the use of human-powered movement, and a continuation of technological reuse. Nyerere also tasked factories with creating spare parts for large trucks in order to reenergize the nation's commitment to rural development through the types of distribution covered in chapter 5. While, in most cases, this required expanding mobilities to regions largely cut off from national economies, a contrast is nevertheless clear: SAPs facilitated the huge growth of personal private vehicles in cities, whereas planners—and much of the public, including drivers—hoped to remake circulations that served and connected predominantly rural populations with reused vehicles.

These divergent possibilities should not mask debates and divisions among Tanzanians about the nature of repair. Many of the users featured in this book felt that planners and politicians failed to grasp the complexity and meaning of their work, at least in part because the latter failed to appreciate the technological possibilities forged through reuse and experientially based expertises. Though this was by no means uniform. As the chapter on oil demonstrates, bureaucrats created a wasteful auctioning system that saw many state vehicles sold for scrap, often to bubu garages, in the 1970s in favor of using new parts and vehicles. That same culture of technical authority led to Brian Ibrick's arrest for building an unregistered roadster composed of parts from twenty-four different models. The politics of remaking in Tanzania after the OPEC crisis thus traversed familiar fault lines between state claims about its prerogative to define and deliver ujamaa and the power of users and maintainers to remake the tools of everyday life, whether daladala, modified vehicles, or the means of distribution. Even at the height of the crisis, the state incorrectly interpreted each of the latter as a threat to its power instead of as an alternative created with broad consensus regarding the need to salvage, repair, or remake the political and economic gains made since 1961. A critique sometimes leveled in bubu garages accuses the state of failing to consider the full spectrum of technological alternatives its citizens forged before and during collapse and thus of missing opportunities to better remake economies and livelihoods.

Regardless, we witness a wide range of groups both willing and able to remake motorized movement. Apart from some resistance to Sunday bans in Dar es Salaam, I cannot recall any public resistance to significantly overhauling modalities of movement or the technologies themselves. At least two parts of Tanzania's earlier history shaped this moment. First, groups could rethink vehicles and car culture in the late 1970s because automobiles had never stabilized as the iconic technology of African-led modernization (a status largely reserved for the hoe)—and thus as something that needed to match external standards—or as an unquestioned part of socioeconomic life. Instead, the automobile was a tool whose use, while necessary in many sectors, could and should be reduced even as the form of the vehicle was continuously altered. Second, consequently, sociotechnical repair went beyond returning a technological thing or social unit to a familiar status quo. Instead, it was about finding ways for breaking and broken social and technological units to work differently and thus toward new technological and economic ends. This constructive nature of "broken world thinking" was not only about finding new ways to configure worlds in the face of both limits and breakdown but also a reassertion of and call to magnify core elements of the city's earlier approach to urban mobility.[17] In 1979, incorporating the private motor vehicle into plans for Dar es Salaam made even less sense than in previous decades. A focus on repair also offers an important corrective to the knowledge politics of unsustainable times. Often connected to places that do not manufacture—or manufacture enough for mass consumption—widespread salvage, reuse, and repair generally function as indications of economic and technological weakness, thus disqualifying places like Tanzania from becoming producers of generalizable knowledge about development or sustainability. Yet the known consequences of and limits to growth that have appeared over the past half century suggest this approach to technology, power, and well-being applies quite poorly to the unsustainable period we inhabit. Donna Haraway and Anna Tsing each identify a tendency to think about unsustainability's opposite—cleaner and sustainable futures—through the very types of technophilia that created worldwide crises. Such approaches look to the same institutions (multinational corporations, states, and nongovernmental organizations), certified bodies and minds, and forms of movement that held power for most of the twentieth century with the hope that they can create the exact opposite result. Tsing and Haraway suggest that alternative presents and futures can be found in and through the debris and wreckage of twentieth-century industrializations. Tsing calls this the "art of noticing," while Haraway writes of "staying with the trouble": working with what we have to remake our worlds, "holding open space" for different possibilities.[18]

That Tanzanian car history might "[hold] open space" for alternatives provides a much different way to view the late 1970s and early 1980s—particularly, the manner in which economic decline can lead almost inevitably to the triumph of privatization on ujamaa's quite literal material ruins. As chapter 4 showed, instead of occupying the cutting edge of efforts to work against the clear limits of growth in oil-based economies, the ideas and plans for this period set the stage for SAPs premised on the notion that Tanzania's state had nothing to offer by way of broader concepts of sustainability or well-being. As many scholars have observed, despite decolonization, Africa still constitutes "an object apart from the world, . . . a failed and incomplete example of something else."[19] A focus on the latter, incompletion, features in the next section as even privatization, that antidote to socialism, failed to bring vernacular automobilities in line with European and American expectations about motoring and development.

There was nothing inevitable about this transition to privatized automobility, particularly from Tanzanian perspectives. Quite the opposite, the state and its citizens, though not always acting or thinking together, were preparing technologically for a transition that either diminished the role of motor vehicles in the economy—in parts of the country, this was already a reality—or kept them at low levels. In evoking a transition that could have been, I am not offering a redemptive narrative about automobility and maendeleo. At least one lesson to take from Tanzanian car history is that certain elements of automobility offer no redemption—or alternatives—in the form of remaking or repair in the face of unsustainability, whether economic or environmental. Had ujamaa's multimodal automobility continued, it would not have offered the type of moral "ecological mode" that Livingston anchors in rainmaking; furthermore, in environmental terms, it would surely constitute what Vinay Lal terms "shallow ecology."[20] However, we can still look at limited motorization for what it was: an achievement that intentionally avoided some of the most destructive tendencies of economies built with and through automobiles. As Arturo Escobar has argued, transitions that emerge "despite limitations and contradictions" retain practices, ideas, and values that are critical to "[establishing] a horizon for the creation of broad political visions beyond the imaginaries of development and progress and the universals of western modernity."[21] Or, to answer a question Lal poses, not all bodies have "become unfit for experiencing other modes of reality" "as a consequence of automobiles."[22]

In *Mobility Justice*, Mimi Sheller asks, "What stories do we tell ourselves about the world becoming ever more mobile and which forms of *demobilization* or forced mobilities do these stories mask?"[23] One way to answer that question is to center Tanzania in a historical epoch that John Robert McNeill and Peter Engelke call the "Great Acceleration." This period, the authors show, saw the greatest increase in GHG emissions associated with the Anthropocene. Those emissions are centered in North America, Europe, India, and China—though the former two have a much longer cumulative history of that destruction. The Great Acceleration, though clearly a helpful framing of some aggregate world-historical processes, tells us much less about alternatives to runaway energy use that occurred either before or within the period it covers.[24] That matters because, as the next section illustrates, Tanzania's much lower carbon emissions have largely been linked to a belief that it was a latecomer to modernization and car culture, not that its users had long put automobile and society together differently. After automobile use rose in Tanzanian cities during privatization, African car use gained international attention for systematic misuse that stemmed from what many considered an immature motoring society. We explore how these vernacular automobilities have become most visible in narratives of death and demise, before concluding with more recent efforts to remake privatized motoring.

TANZANIAN AUTOMOBILITY AFTER SOCIALISM: TRUCK BOMBS, RISK, AND NATIONAL CAR CULTURE AS PATHOLOGY

Sometime in July 1998, an unknown mechanic modified the tank of a Nissan refrigeration truck in a home garage near the city center of Dar es Salaam, Tanzania. On August 7, the truck exploded in front the US embassy located less than a mile away. The blast killed twelve of the embassy's Tanzanian staff and visitors and wounded eighty-five more. Seconds earlier, the same occurred in Nairobi, with even more devastation: over two hundred were killed, and thousands wounded. Together, the bombings killed 232, wounded 4,500, and led to the largest overseas deployment of the Federal Bureau of Investigation (FBI) in the organization's history. The FBI concluded that Osama bin Laden's organization, Al-Qaeda, had organized the attacks to occur on the eighth anniversary of the US troop deployments to Saudi Arabia, but the real significance of the events became apparent later. After three planes flew into the World Trade Center in 2001, the East African bombings became part of an opening act in American narratives of terror. Three American presidents—George W. Bush, Bill Clinton, and Barack Obama—and a secretary of state, Hillary Clinton, have commemorated the bombing at a new embassy in Dar es Salaam. And in 2015 First Lady Michelle Obama visited a memorial to the victims at the city's National Museum.

Titled "Hope from Sadness," the memorial, pictured in figures C.1 and C.2, combines debris from the blast, including a mangled motorcycle and the body of a car, with concrete busts representing the Tanzanian victims. (Readers familiar with statues in Tanzania will note the similarity between the busts and a memorial to the slave trade in Zanzibar; the same Swedish artist created both.) One, whose face is barely visible in the concrete slab, seems to be pulled downward by the explosion's crater; the other depicts a woman who lost both arms in the blast against the backdrop of a shattered embassy window. The message of hope in the memorial's title is difficult to find. The memorial was constructed with the support of the US embassy, and a plaque lists the names of the twelve deceased, along with the following message: "The museum is responsible to protect and preserve this exhibition for the sake of educating [the] Tanzanian community and other stakeholders on the effects of terrorism."

Instead of portraying hope from sadness, the memorial links trucks and automotive debris to terror. Trucks, especially ones continuously modified to keep them roadworthy, are a fixture of everyday life in the city. So, too, is material debris. It is hard to walk much in Dar es Salaam without finding a collection of things that looks somewhat like the mechanical items featured in "Hope from Sadness." Moreover, in 2012 the memorial sat a few yards from an exhibition of significant motor vehicles in Tanzania's nationalist history.[25] Combined with the bombing memorial, visitors look at seven cars with descriptions similar to what follows:

C.1–C.2 (left) Debris from the 1998 US embassy blast, with Julius Nyerere's Mercedes-Benz in the background; (right) a newer memorial to the bombing including a Suzuki Escudo with US embassy plates. Photos by author.

1   Austin A40: The first car used by Tanzania's first prime minister, Julius Nyerere, and his driver, Saidi Tanu, to mobilize against colonial rule.
2   Austin A40 Vanguards: The second vehicle used by Nyerere to create a nationalist movement.
3   Mercedes-Benz (late 1960s): This car was used for the East African Community after independence. It was licensed as "Royal Excellence 1."
4   Rolls-Royce Phantom V State Landaulette: Given to Tanzania by Great Britain as a gift of independence. Only five vehicles of this model were made.
5   Rolls-Royce (1938): The personal state car of the British governor until independence in 1961, at which point Tanzania used it to receive heads of state, including Haile Selassie.
6   Mercedes-Benz (late 1990s): A state car used by Nyerere and his family after he resigned from the presidency. The plaque states that Nyerere took his last drive in Tanzania in this vehicle before boarding a plane to the United Kingdom for cancer treatments. He died shortly thereafter.
7   Debris from the 1998 truck bombing.

Debris from an Al-Qaeda attack may seem like a strange addition to a national collection of cars that includes Rolls-Royces, Mercedes-Benzes, and three vehicles that carried Nyerere, often called "the father of the nation" or simply "teacher" (*mwalimu*).

But a truck bomb not only is perfectly consistent with conventional histories of East African motoring but also provides a fitting ending to conventional stories of misappropriation and misuse. The narrative goes something like this: automobiles, a European technology, were first introduced as a tool of empire to African societies that completely lacked industrial tools and knowledge. Most Africans were either scared or in awe of them, and Africans certainly did not understand how to build or repair them. After decades of British rule, a small number of colonial elites, such as Tanzania's first president, Julius Nyerere, used vehicles to mobilize against colonialism and build a new nation by motoring around the colony. But this type of appropriation was both rare and incomplete. Regardless of the president's ability to build the nation with the help of two used Austin Morris vehicles, this same nation did not acquire the official manufacturing capacity to make its own state vehicles in the 1960s and 1970s, as the presence of foreign luxury vehicles (two Rolls-Royces and two Mercedes-Benzes) attests. As a result, though politically independent, the new nation remained technologically dependent on foreign manufacturers to supply its automotive needs and on domestic informal garages to creatively re-make and modify vehicles in conditions of scarcity.

A central part of this false narrative, and one possible interpretation of the museum exhibit, is the idea that the few Tanzanians who had access to automobiles misused them. Nyerere, of course, not only agreed with this interpretation but was also one of the first to promote it. That a Mercedes-Benz is now enshrined as the last vehicle in which Tanzania's first, and arguably most trusted, political leader motored in his country might seem trivial. For the schoolboy standing next to me in 2011, it was simply unbelievable. When his friend expressed surprise about Mwalimu's "luxury vehicle" (*gari la kifahari*), the boy responded emphatically, "Nyerere didn't have a car." Technically, he was correct; the party had loaned it to him. In addition to listening to civics lessons about Nyerere's role in creating a national community, including his many invectives against corruption, the student had also correctly interpreted the politics of motoring. By 2011 Mercedes-Benzes had given way to the Toyota Land Cruiser VX-V8, popularly known as *mashangingi*, as the vehicle of choice among a political elite. But the point was the same: technology can work in Tanzania, but it has long been used to enrich only part of the nation. As chapter 3 showed, narratives of elite misuse can hide more complex realities about broader patterns of use and more complex genealogies of historical causality (i.e., the notion that motoring politicians and bureaucrats robbed Tanzania of its chance to become self-reliant).

Here I am interested in how narratives of elite misuse in Tanzania can pair with, and even rest on, an assumption of popular incapacity to tell stories about technological pathology, such as "Hope from Sadness" and its debris.[26] Though only two of the suspects were Tanzanian nationals, the FBI's description of the events leading up to the blasts implicates an African culture of technology that made the explosion possible. After renting a house in a downtown neighborhood with a garage and high walls, the perpetrators purchased a used Suzuki Samurai to travel to Arusha to buy TNT and detonators from a mine owner. Upon returning to Dar es Salaam, they hired a mechanic to modify the inside of the refrigeration truck so that oxygen tanks and car batteries—the ignition source—could rest on a shelf.[27] They then removed the refrigeration unit and replaced it with fertilizer. Taking the truck into the ordinary flow of traffic on one of the city's busiest roads, the bombers pulled into the driveway of the embassy compound, where the vehicle exploded. From Dar es Salaam to Arusha and back again, and from regional and urban roads to garages, terrorism emerged out of the everyday flows and places of Tanzanian automobility.

Combined with Nyerere's Mercedes-Benz, the exploded truck tells a history of automobility that has harmed rather than built the nation—extending the story from magendo and HIV in the late 1970s, as described in chapter 5. The exhibit certainly shows that some politicians used motor vehicles toward useful ends—for Nyerere, that was true during at least certain periods of his life—and that we can find pockets of creativity and repurposing in Africa's past. But its main historical message is about a culture of misuse and misappropriation that results in death and debris.[28] Indeed, the most striking aspect of the FBI's description of the 1998 attack is the normalcy of these technological actions in urban life. The same roads, mechanics, and repair techniques used to make automobiles a viable and important technology in everyday life across the country could also be used in an opening act in a global age of terror. The report thus recognizes that a widespread technological appropriation has happened, only to present Tanzanian car culture as an undesirable, incompletely formed culture of technology that Al-Qaeda could exploit because so much activity took place in settings without surveillance, regulation, or licensing.[29]

Since the early 2000s, Tanzania's cars have received attention not for Al-Qaeda–style terror, which remains a singular event, but for high motor vehicle accident and death rates. A 2002 report released by the World Health Organization established that if car use continued to grow without changes in user behavior, monitoring, and infrastructure, motoring in much of Africa would potentially constitute a public health crisis. Though technically less likely to die in a road accident than a motoring citizen of the United States (owing to the latter's higher rates of car use), a citizen of Tanzania nevertheless faces a high risk of death and injury if they commonly use roads, even if they do not use vehicles. Nearly a third of road deaths in Tanzania in 2009 involved pedestrians; another third came from the capacious category "four wheeler," which includes popular urban and rural buses that are often heavily loaded and are mainly manufactured in garages where national safety standards rarely influence design or construction. As someone who spent much time on Tanzania's roads, I do not doubt these risks but want to highlight the way death and risk have become Tanzanian automobility's essence for external observers.[30] Like the FBI report, World Health Organization publications note that one part of motoring culture—car use—had grown in Tanzania without equivalent increases in roads, regulation, or even health services to treat crash victims.[31]

Some reports even concede that that this lack of regulation is a product of privatization efforts that discouraged government entrance into the economy, and they have called for coordinated public-private partnerships that involve the state, financiers, and international development organizations.

As Hecht observes, denigrating discourses like these do technopolitical work.[32] With climate change added to these local safety concerns, a justification for replacing daladala, one of Tanzania's most used vernacular transport systems, emerged in the late 1990s. Overcrowded, operated by drivers whom many call unprofessional, and heavily modified in gereji bubu without regulations on emissions or safety, daladala have been approached by planners as evidence of systematic misuse that implicates owners, garages, drivers, passengers, and the state. In addition to causing road deaths, as already mentioned, daladala have been castigated as overpolluters that foul urban air. Evidence capable of distinguishing daladala fumes from those of other vehicles is thin to nonexistent. I can only surmise that it rests on planners being able to see and smell fumes coming out of buses in ways they cannot with their own vehicles. Nor have I seen estimates about per-capita urban pollution that would at least recognize the huge contributions buses make to mass transit or, conversely, implicate private motoring's large share of toxicity on multiple scales. Planners argue that potential car owners are unlikely to choose available mass-transit options and thus purchase vehicles—further jamming city traffic. Following this logic, daladala become a problem because they channel the mobility aspirations of urban elites into private vehicles that further jam roads. Solve the daladala bus problem with different buses, and the private-vehicle issues go away.

Enter one of the latest mobility trends in urban planning: bus rapid transit (BRT), a system of articulated buses that use their own lane—often in the middle of the road—and are often paired with expanded pedestrian infrastructure. With support from the WB, the European Union, and the hedge fund Simon Group, the project's majority financier, the Tanzanian government agreed to replace daladala with rapid-transit (RT) vehicles. The project, which is not slated to finish until 2025, recently took the name Usafiri Dar es Salaam-Rapid Transit, or UDA-RT. It opened to political fanfare as past presidents and ministers took some of the inaugural rides on the sleek articulated buses. These images, posted to UDA-RT's Facebook page, come along with a short history of the city's urban mobility. Started by a colony-sponsored company, the company was nationalized as Usafiri Dar es Salaam (UDA) while greatly expanding avenues of motorized mobility.

The same will happen as the state steers this project, it claims.[33] Though advertised as a win-win for all of the city's stakeholders, as Matteo Rizzo has chronicled in detail, UDA-RT's construction led to the destruction of roadside dwellings (which are rarely registered with municipalities), has made transport workers' futures uncertain, and promises "imminent" finish dates that are regularly revised.[34] Further, even as more RT routes come online, boosters have backed away from earlier claims that BRT could replace daladala. The latter's scale, more flexible routes (which can quickly respond to urban growth), and lower ticket prices have seemingly secured their place as the staple people's car for the near future.[35]

The construction of UDA-RT is historically significant for at least two reasons. First, though data clearly show that small private cars have increased rapidly since the late 1990s, most reports avoid discussing, let alone targeting, private sedans as the source of gridlock and/or pollution. "[Dar es Salaam Rapid Transit] itself acknowledges this," Rizzo observes, "when it states that in Dar es Salaam there are '120,000 private vehicles that carry only six percent of residents with 480,000 of their seats lacking passengers.'"[36] Second, though funders have offered BRT as the daladala's opposite, the technologies shared an origin story in the late 1970s when different global constituencies wrestled with the limits imposed by raised energy prices. In Dar es Salaam, passengers and operators offered thumni–thumni–turned–daladala as technical assistance to a parastatal heavily impacted by new energy costs. Similarly, BRT and its dedicated bus lines offered cities a way to reduce private-vehicle mobilities without drastically altering a city's landscape and thus without making huge infrastructural outlays—a necessity for a period that saw increased energy prices combine with reduced appetites for centralized planning and intervention.

Why did a Northern solution to the energy crisis win out over an existing vernacular solution? One clue comes from the language used to describe daladala. With the words *paratransit* and *informal*, documents suggested that operators had not created or did not follow a system legible to passengers or regulators. Instead, routes created on the fly continuously responded to customer demand so that drivers, conductors, and owners maximized profits. Moreover, the predominantly male African operators again emerged as hyper- and hypomasculine technological actors. As hypermasculine operators speed and jam their polluting buses full in order to make as much money as possible, hypomasculine mechanics create vehicles not up to international standards—all at the expense of public safety. Meanwhile, reports present daladala as poorly constructed and maintained, and routes as haphazard, thus presenting their users and makers as falling short of a standardized and regulated ideal of technological manhood such interventions implicitly offer.

The notion that daladala had not formed systematic routes by the early 2000s, when plans for the city's BRT schemes first arose, strains credulity. Color-coded buses followed preset routes to stations marked on the front of vehicles. Municipal authorities registered and regulated them, albeit to varying degrees. I rode daladala almost daily during this time. Even though I had no experience with public transport in the United States and had the Kiswahili skills of a toddler, daladala offered a legible system of mobility that allowed me to explore the city. As for the buses themselves, a daladala mechanic, Ali Macosta, noted that the deteriorating conditions of buses stemmed from fare prices that did not rise with increased fuel prices. Owners consequently cut costs in the garage leading to less reliable vehicles. Macosta concluded that daladala could easily be made better and safer with more resources.[37] But planners either did not see daladala as a sociotechnical system that could be improved by existing users and makers and/or considered the vehicles so undesirable and inconsequential that they could be easily replaced by an RT model. Acting as what Timothy Mitchell calls an "object of development," planners used a vernacular system with a deep history to justify intervention and, by extension, did not consider it worthy of investment or improvement.[38]

A clearer answer to the question about solutions comes from the IPCC. In 2007 it stated that "emerging" economies with low motoring rates offered easier targets for redirecting the historical relationship among motorized mobilities, economic growth, and GHG. Seeing nations like Tanzania as latecomers to automobility allows planners to approach them as blanker slates for transitioning to less destructive mass urban mobilities. The idea is that 0.2 metric tons per capita of carbon emissions comes with much less of the infrastructural obduracy found in societies where mass private mobility is an inextricable part of daily life—such as in the United States, with its 15.5 metric tons per capita of carbon emissions. In sum, though the IPCC sees industrial lateness as an attractive opportunity to rework the relationship between mobilities and technology—a return to the idea of Africa as a laboratory—it does not see the history behind the 0.2 figure as something to build on or as an epistemic standpoint capable of centering the experiences of those who have done the least to destroy the world while decentering the voices of those who have done the most to harm it.[39] As the next section illustrates, this history of remaking through breakdown and debate continues to play a central role in Tanzanian automobile politics.

"PEEP, PEEP . . . MOVE OUT OF THE WAY": TRAFFIC, CRITIQUE, AND THE POSSIBILITIES OF TECHNOPOLITICAL REPAIR

As international nongovernmental organizations talk about environmental sustainability, most conversations about cars, roads, and mobility in Tanzania remain focused on issues of political and economic inequality in a time marked by privatization, or *ubinafsishaji,* a term rooted in the Kiswahili word for "self" (*binafsi*). At the same time as car growth has skyrocketed, large parts of the nation have limited access to the social and political resources connected to infrastructures of mobility. This includes roads and vehicles—such as debates about a highway in the Serengeti or about China's investment in road infrastructure—as well as the growing role of combustion engines in supplementing electricity through generators during regularized blackouts. Only 6 percent of urban families have steady access to their own vehicles; in the nation's rural areas, this number plummets to well below 1 percent. Consequently, cars and their specific material conditions and use continue to provide a material technology through which citizens raise and debate broader issues about maendeleo. At stake in these debates, as well as in these final pages, is the extent to which the privatized cultures of technology that followed ujamaa can be remade into something else.

A remake of an old song provides a good place to start this journey. In 2008 Tanzanian hip-hop artist Mr. Nice released a music video for "Bwana Shamba," or "Master Farmer," a remake of a late nineteenth- and early twentieth-century folk song from the Swahili coast. Sung to the tune of "Yankee Doodle," the original version describes the luck of a farmer who finds a diamond while planting potatoes in a rural area. After selling the diamond, the farmer buys a house in town and ultimately makes a claim to move socially from a former slave to a free Swahili patrician through this purchase. The song, Laura Fair illustrates, evidences the importance of urban landownership to claims of social mobility and security in the wake of abolition.[40] A century later, Mr. Nice's motoring version of "Bwana Shamba" follows a similar script. A man in a rural area preparing his land to plant potatoes unearths a diamond with his hoe. He attempts to board a bus from Bagamoyo to Dar es Salaam, but he is kicked out when he cannot pay the fare. After walking barefoot for fifty-eight kilometers, he arrives in Kariakoo, Dar es Salaam's central market, where he sells the diamond for a briefcase of cash before heading to a used-car lot. The video ends with the man in what appears to be a Suzuki Escudo (after he has turned down a Toyota SUV), the culmination of a phrase sung throughout: "He threw the hoe down, he went to town and bought a motor car. Now he is rich. Lo the luck of those with a farm. Lo the luck of those with a farm."[41]

The song describes a subtle but important change in the car's place in Tanzanian history. In previous chapters, young men traveled to cities to learn about motor vehicles. They generally followed the earlier version of this song by using whatever fortune or luck they found through work to invest in land, homes, and farms. Though few owned cars themselves, Mr. Nice's remake of "Bwana Shamba" suggests that car ownership competed with land and urban homeownership, historical signifiers of wealth and security, as a widespread symbol of economic well-being by the late 1990s. Even a used Suzuki or Toyota evidenced one's status and social security because, in addition to meeting the demands of their household, a car owner possessed the resources to purchase, operate, and repair an automobile. Barring an ability to meet each of these demands, the owner also had room to fall. Like coastal urban property at the turn of the twentieth century, cars held their value in the 1990s and 2000s, and even when owners took a loss or used the vehicle to pay a debt, they rarely returned to the destitution represented at the beginning of "Bwana Shamba." One does not become a patrician overnight by buying a vehicle, but car ownership during ubinafsishaji has increasingly signified social distance from vulnerability in an economy that relies heavily on mechanized movement.

Yet the popularity of the car as a symbol of social mobility was not matched by the accessibility of ownership. Because a farmer from Bagamoyo, like most Tanzanians who live in rural and urban areas, is highly unlikely to own a vehicle, the song tells a rags-to-riches story in which entrenched hierarchies are gamed not through wit or skill but by the luck of a persistent farmer. Consequently, as Brad Weiss observed for northwestern Tanzania, car proliferation since the 1990s reflects the highly uneven technoeconomic experiences of ubinafsishaji, as the very symbols of postsocialist economic growth, including cars, roads, and circulating commodities, signify an unlikely or unobtainable social security for most of the nation's citizens.[42] In other words, cars have become a technology of what Lauren Berlant calls "cruel optimism." "Cruel optimism exists," Berlant writes, "when something you desire is actually an obstacle to your flourishing."[43] If, for supporters of free-market reforms, growing car ownership represented a new form of maendeleo not marked by the scarcity of the socialist period, for many others, cars both produced and signified this period's "cruel optimism": growing markets and growing car use have done little to ease economic precarity and, in some cases, have created the conditions for precarity.

One result: as was the case during ujamaa, automobiles offer excellent technologies for identifying and critiquing gendered social and political hierarchies. For example, small Toyota and Nissan sedans—most often the Toyota Vitz and Starlet—received the title "small house" (*nyumba ndogo*), a term usually reserved for talking about an apartment for a mistress.[44] Purchasing a Vitz—cheap, at least for a newer vehicle, and gas efficient— allowed a married man who possibly had a family to reduce the costs of his relationships while also meeting a lover's expectations that she, too, is valued. These roles reverse when we look at the connotation of a "spare tire," a "friend with benefits" who, as in the song "Spare Tairi" by Matonya, recognizes they will never become the single object of their love and yet is content to be available in the metaphorical back of the car, or under the car, in case they are needed. "Spare Tairi" also takes on important class dimensions. The singer in the video takes a literal backseat to a series of potential male partners not because he is not good looking but because he cannot match the wealth of other suitors. It thus references a masculine and working-class philosophy of love: in this man's mind, the real lover is like a spare tire not just out of resignation but because a spare tire is there when you need it—whether because of a metaphorical bump in the road or a worn tire that needs to be replaced. "Please . . . care for me," the chorus implores, before concluding, "There will be a day when I fit you." And thus the "spare tairi" hopes for a puncture.[45]

That a man who compares his virtue to a spare tire and hopes for a puncture likely does not own a vehicle—or that, out of the entire vehicle, the spare tire emerges as a symbol of virtuous manhood—takes us to a central theme in public conversations about car infrastructure: its undeniable growth has not worked for much of the nation. "Pii Pii (Missing My Baby)," a 2009 song by Afropop artist Marlaw, named after the sound of incessant horn honking in bumper-to-bumper traffic, blamed a couple's relationship misfortunes on the amount of time spent away from each other in city traffic and the traveler's frayed nerves when he arrives home tired and angry, needing rest before waiting in the same traffic to return to work the next morning. The lyrics complain, "I want to arrive on time / The way is jammed [*inajam*] / Now, where do I go? / I have sat almost six hours / And now I'm tired of waiting / I am missing my baby."[46] "Tatizo foleni" ("The problem is traffic"), a hip-hop song from 2012, more clearly links the "jam" of automobile excess to diminished expectations for gendered adulthood. Because "the way is jammed" owing to motoring's huge growth, some young people feel disempowered to have what they need: time to move their lives forward. They "have no desire," they sing, to come and struggle in an impossible infrastructural environment during a part of their lives that they call the "time of pushing forward" (*muda wa kukusa*). In the chorus, they charge, "We have a problem to address," but "the government isn't doing its job."[47] A recent study cited by the show *Minibuzz Tanzania* backs up these claims. It estimated that Dar es Salaam residents spent an average of nine hundred hours in traffic per year, which translates to a loss of about 350,000 Tanzanian shillings per capita, an amount that would increase most residents' income by about half.[48]

Few fault the government for the large growth in private vehicle ownership, and many sympathize with the mobility needs of a growing class of private vehicle owners. Yet the outsized role of the traffic jam in everyday life and its longevity in public conversations suggests that the government is either unable or unwilling to address the social and economic issues affecting huge sections of the urban populace. Drawing on Achille Mbembe's "private indirect government," Brian Larkin concludes that the lack of both construction and maintenance is a core feature of neoliberal infrastructural politics in Nigeria. Economic and political elites have accessed funds and markets to insulate themselves from the worst experiences of infrastructural dysfunction—a sort of infrastructural market citizenship—precisely because privatization has led, as chapter 4 showed for Tanzania, to the criminalization of the very state institutions tasked with creating and maintaining a material commons and order for citizens on a national scale.[49] For most users, Larkin observes, a neoliberal infrastructural state creates repeating cycles of breakdown, repair, and subsequent breakdown. In addition to reserving full-fledged experiences of technological function for elites, this process relocates the burden of building and maintaining precarious, soon-to-break material worlds onto the citizens and institutions with the least amount of resources for doing so.[50]

Such images draw power from a contrast that rarely, if ever, needs explicit mention in political conversations: politicians have insulated themselves from most of traffic's harmful effects. In Dar es Salaam, the police block traffic, even during rush hour, so that political convoys can travel an open road at high speeds with no stops—meanwhile annoying huge sections of the city. Outside of Dar es Salaam, politicians have traveled comfortably in large Toyota Land Cruisers, known popularly as *mashangingi*. Tanzania's national language institute defines *shangingi* as "experienced prostitute"; it also refers to women who are beautiful, particularly those with large hips, buttocks, and breasts.[51] While there is no consensus about how Land Cruisers and other large SUVs came to be called *mashangingi*, one linguist suggested that the wide wheelbase and wheel covers of the Land Cruiser—a feature that distinguishes it from other types and models—may mimic a woman's hips.[52] Some I talked to in buses and on streets offered a more obvious interpretation: that in Tanzania's predominantly male political culture, convoys of Land Cruisers have simply taken the place of a harem as a way to legitimize power.

Regardless of the term's origins, the politics of mashangingi mobility spill out of urban traffic debates into conversations about national development. Citizens in rural areas and smaller cities do not have to contend with Dar es Salaam's gridlock, but the contrast between masses stuck in traffic daily and elites moving in long convoys of mashangingi fuels wide speculation that Tanzania's political class works for itself, capably finding resources for its own comfortable mobility even as communities across the country struggle to make ends meet. In 2012 opposition parties and advocates of constitutional reform targeted mashangingi as a huge drain on the country's economy by pointing out that each vehicle costs $119,000 (a conservative estimate that sometimes doubles), even before politicians receive daily fuel and maintenance allowances in addition to per diem for traveling.[53] A fleet of nearly three thousand Land Cruisers was used by leaders in government institutions (excluding parliamentarians). Using budget data from 2013, a 2015 article by the newspaper *Nipashe* estimated the cost of purchasing this fleet with a single year of maintenance, repairs, and operation at $811,145,510—about 1.8 percent of the 2013 gross domestic product.[54] The newspaper then translated these mashangingi costs into other services, including 2.6 million small business loans (at 500,000 shillings per loan), 22,509 secondary school laboratories, 13.1 million school desks, 16,375 rural health clinics, enough water wells for each village in the nation to have four water points, over 17,000 ambulances, no-cost education for the 300,000 students in higher education, or 850 miles of paved road.[55]

Members of Tanzania's ruling party objected to their colleagues' politicization of mashangingi by arguing that the poor conditions of roads in rural districts necessitated their use. But when John Pombe Magufuli ascended to the presidency in 2015, he turned opposition-party car politics into a playbook for cleaning house in government ministries dominated by his own party. Nicknamed "the bulldozer" for his reputation for completing road-building projects on time, in one of his first acts as president, he reduced the number of government ministers from fifty-five to thirty-four. One justification provided was that the reduction in traveling costs alone would contribute to a savings of $11.5 million. At the present, the transition to smaller and more fuel-efficient vehicles is still ongoing. Until his sudden death in 2021, Magufuli himself sometimes toured the country in a convoy of mashangingi.[56] Yet the president and his team also started to reframe the meaning of his own vehicle and national mobility. On tours, he spoke to crowds lining the roads by standing through his vehicle's sunroof, an act analogous to Nyerere giving speeches in villages from the hood of a Land Rover. Moreover, Magufuli used this perch to investigate the political problems he solicited from the residents around him. The accused were called by phone and speakerphone to account for themselves in front of a president who towered over them from his vehicle and traveled with armed security. Some who did not show were fired on the spot.

By turning his Land Cruiser into a mobile presidential office, Magufuli may have reworked the meaning of a vehicle associated almost exclusively with neoliberal excess, corruption and waste (in terms of both gas and tax revenues), and inequality—changing, as frustrated Dar es Salaam residents did before him, the political symbolism of a vehicle by using it in unintended ways. It would be a gross overstatement to suggest that mashangingi are on their way to representing accountability or trust. But the possibility of the president's mobile office becoming part of any locale's politics and a literal seat from which "the bulldozer" fights ineffective governance around the nation with cameras rolling offered a new way to technologically "perform the nation" with automobiles, in contrast to the history of elite motoring visualized at the National Museum.[57] Magufuli's actions suggest that a presidential convoy composed of luxury vehicles is perfectly consistent with transparency and self-reliance as long as it battles the bureaucratic inefficiencies and corruption that have become a hallmark of the nation's political conversation over the past two decades. Consequently, unlike the infrastructural order that is described by Larkin and that frustrated Tanzanian road users—as well as Nyerere's concerns about himself and his colleagues being tied to luxury motor vehicles—Magufuli used his mashangingi to demand and perform government accountability.

Much of this story will continue to unfold in the future, of course. But this technopolitical performance offers one response to widespread complaints about privatization.[58]

The president's supporters, for example, contend that Magufuli's presidential motoring makes possible—or at least constitutes one part of—an alternative form of infrastructural power that addresses the dual technological and political dysfunction characterizing ubinafsishaji. With less waste and a renewed focus on accountability, the government no longer tiptoes around large infrastructural projects, fearing widespread accusations of corruption from the public—a definition of *mradi* (project) that transferred from the late socialist to the neoliberal era. Instead, it pairs huge figures for costs saved with the amount of taxes collected to justify an expansive infrastructural state that builds more roads, railways, and huge dams and purchases Boeing Dreamliners. This approach may appear at odds with earlier forms of technological nation building—in particular, Nyerere's warnings about pursuing multiple large projects. Yet Magufuli's government has made a core element of Nyerere's socialist technopolitics relevant again. After the Second Five Year Plan expanded state power in 1969, Nyerere made explicit connections between technological and political (dys) function as a warning to bureaucrats. When technological things work, bureaucrats and managers are working for the people and toward equality; the opposite holds when systems fail.

For Magufuli, this older technopolitical philosophy of legitimacy offers useful solutions to the outcomes of privatization. Given widespread complaints about the entangled nature of governmental and infrastructural dysfunction—including the clear hierarchies of infrastructural citizenship in which the wealthy and politically powerful have functioning vehicles— his office has tried to pair everyday technological function with bureaucratic reform as evidence of a political system reorienting itself toward national, and not personal, well-being. A song and music video from the hip-hop star Harmonize told precisely this story to celebrate the president's fifth year in office. Opening with the arrival of the Boeing Dreamliner at Dar es Salaam's airport, the video shows Magufuli driving new buses and offers aerial views of new road and rail infrastructure. Harmonize underscores the role of "work" (*kazi*) in Magufuli's political philosophy, and given the images of infrastructure the video shows, the metaphor does not have to be translated: because of Magufuli's work, things are working better. With reduced "annoyances" in life, the singer asks, "Who can oppose" these changes? Harmonize's question certainly ignores the political opposition to Magufuli's administration.[59]

But the song still provides an example of the myriad possibilities of material repair in Tanzanian public culture. In 2016 a writer for the blog *Udaku Special* named Mwanakijiji justified his support of Magufuli by invoking Tanzanian cultures of auto repair. Mwanakijiji asked readers to be patient with the new president by comparing political reform in Tanzania to his own Nissan Maxima, which failed to start after a church service. "When I called the mechanics, they told me the engine had died. Nothing can be done other than replacing the engine. It is true," he added, "that even good cars need regular service. And then there are times when it has much bigger needs." In this situation, engines are removed, and old parts thrown away. Some might even think the car "has met its end." But when the car is put back together after such "big changes," it is often better than when it was first made. The blog post concluded that Magufuli's challenge was to convince people that "fixing this car" (the nation) is for a better future.[60] In comment threads, some readers agreed with the author, while others took issue with the post by extending the author's motoring metaphor. They accused Magufuli of "driving blind" and argued that the nation was more like a "lorry" that "we are all in" than a Nissan Maxima that can fit only a few passengers.

Like generations before them, these readers believed that the type of car representing a national collective mattered because even its most basic material qualities took on dense political meanings. How many people can it fit? And what type of society does a truck build that a Maxima cannot? Regardless of Tanzania's identity as an automobile, a topic that citizens will continue to debate in the future, readers did not challenge the author's mechanical metaphor for political overhaul. Even if Tanzania is more truck than Maxima, technological possibilities in the garage provide some hope that the metaphorical engine of national politics can also be replaced— even if some wish Magufuli was not the head mechanic—and that political inspiration can come from unlikely mechanical places and actors. Here the bubu repair worlds that have modified and remade vehicles for decades provide inspiration for a political philosophy that recognizes that major changes can and should be made and that various parts, whether old or new and whether coming from near or far, can be repurposed into something that works. It suggests that, with time, Tanzania can achieve better political function by drawing inspiration from its own philosophies and histories of technology and repair.

NOTES

Abbreviations

Introduction: Africa, Motors, and a History of Development

1. G. Hecht, *Being Nuclear*, 16.

2. REAAA, "The New Southern Equatorial Route: Nairobi to Lake Nyasa" (Nairobi: East African Standard, 1924), SMLA. Michael Adas notes that nakedness, a common focus of the photographer's gaze in these sources, did not always lead to colonial othering, though most observers still considered that African technology "was at best primitive." Adas, *Machines as the Measure of Men*, 126.

3. "Motoring in East Africa," *New York Times*, March 15, 1927.

4. Adas, *Machines as the Measure of Men*, 153–55.

5. E. W. Hickes, "Power Alcohol," 162, October 12, 1923, CO 323/930, BNA.

6. Chapters 1 and 2 explore specific elements of this mythic antagonism as they relate to motor mobility and car design. Myriad primary-source examples include articles from *Jambo*, a periodical of British East African soldiers that included denigrations of African driving, and car periodicals such as the *Morris Owner* or the *Commercial Motor*.

7. "The Fuel Problem," *Daily Telegraph*, July 13, 1914, CO 323/695, BNA.

8. Hofmeier, *Transport and Economic Development*; and World Health Organization, *Global Status Report on Road Safety*.

9. Ford press release, 1977, author's collection. For more on this topic in Tanzania, see Grace, "Heroes of the Road."

10. Like the drivers who had cars in their blood in Jennifer Hart's *Ghana on the Go* (104).

11. Frank Taylor, interview, Dar es Salaam, August 27, 2012.

12. Igor Kopytoff first wrote about the car as a methodological object of inquiry for African studies in "The Cultural Biography of Things." Jan-Bart Gewald, Sabine Luning, and Klaas van Walraven's "Motor Vehicles and People in Africa" first placed automobiles in African historiography.

13. Sheller and Urry, "City and the Car," 738–39.

14. As Gijs Mom argues in *Atlantic Automobilism*, this applies to historical approaches in many places. Jason Henderson shows the need for and stakes of "de-essentializing automobility" in "Secessionist Automobility" (esp. 295, 296). For excellent examples of how parts of this machinic complex have been taken apart in African studies, see Hart, *Ghana on the Go*; Green-Simms, *Postcolonial Automobility*; Scheele, *Smugglers and Saints*; and Mutongi, *Matatu*. More broadly, see Franz, *Tinkering*; McShane, *Down the Asphalt Path*; Gilroy, "Driving While Black"; and Henderson, "Secessionist Automobility," among many others.

15. Though I have taken much inspiration from scholarship on automobility, readers will notice I have nevertheless limited my use of the term *automobility*. Critical work on this topic has repeatedly shown the necessity of moving beyond the types of technological movement and subjectivities expressed by the term's invocation of "self" (auto) motion or mobility. This includes expectations of automobility as a technological phenomenon capable of producing autonomous, self-generating movement, on the one hand, and as a social and political phenomenon that links concepts of well-being (whether freedom, development, or modernity) to autonomous, individual mobilities, on the other. For example, Sheller and Urry's invocation of automobility's "machinic complex" brings attention to the manner in which the social categories of movement (such as *auto*'s centering of the "self," often read as "individual") are produced by far-flung systems of energy, technology, and capital—an assemblage that overwhelms most definitions of self; see Sheller and Urry, "The City and the Car"; and Featherstone, "Automobilities." Moreover, studies of race, gender, and mobility have demonstrated that the emergence of self-movement (spatially) as an indication of freedom (political autonomy) during the twentieth century

problematically centered white, male, and socially mobile forms of movement as a baseline. Such dominant forms of automobility, studies have shown, often emerged in tandem with marginalized communities' immobility—including the construction of built worlds, legal regimes, and state strength that greatly reduced access to automobility-as-autonomy (and thus, social power) (see Gilroy, "Driving While Black," and Packard, *Mobility Without Mayhem*).

This gets clunky in Kiswahili, too, where one invocation of self, *binafsi*, has an already established negative connotation of bureaucrats and politicians using vehicles only for themselves—only a sliver of the history that follows—and is often associated with more recent histories of privatization. *Kujiendesha*, literally "to drive oneself/selves" (whether mobility or socioeconomic pursuits) loses many of its meanings when channeled into such a specific sociotechnical system. At the same time, the term *automobility* risks locking analysis only into auto-, vehicle-, and transport-centered paradigms of mobility, as Mavhunga has argued and shown by moving beyond "banal" mobilities (*Transient Workspaces*, 26). In sum, following through on Lindsey Green-Simms's example of a "misplaced" automobility may also require distance from the term's apparent invocation of autonomous personhood and self-contained technological function (*Postcolonial Automobility*, 16). When I discuss mobilities that combine car, road, and energy, I stay as close as possible to vernacular terms or their English equivalencies while building on the lessons of scholarship on automobility. I do use the term *automobility* when highlighting clearer links between visions of development and systems of automobility.

16. See Kusimba, *Rise and Fall of Swahili States*, 149–50; and Wynne-Jones, "Public Life of the Swahili Stone House," 769. On the importance of stretched histories of technoscience, see Seth, "Colonial History and Postcolonial Science Studies," 75–76.

17. Schoenbrun, "Conjuring the Modern."

18. Govind Gopakumar made this argument in *Installing Automobility*, 212–20.

19. As Leander Schneider notes in *Government of Development* (21), Tanzanian history has a rich historiography on vernacular concepts of development, progress, and well-being. This also applies to what Andreana Prichard terms "composition of community." Prichard, "'Let Us Swim in the Pool of Love,'" 106.

20. On linkages between cars and modernization theory in different settings, see Patterson, *Automobile Politics*; Green-Simms, *Postcolonial Automobility*; Wolfe, *Autos and Progress*; and Hart, *Ghana on the Go*.

21. Hunter, "History of Maendeleo," 100–101; Hunter, *Political Thought*, esp. chap. 1; Ahearne, "Development and Progress"; Feierman, *Peasant Intellectuals*, 140–50; Koponen, "From Dead End to New Lease on Life"; and Becker, *Politics of Poverty*. As a vernacular category of development, see Decker and McMahon, *The Idea of Development* (5–6). For Kenya, James Smith provides an extensive analysis of maendeleo's meanings as a vernacular category that "permeates all levels of existence, encompassing everything from geopolitics to ice cream." Smith, *Bewitching Development*, xii.

22. Brennan, *Taifa*, 147.

23. Brennan, *Taifa*, 133. Julius Nyerere's early volume of speeches, *Freedom and Development/Uhuru na Maendeleo*, invoked the term as a core part of the independent process.

24. The causative of "to continue" or "to progress," *kuendeleza*, carried similar meanings.

25. In addition to *maendeleo ya haraka*, politicians used the phrase *maendeleo katika muda mfupi* ("development in a short time").

26. In "Drive-In Socialism," Fair provides an example of this multiscalar experience of development.

27. Hawa Ramadhani, "Maisha na maendeleo ya Hawa Ramadhani," unpublished memoir, n.d.

28. Giblin, *History of the Excluded*, 9. He notes the use of *kujenga maisha* (to build life) and a similar term in Kibena and their connection to travel. On "searching for life" (*kutafuta maisha*), see Monson, *Africa's Freedom Railway*; and Callaci, *Street Archives and City Life*, 30. On uses of *uwezo*, see Myers, *Verandahs of Power*, 14; and Prestholdt, *Domesticating the World*, 46–48. On *heshima* (respect), see Moyd, *Violent Intermediaries*. The antonym *maisha magumu* ("life is tough") also applies here. See Vavrus, *Desire and Decline*, 2–3.

29. Fair, "Drive-in Socialism," 1079–83.

30. Dorothy Hodgson observes that ideas and practices later termed *development* and later considered part of development scholarship had been around since the 1860s. Hodgson, *Once Intrepid Warriors*, 10. Juhani Koponen adds that these practices did not arrive in Tanganyika as a package in the late 1800s (or after). Koponen, "From Dead End to New Lease on Life," 38. Both observations open important space to write histories of development outside of European intellectual genealogies. Moreover, unlike the Kiswahili translations for "modern"—which rest on breaks with "tradition" (*desturi*) or the need for newness (*wa kisasa*)—breaking *maendeleo* into movement and its tools/practices does not. On longer histories of ideas and structures of well-being, see Schoenbrun, "Conjuring the Modern," 1410; and Feierman, *Peasant Intellectuals*, 105, 254–56.

31. Centering practice instead of discourse and theory is a central component of recent scholarship in historiographies of both Africa and development and modernization. See Cooper and Packard, introduction to *International Development*; and Miescher, Bloom, and Manuh, "Introduction," esp. 2, 4, 9, and 13. The second part of Joseph Morgan Hodge's "Writing the History of Development" details this move in interdisciplinary literature on development. Ivan Karp and D. A. Masolo, in "African Discourses on Development," and Kwasi Wiredu, in "Our Problem of Knowledge," open intellectual trajectories to tell and imagine long-term histories of development.

32. On perceptions of technological lack, see Landes, "Why Are We So Rich?"; Acemoglu and Robinson, *Why Nations Fail*; and Mokyr, *The Lever of Riches* (vii).

33. J. Fabian, *Time and the Other*, 32–35.

34. Scholars have shown that race played a central role in debates about who/what constituted *African* identities and culture after independence. Those debates do not diminish the term's remaking or its salience for speaking about citizens and technologies in a sovereign African nation. Evidence in this book most closely aligns with Richa Nagar's,

Laura Fair's, and Ronald Aminzade's approaches—recognizing not only the power of racial categories in the colonial and postcolonial periods, but also the way communities and individuals remade, reinterpreted, or simply never (fully) bought in to political categories of race (themselves, contested) in everyday life, technological work, and other concerns related to maendeleo. See Richa Nagar, "The South Asian Diaspora in Tanzania"; Andrew Ivaska, *Culture States;* James Brennan, *Taifa;* Laura Fair, *Reel Pleasures;* Jonathon Glassman, *War of Words, War of Stones;* and Ron Aminzade, *Race, Nation, and Citizenship* (esp. 47).

35. I have in mind the type of Fordist production found in much automobile scholarship. Matthew Patterson provides a good description of this phenomenon in *Automobile Politics.* On the historical and geographic reach of this concept of motors, see Siegelbaum, *Cars for Comrades;* Grandin, *Fordlandia;* and Wolfe, *Autos and Progress.*

36. Oldenziel, *Making Technology Masculine,* 19–42; McGaw, "Why Feminine Technologies Matter," 15–17; P. Edwards, "Industrial Genders"; Edgerton, *Shock of the Old,* xi; Mavhunga, introduction to *Transient Workspaces,* 5–7.

37. Douglas Harper places repair and making on the same "continuum." Harper, *Working Knowledge,* 21. See also Russell and Vinsel, "After Innovation," 5–6; Jackson, "Rethinking Repair"; and Edgerton, *Shock of the Old.*

38. Jackson, "Rethinking Repair," 221–22. On improvisation as a "daily imperative" in cancer wards, see Livingston, *Improvising Medicine,* 181.

39. Miescher, Bloom, and Manuh, "Introduction." This approach has long informed social and cultural histories of Africa. See Terence Ranger's *Dance and Society in Eastern Africa, 1890–1970;* and Nancy Rose Hunt's concept of "mixing" in *A Colonial Lexicon.*

40. Akrich, "De-scription of Technical Objects."

41. I draw inspiration here from Jojada Verrips and Birgit Meyers's recognition that earlier scholarship gave "virtually no attention to car in its materiality." Verrips and Meyers, "Kwaku's Car," 157.

42. For a critique of this view, see Francesca Bray, "Technics and Civilization in Late Imperial China."

43. Historians stress the openness of vehicles to change by users and maintainers at least through the 1930s. See Franz, *Tinkering;* Kline and Pinch, "Users as Agents"; Borg, *Auto Mechanics;* and Lucsko, *Junkyards, Gearheads, and Rust.* Daniel Miller, "Driven Societies," stresses the interpretative flexibility in automobiles. This proliferation of meanings and material compositions echoes Abena Dove Osseo-Asare on histories of "priority"—who or where comes first?—as a problematic horizon; Clapperton Mavhunga's approach to innovation; Emily Osborn on aluminum and narratives of singular points of origin; and Jeremy Prestholdt's definition of "domestication." Osseo-Asare, *Bitter Roots,* 13–14; Mavhunga, "Introduction," 4–10; Osborn, "Casting Aluminum Cooking Pots"; Prestholdt, *Domesticating the World,* 8. With cars in West Africa, Jojada Verrips and Birgit Meyer in "Kwaku's Car" rightly anchor monolithic approaches to automobiles in Western consumers' "alienation" from vehicle production and maintenance.

44. Including narratives in which Africans having "their backs against the wall," even during difficult times, becomes the entirety of their lives, as David Hecht and Maliqalim Simone point out; see D. Hecht and Simone, *Invisible Governance*, 144.

45. Like doctors who must "continually improvise and work empirically." Livingston, *Improvising Medicine*, 20.

46. Mavhunga makes a case for locating the multiplicities of African innovation in much of his work. See, in particular, Mavhunga, "Introduction."

47. On the need for such interscalar approaches, see Gabrielle Hecht, *Being Nuclear*, 22–23, and for things inhabiting "multiple scales," Jessica Barnes, *Cultivating the Nile*, 27.

48. Berlant, *Cruel Optimism*, 19; and Knight and Stewart, "Ethnographies of Austerity."

49. On "impossible choices," see Livingston, *Improvising Medicine*, 177. For approaches to bureaucratic work, see Bierschenk and de Sardan, "Studying the Dynamics of African Bureaucracies," 4; and Eckert, "'We Must Run While Others Walk,'" 217. Feierman explores nationalists' desire for a bureaucracy in *Peasant Intellectuals* (235–44).

50. James Ferguson links informality directly to precarity in *Give a Man a Fish* (15–20). Kenneth King's 1977 *The African Artisan* charts innovative cultures of reuse in Kenya, especially with motor vehicles, but presents them as a constrained technological sphere born of and likely ending with economic precarity; interestingly, it concludes by highlighting the limits of formal/informal as an analytic approach to technical learning (196–97). In *Transient Workspaces*, Mavhunga makes the case for expanding what counts as technology/infrastructure owing to the tendency for colonial practices to become formal while everything else is lowed and othered as informal. Hart opens *Ghana on the Go* by noting the problems with both formal and informal, astutely observing that motor vehicles "operated in the interstices of these binaries" (18). Hart also takes this on in "Of Pirate Drivers and Honking Horns" and in "Informality, Urban Transport Infrastructure, and the Lessons of History in Accra, Ghana." In "The Popular Niche Economy," Michael Stasik covers problems with terminology in detail while adding that transport economies contributed to the original formulation of informal economies. Citing Mavhunga, Hecht and Breckenridge—but particularly Hecht—call for scholars of technology to reevaluate the assumptions embedded in formal/informal through frameworks such as tacit knowledge, in Serlin's interview "Confronting African Histories of Technology" (100). Judith Scheele's research on trans-Saharan transport networks explores exchange through existing vernacular categories and idioms, thereby situating continuities between truck use and much earlier mobilities; see Scheele, *Smugglers and Saints*. In *Markets of Dispossession*, Julia Elychar provides a short history of how informality became part of the developmentalist and academic lexicon; Janet Roitman, in *Fiscal Disobedience* (18), observes that even when *formal/informal* are used well, the boundaries between them often serve as a catchall instead of a sharp analytic term. I've taken much inspiration from a rich literature in Tanzania on informal spheres, including Aili Mari Tripp's *Changing the Rules*, the first book I read on Tanzania, which opens with an illegal bus (I've been hooked since that day). But I, too, find the language of economic informalities limiting

for situating technological histories and for undercutting developmentalist expectations about what sociotechnical change should look like and who, what, or where influences it. Like Mavhunga, who has called on scholars to pay close attention to languages of practice and analysis, I think vernacular lexicons such as *bubu, siyo rasmi, mtaani,* and others used here provide a sharper analytic tool kit than *formal/informal* while drawing attention to the robustness of Tanzania's institutional technological landscape. The latter, in some ways, helps address Asef Bayat's "Un-Civil Society," which recognizes the problematic role of civil society paradigms that "belittle or totally ignore the vast arrays" (55) of activities caught up with the word *informal*. Emily Brownell in *Going to Ground* points out that urbanization often glossed as informal is directly connected to institutional planning, and furthermore, that some spaces that have that generalized informal aesthetic are sometimes government initiatives (64 and 147–48).

51. Stiglitz, "Markets, Market Failures, and Development," 198.

52. Stiglitz, "Markets, Market Failures, and Development," 198. For an update, see Stiglitz and Greenwald, *Creating a Learning Society*. For expanding what counts as a site of analysis in contemporary African history, particularly as it relates to the independent period, I draw from Geiger, TANU *Women* (esp. critiques of linear modernist narratives); Keletso Atkins, *The Moon is Dead! Give Us Our Money,* especially "indigenous imperatives," 54, and continuity of Nguni institutions (60); Moodie and Ndatshe, *Going for Gold,* 2, especially the ideas male migrants brought with them to mines; Schoenbrun, "Conjuring the Modern"; and Englebert, "Pre-Colonial Institutions."

53. Mavhunga, introduction to *What Do Science, Technology, and Innovation Mean from Africa?,* 10.

54. Englebert, "Pre-Colonial Institutions." See also T. J. Tallie's combination of queer theory and indigenous studies in *Queering Colonial Natal,* especially the role of "*queering*" to "unsettle the presumptions of a settler state" ("'queering settlement'") and the marking off of forms of indigeneity, including readings of institutions and practices, as "queer" by colonial authorities (7).

55. Lerman, "Uses of Useful Knowledge," 40; and Marx, "'Technology.'"

56. Latour, *We Have Never Been Modern,* 105; Li, *The Will to Improve,* 10; Rist, *History of Development,* 70.

57. For *siyo rasmi,* see David Mfume, interview, Iringa, December 21, 2011; and Marechulumu Sambala, interview, Iringa, December 21, 2011. David Schoenbrun traces the history of *mtaa* to neighborhoods connected by streets around AD 500 in the lakes region. Schoenbrun, *A Green Place, a Good Place,* 93. It had joined a coastal Kiswahili lexicon by the 1800s where, as Randall Pouwels demonstrates, a mosque stood at the center of social life for a mtaa. Pouwels, *Horn and Crescent,* 79 and 95.

58. On using Kiswahili terms to explore "local frames of awareness," I follow Myers, *Verandahs of Power,* 13–15; and Mavhunga, "Language of Science, Technology, and Innovation."

59. Echoing Ato Quayson's concerns about what constitutes a "top" or "bottom" in urban research and Shadreck Chirikure's negative answer to the question "Should Western

Concepts Always Have Western Equivalents?" (73). Quayson, *Oxford Street, Accra*, 5; and Chirikure, "Metalworker," 73.

60. Guyer, *Marginal Gains*, 164–69. She further notes that the "uniformity" associated with the formal, in contrast to the "diversity" of the informal, "seems so unlikely as to be bewildering" and offers a "coral reef of separate formalities" in place of the "modernist struggle (166–69). Bayat notes in "Un-Civil Society" (54) that such practices are "not extraordinary" but are treated as if they were.

61. James Scott's *Seeing like a State* has rightly received critiques for definitions of authoritarian high modernism. See Cooper, *Colonialism in Question*; and Schneider, *Government of Development*, for good examples. Yet among these critiques, Scott's pivot in the section "The Missing Link" has received much less attention for charting alternative creativities and forms of power.

62. Scott, *Seeing like a State*, 318–29.

63. Quayson, *Oxford Street, Accra*, 6.

64. Palmer, "Ineffective Masculinity," 457–58.

65. I establish the specific contours of these identities in chapters 2, 4, and 5.

66. Laura Fair, Emily Callaci, and Margrethe Silberschmidt chart the dynamic and often difficult political and economic contexts for attaining respectable masculinity in both the colonial and national periods. See Fair, *Reel Pleasures*, 153–77; Callaci, *Street Archives and City Life*, 104–6, 173–75; and Silberschmidt, "Poverty, Male Disempowerment."

67. As statistics on corruption cases show. See Maliyamkono and Bagachwa, *Second Economy*, 143. Indeed, this historical task requires many more sources than are currently available.

68. In emphasizing the relationship between gendered social work and technological function, I draw from a rich history of gender and labor in African studies, including Lindsay, *Working with Gender* (especially notions of laborers "working with gender"); Moodie and Ndatshe, *Going for Gold*, especially descriptions of "practical integrity" and migrant masculinity, 2–3; Miescher, *Making Men in Ghana*, 2–5; and Miescher and Lindsay, introduction to *Men and Masculinities*, especially discussion on the limits of hegemonic masculinities and the continual contestation of their meanings, 16. Kenda Mutongi links men, buses, and pursuits of respectability, and both Fair and Callaci carefully excavate men's identities in antiurban contexts that pathologized the lives of many young men and women. Mutongi, *Matatu*, 63–68; Fair, *Reel Pleasures*; and Callaci, *Street Archives and City Life*, 170–75.

69. On this intersection of social and technological processes, including affect, see de Luna, "Inventing Bushcraft," 55–57. Earlier examples of the intersection of expertise and gendered personhood include Jeff Guy and Motlatsi Thabane's "Technology, Ethnicity, and Ideology" and Sara Berry's work on mechanics in *Fathers Work for Their Sons* (chap. 6).

70. Hart, *Ghana on the Go*, 99. Hart anchors this approach to drivers in Stephan Miescher's foundational work on plural masculinities, *Making Men in Ghana*.

71. This is Lisa Lindsay's term for recognizing commonalities among diverse expressions of manhood in southern Nigeria. Lindsay, *Working with Gender*, 32. See also Moyd, *Violent Intermediaries*, 3; and Weiss, *The Making and Unmaking of the Haya Lived World*, 29.

72. Callaci explores this process through consumer items in *Street Archives and City Life* (104). She notes a form of demasculinization through an absence of things that provides an interesting context for situating mechanics' huge collections of parts. See chapter 2 in this book.

73. U. Beck, *Risk Societies*.

74. Cultural and social history have long noted a relationship between commodities and personhood. See Kopytoff, "Cultural Biography of Things." In Tanzania's history, see Fair, *Pastimes and Politics*; Glassman, *Feasts and Riot*; and Meier, *Swahili Port Cities*.

75. Note Silberschmidt, "Poverty, Male Disempowerment"; and Callaci, *Street Archives and City Life*. See Fair, *Reel Pleasures*; and Hodgson, *Once Intrepid Warriors*.

76. Jackson, "Rethinking Repair." Kevin Borg's *Auto Mechanics* and Douglas Harper's *Working Knowledge* demonstrate that repair/maintenance, and thus breakdown, is part of normal technological life cycles, albeit rarely made visible. Jenna Burrell, in *Invisible Users*, observes that Africanist scholarship—including that of Brian Larkin and Jojada Verrips and Birgit Meyer—pushed forms of this argument when "mainstream STS" approached dysfunction as "out of the ordinary, as sudden and transitory events" instead of an aspect of everyday life (14–15). While crediting Larkin's contributions to repair/breakdown cultures, Burrell also notes a "nonspecificity about form" that risks subsuming myriad breakdowns into a "generic entropic inevitability of things falling apart." Burrell, *Invisible Users*, 15. See also Larkin, *Signal and Noise*, 233.

77. Andrew L. Russell and Lee Vinsel note social continuities in maintenance regimes in "After Innovation" (8–9).

78. In contrast to Daniel Headrick's *The Tools of Empire* or the reprise, *The Tentacles of Progress*.

79. On concerns about actualizing promises in the independent period, see Osseo-Asare, "Scientific Equity," 715; and Cooper, *Citizenship between Empire and Nation*, 3–9, 174–188. Mamadou Diouf, "Senegalese Development," observes that "development was counterpoised to colonial exploitation in deliberate manner" (293).

80. Nyerere, "President's Inaugural Address," in *Freedom and Unity*, 178. His need to redefine nation building suggests scholars should not assume the ideological/discursive nature of nation building as the starting point of analysis. See Callaci, *Street Archives and City Life*, 18–19, for the more intimate social contours of this material-discourse relationship.

81. Nyerere, *Our Economy*, 14; and Bjerk, "Sovereignty and Socialism in Tanzania," 283–84.

82. Tousignant, *Edges of Exposure*, 4–5, and, on the consequences of stretched capacity, 56–57.

83. Lynn Thomas notes the reasons "agency as argument" has long influenced African history and also encourages use of agency as a conceptual tool, rather than a "'safety' argument." L. Thomas, "Historicising Agency," 328–29.

84. On time, "scale as method," and infrastructure, see P. Edwards, "Infrastructure and Modernity," 191–94.

85. Hughes, "Evolution of Large Technological Systems," 51. I first thought of this process with Katherine Verdery's *What Was Socialism and What Comes Next?*, as chapter 3 shows.

86. This is a form of what Verdery describes as power "constituting itself through the effects of austerity." Verdery, *What Was Socialism and What Comes Next?*, 48. See also Howe et al., "Paradoxical Infrastructures," 551. Not building aligns with what Ann Laura Stoler calls an "imperial formation," including its ability to act after the end of empire. Stoler, "Rot Remains," 2, 7–8.

87. This is also a concern of apartheid infrastructure in Antina von Schnitzler's *Democracy's Infrastructure*, in what she calls "the materiality of political claims" (8). See also Cooper, "Africa and the World Economy," 8–13; and Berman and Lonsdale, *Unhappy Valley*.

88. As Daniel Knight and Charles Stewart chart in "Ethnographies of Austerity," and as Ronald Aminzade shows for Tanzania in *Race, Nation, and Citizenship* (93, 131–137).

89. Bjerk, *Building a Peaceful Nation*, 248; Schroeder, *Africa after Apartheid*, 18; and P. Lal, *African Socialism*, esp. chap. 1.

90. Urry, *Mobilities*, 119.

91. See, for example: J. Rweyemamu, *Underdevelopment and Industrialization in Tanzania*; on the enduring impact of struggles to accumulate capital, see Aminzade, *Race, Nation, and Citizenship*, 31–37; and Becker, *Politics of Poverty*, esp. chap. 4.

92. Tsing, *Friction*, 214.

93. Von Schnitzler, *Democracy's Infrastructure*, 8–9.

94. As noted by G. Hecht, *Being Nuclear*; Mavhunga, *Transient Workspaces*; and Donovan, "'Development.'" A large amount of critical development scholarship glosses over technological details, including Escobar, *Encountering Development*; Cowen and Shenton, *Doctrines of Development*; Sachs, *Development Dictionary*; and Rist, *History of Development*. This is even true of what James Ferguson calls "the 'development' apparatus," "institutional apparatus," and the "state apparatus." Ferguson, *The Anti-politics Machine*, 18, 87, and 194. On notions of "work," see Guyer, *Marginal Gains*, 6.

95. MacKenzie and Wajcman, "Introductory Essay," 22.

96. Mavhunga, *Transient Workspaces*, 15–20.

97. I build here on an axiom of car scholarship challenging the inevitability of late twentieth century northern automobilities. *Car Cultures* emphasizes the car's flexibility over space and time. Others include McShane, *Down the Asphalt Path*; Kirsch, *Electric Vehicle*; Wells, *Car Country*; and Mom, *Atlantic Automobilism*.

98. I take inspiration from Hodgson's temporal framing of development in *Once Intrepid Warriors*. Jamie Monson was one of the first to take such an approach in *Africa's Freedom Railway* (9). In *Reel Pleasures* and "Drive-In Socialism," Laura Fair has extended this

approach to show the national subjectivities of development discourse among planners, politicians, and citizens. Kenda Mutongi calls for more approaches that "descend to street level." Mutongi, *Matatu*, 261.

99. Prita Meier, extending other archaeologists of the Swahili coast, makes this case in *Swahili Port Cities* (15–22); Stacey Langwick makes a powerful case for "pluralizing our conceptions of materiality" to explore alternative ontologies of healing; Emily Callaci explores the materialities found in, on, and through popular texts, while Jeremy Prestholdt links *uwezo* (ability and power) to objects in the nineteenth century. Langwick, *Bodies, Politics, and African Healing*, 152; Callaci, *Street Archives and City Life*, 13; Prestholdt, *Domesticating the World*, 46–48.

100. I draw on various approaches to STS materialities often associated with actor network theory (ANT). I hope this book shows there is not a single built world or infrastructure that should occupy our time in thinking about Africa's technological past (and I take inspiration from Mavhunga's *Transient Workspaces* here). With Sheller and Urry's machinic complex, I generally have in mind Anna Tsing's idea of the "open-ended assemblages of entangled ways of life" in *The Mushroom at the End of the World* (20). As Burrell notes in *Invisible Users*, some Africanist scholars have expressed concern about the absence of social and cultural analysis in STS literature because of a "tendency for ANT's human actors to be rendered mute" (16). See also Larkin, "Poetics and Politics of Infrastructure" and "Promising Forms." Indeed, as Warwick Anderson and Vincanne Adams observe, ANT can lead to a "semiotic formalism" (190) that invokes the local without deeply exploring it—an approach that keeps the method from "[embracing] its postcolonial condition." Anderson and Adams, "Pramoedya's Chickens," 191. Still, Jenna Burrell and Richard Rottenburg note respectively that these critiques focus extensively on one form of STS materialism—Bruno Latour's approaches to ANT—and in pushing back against Latour, such critiques sometimes create what Burrell calls "weak materiality." Rottenburg, "Social and Public Experiments," 423; Burrell, *Invisible Users*, 11–12; Latour, *Reassembling the Social*. Since the mid-1980s, STS scholars have raised and written about similar issues—including important questions about where society, politics, technology, and infrastructure begin or end. See MacKenzie and Wajcman, "Introductory Essay," 22; and Bijker, Hughes, and Pinch, *Social Construction of Technological Systems*. The version of ANT popularized by Michel Callon and John Law likely offers a more natural framework for the type of sociocultural analysis of power common in African studies. Callon and Law, "Agency and the Hybrid Collectif." Burrell's use of Law's relational materiality offers one example. Burrell, *Invisible Users*, 15–16. William Storey provides a brief overview of these fields, including hard and soft determinisms, in *Guns, Race, and Power in Colonial South Africa*. For a recent take on the virtues and limits of "people as infrastructure," see Fredericks, *Garbage Citizenship*, 60–68. For a broader discussion, see Paul Edwards et al., "AHR Conversation."

101. LeCain, *Matter of History*.

102. See Mika's exploration of this topic in "The Half-Life of Radiotherapy and Other Transferred Technologies."

103. Haraway, "Situated Knowledges," 583–90.

104. Mukerji, *Impossible Engineering*, 2–12. Osseo-Asare and Mavhunga describe similar processes. Steven Feierman importantly notes that "knowledge was not collective" or centralized but rather distributed according to different roles. Eglash notes a tendency to approach the "professional as the producer." Osseo-Asare, *Bitter Roots*, 13, 45; Mavhunga, *Transient Workspaces*; Feierman, "On Socially Composed Knowledge," 15; and Eglash, "Appropriating Technology," viii.

105. On fusing oral history, technological practice, space, and oral history, see Schmidt, *Iron Technology in East Africa*; Osborn, "Casting Aluminum Cooking Pots"; and G. Hecht, *Being Nuclear*, 341. Luise White, Stephan Miescher, and David William Cohen noted the porousness of the oral and written in their *African Words, African Voices*; so does White in *Speaking with Vampires*. Another interplay occurs between action, training, knowledge production, and history telling.

106. White, Miescher, and Cohen, *African Words, African Voices*; and Thompson, *Voice of the Past*, 233–34.

107. Barber, "Introduction," 18.

108. I draw from Harper, *Working Knowledge*; K. Beck, "Art of Truck Modding"; and Osborn, "Casting Aluminum Cooking Pots."

109. On the "(in)visibilities of history," see G. Hecht, *Being Nuclear*, 341; and G. Hecht, introduction to *Entangled Geographies*, 2–4. I also have in mind Julius Nyerere's statement about "the mass of localized unwritten historical knowledge, which has to be searched for, collected, checked, and written into a comprehensive story." Nyerere, "Congress on African History," in *Freedom and Socialism*, 82.

110. This is a classic issue in histories of technology. Lerman, "Uses of Useful Knowledge"; and Borg, *Auto Mechanics*.

111. Mavhunga, *Transient Workspaces*, 25. Callaci, *Street Archives and City Life*, makes a similar move (58). I draw on Haraway, "Situated Knowledges" (583–90) as well.

112. Allman, "Phantoms of the Archive," 107. This is also taken up in Thomas Bierschenk and Jean-Pierre Olivier de Sardan's *States at Work* and is a key part of what Schneider calls "the world of officials." Schneider, *Government of Development*, 100.

113. See Dumont, *False Start in Africa*; Scott, *Seeing like a State*; and popular postsocialist novels, such as Ruhumbika, *Miradi Bubu ya Wazalendo*.

Chapter 1: Walking to the Car

1. "Carnival Procession Is Week's Climax," *Tanganyika Standard*, June 8, 1953; "Africa through a Lens: Tanzania," CO 1069-160-66 and CO 1069-160-74, BNA.

2. I use Tanganyika to refer to the geographic boundaries of the colony established after the Paris Peace Conference. Though I explore the German period, I do not include the parts of German East Africa that later came under Belgian rule.

3. "Carnival Procession Is Week's Climax," *Tanganyika Standard*, June 8, 1953.

4. Wisnicki, "Interstitial Cartographer," 255.

5. M. Pratt, *Imperial Eyes*, 4.

6. Adas, *Machines as the Measure of Men*, 4, 40, 338.

7. McClintock, *Imperial Leather*, 40.

8. "Carnival Procession Is Week's Climax."

9. Njovu, *Dereva wa Kwanza Tanganyika*, 40.

10. C. Mavhunga, *Transient Workspaces*, 17; the same dictionary referenced earlier in this paragraph supports this latter usage of njia with the saying: "*Njia ya mwongo, ni fupi*" ("The way of the deceitful is short"). Taasisi ya Uchunguzi wa Kiswahili (Dar es Salaam), *Kamusi ya Kiswahili Sanifu*, 310.

11. Recalling Nancy Rose Hunt's phrase "the terms of struggle and *negotiation*" in *A Colonial Lexicon* (11).

12. G. Hecht, *Being Nuclear*, 16. My use of *humanitarian* draws on critical histories of the term, including Barnett, *Empire of Humanity*.

13. On this intersection of slavery, social mobility, and spatial movement, see Glassman, *Feasts and Riot*; Wright, *Strategies of Slaves and Women*, esp. 50–52; 70–74; 83–84; S. Rockel, *Carriers of Culture*; and T. McDow, *Buying Time*, esp. chap. 4. In West Africa, see Filippello, *Nature of the Path*.

14. Rockel, *Carriers of Culture*, 119. On the same theme at the turn of the century, see Sunseri, *Vilimani*, 59.

15. "The Story of Rashidi bin Hassani" is both a product of and evidence of this colonial approach to caravan mobilities. W. F. Baldock (recorder), "The Story of Rashidi bin Hassani."

16. Arnold, "Problem of Traffic."

17. Livingstone, *Last Journals*, 66.

18. Livingstone, *Last Journals*, 62. On mobility and definitions of slavery, see Higgs, *Chocolate Islands*, 24.

19. Roger Price, letter to Rev. Joseph Mullens, September 5, 1877, *London Missionary Society Central Africa: Letters from Missionaries September 1877 to January 1879*, SOAS; Rockel, *Carriers of Culture*; and J. Fabian, *Out of Our Minds*.

20. Thomson, *To the Central African Lakes and Back*, vol. 2, 74; and Farrant, *Tippu Tip*, 108–9, 118.

21. Lugard, *The Rise of Our East African Empire*, Mss. Afr. S. 206, RHO, Oxford University. Thomas McDow examines Swahili and Arab identities, place, mobility, and kinship networks in *Buying Time* (87–97).

22. Christie, *Cholera Epidemics in East Africa*, chs. 7 and 8. Erik Gilbert shows a connection between dhows and "illegal trade" in Zanzibar, and William Bissell explores arguments

about Arab degeneration in more detail. Gilbert, *Dhows*, 64–66; and Bissell, *Urban Design*, 76.

23. Drummond, *Tropical Africa*, 24.

24. Drummond, *Tropical Africa*, 23–25. Ralph A. Austen lists the actual paths of caravan trade as "the initial African contribution" to large-scale nineteenth-century commerce. Austen, *Northwest Tanzania*, 14–15.

25. Livingstone, *Last Journals*, 77.

26. Galbraith, *Mackinnon and East Africa*, 164–65; and Roger Price, letter to Dr. Mullens, Zanzibar, October 1, 1877, *London Missionary Society Central Africa: Letters from Missionaries September 1877 to January 1879*, SOAS. On wagons as indications of "'civilization influence,'" see Timothy Burke, *Lifebuoy Men, Lux Women*, 86. These mobilities undergirded the types of commodity economies Jean Comaroff and John Comaroff explore in *Of Revelation and Revolution* (vol. 2).

27. "Central Africa's First Road," *Washington Post*, June 9, 1907; and Galbraith, *Mackinnon and East Africa*, 49, 54–70.

28. Andrew Denning calls this phenomenon "mobility as civilizing mission" in "Mobilizing Empire" (48).

29. Gregory, *South Asians in East Africa*, 120; and Shell, *Transportation and Revolt*, 46–49. In the two-part article "The Earliest Ox-Wagons in Tanganyika," Edwin Smith provides gruesome details on these transport experiments in 1877–78, including the death of most oxen and the subsequent need for porterage. Smith's data show that while ox wagons replaced porters, a central European aim, they did not carry more cargo or achieve higher speeds (two to seven miles a day) than a six-hundred-person caravan while, in this case, covering less than a quarter of the journey required.

30. Giblin, *Politics of Environmental Control*; White, *Speaking with Vampires*, chap. 7; and Mavhunga, *Mobile Workshop*, chap. 8. Experiments with oxen continued through the 1930s in Sukumaland, albeit with specialized packs for loading instead of carts. See A. H. Savile, *When God Had One Eye Shut*, Mss. Afr.S. 2094, 95, RHO.

31. W. M. to W. Mayes, September 19, 1877, IBEAC, file 4, Special Collections, SOAS; W. Mayes to Mackinnon, September 26, 1877, IBEAC, file 6, Special Collections, SOAS; and W. Mayes to Mackinnon, February 28, 1878, Bungalow No. 1, IBEAC, file 10, Special Collections, SOAS.

32. Thomson, *To the African Lakes and Back*, vol. 2, 291.

33. Thomson, *To the African Lakes and Back*, vol. 2, 59.

34. Thomson, *To the African Lakes and Back*, vol. 2, 276.

35. Thomson, *To the African Lakes and Back*, vol. 2, 105–6, 118.

36. Thomson, *To the African Lakes and Back*, vol. 2, 276.

37. *Slave Trade and Importation into Africa of Firearms, Ammunition, and Spirituous Liquors (The General Act of Brussels)*, in *Treaties and Other International Agreements of the United*

States of America, 1776–1949, Volume I, Multilateral: 1776–1917, accessed at Library of Congress: https://www.loc.gov/law/help/us-treaties/bevans/m-ust000001-0134.pdf.

38. "Making Africa Yours," Outlook, May 7, 1898.

39. Farrant, Tippu Tip, 118. In chapter 3 of Carriers of Culture, Rockel details "professional" porters' continual role during this period. See also Austen, Northwest Tanzania, 35; and Harrison, Pioneer Missionary of the Church Missionary Society to Uganda, 65–67.

40. Gregory, South Asians in East Africa, 118–20; Koponen, Development for Exploitation, 456; and Sunseri, Vilimani, 57.

41. For more on the widening of existing routes, including the role the creation of njia kubwa ("big road[s])" played in European identities, see Harrison, A. M. Mackay: Pioneer Missionary of the Church Missionary Society to Uganda, 55–64. Smith, "The Earliest Ox-Wagons in Tanganyika," observes that when Mackay widened an existing route for wagon travel, it did not last a year for wheeled movement even as it remained a walking route (3–4). T. O. Beidelman, in Culture of Colonialism (58), notes the same for the German period for a road from Sadaani to Mpapwa to Kilosa.

42. Koponen, Development for Exploitation, 445–56; and Parpart and Rostgaard, Practical Imperialist, 101, 155, and 223.

43. Koponen, Development for Exploitation, 448. In Violent Intermediaries, Michelle Moyd excavates the construction of boma (forts) and the settlement of askari, African soldiers who worked for the government, along caravan routes to provide security and encourage trade (165–75).

44. A. C. Madan, English-Swahili Dictionary, 48; and Steere, Handbook of the Swahili Language, 31. The language of gari kubwa may have come from Indian investment in caravans. See Rockel, Carriers of Culture, 91.

45. Graetz, Im Auto, 9.

46. See "35-PS-Spezialwagen der Süddeutschen Automobilfabrik Gaggenau GmbH," M@RS—the Digital Archives of Mercedes-Benz Classic, https://mercedes-benz -publicarchive.com/marsClassic/searchresult/searchresult.xhtml?searchString =spezialwagon&searchId=0&searchType=detailed#prevId=123013.

47. U. Claas and P. Roscoe, "Hot Air and the Colonialist 'Other,'" 134–37. See Austen, Northwest Tanzania, 67–68, 81–82; Gewald, "People, Mines, and Cars," 38; and Koponen, Development for Exploitation, 444–46.

48. Graetz, Im Auto, 14.

49. Graetz, Im Auto, 13. All translations from Graetz are my own.

50. Graetz, Im Auto, 17–19.

51. Graetz, Im Auto, 43 and 51–52.

52. Graetz, Im Auto, 56. This episode was published by the New York Times in "Crossing Africa in an Automobile," December 8, 1907.

53. Graetz, *Im Auto*, 65. On speed, space, and time, see Schivelbusch, *Railway Journey*; and Kern, *Culture of Time and Space*.

54. Graetz, *Im Auto*, 85

55. Graetz, *Im Auto*, 90, 107.

56. Graetz, *Im Auto*, 53.

57. Graetz, *Im Auto*, 35.

58. Mrisho Sulemani Minchande, interview, Mkuranga, March 13, 2012; and "Women Convicts Working on Road, Dar Es Salaam, East Africa," n.d., Library of Congress, https://loc.getarchive.net/media/women-convicts-working-on-road-dar-es-salaam-east -africa. Frank Edward and Mikael Hård note that projects in Dar es Salaam relied heavily on conscripted labor. Edward and Hård, "Maintaining the Local Empire," 39.

59. Great Britain Naval Intelligence Division, *Handbook of German East Africa*, 396–98.

60. "The Covenant of the League of Nations," December 1924, Yale Law School, Lillian Goldman Law Library, https://avalon.law.yale.edu/20th_century/leagcov.asp#:~:text =ARTICLE%2022.&text=Certain%20communities%20formerly%20belonging%20 to,are%20able%20to%20stand%20alone. Helen Tilley connects "mandate" and "trusteeship" to "nineteenth-century ideas of development." Tilley, *Africa as a Living Laboratory*, 93.

61. T.A.B, "The Lorry Goes Pioneering," *Commercial Motor*, August 22, 1918, 558. On porters, see Hodges, *Carrier Corps*.

62. Pesek, "War of Legs." See also Young, *Marching on Tanga*, 65.

63. William E. W. Terrell, *With the Motor Transport in British East Africa*, 104. Accessed at the British National Library. Frederick Johnson, untitled work, chs. 7 and 8, 1916. Private Papers of Lieutenant F. Johnson FRGS, Documents.11136, accessed at Imperial War Museum Archive, London, United Kingdom.

64. "Return of Porters," August 13, 1928, TS 12542, TNA, Dar es Salaam. This occurred despite voluntary porters outnumbering conscripted porters 14,000 to 9,000; "Annual Report of 1924: Transport Department," n.d., 9–10. See also Johnson, untitled work, chs. 8 and 9, for specific examples of porter experiences during the war.

65. "British Mandate for East Africa," quoted in Tanganyika Territory, *Labour: The Recruitment, Employment and Care of Government Labour*, ACC 215/121, TNA.

66. G. Garro Jones, "Note to the Secretary of State for the Colonies on the Subject of Mechanical Transport in Undeveloped Countries," September 29, 1944, TS 12014, TNA.

67. The administration later called this period "the Boom Years." Moffett, *Handbook of Tanganyika*, 96–97.

68. Moffett, *Handbook of Tanganyika*, 40–43; Sunseri, *Vilimani*, 125; and Maddox, "Networks and Frontiers," 447–50.

69. G. Garro Jones, "Note to the Secretary of State for the Colonies on the Subject of Mechanical Transport in Undeveloped Countries," TS 12014 (TNA).

70. Tanganyika Territory, *Annual Report of the Labour Department, 1928*, 34, BC 9/3, ZNA. See also Orde-Browne, *Labour*. For a broad overview, see Monson, *Africa's Freedom Railway*, 17–20.

71. "Motor Lorries in Substitute of Portery," TS, 12542, TNA.

72. Tanganyika Territory, *Annual Report of the Labour Department, 1928*, 34–35. Gordon Pirie, in "Non-urban Motoring in Colonial Africa," first pointed to such usage beyond cities and "grand journeys."

73. Orde-Browne, *Labour*, 32.

74. Amery and Ormsby-Gore, "Problems and Development in Africa," 21–22.

75. Libbie Freed observes for West Africa, "Road work is by nature more easily rendered small scale and local" than railway construction. Stéphanie Ponsavady describes similar aspirations for colonial automobility in French Indochina. Freed, "Networks of (Colonial) Power," 208; and Ponsavady, *Cultural and Literary Representations of the Automobile*, 43–57.

76. Cameron, *My Tanganyika Service*, 53.

77. Bates, *A Fly Switch*, 21. On safari diaries, see Savile, *When God Had One Eye Shut*.

78. Bates, *A Fly Switch*, 16.

79. Cicely Harris, "From Rural England to Tanganyika, c. 1900–1934," 4–5, Mss. Afr. S. 1762, RHO.

80. Tanganyika Territory, *Annual Report of the Labour Department, 1942*, appendix H, BC 9/8, ZNA; Tanganyika Territory, *Annual Report of the Labour Department, 1945*, appendix H, BC 9/11, ZNA; and Tanganyika Territory, *Annual Report of the Labour Department, 1946*, appendix G, BC 9/13, ZNA.

81. Savile, *When God Had One Eye Shut*, 79.

82. Lumley, *Forgotten Mandate*, 86.

83. Barton, *Affair with Africa*, 34.

84. Lumley, *Forgotten Mandate*, 34, 42.

85. Lumley, *Forgotten Mandate*, 34. On motoring, status, and being seen, see Freed, "'Every European Becomes a Chief.'"

86. Lumley, *Forgotten Mandate*, 29. This is a different form of what Jan-Bart Gewald calls "muscle power." Gewald, "People, Mines, and Cars," 24.

87. Lumley, *Forgotten Mandate*, 33.

88. Savile, *When God Had One Eye Shut*, 38. These memoirs provide different material than do colonial guidebooks, which, as Freed demonstrates, taught European motorists how "they ought to be seen" in French Equatorial Africa. Freed, "'Every European Becomes a Chief.'"

89. Sunser, *Vilimani* (59–60), shows that such demand initially responded to increased rail traffic at Lake Victoria after the completion of Kenya's Uganda Railway in 1902. Labour

Commissioner Granville Orde-Browne noted the geographic nature of porterage's transformation by observing that northern coastal areas such as Tanga required fewer porters (and less conscription) and fewer "man days" of work than Mahenge, a mountainous region in south central Tanzania. Granville Orde-Browne, Labour Commissioner to the Chief Secretary, August 13, 1928, TS 12542, TNA.

90. Tanganyika Territory, *Annual Report of the Labour Department, 1927*, 60, BC 9/2, ZNA; Tanganyika Territory, *Annual Report of the Labour Department, 1928*, BC 9/3, ZNA; Tanganyika Territory, *Annual Report of the Labour Department, 1929*, 34, BC 9/4, ZNA; Tanganyika Territory, *Annual Report of the Labour Department, 1930*, 14–15 and 33, BC 9/5, ZNA; Tanganyika Territory, *Annual Report of the Labour Department, 1942*, Annexure H, BC 9/8, ZNA; Tanganyika Territory, *Annual Report of the Labour Department, 1943*, Annexure H, BC 9/9, ZNA; Tanganyika Territory, *Annual Report of the Labour Department, 1945*, Annexure G, BC 9/10, ZNA. See also Iliffe, *Modern History of Tanganyika*, 136–37, 287–88. Gewald describes a similar phenomenon in "People, Mines, and Cars" (22–24). Phillips, in *Ethnography of Hunger* (60–61), observes a link between "hardship" and the government perceiving opportunities to pursue colonial infrastructural projects.

91. Savile, *When God Had One Eye Shut*, 25. In an email to Jan-Bart Gewald, Rockel described an incident in which Chagga conscripted as porters hired a vehicle for their DO to replace them because they could make more money elsewhere. Gewald, "People, Mines, and Cars," 43n73.

92. Savile, *When God Had One Eye Shut*, 27. On porters' sense of importance and influence, see Bakari, *Customs of the Swahili People*; Rockel, *Carriers of Culture*, 78–79; Glassman, *Feasts and Riot*; McDow, *Buying Time*.

93. Sunseri, *Vilimani*, chap. 7.

94. Lumley, *Forgotten Mandate*, 80 and 137; Savile, *When God Had One Eye Shut*, 27. Lumley achieved this speed on the Arusha-Karatu road.

95. Lumley, *Forgotten Mandate*, 80; Savile, *When God Had One Eye Shut*, 34.

96. Lumley, *Forgotten Mandate*, 87–90.

97. Lumley, *Forgotten Mandate*, 80.

98. Gillman, "Short History of the Tanganyika Railways," 14–56.

99. Rodney, *How Europe Underdeveloped Africa*, 209.

100. District Officer A. H. Savile asserted the government's annual profitability relied upon this railway monopoly. Savile, *When God Had One Eye Shut*, 106. See also Stan Pritchard, *Driving Mad*, 24. Pritchard notes that a rail line to Kongwa was replaced by a more "economical" truck service in 1948.

101. J. Lynch, "Professional Engineer," Mss. Afr.S. 1021, RHO, Oxford University. The first estimate is for the Arusha-Makuyuni Road. Director of Public Works, "Notes on Road Construction Costs," June 18, 1958, Acc. CRW 45100, TNA. The subsequent estimates come from Moffett, *Handbook of Tanganyika*, 348.

102. A. J. Mitchell, "Soil Stabilization for Roads in Tanganyika," 134; and McLuckie, "Roads and Road Transport in Tanganyika Territory," 572–73.

103. Lumley, *Forgotten Mandate*, 228.

104. The diminishing possibilities for transport are an important detail for reading these publications. Most all-weather motor roads required materials from "many localities." When the possibility for transport is taken away, discussions about road building with only materials at hand can lead to denials about the possibilities of road building in Tanganyika. Mitchell, "Soil Stabilization," 114–15.

105. "Road Maintenance-Instructions for Travelling Headmen," September 10, 1937, TS 25272, TNA; and Moffett, *Handbook of Tanganyika*, 2nd ed., 96–97. Rolf Hofmeier notes that some postwar estimates reached £18,000 per mile! Hofmeier, *Transport and Economic Development*, 72. For maintenance culture at the PWD, see Edward and Hård, "Maintaining the Local Empire." For similarities in Dahomey, see Alber, "Motorization and Colonial Rule," 86.

106. W. H. McLuckie, "Inspection Notes of Visit of Acting Director of Public Works to Tanga and Northern Provinces in October 1933," 30/MC/37, TNA; and Streit, "Beyond Borders," esp. chap. 3

107. The Secretariat (Dar es Salaam), "Circular No 33 of 1926," May 28, 1926, Acc. 215/121, TNA.

108. "Road Maintenance-Instructions for Travelling Headmen." See also Rose, "Survey and Study of Basic Sufficiency of Territorial and Local Main Roads (1954/1955)," held at the NBA room of TNL.

109. Blaming African cultures of labor and knowledge continued through the mid 1950s. Rose, "Survey and Study of Basic Sufficiency."

110. "Road Maintenance-Instructions for Travelling Headmen."

111. C. C. Fowkes, Headquarters Southern Brigade, King's African Rifles (KAR), July 18, 1935, TS 19639, TNA; and Freed, "Networks of (Colonial) Power," 208.

112. Bates, *Fly Switch*, 179–80. See also Lumley, *Forgotten Mandate*, 228.

113. "Handbook on Field Engineering by Mr. F. Longland, Volume I," TS 23250, TNA.

114. Lumley, *Forgotten Mandate*, 61.

115. Lumley, *Forgotten Mandate*, 60.

116. Bates, *Fly Switch*, 88–89.

117. Lumley, *Forgotten Mandate*, 33, 64.

118. Callahan, *Sacred Trust*, 30.

119. Tanganyika Territory, "Report in Respect of TT for the Period of 1.10.32 to 30.9.33," TNA Library (reports held with accession books in reading room). Freed covers similar "prestations" in French West Africa. Freed, "Networks of (Colonial) Power," 213.

120. Lumley, *Forgotten Mandate*, 33. See also DO Kasulu District to the provincial commissioner (PC) Kigoma, June 23, 1928, AB47—Acc. 1733/5, TNA.

121. DO Biharamulo to PC Bukoba, "Requisition of Labour," January 11, 1928, Acc. 215/121, TNA; and W. E. H. Sartha, "Unpaid Communal Labor on Roads," 1–2, L. 1/14, Acc. 1, box 21, TNA Mwanza.

122. Rose, "Survey and Study of Basic Sufficiency," 26–27.

123. Orde-Browne, "Memorandum on Government Labour," n.d., 2-6, Mss. Afr. Box 2 (1933–37 and 1947), RHO. See also Tanganyika Territory, *Labour: The Recruitment, Employment and Care of Government Labour,* Acc. 215/121, TNA.

124. Philip Harley to the Hon. Secretary of Tanganyika Territory, "The Abolition of Conscripted Labor," February 9, 1927, Acc. 215/121, TNA; and Alber, "Motorization and Colonia Rule," 83–84.

125. Lumley, *Forgotten Mandate,* 118.

126. Musa Mlenga, interview, Ruaha Mbuyuni, December 17, 2012.

127. Saidi Rashidi Matei, interview, Ruaha Mbuyuni, December 16, 2012.

128. As Alber observes in "Motorization and Colonial Rule" (90).

129. Mahija Hamza Chagga, interview, Chogo, March 22, 2012. On the government's denial of women performing hard labor and regulations against it, see also Granville Orde-Brown, Minutes, October 21, 1930, TS 19360, TNA

130. Amina Saluum, interview, Chogo, March 22, 2012.

131. Halima Bakari Mkomwa, interview, Chogo, March 22, 2012; and Simone, "People as Infrastructure," 407. Tasha Rijke-Epstein, "The Politics of Filth," shows how government "choices to implement particular infrastructures" assumed the availability of African maintenance labor and ran afoul of existing moral frameworks (232).

132. "Memorandum by JR Farquharson on Road Policy in Tanganyika Territory," MC/106, "Road Policy in Tanganyika by Mr JR Farquharson, OBE," n.d. (likely 1945), TNA. See also J. Farquharson, *Tanganyika Transport: A Review.*

133. A. J. Mitchell, "Soil Stabilization for Roads in Tanganyika," 134. For seasonal roads in West Africa, see Freed, "Networks of (Colonial) Power," 209. For the Great North Road, see "The Great North Road," CO 822/111/21, BNA.

134. "The Highway . . . ," *Tanganyika Standard,* 28, December 9, 1961, accessed at East African Room, University of Dar es Salaam Library, Dar es Salaam, Tanzania. Increased motor traffic added a new challenge to maintenance. J.F.R. Hill, Letter to the East Africa Road Federation, November 10, 1956, Acc. CRW 45100, TNA.

135. Stoler, "Imperial Debris," 193.

136. This *intentional* form of seasonal breakdown provides an interesting wrinkle to the "unintended consequence" of breakdown in Larkin's *Signal and Noise* (61). It suggests an infrastructural form of Frederick Cooper's "refusal of responsibility," bears out Paul Edwards and Gabrielle Hecht's point that "one form of technopolitical action is to defer a problem into the future," and echoes Tasha Rijke-Epstein's observation about

assumptions about the presence of African maintenance labor in a colonial government's infrastructural choice. Cooper, *Africa since 1940*, 76–83; Edwards and Hecht, "History and the Technopolitics of Identity," 628; Rijke-Epstein, "Politics of Filth," 247. As Aimé Césaire, in *Discourse on Colonialism* (46), and Walter Rodney, in *How Europe Underdeveloped Africa*, observed, not building—and relying on human labor—applied beyond Tanganyika. In chapter 1 of *Reel Pleasures*, Laura Fair analyzes colonial governments' refusal to build public spaces associated with colonial modernity. In *Penetration and Protest*, Isaria Kimambo identifies the failure "to meet the cost" of "increased capitalist production" as a core element of "peripheral capitalism under imperialism" (153). Jennifer Hart writes of a colonial "self-interest" in colonial transport schemes in *Ghana on the Go* (63). Priya Lal covers this process and its influence on the independent period for southeastern Tanzania in *African Socialism* (83). On roads as not an objective technology, see Klaeger, "Introduction"; and J. Livingston, *Self-Devouring Growth*.

137. G. Hecht, *Radiance of France*, 17.

138. S. Barry, "Hegemony on a Shoestring," 329–330. William Bissell, *Urban Design, Chaos, and Colonial Power*, observes that scholarship on colonial weakness and incoherence agrees that, even in these forms, "colonial rule *worked*: it altered the historical terrain, introduced new conditions, impacted consciousness, provoked resistance, and so forth" (71). Kristin Phillips summarizes this literature as saying that there is "an art to not governing." Phillips, *Ethnography of Hunger*, 11.

139. Tanganyika Territory, *Annual Reports: Transport Department, 1929–31*, TS 11789, TNA. Ponsavady links overcoming such restraints to demonstrating to French publics "the viability of the colony." Ponsavady, *Cultural and Literary Representations of the Automobile*, 41.

140. Larkin, *Signal and Noise*, 36. This technopolitical regime contrasts with the role of smoothness and hardness—"language as asphalt"—in colonial ideals of change in Rudolf Mrazek's *Engineers of Happy Land*. Larkin writes that sublimes fall apart by not working or by getting appropriated, thus losing their sociopolitical power. I am interested here in fleeting sublimes that do not arise, spread, or stabilize as instruments of power and in what takes their place. I do so following Moses Ochonu's observation about the importance of histories of "colonial failure" given assumptions of "imperial omnipotence." Ochonu, *Colonial Meltdown*, 166.

141. Bates, *A Fly Switch*, 91–92.

142. Rweyemamu, *Underdevelopment and Industrialization in Tanzania*, 77.

143. Tanganyika Territory, *Annual Report of the Labour Department, 1945*, 32; and Iliffe, *Modern History of Tanganyika*, 306.

144. Mavhunga, *Transient Workspaces*, 17.

145. Ferguson, *Expectations of Modernity*, 38–39.

146. Nkwi and De Bruijn, "'Human Telephone Lines,'" 218–23; on a desire to control African mobility, see Burton, *African Underclass*, 240; and Brennan, *Taifa*, 91–92.

147. Cameron, *My Tanganyika Service*, 63.

148. Feierman, *Peasant Intellectuals*, 46 and 94; Mavhunga, *Transient Workspaces*, 23; Sanders, *Beyond Bodies*, 10. The episode also recalls Schoenbrun, "Conjuring the Modern," and Mavhunga, "Which Mobilities for (Which) Africa?"

149. Wynne-Jones, "Lines of Desire," 224–25.

150. Kimambo, *Penetration and Protest*, 25–27.

151. Rockel, *Carriers of Culture*, 136, 199; and B. Brown and W. Brown, "East African Trade Towns."

152. Monson, "War of Words"; and L. Larson, "Ngindo." On regional "treks" connected to broader processes of social well-being (and not just revolt), see Sunseri, *Vilimani*.

153. Bakari, *Customs of the Swahili People*, 162–63.

154. Sabea, "Limits of Law"; and Miller, "Who Are the Permanent Inhabitants?," chap. 1. In chapter 3 of *Carriers of Culture*, Rockel highlights the association of connectivity and cosmopolitanism with the coast instead of inland regions and the dynamism of mobile cultures in the late 1800s. I hope to build on this here.

155. Ferguson, *Expectations of Modernity*, 53. See also Sunseri, *Vilimani*; Giblin, *History of the Excluded*; and Hodgson and McCurdy, "Introduction"; more broadly, see Swanson, "Sanitation Syndrome"; and Molohan, *Detribalization*.

156. Shell, *Transportation and Revolt*, 4–5.

157. Orde-Browne, *Labour in the Tanganyika Territory*, 32–33, BC/9, ZNA; in Orde-Browne's papers at RHO, see also "The Condition of Native Communities in or near European Centres," Mss. Afr. S. 1117, box 2; and Orde-Browne, "The Condition of Native Communities," 8.

158. Rest camps were also called control camps in the 1920s before being renamed transit centres in the 1950s. Orde-Browne, *Labour in the Tanganyika Territory*, 33, 84–90; "Photographs of Accommodations for Native Labourers: South Africa and the Belgian Congo," Mss. Afr. S. 1117, box 2/1, RHO; Tanganyika Territory, *Annual Report of the Labour Department, 1928*, 19–20.

159. Tanganyika, *Annual Report of the Labour Department, 1953*, 8–9, 92, BC 9/19, ZNA.

160. Tanganyika Territory, *Annual Report of the Labour Department, 1931*, BC 9/5, ZNA.

161. Orde-Browne, *Labour in the Tanganyika Territory*, 34.

162. On this distinction and its history, see Sabea, "Limits of Law," 140.

163. In *Perception of the Environment*, Tim Ingold calls these "taskscapes" because they provide use beyond their initial logic (154, 195).

164. Orde-Browne, *Labour in the Tanganyika Territory*, 32, BC/9, ZNA. Mavhunga calls this "production on the move" in *Transient Workspaces* (85).

165. Mavhunga observes that being "cut off" from colonial transport networks had an "enduring allure" which facilitated social interaction because of the "'cut-offness'" from

colonial technologies. Mavhunga, *Transient Workspaces*, 80. See also Alber, "Motorization and Colonial Rule," 87.

166. Tanganyika Territory, *Annual Report of the Labour Department, 1929*, BC 9/3, ZNA. This echoes Keith Breckenridge's *Biometric State* on the "informational void" of some colonial states in which governance is shaped more by the "absence of information than its presence" (5, 25).

167. Orde-Browne, *Labour in the Tanganyika Territory*, 50–51 and back insert map ("Principal Labour Routes"). See human and fly mobilities in "Crooks Corner" in Mavhunga, *Transient Workspaces*, 83–86.

168. Major Granville Orde-Browne, "Ruanda-Urundi Migration, and Labour Migration Generally," Mss. Afr. S. 117, box 2, RHO.

169. Tanganyika Territory, *Annual Report of the Labour Department, 1945*, appendix F, BC 9/11, ZNA. See also Iliffe, *A Modern History of Tanganyika*, 159.

170. Tanganyika Territory, *Annual Report of the Labour Department, 1929*.

171. Giblin, *History of the Excluded*, 119. Juma Saidi Mlela, interview, Tabora, April 4, 2012.

172. Tanganyika Territory, *Annual Report of the Labour Department, 1957*, 85. In just February and March, ten thousand more laborers proceeded to work than returned; that pattern is apparent in each month of 1957 and in a similar report from 1953. Tanganyika Territory, *Annual Report of the Labour Department, 1953*, 92.

173. Gulliver, "A Report on the Migration of African Workers," A9, TNA.

174. Miller, "Who Are the Permanent Inhabitants?," 41–42. This is the technological extension of Frederick Cooper's observation that the colonial "labeling the African worker as lazy was a way of acknowledging the limits of dominance while attributing these limits to the basic nature of the dominated." A vernacular material world helped produce "the limits of dominance." Cooper, *On the African Waterfront*, 1.

175. Shabani Mohamed Swedi, interview, Tabora, April 6, 2012. Information on decisions not to desert was provided by Juma Saidi Mlela, interview.

176. Rockel, *Carriers of Culture*, 73.

177. Maliko Karumba, interview, Dar es Salaam, July 11, 2012.

178. Ingold, *Perception of the Environment*, 195–99.

179. Lal notes the persistence of these mobilities as survival strategies in the independent period. P. Lal, *African Socialism*, 173–75.

180. Juma Saidi Mlela, interview, Tabora.

181. Zenabu Saluum, interview, Tabora, August 13, 2012.

182. On women's mobility, see M. Mbilinyi, "'Runaway Wives' in Colonial Tanganyika"; Hodgson and McCurdy, "Introduction"; and Rockel, *Carriers of Culture*.

183. Amina Musa, interview, Tabora, August 13, 2012.

184. Hadija Mahomedi, interview, Dar es Salaam, July 12, 2012.

185. Dinani, "Gendered Migrant Labour," 569.

186. See Nichols-Belo, "Uchawi upo." Parsing uchawi's meaning requires context. It can be used to guard and protect, but it here it connotes suspicion and possible harm.

187. On the nexus of trade and spatial and social mobility in East Africa, see Geiger, TANU Women, 32; and Robertson, Trouble Showed the Way, 102–5.

188. Hadija Mahomedi, interview. In Pastimes and Politics, Fair shows that kaniki was most often worn by poor women (and slaves in earlier periods) and was one way clothing acted as a technology of gendered respectability (67, 72, 94–94, 332); see also Dinani, "Gendered Migrant Labour," 577.

189. Sabot, Economic Development and Urban Migration, 43–46; and Molohan, Detribalization, 38.

190. Burton, African Underclass, chap. 5.

191. Secretary of Native Affairs, "Minutes," 16, June 14, 1933, TS 21616, "Repatriation of Unemployed Natives in Townships," TNA; Burton, African Underclass, 281.

192. Provincial Office Dodoma, August 9, 1952, "Repatriation of Unemployed Natives," TS 21616, TNA; on specifics and debates about finding an individual's origins, see "Repatriation of Undesirable Persons to Uganda," A 4/4 Bukoba, TNA Mwanza.

193. Burton, African Underclass, 245–47; Molohan, Detribalization, esp. 38–42; and Brennan, Taifa, 93. The flexibility walking provided thus seems to be to labor desertion what biking was to the identity and goals of East African evangelists in Derek Peterson's Ethnic Patriotism (41–42).

194. W. Fryer (district commissioner, Dar es Salaam), "Annual Report for 1931: General Observations," 54, TNA Library.

195. Isais Chaves, Stanley Engerman, and James Robinson provide a thorough summary of this issue in African economic history in "Reinventing the Wheel" (321–26). For an example in economic history, see Joel Mokyr's discussion of the wheel's absence, especially for society's without draft animals, in The Lever of Riches, 161.

196. Bulliet, Camel and the Wheel, 7. Gilbert makes a similar point with regard to Zanzibari vessels and steamships. Gilbert, Dhows, 5–6.

197. "Report of the Committee Appointed to Examine and Report on the Territory's Requirements for Major Non-recurrent Works," 4–5, CO 691/160, BNA; and Wynne-Jones, "Lines of Desire," 228. Path dependence was not unique to East Africa. See Wells, Car Country, 126; and McShane, Down the Asphalt Path, 6–19. It leads to a different argument than in Gewald, "People, Mines, and Cars," where motoring replaced caravan mobilities and the vernacular socioeconomic networks the latter provided (46). Maddox discusses the significance of a networked approach in East African histories of trade, labor, and environment. Maddox, "Networks and Frontiers," esp. 440.

198. I thus disagree with John Iliffe's assertion that "in the late 1920s the peasant came to Tanganyika on the back of a lorry." Sometimes they did, but this overstates the impact of motorized transport while overlooking the continued relevance of walking and vernacular infrastructure. Iliffe, *Modern History*, 288.

199. Iliffe, *Modern History*, 286–89. On assertions that chiefs did not deserve loans because they received pre-European forms of tribute, see also Lumley, *Forgotten Mandate*, 248.

200. "Purchase of Expensive Articles by Chiefs," Acc. 1, box 44, file 904, TNA Mwanza; Letter to Chief Secretary, June 6, 1933, TS 21627, TNA. Julie Weiskopf generously shared information on this topic.

201. Gregory, *India and East Africa*, 485.

202. See Streit, "South Asian Entrepreneurs in the Automotive Age"; Hofmeier, *Transport and Economic Development*, 101, 109.

203. Gijsbert Oonk, "Karimjee Jivanjee & Co in Tanzania, 1860–2000," 61–66. Car importers to this day (namely, Toyota), the Jivanjee family has shaped Tanzanian automobile history for nearly a century. The political sensitivity of car ownership in socialist Tanzania has made research on this topic difficult. Katie Streit, "Beyond Borders," stands out for this reason.

204. Rolf Hoffmeier, *Transport and Economic Development*, 327.

205. On the persistence of indigenous transport after the introduction of motor vehicles, see also Mavhunga, *Transient Workspaces*, 89.

206. Salum Ede, interview, Morogoro, March 13, 2012; Hamadi Saidi wa Mwenye, interview, Tabora, April 6, 2012; Mrisho Sulemani Minchande, interview, Mkuranga, March 13, 2012; Shabbani Mohamudi, interview, Tabora, April 9, 2012; Ali Issa, interview, Tabora, April 11, 2012; Abrahim Mumba Rihani, interview, Ujiji, April 16, 2012; "Mzee Rashidi Sefu Mpemba: Dreva mwangalifu aacha kazi baada ya kushika Usukani miaka 30," *Nchi Yetu*, March 1972; and "Kamtawa: Tanu's Driver in the Uhuru Struggle," *Daily News*, March 1, 1975.

207. This provides an interesting contrast with Hart's work, where driving offered opportunities for educated men who did not obtain clerical jobs. Hart, *Ghana on the Go*, 84.

208. Njovu, *Dereva wa Kwanza Tanganyika*, 29.

209. "Native Staff Vols. I," March 16, 1936, SF/10, TNA.

210. Leslie, *Survey of Dar es Salaam*, 129.

211. Charles Rajabu, "Kamtawa: Tanu's Driver in the Uhuru Struggle," *Daily News*, March 1, 1975. Many thanks to James Brennan for sharing this document with me.

212. Many maps show this urban concentration. See, for example, *Annual Report of the Public Works Department, 1925; Annual Report of the Public Works Department, 1935*; and *Annual Report of the Public Works Department, 1955*. All maps are an unnumbered foldout. All were accessed at the East African Room, University of Dar es Salaam Library, Dar es Salaam.

213. Mrisho Sulemani Minchande, interview; Shabbani Mohamudi, interview.

214. Mrisho Sulemani Minchande, interview, Mkuranga, March 13, 2012.

215. Hamadi Saidi wa Mwenye, interview, Tabora.

216. H. Walhouse (assistant engineer, PWD Moshi), "Lorry Turn Boys," October 13, 1932, SF/10, Acc. 30, TNA. For a similar structure in the Gold Coast, see Hart, *Ghana on the Go*, 69–78.

217. Juma Ramadhani, interview, Morogoro, December 10, 2012. As Moyd, citing Lisa Lindsay and Stephan Miescher, observes in *Violent Intermediaries* (20).

218. Pier Larson describes a "vernacular life of the street" in *Ocean of Letters* (207). Such a "life of the street" is visible with utingo in Dar es Salaam in the top picture of James Brennan and Andrew Burton, "The Emerging Metropolis," as a truck carries goods and young men on Ring Street in 1949 (43). Though drivers in Hart's *Ghana on the Go* ultimately created unions, many started careers in similar street-side locations (104).

219. Ali Issa, interview; Mrisho Sulemani Minchande, interview, Mkuranga, March 13, 2012; Shabbani Mohamudi, interview; and J. W. Hayfield (transport officer), "Tanganyika Territory—Annual Report of the Transport Department," 1929, TS, 11789, TNA.

220. Fadhili Ramadhani, interview, Tabora, April 4, 2012.

221. Jumanne Sisia, interview, Tabora, April 11, 2012.

222. Yusufu bin Waizi and Noti bin Seju to the director of public works, September 9, 1935, SF/10 Vol. 1, Acc. 30, TNA.

223. Schmidt, *Iron Technology in East Africa*, 209–29.

224. In "Tracing the Itineraries of Working Concepts across African History," de Luna cautions against collapsing our analytic categories over time while exploring thresholds—continuities of sorts—between deep pasts and recent centuries.

225. Leslie, *Survey of Dar es Salaam*, 102–3. On rural areas as colonial sites of technological change, see Arnold, *Everyday Technology*, 60.

226. Leslie, *Survey of Dar es Salaam*, 121, 127–28. Mfaume thus drove to secure a privileged form of the urban entitlements that, as James Brennan shows, were key to postwar urban politics. Brennan, *Taifa*, 105.

227. Tanganyika Territory, *Annual Report of the Transport Department, 1928*, TS 11789, TNA. Most of these offenses come from lists in accession books (which list the offenses for each file). All of the files were unavailable or lost when I requested them in 2012. The ones cited here come from the Mwanza High Court accession lists from 1951 and 1952. They are similar to other places and time periods during the colonial period.

228. Hart, *Ghana on the Go*, 31.

229. J. W. Hayfield (transport officer), "Tanganyika Territory—Annual Report of the Transport Department," 1929, TS, 11789, TNA.

230. "Motor Drivers Recommended for Grade III LCS," SF/10, Acc. 30, n.d. (but other memos from 1946), Native Staff General (Vols. 4 and 5), TNA.

231. "Annual Report: Transport Department, 1923," AB 59, TNA; "Annual Report: Transport Department, 1924," AB 54, TNA; "Annual Report: Transport Department, 1929–1931," TS 11789, TNA; Director of Public Works, "Minutes from Director of PWD," March 10, 1939, SF/10, Acc. 30, TNA; and "Headquarters Southern Brigade KAR," SF/10, Acc. 30, TNA.

232. "Motor Drivers Recommended for Grade II LDS," Native Staff—General (Vols. 3 and 4), SF/10, Acc. 30, TNA. See also Savile, *When God Had One Eye Shut*, 97; and Stan Pritchard, *Driving Mad*, 25.

233. Hart, *Ghana on the Go*, 76–81.

234. Some driver histories are apparent only on these repair cards.

235. "Extract from Tanganyika Territory General Administration Memoranda," 75, Care of Government Motor Vehicles, n.d. (likely 1930), Tanganyika Territory 206, Acc. 215, TNA; and PWD Arusha Divisional Engineer's Office, "Motor Drivers Recommended for Grade II LDS," Native Staff—General (Vols. 3 and 4), n.d. (but other memos from 1946), SF/10, Acc. 30, TNA.

236. J. G. Gardner, "Alifeo Martin Accident," n.d., Tanganyika Public Works, SF/10, Acc. 30, TNA.

237. David Snowden, "The History of the EAR&H Tanganyika Road Services."

238. W. Fairly, Memo, October 12, 1944, SF/10, Acc. 30, TNA.

239. "GT 509—Tanganyika Territory: Bedford Truck WS 30 Cwt Purchased January 1935 Engine No 927073 Chassis No 91107," February 3, 1944, SF/10, Acc. 30, TNA.

240. "PWD Executive Engineer Office Easter Province DSM," May 28, 1937, SF/10, Acc. 30, TNA.

241. Dant, "Driver-Car," 62.

242. Leslie, *Survey of Dar es Salaam*, 127–28. For more about Njovu, see Grace, "Heroes of the Road." On farms as security, see Monson, *Africa's Freedom Railway*, 127.

243. A. B. Chanter, "Preliminary Investigation and Assembly Relevant to an Enquiry into the Question of Competition between Road and Rail in Tanganyika Territory," n.d. (appears to be 1935), accessed at TNL.

244. Cyril Francis, "Appendix B—S.W. Tanganyika Traffic Report by Mr. E. J. Borron," CO 525/151/9, March 23, 1934, BNA.

245. "Company Objects to 'Pirate' Carriers," *Tanganyika Standard*, September 27, 1961.

246. Pritchard, *Driving Mad*, 10–23.

247. Thus my earlier contrast with Gewald's observations about cars and the end of caravan trade. See note 197.

248. Iliffe, *Modern History of Tanganyika*, 415. Hart notes a "plurality" of values brought to driving as work and identity. Hart, *Ghana on the Go*, 99. Following Maddox ("Networks and Frontiers," 449, 452), I hope this brings nuance to histories of transport and

"integration" into global commodity economies that tend to use the former—especially mechanized movement—as evidence of the latter.

249. Elias Mwaifani, interview, Dar es Salaam (traveling from Mbeya), November 12, 2011.

250. "Enlistment of African Motor Drivers with the King's African Rifles," September 22, 1939, TS 27502, TNA.

251. "Enlistment of African Motor Drivers with the King's African Rifles."

252. Njovu, *Dereva wa Kwanza Tanganyika*, 34–36.

253. Brennan describes more tension around racial technopolitics at Tanganyika Railways, including claims by a craftsman that Africans learned more quickly than Europeans. Brennan, *Taifa*, 103–4.

254. I draw from Hecht's "technology of distrust" in "Rupture-Talk" (713–14). Luise White observes that the AK-47 "discomfited ideas about race." White, "'Heading for the Gun,'" 259. See also Hart, *Ghana on the Go*, 99–101, and for bureaucrats and tests, Feierman, *Peasant Intellectuals*, 244.

255. White, *Speaking with Vampires*, 142–43; and Hart, *Ghana on the Go*, 17–18, 96–97.

Chapter 2: Overhaul

1. Campbell, *East Africa by Motor Lorry*, 121. This individual was one of at least forty Africans who worked in the workshop. "Base M.T. Depot, Dar-es-Salaam," para. 113, n.d. (likely 1917), WO 158/882, BNA.

2. Daniel Headrick, in *The Tentacles of Progress* (307–8), endorses this divide between theory and practice, or "manual and intellect," including the necessity of book learning to supplement manual labor. This chapter challenges this approach. For the use of "imported magic" to denigrate societies, see Eden Medina, Ivan da Costa Marques, and Christina Holmes, "Introduction: Beyond Imported Magic," 2.

3. Kline and Pinch, "Users as Agents of Technological Change."

4. See Franz, *Tinkering*; Borg, *Auto Mechanics*; and Lucsko, *Junkyards, Gearheads, and Rust*.

5. Borg, *Auto Mechanics*, 4.

6. For a corollary, see Ponsavady, *Cultural and Literary Representations of the Automobile*, 63–68.

7. "Wheel or Chain Tracks at Option: One Ton Lorry Convertible for Any Use—Tests in England," n.d., Mott 6, SMLA. Nick Baldwin, in *Vintage Lorry Annual*, Number One provides a history of "trucks on tracks."

8. Mott to Cannell, January 21, 1926, Mott 6, SMLA.

9. "Transport: Report on Features and Results Achieved by Various Types of Motor Transport," CO 323/976/5, BNA. For corollaries, see Green-Simms, *Postcolonial Automobil-*

ity, 40–56; Pirie, "Non-urban Motoring in Colonial Africa"; and Ponsavady, *Cultural and Literary Representations of the Automobile*, 66–69.

10. On Africa as a laboratory, see Tilley, *African as a Living Laboratory*.

11. Harper, *Working Knowledge*, 6. I use the *school* in "unschooled" here to refer to the colonial institutions that started with German colonialism and later became national institutions. See the section "From *Bois* to Men" in this chapter for a fuller discussion.

12. Here I draw not only on Harper's excellent visual sociology in *Working Knowledge* but also on Paul Edwards's discussion of knowledge infrastructures in *A Vast Machine* (17–19) and Gabrielle Hecht's definition of a technopolitical regime in *The Radiance of France* (16–17).

13. In "Casting Aluminum Cooking Pots," Emily Osborn explores knowledge transmission outside official channels.

14. Tania Murray Li notes the conflation of expertise with these structures and suggest that scholars sometimes overstate their power. Li, *Will to Improve*, 12.

15. Edwards, *Vast Machine*, 18.

16. Such learning opportunities thus provide a way to explore "male subjectivities," as Stephan Miescher observes. Miescher, *Making Men in Ghana*, 55.

17. Borg, *Auto Mechanics*, 4.

18. Borg, *Auto Mechanics*, 2–4.

19. Harper, *Working Knowledge*, 21.

20. Jackson, "Rethinking Repair," 227.

21. Mbaraka Kassim, interview, Zanzibar Town, Zanzibar, June 8, 2012. Kassim opened a garage sometime in the late 1940s.

22. "Sir Philip Mitchell's Speech Prior to Laying the Foundation Stone, 25 April 1952," TS 39094, TNA.

23. Lugard, *Dual Mandate*, 413.

24. "Industrial Education," ZNA, AB 1/68. The first quote comes from the Director of Public Works' letter to the Chief Secretary while the latter comes from the section of "Education Policy in Tropical Africa" quoted by the director.

25. "Report on Industrial School: General Remarks," 1928, AB 1/68, ZNA.

26. "Memorandum of the Directors of PW and Education Apprenticeship for Town African and Arab Lads in the Skilled Trades of Carpentry and Metalwork in Zanzibar," 1933, AB 1/68, ZNA; Memo, Director of Public Works to Chief Secretary, n.d. (likely 1928), AB 1/68, ZNA.

27. "Training for Demobilized African Soldiers " August 22, 1946, SF/10, Acc. 30, Vols. 4 and 5, TNA.

28. R. Thomas, "Problems of Manpower Development," 116.

29. E. W. Baker, "Memorandum On Proposals for Establishment of a 'Work Service' and on Certain Aspects of Technical Education," March 26, 1951, TS 41619, TNA.

30. "Sir Philip Mitchell's Speech Prior to Laying the Foundation Stone, 25 April 1952." Joseph Hodge discusses the broader limitations and contradictions inherent in postwar development schemes in *Triumph of the Expert* (224–25).

31. Edgerton, "Innovation, Technology, or History," 680–97.

32. In *Alabama in Africa*, Andrew Zimmerman provides a similar discussion about the problems of embodied, uncertified knowledge and labor in the American South, German Togoland, and Germany (esp. chs. 1 and 4).

33. Baker, "Memorandum," and G. W. Hatchell, "Education and Training of Africans," September 8, 1945, TS 22068/III, TNA.

34. Alfred Emms, "Technical Training," 6 and 8, February 17, 1959, Mss. Afr.s. 517, RHO; Alfred Emms, "Trade Training in Trade Schools," 2, July 15, 1959, Mss. Afr.s. 517, RHO. Headrick demonstrates that this "cultural bias" applied broadly in technical education in colonial Africa. He blames it on the social mobility attached to clerical work instead of, as demonstrated here, European misreadings of African technological cultures and histories. Headrick, *Tentacles of Progress*, 306–8. As we saw in chapter 1, Africans had good reasons to be cautious about manual work in colonial spaces.

35. Fabian, *Time and the Other*, 31. See also McClintock, *Imperial Leather*, 54: "The space of empire is figured as a journey backward in time."

36. On this distinction more broadly, see Lerman, "Uses of Useful Knowledge"; and G. Hecht, *Being Nuclear*, 16–21.

37. Arnold, *Everyday Technology*, 60. See also Burton, *African Underclass*, 72.

38. "Handyman Course by WH Percival," 1936, TS 25735, TNA.

39. F. J. Harlow, "Memorandum on the Problem of Training Skilled Craftsmen in East Africa, Chiefly for the Building and Engineering Trades: Apprentices and Trade Testing: The Training of the Rural Craftsman," February 7, 1951, TS 41619, TNA. For an example of such gendered design in French West Africa, see Laura Ann Twagira, "Machines That Cook or Women Who Cook?"

40. "Technical Education of Africans (Makerere Commission)."

41. de Luna, "Collecting Food, Cultivating Persons," 311.

42. For a similar approach, see K. Beck, "Art of Truck Modding"; Schmidt, *Iron Technology in East Africa*; and Harper, *Working Knowledge*. On dynamism within oral histories, see White, Miescher, and Cohen, *African Words, African Voices*.

43. Krieger, *Pride of Men*, 193–95; G. Hecht, *Being Nuclear*, 116. Jojada Verrips and Birgit Meyer note the problematic taken-for-granted status of cars in scholarship on Africa. Verrips and Meyer, "Kwaku's Car," 158–59. On actions, see Eugenia Herbert, *Iron, Gender, and Power*, 3.

44. Kassim Jaha Abdullah, interview, Tabora, April 2, 2012.

45. On space and place in oral histories, see Kodesh, *Beyond the Royal Gaze*, 25; for methodologies of practice, see Harper, *Working Knowledge*; on things as archives, see Morton, *Age of Concrete*.

46. I hope this methodological variety when, taken together, addresses some of the historical challenges of locating skill in historical records identified by William Storey. See Storey, "Guns, Race, and Skill."

47. For a similar educational situation in Nigeria, see Berry, *Fathers Work for Their Sons*, 141.

48. On the popularity of PWD garage work, see Jumanne Sisia, interview, Tabora, April 11, 2012; Mrisho Sulemani Minchande, interview, Mkuranga, March 13, 2012; C. W. Stevenson, "Memorandum on the Training of Africans for Employment in the Lower Graded Technical Posts in the Public Works Department," February 6, 1937, TS 24638, TNA.

49. It appears the government considered only 214 of these individuals as official employees. It lists only 214 "Adult African Males" as mechanics and fitters while recognizing that 3,954 worked in this sector. Government of Tanganyika, *Annual Report of the Labour Division, 1961*, secs. IV and II, BC 9/27.

50. Fadhili Ramadhani, interview, Tabora, April 4, 2012.

51. Ramadhani Saidi Malambo, interview, Iringa, December 15, 2011.

52. Omari Kibwana, interview, Dar es Salaam, May 14, 2012.

53. Suleiman Saidi Sitembo, interview, Morogoro, March 15, 2012.

54. Kassian Duma, interview, Iringa, December 8, 2012. This echoes Stephan Miescher's *Making Men in Ghana* (55, 72) on the importance of apprenticeships for forging ideas of manhood outside of European educational systems.

55. Shabani Ramadhani, interview, Tabora, April 7, 2012.

56. "Annual Report, Transport Department 1926," AB 486, TNA.

57. "Annual Report, Transport Department, 1926," AB 486, TNA; "Annual Report, Transport Department, 1926," AB 485, TNA. Please note there are two separate archival files for this 1926 report.

58. Kassim Jaha Abdullah, interview.

59. Omari Kibwana, interview.

60. Bushiri Ali, interview, Iringa, December 18, 2011.

61. Bushiri Ali, interview.

62. Kondo Mfaume, interview, Morogoro, December 14, 2011.

63. De Luna, "Collecting Food, Cultivating Persons," 311–13. On slaves as fundi, see Glassman, *Feasts and Riot*, 89–91.

64. Suleiman Saidi Sitembo, interview.

65. "Annual Report, Transport Department, 1926," AB 485, TNA.

66. Akrich, "The De-Scription of Technical Objects," 205.

67. Harper, *Working Knowledge*; Henke, "Mechanics of Work Place Order," 75; Dant, "Work of Repair," 1; Krebs, "'Dial Gauge versus Senses 1–0,'" 355. See also Verrips and Meyer, "Kwaku's Car," 171, 177.

68. Collins and Evans, "Third Wave of Science Studies," 238.

69. As Headrick does in *The Tentacles of Progress* (307–8).

70. Suleiman Saidi Sitembo, interview.

71. Suleiman Saidi Sitembo, interview.

72. Kondo Mfaume, interview.

73. Suleiman Saidi Sitembo, interview.

74. Mbaraka Kassim, interview.

75. "Southern Brigade Supply and Transport Corps," March 23, 1930, TS 18964, TNA.

76. "Minutes from Director of Public Works," March 10, 1939," SF/10, Acc. 30, TNA; C. W. Stevenson, Memo, December 18, 1936, TS 24638, TNA; "Memorandum on the Training of Africans for Employment." The clearest definition of permanent versus casual labor categories came in technical education debates in the early 1950s as government laborers moved to private jobs. A 1951 initiative noted that making technical laborers permanent "would clearly be impracticable" due to cost, but suggested they receive benefits, including health care, paid holidays, and payment upon retirement. See "Memorandum On Proposals for Establishment of a 'Work Service' and on Certain Aspects of Technical Education," TS 41619, TNA.

77. "Native Mechanics and Cleaners Transport Section," n.d. (likely 1939), SF/10, Acc. 30, TNA.

78. Mbaraka Kassim, interview.

79. Jumanne Mrisho, interview, Tabora, April 4, 2012.

80. Kassian Duma, interview; and Kassim Jaha Abdullah, interview.

81. Cooper, *Decolonization and African Society*.

82. See, for example, the postwar demands in Cooper, "Industrial Man Goes to Africa."

83. There is a rich literature focusing on "power as knowledge" and the centralization of expert knowledge, including Escobar, *Encountering Development*; T. Mitchell, *Rule of Experts*; and Mehos and Moon, "Uses of Portability." See also Osborn, "Casting Aluminum Cooking Pots"; and Miescher, *Making Men in Ghana*, chap. 3.

84. Ndugu Athumani, "The Development and Organisation of a National Vocational Training System," in *First National Vocational Training Conference*, April 1975, BD14/25,

ZNA. Presence of European teachers information from Shabani Ramadhani, interview, Tabora, April 7, 2012.

85. Klingelhofer, "Occupational Preferences."

86. For the independent period, I use the terms *state*, *party*, and *government* for the remainder of the book. Their meanings overlap because, as Issa Shivji argues, Nyerere aimed to build a "party-state" and because, as Paul Bjerk observes, the president described government as a "machine" that needed to get going to ensure the success of Tanzania's nation-state. I use the term *state* most broadly to refer to the totality of mechanisms that included government and party and to refer to citizens' views of those entities. I follow Kelly Askew's groundbreaking work on the state in *Performing the Nation* to emphasize its subjectivities, blind spots, weaknesses, and the role of citizens in defining it. I use *government* to highlight more specific roles of ministries, departments, and parastatals. The translation between English and Kiswahili works poorly here because much of what academics discuss as the state is bound up in the Kiswahili word for government, *serikali*. I use *party* when it is clear an idea comes from the party apparatus. Shivji, *Development as Rebellion*, 41; Bjerk, "Sovereignty and Socialism," 284.

87. Schuller and Field, "Social Capital, Human Capital, and the Learning Society," 227.

88. Government of Tanganyika, *High-Level Manpower Requirements and Resources in Tanganyika, 1962–1967*, 1; Puaca, *Searching for Scientific Manpower*, 55.

89. For an overview up to 1967, see Resnick, "Manpower Development in Tanzania"; George Tobias, "High-Level Manpower Requirements and Resources in Tanganyika," 1963, BD 14/64, ZNA.

90. Government of Tanganyika, *High-Level Manpower Requirements and Resources in Tanganyika, 1962–1967*, 37–43. Stein, "Theories of the State in Tanzania," 120–21. Tanzanian reports sometimes replaced high, mid, and low with A, B, and C, with mechanical work fitting the latter.

91. Athumani, "The Development and Organisation of a National Vocational Training System," 20, 29; S. R. Makutika, "The Development of Vocational Training in Tanzania," 14–19, in *First National Vocational Training Conference*, April 1975, BD14/25, ZNA.

92. Mohamedi Kibwana Kondo, interview, Dar es Salaam, May 12, 2012.

93. Hamisi Salum Luwango, interview, Morogoro, March 14, 2012; Joseph Raymond Shola, interview, Morogoro, March 15, 2012.

94. Omar Seif Ngomadodo, interview, Dar es Salaam, January 10, 2012.

95. Suleiman Seif Saidi, interview, Dar es Salaam, January 10, 2012.

96. Mohamedi Kibwana Kondo, interview.

97. Geremano Simaliga, interview, Iringa, December 21, 2011.

98. Hamisi Hamadi "Mau," interview, Ujiji, April 16 and 20, 2012; Haji Hamisi Haliyamtu, interview, Ujiji, April 16 and 20, 2012; Fadhili Ramadhani, interview.

99. Musa (surname withheld), interview, Iringa, December 18, 2011.

100. Hamisi Hamadi "Mau," interview.

101. Evans and Collins, *Rethinking Expertise;* and Harper, *Working Knowledge.*

102. Fadhili Ramadhani, interview.

103. Hussein Almasi, interview, Morogoro, March 14, 2012.

104. Mohamedi Kibwana Kondo, interview.

105. Yusufu Ulimwengu, interview, Ujiji, April 17, 2012.

106. Shabani Ramadhani, interview.

107. Hussein Almasi, interview.

108. Mohamedi Kibwana Kondo, interview; Juma (surname withheld), interview, Morogoro, March 15, 2012.

109. Kassian Duma, interview.

110. Hamisi Salum Luwango, interview; Marachelumu Sambala, interview, Iringa, December 21, 2012.

111. Hamisi Hamadi "Mau," interview; Haji Hamisi Haliyamtu, interview; Jumanne Mrisho, interview; and Mohamedi Kibwana Kondo, interview.

112. Siegelbaum, "On the Side."

113. Haji Hamisi Haliyamtu, interview. Musa (surname withheld), interview, added that the "government tried hard" to provide a good environment for work.

114. "Experience of an Engineer in Tanzanian Transport Industries," 5–6.

115. Grace, "Mechanical Expression in a Broken World."

116. Kabura, "Experience of an Engineer," 6.

117. Nyerere, "After the Arusha Declaration," in *Ujamaa: Essays on Socialism,* 151.

118. Fili Karashani, "What Self-Reliance Means," *Sunday News,* March 5, 1978.

119. A. Likoko, "Ubepari lazima upigwe vita: Mafundi walaani magereji ya mitaani . . . ," *Nchi Yetu,* July 1975, 18.

120. Nyerere, "Kila Mtu Afanye Kazi," in *Wafanyakazi na Ujamaa,* 68–69.

121. Bata King (cartoonist), Bwanyenye Cartoon, 1, *Ngurumo,* June 17, 1968.

122. Makutika, "The Development of Vocational Training in Tanzania," 14.

123. The United Republic of Tanzania, "Report of the Working Party on the Establishment of 'The National Training Council,'" November 6, 1978, BD14/27, ZNA.

124. Sabot, *Economic Development and Urban Migration,* 141–47.

125. There is a rich literature on debates about cities and socialism: Brennan, *Taifa;* Callaci, *Street Archives and City Life;* Ivaska, *Cultured States;* and Fair, *Reel Pleasures.*

126. "Maisha Gani Haya Dar es Salaam?," *Nchi Yetu,* April 1975, 22–25.

127. Brennan, *Taifa*, 173; D. H. Mwinge, "Kabwela Mji si Wako," *Nchi Yetu*, December 1974, inside back cover.

128. Nyerere, "Education," 19–21. The term *knowledge import* comes from Parliamentarian C. D. Msuya, in his speech from the same year, "Foreign Aid and Tanzanian Development."

129. Madan, *English-Swahili Dictionary*, 251; Steere, *Handbook of the Swahili Language*, 346; Fabian, *Making Identity on the Swahili Coast*, 22

130. For an example of popular use, see Vincent Mtambo, "Mitaani," *Nchi Yetu*, June 1969.

131. Bushiri Ali, interview.

132. Vitusi Kihanga, interview, Morogoro, December 12, 2011; Musa (surname withheld), interview; Abdallah Suleiman, interview, Tabora, April 5, 2012; Peter William Mabula, interview, Tabora, April 5, 2012; Saidi Hassan, interview, Tabora, April 12, 2012; Yusufu Iddi, interview, Tabora, April 14, 2012; Peja Mboga, interview, Tabora, April 13, 2012; and Mohamed (surname withheld), interview, Stone Town, Zanzibar, May 3, 2012.

133. Juma Katigiro, interview, Morogoro, December 12, 2011.

134. Field notes, Dar es Salaam, January 12, 2012. As James Brennan observes, more than a biological age, *vijana* signified "subordinate status" in a society in which older patrician men controlled important social resources such as bride wealth and employment. In a garage the same occurred except "subordinate status" as *vijana* was indicated by having less knowledge and fewer things. J. Brennan, "Youth, the TANU Youth League, and Managed Vigilantism," 205.

135. Suleiman Abdallah Mwenda, interview, Dar es Salaam, January 16, 2012. Also Hadi Maganza, interview, March 16, 2012, Dar es Salaam.

136. Peter William Mabula, interview.

137. Miescher, *Making Men in Ghana*, 49.

138. Jonas Mbawala, interview, Dar es Salaam, October 29, 2011.

139. Omari Magunda, interview, Dar es Salaam, October 29, 2011; Paul James, interview, Iringa, December 16, 2012; Ramadhani Rashid, interview, Tabora, April 11, 2012.

140. Fair, *Reel Pleasures*, 260–66.

141. Ramadhani Dunda, interview, Dar es Salaam, January 20, 2012; Kibwana, interview.

142. Juma Katigiro, interview.

143. Peter William Mabula, interview; Suleiman Abdallah Mwenda, interview.

144. Hussein Almasi, interview. Also see Samson's linguistic study, *Ufundi (wa) Magari*.

145. For possibilities and limits, see Akrich, "De-scription of Technical Objects," 207–9.

146. Brian Ibrick, interview, Dar es Salaam, July 17, 2012; and Jumanne Mrisho, interview.

147. Yusufu Iddi, interview.

148. Geremano Simaliga, interview, Iringa, December 21, 2011.

149. Suleiman Abdallah Mwenda, interview.

150. Mohamedi Naso, interview, Morogoro, December 13, 2011.

151. Francis Mwakatundu (mechanic), interview, Iringa, December 15, 2011.

152. Patel, *Migritude*, 38.

153. Krieger, *Pride of Men*, 225; and de Luna, *Collecting Food, Cultivating People*, 120.

154. Mtokambali Hassan Saidi, interview, Morogoro, March 13, 2012.

155. Ndeko Jamii, interview, Iringa, December 8, 2011.

156. David Mfume, interview, Iringa, December 21, 2011.

157. Hamisi Salum Luwango, interview. David Kent and Paul Mushi also found this in *The Education and Training of Artisans* (56).

158. Elimu ya Malezi ya Ujana (Jumuiya ya Kikristo Tanzania), "Kijana na Kazi," 16, 1983, TNL.

159. On different articulations of self-reliance, see Fair, *Reel Pleasures*, 231; P. Lal, "Self-Reliance and the State," 220–24; and Callaci, *Street Archives and City Life*, 128–29. Callaci notes the containerized, bootstrap approach foisted on citizens. I use *family* here following David Schoenbrun's definition as "compositions of many different people rather than accumulations of biological relatives." Schoenbrun, *A Green Place, a Good Place*, 99. "Birthing Wealth?" by Rhiannon Stephens, who builds on Schoenbrun, inspired my thinking on mechanical families. Though stretched across hundreds of years and different places, in each of these cases, compositions of family acted as a way to deal with instability and/or create security and mobility.

160. Suleiman Saidi Sitembo, interview; and Omari Kamulika, interview, Tabora, April 7, 2012.

161. Mathias Kayega, interview, Morogoro, December 10, 2011.

162. Mtokambali Hassan Saidi, interview.

163. Mwase, "Supply of Road Vehicles in Tanzania," 83.

164. Fadhili Ramadhani, interview, Tabora, December 17, 2011; and Mohamedi Naso, interview.

165. Kassim Jaha Abdullah, interview.

166. Malambo, interview. See Guyer and Belinga, "Wealth in People as Wealth in Knowledge" (119), for critiques of earlier models of wealth in people without wealth in knowledge. Colleen Krieger provides the nearest corollary to mechanics with both the accessibility of blacksmithing—unlike smelting—and the fluidity of iron economies for social mobility. Krieger, *Pride of Men*, 96–97.

167. Naso, interview; Moshi Omari Abdurahman, interview, Tabora, August 13, 2012.

168. Brian Ibrick, interview; advertisement for Brian Tshaka in *Progress* no. 3 (October 1981), 16.

169. *Daily News*, September 13, 1977.

170. "Diwani Stresses Technology Progress," *Daily News*, August 6, 1976. This recalls Fair's *Reel Pleasures* (265), which identifies the unofficial ways in which citizens achieved ujamaa's principles and the tendency of a political class to misread these moments.

171. Cool told me this story on a nonresearch trip to Dar es Salaam in December 2018.

172. Hadi Maganza, interview.

173. Fadhili Ramadhani, interview.

174. Saidi Hassan, interview.

175. Bushiri Ali, interview; Kazuge, interview, Tabora, April 15, 2012; Hussein Rashid Chambusu, interview, Tabora, April 12, 2012.

176. Juma Katigiro, interview.

177. Omari Kibwana, interview.

178. Harper, *Working Knowledge*, 21.

179. Livingston, *Improvising Medicine*, 20. Richard Sennett calls this "dynamic repair." Sennett, *Craftsman*, loc. 2,140.

180. Geremano Simaliga, interview.

181. Hamisi Salum Luwango, interview. This referenced boring an engine block which some other mechanics did by hand.

182. Juma Katigiro, interview.

183. Mtokambali Hassan Saidi, interview. Verrips and Meyer describe similar approaches to cylinders in "Kwaku's Car" (170–71).

184. Peter William Mabula, interview.

185. Mtokambali Hassan Saidi, interview; Mjomba Kondo, interview, Dar es Salaam, January 22, 2012.

186. Juma Katigiro, interview.

187. Kondo Mfaume, interview.

188. Peter William Mabula, interview; and John Samuel (mechanic), interview, Tabora, April 4, 2012.

189. Mjomba Kondo, interview.

190. Kent and Mushi, "Educational Training of Artisans," 73; Suleiman Abdallah Mwenda, interview; Hussein Almasi, interview.

191. Mtokambali, interview; Mohamed Sagamiko, interview, Iringa, December 17, 2011.

Chapter 3: The People's Car of Dar es Salaam

1. "Special Sunday Interview: UDA Revisited," *Daily News*, June 19, 1977.

2. Fair, "Drive-In Socialism," 1080.

3. Breckenridge, *Biometric State*, 7. On the social meanings of bodies, see Livingston, *Debility and the Moral Imagination*; on residing in not-quite-working infrastructure and its daily modalities, see Larkin, *Signal and Noise*, 235; Gastrow, "Aesthetic Dissent," 378; and Chalfin, "Wastelandia," 666.

4. This is one way of approaching modernization as a historical process. See Miescher, Bloom, and Manuh, "Introduction," 1–16.

5. In *African Socialism in Postcolonial Tanzania*, Priya Lal makes an impassioned case for fighting such declensionist narratives (224–26). This also extends James Brennan's argument in *Taifa* about urban entitlements requiring sustained political engagement (105). David Morton writes about how urban residents' interventions gave "substance to what politics was and what governance should do." Morton, *Age of Concrete*, loc. 205.

6. As Ronald Kline and Trevor Pinch showed in the United States in their "Users as Agents of Technological Change." See also Scott, *Seeing like a State*, esp. the concluding chapter on "metis"; G. Hecht, "Radioactive Excess," 206; and Hadfield and Aerni-Flessner, "Introduction," 3.

7. P. Lal, *African Socialism*, 215.

8. Rizzo, "Being Taken for a Ride."

9. On the emergence of Dar es Salaam as *Bongo* (brain), one of the city's nicknames, see Callaci, *Street Archives in City Life*, 200–206.

10. I thus add technological citizenship and systems to a key theme in the city's history. See Brennan, *Taifa*; Ivaska, *Cultured States*; Fair, *Reel Pleasures*; Callaci, *Street Archives and City Life*; P. Lal, *African Socialism*; and Hunter, *Political Thought*. Both Fair and Emily Callaci argue that reworking discourse required reworking spaces, networks, and sometimes things.

11. Callaci shows, in particular, the important role of taxis for women's nightly mobility. Callaci, *Street Archives and City Life*, 106.

12. David Arnold makes a similar point in *Everyday Technology* (4–5).

13. E. Medina, *Cybernetic Revolutionaries*, 7.

14. Fanon, *Wretched of the Earth*, 176.

15. Nyerere, "Pomposity," in *Freedom and Unity*, 225.

16. Nyerere, *Our Economy*, 16.

17. Nyerere, *Our Economy*, 13.

18. "Naizi na Visa Vyao," *Civil Service Magazine*, November/December 1965, 7.

19. "Family Development Plan: Part II," *Civil Service Magazine*, July/August 1965, 6, TNL. On debates about "Nizer (Naizi) Wealth," including automobiles, see Ivaska, *Cultured States*, 202–3, 132.

20. "Family Development Plan: Part II," 6; and J. A. Namata, "The Role of the Civil Service in a One Party State," *Civil Service Magazine*, July/August 1965, 20, TNL. The magazine's answer to loan problems was for citizens to create credit unions: "Credit unions express in the field of economics the high ideals of *Ujamaa*." See "Money Problems? Government Offers a Solution," *Civil Service Magazine*, March/April 1966, 2, TNL.

21. "Kununua Mamotokaa, Masuti au Taiti—Ni Kutia Maji Katika Pakacha," *Ngurumo*, March 10, 1965. "Cheo ni Dhamana," a poem by Matei Hermani in the November 1969 issue of *Nchi Yetu*, covered these issues by insisting that "status . . . is not a door to income [*pato*]" and thus taxi and Benz ownership.

22. Tanzania Petroleum Development Corporation, "Industry Trade 1970–1990: White and Black Oils," 3, M1128, TPDC archive.

23. To the extent that a poem critical of Africanization called for bureaucrats to keep the process in "first gear" because of danger on the road ahead. D. S. Salum Mkanya, "Gea Moja Nezesheni," *Mwafrika*, July 18, 1964, 10.

24. Nyerere, "President Nyerere's Speech," 15–16.

25. Fair, "Drive-In Socialism," 1089; and Callaci, *Street Archives and City Life*, 164. The statistics are from "The Story of Tanzania's Tiper Refinery," *Tanzania Trade and Industry* no. 25 (1969): 30, TNL. As far as I can tell, registration statistics represent numbers of vehicles categorized as private, not the number of individuals who owned private vehicles. This is supported by oral histories about registration in the final section of this chapter where individuals owning more than one vehicle registered a second vehicle as a taxi (and thus a public serving passenger vehicle) or placed it in a spouse's name.

26. Gaspar Mwacha, interview, Iringa, December 18, 2011; Musa Muikikwa, interview, Iringa, December 18, 2012; Jumanne Sisia, interview, Tabora, April 12, 2012; Hamadi Swedi, interview, Tabora, April 6, 2012. For an example of both views, see Msomaji wa Ngurumo, "Kuhusu Hatua ya Kupunguza Magari ya Binafsi," *Ngurumo*, February 24, 1972.

27. Edwards and Hecht, "History and the Technopolitics of Identity," 622

28. Nyerere, "Arusha Declaration," in *Ujamaa: Essays on Socialism*, 24–25.

29. Nyerere, "Arusha Declaration," in *Ujamaa: Essays on Socialism*, 26–27.

30. Nyerere, "Arusha Declaration," in *Ujamaa: Essays on Socialism*, 29.

31. Hofmeier, *Transport and Economic Development*, 102.

32. Hofmeier, *Transport and Economic Development*, 105. The next highest was Kilimanjaro Region with only 5.9 cars per mile of "classified" road.

33. See Hofmeier, *Transport and Economic Development*, 103.

34. Hyden, *Beyond Ujamaa in Tanzania*. Goran Hyden recognized that many of the state's technological policies and projects stemmed from aspirational, and not realized, power.

This, he shows, meant displacing existing technological livelihoods across the nation, a huge project. I thus disagree with his monolithic presentation of "peasants" but recognize his important contributions to thinking about state power as an aspiration for technological power and thus "state capture." P. Lal charts this more recently in *African Socialism in Postcolonial Tanzania* (80).

35. "The Development of Roads," CRW451000, TNA; East African Transport Study, "Preliminary Findings," 3, n.d., CW45139, TNA.

36. "Roads," *Jenga*, no. 9 (1971): 22–27; "Tanzam Highway Gets New Face," *Tanzania News Review*, 7, August, 1969. See "Bitumen Plant for Tanzania," 9, M00082, TPDC.

37. *Juhudi za Wananchi Kuijenga Tanzania: Waitikia Wito wa Baba wa Taifa, 1967*, BA 26/4, ZNA. For examples of poetry, see "Silaha ni Jembe," *Ngurumo*, February 9, 1968; and "Jembe Silaha ya Nchi," *Nchi Yetu*, June 1969.

38. John Lucas Kampanmbala, interview, Tabora, April 5, 2012.

39. Village Settlement Agency, "Notes on the selection of farmers for Pilot Village Settlements," 2 1965, A.3/294, TNA.

40. Hyden, *Beyond Ujamaa in Tanzania*, 209–36.

41. J. Rweyemamu makes a similar point in *Underdevelopment and Industrialization in Tanzania*, 72–73.

42. Nyerere, "President's Inaugural Address," in *Freedom and Unity*, 82–83.

43. Nyerere, "Education and Law," in *Freedom and Unity*, 131.

44. Nyerere, "To Plan Is to Choose," in *Freedom and Development*, 83; Nyerere, "Tanzania Ten Years After Independence," in *Freedom and Development*, 2–3; Nyerere, "Independence Address to the United Nations," in *Freedom and Unity*, 151–52; Nyerere, "President's Inaugural Address," in *Freedom and Unity*, 179, 181.

45. Nyerere, "The Purpose Is Man," *Ujamaa*, 97.

46. Nyerere, "The Purpose Is Man," in *Ujamaa: Essays on Socialism*, 99; Nyerere, "Socialism and Rural Development," in *Ujamaa: Essays on Socialism*, 143; Nyerere, "After the Arusha Declaration," in *Freedom and Socialism*, 150–51.

47. "Jembe Silaha ya Nchi," published on inside of front cover; see also imagery in *Juhudi za Wananchi Kuijenga Tanzania*, 16, 18.

48. P. Lal, *African Socialism*, 97–98; and author visit to museum in December 2018.

49. "Make It Here in Tanzania," *Tanzania Trade Journal*, January/March 1965, 22–23.

50. Nyerere, "Introduction," in *Freedom and Socialism*, 19; and Nyerere, "Arusha Declaration," *Ujamaa: Essays on Socialism*, 16.

51. "Motokaawalia," *Ngurumo*, July 12, 1972.

52. "Chama cha uchukuzi kitashika njia zote za usafirishaji," *Ngurumu*, March 15, 1965; A. Likoko, "CORETCO inavyowahudumia wananchi," *Nchi Yetu*, October 1975, 12–13. See also

"Wachukuzi wa Magari Waungana," *Ushirika*, November 1965, 4; "Chama Kidogo Kawe Chatoa Mfano Kununua Lori," *Ushirika*, June 1971, 8; "Tatizo la Usafirishaji wa Mazao Kusini," *Ushirika*, January 1974, 7. In one case, the Village Development Bank provided a 1.5 million shilling loan for 18 trucks for Nyanza. "Vyama vya Usafirishaji," *Ushirika Nyongeza*, December 1971, 3.

53. This logic pertained to design, too. A project between the Ministry of Agriculture, the United Nations, and the Soviet Union designed two vehicles specially outfitted to repair farming tools in rural areas: "Magari ya viwanda vijijini," *Ngurumo*, January 31, 1973.

54. "Kununua gari la Tanu," *Ngurumo*, September 7, 1971; and Nyerere, "Arusha Declaration," in *Ujamaa: Essays on Socialism*, 22–24.

55. Government of Tanzania, *Second Five Year Plan*, xvii–xviii, 5–7.

56. Nyerere, *The Arusha Declaration: Ten Years After*, 10–11.

57. On rural-urban articulations in particular, see Nyerere, "To Plan is to Choose," in *Freedom and Development*, 96–97.

58. Government of Tanzania, *Second Five Year Plan*, 177–83. These themes are borne out in the 1968 City Master Plan as well. Armstrong, "Colonial and Neocolonial Urban Planning," 53–57; and Sabot, *Economic Development and Urban Migration*. Callaci rightly calls this process the "ruralization of Dar es Salaam." Callaci, *Street Archives and City Life*, 6.

59. Coulson, *Tanzania*, 279; and Callaci, *Street Archives and City Life*, 187.

60. The United Republic of Tanzania, Uhuru Corridor Regional Physical Plan: Sectoral Studies II, 1–25.

61. Nyerere, "The Varied Paths to Socialism," in *Ujamaa: Essays on Socialism*, 89–90; Government of Tanzania, *Second Five Year Plan*, 37.

62. Nyerere, "Nguzo tano za Ujamaa," in *Ujamaa ni Imani*, 68. Callaci charts an "antiurban turn" between 1972 and 1974 that included expulsions, the movement of the capital to Dodoma, and diminished health services. That the state also expanded UDA during this period shows that a growth in urban entitlements could be paired with a disciplinary antiurban rhetoric and policy that demanded that residents earn everything the state provided through the "communal aspect." Callaci, *Street Archives and City Life*, 57.

63. "Karadha," *Nationalist*, November 19, 1970; "Car Loans and Public Transport," June 17, 1970. Andrew Ivaska notes that politicians jumped on the request of a university student representative requesting reduced national service and access to car loans even as another group of students actively condemned Karadha. Ivaska, *Cultured States*, 136–37, 142.

64. "Combat Conspicuous Consumption," *Nationalist*, May 25, 1970.

65. "No Car Loans," *Tanzania News Review*, January 1973, 11; "NEC Halts Karadha's Plan: People's Money Won't Be Loaned for Buying Cars," *Nationalist*, November 20, 1970; and "Kutononoka kwa magari ya binafsi marufuku sasa!," *Ngurumo*, November 9, 1971.

66. TANU, "TANU Guidelines on Guarding, Consolidating and Advancing the Revolution of Tanzania, and of Africa (*Mwongozo*)," 41–42.

67. Kassum, *Africa's Winds of Change*; M. A. Mgaza, "Pumzisha gari yako Jumapili," *Nchi Yetu*, January 1975, 8–9.

68. TPDC, "Industry Trade," 3. The TPDC blamed the discrepancy between regular and premium fuel sales on advertising campaigns owing to the latter's higher profit margin for marketing companies.

69. Rutayisingwa, *Ngumi Ukutani*, 9.

70. Rutayisingwa, *Ngumi Ukutani*, 22. Callaci explores constructions of womanhood through such encounters. Callaci, *Street Archives and City Life*, 59, 103, 136, and esp. 192–93.

71. See the story of Rama in Eddie Ganzel, "Achane Nae," *Tamasha: Gazeti la Starehe*, July 1971. Accessed at the NBA Room, TNL.

72. This is a steady theme in a bound volume of two issues of *Tamasha: Gazeti la Starehe* from 1971, found in TNL.

73. Ruhumbika, *Silent Empowerment*.

74. *Mfanyakazi*, July 6, 1974, 3.

75. Quoted in Isaac Mruma, "Personal Cars Poor Economics—Nyerere," *Daily News*, December 9, 1980.

76. Brownell describes this planning process and places it within broader global trends in *Gone to Ground* (26–29, 34).

77. Marshall Macklin Monaghan Limited, "Dar es Salaam Master Plan, Part III," October 1979, 59, 79.

78. Armstrong, "Colonial and Neocolonial Urban Planning," 58; and Project Planning Associates, *National Capital Plan, Dodoma, Tanzania*.

79. Ministry of Lands, Housing and Urban Development, "Bus Transport for Site and Service Areas, Dar es Salaam," Dar es Salaam, 1973, accessed in the East Africana Room, UDSM Library, Dar es Salaam, Tanzania.

80. "Dar es Salaam Motor Transport Co. Ltd.—Increase in Fares," TS, 30299/3, TNA.

81. J. M. Mapunda and Habib Shindo, "Wakuu wa DMT," *Mwafrika*, February 29, 1964, 3; Zacharias Kaboja, "Wafanyakazi wa DMT," *Mwafrika*, February 6, 1964, 1; *National Capital Master Plan*, 26, accessed in the East Africana Room, UDSM Library.

82. M. Katunzi, interview, Dar es Salaam, July 14, 2012; anonymous, interview, Dar es Salaam; Hawa Jama, interview, Dar es Salaam, August 9, 2010; Stelar Alfons, interview, Dar es Salaam, August 9, 2010; Hadija (surname withheld), interview, Dar es Salaam; Zana Asmani, interview, Dar es Salaam, August 6, 2010; and Mloka, *Mjini Taabu*, 50–51.

83. Vassanji, *Gunny Sack*, 178–79.

84. Selemani Saidi, interview, Dar es Salaam, August 6, 2012; Veronica Agostin, interview, Dar es Salaam, August 7, 2012.

85. "National Transport Corporation in Formation," *The Nationalist*, March 10, 1970. Lonrho also owned the Motor Service Ltd., Tanzania Motor Corporation, Tanzania

Vehicle Finance Ltd., Mwananchi Tractor Assembly Ltd., and part of Riddoch Motors. See Barker and Wield, "Notes on International Firms."

86. Director of the National Transport Corporation, "Shirika la Taifa la Uchukuzi," December 8, 1973, UDA Offices, Dar Es Salaam, Tanzania; "Towards an Efficient Bus Service," *The Nationalist*, May 8, 1970.

87. Yakob Opita, interview, Dar es Salaam, July 20, 2009. Praising such conduct, see also Charles Mloka, *Mjini Taabu*, 51.

88. Siegelbaum, *Cars for Comrades*, chap. 1.

89. Péteri, "Streetcars of Desire," 22.

90. Charles Mloka, *Mjini Taabu*, 51.

91. Over 20 percent of breakdowns were caused by tires, 13 percent each by brake systems or by the clutch and gearbox, and 10.8 percent by engines. Cited in Banyikwa, "Urban Passenger Transport Problems."

92. Banyikwa, "Urban Passenger Transport Problems," 85; UDA, "Operational Statistics: 1978," UDA; and Berege, "Promotion of an Efficient and Effective Urban Transport Public System in Dar-es-Salaam," 36.

93. Jamhuri ya Muungano wa Tanzania, *Hotuba ya Waziri was Mawasiliano na Uchukuzi, Ndugu A.C. Mwingira, 1980/81*, 26–27; and Jamhuri ya Muungano wa Tanzania, *Hotuba ya Waziri wa Mawasiliano na Uchukuzi, Ndugu A. H. Jamal, 1978/79*, 25.

94. Rizzo, "Being Taken for a Ride," 136; and UDA, "Maelezo Mafupi Kuhusu Mafanikio na Matatizo ya UDA," 1980, UDA.

95. Peter White, "The Coach and Bus Industry," *Bulletin of Tanzanian Affairs*, January 1983, 7–9.

96. Jamhuri ya Muungano wa Tanzania, *Hali ya Uchukuzi na Mawasiliano Nchini Mei, 1980*, appendixes 11 and 12.

97. Mutongi, *Matatu*.

98. National Transport Corporation, "Press Release: Performance of DMT in 1972," March 22, 1973, UDA; and German Technical Aid Project, "List of Routes," 1977. Hans-Peter Torbeck, who worked at UDA as part of West German technical aid projects, provided these materials through email (August 10, 2010).

99. J. M. Mapunda and Habib Shindo, "Wakuu wa DMT," *Mwafrika*, February 29, 1964, 3; Kisele Selemani, "Mabasi Buguruni," *Mwafrika*, March 20, 1964, 3.

100. J. Juma, "Oyster Bay Is No Longer an Exclusive Area, Please," *Daily News*, May 2, 1976.

101. "Sudi, a Short Story by Pili," *Daily News*, July 17, 1980. On cars in novellas, see Callaci, *Street Archives and City Life*, 164.

102. This is a contrast with Kenyan bus passengers, who preferred matatus over the state-run service, as Mutongi notes in *Matatu* (28–29). Interestingly, she later links this to a "defiance of traditional roles" and politics (214).

103. On "infrastructural citizenship," see Kyle Shelton, *Power Moves*; Breckenridge writes of "infrastructures of citizenship" in *Biometric State* (8). I use *technology* because debates about citizenship spilled out of infrastructure to encompass hoes, plows, cars, and scooters.

104. See Ivaska, *Cultured States*, 29. Callaci shows that this engagement was also part of colonial life. See Callaci, "Dancehall Politics."

105. Hodari Likapite, "UDA: The Prodigal Son," *Daily News*, June 20, 1977.

106. L. Thomas, *Politics of the Womb*; and Ivaska, *Cultured States*, 31–34.

107. Ivaska, *Cultured States*, 215.

108. See Condon, "Nation Building and Image"; and Ngonyani, "Tools of Deception." On the grain of these state media sources, see Callaci, *Street Archives and City Life*, 50–51, 210.

109. Woolgar and Grint, "Computers and the Transformation of Social Analysis," 369. Brian Larkin observes a tendency in scholarship for infrastructure to gain political power through its invisibility instead of for its visibility, its intrusions, and the affective politics created by such visibilities and intrusions. Larkin, "Promising Forms," 186.

110. Gastrow, "Aesthetic Dissent," 379. Nate Plageman recognizes newspaper contributors as "tacticians" of urban infrastructural change. Plageman, "'Accra Is Changing, Isn't It?,'" 138.

111. As others have chronicled: Geiger, *TANU Women*; Brennan, *Taifa*; Ivaska, *Cultured States*; and Fair, *Reel Pleasures*.

112. Nyerere, "Uhuru ni Kazi," in *Wafanyakazi na Ujamaa*, 54–55; and Nyerere, *The Arusha Declaration: Ten Years After*, 54, 58.

113. A rich literature has explored this, including Brennan, *Taifa*; Fair, *Reel Pleasures*; Ivaska, *Cultured States*; Callaci, *Street Archives and City Life*; Bjerk, *Building a Peaceful Nation*; and P. Lal, *African Socialism*.

114. Brennan, *Taifa*, 173.

115. Nyerere, *The Arusha Declaration: Ten Years After*, 59.

116. Nyerere, "Ujamaaa: The Basis of African Socialism," in Nyerere, *Ujamaa: Essays on Socialism*, 5.

117. "Nidhamu Tutakayoifuata Haitakuwa ya Mijeledi," *Mfanyakazi*, April 7, 1973; see also Kituma, "Maana ya ufanisi wa kazi," *Mfanyakazi*, December 29, 1973. On discipline in a different urban context in Tanzania, see G. Burgess, "To Differentiate Rice from Grass," 240; on appreciation for in Mozambique, see Drew Thompson, "'Não há Nada' (There is nothing)," s126–28.

118. Hawa Jama, interview, Dar es Salaam, July 15, 2002; L. Chibona, interview, Dar es Salaam, July 2, 2009; Juma Mgema, interview, Dar es Salaam, August 6, 2012; Selemani Saidi, interview, August 6, 2012; Veronica Agostin, interview, August 7, 2012, Dar es Salaam.

119. Juma Mgema, interview, Dar es Salaam, August 8, 2012; Musuguri Msuya, interview, August 6, 2012, Dar es Salaam; Jumanne Issa, interview, Dar es Salaam, July 15, 2009.

120. Musa Ntimizi, "Put More Effort into Solving UDA Problems," *Daily News*, November 13, 1979. Generally, see "DMT Bado Matatizo," *Mfanyakazi*, June 30, 1973.

121. Brownell, *Going to Ground*, 96, 115.

122. Shadrack Swai, "Ni Kweli Foleni Mbaya au Huduma Mbaya?," 5–7, *Nchi Yetu*, April 1973. See also "Special Sunday Interview: On UDA Services," *Sunday News*, June 5, 1977.

123. "Special Sunday Interview: On UDA Services," *Sunday News*, June 5, 1977.

124. Juma Mgema, interview, Dar es Salaam, August 6, 2012; and Mwalim Ruta, interview, Dar es Salaam, July 16, 2010.

125. Toma Toma Jazz Band, "Standi ya Basi," [1970s], YouTube video, 6:39, posted by jphamber, https://www.youtube.com/watch?v=XRyl3xwM5wg.

126. Mikundi E. N. B., "Too Much Time Wasted," *Daily News*, April 3, 1979.

127. Nicholas Kiwale, "UDA Good at Inventing Excuses," *Daily News*, January 22, 1979. See also "Inefficient Services," *Daily News*, June 2, 1977.

128. The problem was reported as early as 1973: "Sisi Tunasema," *Mfanyakazi*, April 14, 1973; "UDA Is to Blame," *Daily News*, April 17, 1977; and D. J. Kyejo, "Hopes for UDA Dwindling," *Daily News*, June 28, 1979. On lines for drive-in theaters, see Fair, "Drive-in Socialism," 1080.

129. Koshuma, "Dar Transport Problems Must Come to an End," *Daily News*, June 4, 1979. See also "UDA Needs Good Leadership," *Daily News*, June 21, 1977; and Adam Masoud (cartoonist), *Mfanyakazi*, August 17, 1974.

130. Harun Machenge, quoted in "Special Sunday Interview: On UDA Services."

131. Nyerere, "Arusha Declaration," in *Ujamaa: Essays on Socialism*, 14.

132. Verdery, *What Was Socialism?*, 48. See also Fredericks, *Garbage Citizenship*, 61: "Austerity works by reconfiguring the relationship between body, infrastructure, and city."

133. King'ei, *Mwongozo wa siku njema*, 4–5.

134. On the gendered structure of (im)mobilities, see Callaci, *Street Archives and City Life*, 192–94.

135. Kyejo, "Hopes for UDA Dwindling."

136. Wambura Mcmbusi Jr., "Boarding Buses with Comfort," *Daily News*, October 6, 1980.

137. A. N. Mloka, "The Big Joke in UDA Buses," *Daily News*, January 11, 1979. See also UDA Passenger, "Police Can Help UDA Repair Buses," June 15, 1977. Mutongi's *Matatu* raises similar concerns about speed, jammed bodies, and the meeting of quotas (93–96).

138. "6 UDA Commuters Fined," *Daily News*, December 16, 1977.

139. "Thugs Enjoy UDA Rides," *Daily News*, December 24, 1977.

140. Quoted in "Commuters Up in Arms," *Daily News*, December 19, 1977.

141. Quoted in "Commuters Up in Arms!," *Daily News*, December 19, 1977.

142. E. G. Munuo, "Passengers Don't Hang on UDA Buses for Fun," *Daily News*, December 19, 1977.

143. Disillusioned Citizen, "Which Way Is the Law?," *Daily News*, December 19, 1977. See also Dennis Ubwe, "UDA Should Go To Court," *Daily News*, May 18, 1978. Chapter 5 in Mutongi's *Matatu* provides a rich example of the politics of boarding, riding, and jumping out in Nairobi.

144. "Maisha Gani Haya Dar es Salaam?," *Nchi Yetu*, April 1975, 22–25; "Madereva," *Nchi Yetu*, November 1974, 6. Callaci explores this very article and a similar framing of the problems of urban life in *Street Archives and City Life* (51–53, 56–57) for policy beyond transport. For a history of the Ministry of Culture, see Askew, *Performing the Nation*, chap. 5.

145. Palmer, "Ineffective Masculinity," 457–58.

146. A. P. Mdoe, "Wasafiri nao, Je?," *Nchi Yetu*, April 1974, 21–22, 63–64.

147. Mutongi describes similar debates about mobility, buses, and regulation. Mutongi, *Matatu*, 74–88, 118–20.

148. Sammy Polly, "UDA Conductors a Menace to Passengers," *Daily News*, May 12, 1977; "KONDAKTA No. 330," *Ngurumo*, September 11, 1972.

149. "Ombi la DMT," *Ngurumo*, December 27, 1971; "Halo Mista, DMT Dereva," *Mfanyakazi*, June 30, 1973; "UDA Conductors a Menace to Passengers," *Daily News*, May 12, 1977; "KONDAKTA No. 330"; "Inefficient Services"; A. R. Chekanae, "D.M.T.," *Ngurumo*, March 18, 1968; M. S. Chambuso, "Wanawake tu," *Ngurumo*, March 20, 1968; C. B. Teikwa, "Something Adds Salt to Wound," *Daily News*, December 27, 1977. On more general pushback against city culture, see also I. G. Mhindi, "Oh No, Ndugu Suleiman!: Dar Workers Are Not Lazy," *Daily News*, June 30, 1977.

150. Bwanyenye, cartoon, *Ngurumo*, July 17, 1970; Allen Silver Mhije, "Nimekutana na nini katika UDA?" *Nchi Yetu*, December 1974, 32. P. Lal, "Militants, Mothers, and the National Family," 9–11; and Aminzade, *Race, Nation, and Citizenship*, 142–45.

151. Mloka, "Big Joke in UDA Buses." The ST cars were renamed SU, Shirika la Umma ("a parastatal organization"), in 1979. "Cars Now Using 'SU' Ante," *Daily News*, April 25, 1979.

152. "Dar Transport Problems Must Come to an End."

153. K. Lujuo, "UDA Stands Accused," *Daily News*, June 6, 1977; "Put More Effort in Solving UDA Problems."

154. "Special Sunday Interview: Indiscipline . . . Negligence . . . Who Is to Blame?," *Sunday News*, May 8, 1977.

155. K. M. Pallangyo, "Did a Bomb Fall on the 41 Buses? UDA Has a Case to Answer," *Daily News*, June 7, 1977; Stan Kakuyu, "UDA Has to Be 'Pushed,'" *Daily News*, May 26, 1977; Zayumba Zayumba, "Situation Beyond Tolerance," *Daily News*, June 16, 1977.

156. Fair, "Drive-In Socialism," 1080.

157. Callaci, *Street Archives and City Life*, 192–93; and Brownell, *Going to Ground*, 102–9.

158. Kapaya Izo, "UDA Is Finished," *Daily News*, May 11, 1977.

159. "On Hiring Cars," *Daily News*, January 25, 1981; "Millions Spent on Car Hires," *Daily News*, January 22, 1981.

160. M. Mtenga, "Our Dying Parastatals," *Sunday News*, June 19, 1977; "UDA," *Daily News*, August 10, 1980; and Izo, "UDA Is Finished."

161. "Don't Hike UDA Fares," *Daily News*, August 25, 1980.

162. "Special Sunday Interview: On UDA Services"; K. Lujuo, "UDA Stands Accused," *Daily News*, June 6, 1977; Kativo Mchomvu, "UDA Services," *Daily News*, June 12, 1977; "UDA Interested in Quick Money," *Daily News*, January 31, 1980; "Unconcerned about UDA Affair," *Daily News*, December 24, 1977; "Matatizo ya UDA," August 5, 1977, UDA; "Consumer Prices Adjusted Upward," *Daily News*, July 17, 1980; "Did a Bomb Fall on the 41 Buses?; and "UDA Needs Good Leadership."

163. "Shirika la UDA," *Ngurumo*, May 24, 1977.

164. M. Mtenga, "Our Dying Parastatals"; E. M. Saga, "Who Is This Devil?"

165. "Umita Is Finished," *Daily News*, April 19, 1977; M. Kinantusi, "Many Might Follow UMITA Way," *Daily News*, April 27, 1977. See also "Mwalimu Declares in Mbeya—Let Sinking State Companies Die," *Daily News*, May 6, 1977.

166. "UDA Fares Don't Match Cost," *Daily News*, July 12, 1980.

167. Obilla, "UDA," *Daily News*, August 10, 1980.

168. Graham and Marvin, *Splintering Urbanism*, 22–23.

169. On technology as "society shaping," see Hughes, "The Evolution of Large Technical Systems," 51. Mutongi describes a similar, albeit more successful, nexus between buses and societal construction with matatus in *Matatu* (66–67).

170. "Tatizo la UDA in la Uongozi," *Ngurumo*, September 27, 1971.

171. Banyikwa, "Urban Passenger Transport Problems," 87.

172. Willy Teikwa, "Let Us Dissolve UDA," *Daily News*, May 23, 1977; "Dar Transport Problems Must Come to an End"; Jamimu Miri, interview, Dar es Salaam, July 16, 2010; Juma Kanimba, interview, Dar es Salaam, July 15, 2010; and Komanda Sefu Mbondei, interview, Dar es Salaam, July 15, 2010.

173. Nyerere, "The Economic Challenge—Dialogue or Confrontation," 243–44; "Understanding Shortages—Nyerere," *Daily News*, October 2, 1980.

174. "Understanding Shortages—Nyerere," *Daily News*, October 2, 1980.

175. Ramadhani Saidi, interview, Dar es Salaam, July 9, 2009.

176. These include Fatuma Hamisi, interview, Dar es Salaam, July 12, 2009; Juma Mgema, interview, Dar es Salaam, August 6, 2012; Musuguri Msuya, interview; Selemani Saidi, interview; Mwaidi Juma, interview, Dar es Salaam, August 10, 2010; anonymous, interview, Dar es Salaam August 9, 2010.

177. Anonymous, interview, Dar es Salaam; Fortini (surname withheld), interview, Dar es Salaam, August 20, 2010. Fatuma Hamisi in her interview (Dar es Salaam), called the buses "very good" for their ability to reduce waiting.

178. Banyikwa, "Urban Passenger Transport Problems," 87.

179. "Twaunga Mkono Taarifa Ya Waziri," *Ushirika*, September 1964.

180. Mohamedi Mpori, interview, Dar es Salaam; Mohamed Hassan, interview, Dar es Salaam, August 6, 2012, Dar es Salaam; Katunzi (surname withheld), interview, Dar es Salaam; Fatuma Hamisi, interview, Dar es Salaam. This provides a technological dimension to the expansion of notions of socialism covered in Ivaska, *Cultured States*; Brennan, *Taifa*; P. Lal, *African Socialism*; Callaci, *Street Archives and City Life*; and Fair, *Reel Pleasures*.

181. Mpole, interview. See also Fair, "Drive-In Socialism"; and P. Lal, *African Socialism*.

182. Tripp, *Changing the Rules*, 1.

183. A. M. Mrema, "UDA Has Failed to Impress," *Daily News*, November 13, 1980. In an "era when state supremacy is on the wane," Brenda Chalfin describes a similar process of remaking as an "infrastructural commonwealth." Chalfin, *Wastelandia*, 666.

184. Mutongi describes a similar relationship among political power, control of working transit, and populist alternatives in *Matatu* (134–36).

185. Sixmund Almasi, "Reply on Dar Buses Irrelevant," *Daily News*, May 24, 1979; Annoyed City Dweller, "UDA's Major Setbacks," *Daily News*, June 15, 1979; W. B. S. Samwell, "The UDA Questioned Not Answered," *Daily News*, June 19, 1979; and "Take Heed of People's Cry," *Daily News*, July 20, 1982.

186. Annoyed Citizen, "UDA Management Should Now Admit Failure," *Daily News*, June 28, 1977.

187. Bill Tekwa, "Let Us Dissolve UDA," *Daily News*, May 23, 1977; "JUWATA Resolution Debatable," *Daily News*, December 24, 1979.

188. "Dar's Transport Problem," *Daily News*, July 6, 1982; Ludovick Ngatara, "Will Somebody Act on UDA?" *Daily News*, January 29, 1978; Helpless Victim, "UDA Must Compete With Private Firms," *Daily News*, December 13, 1977. See also Athumani Kihungandola, quoted in "Special Sunday Interview: On UDA Services." In *Reel Pleasures*, Fair, drawing links between ujamaa and Bruce Lee, argues that citizens fulfillment of Nyerere's principles often went unnoticed by officials (265). Albeit outside debates about socialism, Mutongi in *Matatu* charts similar friction between the Harambee, or nationalist fervor of bus owners hoping to contribute to Africanization, and government regulation (63).

189. Mwajuma Saidi, interview, Dar es Salaam, July 15, 2009; Ufadhili Issa, interview, Dar es Salaam, July 15, 2009; and anonymous, interview.

190. As moviegoers argued in Fair's "Drive-In Socialism."

191. For a similar take on buses with Harambee in Kenya, see Mutongi, *Matatu*, 49.

192. Much like the language of "constitutional means" in Mutongi, *Matatu*, 48–51.

193. Veronica Agostin, interview, Dar es Salaam, August 7, 2012; Mohamed Hassan, interview, Dar es Salaam, August 6, 2012. See also Andreana Prichard, "Let Us Swim in the Pool of Love," on the role of the quotidian in citizens' engagement with ideas of the nation.

194. Jackson, "Rethinking Repair," 221–22. Larkin, *Signal and Noise*, 235. Gregory Mann aptly notes the need to emphasize when something "was *not* a neoliberal moment" but rather drew from much longer logics. Mann, *From Empires to NGOS*, 172.

195. Langwick, *Bodies, Politics, and African Healing*, 174.

196. See Scott, *Seeing like a State*, for example.

197. Rizzo, "Being Taken for a Ride," 137.

198. Fair and Callaci provide important language for recognizing urban life as a "tension" citizens could rework along with the state instead of a contradiction neither party could resolve. Fair, "Drive-In Socialism"; and Callaci, *Street Archives and City Life*, 186–87.

199. Halimoja, *Sokoine*.

Chapter 4: Oily Ujamaa

1. "The Road," *Jenga*, no. 5 (1969) (page numbers appear cut off), accessed at TNL; Gleave, "The Dar es Salaam Transport Corridor," 254; "Clearing Work Is Started for Oil Pipeline in Africa," *New York Times*, April 23, 1967, ProQuest Historical Newspapers.

2. Nyerere, "Tazama Pipeline," in *Freedom and Development*, 53–54.

3. Nyerere, "Tazama Pipeline," 54–56.

4. Nyerere, "Tazama Pipeline," 57.

5. Nyerere, "Tazama Pipeline," 56.

6. Nyerere, "Tazama Pipeline," 52.

7. Jones, *Routes of Power*, 4–5. For such tubular mobilities, see McCormack, "Pipes and Cables"; for an overview, see Sheller, "Global Energy Cultures." Tauri Tuvikene, in "Mooring in Socialist Automobility" (109), writes that the "fixity" of such immobile infrastructure produces mobility.

8. "The Story of Tanzania's Tiper Refinery," *Tanzania Trade and Industry*, no. 25 (1969): 29–31. Accessed at the NBA Room, TNL, Dar es Salaam, Tanzania.

9. Monson, *Africa's Freedom Railway*, 1–4.

10. Chalfin, *Neoliberal Frontiers*, 185–86.

11. See Monson, *Africa's Freedom Railway*; P. Lal, *African Socialism*; and Schroeder, *Africa after Apartheid*.

12. Apter, *The Pan-African Nation*; Watts, *State, Oil, and Agriculture in Nigeria*; Cooper, *Africa Since 1940*; and Appel, *The Licit Life of Capitalism* have richly explored the intersection

among oil production, development, state formation, and citizenship. But there is much less work on the interrelationship among oil, development, and state formation for oil importing nations, as Kairn Klieman observes in "Oil, Politics, and Development in the Formation of a State" (esp. 169–72).

13. See Macekura, *Of Limits and Growth*, chap. 4; and Immerwahr, *Thinking Small*, esp. chap. 2.

14. Huber, *Lifeblood*; and Appel, Mason, and Watts, "Part I: Oil as a Way of Life."

15. T. Mitchell, *Carbon Democracy*, 5; and Sheller and Urry, "City and the Car," 738.

16. One reason to highlight technology, oil, and bureaucratic life is that each encompasses the intersection of domestic and international processes that inform six decades of conversation and debate about the possibilities and limits of independence in Tanzania. Justinian Rweyemamu's *Underdevelopment and Industrialization in Tanzania* (1973), for me, is the best place to start for its early and incisive collapsing of rural and urban issues in domestic policy and for its ability to clearly link colonial development schemes to the limits of independent nation building. In *Class Struggles*, Issa Shivji critiques the Arusha Declaration's focus on rural modernization and its minimization of industrialization— what he interestingly considers a continuation of colonial policies incapable of changing productive forces. This led to a haphazard program of technological transfer, he asserts, and to a bureaucratic class that lacked "efficiency" and "sound expertise" (97–98 and 103–4). Andrew Coulson distinguishes between technological changes that were broadly acceptable among intellectuals and politicians in the 1960s and 1970s, inappropriate projects pursued by bureaucrats, and the necessity of a state to accumulate capital for construction. He concludes by calling ujamaa state capitalism and by suggesting a much different economic outcome would have been possible if the nation's ruling class had "invested in productive projects" (326) and had a more clearly defined industrial strategy. Coulson, *Tanzania*, 272–89, 324–26. In *Beyond Ujamaa in Tanzania*, Goran Hyden adapted Schumacher's "small is"—from the book title *Small Is Beautiful*, referring to intermediate technologies—for each of the book's nine chapter titles. Hyden offers a complex technological narrative that nevertheless links the state's misguided policies to modernist technological arrogance without exploring the manner in which many citizens, including rural citizens, desired forms of citizenship bound up with large technological projects. In *Race, Nation, and Citizenship in Post-colonial Africa*, Ronald Aminzade describes bureaucrats' contradictory locations within debates about and scholarship on socialism, party, and the state. This is part of a broader move underscoring varieties of bureaucratic and policy cultures during ujamaa that includes Schneider, *Government of Development*; P. Lal, *African Socialism* (esp. the critique of ujamaa as "developmentalism"); Bjerk, "Sovereignty and Socialism"; and Fair, "Drive-In Socialism." In *Limited Choices*, Dean McHenry rightly notes that the reasons for ujamaa's downturn are complex and debated (178–81).

17. See Ngalimecha Ngahyoma, *Kijiji Chetu*; and von Freyhold, *Ujamaa Villages in Tanzania*. Hamisi Hamadi "Mau," a mechanic from Ujiji cited in chapter 2, participated in the villagization operation as a mechanic. He emphasized that there were no spare-parts shortages, which contrasts with his subsequent narrative of work at a state ministry.

18. In *Going to Ground*, Emily Brownell fruitfully extends this discussion to South-South technology exchanges and small industries, both of which did not always lead to less capital-intensive projects (140–41).

19. Bjerk, "Sovereignty and Socialism," 284. "The Arusha Declaration" section titled "Let Us Pray and Heed to the Peasant" also includes industries for import substitution. "The Arusha Declaration," 17.

20. Michael Watts and Thomas Bassett call this "public sector deconstruction." Watts and Bassett, "Crisis and Change." On Tanzania specifically, see Scott, *Seeing like a State*, 254; and Dumont, *False Start in Africa*. For some critiques of these approaches, see Schneider, *Government of Development*; P. Lal, *African Socialism*; and Phillips, *Ethnography of Hunger*.

21. Schneider, *Government of Development*, 128. See also Van der Vleuten, "Infrastructures and Societal Change," 399; and Edwards, "Infrastructure and Modernity," 191–92.

22. See Isaacman and Isaacman, *Dams, Displacement and the Delusion of Development*, 1–9, for an overview of dams and large infrastructural projects.

23. Statista, "Average Annual OPEC Crude Oil Prices 1960 to 2020."

24. "Maendeleo ya uchukuzi nchini Tanzania," *Nchi Yetu*, April 1965, 5.

25. Quoted in Ohman, "Taming Exotic Beauties," 132. See also "Giant Power Station for Tanzania," *Tanzania Trade and Industry*, no. 24 (1969): 10, TNL.

26. Sylvester Barongo, "Petroleum Development in Tanzania," *Tanzania Notes and Records*, nos. 79 and 80 (1977): 116.

27. TPDC, "Operation of Petrol Stations by DDCs and Co-operative Unions in Tanzania," 3, March 1977, OMACS. Monthly Sales Summary 1976–1977, M01742, TPDC.

28. Priya Lal and Andrew Coulson note some farmers' disdain for farming with fertilizers. P. Lal, *African Socialism*, 202, 215; Coulson, "Tanzania's Fertilizer Factory," 184.

29. "Hutengenezwa Hapa," *Nchi Yetu*, November 1969, 19–20; and "Fahari ya jikoni," *Nchi Yetu*, July 1970, 20–22. Interviews conducted by Michaela von Freyhold suggest such import-substitution consumption could have broad rural support. Von Freyhold, *Ujamaa Villages*, 140. This focus on basic home goods provides an interesting contrast with the oil culture and "instant development" that Apter, in *The Pan-African Nation*, describes for Nigeria (42–43).

30. Nyerere, *Our Economy*, 14.

31. Critiques of bureaucrats and examples of mismanagement have been more visible than a general agreement among individuals of Tanzania's left (and even its administrative center) about the need for not just industrialization, but also a more coordinated industrial strategy (and thus a more symbiotic relation with rural development strategies), and for an earlier articulation of this strategy to stave off the impact of external forces on the nation's producers and public sector during the first decade of independence, as well as concern over the motives of foreign actors, especially corporations. See Rweyemamu, *Industrialization and Underdevelopment*; and Shivji, *Class Struggles*, 97. For a critique and a denial of

small as beautiful in a letter to Robert Mugabe, see Babu, *Future That Works*, 13. Andrew Coulson, like Shivji, explores industrial projects such as a bread factory and fertilizer factory that, in his opinion, did not fit Tanzania's pursuit of self-reliance by coordinating domestic production with domestic needs or demand and which wasted precious resources on expensive equipment and expatriate management. Coulson, "The Automated Bread Factory"; Coulson, "Tanzania's Fertilizer Factory." On ideological divisions, see Aminzade, *Race, Nation, and Citizenship*, 145.

32. In 1979 a hospital in the village of Kilimatinde used 10,200 liters of diesel on three generators every three months. See TPDC, "S.L.P. 2774—Dar es Salaam," 3, M00106, TPDC.

33. Gasoline is generally called *petroli* (petrol) in Tanzania. I use *gasoline* to clearly distinguish that processed product from petroleum.

34. "The Rural Revolution," *Jenga*, no. 8 (1971): 1, TNL.

35. S. Barongo, "Petroleum Development," 116–17.

36. TPDC, "Petroleum Products Supplies along Tazara Corridor: An On the Spot Survey (15 August 1974)," M01314, TPDC.

37. Nyerere, "Ten Years After Independence," in *Freedom and Development*, 303. This is a technological form of what Hyden calls "capturing the small holder peasants" for economic growth. Hyden, *Beyond Ujamaa in Tanzania*, 259.

38. Nyerere, "After the Arusha Declaration," in *Ujamaa: Essays on Socialism*, 164.

39. All of this language comes from "Saba Saba: International Trade Fair—Official Catalogue and Program, 2nd–8th July 1971," 38–41, TNL.

40. On the emergence of this phrase, see Smith, *We Must Run While They Walk*, 284.

41. Nyerere, "President's Inaugural Address," in *Freedom and Unity*, 181; Nyerere, "McDougall Memorial Lecture—F.A.O.," in *Freedom and Unity*, 239; Nyerere, "The Policies and Purposes of Pan-Africanism," in *Freedom and Unity*, 212; Nyerere, "Africanization of the Civil Service," in *Freedom and Unity*, 101; Nyerere, "Independence Address to the United Nations," in *Freedom and Unity*, 153.

42. Nyerere, "Inauguration of the University of East Africa," in *Freedom and Unity*, 218–21. See Donald Donham's work on the feeling of being behind and "therefore in need of a way to 'catch up.'" Donham, *Marxist Modern*, xv.

43. Msuya, "Foreign Aid and Tanzanian Development," 25. On the need for technological power to overcome this, see Nyerere, "Relations with Private Capital Investment," in *Freedom and Unity*, 209–11; Nyerere, "The Value of Private Investment," in *Freedom and Unity*, 319.

44. Nyerere, introduction to *Freedom and Socialism*, 16–17.

45. Nyerere, "*Ujamaa*—the Basis of African Socialism," in *Ujamaa: Essays in Socialism*, 11.

46. Nyerere, "Rice Means Socialism," in *Freedom and Development*, 45–46; Nyerere, "Introduction," in *Freedom and Socialism*, 17. Abena Dove Osseo-Asare's work on the difficulties

of pursuing "scientific equity" in postcolonial Ghana describes a similar process. See Osseo-Asare, "Scientific Equity," 717.

47. Nyerere, "Introduction," in *Freedom and Socialism*, 17; on a "new synthesis," see Nyerere, "'Groping Forward,'" in *Freedom and Unity*, 121. Here Nyerere was not alone among African leaders. See Ottaway and Ottaway, *Afrocommunism*, on leaders' avoidance of the conflict that drove progress in Marxist dialectics. Issa Shivji, *Development as Rebellion, Book Three*, provides a wonderful description of this philosophy as it pertains to the relationship between people and axes (78–79). This recalls Takyiwaa Manuh's observations in "Building Institutions for the New Africa" about catching up both as an "imperative" and as a "project of recovery and self-assertion" (268, 269).

48. Nyerere, "The Rational Choice," in *Freedom and Development*, 382–83.

49. Nyerere, "President Nyerere's Banquet Speech," 9.

50. Virilio, *Speed and Politics*, 46–47.

51. Nyerere, "The Arusha Declaration," in *Ujamaa: Essays on Socialism*, 18–26.

52. Bwana Twiga, "Msafara Mrefu Kuelekea Ujamaa," *Uhuru*, January 10, 1968. This article pictured the literal "caravan" (*msafara*) which walked in support of the Arusha Declaration while discussing the social obstacles that made "heading toward Ujamaa" a long journey. An article titled "Tanzania yasonga mbele" included a bus moving slowly up a dirt road. *Nchi Yetu*, October, 1966, 16–17. The perception that "we must run" could be done intentionally and with speed is shown in the poem "Nchi yangu yasonga mbele haraka," *Nchi Yetu*, July 1970, back cover. All accessed in the East African Library, University of Dar es Salaam.

53. Nyerere, "'Groping Forward,'" in *Freedom and Unity*, 120.

54. The refinery was constructed by Ente Nazionale Idrocarburi (ENI), an Italian firm that did similar projects in other parts of the socialist and communist world—and that, as Klieman writes, was created by Agip. Klieman observes that Agip's head, Enrico Mattei, attacked the Majors' domination of world oil markets by working with newly decolonized nations. In the case of Tanzania, leaders seemingly appreciated the former, turning down refinery offers by the Majors—as occurred in the Congo. P. Rweyemamu underscores the significance of Mattei offering host nations 75 percent of the profits. Klieman, "Oil, Politics, and Development," 172–77; P. Rweyemamu, *A General Guide to the Oil (Petroleum) Industry*, 167.

55. P. Rweyemamu, *A General Guide to the Oil (Petroleum) Industry*, 184.

56. Stephen Kwetukia, "Kiwanda cha Kusafishia Mafuta Hakina Ubaguzi," *Mfanyakazi*, September 30, 1967. *Jenga* said the same in "Tiper Refinery," no. 8 (1971): 23, TNL.

57. Nyerere, *Our Economy*, 14.

58. Indian Oil Corporation Limited, *Proceedings of the United Nations Interregional Seminar on Petroleum Refining in Developing Countries*, "Introduction," 7.

59. This mix was far from ideal because it made Tanzania reliant upon a single source of energy; TPDC had long-term goals to diversify. Barongo, "Petroleum Development in Tanzania," 115; P. Rweyemamu, *A General Guide to the Oil (Petroleum) Industry*, 198–99.

60. Herman, "Multinational Oligopoly in Poor Countries," 16.

61. TPDC, "Progress Report on Petroleum: Refining," 1, December 1973, M0658, TPDC; S. Barongo, "Petroleum Development in Tanzania," 116.

62. "Progress Report on Petroleum: Refining," 2, December 1973, M0658, TPDC.

63. Government of Tanzania, "Tanzania Petroleum Development Corporation (Establishment) Order, 1969," May 30, 1969, 03127.69.JC, TPDC.

64. "Progress Report: Petroleum Distribution," February 1974, M0657, TPDC. Shares of Agip cost 6.57 million shillings, while Shell and BP cost 17.8 million shillings. Through 1973, the government earned significant dividends on each: about 334,000 shillings on Agip and about 2.4 million shillings on Shell and BP.

65. P. Rweyemamu, A General Guide to the Oil (Petroleum) Industry, 188, 191. TPDC, "Crude Oil Imports: Sources and Problems," 1, December 6, 1983, M00550, TPDC.

66. TPDC, "Crude Oil and Refined Products Imports 1976," 5 October 4, 1975, M553, TPDC; TPDC, "Refining," 3–4, December 1973, M0658, TPDC.

67. "Progress Report: Petroleum Distribution," M0657.

68. On the broader implications of such "strategic infrastructure," see Schroeder, Africa after Apartheid, 17–19.

69. These are average posted prices, which varied wildly, as Jane Guyer notes. Guyer, "Oil Assemblages and the Production of Confusion," 238.

70. TPDC, "Petroleum Products," December 26, 1973, M00550, 4, TPDC.

71. TPDC, "Petroleum Products," 4.

72. Quoted in TPDC, "Purchase of Crude Oil," June 18, 1974, M00548, TPDC.

73. TPDC, "Petroleum Products," 5.

74. Klinghoffer, Oiling the Wheels of Apartheid, 5–10; and Bailey, Oil Sanctions, 7–12. Martin Bailey's work points out that South Africa's "weak link" was not oil. It drew 75 percent of its energy from coal and only 25 percent from oil. See also Sparks, "Between 'Artificial Economics' and the 'Discipline of the Market.'"

75. TPDC, "Petroleum Products," 6.

76. Appel, "Walls and White Elephants," 442. In "Locating the Indian Ocean," Jeremy Prestholdt notes the importance of Indian Ocean oil shipping lanes. He examines whether postcolonial nationalisms foreclosed earlier oceanic connectivities, what he calls "basin consciousness." The imagination behind the plan suggest continuities with early forms of connection—a sort of material form of postcolonial basin consciousness.

77. Tanzania's place on a list of nations "friendly" to OPEC producers meant it did not face restrictions on ordering, albeit it still had to pay new prices. See TPDC, "Hatua za Kupunguza Matumizi za Mafuta," 1, M00845, TPDC.

78. Hodges, *Angola*; and Watts, *State, Oil, and Agriculture in Nigeria*, 8–14. Klieman offers an important departure from the association of oil history in Africa with petroleum exporters. Klieman, "Oil, Politics, and Development."

79. Tanzania provides an alternative approach to what Frederick Cooper calls "the spigot economy" for Nigeria, based as it was in oil wealth. Cooper, *Africa since 1940*, 171–74. Certainly, the TPDC and the Tanzania government hoped to create the metaphorical spigot that would give them increased control over energy resources.

80. Maliyamkono and Bagachwa, *Second Economy in Tanzania*, 3.

81. Cheru, *Silent Revolution in Africa*, 50–51. Some of this came from depressed primary product prices and rises in consumer good costs, but both of those trends, particularly the latter, were linked to higher energy prices as well.

82. TPDC, "Petroleum Products," 4.

83. TPDC, "The Position of Petroleum Products vs Foreign Funds Allocation," April 18, 1979, Bank of Tanzania Import License Application Forms TPDC, July 1982, M01816, TPDC.

84. "Board Paper: Department of Operations and Marketing," Petroleum Products— Import Requirements Crude Oil Import Logs, 1977–1982, M01071, TPDC.

85. Sylvester Barongo, interview, Dar es Salaam, July 2, 2012.

86. "Petroleum Products," 4. On the important role of mobility, see T. Mitchell, *Carbon Democracy*, 28.

87. "Taarifa Kuhusu Hali ya Mafuta Nchini," Kamati ya Waziri, Makatibu Wakuu wa Mipango ya Kujinusuru Kiuchumi—Matatizo ya Mafuta Nchini, 1981, M01896, TPDC.

88. "Supply of Petroleum Products in the Country January–December 1981," 5, M00936, TPDC.

89. "Operation of Petrol Stations by DDCs and Co-operative Unions in Tanzania," 3, 4, March 16, 1977, M1337, TPDC. TPDC felt this stemmed in part from the government's large role as a petroleum consumer and its tendency to use credit instead of cash for payment. This left stations with uncertain liquid assets for infrastructure. Telex from TPDC to Shell and BP, May 31, 1979, M01061, TPDC.

90. TPDC, "Huduma za Mafuta ya Petroli Kando Kando ya Reli ya Uhuru," September, 1973, M00550, TPDC; and P. Lal, *African Socialism*, 148–53.

91. "Taarifa ya Utekelezaji wa Malengo ya Kujinusuru Kiuchumi Uuzaji Mazao Nchi za Nje, Januari 1981—Juni 1981," Kamati ya Waziri, Makatibu Wakuu ya Mipango ya Kujinusuru Kiuchumi: Matatizo ya Mafuta, 1981, M01896; "Mpango wa Taifa Kujihami wa Mwaka 1981/82—Kumbukumbu za Kikao cha Tano (5) cha Kamati ya Makatibu Wakuu Ulipofanyika Wizara ya Mipango, Tarehe 6 Julai, 1981 Saa 4 Asubuhi," Kamati ya Waziri, Makatibu Wakuu ya Mipango ya Kujinusuru Kiuchumi: Matatizo ya Mafuta, 1981, M01896; "Mkutano wa Waziri Mkuu Juu ya Hali ya Chakula Nchini Uliofanyika Siku ya Jumatano Tarehe 27 Mei, 1981 Katika Ofisi ya Waziri Mkuu," Kamati ya Waziri, Makatibu Wakuu ya

Mipango ya Kujinusuru Kiuchumi: Matatizo ya Mafuta, 1981, M01896; TPDC, "Importation of Emergency Cargo From Mombasa," 2, December 7, 1984, M1337, TPDC.

92. Kilimo, "Taarifa ya Utekelezaji wa Mpango wa Taifa wa Kujihami Kiuchumi," 1981, M00936, TPDC.

93. "Refining," 2–6, December 1973, M0658, TPDC.

94. ANIC S.p.a., "Bitumen Plant at Dsm Refinery," April 4–5, 1977, Bitumen Plant Construction Proposal, April 1977, M00105, TPDC.

95. S. Barongo, interview.

96. "Matatizo ya Umeme na Mafuta Kuendesha Viwanda Vya Mutex na Mwatex," Kamati ya Waziri, Makatibu Wakuu wa Mipango ya Kujinusuru Kiuchumi—Matatizo ya Mafuta Nchini, 1981, M01896, TPDC.

97. Maliyamkono and Bagachwa, *Second Economy in Tanzania*, 2.

98. To Governor, Minister of Finance, Minister of Planning from R. H. Green, "A Programme for Survival," 1, March 5, 1981, M01896, TPDC

99. "Report of the Fuel Conservation Committee," Kamati ya Waziri, Makatibu Wakuu wa Mipango ya Kujinusuru Kiuchumi—Matatizo ya Mafuta Nchini, 1981, M01896, TPDC.

100. S. Barongo, interview.

101. T. Mitchell, *Carbon Democracy*, 174.

102. Hughes, "Evolution of Large Technological Systems," 52.

103. Hughes, "Evolution of Large Technological Systems," 77.

104. Hughes, *Networks of Power*, 29.

105. Hughes, *Networks of Power*, 285.

106. Larkin, *Signal and Noise*, 247. As Andrew Russell and Lee Vinsel observe, the absence of maintenance and repair in Thomas Hughes, *Networks of Power*, is a "surprising omission" because it seemingly aligns with his arguments. Russell and Vinsel, "After Innovation," 11.

107. "Hatua za Kupunguza Matumizi ya Mafuta," 1973, M00845, TPDC; TPDC, "Crude Oil and Refined Products Imports 1976," 10, M553, TPDC; "Mpango wa Taifa wa Kujihami Kiuchumi wa Mwaka 1981/82," 2, July 27, 1981, M01896, TPDC. See also P. Rweyemamu, *A General Guide to the Oil (Petroleum) Industry*, 1 and 201–2.

108. TPDC, "Industry Trade 1970–1990: White and Black Oils," Table II, November 1978, M00952, TPDC.

109. September 7, 1981, 1, M01896, TPDC; S. Barongo, interview.

110. The stative term *kunusurika* is commonly used to describe the process of surviving a bad accident, as the next chapter shows.

111. To Governor, Minister of Finance, Minister of Planning from R. H. Green, "A Programme for Survival," 39, March 5, 1981, M01896, TPDC.

112. Gately, "Ten-Year Retrospective," 1101.

113. Telex to TPDC, "Telexes on Fuel Imports, Exports, and Crude Oil Spot Cargo, 1978–1979," May 5, 1979, M00936, TPDC.

114. Nasser Al Salem, "Tanzania Development Corporation," May 5, 1979, M00936, TPDC.

115. Telex from George Kremer to TPDC, December 2, 1978, M00936, TPDC.

116. Telex from Roy Chowdhuri to TPDC, November 9, 1978, M00936, TPDC.

117. Telex from Roy Chowdhuri to TPDC, 18, November 11, 1978, M00936, TPDC.

118. Telex from Abdul Razak Al-Awadi and Abdul Amir Al-Najdi to TPDC, "80,000 MT Crude Oil," May 4, 1979, M00936, TPDC; Telex from George Kremer to TPDC, December 2, 1978, M00936, TPDC.

119. Telex between Roy Chowdhuri and Sylvester Barongo, 15, M00936, TPDC.

120. "Mpango wa Taifa wa Kujihami Kiuchumi wa Mwaka 1981/1982: Maelezo Mafupi Kuhusu Item Na. 4 na 5 za Agenda," 1, July 27, 1981, M01896, TPDC.

121. Kassum, *Africa's Winds of Change*, 80.

122. Al Noor Kassum, interview, Dar es Salaam, August 3, 2012.

123. "Mr. Al Noor Kassum, Mr. Sylvester Barongo: An Apology," *Observer*, April 3, 1983, 34.

124. Kassum, *Africa's Winds of Change*, 135–41.

125. Timothy Mitchell, *Carbon Democracy*, somewhat takes for granted a particular refining capacity in his assessments of petroleum mobilities and political power, but for nations like Tanzania, it was sometimes easier to get and move oil they could not use domestically than to enhance their refining capacity. Mobility was a huge part of oil power, no doubt, but useful petroleum mobilizations required matches between oil types and a refinery's capacity. As a nation with a small refinery and dwindling resources, Tanzania thus struggled to mobilize the right oil.

126. Kassum, *Africa's Winds of Change*, 1127.

127. S. Barongo, interview.

128. Kassum, *Africa's Winds of Change*, 124.

129. Kassum, *Africa's Winds of Change*, 123. We thus need to add the repair techniques that dominate bottom-up approaches, such as those of Brian Larkin, *Signal and Noise*, and Steven Jackson, "Rethinking Repair," to bureaucratic life, too.

130. Barongo, "Petroleum Development in Tanzania," 121.

131. W. Pratt, *Oil in the Earth*, 23–25.

132. Warman, "Future of Oil," 292.

133. Warman, "The Future of Oil," 294; Bardi, "Peak Oil: The Four Stages of a New Idea," 323.

134. Stephen Graham and Simon Marvin provide descriptions of both in *Splintering Urbanism* (181–84). As Bernward Joerges observes, "There is something heroic about

LTS" and those who build them in scholarship on LTSS. Joerges also notes the success/ failure dichotomy that overlooks positions like those explored here. See Joerges, "High Variability Discourse," 260.

135. TPDC, "Annual Report for the Year, 1982," 10, TNL; TPDC, "Annual Report for the Year, 1979," 12; TNL; and TPDC, "Annual Report for the Year, 1985," TNL.

136. TPDC, "Annual Report for the Year, 1982," 13.

137. TPDC, "Annual Report for the Year, 1983," 28, TNL.

138. S. Barongo, interview.

139. S. Barongo, interview.

140. P. Lal, *African Socialism*, 228.

141. Bayart, *State in Africa*, 27.

142. Rweyemamu, *A General Guide to the Oil (Petroleum) Industry*, 193.

143. In part, this is a methodological issue, as Jean Allman points out in "Phantoms of the Archive."

144. World Bank, "Report 3086-TA—Economic Memorandum on Tanzania," http:// documents1.worldbank.org/curated/en/458331468312652459/pdf/multi-page.pdf.

145. World Bank, "Economic Memorandum," 63, 66. See also "DRAFT: BGSanderg/1ta," January 11, 1980, Travel Briefs, Tanzania, folder 1772891, Records of President Robert S. McNamara, WBGA.

146. Stein, *Beyond the World Bank Agenda,* 31.

147. Bengt G. Sandberg, "Office Memorandum," TANZANIA—Mr. McNamara's Visit to President Nyerere, February 11, 1980, WBGA.

148. Anil Gore, "Office Memorandum," February 5, 1980, Travel Briefs, Tanzania, folder 1772891, Records of President Robert S. McNamara, WBGA.

149. Bengt G. Sandberg, "Office Memorandum," 2–3, February 11, 1980, Travel Briefs, Tanzania, folder 1772891, Records of President Robert S. McNamara, WBGA.

150. Sandberg, "Office Memorandum"; Bengt G. Sandberg, "Office Memorandum."

151. W. A. Wapenhans, "Office Memorandum," July 28, 1977, Contacts with Member Countries—Tanzania, folder 1771200, Records of President Robert S. McNamara, WBGA.

152. Sandberg, "Office Memorandum," 2, February 11, 1980.

153. Nyerere, "Economic Challenge," 243.

154. Nyerere, "Economic Challenge," 243; and Appel, "Infrastructural Time," 50–51. On capacity, time, and interruption, see Tousignant, *Edges of Exposure*, 26–27.

155. Nyerere, "Kila Mtu," in *Wafanyakazi na Ujamaa*, 66.

156. Nyerere, "Aid and Development," 9. This recalls Tousignant, "Broken Tempos," (733), on "periodizing tempos," and Eden Medina's point that geopolitics "can play a decisive

role in technological development, regardless of the merits or shortcomings of the system under construction." Medina, *Cybernetic Revolutionaries*, 13.

157. Nyerere, "Address at the Luncheon," in *The President, Mwalimu Julius K. Nyerere*, 2. On a "colonial inheritance of exploitation," see Nyerere, "President Nyerere's Banquet Speech," 11.

158. Nyerere, "Address at the Luncheon," 5.

159. Monson, *Africa's Freedom Railway*.

160. Edwards, "Infrastructure and Modernity," 191–92; see also Appel, Anand, and Gupta, "Introduction," 14–20.

161. Appel, Anand, and Gupta, "Introduction," 16.

162. Hecht, "Rupture Talk in the Nuclear Age," 693.

163. By avoiding monocausality, Nyerere's interpretation mirrors that of actor-network theorists Michel Callon and John Law, particularly their notion of the "hybrid collectif": Callon and Law, "Agency and the Hybrid Collectif." Examples include T. Mitchell, *The Rule of Experts*, chap. 1; and de Leon, *Land of the Open Graves*, 38–43.

164. Coulson, *Tanzania*, 310–11.

165. "The Case for Exceptional Assistance for Tanzania," June 18, 1979, Travel Briefs, Tanzania, folder 1772891, Records of President Robert S. McNamara, the World Bank Groups Archive. This argument appears to have started with a previous Minister of Finance, Edwin Mtei, who served from 1977 to 1979.

166. Cooper, "Africa and the World Economy," 8–13.

167. Lindsay, "Extraversion, Creolization, and Dependency," 139.

168. L. Brown, Flavin, and Norman, "Future of the Automobile," 49. See also Volti, *Car Culture*, chap. 6.

169. Brown, Flavin, and Norman, "Future of the Automobile," 50. These tensions are also underscored in Hart, *Ghana on the Go*, chap. 5; and Green-Simms, *Postcolonial Automobility*.

170. Independent Commission on International Development, *North-South, a Programme for Survival*, 162–69.

171. World Bank, *Tanzania*, xi. Yet David Landes swats aside capital as "the biggest problem" in "Why Are We So Rich and They So Poor?" (9).

172. "The Proposed Expansion of the World Bank's Energy Program," 1, March 14, 1981, Energy Affiliate Correspondence, folder 1771391, Records of President Robert S. McNamara, WBGA.

173. This certainly raises an issue of oil reflexivity for people like me, whose lives are built on access to cheap oil and the capital behind it.

174. Livingston, *Self-Devouring Growth*.

175. McHenry, *Limited Choices*, 168.

Chapter 5: Automobile Domesticities

1. Richard Machary, "Ujanja wa Kutorosha Mali ya Magendo Mpakani," *Nchi Yetu*, November 1975, 20–21. Accessed at East Africana Room, UDSM Library.

2. On the socialist politics of film, see Fair, *Reel Pleasures*, 106–7; and Brennan, "Democratizing Cinema."

3. Machary, "Ujanja wa Kutorosha Mali ya Magendo Mpakani," 20–21.

4. M. M. Komba, *Chakubanga wa Mwenge, 1979–1991* (n.d.), accessed at TNL.

5. Nyerere, "President's Inaugural Address," in *Freedom and Unity*, 185.

6. Bryceson, *Liberalizing Tanzania's Food Trade*, 20–24.

7. Monson, *Africa's Freedom Railway*, 117.

8. Urry, "Inhabiting Cars and Roads," 124–25.

9. See Hart, *Ghana on the Go*, 118, on a similar link between mobility and family, or "chop"; and Monson, *Africa's Freedom Railway*, for links to both family and moral community (esp. 117–22).

10. Hansen, "Introduction," 24. On expanding the problematic boundaries of domestic work and political economy, see White, *Comforts of Home*, 8–12; Geiger, TANU *Women*, 1–19 ; and Robertson, *Trouble Showed the Way*, 5–6.

11. Sheller and Urry, "Mobile Transformations," 116.

12. James Giblin and Priya Lal both note the contested gendered ideals of family that emerged through nation-building projects. Giblin, *History of the Excluded*; and P. Lal, *African Socialism*.

13. Gregory Laurent Kimaro, interview, Iringa, December 16, 2011; Rashidi Mazuri, interview, Morogoro, December 11, 2011; Ibrahim Moses, interview, Morogoro, July 20, 2012; Juma Ramadhani, interview, Dar es Salaam, December 10, 2011; Gaspar Mwacha, interview, Iringa, December 18, 2011; Paul Jonas Kway, interview, Iringa, December 15, 2011.

14. United Republic of Tanzania, Ministry of Planning and Economic Affairs, *Statistical Abstract 1973* (Dar es Salaam: Government Printer, 1974); and United Republic of Tanzania, Ministry of Planning and Economic Affairs, *Statistical Abstract 1973–79* (Dar es Salaam: Government Printer, 1980).

15. Safari Kings advertisement, *Uhuru*, July 28, 1977.

16. See, for example, Feierman, *Shambaa Kingdom*, 52.

17. Fiat advertisement, *Ushirika*, February 1973; and *Ushirika*, January 1973. Emily Callaci notes these gendered embodiments of driving in novellas; see Callaci, *Street Archives and City Life*, 162.

18. Lt. Col. Hiza, CCM Regional Secretary, quoted in Geiger, TANU *Women*, 185. On the role of cars in parliamentary discussions about marriage and divorce reforms, see Ivaska, *Cultured States*, 188–89.

19. On corollaries in West Africa, see Green-Simms, *Postcolonial Automobility*, 164–66; and Hart, *Ghana on the Go*, 114–16.

20. Callaci, *Street Archives and City Life*, 90–98; Geiger, TANU *Women*; and Ivaska, *Cultured States*.

21. Advertisement, *Ngurumo*, September 3, 1973.

22. Zakia Maomba, "Hadisi ya Maisha ya Udereva," Maomba's personal collection shared with author.

23. Ramadhani, "The Life and Development" (*Maisha na Maendeleo*). This comes from Maomba's personal collection. She wrote at least three versions of her life history. This version deals most extensively with her time on regional roads.

24. Rajabu Kilongora, interview, Morogoro, December 14, 2011; Hassan Saidi, interview, Morogoro, December 14, 2011; Gaspar Mwacha, interview, Iringa, December 18, 2011; and Gregory Laurent Kimaro, interview, Iringa, December 16, 2011.

25. Hassan Saidi, interview. *Mapato* most often translates as *revenue* or *income*, but Saidi used the term to include resources beyond just a driver's salary (such as trading opportunities) for reasons that will become clear in the following.

26. Hassan Saidi, interview; Gaspar Mwacha, interview; Gregory Laurent Kimaro, interview; Suleiman Haruna Mgoni, interview, Tabora, April 6, 2012; Rashidi Mazuri, interview, Morogoro, December 11, 2011; Fadhili Ramadhani, interview, Tabora, April 14, 2012; and Abdallah Bitamira, interview, Tabora, April 5, 2012.

27. Kalugila, *Methali za Kiswahili*, 16; and "Fear," *Swahili Proverbs: Methali za Kiswahili*, n.d., http://swahiliproverbs.afrst.illinois.edu/fear.html. Accessed October 17, 2019.

28. Amiri Mussa Mkomwa, interview, Morogoro, December 11, 2011; and Rashidi Mazuri, interview, Morogoro, December 11, 2012.

29. Edwards, "Industrial Genders," 180.

30. Masquelier, "Road Mythographies," 830; and Giles-Vernick, "Na lege ti guiriri (On the Road of History)," 245–75.

31. Maliyamkono and Bagachwa, *Second Economy in Tanzania*, 119; and Hofmeier, *Transport and Economic Development*, 323. The mileage of bitumen roads expanded markedly in the independent period, but they were concentrated in townships.

32. Jamhuri ya Muungano wa Tanzania, *Hali ya Uchukuzi na Mawasiliano Nchini Mei, 1980* (Dar es Salaam: Mpigachapa wa Serikali, 1980), 53, BD/5, ZNA.

33. Hussein Mohamed, interview, Morogoro, December 13, 2011.

34. On the embodiment of competence on the road, see Merriman, *Driving Spaces*, esp. chap. 4.

35. Ibrahim Moses, interview, Morogoro, July 20, 2012.

36. On landscapes of driving, see Zeller, *Driving Germany*.

37. Hassan Saidi, interview.

38. "Waziri Salome Mbatia Afariki Dunia," October 25, 2007, https://bongo5.com/waziri -salome-mbatia-afariki-dunia-10-2007/. The explanation I heard for Mbatia's death likely draws more from public perceptions about the qualities and deficits of smooth roads than the actual details of the accident.

39. This echoes Mimi Sheller's observations about the role of an "emotional agent" in car cultures. Sheller, "Automotive Emotions," 222.

40. Gregory Laurent Kimaro, interview; Amiri Musa Mkomwa, interview, Morogoro; and Taasisi ya Uchunguzi wa Kiswahili, *Kamusi ya Kiswahili Sanifu*, 313.

41. Gaspar Mwacha, interview; and Hussein Mohamed, interview.

42. H. Ramadhani, interview. In "Automobile Masculinities," Morris provides a corollary to these dynamic constructions of manhood through a machinic assemblage.

43. As Jennifer Hart also shows in *Ghana on the Go* (177–78). Sheller calls this "feeling the car." Sheller, "Automotive Emotions," 224. For Tim Dant, this is part of the more-than-hybrid assemblage that constructs the "driver-car"; see Dant, "Driver-Car."

44. Hawa Ramadhani, interview, July 25, 2009, Dar es Salaam, Tanzania.

45. Reginald Regani, interview, July 10, 2009, Dar es Salaam, Tanzania.

46. Livingston, "Insights from an African History of Disability," 111–13.

47. Rashidi Ramadhani, interview, March 2, 2012, Dar es Salaam, Tanzania. See also White, *Comforts of Home*; and K. Beck, "Roadside Comforts."

48. Mohamed Pallo, interview, Morogoro, December 10, 2012. The same tension informs views of the life cycle in Hart's *Ghana on the Go* (118).

49. Suleiman Shabaani, interview, Morogoro, December 11, 2011. He blamed the reputation for starehe on government drivers.

50. Mohamed Shabani Mketo, interview, Dar es Salaam, July 9, 2012; Mohamed Pallo, interview. On the importance of food to maturity, see Kristin Philipps, *An Ethnography of Hunger*, chap. 3; and Weiss, *The Making and Unmaking of the Haya Lived World*, 30.

51. Juma Ramadhani, interview, Dar es Salaam, December 10, 2012. Also Herbert Sebastian Upatu, interview, Dar es Salaam, January 10, 2012.

52. Saidi Rashid Abdallah, interview, Dar es Salaam, December 13, 2012.

53. Hassan Saidi, interview.

54. Rockel, *Carriers of Culture*, 32.

55. Abdallah Mwinyi Mkuu, interview, Dar es Salaam, July 10, 2009.

56. Maomba, "Hadisi."

57. Hawa Ramadhani, interview.

58. Hassan Saluum Said, interview, August 3, 2009, Dar es Salaam.

59. Maomba, "Hadisi."

60. Fadhili Ramadhani, interview. Ramadhani, who features in chapter 2 as a mechanic, stopped driving after these incidents. Also Ramadhani Anzaruni Kiboko, interview, April 16, 2012, Kigoma.

61. Omar Seif Ngomadodo, interview, January 10, 2012, Dar es Salaam, Tanzania.

62. Anonymous driver, interview, Dar es Salaam, March 14, 2012; and Saidi Hussein Abdallah Butani, interview, Dar es Salaam, March 15, 2012. On such roadside routines and the influence of roadside dwellers, see G. Klaeger, "Dwelling on the Road," 448–49.

63. Ndiuma Station Histories.

64. Anonymous, interview; Saidi Hussein Abdallah Butani, interview; field notes, Iringa, December 14, 2011; and Ibrahim Moses, interview, Morogoro, July 20, 2012.

65. Omar Seif Ngomadodo, interview, Dar es Salaam, January 10, 2012.

66. Omar Seif Ngomadodo, interview.

67. Herbert Sebastian Upatu, interview.

68. Herbert Sebastian Upatu, interview.

69. Ndiuma Station Histories.

70. Ndiuma Station Histories.

71. Saidi Hussein Abdallah Butani, interview.

72. Ndiuma Station Histories.

73. Ndiuma Station Histories.

74. Ndiuma Station Histories.

75. Ndiuma Station Histories.

76. This contrasts with the slow speed of reciprocal motoring in Judith Scheele's *Smugglers and Saints of the Sahara* (96–104).

77. Ndiuma Station Histories.

78. Ndiuma Station Histories.

79. Ndiuma Station Histories; and Ibrahim Moses, interview.

80. Ibrahim Moses, interview.

81. Reginald Regani, interview, Dar es Salaam.

82. Jumanne Juma, interview, Dar es Salaam, March 13, 2012.

83. On spirits and sociotechnical systems, see d'Avignon, "Spirited Geobodies," s39. For spirits, roads, and mobility, see Masquelier, "Road Mythographies," 830; Mavhunga, "Which Mobility"; Green-Simms, *Postcolonial Automobility*.

84. On this intersection of masculinity and cattle—including gendered myths about it— see Hodgson, *Once Intrepid Warriors*, 21–22

85. Silberschmidt, "Poverty, Male Disempowerment, and Male Sexuality," 192; and Hodgson, "Being Maasai Men."

86. Mavhunga, *Transient Workspaces*, 69.

87. In *Speaking with Vampires*, Luise White writes, "Genre does not have a status as either/ or but is a strategy of writing and speaking—someone goes in and out of genre to recollect, to comment, to get a point across" (92).

88. Saidi Hussein Abdallah Butani, interview; and Masquelier, "Road Mythographies."

89. Jamie Monson and Callaci describe similar pursuits of social security. Monson, *Africa's Freedom Railway*; and Callaci, *Street Archives and City Life*.

90. U. Beck, *World at Risk*, 7, 27.

91. Guttman, *Meanings of Macho*, 84–85.

92. Owing to the sensitive political nature of the following, I have anonymized all interviewees.

93. "A Worker's View on Shortages," *Nguzo za S.T.C.* 1, no. 1 (1972): 5, accessed at TNL.

94. Fair, "Drive-In Socialism."

95. Callaci, *Street Archives and City Life*, 144. This general attitude contrasts with the suspicion surrounding drivers in Ghana during shortages. Hart, *Ghana on the Go*, 146–47.

96. Maliyamkono and Bagachwa, *Second Economy in Tanzania*, 129; and Bryceson, *Liberalizing Tanzania's Food Trade*, esp. chaps. 6 and 7.

97. All quotations in the text without sources listed come from anonymous interviews.

98. Owomero, "Crime in Tanzania."

99. Ferguson, *Give a Man a Fish*, 90.

100. Hart explores different strategies for navigating fuel shortages in *Ghana on the Go* (142–46).

101. This was the largest national crackdown to date. Regional measures had been taken in places like Mwanza since 1980. See file E 20/14, accession 15, box 17, TNA Mwanza. See Bryceson, *Liberalizing Tanzania's Food Trade*, chap. 1; and Maliyamkono and Bagachwa, *Second Economy in Tanzania*, prelude.

102. "Magendo yanapungua baada ya kufunga mipaka," *Nchi Yetu*, June 1977, 5–7, TNL.

103. As Deborah Bryceson notes in *Liberalizing Tanzania's Food Trade* (100).

104. Emily Brownell shows the specificity of consumer goods listed in newspapers as crackdowns became a "public theatre." Brownell, *Going to Ground*, 143–44.

105. Hart explores similar strategies among drivers in Ghana, noting the "risks of survival." Hart, *Ghana on the Go*, 128.

106. Scheele, *Smugglers and Saints* (104–5).

107. See Owomero, "Crime in Tanzania." Kelly Askew opens the book *Performing the Nation* by describing a group of illegal passengers, who were also strangers, transforming

themselves into mourners complete with a fake corpse when stopped by police in the back of a dump truck after curfew. Both the police and the passengers performed different aspects of the nation. Askew, *Performing the Nation*, 1–3.

108. T. L. Maliyamkono and M. S. D. Bagachwa's study *The Second Economy in Tanzania* found that between 26 percent and 41.5 percent of state cooperative stores were engaged in some form of side activities (167). See Bryceson's analysis of these views by different towns in *Liberalizing Tanzania's Food Trade*, especially the point that views of trading and distribution were shaped by a place's role as producers or consumers in national markets (202–6). This also tracks with Bryceson's description of government aims to take on "big fish," not everyday citizens (100).

109. Kanuti Jonas Mtali, interview, Morogoro, March 13, 2012.

110. Nyerere, "*Ujamaa*—The Basis of African Socialism," in *Ujamaa: Essays on Socialism*, 4.

111. Ferguson, *Give a Man a Fish*, 99.

112. Jamhuri ya Muungano wa Tanzania, *Hotuba ya Waziri wa Mawasiliano na Uchukuzi, Ndugu A. H. Jamal, 1978/79*, 27. This recalls Goran Hyden's observations about ujamaa's founding in aspirational technological power—capable of facilitating state capture—and Andrew Ivaska's discussion of capturing as a two-way street. Hyden, *Beyond Ujamaa in Tanzania*; and Ivaska, *Cultured States*, 211.

113. Fair, "Drive-in Socialism," 1083.

114. United Republic of Tanzania, *Transport Statistics, 1979*, 46. Deaths and accidents rose in the mid-1980s, but unevenly with numbers from 1985 (7,800 accidents and 1,000 deaths) showing changes only in deaths (which increased by 300 for a total of 1,100). A year later, each of these numbers halved to the lowest in a decade. United Republic of Tanzania, *Facts and Figures on Transport and Communications*, 62.

115. Weiss, "Buying Her Grave."

116. Halimoja, *Sokoine*; and Attilio Tagalile, "Special Report: The Life and Times of Edward Sokoine: Man of Firm Action," *Citizen*, April 12, 2015.

117. Tagalile, "Special Report."

118. The virus became known as HIV-1 only after HIV-2 was discovered.

119. Mwizarubi, Cole, and Lamson, "Targeting Truckers in Tanzania," 4. See also Piot et al., "Acquired Immunodeficiency Syndrome"; and Iliffe, *The African Aids Epidemic*, 23.

120. Epstein, *Impure Science*, 11.

121. Piot, *No Time to Lose*, 234.

122. Carswell, Lloyd, and Howells, "Prevalence of HIV-1." The HIV-1 infection rate amongst drivers was thus four times the control group and nearly triple the control group for turners. Laukamm-Josten et al., "HIV and Syphilis Seroprevalence," 4162.

123. This mobilization of a static, hypersexual African masculinity stands in contrast to Shane Doyle's work in East Africa, which emphasizes more dramatic changes to

premarital sexual practices in the late colonial period. Doyle, "Premarital Sex in Great Lakes Africa, 1900–1980."

124. L. Barongo et al., "Epidemiology of HIV-1 Infection."

125. Setel, *Plague of Paradoxes*, 204.

126. Carswell, Lloyd, and Howells, "Prevalence of HIV-1"; and L. Barongo et al., "Epidemiology of HIV-1."

127. L. Barongo et al., "Epidemiology of HIV-1"; Laukamm-Josten et al., "Preventing HIV."

128. Mwizarubi, Cole, and Lamson, "Targeting Truckers in Tanzania," 4. Flora Myula also features in Kilimwiko, "Condoms Hitch Lift with Truckers," 9.

129. Kilimwiko, "Condoms Hitch Lift with Truckers." On a disempowered male figure, see Silberschmidt, "Poverty, Male Disempowerment, and Male Sexuality," 192.

130. Jack Edward, interview, Morogoro, July 27, 2012; Iddi Mohamed, interview, Morogoro, July 27, 2012; and Iliffe, *African AIDS Epidemic*, 1.

131. Epstein, *Impure Science*, 30, 68.

132. As S. Doyle observes in "Premarital Sex in Great Lakes Africa, 1900–1980" (260), there is a tendency to not look further back than the 1970s to examine the HIV/AIDS crisis. In this case, changes in motor transport in the 1960s and 1970s quite literally mobilize epidemiological narratives when combined with perceptions of magendo masculinity.

133. Packard, *Mobility without Mayhem*, 13.

134. U. Beck, *World at Risk*, 6.

Conclusion

1. International Panel for Climate Change (IPCC), *Climate Change 2007: Mitigation. Contribution of Working Group III to the Fourth Assessment Report of the Intergovernmental Panel on Climate Change,* https://archive.ipcc.ch/publications_and_data/ar4/wg3/en/ch5s5-2 .html.

2. Livingston, *Self-Devouring Growth*, 85–88. In addition to the oil used in many roads, Livingston adds sand to the finite resources roads require.

3. IPCC, *Climate Change 2007*. On the hypocrisies of approaches to energy use, see Gabrielle Hecht, "The African Anthropocene," *Aeon*, February 6, 2018, https://aeon.co/essays /if-we-talk-about-hurting-our-planet-who-exactly-is-the-we.

4. Sperling and Gordon, *Two Billion Cars*, 20–24; J. Voelcker, "1.2 Billion Vehicles on World's Roads Now, 2 Billion by 2035." These are estimates. Most estimates have 2021 worldwide vehicle numbers around 1.5 billion.

5. IPCC, *Climate Change 2007*, 328.

6. United Nations, "United Nations Framework Convention on Climate Change," 1.

7. G. Hecht, "African Anthropocene." In *Fossil Capital*, Andreas Malm underscores these hypocrisies.

8. Lekan, *Our Gigantic Zoo*, 252.

9. Rizzo, *Taken for a Ride*, 37; and Cordula Thum, "United Republic of Tanzania: Transport Sector Snapshot."

10. World Bank, "CO_2 Emissions (Metric Tons per Capita)—Tanzania," https://data.worldbank.org/indicator/EN.ATM.CO2E.PC?locations=TZ; and World Bank, "CO_2 Emissions from Liquid Fuel Consumption (kt)—Tanzania," https://data.worldbank.org/indicator/EN.ATM.CO2E.LF.KT?locations=TZ. Accessed February 18, 2021.

11. Malm and Hornborg, "The Geology of Mankind," 63–64.

12. Urry, *Mobilities*, 119.

13. Kirsch, *Electric Vehicle*, 229–34.

14. Patterson, *Automobile Politics*, 226.

15. For a similar argument, see Bekasova, Kulikova, and Emmanuel, "State Socialism."

16. Marshall, Macklin, Monaghan Limited and Tanzania Ministry of Land, Housing and Urban Development, *Dar es Salaam Master Plan*.

17. Jackson, "Rethinking Repair," 223.

18. Haraway, *Staying with the Trouble*, 36–39. Tsing, *The Mushroom at the End of the World*, 20–22. Arturo Escobar also emphasizes the practicality of working through the diversity of existing practices, particularly epistemologies of the South that rarely get recognized by Eurocentric frameworks. See Escobar, *Designs for the Pluriverse*, 67–68.

19. Mbembe and Nuttall, "Writing the World," 348. More broadly, see Comaroff and Comaroff, "Theory from the South."

20. Livingston, *Self-Devouring Growth*, 33; and V. Lal, "Gandhi and the Ecological Vision of Life," 153.

21. Escobar, "Civilizational Transitions," 123.

22. V. Lal, "Gandhi and the Ecological Vision of Life," 156.

23. Sheller, *Mobility Justice*, 18.

24. McNeill and Engelke, *Great Acceleration*, 4–5.

25. The exhibit has moved about thirty yards since my 2012 visit. Visitors now pass the stable of national vehicles before entering a much larger bombing memorial that includes a charred Suzuki Escudo. In 2012, these were the only two outdoor exhibits.

26. This does not mean that function and skill resolve precarity, as Matteo Rizzo's *Taken for a Ride* clearly shows with daladala.

27. The refrigeration unit was taken out after the modifications and sold to a used-car-parts store so that the mechanics would not question the perpetrators.

28. U.S. Department of State, "Report of the Accountability Review Boards: Bombings of the US Embassies in Nairobi, Kenya and Dar es Salaam, Tanzania on August 7, 1998."

29. For Ghana, see Hart, *Ghana on the Go*, 166–68.

30. Livingston, *Self-Devouring Growth*, 90–93.

31. World Health Organization, *Global Status Report on Road Safety*, 216; see also Livingston, *Self-Devouring Growth*, 93.

32. G. Hecht, *Being Nuclear*, 21–22.

33. UDA Rapid Transit—UDART, Facebook Page, https://www.facebook.com /udartTanzania/?ref=page_internal. Accessed 10 October 2019. The posts with pictures of politicians are May 28 and 29, 2016, and June 9, 12, 13, and 17, 2016. The short history was posted May 29, 2016.

34. Rizzo, *Taken for a Ride*; and Rizzo, "Political Economy of an Urban Megaproject."

35. Writing about matatus in Nairobi, Celia Breuer comes to a similar conclusion. See Breuer, "Blind to the Matatus," *Africa Is a Country*, June 13, 2019, https://africasacountry .com/2019/06/blind-to-the-matatu.

36. Rizzo, *Taken for a Ride*, 152.

37. Ali Macosta, interview, Dar es Salaam, January 22, 2012.

38. T. Mitchell, *Rule of Experts*, 231.

39. For a similar take, see Green-Simms, *Postcolonial Automobility*, 199–201.

40. Fair, *Pastimes and Politics*, 40.

41. Mr. Nice, "Bwana Shamba," YouTube video, https://www.dailymotion.com/video /x6fxao (6:28), August 14, 2008.

42. Weiss, *Making and Unmaking of the Haya Lived World*, 183–84, 203.

43. Berlant, *Cruel Optimism*, 1.

44. See Callaci, *Street Archives and City Life*, for a history of the "small house."

45. Matonya, "Spare Tairi," YouTube video, https://www.youtube.com/watch?v =yHdtE2TkHjU (4:01), April 2, 2010.

46. Marlaw, "Pii Pii," YouTube video, https://www.youtube.com/watch?v=8eyAeqkV2gg (4:24), August 26, 2009.

47. Lamar, LWP, and Nature, "Tatizo Foleni," YouTube video, https://www.youtube.com /watch?v=DTBz3pDHYSo (3:55), November 16, 2012. The song, though serious about its critique, drew its title from residents' common usage of *tatizo foleni* to get out of social obligations, explain tardiness, and, according to some, spend dinner with another lover. For drivers, Jennifer Hart calls this the "tension of immobility"; in Tanzania, it applies to urban residents as well. Hart, *Ghana on the Go*, 184–85.

48. *Minibuzz Tanzania*, "Je Tatizo la Foleni Linakuathiri Vipi Wewe Mtanania?," YouTube video, https://www.youtube.com/watch?v=cmfrp9Q6YZk (11:34), October 23, 2013.

It is unclear which study the show cites. However, there is a growing number of studies identifying the costs of Dar es Salaam traffic. In "The Cost of Traffic Congestion and Accidents to the Economy in Tanzania," for example, Jumbe Katala estimates traffic in Dar es Salaam costs the nation about $225,000,000. These studies should be read in a context in which traffic costs and the loss of time is used to justify claims about how the city should function, including interventions like UDA-RT.

49. Mbembe, *On the Postcolony*, chap. 2.

50. Larkin, *Signal and Noise*, 244.

51. Taasisi ya Uchunguzi wa Kiswahili, Dar-es-Salaam, *Kamusi ya Kiswahili Sanifu, Toleo la Pili*, 366.

52. I owe this observation to Professor Aldin Mutembei.

53. "Uchunguzi wa NIPASHE kuhusu 'mashangingi' yanavyofilisi," *Nipashe*, December 3, 2015.

54. "Uchunguzi wa NIPASHE kuhusu 'mashangingi' yanavyofilisi," *Nipashe*, December 3, 2015. *Nipashe* put the estimate of gross domestic product at four percent, but at 1.31 trillion shillings ($811,145,510) for vehicle costs (the newspaper's estimate) and 72.98 trillion shillings of gross domestic produce, an exchange rate of 1,615 shillings to the dollar provides a lower, but still sizable, 1.8 percent estimate.

55. "Uchunguzi wa NIPASHE kuhusu 'mashangingi' yanavyofilisi," *Nipashe*, December 3, 2015.

56. "Siri Kuu 5 Dodoma," *Nipashe*, August 20, 2016.

57. K. Askew, *Performing the Nation*, 12.

58. On recognizing discursive legacies from socialism, see Anne Pitcher and Kelly Askew, "African Socialisms and Postsocialisms," 3.

59. Harmonize, "Magufuli," YouTube video, https://www.youtube.com/watch?v =FrAZ5Lzf5AU (3:41), August 2, 2019.

60. Mwanakijiji, "Ukubali Ukatae . . . Ukweli wa Aliyoyasema Rais JPM Jana; Hili ni Mojawapo . . !!!," *Udaku Special*, April 14, 2017, http://www.udakuspecially.com/2017/04 /ukubali-ukataeukweli-wa-aliyoyasema.html.

BIBLIOGRAPHY

Acemoglu, Daron, and James Robinson. *Why Nations Fail: The Origins of Power, Prosperity, and Poverty*. New York: Crown, 2012.

Adas, Michael. *Machines as the Measure of Men: Science, Technology, and Ideologies of Western Dominance*. Ithaca, NY: Cornell University Press, 1989.

Ahearne, Robert. "Development and Progress as Historical Phenomena in Tanzania: Maendeleo? We Had That in the Past." *African Studies Review* 59, no. 1 (April 2016): 77–96.

Akrich, Madeline. "The De-scription of Technical Objects." In *Shaping Technology/Building Society: Studies in Sociotechnical Change*, edited by Wiebe Bijker and John Law, 205–24. Cambridge, MA: MIT Press, 1992.

Alber, Erdmute. "Motorization and Colonial Rule: Two Scandals in Dahomey, 1916." *Journal of African Cultural Studies* 15, no. 1 (2002): 79–92.

Allman, Jean. "Phantoms of the Archive: Kwame Nkrumah, a Nazi Pilot Named Hanna, and the Contingencies of Postcolonial History-Writing." *American Historical Review* 118, no. 1 (February 2013): 104–29.

Amery, L. S., and Mr. Ormsby-Gore. "Problems and Development in Africa: Addresses before the Society by Mr. L. S. Amery and Mr. Ormsby-Gore." *Journal of the African Society* 28, no. 112 (July 1929): 21–22.

Aminzade, Ronald. *Race, Nation, and Citizenship in Post-colonial Africa: The Case of Tanzania*. New York: Cambridge University Press, 2013.

Anderson, Warwick, and Vincanne Adams. "Pramoedya's Chickens: Postcolonial Studies of Technoscience." In *The Handbook of Science and Technology Studies*, 3rd ed., edited by Edward Hackett, Olga Amsterdamska, Michael Lynch, and Judy Wajcama, 181–204. Cambridge, MA: MIT Press, 2008.

Appel, Hannah. "Infrastructural Time." In *The Promise of Infrastructure*, edited by Nikhil Anand, Akhil Gupta, and Hannah Appel, 41–61. Durham, NC: Duke University Press, 2018.

Appel, Hannah. *The Licit Life of Capitalism: U.S. Oil in Equatorial Guinea*. Durham, NC: Duke University Press, 2019.

Appel, Hannah. "Walls and White Elephants: Oil Extraction, Responsibility, and Infrastructural Violence in Equatorial Guinea." *Ethnography* 13, no. 4 (2012): 439–65.

Appel, Hannah, Nikhil Anand, and Akhil Gupta. "Introduction: Temporality, Politics, and the Promise of Infrastructure." In *The Promise of Infrastructure*, edited by Nikhil Anand, Akhil Gupta, and Hannah Appel, 1–38. Durham, NC: Duke University Press, 2018.

Appel, Hannah, Arthur Mason, and Michael Watts. "Part I: Oil as a Way of Life." In *Subterranean Estates: Life Worlds of Oil and Gas*, edited by Hannah Appel, Arthur Mason, and Michael Watts, 27–30. Ithaca, NY: Cornell University Press, 2015.

Apter, Andrew. *The Pan-African Nation: Oil and the Spectacle of Culture in Nigeria*. Chicago: University of Chicago Press, 2009.

Armstrong, A. "Colonial and Neocolonial Urban Planning: Three Generations of Master Plans for Dar es Salaam." *Utafiti: Journal of the Faculty of Arts and Social Sciences (University of Dar es Salaam)* 8, no. 1 (1986): 43–66.

Arnold, David. *Everyday Technology: Machines and the Making of India's Modernity*. Chicago: University of Chicago Press, 2013.

Arnold, David. "The Problem of Traffic: The Street-Life of Modernity in Late-Colonial India." *Modern Asian Studies* 46, no. 1 (2012): 119–41.

Askew, Kelly. *Performing the Nation: Swahili Music and Cultural Politics in Tanzania*. Chicago: Chicago University Press, 2012.

Atkins, Keletso. *The Moon Is Dead! Give Us Our Money! The Cultural Origins of an African Work Ethic, Natal, South Africa, 1843–1900*. Portsmouth, NH: Heinemann, 1993.

Austen, Ralph A. *Northwest Tanzania under German and British Rule: Colonial Policy and Tribal Politics, 1889–1939*. New Haven, CT: Yale University Press, 1968.

Babu, Abdul Rahman Mohamed. *The Future That Works: Selected Writings of A. M. Babu*. Edited by Salma Babu and Amrit Wilson. Trenton, NJ: Africa World Press, 2002.

Bailey, Martin. *Oil Sanctions: South Africa's Weak Link*. New York: Centre Against Apartheid, 1985.

Bakari, Mtoro bin Mwinyi. *The Customs of the Swahili People: Desturi za Waswahili of Mtoro bin Mwinyi Bakari and Other Swahili Persons*. Berkeley: University of California Press, 1981.

Baldwin, Nick, ed. *Vintage Lorry Annual*, Number One. London: Marshall and Harris Baldwin, 1979.

Banyikwa, William. "Urban Passenger Transport Problems in Dar-es-Salaam, Tanzania." *African Urban Quarterly* 3, nos. 1–2 (1988): 80–93.

Barber, Karin. "Introduction: Hidden Innovators in Africa." In *Africa's Hidden Histories: Everyday Literacy and Making the Self*, edited by Karin Barber, 1–24. Bloomington: Indiana University Press, 2006.

Bardi, Ugo. "Peak Oil: The Four Stages of a New Idea." *Energy* 34 (2009): 323–326.

Barker, Carol, and David Wield. "Notes on International Firms in Tanzania." *Utafiti* 3, no. 2 (1978): 316–41.

Barnes, Jessica. *Cultivating the Nile: The Everyday Politics of Water in Egypt*. Durham, NC: Duke University Press, 2014.

Barnett, Michael. *Empire of Humanity: A History of Humanitarianism*. Ithaca, NY: Cornell University Press, 2013.

Barongo, L. R., M. W. Borgdorff, F. F. Mosha, A. Nicoll, H. Grosskurth, K. P. Senkoro, J. N. Newell et al. "The Epidemiology of HIV-1 Infection in Urban Areas, Roadside Settlements, and Rural Villages in Mwanza Region, Tanzania." *AIDS* 6, no. 12 (December 1992): 1521–28.

Barongo, Sylvester. "Petroleum Development in Tanzania." *Tanzania Notes and Records* nos. 79 and 80 (1976): 115–21.

Barry, Sara. "Hegemony on a Shoestring: Indirect Rule and Access to Agricultural Lands." *Africa* 62, no. 3 (1992): 327–55.

Barton, Donald. *An Affair with Africa: Tanganyika Remembered*. Hertford: Authors OnLine, 2004.

Bates, Darrell. *A Fly Switch from the Sultan*. London: Rupert-Hart Davis, 1961.

Bayart, Jean-François. *The State in Africa: The Politics of the Belly*. 2nd ed. Malden, MA: Polity, 2009.

Bayat, Asef. "Un-Civil Society: The Politics of the 'Informal People.'" *Third World Quarterly* 18, no. 1 (1997): 53–72.

Beck, Kurt. "The Art of Truck Modding on the Nile (Sudan): An Attempt to Trace Creativity." In *The Speed of Change: Motor Vehicles and People in Africa, 1890–2000*, edited by Jan-Bart Gewald, Sabine Luning, and Klaas van Walraven, 151–74. Leiden: Brill, 2009.

Beck, Kurt. "Roadside Comforts: Truck Stops on the Forty Days Road in Western Sudan." *Africa* 83, no. 3 (2013): 426–45.

Beck, Ulrich. *Risk Societies: Toward a New Modernity*. London: Sage Publications, 1992.

Beck, Ulrich. *World at Risk*. Cambridge, UK: Polity, 2014.

Becker, Felicitas. *The Politics of Poverty: Policy-Making and Development in Rural Tanzania*. New York: Cambridge University Press, 2019.

Beidelman, T. O. *The Culture of Colonialism: The Cultural Subjection of Ukaguru*. Bloomington: Indiana University Press, 2012.

Bekasova, Alexandra, Julia Kulikova, and Martin Emmanuel. "State Socialism and Sustainable Urban Mobility: Alternative Paths in St. Petersburg since the 1880s." In *A U-Turn to the Future: Sustainable Urban Mobility since 1850*, edited by Martin Emmanuel, Frank Schipper, and Ruth Oldenziel, locations 4653–5464 of 8338. New York: Berghahn Books, 2000. Kindle.

Berege, Edgar. "Promotion of an Efficient and Effective Urban Transport Public System in Dar-es-Salaam: The Case of Shirika la Usafiri Dar-es-Salaam, Ltd. (UDA)." Master's thesis, University of Nairobi, 1976.

Berlant, Lauren. *Cruel Optimism*. Durham, NC: Duke University Press, 2011.

Berman, Bruce, and John Lonsdale. *Unhappy Valley: Conflict in Kenya and Africa*. Bk. 2. London: James Currey, 2002.

Berry, Sara. *Fathers Work for Their Sons: Accumulation, Mobility, and Class Formation in an Extended Yorùbá Community*. Berkeley: University of California Press, 1984.

Bierschenk, Thomas, and Jean-Pierre Olivier de Sardan, eds. *States at Work: Dynamics of African Bureaucracies*. Boston: Brill, 2014.

Bierschenk, Thomas, and Jean-Pierre Olivier de Sardan. "Studying the Dynamics of African Bureaucracies: An Introduction to States at Work." In *States at Work: Dynamics of African Bureaucracies*, edited by Thomas Bierschenk and Jean-Pierre Olivier de Sardan, 3–34. Boston: Brill, 2014.

Bijker, Wiebe E., Thomas Hughes, and Trevor Pinch, eds. *The Social Construction of Technological Systems: New Directions in the Sociology and History of Technology*. Cambridge, MA: MIT Press, 1987.

Bijker, Wiebe E., and John Law, eds. *Shaping Technology/Building Society: Studies in Socio-technical Change*. Cambridge, MA: MIT Press, 1992.

Bissell, William. *Urban Design, Chaos, and Colonial Power in Zanzibar*. Bloomington: Indiana University Press, 2010.

Bjerk, Paul. *Building a Peaceful Nation: Julius Nyerere and the Establishment of Sovereignty in Tanzania, 1960–1964*. Rochester, NY: University of Rochester Press, 2018.

Bjerk, Paul. "Sovereignty and Socialism in Tanzania: The Historiography of an African State." *History in Africa* 37, no. 1 (2010): 275–319.

Borg, Kevin. *Auto Mechanics: Technology and Expertise in Twentieth-Century America*. Baltimore: Johns Hopkins University Press, 2007.

Bray, Francesca. "Technics and Civilization in Late Imperial China: An Essay in the Cultural History of Technology." *Osiris* 13 (1998): 11–33.

Breckenridge, Keith. *Biometric State: The Global Politics of Identification and Surveillance in South Africa, 1850 to the Present*. New York: Cambridge University Press, 2016.

Brennan, James. "Democratizing Cinema and Censorship in Tanzania, 1920s–1980s." *Africa* 38, no. 3 (2005): 481–511.

Brennan, James. *Taifa: Making Nation and Race in Urban Tanzania*. Athens: Ohio University Press, 2012.

Brennan, James. "Youth, the TANU Youth League, and Managed Vigilantism in Dar es Salaam, 1925–1973." In *Generations Past: Youth in East African History*, edited by Andrew Burton and Hélène Charton-Bigot, 204–28. Athens: Ohio University Press, 2015.

Brennan, James, and Andrew Burton. "The Emerging Metropolis: A History of Dar es Salaam, circa 1862–2000." In *Dar es Salaam: Histories from an Emerging African Metropolis*, edited by James Brennan, Andrew Burton, and Yusuf Lawi, 13–75. Dar es Salaam: Mkuki na Nyota Publishers, 2007.

Brown, Beverly, and Walter Brown. "East African Trade Towns: A Shared Growth." In *A Century of Change in East Africa*, edited by W. Arens, 183–200. Geneva: Mouton, 1976.

Brown, Lester, Christopher Flavin, and Colin Norman. "The Future of the Automobile in an Oil-Short World." Worldwatch Paper 32 (September 1979). Washington, DC: Worldwatch Institute.

Brown, Lester, Christopher Flavin, and Colin Norman. *Running on Empty: The Future of the Automobile in an Oil-Short World*. New York: Norton, 1979.

Brownell, Emily. *Gone to Ground: A History of Environment and Infrastructure in Dar es Salaam*. Pittsburgh: University of Pittsburgh Press, 2020.

Bryceson, Deborah. *Liberalizing Tanzania's Food Trade: Public and Private Faces of Urban Marketing Policy, 1939–1988*. Geneva: United Nations Research Institute for Social Development, 1993.

Bulliet, Richard. *The Camel and the Wheel*. New York: Columbia University Press, 1975.

Burgess, Gary. "To Differentiate Rice from Grass: Youth Labor Camps in Revolutionary Zanzibar." In *Generations Past: Youth in East African History*, edited by Andrew Burton and Hélène Charton-Bigot, 229–44. Athens: Ohio University Press, 2015.

Burke, Timothy. *Lifebuoy Men, Lux Women: Commodification, Consumption, and Cleanliness in Modern Zimbabwe*. Durham, NC: Duke University Press, 1996.

Burrell, Jenna. *Invisible Users: Youth in the Internet Cafés of Urban Ghana*. Cambridge, MA: MIT Press, 2012.

Burton, Andrew. *African Underclass: Urbanization, Crime, and Colonial Order in Dar es Salaam, 1916–1991*. Athens: Ohio University Press, 2005.

Callaci, Emily. "Dancehall Politics: Mobility, Sexuality, and Spectacles of Racial Respectability in Late Colonial Tanganyika, 1930s–1961." *Journal of African History* 52, no. 3 (2011): 365–84.

Callaci, Emily. *Street Archives and City Life: Popular Intellectuals in Postcolonial Tanzania*. Durham, NC: Duke University Press, 2017.

Callahan, Michael. *A Sacred Trust: The League of Nations and Africa, 1929–1946*. Brighton: Sussex Academic Press, 2004.

Callon, Michel, and John Law. "Agency and the Hybrid Collectif." *South Atlantic Quarterly* 94, no. 2 (1995): 481–507.

Cameron, Donald. *My Tanganyika Service and Some Nigeria*. London: George Allen and Unwin, 1939.

Campbell, W. W. *East Africa by Motor Lorry: Recollections of an Ex-Motor Transport Driver*. London: Murray, 1928.

Carswell, J. W., G. Lloyd, and J. Howells. "Prevalence of HIV-1 in East African Lorry Drivers." *AIDS* 3, no. 11 (November 1989): 759–62.

Césaire, Aimé. *Discourse on Colonialism*. New York: Monthly Review Press, 2001.

Chalfin, Brenda. *Neoliberal Frontiers: An Ethnography of Sovereignty in West Africa*. Chicago: Chicago University Press, 2010.

Chalfin, Brenda. "'Wastelandia': Infrastructure and the Commonwealth of Waste in Urban Ghana." *Ethnos* 82, no. 4 (2017): 648–71.

Chaves, Isaís, Stanley Engerman, and James Robinson. "Reinventing the Wheel: The Economic Benefits of Wheeled Transportation in Early Colonial British West Africa." In *Africa's Development in Historical Perspective*, edited by Emmanueal Akyeampong, Robert H. Bates, Nathan Nunn, and James A. Robinson, 321–65. New York: Cambridge University Press, 2014.

Cheru, Fantu. *The Silent Revolution in Africa: Debt, Development, and Democracy*. Harare: Anvil, 1989.

Chirikure, Shadreck. "The Metalworker, the Potter, and the Pre-European African 'Laboratory.'" In *What Do Science, Technology, and Innovation from Africa Mean?*, edited by Clapperton Mavhunga, 63–77. Cambridge, MA: MIT Press, 2017.

Christie, James. *Cholera Epidemics in East Africa: An Account of the Several Diffusions of the Disease in That Country from 1821 till 1872*. London: Macmillan, 1876.

Claas, U. and P. Roscoe. "Hot Air and the Colonialist 'Other': the 'German-English-Dutch Airship Expedition' to New Guinea." *Journal of the Royal Anthropological Institute* 15 (2009): 131–50.

Collins, Harry M., and Robert Evans. "The Third Wave of Science Studies: Studies of Expertise and Experience." *Social Studies of Science* 32, no. 2 (April 2002): 235–96.

Comaroff, John, and Jean Comaroff. *Of Revelation and Revolution.* Vol. 2, *The Dialectics of Modernity on a South African Frontier.* Chicago: University of Chicago Press, 2009.

Comaroff, Jean, and John Comaroff. "Theory from the South: Or, How Euro-America Is Evolving Toward Africa." *Anthropological Forum* 22, no. 2 (2012): 113–31.

Condon, John C. "Nation Building and Image in the Tanzanian Press." *Journal of Modern African Studies* 5, no. 3 (November 1967): 335–54.

Cooper, Frederick. "Africa and the World Economy." *African Studies Review* 24, no. 2/3 (June–September 1981): 1–86.

Cooper, Frederick. *Africa since 1940: The Past of the Present.* New York: Cambridge University Press, 2002.

Cooper, Frederick. *Citizenship Between Empire and Nation: Remaking France and French Africa, 1945–1960.* Princeton, NJ: Princeton University Press, 2017.

Cooper, Frederick. *Colonialism in Question: Theory, Knowledge, History.* Berkeley: University of California Press, 2005.

Cooper, Frederick. *Decolonization and African Society: The Labor Question in French and British Africa.* New York: Cambridge University Press, 1996.

Cooper, Frederick. "Industrial Man Goes to Africa." In *Men and Masculinities in Modern Africa,* edited by Lisa Lindsay and Stephan Miescher, 128–37. Portsmouth, NH: Heinemann, 2003.

Cooper, Frederick. *On the African Waterfront: Urban Disorder and the Transformation of Work in Colonial Mombasa.* New Haven, CT: Yale University Press, 1987.

Cooper, Frederick, and Randall Packard. Introduction to *International Development and the Social Sciences: Essays on the History and Politics of Knowledge,* edited by Frederick Cooper and Randall Packard, 1–41. Berkeley: University of California Press, 1997.

Coulson, Andrew. "The Automated Bread Factory." In *African Socialism in Practice: The Tanzanian Experience,* edited by Andrew Coulson, 179–183. Nottingham: Spokesman, 1979.

Coulson, Andrew. *Tanzania: A Political Economy.* New York: Oxford University Press, 1982.

Coulson, Andrew. "Tanzania's Fertilizer Factory." In *African Socialism in Practice: The Tanzanian Experience,* edited by Andrew Coulson, 184–190. Nottingham: Spokesman, 1979.

Cowen, Michael, and Robert Shenton. *Doctrines of Development.* London: Routledge, 2004.

COWIconsult and Tanzania Ministry of Lands, Housing and Urban Development. *Bus Transport for Site and Services: Dar es Salaam.* Dar es Salaam: Ministry Printer, 1973.

Dant, Tim. "The Driver Car." *Theory, Culture, and Society* 21, nos. 4–5 (2004): 61–79.

Dant, Tim. "The Work of Repair: Gesture, Emotion, and Sensual Knowledge." *Sociological Research Online* 15, no. 3 (2010): 97–118.

d'Avignon, Robyn. "Spirited Geobodies: Producing Subterranean Property in Nineteenth-Century Bambuk, West Africa." *Technology and Culture* 61, no. 2 (2020): S20–48.

Decker, Corrie, and Elisabeth McMahon. *The Idea of Development in Africa: A History.* New York: Cambridge University Press, 2021.

de Leon, Jason. *Land of the Open Graves: Living and Dying on the Migrant Trail.* Berkeley: University of California Press, 2015.

de Luna, Kathryn. *Collecting Food, Cultivating People: Subsistence and Society in Central Africa.* New Haven, CT: Yale University Press, 2017.

de Luna, Kathryn. "Collecting Food, Cultivating Persons: Wild Resource Use in Central African Political Culture, c. 1000 B.C.E. to c. 1900 C.E." PhD diss., Northwestern University, 2008.

de Luna, Kathryn. "Inventing Bushcraft: Masculinity, Technology, and Environment in Central Africa, ca. 750–1250." *RCC Perspectives*, no. 4 (2017): 51–60.

de Luna, Kathryn. "Tracing the Itineraries of Working Concepts across African History." *African Economic History* 44 (2016): 235–57.

Denning, Andrew. "Mobilizing Empire: The Citroën Central Africa Expedition and the Interwar Civilizing Mission." *Technology and Culture* 61, no. 1 (2020): 42–70.

Deutsch, Jan-Georg. *Emancipation without Abolition in German East Africa, c. 1844–1914.* Athens: Ohio University Press, 2006.

Dinani, Husseina. "Gendered Migrant Labour: Marriage and the Political Economy of Wage Labour and Cash Crops in Late Colonial and Post-independence Southern Tanzania." *Gender and History* 31, no. 3 (2019): 565–83.

Diouf, Mamadou. "Senegalese Development: From Mass Nationalism to Technocratic Elitism." In *International Development and the Social Sciences: Essays on the History and Politics of Knowledge*, edited by Frederick Cooper and Randall Packard, 291–319. Berkeley: University of California Press, 1997.

Donham, Donald. *Marxist Modern: An Ethnographic History of the Ethiopian Revolution.* Berkeley: University of California Press, 1999.

Donovan, Kevin. "'Development' as if *We Have Never Been Modern*: Fragments of a Latourian Development Studies." *Development and Change* 45, no. 5 (September 2014): 869–94.

Doyle, Shane. "Premarital Sexuality in Great Lakes East Africa, 1900–1980." In *Generations Past: Youth in East African History*, edited by Andrew Burton and Hélène Charton-Bigot, 237–61. Athens: Ohio University Press, 2010.

Drummond, Henry. *Tropical Africa.* 7th ed. New York: Charles Scribner's and Sons, 1896.

Dumont, Rene. *False Start in Africa.* London: Earthscan, 1988.

Eckert, Andreas. "'We Must Run While Others Walk': African Civil Servants, State Ideologies and Bureaucratic Practices in Tanzania, from the 1950s to the 1970s." In *States at Work: Dynamics of African Bureaucracies*, edited by Thomas Bierschenk and Jean-Pierre Olivier de Sardan, 205–20. Boston: Brill, 2014.

Edgerton, David. "Innovation, Technology, or History: What Is the Historiography of Technology About?" *Technology and Culture* 51, no. 3 (2010): 680–97.

Edgerton, David. *The Shock of the Old: Technology and Global History since 1900.* New York: Oxford University Press, 2007.

Edward, Frank, and Mikael Hård. "Maintaining the Local Empire: The Public Works Department in Dar es Salaam, 1920–60." *Journal of Transport History* 41, no. 1 (2020): 27–46.

Edwards, Paul. "Industrial Genders: Soft/Hard." In *Gender and Technology: A Reader,* edited by Nina Lerman, Ruth Oldenziel, and Arwen Mohun, 177–203. Baltimore: Johns Hopkins University Press, 2003.

Edwards, Paul. "Infrastructure and Modernity: Force, Time, and Social Organization in the History of Sociotechnical Systems." In *Modernity and Technology,* edited by Thomas J. Misa, Philip Brey, and Andrew Feenberg, 185–225. Cambridge, MA: MIT Press, 2003.

Edwards, Paul. *A Vast Machine: Computer Models, Climate Data, and the Politics of Global Warming.* Cambridge, MA: MIT Press, 2010.

Edwards, Paul, Lisa Gitelman, Gabrielle Hecht, Adrian Johns, Brian Larkin, and Neil Safier. "AHR Conversation: Historical Perspectives on the Circulation of Information." *American Historical Review* 116, no. 5 (December 2011): 1393–435.

Edwards, Paul, and Gabrielle Hecht. "History and the Technopolitics of Identity: The Case of Apartheid South Africa." *Journal of Southern African Studies* 36, no. 3 (2010): 619–39.

Eglash, Ron. "Appropriating Technology: An Introduction." In *Appropriating Technology: Vernacular Science and Social Power,* edited by Ron Eglash, Jennifer L. Croissant, Giovanna Di Chiro, and Rayvon Fouche, i–xxi. Minneapolis: University of Minnesota Press, 2004.

Elychar, Julia. *Markets of Dispossession: NGOs, Economic Development, and the State in Cairo.* Durham, NC: Duke University Press, 2005.

Englebert, Pierre. "Pre-Colonial Institutions, Post-Colonial States, and Economic Development in Tropical Africa." *Political Research Quarterly* 53, no. 1 (2000): 7–36.

Epstein, Steven. *Impure Science: AIDS, Activism, and the Politics of Knowledge.* Berkeley: University of California Press, 1998.

Escobar, Arturo. "Civilizational Transitions." In *Pluriverse: A Post-Development Dictionary,* edited by Ashish Kothari, Ariel Salleh, Arturo Escobar, Frederico Demaria, and Alberto Acosta, 121–24. New Delhi: Tulika Books, 2019.

Escobar, Arturo. *Designs for the Pluriverse: Radical Interdependence, Autonomy, and the Making of Worlds.* Durham, NC: Duke University Press, 2018.

Escobar, Arturo. *Encountering Development: The Making and Unmaking of the Third World.* Princeton, NJ: Princeton University Press, 1995.

Evans, Robert, and Harry Collins. *Rethinking Expertise.* Chicago: University of Chicago Press, 2007. Kindle.

"Experience of an Engineer in Tanzanian Transport Industries: An Interview with F. Kabura." *Uhandisi: Journal of the Faculty of Engineering (University of Dar es Salaam)* 4, no. 1 (1978): 5–7.

Fabian, Johannes. *Out of Our Minds: Reason and Madness in the Exploration of Central Africa.* Berkeley: University of California Press, 2000.

Fabian, Johannes. *Time and the Other: How Anthropology Makes Its Subject*. New York: Columbia University Press, 1983.

Fabian, Steven. *Making Identity on the Swahili Coast: Urban Life, Community, and Belonging in Bagamoyo*. New York: Cambridge University Press, 2019.

Fair, Laura. "Drive-In Socialism: Debating Modernities and Development in Dar es Salaam, Tanzania." *American Historical Review* 118, no. 4 (2013): 1077–104.

Fair, Laura. *Pastimes and Politics: Culture, Community, and Identity in Post-Abolition Urban Zanzibar, 1890–1945*. Athens: Ohio University Press, 2001.

Fair, Laura. *Reel Pleasures: Cinema Audiences and Entrepreneurs in Twentieth-Century Urban Tanzania*. Athens: Ohio University Press, 2018.

Fanon, Frantz. *The Wretched of the Earth*. New York: Grove, 1963.

Farquharson, J. R. *Tanganyika Transport: A Review*. Dar es Salaam: Government Printer, 1945.

Farrant, Leda. *Tippu Tip and the East African Slave Trade*. New York: St. Martin's, 1975.

Featherstone, Mike. "Automobilities: An Introduction." *Theory, Culture and Society* 21, nos. 4/5 (2004): 1–24.

Feierman, Steven. "On Socially Composed Knowledge: Reconstructing a Shambaa Royal Ritual." In *In Search of a Nation: Histories of Authority and Dissidence in Tanzania*, edited by Gregory Maddox and James Giblin, 14–32. Athens: Ohio University Press, 2005.

Feierman, Steven. *Peasant Intellectuals: Anthropology and History in Tanzania*. Madison: University of Wisconsin Press, 1990.

Feierman, Steven. *The Shambaa Kingdom: A History*. Madison: University of Wisconsin Press, 1974.

Ferguson, James. *The Anti-politics Machine: "Development," Depoliticization, and Bureaucratic Power in Lesotho*. Minneapolis: University of Minnesota Press, 2009.

Ferguson, James. *Expectations of Modernity: Myths and Meanings of Urban Life on the Zambian Copperbelt*. Berkeley: University of California Press, 1999.

Ferguson, James. *Give a Man a Fish: Reflections on the New Politics of Distribution*. Durham, NC: Duke University Press, 2015.

Ferguson, James. *Global Shadows: Africa in the Neoliberal World Order*. Durham, NC: Duke University Press, 2006.

Filippello, Marcus. *The Nature of the Path: Reading a West African Road*. Minneapolis: University of Minnesota Press, 2017.

Franz, Kathleen. *Tinkering: Consumers Reinvent the Early Automobile*. Philadelphia: University of Pennsylvania Press, 2005.

Fredericks, Rosalind. *Garbage Citizenship: Vital Infrastructures of Labor in Dakar, Senegal*. Durham, NC: Duke University Press, 2018.

Freed, Libbie. "'Every European Becomes a Chief': Travel Guides to Colonial Equatorial Africa, 1900–1958." *Journal of Colonialism and Colonial History* 12, no. 2. https://muse-jhu-edu.pallas2.tcl.sc.edu/article/448308/summary.

Freed, Libbie. "Networks of (Colonial) Power: Roads in French Central Africa after World War I." *History and Technology* 26, no. 3 (2010): 203–23.

Galbraith, John. *Mackinnon and East Africa, 1878–1895: A Study in the "New Imperialism."* Cambridge: Cambridge University Press, 1972.

Gastrow, Claudia. "Aesthetic Dissent: Urban Redevelopment and Political Belonging in Luanda, Angola." *Antipode* 49, no. 2 (2017): 377–96.

Gately, Dermot. "A Ten-Year Retrospective: OPEC and the World Oil Market." *Journal of Economic Literature* 22, no. 3 (September 1984): 1100–114.

Geiger, Susan. TANU *Women: Gender and Culture in the Making of Tanganyikan Nationalism, 1955–1965.* Portsmouth, NH: Heinemann, 1997.

Gewald, Jan-Bart. "People, Mines, and Cars: Towards a Revision of Zambian History, 1890–1930." In *The Speed of Change: Motor Vehicles and People in Africa, 1890–2000,* edited by Jan-Bart Gewald, Sabine Luning, and Klaas van Walraven, 21–47. Leiden: Brill, 2009.

Gewald, Jan-Bart, Sabine Luning, and Klaas van Walraven. "Motor Vehicles and People in Africa: An Introduction." In *The Speed of Change: Motor Vehicles and People in Africa, 1890–2000,* edited by Jan-Bart Gewald, Sabine Luning, and Klaas van Walraven, 1–18. Leiden: Brill, 2009.

Giblin, James. *A History of the Excluded: Making Family a Refuge from State in Twentieth-Century Tanzania.* Athens: Ohio University Press, 2005.

Giblin, James. *The Politics of Environmental Control in Northeastern Tanzania, 1840–1940.* Philadelphia: University of Pennsylvania Press, 1992.

Gilbert, Erik. *Dhows and the Colonial Economy of Zanzibar, 1860–1970.* Athens: Ohio University Press, 2004.

Giles-Vernick, Tamara. "Na lege ti guiriri (On the Road of History): Mapping Out the Past and Present in M'Bres Region, Central African Republic." *Ethnohistory* 43, no. 2 (1996): 245–75.

Gillman, Clement. "A Short History of the Tanganyika Railways." *Tanganyika Notes and Records* 13 (June 1942): 14–56.

Gilroy, Paul. "Driving While Black." In *Car Cultures,* edited by Daniel Miller, 81–104. New York: Oxford University Press, 2001.

Glassman, Jonathon. *Feasts and Riot: Revelry, Rebellion, and Popular Consciousness on the Swahili Coast, 1856–1888.* Portsmouth, NH: Heinemann, 1995.

Glassman, Jonathon. *War of Words, War of Stones: Racial Thought and Violence in Colonial Zanzibar.* Bloomington: Indiana University Press, 2011.

Gleave, M. B. "The Dar es Salaam Transport Corridor: An Appraisal." *African Affairs* 91, no. 3 (1992): 249–67.

Gopakumar, Govind. *Installing Automobility: Emerging Politics of Mobility and Streets in Indian Cities.* Cambridge, MA: MIT Press, 2020.

Government of Tanganyika, *Annual Report of the Labour Division, 1961.* Dar es Salaam: Government Printer, 1962.

Government of Tanganyika, and George Tobias. *High-Level Manpower Requirements and Resources in Tanganyika, 1962–1967—Government Paper No. 2 of 1963.* Dar es Salaam: Government Printer, 1963.

Government of Tanzania. *Second Five Year Plan for Economic and Social Development: 1st July 1969–30th June 1974.* Dar es Salaam: Government Printer, 1969.

Grace, Joshua. "Heroes of the Road: Race, Gender, and the Politics of Mobility in Twentieth-Century Tanzania." *Africa: Journal of the International African Institute* 83, no. 3 (2013): 403–25.

Grace, Joshua. "Mechanical Expression in a Broken World: Repair, Fun, and Everyday Life in Tanzanian Garages." In *Africa Every Day: Fun, Leisure, and Expressive Culture on the Continent*, edited by Oluwakwemi M. Balogun, Lisa Gilman, Melissa Graboyes, and Habib Iddrisu, 287–96. Athens: Ohio University Press, 2019.

Graetz, Paul. *Im Auto quer durch Afrika*. Göttingen, Germany: Hess, 2008.

Graham, Stephen, and Simon Marvin. *Splintering Urbanism: Networked Infrastructures, Technological Mobilities and the Urban Condition*. New York: Routledge, 2001.

Grandin, Greg. *Fordlandia: The Rise and Fall of Henry Ford's Forgotten Jungle*. New York: Metropolitan Books, 2009.

Great Britain Naval Intelligence Division. *A Handbook of German East Africa*. London: H. M. Stationery Office, 1920.

Green-Simms, Lindsey. *Postcolonial Automobility: Car Culture in West Africa*. Minneapolis: University of Minnesota Press, 2017.

Gregory, Robert. *South Asians in East Africa: An Economic and Social History, 1880–1980*. Boulder, CO: Westview, 1993.

Guttman, Matthew. *The Meanings of Macho: Being a Man in Mexico City*. 10th anniversary ed. Berkeley: University of California Press, 2007.

Guy, Jeff, and Motlatsi Thabane. "Technology, Ethnicity, and Ideology: Basotho Miners and Shaft-Sinking on the South African Gold Mines." *Journal of Southern African Studies* 14, no. 2 (1988): 257–78.

Guyer, Jane. *Marginal Gains: Monetary Transactions in Atlantic Africa*. Chicago: University of Chicago Press, 2004.

Guyer, Jane. "Oil Assemblages and the Production of Confusion: Price Fluctuations in Two West African Oil-Producing Economies." In *Subterranean Estates: Life Worlds of Oil and Gas*, edited by Hannah Appel, Arthur Mason, and Michael Watts, 237–52. Ithaca, NY: Cornell University Press, 2015.

Guyer, Jane, and Samuel Eno Belinga. "Wealth in People as Wealth in Knowledge: Accumulation and Composition in Equatorial Africa." *Journal of African History* 36, no. 1 (1995): 91–120.

Hadfield, Leslie, and John Aerni-Flessner. "Introduction: Localizing the History of Development in Africa." *International Journal of African Historical Studies* 50, no. 1 (2017): 1–9.

Halimoja, Yusuf. *Sokoine: Mtu wa Watu*. Dar es Salaam: Tanzania Publications, 1985.

Hansen, Karen Tranberg. "Introduction: Domesticity in Africa." In *African Encounters with Domesticity*, edited by Karen Tranberg Hansen, 1–33. New Brunswick, NJ: Rutgers University Press, 1992.

Haraway, Donna. "Situated Knowledges: The Science Question in Feminism and the Privilege of Partial Perspectives." *Feminist Studies* 14, no. 3 (1988): 575–99.

Haraway, Donna. *Staying with the Trouble: Making Kin in the Chthulucene*. Durham, NC: Duke University Press, 2016.

Harper, Douglas. *Working Knowledge: Skill and Community in a Small Shop*. Chicago: University of Chicago Press, 1987.

Harrison, Alexina Mackay. *A. M. Mackay: Pioneer Missionary of the Church Missionary Society to Uganda*. London: Hodder and Stoughton, 1893.

Hart, Jennifer. *Ghana on the Go: African Mobility in the Age of Motor Transportation*. Bloomington: Indiana University Press, 2016.

Hart, Jennifer. "Informality, Urban Transport Infrastructure, and the Lessons of History in Accra, Ghana." *Routledge Handbook of Urban Planning in Africa*, edited by Carlos Nunes Silva, 297–316. New York: Routledge, 2020.

Hart, Jennifer. "Of Pirate Drivers and Honking Horns: Mobility, Authority, and Urban Planning in Late-Colonial Accra." *Technology and Culture* 61, no. 2 (2020): S49–S76.

Hassani, Rashidi bin. "The Story of Rashidi bin Hassani of the Bisa Tribe, Northern Rhodesia." Recorded by W. F. Baldock. In *Ten Africans*, 2nd ed., edited by Margery Perham, 81–119. Evanston, IL: Northwestern University Press, 1963.

Headrick, Daniel. *The Tentacles of Progress: Technology Transfer in the Age of Imperialism*. New York: Oxford University Press, 1988.

Headrick, Daniel. *The Tools of Empire: Technology and European Imperialism in the Nineteenth Century*. New York: Oxford University Press, 1981.

Hecht, David, and Maliqalim Simone. *Invisible Governance: The Art of African Micropolitics*. Brooklyn: Autonomedia, 1994.

Hecht, Gabrielle. "The African Anthropocene." *Aeon*, February 6, 2018. https://aeon.co/essays/if-we-talk-about-hurting-our-planet-who-exactly-is-the-we.

Hecht, Gabrielle. *Being Nuclear: Africans and the Global Uranium Trade*. Cambridge, MA: MIT Press, 2012.

Hecht, Gabrielle. Introduction to *Entangled Geographies: Empire and Technopolitics in the Global Cold War*, edited by Gabrielle Hecht, 1–11. Cambridge, MA: MIT Press, 2011.

Hecht, Gabrielle. *The Radiance of France: Nuclear Power and National Identity after World War II*. Cambridge, MA: MIT Press, 1998.

Hecht, Gabrielle. "Radioactive Excess: Modernization as Spectacle and Betrayal in Postcolonial Gabon." In *Modernization as Spectacle in Africa*, edited by Peter J. Bloom, Stephan F. Miescher, and Takyiwaa Manuh, 205–28. Bloomington: Indiana University Press, 2014.

Hecht, Gabrielle. "Rupture-Talk in the Nuclear Age: Conjugating Colonial Power in Africa." *Social Studies of Science* 32, nos. 5–6 (2002): 691–727.

Henderson, Jason. "Secessionist Automobility: Racism, Anti-urbanism, and the Politics of Automobility in Atlanta, Georgia." *International Journal of Urban and Regional Research* 30, no. 2 (June 2006): 293–307.

Henke, Christopher. "The Mechanics of Workplace Order: Toward a Sociology of Repair." *Berkeley Journal of Sociology* 44 (1999–2000): 55–81.

Herbert, Eugenia. *Iron, Gender, and Power: Rituals of Transformation in African Societies*. Bloomington: Indiana University Press, 1993.

Herman, Barry. "Multinational Oligopoly in Poor Countries: How East Africa Got Its Petroleum Refineries." Center for Research on Economic Development, Discussion Paper 39, University of Michigan, Ann Arbor, 1974.

Higgs, Catherine. *Chocolate Islands: Cocoa, Slavery, and Colonial Africa*. Athens: Ohio University Press, 2013.

Hodge, Joseph Morgan. *Triumph of the Expert: Agrarian Doctrines of Development and the Legacies of British Colonialism*. Athens: Ohio University Press, 2007.

Hodge, Joseph Morgan. "Writing the History of Development (Part 2: Longer, Deeper, Wider)." *Humanity: An International Journal of Human Rights, Humanitarianism, and Development* 7, no. 1 (2016): 125–74.

Hodges, Geoffrey. *The Carrier Corps: Military Labour in the East African Campaign, 1914–1918*. Westport, CT: Greenwood, 1986.

Hodges, Tony. *Angola: Anatomy of an Oil State*. Bloomington: Indiana University Press, 2004.

Hodgson, Dorothy. "Being Maasai Men: Modernity and the Production of Maasai Masculinites." In *Men and Masculinities in Modern Africa*, edited by Lisa Lindsay and Stephan Miescher, 211–29. Portsmouth, NH: Heinemann, 2003.

Hodgson, Dorothy. *Once Intrepid Warriors: Gender, Ethnicity, and the Cultural Politics of Maasai Development*. Bloomington: Indiana University Press, 2006.

Hodgson, Dorothy, and Sheryl McCurdy. "Introduction: Wicked Women and the Reconfiguration of Gender in Africa." In *"Wicked" Women and the Reconfiguration of Gender in Africa*, edited by Dorothy Hodgson and Sheryl McCurdy, 1–26. Portsmouth, NH: Heinemann, 2001.

Hofmeier, Rolf. *Transport and Economic Development in Tanzania: With Particular Reference to Roads and Road Transport*. Munich: Weltforum, 1973.

Howe, Cymene, Jessica Lockrem, Hannah Appel, Edward Hackett, Dominic Boyer, Randall Hall, Matthew Schneider-Mayerson, Albert Pope, Akhil Gupta, Elizabeth Rodwell et al. "Paradoxical Infrastructures: Ruins, Retrofit, and Risk." *Science, Technology, and Human Values* 41, no. 3 (2015): 547–65.

Huber, Matthew. *Lifeblood: Oil, Freedom, and the Forces of Capital*. Minneapolis: University of Minnesota Press, 2013.

Hughes, Thomas. "The Evolution of Large Technological Systems." In *The Social Construction of Technological Systems: New Directions in the Sociology and History of Technology*, edited by Wiebe Bijker, Thomas Hughes, and Trevor Pinch, 51–82. Cambridge, MA: MIT Press, 1987.

Hughes, Thomas. *Networks of Power: Electrification in Western Society, 1880–1930*. Baltimore: Johns Hopkins University Press, 1983.

Hunt, Nancy Rose. *A Colonial Lexicon: Of Birth Ritual, Medicalization, and Mobility in the Congo*. Durham, NC: Duke University Press, 1999.

Hunter, Emma. "A History of Maendeleo: The Concept of 'Development.'" In *Developing Africa: Concepts and Practices in Twentieth-Century Colonialism*, edited by Joseph Hodge, Gerald Hödl, and Martina Kopf, 87–107. Manchester: Manchester University Press, 2014.

Hunter, Emma. *Political Thought and the Public Sphere in Tanzania: Freedom, Democracy, and Citizenship in the Era of Decolonization*. New York: Cambridge University Press, 2015.

Hyden, Goran. *Beyond Ujamaa in Tanzania: Underdevelopment and an Uncaptured Peasantry*. Berkeley: University of California Press, 1980.

Iliffe, John. *The African AIDS Epidemic: A History*. Athens: Ohio University Press, 2007.

Iliffe, John. *A Modern History of Tanganyika*. Cambridge: Cambridge University Press, 1979.

Immerwahr, Daniel. *Thinking Small: The United States and the Lure of Community Development*. Cambridge, MA: Harvard University Press, 2015.

Independent Commission on International Development. *North-South, a Programme for Survival: Report of the Independent Commission on International Development Issues*. London: Pan Books, 1980.

Indian Oil Corporation Limited. *Proceedings of the United Nations Interregional Seminar on Petroleum Refining in Developing Countries, New Delhi, 22 January—3 February 1973, Volume I*. Thompson Press Ltd.: Haryana, India, 1973.

Ingold, Tim. *The Perception of the Environment: Essays on Livelihood, Dwelling, and Skill*. New York: Routledge, 2000.

Intergovernmental Panel on Climate Change (IPCC). *Climate Change 2007: Mitigation of Climate Change*. New York: Cambridge University Press, 2007.

Isaacman, Allen F., and Barbara Isaacman. *Dams, Displacement and the Delusion of Development: Cahora Bassa and Its Legacies in Mozambique, 1965–2007*. Athens: Ohio University Press, 2013.

Ivaska, Andrew. *Cultured States: Youth, Gender, and Modern Style in 1960s Dar es Salaam*. Durham, NC: Duke University Press, 2011.

Jackson, Steven. "Rethinking Repair." In *Media Technologies: Essays on Communication, Materiality, and Society*, edited by Tarleton Gillespie, Pablo J. Boczkowski, and Kristen A. Foot, 221–40. Cambridge, MA: MIT Press, 2014.

Jamhuri ya Muungano wa Tanzania. *Hotuba ya Waziri wa Mawasiliano na Uchukuzi, Ndugu A. H. Jamal, Mbunge, kuhusu Makadirio ya Fedha kwa Mwaka 1978/79*. Dar es Salaam: Mpigachapa wa Serikali, 1978.

Jamhuri ya Muungano wa Tanzania. *Hotuba ya Waziri was Mawasiliano na Uchukuzi, Ndugu A.C. Mwingira, Mbunge, kuhusu Makadirio ya Fedha kwa Mwaka 1980/81*. Dar es Salaam: Mpigachapa wa Serikali, 1980.

Jamhuri ya Muungano wa Tanzania. *Hali ya Uchukuzi na Mawasiliano Nchini Mei, 1980*. Dar es Salaam: Mpigachapa wa Serikali, 1980.

Joerges, Bernward. "High Variability Discourse in the History and Sociology of Large Technical Systems." In *The Governance of Large Technical Systems*, edited by O. Coutard, 259–90. London: Routledge, 1999.

Jones, Christopher. *Routes of Power: Energy and Modern America*. Cambridge, MA: Harvard University Press, 2014.

Jones, Toby. *Desert Kingdom: How Oil and Water Forged Modern Saudi Arabia*. Cambridge, MA: Harvard University Press, 2010.

Kalugila, Leonidas. *Swahili Proverbs from East Africa = Methali kiswahili toka Afrika Mashiriki*. Uppsala: Scandinavian Institute of African Studies, 1977.

Karp, Ivan, and D. A. Masolo. "African Discourses on Development: Introduction to Part 3." In *African Philosophy as Cultural Inquiry*, edited by Ivan Karp and D. A. Masolo, 175–80. Bloomington: Indiana University Press, 2000.

Kassum, Al Noor. *Africa's Winds of Change: Memoirs of an International Tanzanian*. New York: I. B. Tauris, 2007.

Katala, Jumbe. "The Cost of Traffic Congestion and Accidents to the Economy in Tanzania." Unpublished report for Dar es Salaam Rapid Transit. Accessed January 5, 2020. https://iekenya.org/forms/papers/Jumbe%20N.Katala%20[The%20cost%20of%20traffic%20congestion.....]DART.pdf.

Kent, David, and Paul Mushi. *The Education and Training of Artisans for the Informal Sector in Tanzania.* London: Overseas Development Administration, 1995.

Kern, Stephen. *The Culture of Time and Space, 1880–1918.* Cambridge, MA: Harvard University Press, 2003.

Kilimwiko, L. "Condoms Hitch Lift with Truckers." *WorldAIDS* 17 (1991): 9.

Kimambo, Isaria. *Penetration and Protest in Tanzania: The Impact of the World Economy on the Pare, 1860–1960.* Athens: Ohio University Press, 1991.

King, Kenneth. *The African Artisan: Education and the Informal Sector in Kenya.* Nairobi: Heinemann, 1977.

King'ei, Kitula. *Mwongozo wa siku njema.* Dar es Salaam: East African Educational Publishers, 1999.

Kirsch, David. *The Electric Vehicle and the Burden of History.* New Brunswick, NJ: Rutgers University Press, 2000.

Klaeger, Gabriel. "Dwelling on the Road: Routines, Rituals and Roadblocks in Southern Ghana." *Africa* 83, no. 3 (2013): 446–69.

Klaeger, Gabriel. "Introduction: The Perils and Possibilities of African Roads." *Africa* 83, no. 3 (2013): 359–66.

Klieman, Kairn. "Oil, Politics, and Development in the Formation of a State: The Congolese Petroleum Wars, 1963–1968." *International Journal of African Historical Studies* 41 2 (2008): 169–202.

Klieman, Kairn. "U.S. Oil Companies, the Nigerian Civil War, and the Origins of Opacity in the Nigerian Oil Industry." *Journal of American History* 99, no. 1 (2012): 155–65.

Kline, Ronald, and Trevor Pinch. "Users as Agents of Technological Change: The Social Construction of the Automobile in the Rural United States." *Technology and Culture* 37, no. 4 (1996): 763–95.

Klingelhofer, E. L. "Occupational Preferences of Tanzania Secondary School Pupils." *Journal of Social Psychology* 72 (1967): 153–57.

Klinghoffer, Arthur Jay. *Oiling the Wheels of Apartheid: Exposing South Africa's Secret Oil Trade.* Boulder, CO: Lynne Rienner, 1989.

Knight, Daniel, and Charles Stewart. "Ethnographies of Austerity: Temporality, Crisis, and Affect in Southern Europe." *History and Anthropology* 27, no. 1 (2016): 1–18.

Kodesh, Neil. *Beyond the Royal Gaze: Clanship and Public Healing in Buganda.* Charlottesville: University of Virginia Press, 2010.

Koponen, Juhani. *Development for Exploitation: German Colonial Policies in Mainland Tanzania, 1884–1914.* Hamburg: Finnish Historical Society, 1994.

Koponen, Juhani. "From Dead End to New Lease on Life: Development in South-Eastern Tanganyika from the Late-1930s to the 1950s." In *Developing Africa: Concepts and Practices in Twentieth Century Colonialism,* edited by Joseph Hodge, Gerald Hödl, and Martina Kopf, 37–62. Manchester: Manchester University Press, 2014.

Kopytoff, Igor. "The Cultural Biography of Things: Commoditization as a Process." In *The Social Life of Things: Commodities in Cultural Perspective*, edited by Arjun Appadurai, 64–91. Cambridge: Cambridge University Press, 1986.

Krebs, Stefan. "'Dial Gauge versus Senses 1–0': German Car Mechanics and the Introduction of New Diagnostic Equipment." *Technology and Culture* 55, no. 2 (April 2014): 354–89.

Krieger, Colleen. *Pride of Men: Ironworking in 19th Century West Central Africa*. Portsmouth, NH: Heinemann, 1999.

Kusimba, Chaparukha. *The Rise and Fall of Swahili States*. Walnut Creek, CA: Alta Mira, 1999.

Lal, Priya. *African Socialism in Postcolonial Tanzania: Between the Village and the World*. New York: Cambridge University Press, 2015.

Lal, Priya. "Militants, Mothers, and the National Family: Ujamaa, Gender, and Rural Development in Postcolonial Tanzania." *Journal of African History* 51, no. 1 (2010): 1–20.

Lal, Priya. "Self-Reliance and the State: The Multiple Meanings of Development in Early Post-colonial Tanzania." *Africa: Journal of the International African Institute* 82, no. 2 (2012): 212–34.

Lal, Vinay. "Gandhi and the Ecological Vision of Life: Thinking beyond Deep Ecology." *Environmental Ethics* 22, no. 2 (2000): 149–68.

Landes, David. "Why Are We So Rich and They So Poor?" *American Economic Review* 90, no. 2 (1990): 1–13.

Langwick, Stacey. *Bodies, Politics, and African Healing: The Matter of Maladies in Tanzania*. Bloomington: Indiana University Press, 2011.

Larkin, Brian. "The Politics and Poetics of Infrastructure." *Annual Review of Anthropology* 42 (2013): 327–343.

Larkin, Brian. "Promising Forms: The Political Aesthetics of Infrastructure." In *The Promise of Infrastructure*, edited by Nikhil Anand, Akhil Gupta, and Hannah Appel, 175–202. Durham, NC: Duke University Press, 2018.

Larkin, Brian. *Signal and Noise: Media, Infrastructure, and Urban Culture in Nigeria*. Durham, NC: Duke University Press, 2008.

Larson, Lorne. "The Ngindo: Exploring the Center of the Maji Maji Rebellion." In *Maji Maji: Lifting the Fog of War*, edited by James Giblin and Jamie Monson, 71–114. Leiden: Brill, 2010.

Larson, Pier. *Ocean of Letters: Language and Creolization in an Indian Ocean Diaspora*. New York: Cambridge University Press, 2009.

Latour, Bruno. *Reassembling the Social: An Introduction to Actor-Network-Theory*. Oxford: Oxford University Press, 2008.

Latour, Bruno. *We Have Never Been Modern*. Cambridge, MA: Harvard University Press, 1991.

LeCain, Timothy. *The Matter of History: How Things Create the Past*. New York: Cambridge University Press, 2017.

Laukamm-Josten, U., B. K. Mwizarubi, A. Outwater, C. L. Mwaijonga, J. J. Valadez, D. Nyamwaya, R. Swai, T. Saidel, and K. Nyamuryekung'e. "Preventing HIV Infection Through Peer Education and Condom Promotion Among Truck Drivers and Their Sexual Partners in Tanzania, 1990–1993." *AIDS Care* 12, no. 1 (2000): 27–40.

Laukamm-Josten, U., O. Ocehng, B. K. Mwizarubi, C. L. Mwaijonga, R. Swai, and M. Trupin, "HIV and Syphilis Seroprevalence and Risk Factors in Truckstops and Nearby Communities in Tanzania." *Eighth International Conference on AIDS*. Amsterdam, PoC 4162.

Lekan, Thomas. *Our Gigantic Zoo: A German Quest to Save the Serengeti*. New York: Oxford, 2020.

Lerman, Nina. "The Uses of Useful Knowledge: Science, Technology, and Social Boundaries in an Industrializing City." *Osiris* 12, no. 1 (1997): 39–59.

Leslie, J. K. *A Survey of Dar es Salaam*. New York: Published on behalf of East African Institute of Social Research by Oxford University Press, 1963.

Li, Tania Murray. *Governmentality, Development, and the Practice of Politics*. Durham, NC: Duke University Press, 2007.

Li, Tania Murray. *The Will to Improve: Governmentality, Development, and the Practice of Politics*. Durham, NC: Duke University Press, 2007.

Lindsay, Lisa. "Extraversion, Creolization, and Dependency in the Atlantic Slave Trade." *Journal of African Studies* 55, no. 2 (2014): 135–45.

Lindsay, Lisa. *Working with Gender: Wage Labor and Social Change in Southwestern Nigeria*. Portsmouth, NH: Heinemann, 2003.

Lindsay, Lisa, and Stephan Miescher, eds. *Men and Masculinities in Modern Africa*. Portsmouth, NH: Heinemann, 2003.

Livingston, Julie. *Debility and the Moral Imagination in Botswana*. Bloomington: Indiana University Press, 2005.

Livingston, Julie. *Improvising Medicine: An African Oncology Ward in an Emerging Cancer Epidemic*. Durham, NC: Duke University Press, 2012.

Livingston, Julie. "Insights from an African History of Disability." *Radical History Review* 94 (2006): 111–26.

Livingston, Julie. *Self-Devouring Growth: A Planetary Parable as Told from South Africa*. Durham, NC: Duke University Press, 2019.

Livingstone, David, and Horace Waller. *The Last Journals of David Livingstone in Central Africa, from 1865 to His Death: Continued by a Narrative of His Last Moments and Sufferings, Obtained from His Faithful Servants, Chuma and Susi, Volume I*. London: John Murray, 1874.

Lucsko, David. *Junkyards, Gearheads, and Rust: Salvaging the Automotive Past*. Baltimore: Johns Hopkins University Press, 2016.

Lugard, Frederick. *The Dual Mandate in British Tropical Africa*. London: F. Cass, 1965.

Lumley, Edward K. *Forgotten Mandate: A British District Officer in Tanganyika*. London: Hurst, 1976.

Macekura, Stephen. *Of Limits and Growth: The Rise of Global Sustainable Development in the Twentieth Century*. New York: Cambridge University Press, 2015.

MacKenzie, Donald, and Judy Wajcman. "Introductory Essay: The Social Shaping of Technology." In *The Social Shaping of Technology*, edited by Donald MacKenzie and Judy Wajcman, 1–49. 2nd ed. Philadelphia: Open University Press, 2002.

Madan, A. C. *English-Swahili Dictionary*. 2nd ed., rev. Oxford: Clarendon Press, 1902.

Maddox, Gregory H. "Networks and Frontiers in Colonial Tanzania." *Environmental History* 3, no. 4 (1998): 436–59.

Maddox, Gregory, and James Giblin, eds. *In Search of a Nation: Histories of Authority and Dissidence in Tanzania*. New York: James Currey, 2005.

Maliyamkono, T. L., and M. S. D. Bagachwa. *The Second Economy in Tanzania*. Athens: Ohio University Press, 1990.

Malm, Andreas. *Fossil Capital: The Rise of Steam Power and the Roots of Global Warming*. New York: Verso, 2016.

Malm, Andreas, and Alf Hornborg. "The Geology of Mankind: A Critique of the Anthropocene Narrative." *Anthropocene Review* 1, no. 1 (2014): 62–69.

Mann, Gregory. *From Empires to NGOs in the West African Sahel: The Road to Nongovernmentality*. New York: Cambridge University Press, 2015.

Manuh, Takyiwaa. "Building Institutions for the New Africa: The Institute of African Studies at the University of Ghana." In *Modernization as Spectacle in Africa*, edited by Peter Bloom, Stephan Miescher, and Takyiwaa Manuh, 268–84. Bloomington: Indiana University Press, 2014.

Marshall, Macklin, Monaghan Limited. *Dar es Salaam Master Plan*. Don Mills, Ontario, Canada: Marshall Macklin Monoghan Ltd., 1979.

Marx, Leo. "'Technology': The Emergence of a Hazardous Concept." *Technology and Culture* 51, no. 3 (2010): 561–77.

Masquelier, Adeline. "Road Mythographies: Space, Mobility, and the Historical Imagination in Postcolonial Niger." *American Ethnologist* 29, no. 4 (2002): 829–56.

Mavhunga, Clapperton. "Introduction: What Do Science, Technology, and Innovation Mean from Africa?" In *What Do Science, Technology, and Innovation Mean from Africa?*, edited by Clapperton Mavhunga, 1–27. Cambridge, MA: MIT Press, 2017.

Mavhunga, Clapperton. "The Language of Science, Technology, and Innovation: A *Chimurenga* Way of Seeing from *Dzimbahwe*." In *What Do Science, Technology, and Innovation Mean from Africa?*, edited by Clapperton Mavhunga, 45–62. Cambridge, MA: MIT Press, 2017.

Mavhunga, Clapperton. *The Mobile Workshop: The Tsetse Fly and African Knowledge Production*. Cambridge, MA: MIT Press, 2019.

Mavhunga, Clapperton. *Transient Workspaces: Technologies of Everyday Innovation in Zimbabwe*. Cambridge, MA: MIT Press, 2014.

Mavhunga, Clapperton, ed. *What Do Science, Technology, and Innovation Mean from Africa?* Cambridge, MA: MIT Press, 2017.

Mavhunga, Clapperton. "Which Mobilities for (Which) Africa? Beyond Banal Mobilities." In *Mobility in History: Reviews and Reflections—T2M Yearbook*, edited by Peter Norton, Gijs Mom, Liz Millward, and Mathieu Flonneau, 73–84. Neuchâtel: Editions Alphil, 2012.

Mbembe, J.-A., and Sarah Nuttall. "Writing the World from an African Metropolis." *Public Culture* 16, no. 3 (2004): 347–72.

Mbilinyi, Marjorie. "'Runaway Wives' in Colonial Tanganyika." *International Journal of the Sociology of Law* 16, no. 1 (1988): 1–29.

McClintock, Ann. *Imperial Leather: Race, Gender, and Sexuality in the Colonial Conquest*. New York: Routledge, 1995.

McCormack, Derek. "Pipes and Cables." In *The Routledge Handbook of Mobilities*, edited by Peter Adey, David Bissell, Kevin Hannam, Peter Merriman, and Mimi Sheller, 225–32. New York: Routledge, 2014.

McDow, Thomas. *Buying Time: Debt and Mobility in the Western Indian Ocean*. Athens: Ohio University Press, 2018.

McGaw, Judith. "Why Feminine Technologies Matter." In *Gender and Technology: A Reader*, ed. by Nina Lerman, Ruth Oldenziel, and Arwen Mohun, 13–36. Baltimore: Johns Hopkins University Press, 2003.

McHenry, Dean E. *Limited Choices: The Political Struggle for Socialism in Tanzania*. Boulder, CO: Lynne Rienner, 1994.

McLuckie, A. J. "Roads and Road Transport in Tanganyika Territory." *Journal of the Institution of Civil Engineers 6*, no. 8 (1937): 572–74.

McNeill, John Robert, and Peter Engelke. *The Great Acceleration: An Environmental History of the Anthropocene since 1945*. Cambridge, MA: Belknap Press of Harvard University Press, 2014.

McShane, Clay. *Down the Asphalt Path: The Automobile and the American City*. New York: Columbia University Press, 1994.

Medina, Eden. *Cybernetic Revolutionaries: Technology and Politics in Allende's Chile*. Cambridge, MA: MIT Press, 2014.

Medina, Eden, Ivan da Costa Marques, and Christina Holmes. "Introduction: Beyond Imported Magic." In *Beyond Imported Magic: Essays on Science, Technology, and Society in Latin America*, edited by Eden Medina, Ivan da Costa Marques, and Christina Holmes, 1–23. Cambridge, MA: MIT Press, 2017.

Mehos, Donna, and Suzanne Moon. "The Uses of Portability: Circulating Experts in the Politics of Cold War and Decolonization." In *Entangled Geographies: Empire and Technopolitics in the Global Cold War*, edited by Gabrielle Hecht, 43–74. Cambridge, MA: MIT Press, 2011.

Meier, Prita. *Swahili Port Cities: The Architecture of Elsewhere*. Bloomington: Indiana University Press, 2016.

Merriman, Peter. *Driving Spaces: A Cultural-Historical Geography of England's M1 Motorway*. Malden, MA: Blackwell, 2007.

Miescher, Stephan. *Making Men in Ghana*. Bloomington: Indiana University Press, 2005.

Miescher, Stephan, Peter Bloom, and Takyiwaa Manuh. "Introduction." In *Modernization as Spectacle in Africa*, edited by Peter Bloom, Stephan Miescher, and Takyiwaa Manuh, 1–16. Bloomington: Indiana University Press, 2014.

Miescher, Stephan, and Lisa Lindsay. "Introduction: Men and Masculinities in Modern African History." In *Men and Masculinities in Modern Africa*, edited by Lisa Lindsay and Stephan Miescher, 1–29. Portsmouth, NH: Heinemann, 2003.

Mika, Marissa. "The Half-Life of Radiotherapy and Other Transferred Technologies." *Technology and Culture 61*, no. 2 (2020): S135–37.

Miller, Charlotte. "Who Are the 'Permanent Inhabitants' of the State? Citizenship Policies and Border Controls in Tanzania, 1920–1980." PhD diss., University of Iowa, 2011.

Miller, Daniel, ed. *Car Cultures*. New York: Berg, 2001.

Miller, Daniel. "Driven Societies." In *Car Cultures*, edited by Daniel Miller, 1–33. New York: Berg, 2001.

Mitchell, A. J. "Soil Stabilization for Roads in Tanganyika." *Journal of the Institution of Civil Engineering* 24, no. 6 (April 1945): 134–44.

Mitchell, Timothy. *Carbon Democracy: Political Power in the Age of Oil*. 2nd ed. New York: Verso, 2013.

Mitchell, Timothy. *Rule of Experts: Egypt, Techno-Politics, Modernity*. Berkeley: University of California Press, 2002.

Mloka, Charles. *Mjini Taabu*. Peramiho: Benedictine Publications Ndanda, 1985.

Moffett, J. P. *Handbook of Tanganyika*. Dar es Salaam: Government Printer, 1958.

Mokyr, Joel. *The Lever of Riches: Technological Creativity and Economic Progress*. New York: Oxford University Press, 1990.

Molohan, M. J. *Detribalization: A Study of the Areas of Tanganyika Where Detribalized People Are Living, with Recommendations as to the Administrative and Other Measures Required to Meet the Problem Arising Therein*. Dar es Salaam: Government Printer, 1959.

Mom, Gijs. *Atlantic Automobilism: The Emergence and Persistence of the Car, 1895–1940*. New York: Berghahn Books, 2015.

Monson, Jamie. *Africa's Freedom Railway: How a Chinese Development Project Changed Lives and Livelihoods in Tanzania*. Bloomington: Indiana University Press, 2011.

Monson, Jamie. "War of Words: The Narrative Efficacy of Medicine in the Maji Maji War." In *Maji Maji: Lifting the Fog of War*, edited by James Giblin and Jamie Monson, 33–69. Leiden: Brill, 2010.

Moodie, T. Dunbar, and Vivienne Ndatshe. *Going for Gold: Men, Mines, and Migration*. Berkeley: University of California Press, 1994.

Morton, David. *Age of Concrete: Housing and the Shape of Aspiration in the Capital of Mozambique*. Athens: Ohio University Press, 2019.

Moyd, Michelle. *Violent Intermediaries: African Soldiers, Conquest, and Everyday Colonialism in German East Africa*. Athens: Ohio University Press, 2014.

Mrazek, Rudolf. *Engineers of Happy Land: Technology and Nationalism in a Colony*. Princeton, NJ: Princeton University Press, 2002.

Msuya, C. D. "Foreign Aid and Tanzanian Development." *Mbioni* 7, no. 4 (1974): 38–42.

Mukerji, Chandra. *Impossible Engineering: Technology and Territoriality on the Canal du Midi*. Princeton, NJ: Princeton University Press, 2009.

Mutongi, Kenda. *Matatu: A History of Popular Transportation in Nairobi*. Chicago: University of Chicago Press, 2017.

Mwase, Ngila. "The Supply of Road Vehicles in Tanzania: The Problem of Suppressed Demand." *Journal of Transport Economics and Policy* 17, no. 1 (1983): 77–89.

Mwizarubi, B., L. Cole, and N. Lamson. "Targeting Truckers in Tanzania." *AIDS and Society* (April/May 1991): 4.

Myers, Garth. *Verandahs of Power: Colonialism and Space in Urban Africa*. Syracuse, NY: Syracuse University Press, 2003.

Nagar, Richa. "The South Asian Diaspora in Tanzania: A History Retold." *Comparative Studies of South Asia, Africa, and the Middle East* 16, no. 2 (1996): 62–80.

Ngahyoma, Ngalimecha. *Kijiji Chetu*. Dar es Salaam: Tanzania Publishing House, 1977.

Ngonyani, Deogratias. "Tools of Deception: Media Coverage of Student Protests in Tanzania." *Nordic Journal of African Studies* 9, no. 2 (2000): 22–48.

Nichols-Belo, Amy. "Uchawi upo: Embodied Experience and Anti-Witchcraft Practice in Mwanza, Tanzania." PhD diss., University of Virginia, 2014.

Njovu, Vincent. *Dereva wa Kwanza Tanganyika*. Dar es Salaam: Tanzania Publishing House, 1981.

Nkwi, Gam W., and M. De Bruijn. "'Human Telephone Lines': Flag Post Mail Relay Runners in British Southern Cameroon (1916–1955) and the Establishment of a Modern Communications Network." *International Review of Social History* 59, no. 22 (2014): 211–35.

Nyerere, Julius. "Aid and Development from a Recipient's Point of View." *Mbioni* 7, no. 4 (1974): 5–23.

Nyerere, Julius. *The Arusha Declaration: Ten Years After*. Dar es Salaam: Government Press, 1977. Accessed at https://www.juliusnyerere.org/resources/view/the_arusha _declaration_ten_years_after_julius_k._nyerere_1977.

Nyerere, Julius. "The Economic Challenge: Dialogue or Confrontation." *African Affairs* 75, no. 299 (1976): 242–49.

Nyerere, Julius. "Education: A Tool for Liberation and Development of Man." *Mbioni* 7, no. 7 (1975): 19–21.

Nyerere, Julius. *Freedom and Development, Uhuru na Maendeleo: A Selection from Writings and Speeches, 1968–1973*. Dar es Salaam: Oxford University Press, 1973.

Nyerere, Julius. *Freedom and Socialism, Uhuru na Ujamaa: A Selection from Writings and Speeches, 1965–1967*. New York: Oxford University Press, 1968.

Nyerere, Julius. *Freedom and Unity, Uhuru na Umoja: A Selection from Writings and Speeches, 1952–1965*. Dar es Salaam: Oxford University Press, 1966.

Nyerere, Julius. *Our Economy, 1965–1967: Speech by the President Mwalimu Julius K. Nyerere to the National Assembly, June 13, 1966*. Dar es Salaam: Ministry of Information and Tourism, 1966.

Nyerere, Julius. *The President, Mwalimu Julius K. Nyerere: Speeches in United Kingdom, March 1985*. Accessed at The Mwalimu Nyerere Foundation. Published December 8, 2009. https://www.juliusnyerere.org/resources/view/speeches_of_j.k._nyerere_in _the_uk_1985.

Nyerere, Julius. "President Nyerere's Banquet Speech in Bucharest-Rumania." *Mbioni*, 7, no. 9 (1975): 8–12.

Nyerere, Julius. "President Nyerere's Speech at the Return Banquet in China." *Mbioni* 7, no. 8 (1975): 14–19.

Nyerere, Julius. *Ujamaa: Essays on Socialism*. Dar es Salaam: Oxford University Press, 1968.

Nyerere, Julius. *Ujamaa ni Imani, 1: Moyo kabla ya silaha*. Dar es Salaam: East Africa Publishing House, 1973.

Nyerere, Julius. *Wafanyakazi na Ujamaa Tanzania*. Dar es Salaam: Makao Makuu ya NUTA, 1977.

Ochonu, Moses. *Colonial Meltdown: Northern Nigeria in the Great Depression*. Athens: Ohio University Press, 2009.

Ohman, May-Britt. "Taming Exotic Beauties: Swedish Hydropower Constructions in Tanzania in the Era of Development Assistance." PhD diss., Royal Institute of Technology-Stockholm, 2007.

Oldenziel, Ruth. *Making Technology Masculine: Women, Men, and the Machine in America, 1880–1945*. Amsterdam: Amsterdam University Press, 1999.

Oonk, Gijsbert. "Karimjee Jivanjee and Co. in Tanzania, 1860–2000: A Case for 'Diasporic Family Firms.'" In *Mobility between Africa, Asia and Latin America: Economic Networks and Cultural Interactions*, edited by Ute Röschenthaler and Alessandro Jedlowski, 46–71. London: Zed Books, 2017.

Orde-Browne, G. St. J. *Labour: The Recruitment, Employment, and Care of Government Labour*. Dar es Salaam: Government Printer, 1930.

Orde-Browne, G. St. J. *Labour Conditions in East Africa*. London: His Majesty's Stationery Office, 1946.

Osborn, Emily. "Casting Aluminum Cooking Pots: Labour, Migration, and Artisan Production in West Africa's Informal Sector, 1945–2005." *African Identities* 7, no. 3 (Fall 2009): 373–86.

Osseo-Asare, Abena Dove. *Bitter Roots: The Search for Healing Plants in Africa*. Chicago: University of Chicago Press, 2014.

Osseo-Asare, Abena Dove. "Scientific Equity: Experiments in Laboratory Education in Ghana." *Isis* 104, no. 4 (December 2013): 713–41.

Ottaway, Marina, and David Ottaway. *Afrocommunism*. New York: Holmes and Meier, 1986.

Owomero, Basil. "Crime in Tanzania: Contradictions of a Socialist Experiment." *International Journal of Comparative and Applied Criminal Justice* 12, no. 2 (Winter 1988): 177–89.

Packard, Jeremy. *Mobility without Mayhem: Safety, Cars, and Citizenship*. Durham, NC: Duke University Press, 2008.

Palmer, Jamie. "Ineffective Masculinity: Intersection of Masculinity and Nationhood in Portraits of Cuban Men from *Time* and *Newsweek*." *Men and Masculinities* 21, no. 4 (October 2018): 455–78.

Parpart, Jane, and Marianne Rostgaard. *The Practical Imperialist: Letters from a Danish Planter in German East Africa, 1888–1906*. Leiden: Brill, 2006.

Patel, Shailja. *Migritude*. New York: Kaya Press, 2014.

Patterson, Matthew. *Automobile Politics: Ecology and Cultural Political Economy*. New York: Cambridge University Press, 2007.

Pesek, Michael. "The War of Legs: Transport and Infrastructure in the East African Campaign of World War I." *Transfers: Interdisciplinary Journal of Mobility Studies* 5, no. 2 (2015): 102–20.

Péteri, György. "Streetcars of Desire: Cars and Automobilism in Communist Hungary (1958–70)." *Social History* 34, no. 1 (2009): 1–28.

Peterson, Derek. *Ethnic Patriotism and the East African Revival: A History of Dissent c. 1935–1972*. New York: Cambridge University Press, 2012.

Phillips, Kristin. *An Ethnography of Hunger: Politics, Subsistence, and the Unpredictable Grace of the Sun*. Bloomington: Indiana University Press, 2018.

Piot, Peter. *No Time to Lose: A Life in Pursuit of Deadly Viruses*. New York: Norton, 2013.

Piot, Peter, Henri Taelman, Kapita Bila Minlangu, N. Mbendi, K. Ndangi, Kayembe Kalambayi, Chris Bridts, Thomas Quinn, Fred Feinsod, Odio Wobin et al. "Acquired Immunodeficiency Syndrome in a Heterosexual Population." Lancet 324, no. 8394 (July 1984): 65–69.

Pirie, Gordon. "Non-urban Motoring in Colonial Africa in the 1920s and 1930s." South African Historical Journal 63, no. 1 (2011): 38–60.

Pitcher, Anne, and Kelly Askew. "African Socialisms and Postsocialisms." Africa: Journal of the International African Institute 76, no. 1 (2006): 1–14.

Plageman, Nate. "'Accra Is Changing, Isn't It?': Urban Infrastructure, Independence, and Nation in the Gold Coast's Daily Graphic, 1954–1957." International Journal of African Historical Studies 43, no. 1 (2010), 137–59.

Ponsavady, Stéphanie. Cultural and Literary Representations of the Automobile in French Indochina: A Colonial Roadshow. Cham, Switzerland: Palgrave, 2018.

Pouwels, Randall. Horn and Crescent: Cultural Change and Traditional Islam on the East African Coast, 800–1900. New York: Cambridge University Press, 1987.

Pratt, Cranford. The Critical Phase in Tanzania: Nyerere and the Emergence of a Socialist Strategy. Cambridge: Cambridge University Press, 1976.

Pratt, Mary Louise. Imperial Eyes: Travel Writing and Transculturation. London: Taylor and Francis, 2008.

Pratt, Wallace. Oil in the Earth. Lawrence: University of Kansas Press, 1943.

Prestholdt, Jeremy. Domesticating the World: African Consumerism and the Genealogies of Globalization. Berkeley: University of California Press, 2008.

Prestholdt, Jeremy. "Locating the Indian Ocean: Notes on the Postcolonial Reconstitution of Space." Journal of Eastern African Studies 9, no. 3 (2015): 440–67.

Prichard, Andreana. "'Let Us Swim in the Pool of Love': Love Letters and Discourses of Community Composition in Twentieth-Century Tanzania." Journal of African History 54, no. 1 (2013): 103–22.

Pritchard, Stan. Driving Mad. n.p.: n.p., n.d.

Project Planning Associates. National Capital Master Plan, Dar es Salaam United Republic of Tanzania. Toronto: The Associates, 1968.

Project Planning Associates. National Capital Master Plan, Dodoma, Tanzania. Toronto: The Associates, 1976.

Puaca, Laura. Searching for Scientific Manpower: Technocratic Feminism and the Politics of National Security, 1940–1980. Chapel Hill: University of North Carolina Press, 2014.

Quayson, Ato. Oxford Street, Accra: City Life and the Itineraries of Transnationalism. Durham, NC: Duke University Press, 2014.

Ranger, Terence. Dance and Society in Eastern Africa, 1890–1970: The Beni Ngoma. Berkeley: University of California Press, 1975.

Resnick, Idrian. "Manpower Development in Tanzania." Journal of Modern African Studies 5, no. 1 (May 1967): 107–23.

Rijke-Epstein, Tasha. "The Politics of Filth: Sanitation, Work, and Competing Moralities in Urban Madagascar, 1890s–1977." Journal of African History 60, no. 2 (2019): 229–56.

Rist, Gilbert. The History of Development: From Western Origins to Global Faith. 3rd ed. New York: Zed Books, 2013. Kindle.

Rizzo, Matteo. "Being Taken for a Ride: Privatisation of the Dar es Salaam Transport System, 1983–1998." *Journal of Modern African Studies* 40, no. 1 (2002): 133–57.

Rizzo, Matteo. "The Political Economy of an Urban Megaproject: The Bus Rapid Transit Project in Tanzania." *African Affairs* 114, no. 455 (April 2015): 249–70.

Rizzo, Matteo. *Taken for a Ride: Grounding Neoliberalism, Precarious Labour, and Public Transport in an African Metropolis.* Oxford: Oxford University Press, 2017.

Robertson, Claire. *Trouble Showed the Way: Women, Men and Trade in the Nairobi Area, 1890–1990.* Bloomington: Indiana University Press, 1997.

Rockel, Stephen. *Carriers of Culture: Labour on the Road in Nineteenth-Century East Africa.* Portsmouth, NH: Heinemann, 2006.

Rodney, Walter. *How Europe Underdeveloped Africa.* Dar es Salaam: Tanzania Publishing House, 1972.

Roitman, Janet. *Fiscal Disobedience: An Anthropology of Economic Regulation in Central Africa.* Princeton, NJ: Princeton University Press, 2005.

Rottenburg. Richard. "Social and Public Experiments and New Figurations of Science and Politics in Postcolonial Africa." *Postcolonial Studies* 12, no. 4 (2009): 423–40.

Ruhumbika, Gabriel. *Miradi Bubu ya Wazalendo.* Dar es Salaam: Tanzania Publishing House, 1992.

Ruhumbika, Gabriel. *The Silent Empowerment of the Compatriots.* Dar es Salaam: E&D, 2009.

Russell, Andrew L., and Lee Vinsel. "After Innovation, Turn to Maintenance." *Technology and Culture* 59, no. 1 (January 2018): 1–25.

Rutayisingwa, John. *Ngumi Ukutani.* Dar es Salaam: Ben, 1979.

Rweyemamu, Justinian. *Underdevelopment and Industrialization in Tanzania: A Study of Perverse Capitalist Industrial Development.* Nairobi: Oxford University Press, 1973.

Rweyemamu, Paul. *A General Guide to the Oil (Petroleum) Industry (with Special Reference to the Tanzanian Oil Industry).* Dar es Salaam: Tanzanian and Italian Petroleum Refinery, Ltd., 1988.

Sabea, Hanan. "The Limits of Law in the Mandated Territories: Becoming Manamba and the Struggles of Sisal Plantation Workers in Tanganyika." *African Studies* 68, no. 1 (2009): 135–61.

Sabot, R. *Economic Development and Urban Migration: Tanzania, 1900–1971.* Oxford: Clarendon, 1979.

Sachs, Wolfgang, ed. *The Development Dictionary: A Guide to Knowledge as Power.* 2nd ed. New York: Zed Books, 2010.

Samson, Ridder. *Ufundi (wa) Magari: Mfano wa Ukuzajo wa Istilahi za Kiswahili Nchini Tanzania, Matumizi na Usanifishaji Wake.* Leiden: Isimu ya Lugha za Kiafrika, 1988.

Sanders, Todd. *Beyond Bodies: Rain-making and Sense Making in Tanzania.* Buffalo, NY: University of Toronto Press, 2008.

Scheele, Judith. *Smugglers and Saints of the Sahara: Regional Connectivity in the Twentieth Century.* New York: Cambridge University Press, 2012.

Schivelbusch, Wolfgang. *The Railway Journey: The Industrialization of Time and Space in the Nineteenth Century.* Berkeley: University of California Press, 2014.

Schmidt, Peter. *Iron Technology in East Africa: Symbolism, Science and Technology.* Bloomington: Indiana University Press, 1997.

Schneider, Leander. *Government of Development: Peasants and Politicians in Postcolonial Tanzania*. Bloomington: Indiana University Press, 2014.

Schoenbrun, David. "Conjuring the Modern in Africa: Durability and Rupture in Histories of Public Healing between the Great Lakes of East Africa." *American Historical Review* 111, no. 5 (2006): 1403–39.

Schoenbrun, David. *A Green Place, a Good Place: Agrarian Change, Gender, and Social Identity in the Great Lakes Region to the 15th Century*. Portsmouth, NH: Heinemann, 1999.

Schroeder, Richard. *Africa after Apartheid: South Africa, Race, and Nation in Tanzania*. Bloomington: Indiana University Press, 2012.

Schuller, Tom, and John Field. "Social Capital, Human Capital and the Learning Society." *International Journal of Lifelong Education* 17, no. 4 (1988): 226–35.

Schumacher, E. F. *Small Is Beautiful: A Study of Economics as If People Mattered*. London: Blond and Briggs, 1973.

Scott, James. *Seeing like a State: How Certain Schemes to Improve the Human Condition Have Failed*. New Haven, CT: Yale University Press, 1998.

Sennett, Richard. *The Craftsman*. New Haven, CT: Yale University Press, 2008. Kindle.

Serlin, David. "Confronting African Histories of Technology: A Conversation with Keith Breckenridge and Gabrielle Hecht." *Radical History Review* 1, no. 127 (2017): 87–102.

Setel, Philip. *A Plague of Paradoxes: AIDS, Culture, and Demography in Northern Tanzania*. Chicago: University of Chicago Press, 1999.

Seth, Suman. "Colonial History and Postcolonial Science Studies." *Radical History Review* 2017, no. 127 (2017): 63–85.

Shell, Jacob. *Transportation and Revolt: Pigeons, Mules, Canals, and the Vanishing Geographies of Subversive Mobility*. Cambridge, MA: MIT Press, 2015.

Sheller, Mimi. "Automotive Emotions: Feeling the Car." *Theory, Culture, and Society* 21, no. 4–5 (2004): 221–42.

Sheller, Mimi. "Global Energy Cultures of Speed and Lightness: Materials, Mobilities and Transnational Power." *Theory, Culture, and Society* 31, no. 51 (2014): 127–54.

Sheller, Mimi. *Mobility Justice: The Politics of Movement in an Age of Extremes*. New York: Version, 2018.

Sheller, Mimi, and John Urry. "The City and the Car." *International Journal of Urban and Regional Research* 24, no. 4 (December 2000): 737–57.

Sheller, Mimi, and John Urry. "Mobile Transformations of 'Public' and 'Private' Life." *Theory, Culture, and Society* 20, no. 3 (2003): 107–25.

Shelton, Kyle. *Power Moves: Transportation, Politics, and Development in Houston*. Austin: University of Texas Press, 2018.

Sheriff, Abdul. *Slaves, Spices, and Ivory in Zanzibar: Integration of an East African Commercial Empire into the World Economy, 1770–1873*. Athens: Ohio University Press, 1987.

Shivji, Issa. *Class Struggles in Tanzania*. New York: Monthly Review Press, 1976.

Shivji, Issa. *Development as Rebellion, Book Three: Rebellion Without Rebels—A Biography of Julius Nyerere*. Dar es Salaam: Mkuki na Nyota Press, 2020.

Shivji, Issa. *The Silent Class Struggle*. Dar es Salaam: Tanzania Publishing House, 1973.

Siegelbaum, Lewis. *Cars for Comrades: The Life of the Soviet Automobile*. Ithaca, NY: Cornell University Press, 2008.

Siegelbaum, Lewis. "On the Side: Car Culture in the USSR, 1960s–1980s." *Technology and Culture* 50, no. 1 (January 2009): 1–23.

Silberschmidt, Margrethe. "Poverty, Male Disempowerment, and Male Sexuality: Rethinking Men and Masculinities in Rural and Urban East Africa." In *African Masculinities: Men in Africa from the Late Nineteenth Century to the Present*, edited by Lahoucine Ouzgane and Robert Morrell, 189–203. New York: Palgrave Macmillan, 2005.

Simone, AbdouMaliq. "People as Infrastructure: Intersecting Fragments in Johannesburg." *Public Culture* 16, no. 3 (2004): 407–29.

Smith, Edwin. "The Earliest Ox-Wagons in Tanganyika—An Experiment Which Failed." *Tanganyika Notes and Records* 40 (1955): 1–14.

Smith, James. *Bewitching Development: Witchcraft and the Reinvention of Development in Neoliberal Kenya*. Chicago: University of Chicago Press, 2008.

Smith, William Edgett. *We Must Run While They Walk: A Portrait of Africa's Julius Nyerere*. New York: Random House, 1971.

Snowden, David. "The History of the EAR&H Tanganyika Road Services." Accessed July 1, 2020. https://www.britishempire.co.uk/article/tanganyikaroadservices.htm.

Sparks, Stephen. "Between 'Artificial Economics' and the 'Discipline of the Market': Sasol from Parastatal to Privatisation." *Journal of Southern African Studies* 42, no. 4 (2016): 711–24.

Sperling, Daniel, and Deborah Gordon. *Two Billion Cars Driving toward Sustainability*. Oxford: Oxford University Press, 2009.

Stasik, Michael. "The Popular Niche Economy of a Ghanaian Bus Station: Departure From Informality." *Africa Spectrum* 53, no. 1 (2018): 37–59.

Statista. "Average Annual OPEC Crude Oil Prices 1960 to 2020." Accessed February 25, 2021. https://www.statista.com/statistics/262858/change-in-opec-crude-oil-prices-since-1960/.

Steere, Edward. *A Handbook of the Swahili Language, as Spoken at Zanzibar*. 3rd ed. London: Society for Promoting Christian Knowledge, 1884.

Stein, Howard. *Beyond the World Bank Agenda: An Institutional Approach to Development*. Chicago: University of Chicago Press, 2008.

Stein, Howard. "Theories of the State in Tanzania: A Critical Assessment." *Journal of Modern African Studies* 23, no. 1 (1985): 105–23.

Stephens, Rhiannon. "Birthing Wealth? Motherhood and Poverty in East-Central Uganda, c. 700–1900." *Past and Present* 215, no. 1 (2012): 235–68.

Stiglitz, Joseph. "Markets, Market Failures, and Development." *American Economic Review* 70, no. 2 (1989): 197–203.

Stiglitz, Joseph, and Bruce Greenwald. *Creating a Learning Society: A New Approach to Growth, Development, and Social Progress*. New York: Columbia University Press, 2015.

Stoler, Ann Laura. "Imperial Debris: Reflections on Ruins and Ruination." *Cultural Anthropology* 23 (2008): 191–219.

Stoler, Ann Laura. "'The Rot Remains': From Ruins to Ruination." In *Imperial Debris: On Ruins and Ruination*, edited by Ann Laura Stoler, 1–35. Durham, NC: Duke University Press, 2013.

Storey, William. *Guns, Race, and Power in Colonial South Africa*. Cambridge: Cambridge University Press, 2012.

Storey, William. "Guns, Race, and Skill in Nineteenth-Century Southern Africa." *Technology and Culture* 45, no. 4 (2004): 687–711.

Streit, Katie. "Beyond Borders: A History of Mobility, Labor, and Imperialism in Southern Tanzania." PhD diss., University of Houston, 2016.

Streit, Katie. "South Asian Entrepreneurs in the Automotive Age: Negotiating a Place of Belonging in Colonial and Post-Colonial Tanzania." *Journal of Eastern African Studies* 13, no. 3 (2019): 525–45.

Sunseri, Thaddeus. *Vilimani: Labor Migration and Rural Change in Early Colonial Tanzania*. Portsmouth, NH: Heinemann, 2002.

Swanson, Maynard. "The Sanitation Syndrome: Bubonic Plague and Urban Native Policy in the Cape Colony, 1900–1909." *Journal of African History* 18, no. 3 (1977): 387–410.

Taasisi ya Uchunguzi wa Kiswahili, Dar-es-Salaam. *Kamusi ya Kiswahili Sanifu, Toleo la Pili*. Dar es Salaam: Oxford University Press, 2004.

Tallie, T. J. *Queering Colonial Natal: Indigeneity and the Violence of Belonging in Natal*. Minneapolis: University of Minnesota Press, 2019.

Tanzania African National Union, "TANU Guidelines on Guarding, Consolidating and Advancing the Revolution of Tanzania, and of Africa (*Mwongozo*)." In *African Socialism in Practice: The Tanzanian Experience*, edited by Andrew Coulson, 36–42. Nottingham: Spokesman, 1979.

Thomas, Lynn. "Historicising Agency." *Gender and History* 28, no. 2 (2016): 324–39.

Thomas, Lynn. *Politics of the Womb: Women, Reproduction, and the State in Kenya*. Berkeley: University of California Press, 2003.

Thomas, Robert. "Problems of Manpower Development." In *Tanzania: Revolution by Education*, edited by Idrian Resnick, 106–122. Arusha: Longmans, 1968.

Thompson, Drew. "'Não há Nada' (There is nothing): Absent Headshots and Identity Documents in Independent Mozambique." *Technology and Cultures* 61, no. 2 (2020): S104–S134.

Thompson, Paul. *The Voice of the Past: Oral History*. 3rd ed. New York: Oxford University Press, 2000.

Thomson, Joseph. *To the Central African Lakes and Back: the Narrative of the Royal Geographic Society's East Central African Expedition, 1878–1880*. London: Sampson Low, Marston, Searle, & Rivington, 1881.

Thum, Cordula. "United Republic of Tanzania: Transport Sector Snapshot." World Bank: Washington, D.C., 2004. http://www.worldbank.org/transport/transportresults /regions/ africa/tanzania-thum.pdf.

Tilley, Helen. *Africa as a Living Laboratory: Empire, Development, and the Problem of Scientific Knowledge, 1870–1950*. Chicago: University of Chicago Press, 2011.

Tousignant, Noemi. "Broken Tempos: Of Means and Memory in a Senegalese University Laboratory." *Social Studies of Science* 43, no. 5 (2013): 729–53.

Tousignant, Noemi. *Edges of Exposure: Toxicology and the Problem of Capacity in Postcolonial Senegal*. Durham, NC: Duke University Press, 2018.

Tripp, Aili Mari. *Changing the Rules: The Politics of Liberalization and the Urban Informal Economy in Tanzania.* Berkeley: University of California Press, 1997.

Tsing, Anna Lowenhaupt. *Friction: An Ethnography of Global Connection.* Princeton, NJ: Princeton University Press, 2004.

Tsing, Anna Lowenhaupt. *The Mushroom at the End of the World: On the Possibility of Life in Capitalist Ruins.* Princeton, NJ: Princeton University Press, 2015.

Tuvikene, Tauri. "Mooring in Socialist Automobility: Garage Areas." In *Mobilities in Socialist and Post-Socialist States,* edited by Kathy Burrell and Kathrin Hörschelmann, 105–21. London: Palgrave Macmillan, 2014.

Twagira, Laura Ann. "Machines That Cook or Women Who Cook? Lessons from Mali on Technology, Labor, and Women's Things." *Technology and Culture* 61, no. 2 (2020): S77–S103.

United Nations. "United Nations Framework Convention on Climate Change." https://treaties.un.org/doc/Treaties/1994/03/19940321%2004–56%20AM/Ch_XXVII_07p.pdf.

United Republic of Tanzania. *Facts and Figures on Transport and Communications, 1978–1987.* Dar es Salaam: Ministry of Communication and Works, 1988.

United Republic of Tanzania, Ministry of Lands, Housing, and Urban Development. *Uhuru Corridor Regional Physical Plan: Sectoral Studies II, 1–25.* Ministry of Foreign Affairs of Finland, Department for International Development Cooperation: Helsinki, 1979.

United Republic of Tanzania, Ministry of Planning and Economic Affairs. *Statistical Abstract 1973.* Dar es Salaam: Government Printer, 1974.

United Republic of Tanzania, Ministry of Planning and Economic Affairs. *Statistical Abstract 1973–79.* Dar es Salaam: Government Printer, 1980.

United Republic of Tanzania. *Transport Statistics, 1979.* Dar es Salaam: Bureau of Statistics, 1982.

United States Department of State. "Report of the Accountability Review Boards: Bombings of the US Embassies in Nairobi, Kenya and Dar es Salaam, Tanzania on August 7, 1998." January, 1999. https://1997–2001.state.gov/regions/africa/accountability_report.html.

Urry, John. "Inhabiting Cars and Roads." In *Mobilities,* 114–34. Malden, MA: Polity, 2007.

Urry, John. "Inhabiting the Car." *Sociological Review* 54, no. 1 (2006): 17–31.

Urry, John. *Mobilities.* Malden, MA: Polity, 2007.

Van der Vleuten, Erik. "Infrastructures and Societal Change: A View from the Large Technical Systems Field." *Technology Analysis and Strategic Management* 16, no. 3 (2004): 395–414.

Vassanji, M. G. *The Gunny Sack: Africa's Answer to "Midnight's Children."* Portsmouth, NH: Heinemann, 1989.

Vavrus, Frances. *Desire and Decline: Schooling amid Crisis in Tanzania.* New York: Peter Lang, 2003.

Verdery, Katherine. *What Was Socialism, and What Comes Next?* Princeton, NJ: Princeton University Press, 1996.

Verrips, Jojada, and Birgit Meyer. "Kwaku's Car: The Struggles and Stories of a Ghanaian Long-Distance Taxi-Driver." In *Car Cultures*, edited by Daniel Miller, 153–84. London: Berg, 2001.

Virilio, Paul. *Speed and politics: An Essay on Dromology*. New York: Columbia University Press, 1986.

Voelcker, John. "1.2 Billion Vehicles on World's Roads Now, 2 Billion by 2035." Green Car Reports. July 29, 2014. https://www.greencarreports.com/news/ 1093560_1-2-billion-vehicles-on-worlds-roads-now-2-billion-by-2035-report.

Volti, Rudi. *Car Culture: The Life and Story of a Technology*. Baltimore: Johns Hopkins University Press, 2006.

von Freyhold, Michaela. *Ujamaa Villages in Tanzania: Analysis of a Social Experiment*. New York: Monthly Review Press, 1979.

von Schnitzler, Antina. *Democracy's Infrastructure: Techno-Politics and Protest after Apartheid*. Princeton, NJ: Princeton University Press, 2016.

Warman, H. R. "The Future of Oil." *Geographic Journal* 138, no. 3 (1972): 287–97.

Watts, Michael. *State, Oil, and Agriculture in Nigeria*. Berkeley: University of California Press, 1987.

Watts, Michael, and Thomas Bassett. "Crisis and Change in African Agriculture: A Comparative Study of the Ivory Coast and Nigeria." *African Studies Review* 28, no. 4 (1985): 3–27.

Weiss, Brad. "Buying Her Grave: Money, Movement and AIDS in North-West Tanzania." *Africa: Journal of the International African Institute* 18 (1993): 19–35.

Weiss, Brad. *The Making and Unmaking of the Haya Lived World: Consumption, Commoditization, and Everyday Practice*. Durham, NC: Duke University Press, 1996.

Wells, Christopher. *Car Country: An Environmental History*. Seattle: University of Washington Press, 2012.

White, Luise. *The Comforts of Home: Prostitution in Colonial Nairobi*. Chicago: University of Chicago Press, 1990.

White, Luise. "'Heading for the Gun': Skills and Sophistication in an African Guerrilla War." *Comparative Studies in Society and History* 51, no. 2 (2009): 236–59.

White, Luise. *Speaking with Vampires: Rumor and History in Colonial Africa*. Berkeley: University of California Press, 2000.

White, Luise, Stephan Miescher, and David William Cohen. *African Words, African Voices: Critical Practices in Oral History*. Bloomington: Indiana University Press, 2002.

Wiredu, Kwasi. "Our Problem of Knowledge: Brief Reflections on Knowledge and Development in Africa." In *African Philosophy as Cultural Inquiry*, edited by Ivan Karp and D. A. Masolo, 181–243. Bloomington: Indiana University Press, 2000.

Wisnicki, Adrian S. "Interstitial Cartographer: David Livingstone and the Invention of South Central Africa." *Victorian Literature and Culture* 37, no. 1 (2009): 255–71.

Wolfe, Joel. *Autos and Progress: The Brazilian Search for Modernity*. New York: Oxford University Press, 2010.

Woolgar, Steve, and Keith Grint. "Computers and the Transformation of Social Analysis." *Science, Technology, and Human Values* 16, no. 3 (1991): 368–78.

World Bank. *Tanzania: Issues and Options in the Energy Sector.* Washington, DC: World Bank Group, 1984. http://documents.worldbank.org/curated/en/403251468778743225 /Tanzania-Issues-and-options-in-the-energy-sector.

World Health Organization. *Global Status Report on Road Safety: Time for Action.* Geneva: World Health Organization, 2009.

Wright, Marcia. *Strategies of Slaves and Women: Life-Stories from East/Central Africa.* London: James Currey, 1993.

Wynne-Jones, Stephanie. "Lines of Desire: Power and Materiality along a Tanzanian Caravan Route." *Journal of World Prehistory* 23 (2010): 219–37.

Wynne-Jones, Stephanie. "The Public Life of the Swahili Stone House, 14th–15th Centuries AD." *Journal of Anthropological Archaeology* 32, no. 4 (2013): 759–73.

Young, F. B. *Marching on Tanga.* Gloucester: Alan Sutton, 1917.

Zeller, Thomas. *Driving Germany: The Landscape of the German Autobahn, 1930–1970.* New York: Berghahn Books, 2006.

Zimmerman, Andrew. *Alabama in Africa: Booker T. Washington, the German Empire, and the Globalization of the New South.* Princeton, NJ: Princeton University Press, 2010.

INDEX

Page numbers in italics refer to figures and tables.

automobiles (continued)
exhibitions, 285, 287–88, 367n25; *njia*,
44–45, 50, 81; Nyerere's criticisms,
147–50; Nyerere's uses, 159–60, 287–88;
political hierarchies, 147; pulled by
African laborers, 48–49; remaking, 15;
replacing porters, 46; representing the
nation, 300; roadless trucks, 83–85;
"small house," 295; socialist imports,
163; societies remaking, 278; state-
owned, 111–12; Tanzanian perspectives
on, 14–15; as technologies of trust, 80;
"tools of fire" *(chombo cha moto)* term,
74; villages buying *(gari la TANU)*,
154–55. *See also* automobiles and Africa;
Dar es Salaam private automobiles; *gari*
(automobiles); *utingo*
automobiles and Africa discourses: incompatibility, 1, 4, 277–78, 287; misuse,
287–88; technological stasis, 5–6, 7
automobility: overview, 8, 302n15; African
creativity, 15; African views of, 12;
changeability, 292; changing state
approaches to, 235, 238; creating communities, 238–39; deregulation, 277;
destruction discourses, 273; destructiveness, 275–80, 289; developmental
limits of, 25; dynamism, 13–14; as failed
modernization, 238; failed modernization discourses, 269, 273–74; false
historical narratives, 287–88; HIV/AIDS,
238, 366n132; Kiswahili terms, 302n14;
limited, 283–84; *magendo*, 235, 238;
motorized domesticities, 239; privatized
transition, 283; remaking, 281–82; sanctioned circulation of goods, 242; social,
302n14; unmaking, 280–81; and vernacular complexes, 9. *See also* accidents
and deaths on the road; drivers; roads
axes, 153–54

Bagachwa, M. S. D., 364n108
Bailey, Martin, 354n74
bananas, 59
Barber, Karin, 28

Barongo, Sylvester: oil consumption
increase views, 195; oil procurement,
208, 211, 217–20; oil refinery, 200; oil
shortness concerns, 199; technological
self-reliance views, 221–22; TPDC, 203,
221–22
Barry, Sara, 56
Barton, Donald, 48
Bates, Darrell, 52–53, 57
Bayart, Jean-François, 222
Bayat, Asef, 306n50
Beck, Ulrich, 257–58, 273
Berlant, Lauren, 294–95
Bibi Benzi (Maomba, Zakia), 244,
250–52
bicycles, 148–49
Bissell, William, 321n138
boi (boy) term, 72, 97, 240
Bongoland. *See* Dar es Salaam
Borg, Kevin, 86, 309n76
Brandt, Willy, 230
breakdown, 13, 22, 87, 182, 282, 309n76,
320n136
Breckenridge, Keith, 145, 323n166
Brennan, James, 116, 335n134, 338n5
broken world thinking, 13, 22, 87, 182, 282
Brownell, Emily, 160, 171, 176, 306n50,
351n18, 364n104
Bryceson, Deborah, 365n108
bubu (muteness, silence), 18, 29
bubu archives, 28
bubu garages (street garages): as archives,
28; criticisms of, 113–14; definition, 6, 9;
family-knowledge-things intersections,
125, 126; fundi, 118, 120; masculinities,
118–19, 125; modification practices, 121,
124; part terms, 121; as social spaces, 121;
spare parts availability, 124; terms for,
9; views on, 113, 117, 120. See also *bubu*
mechanics
bubu masculinities, 20
bubu mechanics: apprentice *(vijana)*,
117–22, 335n134; critiques of the state,
282; economic success, 124–25; official
education access, 123; restful work,

124–25; uncles (*wajomba*), 118, 120, 125; wealth and security discourses, 125

Bulliet, Richard, 67

bureaucrats: automobile loans, 149–50, 157–58; blame for economic problems, 223, 231; business and automobile ownership restrictions, 158; corruption imaginaries, 158–59; technological choices, 157; technologically heavy, 190; transportation choices, 148–49, 176; *wabenzi* (wealthy Benz owners), 148, 235, 242

Burrell, Jenna, 309n76, 311n100

buses, 62, 66, 163, 264. *See also* Dar es Salaam buses

bus rapid transit (BRT), 290–92

"buy local" campaigns, 193, 351n29

Callaci, Emily: antiurbanism, 168, 341n62; automobile ownership, 149; demasculinization, 124, 309n72; drivers distributing novels, 258; driving, 360n17; mobility and power, 176; Nyerere's principles, 348n188; reworking discourse, 338n10; Second Five Year Plan, 341n58; self-reliance, 336n159; *ujamaa* urban, 156; urban life tensions, 349n198

Callon, Michel, 311n100

Cameron, Donald, 47, 58–59

Campbell, William, 82, 91

caravans: European complaints about, 39; persistence post-European projects, 42; reliability, 45; route widening, 41, 315n41; slavery roles, 37–38; travel writing on, 37–38, 313n15. *See also* porterage

cars. *See* automobiles

casual labor, 102–3, 332n76

cattle, 254, 256

Césaire, Aimé, 320n136

cha ajabu (stories of awe and the miraculous), 251–58

chombo cha moto (tools of fire), 74

Chowdhuri, Roy, 216–17

Christie, James, 39

chronopolitics, 221, 223–24, 227–29

cities: antiurbanism, 168, 341n62; daily life tensions, 349n198; development *versus* rural areas, 189; Dodoma, 160; drivers, 71; immigration to, 156; mechanics from (*pwani*), 136–37; migrant laborers, 65; socialist perspectives on, 115; streets (*mitaani*), 115, 117. *See also* Dar es Salaam; urban socialism

citizenship: technological, 167, 344n103; *ujamaa* and infrastructure, 156; urban socialist, 167, 169–70, 175

civil servants. *See* bureaucrats

Civil Service Magazine, 148, 338n20

climate change, 275–77, 284

collective work (*kazi*), 153

Collins, Harry, 100, 109

colonialism: and automobiles, 45–46, 145, 147; car-driver relationships, 75–77, 79; casual labor, 103; the colonial sublime, 56–57, 321n140; infrastructural impermanence, 51–52, 55–56, 320n136; rural society emphasis, 91; technological change, 90–92. *See also* Tanganyika

colonial progress narratives, 35

commodities, 40

condoms, 271–73

conjugation, 228–29

conscripted porters, 46–48, 50, 316n64

contraband. See *magendo*

Cooper, Frederick, 103, 323n174, 355n79

cooperatives, 154–55, 267, 364n108

Coulson, Andrew, 350n16, 351n31

cowards. *See* driver-cowards

craft-mechanics distinctions, 87–91

creativity. See *ubunifu*

cruel optimism, 294–95

daladala. See *thumni-thumni*

Dant, Tim, 77, 100, 362n43

Dar es Salaam: bunkering port plans, 204; colonial racial zones, 166; forced returns from, 66; government relocation from, 160; immigration to, 156; "Lords of Travel" joke, 33–35; motoring culture, early, 66; traffic problems, 296–97,

famine, 229
Fanon, Frantz, 147
Farquharson, J. R., 55
Feierman, Steven, 59, 312n104
Ferguson, James, 58, 259, 268
field engineering, 52–53
foleni (queues), 170–73, 258, 296, 368n47
forced villagization, 190, 229, 350n17
formal/informal analytic divides, 17,
    305–6, 306n50
Freed, Libbie, 317n75
Frehold, Michaela von, 351n29
Fryer, W., 66
fuel sale declines, 158, 341n68
full idea of a car, 99, 141–42
fundi (holder of skill or expertise), 93, 99,
    118, 120

Galton-Fenzi, Frederick, 4
garages: access routes, 96–97; as archives,
    93–95; broken machine ubiquity,
    97; dependence on dysfunction, 86;
    expertise signaling, 94; home-based,
    102–3; institutional contexts, 103–4;
    laborers (non-mechanics), 97–102, 118;
    languages used, 98; manuals in, 141;
    specialization, 141; spread of, 95–96;
    state, 105, 107–13. See also *bubu* garages;
    mechanics
garages, street. See *bubu* garages
Gardner, J. G., 77
gari, 42–43, 45, 74. See also automobiles
gari (animal-drawn carts), 40, 42, 43
gari la moshi (railways), 42. See also
    railways
gari la TANU, 154–55
Gastrow, Claudia, 169
gender: advertising uses, 240–43; drivers,
    249–51, 258; hierarchies reflected in au-
    tomobile terms, 295; labor, 240, 245–46;
    roles in the independent period, 243;
    technological personhood, 21. See also
    masculinities; women
geological surveys, 219
gereji bubu. See *bubu* garages

Giblin, James, 62
Graetz, Paul, 43–45, 80–81
Graham, Stephen, 178
the Great Acceleration, 284
Great North Road, 187
Green, Reginald, 211
Green-Simms, Lindsey, 302n14
growth and sovereignty, 231
Guyer, Jane, 18–19, 308n60, 352n69

Hamadi "Mau," Hamisi, 107
Hamed bin Mohammed bin Juma bin
    Rajab el Murjebi (Tippu Tip), 39, 42
hands and labor, 122
Handyman training courses, 91–92
Hansen, Karen Tranberg, 239
Haraway, Donna, 27, 282–83
Harley, Philip, 54
harmful sociotechnical systems, 54–55,
    196–97, 279–80
Harmonize, 299–300
Harper, Douglas, 86–87, 100, 136, 309n76
Harris, Joe and Cicely, 47
Hart, Jennifer: driving and identity,
    327n248; formal-informal binaries,
    306n50; Ghanaian drivers, 325n206;
    326n218; Gold Coast automobiles,
    67, 80; plural masculinities, 20; traffic
    violations, 75
Hatchell, G. W., 89
headmen, 52, 62, 98–99
Headrick, Daniel, 328n2, 330n34
Hecht, Gabrielle: conjugation, 228;
    European attitudes toward Africa, 1,
    4, 37; national identity, 150; safety,
    290; technopolitical action, 320n136;
    technopolitical regimes, 55; Volkswagen
    emissions scandal, 276
hegemony on a shoestring, 56
Hell's Road, 185–87
Henderson, Jason, 302n14
Henke, Christopher, 100
Hermani, Matei, 339n21
HIV/AIDS, 238, 270–73, 365n118, 365n122,
    366n132

Hodgson, Dorothy, 304n30
hoes, 153–54, 282
Hofmeier, Rolf, 319n104
Hornborg, Alf, 277
Hughes, Thomas, 24, 27, 212–13, 220, 356n106
human capital, 105
Hyden, Goran, 339n34, 350n16, 352n37, 365n112
hyper- and hypomasculinity, 19–20, 291

Ibrick, Brian (mechanic), 125, *127*, 128–32, 142, 281
identity: drivers, 77, 80, 327n248; mechanics, 136; national, 150; and race, 304n34; technological, 19–20
Ikarus bus manufacturer, 163
Iliffe, John, 325n198
import-substitution consumption, 193, 351n29
Industrial Revolution ideologies, 89
inequality from privatization, 293–96
informality: overview, 16–17; improvisation, 97; mechanic training, 85–86, 96, 103–4; scholarship on, 306n50; *versus* vernacular institution terms, 18. See also *magendo*
infrastructural constraints, 22–25
infrastructural impermanence, 51–52, 55–56, 320n136
infrastructure: absences, 23–24, 231, 310n86; automobility's changeability, 292; chronopolitics, 223, 228; community creation, 178, 184; European views of African, 41–42; growth of, for automobiles, 295–96; long-distance walking, 60–61; of mobility, 293; neoliberal politics, 296; people as, 55, 320n131; political roles, 168–69, 344n109; rural migration, 156; state projects, 299; Tanganyika's colonial, 50–56, 319n104, 319n109, 320n131; temporality, 228; *ujamaa* citizenship forms, 156; vernacular, 59–64, 86, 116–17, 178–79. See also *njia* (ways); railways; roads

infrastructures of expertise, 85–86, 92, 94, 103, 136
Ingold, Tim, 322n163
inherited mechanics, 93, 96, 124
inscription *versus* de-scription, 14
invention narratives, 15
Ivaska, Andrew, 168, 341n63, 365n112

Jackson, Steven, 13, 22, 87, 182
Jamal, Amir H., 229, 268
Joerges, Bernward, 357n134
joking relationships, 250
Jones, Christopher, 188

Kabura, F. (mechanical engineer), 111–13
KAMATA bus network, 264
Kaniki, 64–65, 324n188
Karadha loan scheme, 157–58, 341n63
Karumba, Maliko, 62–63
Kassum, Al Noor, 217–19, 221
Kaunda, Kenneth, 185–87, 189
Kikwete, Jakaya, 277
Kilosa rest camp, 60
King, Kenneth, 306n50
King's African Rifles, 76
Kirsch, David, 279
Kiswahili: analytic value, 306n50; automobility terms, 302n14; *bubu* (muteness, silence), 18, 29; creativity, innovation and making terms, 12–13; *matengenezo* (maintenance, repair, production), 13–14, 16; *mitaani* (city streets and spaces), 20, 115–17; socialist lexicon, 196; *ubunifu* (creativity, innovation), 13, 16–17; vernacular institution terms, 12, 18. See also *maendeleo*
Kiwale, Nicholas, 172
Klieman, Kairn, 353n54
Kline, Ronald, 83
knowledge: embodied production, 100; imports, 116, 335n128; mobility, 92; power, 17–18; spread of, 19; as unfinished, 12, 134–36, 222. See also expertise
Koponen, Juhani, 304n30
Krebs, Stefan, 100

colonial infrastructure, 52–54, 319n109. *See also* mechanics

Maji Maji Rebellion, 59

Makutika, S. R., 115

Maliyamkono, T. L., 364n108

Malm, Andreas, 277

Mann, Gregory, 349n194

manpower planning, 105–6, 113

Manuh, Takyiwaa, 353n47

Maomba, Zakia (Bibi Benzi), 244, 250–52

mapato (revenue, income, resources), 245, 361n25

Marcotrade, 218

Marlaw, 295–96

Marvin, Simon, 178

Marxist development phases, 197–98

masculinities: automobiles signifying, 295; *boi* term, 72; *dume* (sanctioned public), 240–43, 246, 257; effective manhood, 20–21; effective technological, 78–79, 86; garage labor, 118; and HIV's spread, 271–72; hyper- and hypo-, 19–20, 291; industrial, 103; ineffective, 175; knowledge mobility, 92; ownership, 124; rites of passage, 256; technological, 20, 125, 308n68; technological remaking as gendered remaking, 86–87, 124–30

mashangingi (Land Cruisers), 288, 297–98, 369n54

"Master Farmer" ("Bwana Shamba") song, 293–94

matengenezo (maintenance, repair, production), 13–14, 16

materiality as method, 26–27, 311nn99–100

material *maendeleo*, 25–26

Matonya, 295

Mattei, Enrico, 353n54

Mavhunga, Clapperton: automobility, 302n14; cut-offness from colonial technologies, 322n165; European views of African knowledges, 17; hydrological mobility, 59; innovation, 305n14, 306n46; language, 307n50; migrant laborers, 322n164; mobility as creative work, 58; *nzira* (ways), 37; technology

definitions, 26; technology/infrastructure, 306n50

Mbatia, Salome, 247, 361n38

mbioni ("we must run while others walk"), 196, 198, 228

McNamara, Robert, 224–25, 277

McNeill, John Robert, 284

mechanical families, 124, 336n159

mechanics: adaptations to technological change, 141–42; automobiles built by, 130, 142; career desirability, 105; certification, 109–10; challenges faced, 13–14; economic concerns, 111; European views of, 82–83, 87–90, 92; expertise, 85–86, 94, 103, 136; full idea of a car, 99, 141–42; government-employed, 95–96, 331n49; hands as status symbols, 122; historical demonstrations, 93–94; Ibrick, Brian, 125, *127*, 128–32, 142, 281; improvisation and flexibility, 97, 103; inherited, 93, 96, 124; language, 98; manpower planning views, 113; masculinities, 19; nicknames, 119; numerical growth, 95–96; passion for their work, 121; pay, 102; photographs of, *104*, *112*; practical and theoretical education, 121–23; practice *versus* theory perspectives, 121–22; regional differences, 136–37; remaking technologies, 87; roles, 15; rural (*mikoani*), 136–37; school leavers becoming, 117; scrap and parts collecting, 124, *126*; self-reliance, 110–13; skill levels, 106; social mobility, 102; specializations, 141; state garage, 109; status, 101–2; street, 116; technical authority, 109–10, 281; tools and status, 120; urban (*pwani*), 136–37; white uniforms, 97–98, 102. See also *bubu* garages; garages; mechanics training; modification of bodies and parts; repair

mechanics training: apprentices (*vijana*) in *bubu* garages, 117–22, 335n134; Department of Works (Ujenzi), 104–9; formal colonial programs, 88–90, 92; informal, 85–86, 96, 103–4

about, 39–40; long-distance walking, 60–62, 67, 68, 69; migrant laborer use, 61–63; parallel to railways, 50–51; porters, 41; security, 315n43; slavery's spread, 37; walking, 60–62, 67, 68, 69; widening, 42, 315n41. *See also* roads

Njovu, Vincent (driver), 36, 77–80

Nyerere, Joseph, 270

Nyerere, Julius: African socialism, 24, 110–11, 115, 235; automobiles used by, 159–60, 287–88; *bubu* garage criticism, 114; bureaucrat views, 157; distribution, 195, 268; education approach, 116; effective freedom, 187; exploitation, 169; government views, 333n86; historical knowledge, 312n109; Ikarus visit, 163; infrastructure projects, 23–24; legacy, 288; *maendeleo* invocations, 304n23; manpower planning, 105–6; master plan of 1979, 280–81; meetings with McNamara, 224–25; National Economic Survival Programme, 179; nation building, 23–25; newspaper nationalization, 168; oil pipeline opening speech, 186–88; oil refinery opening, 199–200; OPEC crisis impacts on growth, 226–30; private automobile criticisms, 147–50; Rhodesia embargo, 185–86; saboteur economies, 265; self-reliance ideology, 110–11, 113; services approach, 177; socialist theory, 196–99; Sokoine's death, 270; technological determinism, 191; technological minimalism, 152–54, 189; technological-political power connections, 299; technological sovereignty speeches, 225–26; travels, 79, 154; trip from Tabora to Dar es Salaam, 80–81; underdevelopment theory, 229–30; urban-rural social services networks, 155–56; village modernization, 195; "we must run while others walk" slogan, 196; workers, 169

nyumbani garages. See *bubu* garages

Ochonu, Moses, 321n140

oil: advantages *versus* other energy sources, 191–92; bartering goods for, 217; consumption rate increases, 193, 195; dependence, 199, 353n59; development and nation building, 186, 206–7, 211–13, 230–31, 275; development roles, 230; effective freedom relationship, 187–88, 230–31; energy production use, 192; exploration, 218–19; exports to Zambia, 185–87; imports, 199–201, 206–7, 214, 355n81; indigenous economies, 200–1, 203; infrastructural self-reliance, 191; international relationships, 201, 202–3*t*; Iran-Iraq War, 207–8; light distillates, 201; major companies (majors), 206–8; need for self-reliance, 226; origin and type importance, 218; peak oil concerns, 219; petroleum swapping, 217–18; pipeline to Zambia, 186–88; power generation, 193; primary product transformation, 193; refinery (TIPER), 199–201, 210–11, 213, 353n54; Report on the Plan for Saving the Economy, 210; reserves in 1981, 213*t*; Rhodesia embargo scarcity, 185–86; rural modernization, 189–91, 193–95, 205, 210; social services, 193, 352n32; sovereignty entanglements, 231; spot markets, 216–17; state investments in foreign companies, 200–1, 354n64; traders, 19–20; *ujamaa* roles, 191, 193, 205, 210; "we must run while others walk" slogan, 196. *See also* OPEC crisis; Tanzania Petroleum Development Corporation

oil distribution and mobility: amounts by region, 209*t*; difficulties, 209–10; majors, 208; political power, 218, 357n125; railway, 203, 208–10; state, 195, 208

oil economies, 14, 200

OPEC crisis (1973): overview, 203; automobility impacts, 280–81; busing impacts, 164, 166; chronopolitics following, 224, 227–28; developing countries, 203–5, 226; economic changes caused

seasonal infrastructure, 50–51
Second Five Year Plan (SFYP), 155–57
self-devouring growth, 276, 278
self-reliance *(kujitegemea)*: automobiles,
159–60; community, 153; gendered personhood, 124; industrial development
working against, 351n31; infrastructural, 191; mechanics', 110–13, 116; oil
as necessary for, 226–27; repair and
maintenance's roles in pursuing, 110–13,
181–82, 221–22; road farming, 152; rural
versus urban, 115–16, 169; technological,
116–17, 196, 221; types of, 221–22; *ujamaa*
villages, 153, 155; urban socialism, 161
sex work, 249, 270
Shell, Jacob, 60
Sheller, Mimi, 8, 189, 284, 302n15, 311n100
Shivji, Issa, 333n86, 350n16
situated knowledges, 27
skill definitions, 106
slavery, 37–39, 41
Smith, Edwin, 314n29
Smith, James, 303n21
smuggling. See *magendo*
soap production, 210
socialism. See *ujamaa*
social mobility, 102–3
social services, 155–56, 193, 352n32
sociotechnical systems, harmful, 279–80
Sokoine, Edward, 147, 183, 269–70
Songo Songo gas mine, 219
South Africa, 217–18, 354n74
spare parts, 124
"Spare Tairi" song, 295
speeding, 247, 254–55
Stasik, Michael, 306n50
states of deferral, 55
ST cars *(sitaki tabu)*, 176, 346n151
Stein, Howard, 223–24
Stevenson, C. W., 92
Stiglitz, Joseph, 17
stitch-in-time maintenance, 52, 56, 319n109
Stoler, Ann Laura, 55
stories of awe and the miraculous *(cha
ajabu)*, 251–58

street garages. See *bubu* garages
structural adjustment policies (SAPs), 276,
280–81, 283
sustainability as technophilia, 282–83

Tallie, T. J., 307n54
Tanganyika (colonial period): automobiles, 45, 50, 67, 80–83, 85; first
registered vehicle (Albion GT 1), 33–35;
gari (animal-drawn carts), 40, 314n29;
geographic area, 312n2; infrastructure,
50–56, 319n104, 319n109, 320n131; long-
distance walking problems, 60; "Lords
of Travel" joke, 33–35; motoring culture,
66; road trains, 85. *See also* Public
Works Department; Tanganyika's British colonial authority
Tanganyika African National Union
(TANU): automobile ownership
prohibitions for bureaucrats, 158; automobiles provided to Nyerere, 159–60;
bus company employee training, 162;
national development, 153; newspaper
nationalization, 168; vehicles purchased
by villages, 154
Tanganyika National Transport Co-
operative Ltd., 154
Tanganyika's British colonial authority:
administrative mobilities, 48, 56; automobiles, 45–50; conscripted porters,
46–50; drivers' status with, 79–80; end
of, 81; migrant labor, 58–62; tax collection, 53–54
tanibois. See turners
TANU. See Tanganyika African National
Union
Tanu, Saidi (driver for Nyerere), 79–81,
287
Tanzania (independent period): aspirational power, 339n34; carbon output,
277–78, 292; historiography on vernacular concepts, 303n19; mineral wealth,
219; nation building, 23–25; party-
state, 333n86; postcolonial economic
situation, 196–97; primary education

expansion, 115; road building, 151–52; *utingo* (driver training), 240; war with Uganda, 229. *See also* development; modernization; OPEC crisis's impacts on Tanzania; *ujamaa*

Tanzania Petroleum Development Corporation (TPDC): bituminization plant plans, 211; directors, 195; distribution, 208; employee benefits, 221–22; financial health, 221; goals, 201, 203, 355n79; importing, 201; infrastructural acceleration hopes, 205; infrastructural self-reliance concerns, 191; oil price increase responses, 16; OPEC crisis responses, 16, 204–7, 222–23; procurement methods, 216–20; sales, 201; self-reliance, 222; survival *(kujinusuru)*, 216–20

Tanzania-Zambia highway (Tanzam), 151–52, 200

"Tatizo foleni" (song), 296, 368n47

Taylor, Frank: automobile, 1, 2, 3, 6, 11, 15; family, 6; garage business, 6, 8; knowledge, views of, 18; mechanical interests, 15; rally competitions, 1; spare parts collection, 127

technical authority, 72, 109–10, 115, 281

technical education cultural biases, 89–90, 330n34

technological abolitionism, 39–40

technological citizenship, 167, 344n103

technological dysfunction and political independence, 145

technological history, 89–90

technological inertia, 212

technological minimalism, 152–54, 189, 280

technological personhood, 21–22, 109

technological sovereignty, 225–26

technological worth discourses, 245–46

technology definitions, 26

technopolitics, 55, 150, 290, 320n136

temporal distancing, 90

terrorism, 284–87

Thomas, Lynn, 309n83

Thomson, Joseph, 41–42

thumni-thumni (daladala): overview, 145–46; broken world thinking, 182; emergence of, 178–79; legalization, 183; legibility, 292; planner attitudes toward, 290–92; public approval, 180, 182, 347n177; public discussions about in newspapers, 181–82; replacement efforts, 290; routes, 291–92; social reciprocity, 180–81; *versus* the UDA, 181; urban socialism, 145–46, 179, 181–83; vehicle registrations, 179, 182; vehicle types, 180

Tippu Tip (Hamed bin Mohammed bin Juma bin Rajab el Murjebi), 39, 42

Tousignant, Noemi, 23

TPDC. *See* Tanzania Petroleum Development Corporation

tracks, 36–37

tractorization, 157

traffic violations, 75, 326n227

training. *See* education

Transport Department, 95–96

travel writing, 35, 37–38, 41–42, 313n15

truckers. *See* drivers

Truman, Harry, 17

Tsing, Anna s, 25, 282–83, 311n100

turners *(taniboi)*, 71–72, 96, 240, 271. See also *utingo*

ubunifu (creativity, innovation), 13, 16–17

ufundi wa kurithi. See inherited mechanics

Uhuru Corridor, 156

ujamaa: automobiles' roles in, 155; citizenship forms, 156; collective work *(kazi)*, 153; critiques of, 193, 351n31; distribution, 268, 274; drivers' status, 242; failure, 190, 273–74, 350n16; infrastructural expansion, 156; international attention to, 189–90; large technological systems, 190; means of production control, 150; mechanization, 153–55; political *versus* sociotechnical understandings, 180; privatized transportation, 145–46; public transportation, 144–45; road farming, 152; rural modernization,